THE WASHINGTON WAR

THE
WASHINGTON WAR

FDR's Inner Circle and the Politics

of Power That Won World War II

JAMES LACEY

Bantam Books
New York

Copyright © 2019 by James Lacey

Published in the United States by Bantam Books, an imprint of Random House, a division of Penguin Random House LLC, New York.

BANTAM BOOKS and the HOUSE colophon are registered trademarks of Penguin Random House LLC.

LIBRARY OF CONGRESS CATALOGING-IN-PUBLICATION DATA
Names: Lacey, Jim, author.
Title: The Washington war : FDR's inner circle and the politics
of power that won World War II / James Lacey.
Description: First edition. | New York : Bantam Books, [2019] | Includes
bibliographical references and index.
Identifiers: LCCN 2018053679| ISBN 9780345547583 (hardcover) |
ISBN 9780345547590 (ebook)
Subjects: LCSH: Roosevelt, Franklin D. (Franklin Delano), 1882–1945. | Roosevelt,
Franklin D. (Franklin Delano), 1882–1945—Military leadership. | Roosevelt, Frank-
lin D. (Franklin Delano), 1882–1945—Friends and associates. | Cabinet officers—
United States. | Marshall, George C. (George Catlett), 1880–1959. | Morgenthau,
Henry, 1891–1967. | Stimson, Henry L. (Henry Lewis), 1867–1950. | Byrnes, James F.
(James Francis), 1882–1972. | King, Ernest Joseph, 1878–1956. | Hopkins, Harry L.
(Harry Lloyd), 1890–1946. | World War, 1939–1945—United States. | United States—
Politics and government—1933–1945.
Classification: LCC E806 .L24 2019 | DDC 973.917092—dc23
LC record available at https://lccn.loc.gov/2018053679

Printed in the United States of America on acid-free paper

randomhousebooks.com

2 4 6 8 9 7 5 3 1

First Edition

Book design by Virginia Norey

To Sharon
who made this book possible.
And
the Brood
Allison, James, Edmund, Anastasia, Adam, and Ethan
who made this book necessary.

CONTENTS

THE WASHINGTON WARRIORS

Henry Harley "Hap" Arnold—Chief of staff of the Air Force and the driving force behind the creation of the great air armadas that bombed Germany and France into submission. His idea of getting things done was to tell someone to do it, and he ensured long-term success by making sure no one ever stayed around to disappoint him twice.

Bernard Baruch—A self-made multimillionaire, he had been the production czar during the mobilization for World War I and expected to get the call again. It never came. Roosevelt liked Baruch, and valued his advice, but Hopkins, who saw him as a threat to his own power, always kept him at arm's length. Baruch spent most of the war offering valuable advice to whoever came calling.

Alan Brooke—A British field marshal and chief of the Imperial General Staff. Brooke had three enemies during the war: Churchill, Marshall, and the Axis powers. His barely concealed disdain for the military capacity of the first two sometimes got in the way of defeating the third.

William C. Bullitt, Jr.—The most brilliant graduate of Yale's 1912 class, he wasted his talent on petty jealousies and revenge plots. He was the first U.S. ambassador to the Soviet Union, and at the start of the war the ambassador to France. He always judged himself as ready to play at the highest levels and certainly saw himself as FDR's wartime secretary of state, a job he coveted.

James F. "Jimmy" Byrnes—For years he was the president's go-to man in the Senate. If there was something important to get through the Senate, FDR handed the job to Byrnes, whose technique, a combination of iron fist and velvet glove, shepherded through many difficult legislative proposals. In midwar he was brought to the White House, where he quickly established himself as the "assistant president" and took over running the country.

Neville Chamberlain—British prime minister at the war's onset. Upon returning from the Munich talks with Hitler, he had famously promised "peace in our time," to which Churchill retorted, "The government had a choice between shame and war. It chose shame; it will get war."

Winston Churchill—British prime minister throughout most of the war. He was moody, argumentative, and often difficult to bear, and he drank too much, but, in Britain's darkest hour, he was the indispensable man.

Grenville Clark—As a confidant to presidents, Clark was the master of wielding power from behind the scenes, mobilizing both the Republican and Democratic establishments to an overriding cause: winning two world wars.

Father Charles Coughlin—A bigoted, anti-Semitic priest who went from being an early Roosevelt supporter to railing against everything FDR stood for. His support of Hitler, Mussolini, and Hirohito finally caused the cancellation of his nationally syndicated radio show in 1939.

Charles de Gaulle—The leader of the Free French, and a thorn in both Churchill's and Roosevelt's sides throughout the war. Through arrogance and force of will he played a weak military, political, and diplomatic hand with consummate skill.

Thomas Dewey—As a district attorney in New York City and governor of New York State, he waged a relentless war against organized crime. But when he ran against FDR in 1944, he proved no match for the Champ.

John Dill—A British field marshal and former chief of the Imperial Staff. After a falling-out with Churchill he was sent to the United States as a liaison to the American Joint Chiefs. He became a close friend to General Marshall, and did yeoman's service explaining the Americans to the British and the British to the Americans.

Ferdinand Eberstadt—Co–vice chairman of the War Production Board (WPB), he almost single-handedly brought order out of chaos in the allocation of scarce raw materials. Unfortunately, he was a neophyte in the ways of Washington—a fatal weakness in the ensuing power struggles.

Dwight Eisenhower—He began the war as General Marshall's chief planner and ended as the supreme Allied commander in Europe.

Felix Frankfurter—A Supreme Court justice and Roosevelt administration talent scout. His acolytes populated almost all the rungs of government just below the secretary level, and were commonly referred to as "Felix's Happy Hot Dogs."

John Nance Garner—As vice president for Roosevelt's first two terms, he famously observed that "the vice presidency is not worth a bucket of warm spit." (He really said "warm piss.")

Leon Henderson—A man without friends or the desire to make any. When there was a dirty and unpopular job to be done, it went to the always bellicose Henderson. During the war he was tasked with keeping inflation in check through the Office of Price Administration, where he accumulated enemies while almost single-handedly turning the tide of some of the most vicious Washington disputes.

Sidney Hillman—A full-time labor leader, part-time communist, and the man Roosevelt kept on every production organization as a foil to the more belligerent labor titan John L. Lewis.

Harry Hopkins—By living in the White House, Hopkins became Roosevelt's most powerful and trusted adviser. He was hugely capable, but just as hugely insecure and protective of his influence and position.

Cordell Hull—As secretary of state he was rarely able to get beyond the picayune and rise to the level of wartime consigliere, a role he coveted. Hull was the perfect secretary for a stable world but was unable to cope with a world in crisis.

Harold Ickes—The "great curmudgeon" and FDR's political attack dog. He hated Harry Hopkins and disliked everyone else. His inability to get along with anyone sidelined him during the great policy debates of the war, but Roosevelt kept "Horrible Harold" close as secretary of the interior and used him as a cudgel against his political opponents and enemies.

William "Bill" Jeffers—He ran the Union Pacific Railroad through the time-tested methods of fear and physical intimidation and did the same in Washington, where he was the rarest of things: a man who came to do a job—rubber czar—accumulated the power necessary to do it, and then gave it up when the job was done.

Jesse Jones—The head of the Reconstruction Finance Corporation (RFC) and the secretary of commerce. If one needed money for a major project, Jones was the go-to guy. As he handed out money without regard to political affiliation, he was beloved by both parties. His feud with Vice President Wallace was the stuff of Washington legend.

Joseph Kennedy—At the start of the war he was ambassador to Great Britain (the Court of St. James's). Churchill thought him a traitor and Roosevelt despised him, but he was kept around to help secure the Irish vote.

Ernest King—Commander in chief, United States Fleet, and chief of naval operations for most of the war. He was roundly hated by nearly everyone with whom he came in contact, and even the amiable Eisenhower thought the war effort would significantly benefit if someone shot him. But he was the perfect man to kick the Navy out of its post–Pearl Harbor funk and drive the fleet toward his one burning ambition: the defeat of Japan.

Frank Knox—A Republican who deserted his party for the higher cause of confronting Hitler. As secretary of the navy he proved a match for Admiral King.

William Knudsen—A production genius brought in from the automobile industry to manage the shift to a war economy. His inability to play or even understand the political dimensions of his role guaranteed his fate as ineffective roadkill steamrollered by those who played the Washington game without mercy.

Simon Kuznets—A Nobel Prize–winning economist whose planning documents turned the Victory Program as envisioned by Stacy May into the American production miracle.

William Leahy—An American admiral and chairman of the Joint Chiefs of Staff. He placed his main office in the White House and became FDR's closest adviser in the final two years of the war. He did his job without flash, but with supreme competence.

Marguerite "Missy" LeHand—Roosevelt's private secretary and a functional chief of staff to FDR for much of his presidency. Many considered her the president's second wife.

John L. Lewis—He ruled labor with an iron fist, and although he was fully committed to the war effort, he saw no reason that labor could not make major permanent wage gains as the nation transitioned to a war economy. He was a perpetual thorn in Roosevelt's side, and each nursed a strong antipathy for the other.

Charles Lindbergh—Using the residual fame from his celebrated flight, Lindbergh became the public face of the antiwar and neutrality movement. FDR sent Harold Ickes out to stalk his every move in the prewar years, using Lindbergh's personal friendship with Hermann Goering and other Nazi high officials to good effect. After Pearl Harbor, he became an active supporter of the war effort and did great service for the nation in the Pacific.

Breckinridge Long—A State Department official who, through lies and deceit, did more than any other American to keep European Jews out of the country, and thereby sentenced them to near extinction by the Nazi extermination apparatus.

Douglas MacArthur—Commanding general in the Philippines and later supreme commander, South West Pacific Area. In 1932 Roosevelt had declared him the most dangerous man in the country, but in 1944 he had little trouble crushing a political insurrection aiming to make MacArthur president.

George C. Marshall—U.S. Army chief of staff and the "architect of victory." If any single man can be credited with directing the war effort by force of personality, it was Marshall. His single-minded focus on victory in the shortest possible time drove battlefield commanders to achieve the seemingly impossible.

Stacy May—An unassuming statistician on loan to the government from the Rockefeller Foundation. At the start of the war he built the Consolidated Balance Sheet. This detailed inventory of U.S. production, as well as an analysis of future potential, became the foundation of the Victory Program.

John McCloy—During the war he was one of Stimson's deputies in the War Department. After the war he would become a pillar of the policy-making establishment and one of the "wise men." He would spend much of his time defending his wartime decisions to intern Japanese Americans and his refusal to bomb Auschwitz.

Paul McNutt—The Adonis of American politics, he took pride in his spectacular physique, and he was a reasonably competent manpower administrator, despite the nearly continuous war waged against him by the Army.

Vyacheslav Mikhailovich Molotov—"Old Iron Pants" was one of Stalin's most trusted confidants. Through most of the war he was minister of foreign affairs and the public face of the Soviet Union in Western capitals, despite his reputation back home as a "small-minded intriguer."

Jean Monnet—After the war he would be the driving force behind the creation of the European Union. But at the start of World War II he was the indefatigable force that secured American industrial might for France and Great Britain. To keep things moving at a brisk pace he would often write and send memos from Roosevelt to Churchill, and then write and send Churchill's reply back to Roosevelt.

Henry Morgenthau, Jr.—He was secretary of the treasury, one of FDR's Hyde Park neighbors, an early hater of Hitler and the Nazis and an early supporter for doing whatever was necessary to prepare America for war. He was a man of great passion and huge dedication, but of only mediocre ability. He was manipulated throughout the war by his second in command, and communist spy, Harry Dexter White.

Robert R. Nathan—The tough-as-nails political brawler who pushed the Victory Program, as envisioned and designed by Stacy May and Simon Kuznets, past a resistant U.S. military.

Donald Nelson—The czar of all war production through the first years of the war, a job for which he was totally unsuited. He was decisive and dogmatic in minor matters where flexibility was required, but weak and plagued with indecision on major points. The military hated him and continually schemed to destroy him. He may have been a poor administrator, but he had an instinct for political brawling when his survival was at stake and was a prime example of the truism that "good people don't survive; survivors survive."

Robert P. Patterson, Sr.—Undersecretary of war and a man who went to bed every night worrying that some civilian somewhere in the country was being coddled at the expense of the war effort. His single-minded ambition was to increase war production, and he was tough enough to force his will on most, which he did with reckless abandon.

Eleanor Roosevelt—First lady and Roosevelt's connection to the feelings and pulse of the American people.

Franklin Delano Roosevelt—President of the United States.

Samuel Rosenman—A judge, a Roosevelt confidant, a presidential speechwriter (he coined the term "New Deal"), a high-level fixer, and the man FDR often sent when there was bad news to deliver. Taking a meeting with Rosenman rarely ended in the other party having a good day.

Harold D. Smith—As director of the budget he directed the accountants who looked into every facet of the war to make sure the American people were getting their money's worth. His inspectors were so feared that they became known as Roosevelt's Gestapo.

Brehon Somervell—The Army general responsible for running the Army Service Forces, which ran the logistics for the land and air war in both the Pacific and Atlantic theaters. He was a tough man in a job that required toughness, but his obstinacy almost single-handedly wrecked the nation's nascent mobilization for war.

Joseph Stalin—Premier of the Soviet Union. Despite his prominent role in Hitler's defeat, it is difficult to state with any certainty which man was worse or had a higher body count.

Harold Stark—At the start of the war he was the chief of naval operations. He was well liked and competent, but the blame for Pearl Harbor required a sacrificial lamb, and Stark was chosen.

Edward Stettinius, Jr.—Smart, wealthy, and ambitious, although he was not tough enough to take a leading role in anything, he was an able assistant to the great men who directed the war effort. Hopkins gave him the powerful position of running the Lend-Lease program because he never considered him a political threat.

Henry L. Stimson—As secretary of war his unique partnership with General Marshall proved a winning combination. Throughout the war he was the steady hand on the tiller, and a voice for moral concerns in an increasingly brutal conflict.

Harry Truman—A U.S. senator and head of the Truman Committee, which had oversight of all war-related spending and saved the nation many billions that would otherwise have been wasted. He was as shocked as anyone when FDR chose him as his 1944 running mate.

Henry Wallace—A committed New Dealer and Roosevelt's vice president in his third term. He believed in mysticism and in giving away money, and was famous for his new age meanderings at important meetings. When he tried to build an independent power base and then lied to Roosevelt about his intrigues, FDR crushed him.

Edwin "Pa" Watson—An Army major general and a close personal friend of the president. Until his death in 1944 he was Roosevelt's gatekeeper, where he proved remarkably adept at keeping people FDR wished to avoid away from the president without antagonizing them. Quick with a quip or a story, he was liked by everyone except General Hap Arnold, who despised him.

Sumner Welles—As undersecretary of state he was a Roosevelt confidant and the president's go-to person in the State Department. His close relationship with FDR bred powerful enemies determined to bring him down.

Wendell Willkie—Republican Party candidate for president in 1940. His stance on the war was contrary to most of his party's establishment but gave Roosevelt much-needed political cover to prepare the nation for war.

Charles Edward "Charlie" Wilson—A co-chairman of the War Production Board (WPB), he was responsible for fixing the scheduling problems that were holding up the production miracle. He worked hard, was diligent and capable, but was petty and insecure. His ruthless determination to crush his opponents served him well in the Washington war.

PREFACE

WHILE MILLIONS OF AMERICAN SOLDIERS, SAILORS, AND MARINES fought savage battles around the globe, another war raged in Washington, D.C. This war was not waged with guns and bombs, nor were there broken bodies and ruined cities in its wake. Nevertheless, the battles of the Washington war were fought with tremendous intensity and influenced the war's course as critically as those fought on any military battlefield. It was a war conducted on many fronts: political, industrial, diplomatic, and military, and it engaged all of official Washington. The contestants agreed on two things: they wanted what was best for the country, and they wanted to win the war as quickly as possible. Unfortunately, that is where consensus ended, as no two parties agreed on how best to accomplish either goal.

While some of the participants in these struggles remain household names, many of the most consequential players are all but forgotten, despite their having had as profound an impact on World War II as Eisenhower, Patton, Nimitz, or MacArthur. Writing this story has led me down many pathways familiar to historians, and a few that had not been previously traversed. During my research, I unearthed many surprises, even in areas I thought I knew well. Focusing closely on the perspective of those making the decisions in Washington, I was forced to re-examine every historical strand in its relation to every other element of what it takes to ready a great nation for war and to then prosecute such a monumental endeavor. *The Washington War* is the story of how a nation whose military in 1940 was on a par with Bulgaria's, and which lost much of its Pacific fleet at the end of 1941, was, in only thirty months, able to fling huge armies onto the European continent, and shortly thereafter shatter Japanese naval power in the Pacific. Ideally, readers will never again consider D-Day without thinking about what a near-run thing it was—and I am not talking about the ferocious struggle to gain a beachhead on June 6, 1944, as fraught with peril as that day was. Rather, this book presents a behind-the-scenes look at the remarkable story of what it took to make the invasion—and other achievements like it—possible.

Between the start of the war and the beginning of the great Allied offensives of 1944 there were many occasions where the misapplication of limited resources or the wrong strategic decisions could have derailed or long delayed our fleets and armies on the road to victory. That many of these mischances were avoided and the tide of war was reversed in such a remarkably short time was not an accident. Rather, it was the result of many months of brutal internecine warfare, as bureaucrats, military officers, business leaders, and politicians converged on Washington to fight for their own interests to the exclusion of all others. In the great majority of such cases self-interest did not translate to self-promotion, nor did it betray any failure to fully support the war effort. Instead it reflected what happens when serious men (they were all men at this period of history) who were used to getting their way were given big tasks to accomplish. Typically, they adopted a take-no-prisoners attitude and attempted to steamroller whoever was in their way, not for their personal aggrandizement, but because that was what the job required. Often, this involved run-ins with other serious men who were just as determined to accomplish their own assigned tasks. In an environment where resources were always short and demands high, strife was unavoidable.

My assumption when I began this book was that such fights hampered the war effort. But the more I delved into the clashes that made up the Washington war, the clearer it became that these titanic rows almost always led to better outcomes than would have prevailed had there been a single man or apparatus directing events. These pitched bureaucratic battles, so fraught at the time, allowed every party to air its side of the argument, which usually led to grudging compromises. No one came away happy and results were rarely optimal, but the big jobs were accomplished, and for the most part resources were used as efficiently as possible.

The same was true of the great strategic debates, the resolution of which would dictate the course of the war. No general or admiral ever got everything he wanted, but the overall direction and conduct of the war was good enough to win on two fronts against powerful and determined enemies. Moreover, these victories were achieved without making the catastrophic mistakes that often happen in the absence of such debates. For instance, how might the course of the war have changed if Hitler had let the German general staff debate the pros and cons of declaring war on the United States, at a time when Britain remained undefeated and the Wehrmacht was stalled in front of Moscow? The battles of the Washington war were never pleasant, they were always messy, and bad blood often persisted for a lifetime, but in the end they were a precondition of victory.

Given the large and dynamic cast of characters who would play key roles at critical junctures throughout the war years, I briefly entertained the idea that it might be possible to avoid featuring Franklin Delano Roosevelt as the dominant central figure around whom everything and everyone revolved. But of course the president was, by his own calculated design and political genius, the center of the Washington universe, a master manipulator who generated results via conflict and always resisted delegating ultimate authority. Over the course of his first two terms, he established an administrative apparatus and style that horrified efficiency experts. Prewar and wartime Washington was a bureaucratic nightmare in which identical tasks were often assigned to different subordinates and organizations, making turf squabbles unavoidable and guaranteeing that all such disputes eventually reached FDR's desk. Nothing important could be decided without the president's knowledge and approval.

This book aims to capture the most consequential of the Washington battles and a good number of the lesser ones, and it does not linger on events around which there was broad general consensus, such as the Bretton Woods and Dumbarton Oaks conferences, or on matters conducted outside the purview of the doyens of Washington, such as the Manhattan Project. My hope is that by drawing together in one fresh, comprehensive narrative the political, diplomatic, military, and economic elements of

World War II and revealing in unprecedented depth the fiery clashes and monumental bureaucratic strife that underpinned every turn of these great events, *The Washington War* might provide a new and deeper understanding of how the issues that sealed the fate of millions were resolved, often by all-too-fallible men working under the most severe stress imaginable, ultimately to the greater good of the country and of the world.

PART ONE

PREPARING

THE BATTLEFIELD

No man can tame a tiger into a kitten by stroking it. There can be no appeasement with ruthlessness. There can be no reasoning with an incendiary bomb. We know now that a nation can have peace with the Nazis only at the price of total surrender.

President Franklin Roosevelt, fireside chat, December 29, 1940

1

INCHING TOWARD WAR

I N LATE SEPTEMBER 1938, THE WORLD STOOD ON THE PRECIPICE OF war. Japanese armies were on the march in China, and a revanchist Germany had set itself on a path aimed at overthrowing the World War I peace settlement, if need be by force of arms, and was engaged in a game of diplomatic brinkmanship with Britain and France over the fate of Czechoslovakia. When, at the last moment, Britain and France infamously blinked and handed the Sudetenland over to the Third Reich in exchange for Hitler's promise of European peace, an ebullient Neville Chamberlain, British prime minister, returned from the Munich Conference to the cheers of a rapturous public. It was left to Winston Churchill to throw water on the celebration, commenting, "The government had a choice between shame and war. It chose shame; it will get war."

On the other side of the Atlantic, President Franklin Roosevelt, like Churchill, was acutely aware that another European conflict was looming, and that America needed to start preparing for war. This was a complete reversal from the early days of Roosevelt's presidency when he planned draconian reductions to the Army's budget. The distraught Army chief of staff at the time, Douglas MacArthur, had bitterly opposed the cuts, later recounting that he had shouted at the president that "when we lost the next war, and an American boy, lying in the mud with an enemy bayonet through his belly and an enemy foot on his dying throat, spat out his last curse, I wanted the name not to be MacArthur, but Roosevelt." A livid Roosevelt icily replied: "You must not talk that way to the President." The exchange likely saved the Army from complete ruin, but the budget axe could not be avoided entirely during the Great Depression, when FDR had more pressing domestic uses for those funds.

Years of neglect had left the U.S. Army little more than an underfunded constabulary force. As the Munich Conference drew to a conclusion, Roosevelt knew it was past time to rehabilitate American military power; he was already wondering if it was too late. His instincts, as always, were to move rapidly upon his objective and seize the commanding ground before his opponents could mobilize to beat him. But he was leading a nation still mired in the Great Depression and a people who passionately believed that Europe's problems were not their concern. Roosevelt, always acutely attuned to the voter's psyche, understood that if he was going to move America toward war it needed to be done gradually and with a great deal of subterfuge. Later he would explain to his son James why he had lied to the American people about the likelihood of America entering the war: "I could not come out and say a war was coming, because the people would have panicked and turned from me. I had to educate the people to the inevitable, gradually, step-by-step, laying the groundwork for the programs which would allow us to prepare for the war that was drawing us into it."

Although most Americans fervently believed that Great Britain had led them into the First World War through trickery and propaganda, the British did not stand alone in the docket. Americans also held industrialists and bankers, whom they perceived as having reinforced British manipulations, just as guilty. In September 1934, only a few months after MacArthur's run-in with the president, North Dakota senator Gerald Nye stood before the Senate to condemn the banking and munitions industries as "merchants of death" motivated only by greed, who had pressured President Woodrow Wilson into entering the Great War. A steady diet of such innuendo and lies sparked a surge of isolationism and overwhelming public support for a series of neutrality laws, the first passed in 1935, that made it illegal for the United States to trade with "any" warring power, ostensibly to keep America from being dragged into the next European conflict.

But there were a few men, close to the president, who saw the threat posed by Hitler as clearly as Roosevelt did. Over time, this group would grow and coalesce into an internal government pressure group—tagged by the press as the "all-outers"—who increasingly prodded and coaxed Roosevelt to do more to help the Allied cause and to prepare the nation for war. One of the first of this group, Secretary of State Cordell Hull, managed to convince the president to risk getting ahead of public opinion and take a tentative first step toward breaking free of the Neutrality Acts by making a speech on the need for international cooperation. Moreover, he persuaded FDR to make the speech in a large city firmly entrenched in isolationism: Chicago. A year before the Munich Conference, on October 5, 1937, Roosevelt told a large crowd, "The present reign of terror and international lawlessness . . . has reached a stage where the very foundations of civilization are seriously threatened." He then asked for the peaceful nations of the world to unite to "quarantine" the aggressors.

The reaction to what was quickly branded Roosevelt's "Quarantine Speech" had been immediate and violent. Every major pacifist organization—and in 1937 there were already a great number of them—attacked what they all perceived as a first step toward war. Leading the outcry were the vehemently anti-Roosevelt Hearst and McCormick newspaper chains. But before the week was out, even the Veterans of Foreign Wars had launched a petition drive with the goal of collecting twenty-five million signatures to "Keep America Out of War." Stunned by the speed and virulence of the public reaction, Roosevelt pulled back from his comments. In a press conference a couple of days later he dodged the issue by stating that he was not advocating any set program or policy. Rather he was trying to set an attitude.

Sumner Welles, the number two man in the State Department and a close Roosevelt intimate, described the president as "dismayed by the widespread violence of the attacks." Welles's impression likely did not reflect Roosevelt's deeper thoughts. Such attacks rarely dimmed Roosevelt's essential optimism for long, as was apparent a few days later when he told Secretary of the Interior Harold Ickes—who also functioned as his political attack dog—"I frankly thought there would be more criticism and I verily believe that . . . we can slowly but surely make people believe that war is a greater danger to us if we close all of our doors and windows." Nor did he seem much concerned with the continuing attacks of the isolationist press, writing to Welles, "Frankly I do not believe any of these newspapers carry any particular weight as expressions of public opinion."

Roosevelt was a master of an attack-and-retreat style of politics, adept at first offering a new initiative, gauging the resistance, then temporarily withdrawing to formulate the best way forward. Although he clearly pulled back from taking any substantive action after the speech, this was part of a pattern Roosevelt would repeat many times over the next two years. After each such retreat, he would sit patiently, waiting for another opportunity—always sure one would come—to make his next provocative statement. Even when polls demonstrated clear majorities supporting his position, Roosevelt continued to move cautiously, waiting weeks or months before once again pushing his agenda forward. As war edged closer these tactics drove the growing number of "all-outers" in his government to distraction, but Roosevelt recognized that public support was much wider than it was deep. He was clearly playing a long game, while he waited for America to conclude what he already knew: war was coming.

President Franklin D. Roosevelt.

In the final analysis, Roosevelt's "Quarantine Speech" was a landmark event that marked the moment when the president irrevocably committed himself to stand against Hitler and the Axis powers. He was advancing by inches, but his determined advance never ceased.

What the presidential advisers urging more dramatic action failed to grasp, but Roosevelt knew only too well, was how much his political power had ebbed since his reelection. The Roosevelt of 1932, or even 1936, would certainly have moved faster and dared more. But by 1938, FDR had incurred grievous political damage, much of it self-inflicted. Convinced by his landslide victory in 1936 that he was politically invincible and possessed a public mandate to do as he wished, Roosevelt, against the advice of his closest advisers, embarked on two disastrous initiatives: packing the Supreme Court and purging the Democratic Party of those whose support was not sufficiently enthusiastic.

Pushing New Deal legislation through a compliant Congress had been easy. Much harder was keeping the Supreme Court—a last bastion of conservatism—from neutering those laws once passed. For three years, a furious Roosevelt fumed as the court struck down one after another of his New Deal initiatives. Unable to push aging justices into retirement, Roosevelt determined to dilute their power by increasing the number of justices.

In a city where leaks were the currency of the realm, Roosevelt kept his strategy a secret from all but a few advisers until he was ready to pounce. Finally, in February 1937, he assembled key members of his cabinet and the Democratic congressional leadership to outline his proposed legislation to "reform" the judiciary by authorizing him to appoint not only additional Supreme Court justices but also additional judges to the lower federal courts. In the first of many tactical mistakes, he neglected to invite the one senator who had been his workhorse throughout his first term: Senator James F. Byrnes. On the ride back to Capitol Hill, congressional leaders sat in stunned silence, until the chairman of the House Judiciary Committee, Democrat Hatton W. Sumners—up to then a staunch New Dealer and presidential supporter—announced, "Boys, here is where I cash in my chips."

From the start, the bill was in serious trouble. Still, Roosevelt persisted, even refusing to compromise when Vice President John Nance Garner pleaded with him to find a middle way so as to avoid a highly public defeat. Rebuffed and disgusted, Garner, who coined the phrase that the vice presidency "was not worth a bucket of warm spit," departed for Texas, where he remained for the duration of the Senate debate.

Roosevelt then made an irreparable political mistake. Having collapsed under the strain of vehemently supporting a bill he did not believe in, Majority Leader Joseph "Scrappy Joe" Robinson was found dead by his maid.

Robinson, despite his nickname, was one of the most admired and liked men in the Senate. But Roosevelt, holding him personally accountable for failing to convince his colleagues to vote for the bill, refused to attend the funeral. Many senators never forgave Roosevelt's petty and deliberate slight of a man who had literally died in harness fighting for the president's scheme. Afterward, financier Bernard Baruch, a charter New Dealer and trusted adviser, called the White House and begged FDR to give up the fight and not to "kill any more senators."

John Nance Garner, 32nd vice president of the United States.

A few days later the court bill was defeated by a vote of 70 to 2. Roosevelt, disastrously, came away from his humiliating loss with the wrong lesson. Instead of examining his own mistakes, something he may have been congenitally unable to do, he blamed the loss on an alliance of conservative southern Democrats and Republicans. There was not much he could do to punish the Republicans, but the Democrats were another matter. He proceeded to target those wayward Democrats who had defied him, and whom he thought vulnerable to primary challenges in the 1938 elections. When rumors of his plans to get rid of members of his own party

Jimmy Byrnes,
senator from South Carolina.

leaked, previously loyal lieutenants—Bernard Baruch, Vice President Garner, and Senator Byrnes—were propelled into opposition. By the time
Roosevelt publicly announced his intentions during a June fireside speech,
the counter forces, backed by Baruch's millions, were united behind a plan
to curtail the vendetta.

Roosevelt's so-called "great purge of 1938" was an unmitigated disaster,
which undermined the rest of his presidency. In the end, all he had to show
for the tremendous effort he had expended was the primary defeat of a
single New York congressman—and another public failure that signaled to
many that Roosevelt was a spent political force. Rather than devoting his
energies to uniting the country behind a preparedness platform, the president had squandered years of stored-up political capital on destructive
power plays. Roosevelt eventually came to his senses and admitted defeat,
telling Senator Byrnes, "We'll forget about it." But congressional barons,
with their famously elephantine memories, nursed their grudges.

Roosevelt's troubles, unfortunately, did not end on Capitol Hill. After an
economic upturn that convinced many that the Great Depression was ending, hard times had returned with a vengeance in mid-1937. Even as Roosevelt was consumed by political turmoil, unemployment skyrocketed
from 14.3 percent to 19 percent in 1938, while manufacturing fell 34

percent—back to 1934 levels. Although the reasons for the downturn were complex, everyone in Washington was certain that it was the natural result of Roosevelt's insistence, after years of deficits, on cutting relief spending to balance the 1938 budget, among other contractionary adjustments in fiscal policy. The cuts were too large and too sudden for the fragile civilian sector to adjust, and without the government stimulus the nascent recovery was wrenched into reverse. For too long Roosevelt did nothing, insisting that the economy was fundamentally sound and would soon right itself. But in the spring of 1938, Congress, despairing of presidential action, approved $3.5 billion in new spending, allowing the economy to slowly regain momentum.

So, as the world edged toward war we find Roosevelt, the once unstoppable political dynamo, chastened and nursing his wounds. According to Harold Ickes, FDR was "punch drunk from the punishment" and "distinctly more nervous than he had formerly been." Still, the old warrior was a long way from done. Two years of political bruising was humiliating, but it was also instructive. Shrewdly, he pulled back and recalibrated his approach. He became less impulsive, more careful and methodical. Before advancing an initiative, he first secured strong popular backing, and ensured that powerful Capitol Hill supporters were firmly aboard. Roosevelt also became far readier to take advice and to allow others to take the lead in muscling bills through Congress. He remained ready to push forward on bold proposals, and to continue to shape public opinion, but only with an abundance of caution and at a glacial pace.

2

WARS ARE WON IN THE DETAILS

B ATTLES ARE WON ON THE FIGHTING FRONTS, BUT WARS ARE WON in conference rooms. Overseeing the minutiae of war involves a host of routine tasks, requiring a huge and well-managed organization just to process the paperwork and monitor the moving pieces. Such mundane activities pale amid the grand panorama of global war, and are little noted by historians. Still, if one wants to win a global war one needs an organization capable of efficiently handling administrative burdens that would overwhelm even the most active intellect. On the eve of World War II this was something Roosevelt lacked.

Before leading the nation into war, FDR wanted the executive branch slimmed down, reorganized, and placed more firmly under his control. It had long been clear that the powers and responsibilities of the office of the president had grown far beyond the antiquated administrative structure that supported it. Roosevelt had combatted this deficiency in several ways, the most ambitious of which was his famous "brain trust" of advisers who followed him to Washington in his first term. He placed these men in the White House, as well as in assorted government offices, where he hoped they would bring the government's creaky administrative apparatus to heel. The "brain-trusters" were a spectacular failure, spending most of Roosevelt's first four years getting in one another's way and creating bad will in the agencies in which they were planted. Even Roosevelt, who hated to admit error, soon recognized that his unpopular coterie was sowing seeds of resentment and setting him up for political disaster.

By the time FDR's second term got under way, most of the brain trust was gone, leaving behind an unbowed administrative structure incapable of moving with the speed and efficiency Roosevelt demanded. In a final attempt to get control of the government he ostensibly led, FDR asked Professor Louis Brownlow to form a presidential reorganization committee to advise on the restructuring of the civil service, as well as the president's executive office. When the committee reported its findings, Roosevelt sent them, in toto, to Congress and asked that they be turned into law. Unfortunately, while Congress accepted the report's bottom line—"the President needs help"—there were few legislators disposed to give it to him.

Even had there been a plurality for reform in Congress, Brownlow's proposal to reorganize the civil service and other managerial agencies and place them under the control of the executive branch—thereby gutting their power—was a foolish overreach. Branding Brownlow's proposal as the "Dictator Bill," the anti-Roosevelt press attacked with all the vehemence it could muster. On the radio, the notorious anti-Semitic rabble-rouser Father Charles Coughlin exhorted his millions of listeners to bombard Congress with letters and telegrams opposing the bill; Congress received seventy-five thousand such missives in a single day. Desperate to get the bill passed, Roosevelt finally called on his top political fixer, Senator James F. "Jimmy" Byrnes, to shepherd it through. But as the administration was already waging other political battles with Congress, Byrnes asked Roosevelt to put the bill on hold until after the summer adjournment, sage advice that Roosevelt quickly accepted.

When Congress reconvened Byrnes presented a slimmed-down bill aimed squarely at fixing only the government's executive agencies. Recognizing threats to their influence and turf, various agency and department heads besieged Byrnes's office, forcing him to involve himself in their internecine battles as he simultaneously navigated the congressional gauntlet. The always combative Harold Ickes, secretary of the interior, and Secretary of Agriculture Henry Wallace were cases in point: when they got into a heated row over how their fiefdoms should be divided under the new legislation, Wallace stormed in to see Byrnes, an incendiary letter from Ickes in hand, threatening to take his dispute with Ickes public if Byrnes didn't curb Ickes's depredations immediately. Byrnes, after reading the letter—in which Ickes pressed for the Forestry Service to be removed from Wallace's Agriculture Department and placed under his Interior domain—

advised Wallace to either pretend not to have seen it or go punch Ickes in the face. He finished by counseling Wallace against any public display, as Wallace was certainly no match for Ickes in a name-calling contest—nor was anyone else. When Byrnes informed FDR that Ickes had threatened to resign if *his* powers were curtailed, Roosevelt laughed and confided that he already had three of Ickes's resignation letters in a drawer. After several months of arm-twisting Byrnes prevailed, and the bill passed both houses on April 3, 1939.

The bill's passage marked the birth of the modern institutional presidency, as it established for the first time the infrastructure for the presidential management and oversight of the government's burgeoning executive departments—and handed Roosevelt a powerful tool for controlling the federal response to the growing world crisis. Its vital mechanism was a well-staffed Executive Office of the President, which Roosevelt would employ to manage the war. The law also gave the president authority, in the event of a national emergency, to create an emergency management office, which Roosevelt did immediately after Germany's invasion of France in May 1940. Within this office he housed the plethora of wartime agencies he was soon creating.

The law also allowed Roosevelt to make a critical move that was little noted at the time: placing the Bureau of the Budget, run by Harold D. Smith, in the Executive Office of the President. Smith, although modest and self-effacing, was tenacious in his quest to eliminate wasteful spending. During the war, Smith's budget team grew from fifty individuals to more than five hundred, providing Roosevelt with the "shock troops" necessary to control a sprawling bureaucracy. Smith and his teams of bookkeepers fought a different kind of war; authorized to visit any department, agency, mission, or theater of war, at any time, they kept Roosevelt informed as to how much was being spent, who was spending it, and on what. For Roosevelt, the Bureau of the Budget acted as a private intelligence service. Those who came under its scrutiny referred to it as "Roosevelt's Gestapo."

3

ROOSEVELT FINDS

A WAR CONSIGLIERE

WITH HIS ADMINISTRATIVE APPARATUS IN PLACE, ROOSEVELT was better positioned to do as the "all-outers" advising him wanted and lead the nation toward rearmament and, if necessary, war. Still, his watchword remained caution. A slow advance did not, however, preclude his taking measured risks. Even before the Munich crisis, Roosevelt chanced a further weakening of his political position by covertly but quite deliberately preparing the nation for war, while also maneuvering closer to the Allied camp. And as he did so, those core advisers who would see him, and the country, through that coming war began to emerge from the ever-present throng around him.

After listening to a particularly vile speech Hitler gave at Nuremberg, in mid-September 1938 Roosevelt tapped the man who would become his closest wartime confidant for an initial foray into the national security arena. Already preoccupied with airpower, he dispatched Harry Hopkins on a tour of the western aircraft plants, to assess how fast and how effectively they could increase capacity in the event of war. This was the first time Roosevelt had used Hopkins in an investigatory role, a sensitive undertaking typically reserved for those whom he most trusted, such as his wife, Eleanor. The inaugural assignment in Roosevelt's tutelage of his new protégé in the intricacies of national and foreign affairs would lead to a significant new brief for the man whose drive and energy had powered much of the New Deal.

Why was Hopkins chosen for this role? According to Hopkins himself, Roosevelt, toward the end of 1938, was certain of three things: war would erupt in Europe, the United States would eventually enter that war, and finally, that airplanes would be the instrument of victory. FDR, on some level, must also have sensed that to meet the challenges ahead he would need a trusted confidant. Hopkins had already demonstrated a capacity to get big jobs done, and the aircraft assignment was likely a trial run by the president to test his suitability for a far more sensitive and consequential role. While Hopkins's path from social worker to wartime adviser may, on the face of it, have seemed unlikely, his preternatural ability to divine Roosevelt's intent and give him what he desired made him a perfect intermediary.

Harry L. Hopkins, secretary of commerce.

Hopkins was born on August 17, 1890, in Sioux City, Iowa, the fourth of five children. His father, after a series of dead-end endeavors, finally settled in Grinnell, Iowa, as a harness maker. Hopkins's mother, a deeply religious woman, imparted her concern for the welfare of the less fortunate upon her son. After graduating from Grinnell College in 1912, Hopkins moved to New York City, taking a job in a settlement house in the slums of New York's Lower East Side. From there he progressed through a succession of social welfare jobs, developing a reputation as a man who got things done, but never on the cheap. Along the way, he married Ethel Gross, a Hungarian immigrant, and had three sons. By 1930, they had drifted apart. She sued for divorce and was awarded half of his salary. Hopkins rarely paid her, and most of Hopkins's friends believed he treated her rather shabbily.

His big break came at the start of the Great Depression, when, in 1931, New York's Governor Roosevelt established a precursor to his later New Deal agencies—the Temporary Emergency Relief Administration— funded with $20 million. Hopkins was the number two man for the first year, running the agency's day-to-day operations, where his speed of action made a favorable impression on the similarly aggressive governor. When Roosevelt once mentioned in passing that it would be nice to take young men out of the slums and put them to work maintaining the state's forests, Hopkins acted. Future secretary of the treasury Henry Morgenthau, a Dutchess County neighbor and close friend of Roosevelt, chose the forests and set up the support infrastructure, while Hopkins supplied the workers and the money. Within weeks Hopkins had ten thousand men and boys working in New York's forests. It was Hopkins's first demonstration of his talent for quick and effective action, an ability to handle big projects, and, most crucially, a knack for reading what Roosevelt wanted and then giving it to him. For Roosevelt, there was no better quality in a person than this last.

During this early period, Hopkins also met and learned to work with those closest to Roosevelt, particularly Eleanor. He once explained to his fellow New Dealer Harold Ickes the key to successfully operating within the president's circle: "Cultivate the President's family—Mrs. Roosevelt, the President's mother . . . and Missy LeHand [Roosevelt's private secretary]. You will not have to pay attention to anyone else." Such ingratiating tactics, however, would have done little to bind Hopkins to Roosevelt had he not also been brutally effective in achieving their mutual objectives. As one journalist wrote, Hopkins possessed "a mind like a razor, a tongue like a skinning knife, a temper like a Tartar and a sufficient vocabulary of parlor profanity . . . to make a mule skinner jealous."

* * *

When Roosevelt went to the White House, Hopkins followed. Placed in charge of the newly minted Federal Emergency Relief Administration, Hopkins busied himself spending the first $500 million he was allotted, and drawing yet closer to Roosevelt; joining him for trips on the presidential yacht and for sojourns to Roosevelt's home at Hyde Park, New York. Roosevelt not only appreciated Hopkins's work, but enjoyed his company. As one biographer noted, "He did not bore FDR, ever."

Roosevelt enjoyed Hopkins's quick wit, and like FDR's personal secretary, General Edwin "Pa" Watson, Hopkins had a seemingly inexhaustible supply of anecdotes and stories, drawn from the high life he enjoyed leading when he was healthy. He was often in the company of beautiful women, was at all the right parties, liked the track, and though he advocated for the poor, he hugely enjoyed palling around with the rich. As Roosevelt's confidant and lead speechwriter, Samuel Rosenman, noted, although he was a rabid New Dealer, and had grown up in very modest circumstances, he was a fellow who loved the fleshpots very much in private life. His close friends were all multimillionaires: Vincent Astor, Averell Harriman, Marshall Field, and a great many of the Long Island set. Roosevelt rarely concerned himself with the personal habits of his underlings, but he avidly took in Hopkins's recounting of his latest adventures. Hopkins was living the kind of life the polio-stricken Roosevelt often yearned for. It was a lifestyle that cost many times Hopkins's salary, and if not for the gracious generosity of his many rich friends picking up his tabs and, rumor had it, even quietly taking care of his gambling losses, Hopkins would have had far fewer stories with which to entertain Roosevelt.

When Hopkins later established the Works Progress Administration (WPA), he went from spending millions to billions. It was in this capacity that he began a long and public feud with Harold Ickes, who in addition to being secretary of the interior also ran Roosevelt's Public Works Administration (PWA). The two men shared an objective—ending the Great Depression—but differed as to methods. That did not necessarily mean there had to be a feud. That one arose and was sustained vehemently for over a decade had little to do with policy disagreements and much to do with the fact that each thoroughly despised the other. One historian claimed that their problems were personality driven: "Hopkins was given to confident self-righteousness, Ickes to paranoia." Moreover, they shared "irreconcilably low opinions of each other's skills as relief organizers." Though Hopkins could be tough and often unleashed a volcanic temper, he was generally genial, made friends easily, and was considered pleasant company by most people. Ickes, on the other hand, had a talent for rubbing nearly everyone he met the wrong way, and actually reveled in his reputation as a curmudgeon, although that term significantly underplayed the less charitable descriptions of a number of his contemporaries. He was famously described by Clare Boothe Luce as having the "mind of a commissar and the soul of a meat axe." *Time* magazine described him as:

> Honest, fearless, tough and shrewd—and loyal to his boss—Harold Ickes long ago earned his post as dog robber to the New Deal. But he expanded this job, as he does all the jobs he can lay his hands on. He is the Scout who goes ahead, trial balloon in hand, prowling the unexplored bushes of public opinion, whipping up sentiment pro or con whatever the President has decided the U.S. should be for or against. He is the Whipping Boy who takes the blame whenever anything goes wrong. He is the New Deal's Janitor, who cleans out the goboons and sweeps up the floor (usually using some victim as the broom). He captains the Purity Squad that keeps his colleagues honest. He is the Public Executioner, the Court Poisoner and the Bouncer. In short, if there is on the docket a hard, nasty, grinding job, Ickes gets the assignment.

Ickes believed the best way to revive the economy was through "prime the pump" infrastructure projects that would enhance growth for generations to come. He advocated huge initiatives requiring substantial expertise and tremendous lead time, such as the Grand Coulee Dam and the Triborough Bridge. All of "Honest Harold's" projects were expensive, but not a single dollar escaped his grasp until he was personally convinced it needed to be spent and there was no corruption involved. He was, in short, an able administrator, but his snail's pace did little to achieve Roosevelt's most urgent goal: putting Americans across the country back to work, quickly.

Harold Ickes,
secretary of the
interior.

Hopkins, in contrast, believed dollars were for spending. He pushed money out the door at astonishing speed, providing employment for millions. Economic historians still debate the economic wisdom of such policies, but the effect on the nation's morale is indisputable. For the first time in years, men who wanted to work, and had been raised to judge their worth by being able to provide for themselves and their families, had jobs. Economically shortsighted it might have been, but in the depths of the Depression it restored hope to those who had lost it. And Roosevelt, in addition to his genuine concern for those enduring hard times, also recognized that Hopkins's rapid-fire spending was good politics.

When Roosevelt began taking money from Ickes's PWA and giving it to Hopkins's WPA, the war was on, with the president often thrust into the role of referee. Ickes repeatedly threatened to resign—a trump card he played so often that Hopkins derisively nicknamed him "The Great Resigner"—a position from which Roosevelt reliably talked him down. Despite Hopkins's growing closeness to the president, and his undeniable effectiveness at putting paychecks in the hands of the unemployed, Ickes finally achieved what he thought was a decisive victory when he persuaded

Roosevelt to order that all projects over $25,000 would go to him, with anything under that threshold going to Hopkins's WPA. Hopkins simply broke big projects into dozens of $25,000 sub-projects, and kept the money flying out the door.

In an effort to instill harmony—or at least a truce—between the two men, Roosevelt took them on a fishing cruise with him aboard the cruiser USS *Houston*. The ship's paper, *The Blue Bonnet*, captured the results:

> The feud between Hopkins and Ickes was given a decent burial today. With flags at half-mast . . . the President officiated at the solemn cere-mony which we trust will take these two babies off the front page for all time . . .
>
> Hopkins expressed regret at the unkind things Ickes had said about him and Ickes on his part promised to make it stronger—only more so.
>
> The President gave them both a hearty slap on the back—pushing them both into the sea. "Full steam ahead," the President ordered.

Harry Hopkins and Harold Ickes.

* * *

Notwithstanding such presidential flourishes, over the next decade Ickes and Hopkins continued to find much to fight about. In elevating Hopkins to an increasingly prominent national security portfolio, which brought him even closer to Roosevelt, the president enraged Ickes, who had always imagined he would fill the roles Hopkins was moving into and was dismayed to often find himself far from the circle of power. The explosive antagonism of these two pillars of the Roosevelt regime, already enemies, would shape or skew Washington dynamics throughout the war.

As both men were loyal to him personally, and crucial to achieving his goals, Roosevelt resolved to live with their quarrels. Significantly, there was one fundamental point on which Hopkins and Ickes saw eye to eye: both men recognized early on the threat Hitler posed, and moved into the "all-outer" camp. They would be among the few New Dealers who remained at Roosevelt's side until his death in 1945.

4

EARLY MANEUVERS

THROUGHOUT 1938 ROOSEVELT MAINTAINED HIS GLACIAL PACE on international and military issues, and he clothed the limited moves he made in secrecy. The all-outers were multiplying, but most of them remained on the fringes of real power. Within his own cabinet, only Harold Ickes and Treasury Secretary Henry Morgenthau recognized the extent of the European crisis and were reconciled to the idea of the United States being dragged into a general war. Opposing the all-outers was Secretary of War Harry Woodring, a committed isolationist, who saw no reason to waste money on the military he headed. Secretary of the Navy Charles Edison was a bit more hawkish, but he was weak, ineffectual, and incapable of advancing Roosevelt's agenda. At State, Cordell Hull remained a committed anti-fascist, but resisted any initiatives he thought would provoke the Axis powers. Hull firmly believed war could only be avoided if the Axis powers were cajoled toward a policy of self-restraint, to which they surely would not accede if they constantly perceived new threats. Roosevelt reacted to such cabinet obstructionism by moving ever greater amounts of national defense work from the agencies and departments normally responsible for such activities to Morgenthau's Treasury.

As he began to actively assess the nation's military capacity, by way of Hopkins's trip and other means, Roosevelt was also looking for concrete ways to help the Allies. On October 13, 1938, he met with Ambassador William Bullitt, recently returned from Paris. Bullitt painted a bleak picture of the Allied situation and convinced Roosevelt that France's most pressing need was for first-line combat aircraft capable of standing up to

Harry Woodring, secretary of war.

overwhelming German numbers. Making liberal use of statistics he had received from American hero Charles Lindbergh, Bullitt horrified Roosevelt with the news that Germany possessed several times more combat aircraft than the combined Allied air forces.

Three days later, Roosevelt met with Bullitt and Hopkins, fresh from his tour of aircraft production facilities, at Hyde Park. He and Hopkins laid out a scheme whereby the Works Progress Administration, which Hopkins still headed, would "secretly" fund the construction of eight aircraft plants capable of building 15,000 aircraft a year, a full order of magnitude greater than the current annual production of approximately 1,500 aircraft.

As with other defense-related projects, Roosevelt housed the effort under Treasury's burgeoning auspices. Just four days after Hopkins's return from his fact-finding mission, Roosevelt informed Morgenthau that he was now responsible for expanding the production of military aircraft. The treasury secretary was elated. Rushing back to his office, he told his staff that he was "tickled pink that the President is thinking of making this country so strong that nobody can attack us." Morgenthau ordered his staff to get to work immediately on plans to make Roosevelt's proposals a reality. On November 12, 1938, Morgenthau trooped over to the White House to deliver his completed plan. Two days later Roosevelt summoned his military team—Assistant Secretary of War Louis Johnson, Army Chief of Staff General Malin Craig, Army Air Corps Chief General Hap Arnold, and Army Vice Chief of Staff General George C. Marshall—to discuss his current plan to purchase thousands of new aircraft. Waiting for them in the president's office were Morgenthau and Harry Hopkins.

The president began the meeting by declaring that the Army's current plans for expansion were inadequate. He also announced that he could not care less about a few extra outposts out west, or adding a few new divisions in some western states. In his mind, planes were the decisive element of modern war, and he wanted a lot of them. Following up on earlier meetings in which he had emphasized aircraft production, Roosevelt told the assembled audience that he wanted twenty thousand planes, but that Congress would likely cut such a request in half. Therefore, the Army should plan for ten thousand aircraft, most of which would be built by new plants funded by Hopkins's WPA. Roosevelt was in top rhetorical form, and to Marshall it appeared as if everyone present was primarily looking to please him, ignoring the imbalances such a concentration on aircraft would create. When the president finished talking, he polled the audience for comments, pleased to find that everyone agreed with him. That was until he came to Marshall: "I think I have made a good case for my program. Don't you think so, George?" Roosevelt pressed, smiling broadly.

In this, possibly their first official meeting, Marshall responded coldly, "I am sorry, Mr. President, but I don't agree with that at all." Startled, Roosevelt abruptly ended the conference, without asking Marshall to explain. Marshall later recalled that out in the anteroom, as they left, his fellow attendees bade him farewell, certain that his Washington tour had just come to an abrupt end.

Marshall, of course, did survive to fence repeatedly with the president for many more years, his longevity owed to several factors. First, and probably foremost, Roosevelt did not mind criticism based on professional knowledge and when he perceived no personal attack. Marshall later commented that Roosevelt was much like General Pershing, another man Marshall had often stood up to, who could accept criticism and appreciated

forthright honest opinions. As for Marshall, he had for the first time witnessed how Roosevelt seduced those around him to his point of view. At
that moment, he decided to make a point of not humoring the commander
in chief, a tactic he would repeatedly employ during the war, even taking
the extreme position of refusing to smile at the president's jokes. Later he
said that he never went to Hyde Park or Warm Springs for private talks, as
he had discovered that "informal conversations with the President would
get you into trouble." Roosevelt, with a master politician's feel for people,
seamlessly accommodated Marshall's taciturn demeanor. In fact, this
meeting was the last time Roosevelt ever referred to Marshall as George.
But Marshall also learned to read his man, advising a subordinate who was
preparing for a presidential visit not to press the president in order to make
a point or hand him lengthy paperwork. Marshall told him that "a little
sketch . . . is the most effective method, as he is quickly bored by papers, by
lengthy discussions, and anything short of a few pungent sentences of description. *You have to intrigue his interest, and then it knows no limit.*"

As World War II began and their relationship deepened, Marshall demonstrated two other traits that Roosevelt deeply appreciated. Unlike his
dealings with previous Army chief of staff General Douglas MacArthur,
Roosevelt never detected any political ambition in Marshall. Even more
valued, in the political circus that was Roosevelt's daily existence, Marshall
never fought his battles through leaks to the press. Instead, he gave Roosevelt his best military advice and then did his best to carry out the president's orders, although there were many times he did not agree with them.
It would, however, take some time for Roosevelt to fully appreciate Marshall's qualities. In the meantime, Marshall's survival rested upon Hopkins's influence.

On his tour of aircraft production facilities Hopkins had taken along
Colonel Arthur Wilson, his WPA liaison to the War Department. Wilson
had written Marshall that Hopkins thought the president was ready to use
a significant portion of the next relief appropriation to jump-start military
procurement . . . if he could be convinced of the necessity. To help convince him Wilson advised Marshall to meet with Hopkins as soon as possible. Marshall was slow to act on Wilson's advice, but soon after Christmas
1938, Hopkins, who became secretary of commerce on Christmas Eve,
took the initiative and asked for a meeting. For their first one-on-one
meeting Marshall went to Hopkins's office at the Commerce Building,

where he outlined the state of the Army and Army Air Forces in such stark terms that a shocked Hopkins begged him to go to Hyde Park and brief Roosevelt. Marshall, not yet Army chief of staff, demurred. Still, he had converted Hopkins to the Army's cause and gained a firm and important ally. From this point forward, Hopkins not only pushed Roosevelt toward paying more attention to Army requirements, he also never missed a chance to build up Marshall in Roosevelt's eyes. Later, Marshall credited Hopkins as the man who tipped the balance in Roosevelt's decision to appoint him as chief of staff.

But in late 1938, Marshall and air chief Hap Arnold were more concerned about Roosevelt's myopic focus on manufacturing tens of thousands of airplanes rather than creating a balanced force. Arguments that the Air Corps could not live on planes alone, but also needed bases, training schools, pilots, mechanics, countless tons of spare parts, and replacement personnel, fell on deaf ears. None of these concerns mattered to Roosevelt. As he saw it, the first step was to get Congress to pay for the planes. Once the planes were in the pipeline Congress would have little choice but to fund everything else, or risk the press discovering that they had just bought ten thousand expensive paperweights. More crucially, both Marshall and Arnold mistakenly believed that Roosevelt wanted these aircraft solely for the U.S. Army Air Corps. Nothing could have been further from the truth, as from the start Roosevelt intended to sell or give a significant portion of these new aircraft to France and England. In addition to his alarming meeting with Ambassador Bullitt, which buttressed his own concerns about airpower, he had been hugely impressed on meeting the influential French diplomat Jean Monnet, who during the First World War had run inter-allied transport and food distribution and would later become the driving force behind what is now the European Union. He was fifty years old, balding, bespectacled, and bookish looking. He was also precise, forceful, and passionate about the military needs of the Allies, and the president had promised to use his full executive powers to expedite aircraft deliveries to France.

This was something that the combative air chief, Hap Arnold, who sorely felt the loss of every plane, would have gone to mattresses over—had he known of the plan.

* * *

Arnold, having learned to fly from the Wright Brothers in an eleven-day training course, was a true pioneer of flight. He made his first solo flight on May 13, 1911, and received pilot certificate no. 29 and military aviator certificate no. 2. It was a time when many considered boarding an aircraft as near suicidal. Of the first twenty-four qualified pilots, eleven were killed before they completed training and seven of the remainder died in later crashes. Given the two-out-of-three mortality rate Arnold counted himself lucky to have survived.

Shaken by the deaths of two close friends and a near-fatal crash of his own, from November 1912 he avoided flying for almost four years, instead taking an infantry assignment in the Philippines, where he and his wife were assigned a house next door to Lieutenant George Marshall. Soon after Arnold's return to the United States, Captain William "Billy" Mitchell called with an offer Arnold could not refuse: volunteer to return to aviation as a captain, or be ordered to return as a lieutenant. By mid-December 1916, with the war raging in Europe, Arnold had conquered his fears and was back on flying duty.

When America entered the First World War, Arnold was ordered to Washington to help build an air force equal to that of France and Britain. For Arnold, the next eighteen months were a whirlwind of activity, but also a time of growing frustration. Despite rapid promotions, making him, at thirty-two, the youngest colonel in the Army (when Marshall was still a captain), he did not have the power or institutional knowledge to harness the system to support his vision. His tireless efforts were falling well short of the goals he had established for expanding the nation's air arm. When the armistice was declared, Arnold was dismayed that all 2,768 American pilots in France were flying French and British aircraft.

Though missing out on the actual experience of combat, Arnold finished the war with a keen appreciation of what it took to build an air force from scratch, knowledge that would serve him well when he again led a massive and unparalleled expansion of airpower—and possessed the rank and power to bend people and organizations to his will. But there was one area where Arnold demonstrated no talent: administration. He hated the grunt work necessary to get anything done. Robert Lovett, who became assistant secretary of war for air affairs and a key Arnold ally during World War II, later said that Arnold's idea of how to get something accomplished never went far beyond just telling someone to do it.

Throughout the interwar years Arnold slowly but steadily climbed the ranks, but his chance to break out from the pack came when he was commanding March Field in California. Asked if the base could handle three thousand men from the New Deal's nascent Civilian Conservation Corps (CCC), Arnold threw his full support behind an effort that eventually grew to seven thousand men in over thirty widely dispersed camps. Despite the huge amount of time he spent managing the CCC camps, Arnold also found time to entertain a constant cavalcade of political and Hollywood visitors. Visitors not only were treated to carefully choreographed aerial reviews, but were also taken to see what he considered model CCC camps. Arnold was both learning how to sell airpower to the public and becoming adept at shoring up his political support. Thus, every politician that mattered regarded him as one of the few Army officers friendly to the New Deal. It did not hurt that many of Hollywood's most famous stars sang his praises, especially given that there was one New Dealer who liked to surround himself with celebrities: Harry Hopkins.

In September of 1938, Major General Oscar Westover, the current air corps chief of staff, was killed in a plane crash while en route to the West Coast. Arnold should have been an easy choice for the position, but rumors had reached Roosevelt that he was a drunk. Arnold always suspected these rumors came from the president's close intimate, military aide, and personal secretary Colonel Edwin "Pa" Watson. Watson had been a West Point classmate of Arnold's, and there was a long-standing but never revealed grudge between them. In his memoirs, Arnold mentions a smear campaign to keep him from getting the job, but does not identify a culprit. Arnold, however, had powerful persons in his corner, including Harry Hopkins and Army Chief of Staff Malin Craig, who, it was rumored, threatened to resign if Arnold was not appointed. Roosevelt made the final decision the day after a September White House meeting on airpower, which included Arnold supporters Harry Hopkins; General Craig with his new assistant chief of staff, George Marshall; and a close friend of both Arnold and Hopkins, Colonel James Burns. When Roosevelt announced his plans to hugely increase aircraft production, Arnold pounced, suggesting that the Air Corps be expanded by 7,500 combat planes and 2,500 training planes. A pleased Roosevelt named Arnold as the next Air Corps chief of staff on September 29, 1938.

As Arnold assumed his new position Prime Minister Neville Chamberlain was in Munich handing half of Czechoslovakia to Hitler.

In mid-December 1938, Jean Monnet returned to the United States, leading a team of French aircraft experts who would examine America's topline military aircraft as well as arrange financing for hundreds of purchases. This time the entire War Department was united in opposition to Treasury's meddling, including Secretary of War Woodring and Assistant Secretary Johnson, who rarely saw eye to eye on any matter.

Arnold, fearful that priority French orders would hinder his own buildup, had little problem parrying Treasury's requests to let the French inspect Air Corps planes. Morgenthau, however, had an ace card to play: Roosevelt's full support. On January 16, Roosevelt summoned Morgenthau, Navy Secretary Edison, Woodring, and Louis Johnson to the White House to lay down the law. The issue was settled when Johnson point-blank asked Roosevelt if he wanted the planes released to the French. Roosevelt replied, "That is exactly what I want." The meeting broke up soon thereafter. For Arnold, the shock was complete, as he at last realized that the president planned to send as many aircraft as possible to England and France and enlist those nations as America's first line of defense.

Morgenthau was now able to expedite the French contracts, which were let a full six months before Congress appropriated money for Army Air Corps procurement and nearly a year before the Air Corps could make major orders. Roosevelt's and Morgenthau's true achievement, hidden at the time, was that the French orders forced the construction of new plants and the creation of assembly lines that jump-started U.S. aircraft production for the day when Arnold's Army Air Forces orders eventually came in. Over the next year the production of aircraft engines tripled, and airframe production more than doubled.

5

Hot Dogs at Hyde Park

A S THE WORLD MOVED INEXORABLY TOWARD WAR, THERE WAS little Roosevelt, with few options and politically hemmed in on all sides, could do to influence affairs. By the end of March 1939, the Spanish Civil War was over, leaving General Francisco Franco firmly in charge; the French premier Édouard Daladier had received the power to rule by decree; Germany annexed the rest of Czechoslovakia; and Lithuania, under heavy German pressure, had turned the city of Memal over to the Reich. Chamberlain, pressured by a storm of public outrage, on the final day of March roused himself from his geopolitical stupor to inform Parliament that Britain had given Poland a unilateral and unconditional guarantee of support if Germany attacked. Having witnessed the Allies' serial failures to contest earlier provocations, Hitler was not inclined to believe Chamberlain would go to war over Poland.

In the end, all Roosevelt felt able to do was to write a letter to Hitler (an exact copy was sent to Mussolini from Secretary of State Hull) asking him to forswear all attempts at military conquest for ten or twenty-five years. Taken on its face, such a letter could imply a dangerous naïveté about Hitler and the threat he presented. But Roosevelt was playing a longer game. He fully expected Hitler to scorn his missive and was delighted when the Führer launched a blistering attack on the letter's presumption, and on Roosevelt himself.

The actual targets of Roosevelt's letter were, in fact, his political opponents: the isolationists on Capitol Hill, who wasted no time stepping into the trap. The communiqué neatly established the differences between the democracies desiring peace and the warmongering Axis tyrants. The Führer's insulting response offended most Americans while also underscoring the danger Hitler posed to Europe. When the leading isolationist senators— William E. Borah, Gerald Nye, Hiram Johnson, and Burton Wheeler— condemned Roosevelt's initiative and demanded a more conciliatory approach to Hitler, many Americans who had previously supported the isolationist bloc began moving in another direction. Equally important, the senators' comments, coming so soon after Kristallnacht and the subjugation of Czechoslovakia, opened them up for attacks as Nazi sympathizers, not just appeasers—a corner Roosevelt clearly intended to paint them into.

Meanwhile in Europe, observers noted that there had been a tremendous slackening in Germany's anti-Soviet rhetoric in recent months, causing an observant few to worry about a German-Russian rapprochement that would fundamentally redraw Europe's political map. Allied concerns were somewhat relieved when on April 17, 1939, Soviet foreign minister Maxim Litvinov summoned the British ambassador to the Kremlin to offer a triple alliance between France, Britain, and the Soviet Union. Here was a golden opportunity to place Hitler between powers on two fronts, and deliver a real check on his further ambitions—one that might have been fatal to him personally. What was required on Britain's part was resoluteness and quick action. Neither was forthcoming. Distrusting Soviet motives and unsure of Soviet military effectiveness, the British went into consultation with anyone available to consult. When they emerged three weeks later, Litvinov was not there to receive the reply. Disgusted by British dithering, Stalin told Molotov to approach Germany with the offer that led to the German-Soviet Nonaggression Pact. Chamberlain's diplomatic incompetence had squandered the last best chance to stop Hitler short of a conflagration that would consume Europe.

Two events brightened the American landscape in the spring and summer of 1939, as Europe slid toward war. The first, the opening of the New York World's Fair, gave tens of thousands of Americans a dazzling glimpse of the technological marvels on the near horizon. With the economy rebounding somewhat from 1938's "Roosevelt Depression," the World's Fair did its part in lifting the popular mood. Only Germany's absence from the Court of Peace, where the flags of recently conquered Czechoslovakia and Albania were at half-mast, offset the fair's buoyant optimism.

It was, however, the second event that thrilled the nation. Britain's King George VI and the fashionable Queen Elizabeth arrived in Washington on June 7. After a brief reception and a few requisite ceremonial activities, including laying a wreath on the Tomb of the Unknown Soldier, Roosevelt spirited the royal couple away for a weekend at Hyde Park. The king and queen's arrival, a political godsend, had been purposefully engineered by the president. Aware that a visit by Britain's inept politicians, particularly Chamberlain, would not move public opinion, FDR wrote to the king, ". . . Frankly, I think it would be an excellent thing for Anglo-American relations if you could visit the United States." When the king assented, Roosevelt personally planned every detail of the visit, including services at the local Episcopal church and a lunch featuring America's greatest culinary delicacy: the hot dog. The visit was a smashing success, as the king and queen captivated American audiences. Millions of Americans, some for the first time, reflected on the heritage their country shared with Britain. When they compared this to what they saw coming out of Hitler's Germany, many were at last convinced that Britain deserved American support, and if necessary salvation. It was an important, if still mostly incremental, turn in the tide of isolationism. Public support for a more interventionist policy was growing, but it remained extremely fragile, and Roosevelt planned to continue moving cautiously.

World fairs and visiting royalty remained mere distractions from the great events unfolding amid the tense geopolitical pause. As the Roosevelts enjoyed hot dogs with the king, Wehrmacht planners were finalizing details for the invasion of Poland. Against the ominous backdrop, Roosevelt judged the risk of war great enough to ask Congress to amend the Neutrality Act, which made it illegal to sell goods to "all" warring nations. The new bill, as written by the State Department, asked Congress for an outright repeal of the act. Outraged isolationists, led by Roosevelt's own Hyde Park congressman, Hamilton Fish, fought it tooth and nail.

Fish failed to stop the bill's passage through the House, but his amendments substantially damaged it. The final bill retained the embargo on arms and ammunition, while allowing dual-use items, such as aircraft, to be sold only on a cash-and-carry basis. The bill then went to Senator Key Pittman's Foreign Relations Committee, where Pittman's support had been secured for his usual price, a presidential promise to increase the official price of silver. But the slow-moving Pittman failed to pass the bill out

of committee before the isolationist bloc rounded up enough votes to fili-
buster it.

Desperate to salvage the bill, Roosevelt held a small reception for six
carefully chosen senators, three Republicans and three Democrats, including one of the Senate's leading isolationists, William E. Borah. Trying to
create a more convivial atmosphere, Roosevelt invited his guests to remove
their suit jackets, as he plied them with drinks. When everyone was comfortable, Roosevelt launched into a nonstop hour-long tirade about how
the Nazis had brought Europe to the edge of war, and that his own efforts
to forestall the conflict were being hindered by the Neutrality Act. Next he
invited Secretary Hull, his co-host for the evening, to speak.

Hull spoke with eloquence and a rare level of emotion. He concluded by
telling the assembled senators that unless the Neutrality Act was repealed,
war was certain. Even then, he told them the chances for peace were only
50-50 at best. At this the "Lion of Idaho," Senator Borah, roused himself
and thundered: "There is not going to be any war in Europe . . . all this
hysteria is manufactured and artificial."

Hull, visibly fighting for control, exploded: "I wish the Senator would

John Nance Garner.

come back to my office and read the cables. I'm sure he would come to the conclusion that there is far more danger than he thinks."

Borah, far from being dissuaded, pompously replied that he had his own sources, and that they were "more reliable than those of the State Department."

An ashen Hull, tears brimming, retreated to a corner of the room, where he tried to compose himself and get control of his well-known temper. After an uneasy quiet, Vice President Garner canvassed the senators. It was just after midnight when he turned to Roosevelt and said: "Well, Captain, we might as well face facts. You haven't got the votes and that's all there is to it."

Roosevelt accepted the news stoically, but he also took away a valuable lesson. When he next acted to push America closer to the Allied cause, he would make damn sure he had the votes.

It was now early in the morning of July 19, 1939. World War II, which Senator Borah confidently proclaimed impossible, would start in just over six weeks.

PART TWO

OPENING ROUNDS

Hold what you've got and hit them where you can.

Admiral Ernest King, memo to
Secretary of the Navy Frank Knox, February 8, 1942

6

FIRST SALVOS

JUST BEFORE 3:00 A.M. ON FRIDAY, SEPTEMBER 1, 1939, FRANK-
lin Delano Roosevelt was roused from a sound sleep when an emergency call from Ambassador William Bullitt, in Paris, was put through to his bedroom. Bullitt got right to the point. He had just heard from Ambassador Joseph Biddle in Warsaw, who reported that German bombers were over the city and several Wehrmacht divisions had already penetrated deep into Polish territory.

"Well, Bill, it has come at last. God help us all," Roosevelt responded, before calling Hull, Woodring, Welles, and several others to inform them of the news. Then, with an unflappability that never failed him, he went back to sleep. A second call from Bullitt awakened him again. This time, FDR learned that France planned to honor its commitments to Poland and declare war if Germany did not immediately halt its attack. Having witnessed France's and Britain's abandonment of Czechoslovakia, Roosevelt did not quite believe his ambassador and returned to sleep. When Joseph Kennedy called from London to inform him that Britain also planned to declare war, Roosevelt gave up on sleep and called his butler. It was time to greet what promised to be a long day. Three hours later, he appeared before the press. After the usual jocular exchanges, the big question was finally put to the president: "Can we stay out?" The smile that had been playing on Roosevelt's lips vanished, as he solemnly answered: "I not only sincerely hope so, but I believe we can, and every effort will be made by this Administration to do so."

Thereafter, the pace of events quickened. On September 2, Mussolini offered to mediate between the warring parties. Roosevelt and others saw this for what it was; Il Duce was looking to distance himself from the "Pact of Steel" he had negotiated with Hitler, in case the Führer's gamble went disastrously wrong. Almost simultaneously Prime Minister Chamberlain, after twice delaying his appearance in Parliament, arrived to deliver an anguished, self-pitying speech that left him isolated even within his own party. How far he had misjudged the mood of the moment became apparent when the deputy opposition leader, Arthur Greenwood, rose to speak. Greenwood had come to Parliament that day ready to cheer Chamberlain's ultimatum to Germany, but when Chamberlain failed to offer an ultimatum Greenwood had no prepared remarks. Moreover, he had had a few whiskeys before entering the chamber. Swaying a bit as he rose, he had only uttered a few words before he was interrupted by Leo Amery, a member of Chamberlain's Conservative Party and a strong opponent of appeasement, who rose and shouted, "Speak for England, Arthur!" Greenwood did just that, delivering the shortest and most eloquent speech of his career. He ended to thunderous applause: "I wonder how long we are prepared to vacillate at a time when Britain and all that Britain stands for—and human civilization—are in peril."

The next day, Chamberlain, warned by his whips that he faced a revolt in his own party, accepted the inevitable. The British government issued an ultimatum to Germany demanding that it begin withdrawing from Poland by 11:00 A.M. At fifteen minutes past that hour, Chamberlain went on the radio to announce that Britain was at war. Five hours later, a similar ultimatum from France expired, and France too declared war.

That night Roosevelt gave a fireside speech in which he announced: "I have said not once but many times that I have seen war and that I hate war. I say that again and again. I hope the United States will keep out of this war. I believe that it will. And I give you assurance and reassurance that every effort of your Government will be directed toward that end." But after promising that America would remain neutral, he finished by declaring that he could not ask Americans to remain neutral in thought. Slowly but surely Roosevelt was bending American opinion, if not toward war, at least toward helping the Allied cause. A week later, Roosevelt sent his first wartime note to Winston Churchill, whom Chamberlain had just brought out of a long political exile to resume the position he held at the start of World War I: First Lord of the Admiralty. Churchill replied by phone, beginning one of the most remarkable wartime political relationships in history.

Understanding the full implications of renewed war in Europe, at a time when few Americans did, Roosevelt returned with renewed vigor to the problem of breaking free of the Neutrality Acts. It was going to be a long uphill struggle, for the forces of isolationism were already rallying. The most potent of these was "The Lone Eagle"—Charles Lindbergh, who despite having lived in Germany, or perhaps because of it, praised the Nazi

Colonel Charles Lindbergh.

system, and proudly displayed the decorations Reich Minister Hermann Goering had presented to him. Still hugely popular throughout the country, Lindbergh spoke to a national radio audience on September 15. As he spoke, the Germans tightened their siege around Warsaw, which did not stop Lindbergh from insisting that there was no moral difference between Hitler and the leaders of Europe's democracies. Coming at a time when pictures of German atrocities in Poland and stories of new roundups of Jews were appearing in every American newspaper, the speech had an air of unreality. Still, for a large slice of the population, fearful of getting dragged into a foreign war they continued to consider none of America's concern, Lindbergh's words struck a chord.

Roosevelt muted his own reply but sent Harold Ickes out to dog Lindbergh's steps. Ickes offered administration rebuttals in his typical hard-hitting style, in a tone and language beneath the dignity of the presidency, but it would take time for his efforts to have an effect. In the meantime, Lindbergh's speech reversed almost all the progress Roosevelt had made against the isolationists, as a deluge of letters demanding the retention of the Neutrality Acts landed upon an already balking Congress. Many on the Hill who had been leaning toward lifting the bill now repudiated or hedged their positions. Roosevelt let the worst of the storm pass before calling a special session of Congress on September 21, 1939. In the meantime, Stalin, who had stunned the world by agreeing to a nonaggression pact with Hitler the previous month, doomed Poland's chances by ordering his forces to invade that beleaguered nation from the east. Several days later, Roosevelt went before a subdued Congress and demanded revisions to the 1937 Neutrality Act while continuing to emphasize peace: "Let no group assume the exclusive mantle of 'peace bloc.' We all belong to it." He then asked for the power to help the Allies by lifting many of the Neutrality Act's embargo restrictions. It was a bravura performance, one of Roosevelt's best.

Thousands of letters of support flooded the White House and congressional offices as the tide slowly turned. Roosevelt's cause was helped along by two other factors. Having been battered for two years whenever he interfered on the Hill, Roosevelt wisely stepped back and let his supporters take the fight to the isolationists in Congress. At the same time, a well-organized movement among society's elites in favor of actively supporting the Allies began to stir; it soon provided a powerful counterweight to the burgeoning "America First" isolationist movement. The cause was also ably assisted by Henry Stimson, one of the great old men of the Republican establishment, who in an October 5 radio speech that horrified Hull with its candor, but provided some interventionist Republicans with political cover, told the American people that the neutrality laws had been "a wanton encouragement of aggression and that their repeal would be morally and materially a step forward." By mid-October defections from the isolationist cause were increasing, as polls favoring repeal tipped over 80 percent. At the same time, big business, smelling an opportunity for profit and putting people back to work, began pressing the case for repeal. After a long and contentious debate a bill modifying the acts was finally passed on November 3 and signed into law the next day.

Long before Roosevelt won his victory on Capitol Hill, the city of Warsaw, after a gallant but hopeless stand, succumbed to the invading Germans on September 28. On October 6, Poland's last divisions surrendered near Lublin. Poland was lost. Soon to join it, Lithuania, Estonia, and Latvia were all forcibly incorporated into the Soviet Union. Stalin, addicted to the taste of easy victories, was soon pressuring Finland for territorial concessions. At first the Finns, intimidated by the fate of Poland and their Baltic neighbors, were inclined to give in. But this only encouraged Stalin to increase his demands. When the Finns resisted, he unleashed the Red Army, which promptly ran into a buzz saw. Exploiting the bitter cold (temperatures plunged below minus 40 degrees Fahrenheit), long hours of darkness, and Russian unpreparedness for a bitter winter war, thousands of Finns on skis slashed into the huge, lumbering Soviet columns, slicing them into pieces that were then eradicated piecemeal. After these initial setbacks the Soviets, for the most part, gave up on a war of maneuver, opting instead for the tried-and-true method of overwhelming an enemy with sheer numbers and firepower. The Finns fought bravely through February, as their fortified Mannerheim Line was slowly but inexorably ground out of existence. In early March, after enduring horrific losses, the Soviets broke through, forcing Finland to sue for peace on Stalin's terms.

The "Winter War" had a lasting effect on the wider conflict beyond Finland. Only by the slimmest of margins was a proposal by French premier Édouard Daladier to send troops to Finland defeated. In a mark of the continuing instability of the Third Republic, Daladier's government soon fell and was replaced by one led by the determined Paul Reynaud. A proposal to help the Finns was also offered by Churchill, who wanted to gain a foothold in Scandinavia but not to go so far as to risk war with the Soviet Union. It was not acted upon before the Finnish collapse and was soon thereafter shelved. These Allied failures of will were probably for the best. It is hard to conceive how the Allies could have built, transported, and supplied a force of sufficient combat power to have halted the Soviets once the Red Army juggernaut hit its stride. The most likely outcome was a humiliating Allied reversal that would have shaken both the French and British governments.

Hitler, too, was closely observing events in Finland. For him, the Winter War demonstrated just how weak and demoralized the Red Army truly was. Though it was numerically huge, the Soviet army was apparently no-where near as efficient and capable as the Wehrmacht. Hitler also noted the inferiority of Soviet military leadership, which having been decimated by Stalin's purges was clearly subpar. For Hitler, who already viewed the Slavs as *Untermenschen,* the Red Army's performance confirmed his opinion that the Soviet Union was a house of sticks, ready to crash down with a single hard kick. Notwithstanding the fact that Britain and France re-mained unbowed, Hitler's gaze began turning toward the east.

In the United States, Finland's plight provided the opportunity for countless supreme rhetorical gestures of support. But except for some loan credits, Roosevelt did little to aid Finland in its moment of dire need. Per-haps he already saw that no less than a great battle for civilization was de-veloping and that tiny Finland was too small a prize if it meant risking the long-term support of the Soviet Union. More likely, Roosevelt realized there was little the United States could do to change the outcome, and dis-playing a ruthlessness that would serve him well during the war, he opted to preserve his limited resources for the big show to come.

7

THE STATE DEPARTMENT

AT WAR . . . WITH ITSELF

A S THE EUROPEAN CRISIS INTENSIFIED, THE STATE DEPARTMENT, which should have played a leading role in guiding U.S. diplomacy, was increasingly sidelined. There were many reasons why State was cast into near oblivion in the great affairs of nations, but they start with how Cordell Hull organized and ran his department. Since the Wilson presidency, State had considered its primary role to be the maintenance of peace internationally and, failing that, to keep the United States as removed from a European or Asian war as possible. Few within the State Department, and certainly not Hull, believed State had a vital wartime role to play, except to push for peace. Consequently, the structures and processes necessary to maintain State's usefulness and engagement while a war was under way had atrophied.

State's capacity to move to a war footing was also hampered by Hull's risk-averse nature. He was extremely proud of the fact that he was the only senior member of the administration who had never made a mistake large enough to attract unwanted press attention or Roosevelt's wrath. But during war, when risks are necessary and immediate action is the norm, Roosevelt had little use for a cabinet member whose primary concern was maintaining "a personal record of no runs–no hits–no errors." But there was more to it than just professional frustration. Roosevelt's inclination to skip Hull and employ Undersecretary of State Sumner Welles on sensitive assignments was just as much a result of the president's personal affinity for Welles, who was of a similar background and pedigree, as his inability to bond with Hull on a personal level.

Cordell Hull was past sixty when he became secretary of state in 1933. He had already had a long and distinguished career in Congress before Roosevelt offered him the cabinet position. Born in a log cabin, to a hardscrabble farmer, Hull had risen from a hard life in the mountains of Tennessee. He was the only one of five brothers to receive an education, mostly due to his own drive, and was already a practicing lawyer before his twenty-first birthday. At the start of the Spanish-American War, Hull temporarily abandoned his law practice to raise a company of infantry. As the fighting ended before his regiment's arrival, Hull's time on active service was spent mostly as part of the occupying force in Cuba.

Cordell Hull, secretary of state.

Upon his return to Tennessee, Hull took a greater interest in local politics, first as a judge and then in Congress. He served in Congress for a total of twenty-two years, with only one break, from 1920 to 1922, when he served as chairman of the Democratic National Committee. As a member of the powerful Ways and Means Committee, Hull took a keen interest in taxes and tariffs, and his Hill colleagues considered him a fanatic on the issue. A rumor, current at the time, had it that Hull had once passed on a seven-course gourmet dinner in favor of studying a pamphlet on tariff statistics. Hull's near obsession with dismantling restrictive trading practices became a source of Allied wartime tensions, as he used every opportunity to press the British to dismantle their system of imperial preferences in return for U.S. aid and support.

It was early in his tenure in Congress that Hull began developing the work habits that would mark his career. Still a bachelor (he did not marry until age forty-five in 1917), Hull turned down almost all invitations and was only rarely seen at social events. Instead, he stayed in his rooms studying the issues before Congress, or if he did venture out, it was to meet other congressmen at the Cochran Hotel to discuss these same issues. Hull may have been a master of the issues, but he was never a great orator, as his voice was too weak to hold an audience spellbound. In private, though, a different Hull emerged—earnest, lively, and a master of colorful vernacular. If Hull had a personal weakness it was a tendency to view those who disagreed with him as personal foes. He also had a short fuse and a hot temper, and once had to be restrained from physically assaulting a Republican congressman on the floor of the House.

Why Roosevelt appointed Hull as secretary of state is still a matter of debate, and even Hull claimed he was thunderstruck when the position was offered. A long political acquaintance, if not friendship, played some part. More important, however, was that Hull was a relatively conservative Democrat, with close personal ties to everyone on the Hill who mattered. In other words, he had his own political constituency, which was particularly strong in many of the areas where Roosevelt's support was wavering. Unfortunately, his almost two dozen years in Congress had done little to prepare Hull for the role of secretary of state. This, however, was a minor matter for Roosevelt, who from the start intended to function as his own secretary of state in all but routine matters.

As the world darkened and drifted toward war, international issues moved to the forefront of FDR's concerns. Tensions with Hull soon developed, and the president became increasingly prone to bypass the State Department when dealing with foreign powers. Worse, as far as Hull was concerned, when Roosevelt did employ the State Department he did so through Hull's undersecretary, Sumner Welles, often leaving Hull completely out of the loop. Unfortunately, Roosevelt allowed the resulting tension between State's two doyens to fester for several years, until their animosity erupted in a blood feud that shook both the State Department and the White House.

Sumner Welles was more than twenty years Hull's junior and had spent his entire professional life in the Foreign Service. Early on, he impressed Roosevelt by instigating and nurturing the Good Neighbor Policy, which placed previously strained United States–Latin America relations on a new playing field. Within the State Department, Welles was everything Hull was not. Where Hull was increasingly frail and sickly, Welles was at his physical peak. Where Hull was loath to tackle State's mountains of administrative minutiae, Welles dove in. Hull was always deliberate and slow to act; Welles, by contrast, moved with dispatch. Moreover, when Hull disagreed with the president he was never shy about stating his opinions forcefully and, far worse in Roosevelt's eyes, repeatedly. Welles, on the other hand, was always quick to please the president, even if he had personal qualms about Roosevelt's desires—a trait Roosevelt greatly prized in his subordinates. Further, Welles was the personification of a professional diplomat. According to *Time,* "Welles was first and foremost tough minded with a mental resilience to absorb shocks . . . He has a firm hold of every one of the diplomatic virtues: he is absolutely precise, imperturbable, accurate, honest, sophisticated, thorough, cultured, travelled and financially established." *Time* continued that the only surprises left to Welles were destiny. Destiny, however, would not be kind.

Just as important to FDR as Welles's professional qualities was that Welles was one of his own: born to wealth, and with a superb pedigree dating back over three hundred years. Welles and Eleanor even had a grandmother in common. Welles also went to all the right schools: Roosevelt's alma maters Groton and then Harvard. Moreover, they shared many of the same friends, had cousins in common, and both spoke the language of old wealth and privilege. He was the president's kind of person, someone FDR could relax with, which he often did during sojourns to Welles's forty-nine-room mansion, Oxon Hill Manor. FDR always preferred conducting policy in a convivial atmosphere, where he eschewed formality in favor of small intimate gatherings. And Welles and Roosevelt were nothing if not convivial.

Welles did, however, have two vulnerabilities. First, he was a "cold fish" who did not make friends easily, nor did he try to. While he was respected

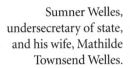

Sumner Welles,
undersecretary of state,
and his wife, Mathilde
Townsend Welles.

at State he was also feared. It was said that being dressed down by Welles was like being "stabbed in the heart by an icicle." Thus, when his moment of personal crisis arrived, he had no friends or supporters to rush to his defense. Second, and ultimately fatal to his career—and his further usefulness to Roosevelt—Welles was bisexual, at a time in U.S. history when same-sex relationships were illegal. Unfortunately, Welles, typically the epitome of restraint, would from time to time go on drunken benders. When he did so, he was prone to make advances to any available men, usually those well below his social caste. As Welles's enemies accumulated, it was only a matter of time before his indiscretions would be revealed with cataclysmic impact.

In addition to bypassing Hull in favor of Welles, Roosevelt added fuel to the tinder by transferring many of State's functions to the Treasury and War Departments, "or any agency that could get things done." A disgruntled Hull often complained to others about how he and his department were treated and became visibly upset when discussing Roosevelt's pack of special envoys who reported only to the president. Hull deeply resented being bypassed in favor of such personal diplomacy, and was disturbed by the havoc these presidential emissaries created wherever they went. Hull also took offense that certain of State's ambassadors—Bullitt, Kennedy, and Joseph E. Davis—believed they had the right to correspond directly with the president (who encouraged such behavior) without informing the State Department.

Despite all of this, Hull still commanded Roosevelt's respect, or, probably more accurately, Roosevelt respected his continuing influence on the Hill. But respect never translated into intimacy, and Hull never became one of the president's inner circle. As Hull complained later: "In general, I was not a social intimate with the President. I was not invited to the White House dinners except on official occasions, or on weekend excursions on Mr. Roosevelt's yacht or visits to Hyde Park."

As most of the president's friends were beyond Hull's reach, his growing resentment was increasingly focused on Sumner Welles. FDR was aware of their growing enmity, but typically, he failed to intervene. Hull himself noted that Roosevelt often appeared to "take a boyish delight in seeing two of his assistants at odds." His characteristic response to such quarrels was always the same: "settle it between yourselves." Roosevelt, of course, knew that many of these disputes were, without his active involvement, beyond resolution, which is how he wanted it. By establishing rivals and giving them overlapping tasks and authorities, FDR ensured that there would always be disagreements over the big issues—differences that only he could solve. In this way, Roosevelt kept his finger on the bureaucratic levers and thoroughly dominated the nation's decision-making process. The cost of this dominance was often managerial chaos, never-ending bureaucratic warfare, and delayed decisions when speed was essential. All too often these disputes spilled into the press, embarrassing the administration. In other cases, resentments would fester until they reached a breaking point, forcing Roosevelt to take drastic action. Clearer lines of authority established from the start would almost certainly have circumvented most of the mini-crises.

Unfortunately, the war could not be placed on hold while State realigned its priorities and established a new internal cultural paradigm. But for the time being there was a lull in military action. Severe cold, the temporary unpreparedness of the German Army, and a looming economic crisis all conspired to force Hitler to postpone a planned winter assault on France.

Roosevelt, sensing a limited opportunity, took advantage of the pause, already being called "the Phony War," to undertake a round of peacemaking diplomacy. Here was an opportunity for Hull to step forward and thrust State into the center of great events. He failed to do so, and on February 9, 1940, Roosevelt announced that he was sending Sumner Welles to Italy, Germany, Britain, and France as his personal envoy. Ever since, Roosevelt's motives have remained clouded. Was it, as he publicly claimed, a fact-finding mission? If so, what was wrong with the facts already flooding in from the U.S. embassies in those nations? Roosevelt's answer to that was that he wanted an assessment from one trusted voice rather than four disparate opinions. Roosevelt had made using trusted advisers as his eyes and ears part of his modus operandi since he was stricken with polio. In the domestic sphere, he sent Eleanor crisscrossing the country, trusting implicitly her judgment on the people's moods; in national security matters he increasingly employed Hopkins, and in international affairs he turned to Welles.

Still, many have theorized that Roosevelt had other reasons for dispatching Welles. Ever sure of his own deft hand in making people see reason—as he defined it—it is possible that Roosevelt was trying to pull a rabbit out of a hat and broker an eleventh-hour peace. The truth will never be known. But given known Rooseveltian methods it is fair to speculate that Welles's trip was simply a shot in the dark. If it spurred some type of peace initiative Roosevelt stood ready to take the credit. If it failed to do so, it was of little consequence, given that, after all, Welles was ostensibly in Europe just to assess the situation and report back to the president. Whatever Roosevelt's intent, his penchant for secrecy caused him to keep Secretary Hull in the dark, adding to an already damaging rift between Welles and Hull and irreparably harming Welles's mission before it even got under way.

Roosevelt's announcement that Welles would soon depart on a tour of Europe's great capitals further inflamed Hull's resentment of Welles. Moreover, the timing of the announcement was awful, given that the nation's ambassadors to England and France—Joseph Kennedy and William Bullitt, respectively—were both in the United States when the announcement was made. On hearing the news Kennedy flew into a rage, shouting: "You would think I had been pouring tea over there instead of working my head off." Bullitt, a brilliant but mercurial diplomat, who had been the nation's first representative to the Soviet Union, considered himself not only Roosevelt's representative to France but also his "viceroy to all of Europe." Consequently, when he learned of Welles's planned trip, he too became enraged and infuriated Roosevelt by complaining loudly and publicly. In a fit of pique Bullitt refused to return to France until Welles had left Europe. According to Bullitt's deputy, Robert Murphy, this perceived slight was the start of Bullitt's insane jealousy toward Welles, whose professional demise Bullitt would relentlessly pursue for the next three years.

In the meantime, Welles still had a mission—however ambiguous—to complete. On February 17, 1940, he departed for Naples on the Italian liner *Lex*—the Riviera afloat. In his briefcase was a numbered codebook, allowing him to communicate directly with the president. With him were several State Department European experts, his wife, her cousin, a traveling companion, assorted maids, a valet, and a West Highland terrier named Toby. At Naples, he and his party boarded a special train Mussolini had sent to speed him to Rome. Welles first met with Mussolini's son-in-law, Foreign Minister Galeazzo Ciano. The meeting got off to an inauspicious start when Toby the terrier relieved himself on the ceremonial decorations. Still, both men came away impressed with the other's commitment to peace, but Ciano held out little hope for their common goal, confiding in Welles that there might have been a time when Hitler would have negotiated a peace, but that time had passed.

The next day, after hearing much the same thing from Mussolini, Welles lowered his sights and aimed at keeping Italy out of the war. On this point, Mussolini was evasive, and Welles perceived that he was laboring under an enormous strain. Welles attributed this to the unfit Mussolini having to keep up with a new young mistress, as the relationship was not even two weeks old. More likely, Mussolini was being pressured by Hitler—far more demanding than any mistress—to enter the war. Unbeknownst to Welles, Il Duce was to meet the Führer in just a few days, where the pressure was sure to double and double again.

Disappointed, Welles departed for Germany by way of Switzerland. In a Zurich hotel he was besieged by reporters, including one female reporter from a New York paper who tried to seduce his secrets from him. She had no better luck than a mysterious Austro-Hungarian princess who claimed she was carrying a message from Goebbels; Welles refused to meet her.

Upon arriving in Germany, Welles had an initial and very unpleasant meeting with Foreign Minister Joachim von Ribbentrop. For two hours

Ribbentrop, his arms gesticulating wildly, held forth without interruption, concluding that there was no hope of peace "until the will of England to destroy Germany is killed once and for all." Welles wrote Ribbentrop off as a man with "a very stupid mind . . . saturated with hate for England." Late the next morning, Hitler greeted Welles pleasantly but with great formality. Their ninety-minute conversation was sociable, as Hitler provided his own view of the conflict, concluding with "I did not want this war. It has been forced upon me against my will. It is a waste of time. My life should have been spent constructing and not destroying." When Welles tried to use this as a basis for further peace negotiations, Hitler concluded the conference on a sour note: "I can assure you that Germany's aim, whether it must come through war or otherwise, is a just peace."

Welles received scant encouragement from other German leaders, though he thought Hermann Goering polite and welcoming. He was also amused to see firsthand that Goering looked just like caricatures he had seen: "His thighs and arms are tremendous, and his girth tremendous. His face gave the impression that it had been heavily rouged." Goering, playing his part, proudly boasted about how much more powerful Germany was now than in 1914, and stated that he was convinced the war would be a short one. More ominously he added that even if the war went five or ten years "Germany would strengthen . . . as every month passed."

Deeply depressed at discovering Germany hell-bent for war, Welles boarded a train for France. In Paris, he discovered a city overtaken by sullen apathy. The first Parisians he met were laughing about a new Hôtel Crillon drink, created in his honor and consisting only of ice water. In Paris everyone was ready to make a deal, but none held out any hope that Hitler would oblige them with anything less than ruinous terms. It was only after meeting with former premier Léon Blum that Welles discovered where popular sentiment lay, as in the wake of the meeting the American embassy was flooded with thousands of letters asking why Welles had dared meet with a Jew. As Welles departed for the United Kingdom, Bullitt's vendetta against Welles got under way, as he informed Roosevelt that Welles was poorly received in France and spread defeatism wherever he went.

In Britain, Welles naïvely pushed for a disarmament agenda that would reassure Germany. Chamberlain, made much wiser by Hitler's double-dealing at Munich, rebuffed Welles, telling him that as His Majesty's government had no confidence in Hitler's peaceful intentions, no disarmament

William Bullitt,
ambassador to France (left),
and Sumner Welles.

was possible. Looking for support elsewhere, Welles turned to the British foreign secretary, Lord Halifax, a leading supporter of the appeasement policy, who was still actively looking for some way to accommodate Hitler. Welles was surprised when he got little from Halifax except a confidential warning to be circumspect in his consultations with Chamberlain, as he had undergone a most harrowing experience in his dealing with Hitler at Munich. Anthony Eden, who would be Churchill's number two throughout the war, removed the last underpinnings of Welles's hopes for peace by declaring that the only path to peace was through "the destruction of Hitlerism, and forcing on the German people a government that was not a threat to the rest of Europe."

Upon Welles's return to Rome, Mussolini informed him that Germany was unwilling to consider any solution "other than military victory, and that peace negotiations were impossible." Discouraged, Welles and his personal entourage on March 20 boarded the elegant *Conte de Savoia* for the trip home. He had traveled nearly fifteen thousand miles and met with kings, diplomats, politicians, and the leaders of every nation involved in the ongoing crisis, except the Soviet Union. Welles knew more about the current state of European politics than any other American; and to get at these insights the press was willing to pay handsomely, offering Welles the then princely sum of $50,000 for a copy of his findings. Welles ignored the clamor and produced only two copies of his report. One went to Hull and the other to the president. Hull later wrote that it was a superb report, but it provided nothing on which to base any further action. On the other hand, Roosevelt found the report invaluable, as he always prized personal insights into those he was dealing with, and Welles's report was filled with the kind of anecdotal reporting that Roosevelt delighted in.

8

BLITZKRIEG

ROOSEVELT WAS PREPARING FOR BED ON THE NIGHT OF MAY 9, 1940, when his ambassador to Belgium, John Cudahy, called to excitedly inform him that the "blitzkrieg" in the west had begun, and that German tanks were streaming into the Netherlands and Belgium. No further news was available until a bit after midnight, when Roosevelt's press secretary arrived with a collection of press reports coming out of Europe. After scanning them, Roosevelt phoned Morgenthau and ordered him to freeze all Belgian, Dutch, and Luxembourgian assets in the United States to keep them from the Germans. As there was little more he could do, and it being well after 2:00 A.M., Roosevelt went off to, by all accounts, a deep and restful sleep. At midmorning, a rested and alert president called a meeting of what amounted to his national security staff: General Marshall, Admiral Harold Stark, Attorney General Robert Jackson, Secretary of the Treasury Morgenthau, Secretary of State Hull, and Undersecretary Sumner Welles. Except for ordering the Army and Navy to submit new estimates of what they required to match Germany's military strength, the meeting accomplished little.

That afternoon, Roosevelt met with his entire cabinet. Slightly recovered from another long bout of illness, Hopkins was also in attendance. After Hull updated the attendees on the recent cables sent from Europe, Hopkins took over the meeting. Everyone, including his major cabinet antagonist, Harold Ickes, was impressed by Hopkins's command of the state of U.S. war production, particularly as it came to raw materials, where he broke the news that there was already a rubber and tin crisis that would only get worse. As the meeting was winding down, word arrived that Chamberlain was out and Churchill was the new prime minister. Roosevelt said he was pleased at the news, commenting: "I suppose that Churchill was the best man that England had." Afterward FDR held a quick meeting with the Belgian ambassador, before "cocktail hour"—one of the White House's most important rituals, during which anyone speaking about politics or the concerns of the day was banished, often forever. Rather, it was a time when Roosevelt and his "official family" (Eleanor rarely attended) could relax, tell jokes, and gossip. Roosevelt himself always mixed the drinks, something he claimed to be a master of, though his guests rarely gave him high marks in that department.

That evening, Hopkins remained for the cocktail hour, as he did whenever he was at the White House.

At the end of the cocktail hour, FDR invited Hopkins to stay for dinner. Noting that his guest looked drained, Roosevelt then insisted he stay the night. Hopkins stayed for three and a half years, becoming Roosevelt's most trusted intimate, filling a spot in Roosevelt's life that had been empty since the death of his longtime friend and political guru Louis Howe. Howe, who had remained at Roosevelt's side through the trials of adapting to life in a wheelchair and was more than any man responsible for making him governor of New York, and then president, may have been irreplaceable, but Hopkins was the next best thing. If Hopkins could not get angry and yell at the president when he was making a wrong move, as Howe often had, he could at least speak frankly to him.

Commenting on their relationship, one observer noted: "Many New Dealers have bored Roosevelt with their solemn earnestness, Hopkins never does. He knows instinctively when to ask, when to keep still, when to press, when to hold back; when to approach Roosevelt direct, when to go at him roundabout." Another said: "Hopkins had an almost feminine sensitivity to Roosevelt's moods. He seems to know precisely when Roosevelt wants to consider affairs of state and when he wants to escape from the awful consciousness of the Presidency." But for the many enemies Hopkins acquired over the years, and others jealous of his closeness to the president, Hopkins was a Rasputin, bending the president to his will. Inevitably, whenever Roosevelt decided contrary to the advice of one or another of his advisers, Hopkins's malevolent counsel was the cause.

The reality was quite different. What made Hopkins invaluable to the president, and the reason for his longevity as FDR's top adviser, was that he never got out ahead of Roosevelt and then tried to drag the president along with him. What Hopkins did better than anyone was interpret Roosevelt's desires and then make them happen. Samuel Rosenman said that the source of Hopkins's power was "that he was there . . . He lived there, he had dinner and lunch with Roosevelt. There was time to argue and debate, and create a common vision without the crunch of time rushing everything."

A more troubling aspect of Hopkins's dealings with the president was his power as gatekeeper. According to Rosenman: "During the years when Harry was at the height of his influence, he often went to great extremes to keep people from seeing the President. For example, some military people who did not quite agree with what the two men destined to run the war, General George Marshall and Admiral Ernest King, wanted done—and they were Hopkins's heroes—he would go to all kinds of lengths to keep them from seeing the President." Hopkins jealously guarded his relationship with FDR, viewing anyone else who enjoyed the president's confidence as a mortal threat to his own position. Roosevelt was apparently blind to this, and saw only Hopkins's unquestioned loyalty to him personally. During a White House visit, his erstwhile Republican opponent Wendell Willkie mentioned that he was soon heading for Britain, to which Roosevelt replied that he must visit with Hopkins when he got to London. Willkie, his evident dislike of Hopkins showing on his face, rather rudely inquired: "Why do you keep Hopkins so close to you? You must realize that people distrust him and they resent his recent influence." Roosevelt gave a thoughtful reply: "Someday you may be sitting where I am now as President of the United States. And when you are, you'll be looking at that door over there and knowing that practically everyone who walks through it wants something out of you. You'll learn what a lonely job this is, and you'll discover the need for somebody like Harry Hopkins who asks for nothing except to serve you."

As Hopkins made himself at home in the White House, the pace of events in Europe quickened. On May 20, German panzers reached the English Channel, trapping the British Expeditionary Force and a large portion of the French Army. Then, in one of the most remarkable achievements in the annals of warfare, the British, under intense pressure from land and sea, somehow evacuated their army and a significant contingent of French soldiers off the beaches near Dunkirk. When the evacuation ended on June 4, nearly 340,000 men had been rescued. Unfortunately, they left behind much of their equipment, so while England had her soldiers back, she did not have an army. Though by any standard Dunkirk was a miracle, one must not lose sight of the fact that it was also a major Allied military defeat. The Germans had ignominiously thrown British arms off the Continent, and it was increasingly clear that France was doomed.

The following week, on June 10, Roosevelt delivered his most bellicose speech yet. On the same day that Mussolini, wanting a piece of Germany's conquests for himself, declared war on France, Roosevelt took advantage of an already scheduled speech at the University of Virginia in Charlottesville to attack the Axis powers. Standing before the graduating students and their families, Roosevelt, reading from a hastily rewritten speech, contemptuously said of Italy and Mussolini: "On this tenth day of June, 1940, the hand that held the dagger has struck it into the back of its neighbor." He then promised, without any congressional approval, to "extend to the opponents of force the material resources of this nation; and at the same time, we will harness and speed up the use of those resources in order that we ourselves may have equipment and training equal to the task . . . full speed ahead."

But it was not full speed ahead. The United States was still caught in the grip of isolationism, and Roosevelt remained loath to get too far ahead of public opinion. Some have argued that many of the polls taken at the time indicated there was a growing majority supporting plans to help the Allies. Roosevelt, however, knew that this support was shallow, and likely to vanish upon the first setback. In the political atmosphere of the time, a defeat of any one of his initiatives could have spelled disaster for his entire preparedness plan and might eliminate any chance of the United States providing substantial support to Britain. For Roosevelt, "full speed ahead" was always defined as "going as fast as the politics of the situation allowed." Could he have moved faster or brought the American public along at a quicker pace? Probably, but only by taking risks he was clearly no longer willing to chance.

Roosevelt also had to calculate on it being an election year in which he was a lame duck president. When the Germans invaded France he was already in his final months in office, and in political terms a ninety-eight-pound weakling. Given such circumstances he had little chance of pushing through any major initiative, unless it had vocal and overwhelming public support. There was only one way for Roosevelt to regain his political power, but it meant doing what no other president had dared to do: break the two-term tradition established by George Washington.

9

ROOSEVELT'S GENERAL

GEORGE MARSHALL HAD ALWAYS BEEN DIFFERENT. FROM THE very start of his career many marked him as the most competent officer in the service. In 1914, while still a lieutenant, Marshall was assigned as adjutant to the "White Force" for a major field training exercise in the Philippines. Despite his junior rank, he threw himself into the planning for the operation. When the White Force commander arrived drunk on the exercise's first day, Marshall, the youngest officer present, was put in charge of a brigade-size force for the remainder of the exercise. Another even more junior lieutenant, Hap Arnold, watched Marshall's performance with keen appreciation, later relating to his wife, "That man will one day be the Army Chief of Staff."

Marshall's early life was in most ways unremarkable. Born in Uniontown, Pennsylvania, in 1880, he was, at first, raised in an affluent if not truly wealthy home. When he was ten, however, his father lost most of the family fortune speculating in land. Although the family was not destitute, Marshall was stung by the humiliation of carrying food scraps home from the local hotel, which decades later he called a "black spot on my boyhood." At some point, he decided on a career in the Army, but as his academic preparation was far below what West Point required, he never applied to West Point, choosing instead the Virginia Military Institute (VMI) as the best path for an Army commission.

Marshall's real chance to shine came during World War I. There he had attracted the attention of General John "Black Jack" Pershing, who pulled him out of the First Division onto his Army planning staff. Here Marshall displayed a talent for organization far above his peers, planning America's first major offensive at Saint-Mihiel, and while that was still in progress, he planned and organized the greatest American operation of the war at Meuse-Argonne. In all, Marshall had to plan for the simultaneous march of well over a million troops, constructing eighty massive supply dumps and forty-four hospitals, while also extending rail lines, emplacing 3,000 artillery pieces, and moving 900,000 tons of supplies and ammunition. When it was done Marshall had earned the nickname "the Wizard."

After the armistice, Pershing retained Marshall as his aide. He was still in that position in 1921, when Pershing became Army chief of staff. It was during this time that Marshall became accustomed to dealing with Congress and the White House. More important, he began enlarging his circle of friends well beyond the military sphere, including financier and World War I production czar Bernard Baruch, a man who was to wield great influence during the next war. Marshall always enjoyed his time with Baruch and considered him one of the most fascinating men in Washington. As Pershing was often away from Washington, Marshall assumed many of his day-to-day duties and was the de facto chief of staff from late 1923 into 1924, during Pershing's six-month trip to France. When Pershing's tenure

General John J. Pershing (left) and General George Marshall.

Bernard Baruch, financier and
trusted adviser to President
Franklin D. Roosevelt.

as chief of staff ended in 1924, so did Marshall's residence in Washington. He was now probably the most experienced and knowledgeable officer in the Army and, in the eyes of many, poised to become the next Army chief of staff. Unfortunately, his rank had not kept up with his experience.

Following a stint at Fort Benning, where he revolutionized the curriculum and started instilling the "Benning spirit" throughout the Army, Marshall took a series of assignments in Screven, Georgia; Columbia, South Carolina; Chicago; and Vancouver, Washington. The two most important aspects of these assignments were that Marshall, though remaining apolitical, made it known that he was a strong supporter of several major New Deal initiatives; and that they vastly expanded the number of his civilian contacts across the country. Foremost among these was the close relationship Marshall developed with the powerful South Carolina senator Jimmy Byrnes while he was assigned to the senator's home state.

In 1938, Marshall, now finally a brigadier general, had his tour of duty at Vancouver, Washington, cut short by Army Chief of Staff Malin Craig, who wanted him to head the War Plans Division (WPD) in Washington. As it turned out, Marshall was not to head WPD for long, and even before he took the job it was rumored he had been selected for the position as a

stepping-stone to becoming deputy chief of staff. Still, Craig, wary of upsetting a number of officers senior to Marshall, hesitated in making the
appointment. The issue was finally forced by Assistant Secretary of War
Louis Johnson, who asked Craig to immediately promote Marshall to vice
chief, in order to forestall the seemingly inexorable rise of General Hugh A.
Drum, whom Johnson detested.

Marshall spent a year in the deputy position before Roosevelt, at Hopkins's and Baruch's urging, appointed him the Army's fifteenth chief of
staff. He was sworn in to the job on the same day that the Germans unleashed their panzers on Poland. Witnessing the speed at which Poland's
large but obsolete army was pulverized by the Wehrmacht's hammer blows,
Marshall became more convinced than ever that in addition to its pitiful
size the United States Army was hopelessly antiquated. Fixing it required
money and time. Unsure of how much time events would allow him, he
turned to the pressing problem of getting Congress and the president to
pony up the money. Uncertain of his influence with the president at this
early point in their relationship, Marshall planned to first approach Hopkins and later Morgenthau, men he knew had the president's ear.

But in early 1940, just before the German invasion of France, Congress,
not the president, was the obstacle to a larger and more modern army.
Legislators had already taken a knife to FDR's budget request, particularly
the parts pertaining to the Army. To get Congress to reverse itself Marshall
turned to his old friend, financier Bernard Baruch, for help.

After his joint campaign with Senator Byrnes to frustrate Roosevelt's
purge of the Democratic Party, Baruch had turned his energy toward alerting anyone who would listen to the magnitude of the threat posed by Germany. His greatest convert to date was Harry Hopkins, who had spent
some time at Baruch's sprawling South Carolina estate, Hobcaw, in early
1939. At the time Hopkins, unsure of Roosevelt's intentions regarding a
third term, was starting to nurse his own presidential ambitions. In fact, he
had come to Hobcaw hoping to solicit political advice and, more crucially,
campaign funding. Baruch, however, wanted only to discuss the war clouds
gathering on the horizon and what America had to do to prepare itself.
Hopkins was slow to embrace the theme, but Baruch persisted. Eventually,
Hopkins came around, and before he left Hobcaw, Baruch claimed, "he
was all out for a total effort." Hopkins had gone to Hobcaw a committed
New Dealer; he left as an apostle of military preparedness, ready to take his

place among the growing number of "all-outers" around the president. If this had been all Baruch did to help the United States win World War II, it was enough.

Baruch took Marshall's problems to his political partner and FDR's political fixer, Jimmy Byrnes. Getting right to work, Byrnes, a friend of Marshall's since the general's earlier assignment in South Carolina, arranged a dinner for April 10, 1940, where Marshall could meet with a dozen of the most powerful senators on the Hill. In a discussion that stretched well into the morning hours the Army chief made his case. At the end, Marshall, who had spoken for hours without notes, could not read his audience. Disconsolately he ended with "My job as Chief of Staff is to convince you of our needs, and I have utterly failed. I don't know what to do." He had, however, misjudged his audience. Senator Alva B. Adams from Colorado, while laughing at Marshall's statement, replied: "You came before us without even a piece of paper and you got everything you asked for."

Baruch and Byrnes had come through for Marshall. Congress would not stymie the Army or the Army Air Forces' methodical buildup. It was now time to go to work on the president, who remained reluctant to move far ahead of public opinion. As Hopkins was still recovering from his latest serious bout of illness, Marshall went to see Morgenthau. They met on May 1, 1940, when, in a long meeting, Marshall laid out in minute detail the Army's many needs. Morgenthau listened intently, asking Marshall to explain everything as it was "all new to him." When he was finished, Marshall announced that the total bill was $640 million.

Morgenthau, after a brief pause, said, "I don't scare easily. I am not scared yet."

Marshall responded, "It makes me dizzy."

To which Morgenthau answered, "It makes me dizzy if we don't get it."

Besides alerting the "all-outer" Morgenthau that the U.S. Army was far from ready to enter the war, the meeting had another salutary effect. As the historian John Morton Blum notes, Morgenthau had discovered a wise and temperate Army spokesman: "His respect for Marshall and his confidence in him were complete then and thereafter."

Both men met with the president two days later. Also present were Budget Director Harold Smith, Secretary of War Harry Woodring, and Assistant Secretary Louis Johnson. From the start the meeting was a fiasco. Immediately after Marshall made his requests, the isolationist Woodring and the all-outer Johnson started bickering over what was required and the costs. Roosevelt, incredulous that the Army secretaries had not hashed out a common vision before entering his office, moved to put off any decision. Marshall, a strong believer in the chain of command, hesitated to contradict his boss. Morgenthau stepped in to press Marshall's position, but Roosevelt snapped: "I am not asking you. I am telling you." Morgenthau protested further: "Well, I still think you are wrong." The president, unmoved, responded, "Well, you filed your protest."

Morgenthau begged Roosevelt to hear General Marshall out, but Roosevelt, claiming he already knew what Marshall would say, refused. Marshall, remembering an earlier Morgenthau comment that few ever stood up to Roosevelt but he liked it when someone did, decided to risk angering Woodring rather than miss a possibly fleeting chance to impress Roosevelt with the seriousness of the Army's needs. He stepped forward and asked Roosevelt for a few moments. When the president graciously agreed, Marshall unleashed an emotional torrent. When he had finished, Roosevelt asked him to return the next day with a detailed list of his requirements. Morgenthau knew Roosevelt would cut the list, but he also realized that Marshall was slowly convincing FDR that preparedness involved much more than fifty thousand aircraft.

Marshall had won the first skirmish, but harder fights were ahead.

10

A Reluctant

Industrial Complex

F OR THE MOMENT, MARSHALL AND HIS ALLIES WERE RIDING A RIS-
ing tide. Congress, rattled by the German blitzkrieg through France,
appropriated over a billion dollars by the end of May 1940, with much
more to follow before the year was out.

Ironically, the Hill's sudden largesse ignited the first great crisis of the
war. It was one thing to drop a mountain of money on the military; quite
another to spend it. Despite having increased the base level of wartime
production to supply French and British orders, American industry was
incapable of meeting exploding U.S. military requirements. Nor was it in a
hurry to do so. One might have assumed that most businesses would leap
at the chance to secure guaranteed government contracts totaling over a
billion dollars. But many factors discouraged business leaders from seizing
the ostensible windfall.

In the aftermath of World War I American businessmen had been badly
burned. Prior to the Great War, America had no war industries worthy of
the name, certainly nothing to rival Germany's Krupp or Britain's Vickers.
After three years of Allied war orders, followed by Bernard Baruch's 1917
mobilization of American industry to support America's entry into the
war, much had changed. By 1918 the Allies were being kept afloat by a
flood of U.S. financing and American industrial muscle. German field
marshal Paul von Hindenburg later lamented that U.S. industrialists were
the only ones who truly understood modern war, and to win it they had

created a war industry that was both "brilliant and pitiless." After the war, however, the idea spread that the British had tricked the nation into joining a European war, and had done so with the full support of the industrialists who were supposedly salivating for increased profits. America turned away from these "merchants of death" and demanded the destruction of the nation's first modern military-industrial complex, which was accomplished neatly by the passage of onerous tax laws that limited machinery write-offs and made underutilized facilities too expensive to maintain.

Donald Nelson, who would become World War II's production czar, cited the all-too-representative example of Bethlehem Steel, which as America entered World War I was alone producing nearly all the munitions American forces would require. The postwar tax levies forced Bethlehem to destroy its entire munitions business: every building razed, thousands of machine tools scrapped. This destruction was repeated all over the country, as the industries that had powered the Allies to victory were demolished by their owners in order to avoid the ruinous taxes. As Nelson stated, "Here, one month was a blood-sweating behemoth of munitions production. . . . The next month the wreckers moved in and left not a trace." The industrial plant that had made Hindenburg shudder vanished in a mere twinkling.

If demolishing billions of dollars' worth of capital stock had been the end of the matter, American business would likely have put the matter behind it and grabbed the government contracts. Unfortunately, it did not end there. Articles such as those by Charles Beard in *The New Republic* and bestsellers such as George Seldes's *Iron Blood and Profits* exacerbated the popular revulsion not only at war industries, but also at the men who ran them. Sensing easy notoriety and political gain, Senator Gerald Nye, the champion of the neutrality laws, launched Senate hearings on the matter of war profits. One historian described the process as "more of a court than a congressional investigation, hearing the hypothetical case of *Peace Loving and Moral People v. Manufacturers and Salesmen of Implements of War*. True to this interpretation, Nye opened the hearings by declaring: "I confidently predict that when the Senate investigation is over, we shall see that war and preparation for war is not a matter of national honor and national defense, but a matter of profit for few." Starting in September 1934, he called before his inquisition a who's who of American industrialists and bankers, including J. P. Morgan, Jr., and Pierre du Pont. For eighteen months and ninety-three hearings Nye plunged on, never finding any evidence of war profiteering, but also never letting his lack of results slow his constant stream of invective and accusations.

Nye finally overstepped his bounds when he accused President Wilson of having lied about his knowledge of secret treaties for the Allies to carve up Europe at the end of World War I. Senator Tom Connally of Texas rose to Wilson's defense. Smashing his fist into the podium so hard that he fractured a knuckle, Connally shouted: "Some checker-playing, beer-drinking back room of some low house is the only place fit for the kind of language which the Senator from North Dakota puts into the Record about a dead man, a great man, a good man, a man who, when alive, had the courage to meet his enemies face to face and eye to eye." The Senate promptly cut off the committee's funding. The Nye Committee was dead, but the damage was done. Americans, already prejudiced against greedy men who profited from death and destruction, had their biases confirmed, and were inspired to overwhelmingly support the subsequent Neutrality Acts of 1935–1937. Senator Harry Truman later called the committee an exercise in "pure demagoguery" and thought it did inestimable damage to U.S. efforts to prepare for World War II.

The effects of the Nye Committee remained evident even as the nation began mobilizing for war. Many congressmen were wary of giving businesses any kind of tax relief for new construction, or making any other allowance that permitted firms to turn a profit on war contracts. It was left to Republican and former secretary of war Henry Stimson to remind them that "if you are going to go to war in a capitalist country . . . you have to let business make money out of the project or business won't work . . . Many in Congress think that they can tax business out of all proportion and still have businessmen work diligently and quickly. This is not human nature." Businesses were, in the end, permitted to make a profit, but allowing them to do so remained a political struggle throughout the war.

Given this poisoned political atmosphere, many businessmen refused contracts, fearing they would later be demonized as merchants of death. Understandably, they loathed the idea that their personal reputations would again be pilloried by a populace that remained adamant that the United States steer clear of involvement in any new war. Moreover, the national mood, fed by Charles Lindbergh's gospel of non-involvement and huge America First rallies, suggested the strong possibility that America was not going to enter the war. Business interests were understandably reluctant to add billions of dollars of industrial capacity that would become an albatross around their necks if America steered clear of the conflict.

Finally, American businesses were making money again—a lot of money—without the benefit of military contracts. As the economy picked up after the 1938 downturn, Americans were spending again. Cars were rolling off the lots as fast as they were built, and people were queueing up for refrigerators, washing machines, and countless other items in a frenzy of pent-up demand. As it became clearer that this was not just another false economic dawn, the buying pace picked up. After a long and grueling depression, American businesses were reluctant to divert resources on the iffy chance they could profit from war contracts.

Ultimately, however, the lure of profits was irresistible, and the German invasion of Poland provided the necessary impetus for the business community to begin taking war orders in earnest. Within weeks, American industry accelerated their acceptance of Allied orders, as well as some orders from the American military, as long as they did not conflict with the production of ever greater quantities of consumer goods. Problems, however, were not slow in coming: not enough raw materials, a lack of machine tools, no spare factory capacity, and to top it all off the military had no idea what to spend their newly acquired riches on.

Having seen this same thing happen in the First World War, the military had developed various plans, most notably the Industrial Mobilization Plan, authored primarily by World War I production czar Bernard Baruch, which outlined how the Army and Navy would take control of all American industry at the start of the next war. The plan had done a good job incorporating the lessons of 1918—but it gloriously failed to make allowances for the much-changed world and economy of 1940. It also assumed that America would go from peace to war in an instant. In reality, America's war mobilization took place in fits and starts and had been under way for almost two years before the country actually entered the war. Finally, even if the mobilization plan had been perfect, the military should have realized from the start that it had zero chance of implementation, given that it called for a czar to take the reins of the entire economy. This, of course, was a job Roosevelt reserved for himself, and he was never going to hand such immense domestic power to someone else unless it became absolutely necessary. Nor had the president yet focused on establishing the agencies that would save the day.

In fact, no one even knew if Roosevelt would remain in Washington long enough to address the issue.

11

THE SPHINX

WOULD ROOSEVELT RUN FOR A THIRD TERM? By May 1940 the uncertainty was seizing up Washington's political machine. Roosevelt himself gave no public indication about his plans, although he did confide to some intimates that he was tired and looking forward to retiring to Hyde Park. Within his closed social circle, he repeatedly talked about working on his stamp collection, and repairing the family finances by doing some writing. In fact, plans were already going forward for his presidential library—Harry Hopkins planned on running it—and a new retirement cottage was under construction. The problem was that no one outside of his "official family" believed he was through, and even those closest to him were often not sure.

As Roosevelt's public silence continued, others began jockeying for position. Many of these potential candidates thought they had either Roosevelt's strong support or at least his tacit approval to make a run at the nomination. This was the inevitable result of Roosevelt's modus operandi, as many of those who left his presence believed that he agreed with everything they had said—when nothing could have been further from the truth. This often led to a sense of betrayal when one or another visitor later learned that FDR had decided a matter in a contrary manner. Usually the residual bitterness at such slights could be erased by a subsequent Roosevelt charm offensive, but at times the personal damage was lasting.

Eighteen months before, Harry Hopkins was to all appearances FDR's anointed successor. Roosevelt saw in Hopkins the one man with national stature who was totally committed to the same causes that he was. In fact,

Roosevelt's primary reason for elevating Hopkins to secretary of commerce was to place him in a position where he would deal with businessmen on a regular basis, to begin mending fences with those angered by his New Deal initiatives. Plans for Hopkins's candidacy always turned on his uncertain health, and in the spring of 1939 it was failing. By late summer, Hopkins could no longer go to work and was soon in the Mayo Clinic fighting for his life. The doctors had given up hope and expected him to pass on within a month, until Roosevelt intervened. Hopkins moved to Washington, where Roosevelt personally tasked the Navy's surgeon general with his care. As spring 1940 approached, Hopkins was on the mend. But his health was never secure, and consequently his presidential ambitions vanished. In their place came new ambitions: to dedicate himself to Roosevelt's needs, and to push the president toward a third term.

With Hopkins removed from the electoral landscape, the door opened for other Democratic notables. While most of them believed that Roosevelt approved of their ambitions, in the case of Secretary of Agriculture Henry Wallace it was probably true. Wallace was smart, well informed, and a great communicator. He also had many political liabilities, such as a partiality to new spiritual fads. But as he was an internationalist and a committed New Dealer, Roosevelt ignored what he considered slight character peccadilloes and encouraged Wallace's presidential ambitions. Unfortunately for Wallace's chances at the nomination, Roosevelt was also encouraging Cordell Hull, whom many considered the Democratic Party establishment's favored candidate. Moreover, Roosevelt had specifically told party boss Jim Farley that he would not run for a third term; leaving Farley with the impression that the field was open for his own run, completely unaware that Roosevelt, for reasons never explained, was already maneuvering to make sure Farley could never gain the nomination.

Of course, until Roosevelt publicly announced his intentions the field was frozen, keeping donors' wallets sealed and the populace uninterested. Roosevelt, for his part, was in no hurry to let anyone know his plans. He loved the suspense and relished the mounting pile of political cartoons portraying him as a sphinx—eternal and silent. He gave little thought to the new political schisms he was creating at a time when he should have been trying to heal party wounds still festering from his attempted purge of Democratic conservatives.

In truth, while his inclination was not to run, Roosevelt probably did not know his own mind and remained undecided for many months. In January 1940, for instance, he signed a contract to write articles for *Collier's* magazine in exchange for an annual salary of $75,000. He told Harold Ickes that he was tired, and Eleanor shared with Hopkins that "he has not the same zest for administrative detail that he had and is probably quite frankly bored." Eleanor herself was strongly against his running, as were most of the Democratic Party's power brokers. Though Roosevelt fretted over the New Deal's fate, if domestic issues had remained his only concern he likely would have left office. But by spring 1940 he could see that a world in flames directly threatened the well-being of the nation. Hopkins, and many of his intimates, believed that it was the rapid defeat of France that finally drove Roosevelt to a decision. By the time the British were evacuating Dunkirk, he understood that it was highly unlikely that America could hide behind its ocean moats forever, and with some justification he saw himself as the indispensable man to lead the nation through the gathering storm.

Having made his decision, Roosevelt continued to act as if he did not want the nomination, but he also flatly refused to make a Shermanesque statement refusing it. Gradually it dawned on even the most dim-witted party power broker that the president was not ready to ride into the sunset. Still, he remained reluctant to actively seek an unprecedented third term; he wished to be drafted and proceeded to choreograph an elaborate dance designed to lead to his accepting the nomination only if the party demanded he take it. He wrote a letter to be read to the delegates at the party convention in July, informing them that he had a "fervent desire not to run." The historian Kenneth Davis called this Roosevelt's most "sincere statement of untruth."

Hopkins, who had just recently moved into the White House, took it upon himself to go out to Chicago and take charge of coordinating the party's "spontaneous drafting" of Roosevelt. His presence only added another layer of confusion to a convention that was rapidly becoming a fiasco. When Hopkins, Byrnes, and Chicago mayor Edward Kelly begged the president to put in a personal appearance and make his desires known, Roosevelt flatly refused, saying, "Too many promises will be extracted from me if I go."

On the convention floor, resentful delegates, unhappy about being used as Roosevelt's puppets, were in a foul mood. The very sense of the fix being in that Roosevelt had tried to avoid pervaded the hall. Most of the delegates just wanted to get it over with and go home. Worse, Hopkins, who saw everything in black and white, was angering many of the party faithful. In his Roosevelt-centric worldview, one either supported FDR's nomination for a third term or one was an enemy to be steamrollered and beaten down. The mood got so ugly that the president, at the urging of Labor Secretary Frances Perkins, decided to send Eleanor to Chicago to smooth ruffled feathers.

When the mood of the delegates did not improve on the second day, Mayor Kelly put the Chicago machine to work, packing the galleries with his people and calling in the Chicago Police Department to block entry of third-term doubters. A little after 9:00 P.M., Senate Majority Leader Alben Barkley, in the course of a stem-winder speech, invoked Roosevelt's name. On cue, Kelly's plants erupted in joyous pandemonium, as "Happy Days Are Here Again" blared through loudspeakers and confetti rained down. Catching the mood, suddenly jubilant delegates roared in delight.

When the crowd finally settled down, Barkley told them he had a message from Roosevelt and solemnly read: "The President has never had, and has not today, any desire or purpose to continue in the office of President . . . He wishes in all earnestness and sincerity to make it clear that all the delegates to this convention are free to vote for any candidate." Stunned, the delegates began turning to each other, all of them wondering what they were supposed to do next. Did Roosevelt want the nomination or not?

Kelly had an answer for them.

A voice, the "voice of God," bellowed through the speaker system: "ROO-SEVELT . . . ROOSEVELT . . . ROOSEVELT . . . AMERICA WANTS ROO-SEVELT . . . EVERYONE WANTS ROOSEVELT." On and on the voice continued. Delegates soon started chanting the same phrases. The Chicago Police band magically marched in from a side entrance, joining the revelry. Shouting at the top of their lungs, thousands of plants from the Kelly political machine burst from the galleries and stormed onto the convention floor, all of them shouting Roosevelt's praises. Through it all there was the steady drumbeat from the speakers: "THE WORLD NEEDS ROO-SEVELT . . . ROOSEVELT . . . ROOSEVELT." Only later did a journalist discover that the "voice of God" was a Kelly operative named Thomas D.

McGarry, Chicago's superintendent of sewers. It was not long before the Republicans dubbed his chants, heard by tens of millions of radio listeners, "the voice from the sewers." But that would be later. In Chicago that evening, "the voice of God" went on without letup for nearly an hour. When he and the crowd finally wore themselves out, Jimmy Byrnes took to the podium and announced that the convention was finished for the evening and that "tomorrow night, you can finish the job of drafting Franklin D. Roosevelt."

Eight hundred miles to the east FDR finished dinner, turned off his radio, and went to sleep. But the drama had not yet ended. For decades, it had been the delegates' right to nominate a vice president, with little regard for the presidential nominee's desires. But Roosevelt insisted they nominate Henry Wallace. As he explained to Frances Perkins: "I like him. He is the kind of man I like to have around. . . . He thinks right." Unfortunately, there were few Democrats who agreed with the president about the controversial, mercurial agriculture secretary.

Roosevelt would have been denied his choice if not for the intervention of Jimmy Byrnes, who although nursing his own vice presidential ambitions told Roosevelt he would "go down the line" for the president's choice.

Henry Wallace,
33rd vice president
of the United States.

All that day Byrnes moved among the rebellious delegates twisting arms, and repeatedly shouting: "For God's sake, do you want a president or a vice president?" He was ably supported by Eleanor, whose speech soothed many restive delegates and persuaded them to see that this was "no ordinary time," and so they should give the president what he desired. When Roosevelt made it known that if Wallace was not nominated, he would refuse his own nomination, the tide turned. Given a choice between Wallace and political annihilation without Roosevelt at the head of the ticket, the delegates grudgingly obliged FDR. But they were in such a foul state that when Wallace went to deliver his acceptance speech, Jimmy Byrnes grabbed him: "Don't do it, Henry. Don't go out there. You'll ruin the party if you do."

Roosevelt's election was not a foregone conclusion. In 1940 the Republicans discovered they also had a man of the people in their midst.

Wendell Willkie was a small-town boy who discovered he liked the big stage. He had made his reputation when he gave up his membership in the Democratic Party and began crisscrossing the country fighting parts of the New Deal where he thought the government was taking too heavy a hand in the marketplace. He thrived on meeting politicians, local businessmen, and even, from time to time, celebrities. After a radio debate one commentator said of his skillful manipulation of the audience: "If Willkie is an amateur, so is Babe Ruth." As he grew in stature and redefined himself on the national stage, he and his wife, the former Edith Wilk, became increasingly estranged. There were many causes for the estrangement, but high on the list was the fact that Willkie was not immune to the charms of other women. He also possessed the looks, charm, and aw-shucks innocence that attracted numerous women into his orbit. One of them, Irita Van Doren, was a New York socialite and the *New York Herald Tribune*'s influential book editor. Van Doren, whom Willkie met in 1937, was smart, slim, and articulate, and exuded charm with every breath. Willkie was instantly enamored of her, as was she of him. Almost immediately they became an item, and although Van Doren tried to maintain some degree of circumspection, Willkie never went out of his way to keep the affair discreet.

Van Doren not only fell in love with Willkie, she made him her project. With her encouragement Willkie started putting himself forward as an al-

Wendell Willkie,
Republican presidential candidate.

ternative to the Republican establishment candidates, all of whom were committed isolationists. At the turn of the year, three candidates besides Willkie were vying for the nomination. Thomas E. Dewey, the youngest at thirty-seven, came to national attention when he broke up the powerful New York–based crime rackets, locking up Lucky Luciano and Dutch Schultz. He was leading in the polls, but the other two contenders, Senator Arthur Vandenberg and the recently elected Senator Robert A. Taft, the son of a former president, were not far behind.

Willkie was a true dark horse, but he had a few advantages. For one, Republican business leaders and publishers were alert to the dangers Germany and Japan posed to the United States. For them Willkie was a tailor-made candidate: a businessman like themselves and an outspoken internationalist, and, most crucial of all, he had a folksy appeal that won over audiences. Willkie was also a liberal, and despite becoming a Republican he strongly supported those parts of the New Deal that remained popular with the general public.

The convention itself was a raucous affair, with Willkie finishing a distant third on the first ballot. But by the third ballot, with his supporters raising the roof, Willkie passed Taft. Four ballots later Willkie was the Republican nominee for president.

Republicans had nominated a candidate with the vote-getting appeal of

Roosevelt himself, and the president clearly recognized the danger. When Harold Ickes mentioned in a cabinet meeting that Willkie's favorable image with the public should not go unchallenged, Roosevelt agreed, and loosed his favorite attack dog to hit Willkie over the airwaves. He could not have made a better pick. In attacking Willkie, Ickes was in his element, and he relished his new assignment.

Even before the convention Roosevelt made another key decision as to how to conduct an unprecedented third-term campaign. Because of the rapidly developing national emergency he announced that he needed to remain near Washington as much as possible. Instead of campaigning, Roosevelt shrewdly put himself above squalid partisan politics by clothing himself in the mantle of commander in chief. If Americans wanted a competent man at the helm during this time of crisis they would have to come to that decision on their own; Franklin Delano Roosevelt would be too busy protecting the nation to beg them for their votes. After all, he had

Harold Ickes.

Ickes and a veritable host of other political infighters to wage political war for him.

At the same time, Roosevelt knew that Willkie's nomination had greatly eased the way for his own plans to prepare the nation for war. As Willkie was an interventionist and supported all-out aid for Britain, Roosevelt could push preparation programs forward with little fear that the Republican candidate would stir up isolationist antagonisms. Interestingly, papers in both Britain and Germany cheered Willkie's nomination. The Germans did not know their man.

12

REPUBLICANS SEIZE

THE WAR DEPARTMENT

T HE TEMPO OF EVENTS INTENSIFIED DRAMATICALLY THROUGH 1940 as panzers rampaging deep into France galvanized official Washington. At the beginning of the year Roosevelt had asked Congress for the then astronomical sum of $1.8 billion in defense-related spending, convinced that he had requested a sufficient amount to jump-start war production. But by early April the appropriation bill was stalled, and Congress was taking a carving knife to it. Attitudes changed a bit on April 9, when Hitler attacked Norway and Denmark. Then on May 16, six days after Hitler launched the Wehrmacht into France, Roosevelt, convinced that Congress was finally alert to the broader danger Hitler represented, asked for an additional $1.4 billion. The sea change in congressional attitudes was made clear when by mid-October Congress had appropriated an astounding $17.7 billion for defense, almost double the entire government budget for the previous year.

For the most part, Roosevelt was satisfied with his military team, at least for the moment. He was far less content with the civilians in positions that significantly impacted national preparedness. Only Morgenthau's Treasury Department—where Roosevelt was already sending much of the work that should have been undertaken by other departments—was on anything resembling a war footing. The president remained relatively unconcerned by the inadequacies and antiquated diplomatic processes of Hull's State Department. The secretary's sympathies dovetailed with Roosevelt's and if

delicate diplomatic work became necessary—beyond his own efforts—
Roosevelt knew he could count on Sumner Welles or a number of other
trusted envoys to take care of it. He had no intention of expending precious time and political capital trying to dramatically reform State or most
of the other cabinet-level departments, unless it became apparent that they
were actively hindering the war effort.

Recognizing that most of the constitutionally established government
departments were incapable of dealing with the demands of all-out war,
during the spring and summer of 1940 Roosevelt created and staffed new
organizations designed to deal with problems as they arose. Unlike cabinet-
level organizations, when these new institutions failed him, the president
simply eliminated them, or, more often, added to the growing chaos by
establishing new organizations in their place without ever dissolving the
earlier creations.

One department was essential to running any future conflict: the irreplaceable War Department, which became Roosevelt's primary concern.
His first priority was fixing the relationship between Secretary of War
Harry H. Woodring and Assistant Secretary Louis A. Johnson, who detested one another. Woodring was a poor administrator, a terrible leader,
and in the judgment of all who dealt with him, wholly unfit for his responsibilities. Johnson, on the other hand, was a better administrator and
leader. Unfortunately, he was a born intriguer who never missed a chance
to belittle Woodring or to undermine his authority. The situation was not
helped by the fact that Woodring was an isolationist who saw little need to
enlarge the military and was dead set against sending military aid to the
Allies. As for Johnson, he was an all-outer and passionately convinced that
every effort should be made to give the Allies whatever they needed.

Into this snake pit stepped one of those rare men, mostly overlooked by
history, who quietly have an outsized impact on affairs: Grenville Clark.
One historian said of him: "He appeared, in critical or confusing times, as
a lobby for particular impulses of national conscience." Clark was always
content to work behind the scenes, and always shunned publicity. One
writer referred to him as "statesman incognito" because he was unknown
to the public but very well known to "a few thousand persons of considerable influence in national affairs." Among those in his circle was Franklin
Roosevelt, who called him "Grenny," as did Teddy Roosevelt. The two had
known each other at Harvard and stayed in touch over the years. Clark, in

fact, was instrumental in developing much of Roosevelt's early economic agenda. He also organized the American Bar Association's vocal and effective protests to kill Roosevelt's court-packing scheme.

Earlier in his career, in 1915, Clark had devised the idea for what became the Plattsburg Movement, which provided tens of thousands of trained officers for the American Expeditionary Force in World War I. Now, as he watched newsreels of German panzers rolling across the fields of France, it was for him once again 1915. After deciding that it was time for the first peacetime draft in American history, Clark began rallying the most influential of the Plattsburg alumni to his cause. With their backing, Clark took his message to Washington.

Roosevelt, knowing the purpose of Clark's visit, had his gatekeeper, General "Pa" Watson, shunt him off to Hopkins. At the time, late May, Roosevelt did not yet know who the Republicans were going to run against him, or how the Republicans would use his support for a peacetime draft as political ammunition, and he was not prepared to commit himself. Clark, believing Hopkins would also try to put him off, refused the proffered meeting. But, two weeks later, when he and Hopkins did meet, Hopkins assured him that Roosevelt approved of the draft effort and would come out in support when it was politically opportune.

Somewhat buoyed by Roosevelt's tacit endorsement, Clark next took his message to Capitol Hill, where Jimmy Byrnes told him that it did not have a "Chinaman's chance" of passing. He had better luck with Congressman James Wadsworth and Senator Edward Burke, neither of them FDR allies. Both agreed to put the measure before Congress as soon as the completed draft bill, currently being written by another Plattsburg alumnus, was in their hands. In the meantime, Clark turned his attention to the War Department, where his first stop was Army chief of staff George Marshall. To his dismay, he discovered that Marshall was lukewarm, and possibly hostile, to a peacetime draft. Marshall was aware of Roosevelt's position and was unwilling to get ahead of the president in advocating a draft; and he flatly refused to lobby the commander in chief on behalf of the measure, believing involvement in the political debate was far outside his brief.

Clark was further taken aback—horrified—to discover that Marshall was preoccupied with the defense of the Western Hemisphere, convinced that the Nazis' next move would be the invasion of South America. Astonished at the general's strategic naïveté, Clark tested Marshall's patience by ridiculing that priority at a time when France was on the verge of military collapse. Marshall's fallback position was that a sudden flood of raw recruits would disrupt the careful schedules the War Department had created for the methodical expansion of the Army. Again, Clark could only listen in disbelief, astounded at Marshall's inability to grasp the gravity and extent of the unfolding global crisis. Clearly, Marshall was still growing into the job of chief of staff, and was only slowly beginning to comprehend the magnitude of the tasks before him. Clark swallowed his disappointment and moved on. He understood that Marshall was a soldier and thought like a soldier. The only way to gain his wholehearted support of the draft legislation was through the president.

As Clark continued to call on various denizens of the War Department, he began to fully apprehend the sordid mess at the top of the organization. Of course, like anyone who read a newspaper, he knew there was bad blood between Woodring and Johnson, but this was the first time he got an insider's look at the morale-sapping, corrosive dysfunction, which clearly precluded forward momentum in general, let alone progress on a military draft. He left the War Department convinced it was time for new blood at the top.

Clark's next step was to visit Supreme Court justice Felix Frankfurter. Frankfurter, a liberal jurist and one of the founders of the American Civil Liberties Union (ACLU), had spent many years alternating between the Harvard faculty and government service. Roosevelt considered him a valuable adviser and counted on him to recommend bright young persons to fill crucial but normally second-tier positions within the government. During the New Deal years, Frankfurter had staffed many of the key administrative positions within the government with his acolytes, who were collectively known as "Felix's Happy Hot Dogs." Even after Roosevelt appointed him to the Supreme Court in 1938, he continued to proffer advice and recommend appointments. Although as a justice he needed to maintain a degree of circumspection, he stayed close to Roosevelt and had his ear on many matters throughout the war.

Frankfurter had already discussed with Roosevelt pending changes within the War Department, and assured Clark that the president would welcome the departure of Woodring, if the right replacement could be found. Clark and Frankfurter considered many candidates, but kept coming back to Henry Stimson, who had served past administrations as secre-

Confirmation hearing of Professor Felix Frankfurter,
later associate justice of the Supreme Court.

tary of state and secretary of war. Though a Republican, Stimson was no
isolationist. He had, in fact, come out strongly in support of Roosevelt's
initiatives to assist the Allies, and was even running ahead of the administration in many areas. Clark, however, was worried about Stimson's age,
and thought he appeared to be a tired old man when last they met. Frankfurter correctly surmised that he was merely bored, and that the challenge
of running the War Department would revitalize him. On June 3, Frankfurter visited the White House, where Roosevelt inquired as to whether he
had any ideas about the War Department. Frankfurter leaped into the
opening, suggesting that the president consider Stimson for the top job.
Roosevelt was noncommittal, but Frankfurter recalled later that his face lit
up at the mention of Stimson's name.

Initially reluctant when Clark finally asked him if he wanted the job,
after discussing the matter with his wife Stimson said he would serve on
certain conditions: he would not take part in administration politics; he
would push for a draft; and he demanded the right to choose his own subordinates. Frankfurter relayed the news to the White House, and being
assured of Stimson's excellent health, Roosevelt accepted Stimson, as well
as his choice for the job of assistant secretary: Robert P. Patterson.

Patterson, a former Plattsburger and a major in World War I, is one of the great but forgotten men of World War II. A successful lawyer, he gave up his practice to serve as an infantry officer in World War I, where he was gassed, temporarily blinded, and awarded the Distinguished Service Cross (second only to the Medal of Honor) and Silver Star for bravery, after leading his company through some of the most horrific fighting of the war. His troops idolized him, and one later remembered they would often see him carrying his own pack, along with that of one or two tired soldiers, during long marches.

Patterson returned to the law after the armistice, but his devotion to his men endured. As many of those who had served with him related, when-

Robert Patterson, undersecretary of war (left), shakes hands
with Henry Stimson as General Jacob Devers looks on.

ever any of his former comrades in arms went to see him he dropped everything to talk with them and help with their problems, no matter how trivial or modest they might be. In 1940, he was a federal judge, but at forty-nine years old he had taken a leave of absence to return to Plattsburg for a military refresher course, in anticipation of once more serving in the infantry. He was a private on KP duty, emptying trash cans, when he got the cable offering him the job of assistant secretary of war. After accepting the job, he asked to leave the camp, but his sergeant refused permission until he finished emptying the trash cans.

Two weeks after Roosevelt had agreed to bring Stimson into the cabinet, there had been no call from the president. Clark, Stimson, and Patterson all wondered if Roosevelt had changed his mind. Only when Woodring twice refused a direct presidential order to ship B-17 bombers to Britain did matters come to a head. Furious, Roosevelt, who had been reluctant to fire Woodring and then have him out attacking him on the campaign trail, demanded his resignation on June 19. Making a clean sweep, Roosevelt also moved to replace Acting Secretary of the Navy Charles Edison, whom he had long considered out of his depth, convincing the son of the great inventor to run for governor of New Jersey with the administration's full political support.

Roosevelt had already decided on another Republican, Frank Knox, to fill the Navy position. Knox, a former Rough Rider and subsequently a newspaper publisher, was no fan of the Roosevelt administration. He had even run for vice president with Alf Landon on the Republican ticket in 1936. But like Stimson he was a committed internationalist, and his newspaper strongly advocated giving all possible aid and support to the Allies. When Roosevelt called him on June 19, Knox accepted the post without hesitation. Roosevelt then called Stimson and offered him the War Department. After getting Roosevelt's assurance that Patterson would soon replace Louis Johnson, Stimson accepted.

Roosevelt was never reluctant to fire anyone who he believed had betrayed or purposely disobeyed him to achieve their own personal ends. But firing people loyal to him was a different matter. Eleanor had once observed that he "had a great sympathy for people and a great understanding, and he couldn't bear to be disagreeable to someone he liked. . . . And he just couldn't bring himself to really do the unkind thing that had to be done unless he got angry."

She also noted that when pushed beyond a certain point Roosevelt could easily become icily detached from almost everyone. He could inflict punishment with vindictive cruelty, unless, of course, there were political reasons to be gentle, as there were in Woodring's case. But when someone had remained loyal and dutiful but still had to go, Roosevelt turned soft

William Franklin "Frank" Knox, secretary of the navy.

and found it almost impossible to fire that someone. Louis Johnson was such a case. It was not until Stimson enlisted Morgenthau's intervention that Roosevelt finally tasked Pa Watson to deliver the news. When Watson told him he was fired, the assistant secretary "broke down and cried like a baby."

For Roosevelt, bringing two men who embodied the Republican establishment—Stimson and Knox—into the cabinet was a multifaceted coup. Not only did he get to replace two incompetent cabinet members with men possessing the drive, foresight, and intelligence to lead huge organizations through the coming crisis; during an election year he clearly demonstrated that preparedness was not a partisan issue. He was delighted to announce Knox's and Stimson's appointments on the very eve of the Republican convention.

In Washington, Stimson put Patterson in charge of all production and supply matters. It made little difference that he knew nothing about either. As he dove into the job and began to bring order to chaos, Patterson garnered a reputation as the "toughest man in Washington," befitting someone who considered the greatest moment of his life the day he killed two Germans in hand-to-hand combat. He was one of those rare individuals who only came fully alive in combat, and for most of his life he wore the belt of a German soldier he had killed. Taking the helm of a vast, complex structure, Patterson eschewed the spirit of enlightened compromise in favor of "force unqualified by reasonable doubt." He brought to his task a single-minded purpose, an intolerance of fools, a penetrating intellect, a capacity for hard work, and a fervent belief that if soldiers needed something they should have it. If there was one thing that ate at Patterson's soul, it was the suspicion that somewhere there was a civilian being coddled. For Patterson, denied a chance for further battlefield combat, the Washington war was almost as good.

For Clark's part, he now had a powerful supporter of a national draft running the War Department. Clark was immensely cheered when, even before his Senate confirmation, Stimson had Clark, Patterson, Marshall, and assorted staff officers out to Woodley—Stimson's Washington mansion—for a "peace conference." Here Stimson laid down the law, and told his assembled guests he expected them to give Burke and Wadsworth's draft legislation their full support. Assured that Roosevelt had given the measure his tacit approval, Marshall duly appeared before a Senate committee on July 12 and placed his already considerable authority behind the draft. Roosevelt's public support, however, remained tepid and it took considerable prodding before he made a single public remark in its favor. For the next two months the battle thundered on Capitol Hill, even as a tremendous second battle raged, aimed at swaying public opinion. In this second fight, Clark's well-funded organization was clearly winning. By early August, opinion polls that had indicated scant support for a draft in June showed that over 70 percent of the public was now in favor. What turned the tide? As one commentator noted, every time the Germans bombed London the draft gained support.

Roosevelt, at last confident that he would not suffer an electoral backlash, announced his support for the draft bill and told Jimmy Byrnes to actively start rounding up the votes. Byrnes then did what he did best, convincing reluctant senators to join him on the side of the angels . . . or else. When Willkie, at Clark's urging, came out in favor of a draft, the deal was sealed. By the time the United States entered the war it would have 1,650,000 men under arms in thirty-six combat divisions, almost as large an American force as had been in France at the end of World War I—a huge reservoir of trained manpower that proved vital in the months and years after Pearl Harbor.

13

YOUR BOYS ARE NOT GOING TO

BE SENT INTO ANY FOREIGN WARS

A S THE PARTY CONVENTIONS CONCLUDED, MUCH OF THE POLITICAL
stasis that had gripped Washington loosened. Roosevelt ordered that
every spare rifle, cannon, and round of ammunition be sent to Britain in
the wake of the costly evacuation from Dunkirk. Marshall and Chief of
Naval Operations Harold Stark offered no objections, and the matériel was
quickly declared surplus and transported to ports for emergency shipping.
Soon thereafter, however, both service chiefs asked Roosevelt to suspend
further shipments of munitions until Army stocks had been replenished.
By this time as much as a quarter of all the ammunition stored in the
United States was already on its way to Britain. Roosevelt refused the request. But on July 2 he was forced to sign into law a naval appropriations
bill into which the isolationists had slipped an amendment forbidding any
further shipments of munitions unless Marshall and Stark certified that
the U.S. military had no use for the matériel. This put both officers in the
untenable position of being able—being *required*—to countermand an
order from their commander in chief. The law could not have come at a
less opportune time: the British were requesting fifty aged U.S. destroyers,
and Roosevelt was leaning toward giving them the ships. Stark, however,
could not certify that the U.S. Navy did not need ships, as he had just recently told Congress the opposite to keep them from being scrapped.

Churchill had first requested the ships on May 15, only five days after the
German invasion of France and his own elevation to prime minister. He

Admiral Harold
Rainsford Stark,
chief of naval
operations.

had cabled: "Immediate needs now are: first of all the loan of forty or fifty of your older destroyers." Two months later he cabled again: "It has now become most urgent for you to give us the destroyers." Roosevelt had two concerns: Could he legally send the ships without congressional approval; and, more crucially, would Britain continue the struggle in the wake of France's surrender? His military advisers, stunned at the ease of the German conquest of France, held out little hope for Britain, most agreeing with French general Weygand's appraisal that Britain would in three weeks have its neck wrung like a chicken. Even more gloomy predictions of Britain's inevitable doom arrived at regular intervals from Ambassador Joseph Kennedy. Fortunately, Roosevelt was well aware of Kennedy's anti-British and pro-German sentiments, and discounted much of his commentary.

To gain some degree of certainty, Roosevelt sent William Donovan, World War I hero and later the founder of the Office of Strategic Services (OSS)—forerunner of the CIA—to evaluate the commitment of British leaders to fight on. Churchill rolled out the red carpet, and Donovan's glowing reports of British determination, the miracle at Dunkirk, and the spirited resistance of the Royal Air Force (RAF) in the face of the German air blitz convinced Roosevelt that Britain would fight on.

The legal restrictions were more formidable. Not only did Roosevelt have to overcome the need to get Stark's approval, but the Espionage Act of 1917 made delivering a naval vessel to a nation at war a criminal offense. Help came from two unexpected sources. At a mid-July dinner at New York City's Century Club, hosted by Roosevelt intimate Lewis Douglas, thirty of America's most distinguished and well-connected individuals decided to form a group dedicated to alerting Americans to Britain's peril, as well as the growing danger to the United States. During this meeting—the first of the Century Club—someone broached the idea of trading the fifty destroyers in exchange for British-owned naval bases in the Western Hemisphere. After checking with the British ambassador, Lord Lothian, publisher Henry Luce proposed the idea to Roosevelt. Roosevelt liked it and brought the scheme up at the next cabinet meeting, which Stimson at the time called one of the most important debates in which he ever participated. The cabinet was unanimously behind the proposal, but they were also all confirmed in the opinion that sending the destroyers required congressional approval. Roosevelt, who did not want a long debate that he might lose, remained committed to circumventing Congress.

Again, the Century Club came through for him. One of their members, Dean Acheson, produced a detailed legal opinion stating that the president could, on his own authority, make the destroyers-for-bases deal. In 1933 Roosevelt had fired Acheson, then serving as undersecretary of the treasury, and banished him from his official circle. At the time Acheson had opposed Roosevelt's personal manipulation of the price of gold, which somewhat ironically he had considered an abuse of presidential powers. Looking to regain Roosevelt's good favor, and wanting to play a role in the unfolding global crisis, Acheson was now ready to expand those same powers into untested waters. Acheson had been one of Frankfurter's prize students at Harvard, and among the first of the "Happy Hot Dogs." Turning to his old mentor, Acheson presented Frankfurter with a copy of his analysis, before having it printed on the *New York Times* editorial page. After thinking about it for a few days, Frankfurter was convinced the argument would withstand legal challenges and called Stimson to let him know he had a solution to the destroyer problem. Roosevelt declared himself "very much encouraged" when Stimson relayed the idea to him. The matter was discussed at the next day's cabinet meeting, where the attorney gen-

Felix Frankfurter and his counsel, Dean Acheson (later secretary of state).

eral, who had been reviewing Acheson's legal reasoning since it appeared in *The New York Times* several days before, declared the idea sound.

That left Roosevelt with one final problem: Willkie. To help ensure Willkie did not make the destroyer deal a major campaign issue, the Century Club had convinced General Pershing to make a national radio speech trumpeting the deal's necessity. The speech was the kickoff of a national campaign that effectively shifted public opinion in favor of the deal. Roosevelt, looking for further assurance that the deal would not hurt him at the polls, asked William Allen White to request Willkie's support for the deal. White—the Sage of Emporia—was a renowned American newspaper editor and was considered by many, including himself, to be the voice of "middle America." Though a Republican, he was on the left of the party, as was Willkie, and supported much of the New Deal. When the Germans struck into France, White formed the Committee to Defend America by Aiding the Allies. It was this group, with its over six hundred local chapters, that took on the political fight with the isolationist America First Committee. White approached Willkie and asked him to lobby Republican senators to support the bill. This was a step too far for Willkie, but he did promise not to make it a campaign issue. In fact, Willkie did not believe fifty destroyers were sufficient to meet Britain's pressing needs and asked White why so few were being sent.

On August 13, Roosevelt cabled Churchill that he would send the fifty destroyers under certain conditions. The ships would be exchanged for bases in Newfoundland, Bermuda, the Bahamas, Jamaica, St. Lucia, Trinidad, and British Guiana. Furthermore, Churchill had to promise that, in the event Britain fell to a German assault, the Royal Navy would not be surrendered or scuttled. Churchill grew increasingly incensed as he read the cable and raged to one of his assistants that "Roosevelt wants to put a lien on the fleet." Not able to spare ships to defend the Western Hemisphere, he had already planned to present—as a gift—the bases that the Americans were demanding. He disliked the idea of turning them over in a tawdry deal that made Britain look desperate, which, in fact, it was. Beyond that, Churchill believed Britain's fall was impossible as long as its navy still existed and intended, if it came to that, to sacrifice the entire fleet in one final glorious battle to stop an invasion. Roosevelt's idea that the storied Royal Navy would survive the loss of England was profoundly insulting.

Churchill took two days to reply, and by then he had calmed down. Realizing that by sending the destroyers the United States had inched closer to entering the war, he gratefully accepted the ships. The deal was soon done. No mention was made of sending the fleet to the Dominions in the event of Britain's fall, and bases in Newfoundland and Bermuda were presented as gifts separate from those bases that were made part of the destroyer deal. Stark and Marshall, recognizing the benefits the bases had for U.S. security, had no trouble signing off on the deal. As for the destroyers themselves, the first eight arrived in Britain in early September, but due to their antiquated design and years of limited maintenance it was many months before their presence was felt in the North Atlantic.

Because Willkie twice chose principle over scoring campaign points, Roosevelt had a clear field for his big initiatives. That, however, did not mean the respective campaigns had called an overall truce. All through the summer and fall Willkie was out on the hustings, traveling nearly 19,000 miles and delivering 5,621 speeches in 31 states. But "the Champ" refused to come out of his corner and fight, leaving Willkie alone, shadowboxing in the center of the ring. He was also hampered by the fact that he was an internationalist, while most Republicans remained firmly in the isolationist camp. Many voters were asking how Willkie could impose an internationalist program when most of his own party would refuse to follow his lead. But there were other reasons he was failing to gain traction. The biggest one was clearly apparent to Willkie as he traveled the nation assailing Roosevelt's record: people were back at work. As military orders took up the economy's remaining slack, voters, who could see and feel the improvement in their situations, stopped listening to Willkie's message.

Trailing in every major poll, Willkie, at the urging of establishment Republicans, switched tactics in September. By this time, it was clear that Britain was winning the air war, a fact confirmed by Reichsmarschall Hermann Goering's decision to give up the Luftwaffe's direct assault on the Royal Air Force in favor of indiscriminate terror bombing of British cities. With the immediate threat of an invasion removed by Germany's failure to gain air supremacy, it was clear that Britain's ultimate defeat was indefinitely delayed. This opened a window for Willkie to start accusing Roosevelt of being a warmonger, a complete reversal from his weeks of accusing Roosevelt of supporting appeasement at the start of the European crisis. Willkie scored points with his oft-repeated pitch line: "If his promise to keep our boys out of foreign wars is no better than his promise to balance the budget, they're already almost on the transports." Willkie was renouncing everything he had stood for since entering the race. Now, by standing squarely with the isolationists, he was sure he had finally found the winning formula. With almost every newspaper in the country blaring his new message, the polls rapidly narrowed.

Democrats panicked. Tens of thousands of letters and telegrams poured into the White House begging the president to get out and fight. For a time, although angered by what he considered Willkie's unfair attack, Roosevelt held back. But then in mid-October, Eleanor, who was traveling the country, wrote: "I hope you will make some speeches. It seems to me pretty essential that you make them now. . . ." If Eleanor, the ever-reliable barometer of the public mood, sensed trouble, it was time to act.

Just as Roosevelt made up his mind to go on the offensive, another crisis struck. The White House learned that a Republican newspaper had gotten its hands on letters between vice presidential candidate Wallace and his onetime "guru," the mystic Nicholas Roerich. Harry Hopkins, who had also managed to get copies, informed Roosevelt that they were not just embarrassing, they could destroy the campaign. The "dear guru" letters, filled with mystical language and codes, could surely cast doubt on Wallace's mental fitness to be president if something happened to Roosevelt. But Roosevelt had his own secret weapon. His campaign staff informed their Republican counterparts that if the "guru letters" were published they would publicize Willkie's continuing affair with Irita Van Doren. Every jaded New York journalist may have known of the affair, but the millions in middle America, who saw Willkie's wife dutifully following him on every campaign stop, remained ignorant. In the end, both sides kept their doomsday arsenal under wraps.

On October 18, the White House announced that Roosevelt would make five major speeches to "set the record straight." Historian James Mac-Gregor Burns captured the effect of the Roosevelt campaign blitz: "No commander has ever sized up the terrain more shrewdly, rallied his demoralized battalions more tellingly, probed the enemy's weak spots more unerringly, and struck more powerfully than did Roosevelt against the Republican Party during the climactic two weeks before the election." Roosevelt struck first in Philadelphia, telling the crowd: "I am an old campaigner, and I love a good fight," before eviscerating Willkie's charges. He continued the attack five days later in New York City, this time focusing on Republican leaders who had opposed American rearmament at every step, but now accused him of not having done enough when Hitler first emerged as a threat. He proclaimed it a "remarkable somersault," archly inquiring: "I wonder if the election could have something to do with it?"

The turning point came on October 30. Roosevelt's previous two speeches had stanched his campaign's bleeding and staggered Willkie. But like many a novice gambler, Willkie doubled down. One day after the first numbers were drawn in the Selective Service draft, he announced: "On the basis of Roosevelt's record of broken promises, his election would mean war within six months." Soon thereafter, a telegram from Ed Flynn, Roosevelt's campaign manager, implored Roosevelt to emphasize a "no foreign wars" pledge in his next speech. Exasperated, Roosevelt asked his speechwriters "how often do they expect me to say that . . . I've repeated it a hundred times." Off the cuff Robert Sherwood replied: "Evidently, you've got to say it again and again, and again"—words Roosevelt would memorably make his own.

That night in Boston, Roosevelt unleashed the most famous phrase of the campaign: "I have said this before, but I shall say it again and again and again: Your boys are not going to be sent into any foreign wars." In the past, Roosevelt had always added a caveat along the lines of "except in the case of attack." This time he dropped it, explaining to his key speechwriter and close confidant Judge Samuel Rosenman: "It's not necessary. If we're attacked, it's no longer a foreign war."

Willkie, listening on the radio, exclaimed to his brother, "That hypocritical son of a bitch! This is going to beat me." He was right. Though Willkie's attacks continued, the tide had swung irreversibly back toward Roosevelt. The following two campaign speeches were anticlimactic, and Roosevelt on the eve of the election returned to Hyde Park to await the returns. By 10:00 P.M. a beaming Roosevelt was confident enough to greet visitors streaming in to congratulate him on winning an unprecedented third term. While Americans wanted a change in domestic politics, with Europe burning they wanted a president they knew. As New York mayor Fiorello La Guardia noted, Americans preferred "Roosevelt with his known faults to Willkie with his unknown virtues."

Late that night, an exhausted Harry Hopkins made his way to the home of Russell Davenport, Willkie's campaign manager. The two men talked into the early morning, burying a lot of hatchets. A few days later, Willkie went on the radio to announce: "We have elected Franklin Roosevelt president. He is your president. He is my president . . . We will support him."

14

BUSINESS GETS

ITS FIELD MARSHALS

ALL THROUGH THE ELECTION CAMPAIGN, WHILE THE BATTLES OVER destroyers for Britain and the Selective Service draft raged, Roosevelt was often preoccupied with military production. He knew he needed help, but remained unwilling to trust one man with the job. Besides, because of Congress's 1939 reorganization of the president's executive office, Roosevelt believed he had the perfect tool for bringing order to the growing production bedlam. On May 25, 1940, he established the Office of Emergency Management (OEM). As new agencies proliferated during the war years, Roosevelt would shoehorn each into the OEM, where he could keep a close eye on them and direct their actions without intermediaries, such as cabinet officers, getting in the way. This concentration of power alarmed Congress and annoyed cabinet members who saw their powers transferred into agencies they could not control. But Roosevelt regarded the glacial pace of the cabinet departments as roadblocks to be maneuvered around, not worked with, and saw no other way forward.

Three days after establishing the Office of Emergency Management, Roosevelt created by executive order the National Defense Advisory Commission (NDAC), the first of a series of war production agencies. Implicit in its title was the fact that the seven-member board had no power to direct anything; it was there merely to "advise." Nor did it have anyone at its head who might consolidate power. Each of its members was equal, although only three—William Knudsen, Edward Stettinius, and Sidney Hillman—

worked full-time. About a month after the commission's creation, Sears's executive vice president in charge of purchasing, Donald Nelson, joined as a full-time member. Finding four more disparate personalities would have been difficult.

William Knudsen was a Danish immigrant who never quite lost his accent. He was a huge man, a former boxer who loved to dance and play the piano. He had a quick wit and a ready smile, and was typically amiable and direct. He loved numbers and considered a well-drawn chart the supreme management tool. When he wanted to think, he went to his desk, put his hat on, and sat there pondering, undisturbed by subordinates who quickly learned that his "indoor hat" precluded interruptions.

William Knudsen, president of General Motors Group
(right, wearing bow tie).

A production genius who got his start producing bicycles, Knudsen moved on to automobiles, building Henry Ford's assembly lines. After falling out with Ford, Knudsen proceeded to turn Chevrolet into an automobile powerhouse. His sole focus was putting men and material together to rapidly produce whatever he was charged with building. Unfortunately, he

Edward Stettinius, Jr., secretary of state.

cared little—and had less aptitude—for policy or politics. When "the Great Dane" gave up his princely $300,000-a-year salary to work for free in Washington, he thought Roosevelt was going to put his production expertise to good use. Instead, he was plunged headfirst into the policy arena, where everything revolved around politics. Few in Washington worked as hard as Knudsen, but he was placed squarely in the middle of a game he did not understand and had no interest in playing. While everyone liked Knudsen, it was not long before his incapacity, bordering on incompetence, to negotiate the political obstacles that came with the job became apparent to all of official Washington.

Edward Stettinius, unlike Knudsen, came from wealth, his father having been a full partner in J. P. Morgan. Handsome, silver-haired, possessed of perfect aristocratic posture, for most of his professional career he had alternated between business and government service. But in 1934 he returned to private enterprise and eventually became chairman of the board of U.S. Steel. In 1939 he returned to head the short-lived War Resources Board, which did nothing during its six-week existence other than reviewing the military's Industrial Mobilization Plan. Because of his pedigree, Stettinius was assumed to represent business and money interests within NDAC.

Although Stettinius was ambitious, he was not a tough man. In both the business world and in Washington politics he had gotten along by going

along. Hopkins considered him weak, and there were many who believed
Hopkins later supported Stettinius taking over Lend-Lease responsibilities
because he posed no threat to Hopkins's authority. Within NDAC, however, he had been given the job on which all else rested: finding sufficient
raw materials to supply a rapidly expanding military, particularly Roosevelt's fifty thousand aircraft. Why Roosevelt, having witnessed his lack-
luster performance as head of the War Resources Board, put him in this
crucial position is inexplicable.

Roosevelt's choice of Sidney Hillman as labor adviser for the committee
is easier to fathom. If war production was going to get off the ground, hundreds of thousands of workers would soon have to transfer from civilian-
oriented manufacturing to munitions production. Such an unprecedented
labor disruption would be impossible unless the great unions agreed to
maintain at least a modicum of peace. In 1940 America, two powerful men
ran labor—Hillman and John L. Lewis—and only they could bring labor
to heel during a national emergency. As Lewis and Roosevelt shared a deep
mutual antipathy, Hillman was the logical choice.

Lord Beaverbrook at the Office of Production Management (OPM) in
Washington, D.C., 1941. From left: Sidney Hillman, associate director, OPM;
John Lord O'Brian, general counsel, OPM; Edward Stettinius, Jr., director
of priorities, OPM; Lord Beaverbrook, British minister of supply;
and William Knudsen, director-general, OPM.

Hillman was a round-faced, compact bundle of energy. Born in Lithuania, he was training as a rabbi when he opted to become a revolutionary instead in the wake of Russia's disastrous defeat in the 1905 Russo-Japanese War. After his arrest by the czar's police and ten months in jail he rejoined the cause, but soon despaired of progress and immigrated to Britain and then to the United States. After a series of menial jobs in the garment industry, by 1910 Hillman was heavily involved in union agitation. His tremendous drive, steel-trap memory, and a "special ability" to bring diverse groups into harmony led to his rapid rise through the labor hierarchy. He was a founding member of the Congress of Industrial Organizations (CIO), and the driving force behind its joining with the American Federation of Labor (AFL). By 1940, he was the number two man in the American labor movement, working directly for John L. Lewis. The only downside to selecting Hillman was that most of Congress considered him a communist who only got the job because he was a Roosevelt sycophant. But sycophancy was never a disqualifier for Roosevelt.

Lewis, whom Hopkins called the "worst Roosevelt hater of them all," considered FDR's appointment of Hillman to NDAC, without consulting him, as a deliberate and mortal insult. Probably worse in Lewis's mind was that he believed, rightly, that Roosevelt, fearing Lewis would support Willkie (which he did), was trying to split the labor vote, which is what

Donald Nelson.

Leon Henderson, 1938;
later the director of the
U.S. Office of Price
Administration (OPA).

happened. By appointing Hillman, Roosevelt, the most Machiavellian of U.S. presidents, brought labor and big business together for a common objective; ensured an unprecedented, if far from perfect, degree of labor peace; and reduced to irrelevance the labor bloc that opposed his policies. Not that Hillman and Big Labor did not gain; all through the war years Hillman made sure that labor continually enhanced its power as a reward for a general peace.

Donald Nelson was a study in contrasts, decisive and dogmatic when a matter was small and flexibility was required, but weak and plagued with indecision on major points. Coming from the comparatively orderly world of Sears, Roebuck, where he spent thirty years patiently working his way up the ladder, Nelson was ill prepared for the fast-moving rough-and-tumble of wartime Washington. He was a big man, "allergic to exercise," who concentrated on his job and expected the same of everyone else. Quite possibly, he was the only highly placed man in Washington with neither a hidden agenda nor a ruthless will to power. Consequently, he soon found himself at the mercy of those who were not lacking in either. So how did he survive as long as he did? Some wit once said, "Good people don't survive; survivors survive." Nelson, if nothing else, was a survivor. David Brinkley, in his portrait of wartime Washington, noted: "He was pleasant, patient and conciliatory. He ruffled no feathers, and no one—including, most importantly, the president—considered him a threat."

There was one part-time committee member who soon proved himself a force to be reckoned with: Leon Henderson. Loud, short, large-framed, and bellicose, Henderson reveled in a hard-fought fight. On Washington's hottest days he worked in his underwear, only deigning to dress on those occasions when he had to leave his office to step on someone's toes. Belying this rough-edged affect was the fact that he was a brilliant economist and a voracious reader, who set aside days at a time to immerse himself in books. He was also a New Dealer from the start, and one of the few of his breed to make the full transition to "all-outer." Before the war, he had held several important economic postings for Roosevelt, culminating with replacing Joseph Kennedy as the head of the Securities and Exchange Commission. By 1939 Henderson was certain that the United States would enter the war and he became driven by one goal: that when America did enter the war it would do so with everything it needed to smash the Axis powers on the battlefield. As he wrote in his diary at the time, any letup would "just be a period in which Germany got ready for the complete annihilation of England."

Henderson's responsibility within NDAC was price controls, which after Pearl Harbor morphed into a position as head of the Office of Price Administration. Before he took the job, Baruch had tried to warn him off, predicting that "you will become the most hated man in America." Knowing that someone had to do the job, Henderson ignored the warning and plunged in. Baruch was right; for many Americans, particularly those in Congress, business leaders, and labor leaders, Henderson was soon public enemy number one. Why did they hate him? Because to a substantial degree he was successful. Henderson knew from the start that once the nation undertook full economic mobilization inflation was inevitable. His goal, then, was to hold it in check, hoping the country could avoid the crushing inflation brought on by the First World War. Undeterred by the fact that NDAC did not give him the requisite legal powers to fight inflation, Henderson nevertheless went to work doing just that. Day after day, he worked the phones, politely asking executives to not raise prices, or, if they already had, to roll them back. His most common refrain was "I hear you are going to raise prices; I trust you won't." When that failed, he resorted to threats, upon which he never bothered to place a veil. Executives who ignored him soon discovered, to their detriment, that few could work the power of the executive branch as well as Henderson.

Henderson was making enemies, but he was succeeding. Roosevelt was so pleased with his work that he once quipped to the great economist Lord Maynard Keynes: "Just look at Leon—when I got him he was only an economist."

It was said of Henderson that he had five extra fingers so that he could put them into more pots. Within weeks, Henderson had inserted himself into just about everything NDAC did. As Knudsen (business) and Hillman (labor) kept each other's constituencies in check, Henderson accumulated power by adroitly positioning himself to tip the balance. This was greatly facilitated by the fact that Henderson and Donald Nelson got along well, and that Nelson typically saw things the same way he did. Henderson always got along well with those who were malleable to his wishes.

Through sheer force of personality, the blunt-spoken Henderson became the driving force of NDAC. Here was a New Dealer who understood business, and although he could be tenacious in a struggle, he also recognized the need to compromise. Unlike their feelings about many New Dealers, businessmen did not consider Henderson an enemy—at least at the start. But it was his single-minded drive to do everything possible to prepare America for war that most struck those who dealt with him.

As Henderson never considered making friends crucial to his success, he was often like a bull in a china shop as he went about his appointed mission. One example from the early days of the nation's mobilization phase is typical of many of his interactions. During World War I, Roosevelt, in his role as assistant secretary of the navy, had mostly cornered the market for copper in the United States. It took Baruch some time to get Roosevelt to release a portion of it to the other services, who were already facing dangerous shortages. When NDAC was created, Roosevelt, who now fancied himself an authority on the copper market, let it be known that he considered it essential that America get its hands on as much copper as possible. Henderson, taking time from his price control duties, took on this mandate as well. Taking Stettinius with him, he went to see Reconstruction Finance Corporation (RFC) head Jesse Jones.

Jones politely listened to the two men and then ushered them out, assuring them that he would buy some copper. Realizing Jones had no intention of acting on their suggestion or that at most he would purchase only a minuscule amount, Henderson told Jones not to worry about it, that he would find another way to get the copper. Jones, sensing a threat to his own prerogatives and power, pressed Henderson to explain. "I am going to get the law changed so that my organization can buy copper," Henderson replied, making it crystal clear that he was going to cut off a piece of Jones's fiefdom. Urging Henderson not to be so hasty, Jones took him to see one of his subordinates, Will Clayton.

Clayton was a self-made multimillionaire who had made his fortune as a commodities trader and was now working in Washington for a dollar a year helping the government establish a purchasing program to guarantee sufficient raw materials to keep the factories humming. He was a no-nonsense professional who, like Henderson, did not suffer fools or incompetence gladly. Clayton heard Henderson out, and nodded agreeably. When Henderson, unsure if Clayton understood the urgency of the matter, pressed him as to how much copper he planned on buying, Clayton matter-of-factly replied: "The entire global supply." He then returned to work. Henderson, for once, was satisfied. As for Jesse Jones, he had seen off a threat, as contained as it was, to his substantial power base.

The NDAC board had learned early on that if they were going to accomplish anything they eventually had to go through Jesse Jones, the most powerful man in the world of finance. Jones, born in 1874 in Tennessee, had made his fortune in Texas. Starting in his uncle's lumber business, Jones soon established his own lumberyards before expanding into banking, real estate, construction, and a host of other businesses. Standing well over six feet, Jones was dubbed by *Time* magazine as "Biblically big" with a face that looked like "The Ten Commandments." He coupled his size with driving ambition and a capacity for hard work and long hours that never left him. He was almost always calm, a bit profane when excited, and a good storyteller, and he had a substantial number of friends in Congress. Only those who had no attachment to their money played poker with him, and after a full day's work only a good poker game could entice him away from a long evening of more work. Jones was also a superb bridge player, who met his match only when Knudsen entered the game. They played for a dollar a hand, which Jones thought was rather reckless of Knudsen, as he was betting his entire annual salary on a single turn of the cards. Despite

Knudsen's continual declarations that he was just learning the game, he habitually walked away with $50 or more of Jones's money.

Like Baruch, Jones established himself as a power within the Democratic Party by freely giving of his fortune, having in 1928 brought the

Jesse Jones, 1939; later secretary of commerce and
chair of the Reconstruction Finance Corporation.

Democratic convention to Houston by offering a blank check to pay for expenses (the Democrats filled it in for $200,000). Although Jones was a Democrat, President Hoover put him on the board of the RFC, a new organization established to fight the Great Depression. Roosevelt, seeing the RFC's value to the New Deal, kept the organization and its leader.

Jones turned the RFC into an empire. Through a collection of subordinate agencies such as the Commodity Credit Corporation and the Federal National Mortgage Association (now Fannie Mae) the RFC's tentacles spread into almost every area of American business. It made loans to banks and businesses in every state, and one of its divisions even made loans to states. Roosevelt used RFC funds to manipulate the price of gold, prop up a tottering banking sector, and assist farmers, and he even set up the Export-Import Bank under the RFC to jump-start trade with the Soviet Union.

By 1940, Jones was boasting that he had made over $10 billion in credit available—a fantastic sum for the time—and that "there was no line of business that we have not aided, and probably every man, woman, and child in the United States has benefited from RFC operations." In the process, Jones amassed political power, as every politician knew that if you needed cash to fund a project or government initiative there were only two persons to go to: Harry Hopkins or Jesse Jones. Hopkins, however, preferred supporting Democratic politicians, becoming notorious for a phrase that he lived by, although whether he actually said it is disputed: "We will spend and spend and tax and tax and elect and elect." Jones, on the other hand, was a businessman at heart, and his first interest was always the quality of the collateral put up to secure one of his loans. If you had the collateral, he was blind to your political affiliation. Moreover, throughout the Depression the RFC always turned a profit, returning substantial funds each year to the Treasury. The combination of political neutrality and profits made Jones extremely popular on Capitol Hill. *Time* even once referred to the entire U.S. Senate as his "admiring friends."

In 1940, Jones, led on by Roosevelt, believed he was a strong contender to get the vice presidential nod. When it went to Wallace, Jones was offered the job of secretary of commerce—recently vacated by Harry Hopkins—as a consolation. Little interested in consolation offers but prizing power, he refused to take the job unless he could bring the Federal Loan Administration—of which the RFC was now a part—under Commerce's purview. Roosevelt, knowing that Jones could get more money out of Congress through a simple request for funding than he himself could get after a long political fight, was glad to let him have his way. At the moment, the Texas titan suited Roosevelt's needs, but Roosevelt had overlooked a major liability in placing Jones in the cabinet. Jones blamed Wallace for Roosevelt's not selecting him for the vice presidency and placed Wallace in the top slot on his enemies list. Their feud would have huge repercussions in wartime Washington.

After passing a special law allowing Jones to hold both Commerce and the RFC job simultaneously, Congress in June 1940 gave him the power to finance defense production facilities. Within a week he had established within the RFC the Rubber Reserve Company and the Metals Reserve Company. By summer's end he had also created the Defense Supplies Corporation and the Defense Plants Corporation. The Rubber Corporation was formed to finance the creation of a synthetic rubber industry, as shortages were already developing. These shortages would turn critical in mid-1941 when the Japanese, exploiting France's collapse, marched into the southern half of French Indochina, where much of the world's natural rubber was harvested. Other companies were established to purchase commodities, increase the production of aviation fuel, and finance the building of new industrial plants to support war production.

Though Jones took his war mobilization duties seriously, the NDAC board found him frustrating to work with. When Knudsen first went to Morgenthau with the idea of using RFC funds for the production effort, Morgenthau advised him to "take a bodyguard with him when he went to ask Jones for money." At a time when speed was essential, Jones demanded careful scrutiny of major loans, just as he had during the Depression, determined not to give anything away without a return. He remained proud of his record of turning a profit and was not about to let something as minor as an impending global war place that record at risk. Jones became a "one-man bottleneck" whose stranglehold on the release of money was seizing up the nation's nascent mobilization drive.

Fortunately for the country, Jones always hired the best. By the summer of 1940 he had assembled a "collection of tough-minded younger men" on his immediate staff. Unlike their boss, these men understood that mobilization was an emergency and undertook to do what no bank or other government organization could do: rapidly finance the creation of new production facilities. While Jones bargained for the best deal, they conducted an end run with what he considered "his money." Each morning Deputy Secretary of War Patterson would call over with the War Department's latest requirements. Without ever informing Jones to what they were doing, the RFC staff would, by the end of the day, approve the contracts and transmit them to the War Department for immediate signature. Within twenty-four hours the firm requesting the cash would have its contract and the cash to build a plant and tool it up. As a model of government efficiency, the speed at which Jones's subordinates got things done has probably never been equaled.

This backroom conspiracy was three months old before Jones learned of it. He immediately sprang into action, removing almost all of the participants from the RFC. But the damage, as Jones saw it, had been done. Billions of dollars of RFC financing had gone out the door and could not be clawed back. Worse, from Jones's point of view, he now had to support this first tranche of loans with billions of dollars in new loans. As the initial plants that the conspirators had financed came online, they needed new financing for hiring, purchasing commodities, and building out the infrastructure required to run a major operation. Jones confronted a choice: finance this expansion, or hold up the money and see all of the billions already spent lost. If he wanted to turn a profit on the first tranche of loans, he had to agree to the second, third, and fourth tranches. With no other choice, Jones turned to Congress for a cash injection to the RFC. Congress, its isolationist wing temporarily neutered, was in a new mood and rapidly approved the money. In fact, Jones was told not to hesitate to come back for more whenever he needed it. From that point on, Jones was all in. He had no other choice: his employees had committed "his money" and put his reputation on the line, a reputation Jones was willing to spend every dollar Congress could raise to defend.

Despite the strenuous efforts of its members, many judged NDAC a failure. It could hardly be otherwise for an organization whose only role was to give advice, and whose only power over industry rested upon its members' ability to cajole and bluff. In mid-October, Secretary of War Stimson, visiting the White House for a photo op, was asked to stay for an NDAC meeting. In front of Roosevelt, Stimson laid into the NDAC board for their slowness in approving contracts and general inability to get much done. Predictably, this got a "howl and an uproar from Leon Henderson," but Stimson proudly told his diary that he had "held his own."

By November 1940, everyone involved with NDAC was ready to throw in the towel. Knudsen went to Roosevelt and begged him to reset the organization by creating a director of industrial mobilization who would have real power over industry and the military. Knudsen was, in effect, asking Roosevelt to create a co-president, empowered to control the home front. Roosevelt had not been ready to do this when he quashed the military's attempt to start their Industrial Mobilization Plan, nor was he even close to ready to do so now.

A month later, the problems could no longer be ignored. On December 14, Stimson spent the entire morning with Baruch detailing NDAC's failures and his conviction that nothing would get better until the commission had a responsible single head with the powers to do the job Baruch himself had done twenty-three years before. As Stimson phrased it, "industry would not work . . . until the Commission [NDAC] has reached a war psychosis." On December 18, in a series of meetings with General Marshall, Admiral Stark, James Forrestal (deputy secretary of the navy), and Frank Knox, Stimson discovered they were all in agreement on the imperative that Roosevelt appoint someone with real power to direct the American economy. The consensus was that "the President has been advised that giving it [NDAC] a head would create a super-Government" beyond his control.

After consulting with Morgenthau, who gave him some good advice on presenting a compromise that Roosevelt might accept, Stimson moved on to Jesse Jones, who informed him that he too had been distressed by the problem for weeks. Jones signed on to the cabal, and made a call to the head of the American Federation of Labor to get labor's support. The next morning Stimson reached out to Felix Frankfurter to garner his aid. It was freely given, and Frankfurter took the additional step of corralling Sidney Hillman and asking him to sign on to the change. Hillman first demanded a conversation with both Stimson and Knox, to get their assurances that labor's interests were going to be safeguarded. Both men took the meeting and recorded that Hillman was delighted at the prospect of creating a truly effective agency, but that he was against making Knudsen the boss, as he doubted his capacity to manage such an organization or "to push things hard."

With support shored up on all fronts, Stimson, Patterson, Knox, and Forrestal headed for the White House. Stimson's notes on the subsequent meeting reflect the dynamics of dealing with Roosevelt: "Conferences with the President are very difficult matters. He does not follow easily a consecutive chain of thought but he is full of stories and incidents and hops about in his discussions from suggestion to suggestion and it is very much like chasing a vagrant beam of sunshine around a vacant room." When he finally did get around to the point of the meeting, Stimson was gratified to discover that Roosevelt had already given the matter considerable thought and agreed that there needed to be a concentration of responsibility at the top.

What caused Roosevelt's change of mind? Probably two things in combination: the undeniable fact that the production machinery had broken down and, more important, that Congress had taken note. In late November, isolationist senator Robert Taft announced he would sponsor a bill creating a single administrator to lead a War Resources Board that would direct America's mobilization effort. Always alert to any measure that might limit or circumvent his own powers Roosevelt began formulating a preemptive strike. Too, with the election behind him, Roosevelt believed he had a mandate to move the nation to providing greater assistance to Britain. The final collapse of NDAC could not have come at a more awkward moment. How could he argue that the United States could shoulder Britain's needs as well as its own, when the system clearly could not even handle the latter?

Roosevelt's solution was typical. He created a new organization and placed both Knudsen and Hillman in charge of it. At a December 20 press conference, Roosevelt announced the opening of the Office of Production Management (OPM), in the process ridiculing the idea that a single economic czar was necessary. The country, he informed the assembled journalists, did not need a "Czar, Poobah or Akhoond of Swat," nor did the Constitution make any allowance for a second president. In a hat tip to the military, Roosevelt also placed Stimson and Knox on the OPM board.

Roosevelt gave OPM a sweeping mandate to determine military needs, secure raw materials, plan new industrial plants, and mobilize civilian industries for defense needs. He did not, however, confer upon it the power to accomplish any of these responsibilities. By once again limiting the new organization to an advisory role, he gave OPM no more authority than NDAC had to compel anyone to do anything, dooming it from the start.

Things broke down almost immediately. First, Knox and Stimson quickly lost interest, preferring to go their own way to accomplish what they believed had to be done. Next, Knudsen, for reasons known only to him, began keeping Hillman in the dark about production matters. Hillman retaliated by not informing Knudsen about any matters having to do with labor. The only reason any progress was made at all was that OPM's executive secretary, Herbert Emmerich, moved into the power vacuum to conduct much of the coordination work within OPM. Without Emmerich the entire apparatus would have collapsed months before it actually did. As it was, OPM trundled on, without accomplishing much until Roosevelt undertook another major reorganization in August 1941.

15

BANKROLLING BRITAIN

WITH A RENEWED LEASE ON THE OVAL OFFICE, ROOSEVELT SHOOK off his lame-duck status and planted himself firmly at the pinnacle of Washington's power structure. The election behind him, Roosevelt believed he had a mandate to move the nation toward providing greater assistance to Britain. As Hopkins explained to Robert Sherwood when he enlisted him as a speechwriter: "So far as he [Roosevelt] is concerned there is absolutely nothing important in the world today except to beat Hitler."

Churchill, among his many pressing concerns at the forefront of that fight, worried most about two things. The first was the continuing carnage in the North Atlantic. The day before Roosevelt's reelection, Britain lost its five hundredth merchant ship. That loss added to the nearly two million tons of shipping—10 percent of Britain's merchant fleet—that had gone to the bottom since the start of the war. As a result, Britain's food imports fell 200,000 tons short of what it took to keep widespread starvation at bay. As Churchill well knew, all else was for naught if Britons starved. The second crisis, while not as dramatic as the brutal North Atlantic struggle, was just as deadly to British hopes of victory. The empire was nearly broke. In early November, it had less than $2 billion in reserves, to pay for at least $5 billion worth of orders placed with American firms. As the revised Neutrality Act decreed that all British purchases had to be cash-and-carry, the day was rapidly approaching when war matériel might never leave American ports. Without cash, Britain's war machine would soon face crippling shortages, and the United States would be lost as a source of vital munitions.

The week before the election, Roosevelt had Morgenthau and Arthur

Purvis, the head of the British Purchasing Commission, join him for lunch. Purvis outlined the dire state of British merchant shipping—they were losing more ships than they were building—and strongly hinted at Britain's perilous financial condition, most of which Morgenthau already knew. Unfortunately, Roosevelt had no answers to give him. At one point, the president off-handedly commented: "Might it not be possible for the United States to build cargo vessels and lease them to Britain?" The suggestion went nowhere that day, and although it also was mentioned at the next cabinet meeting the notion was rapidly shelved. But an idea had taken root in Roosevelt's mind.

A measure of good war news brightened prospects in the two weeks after the election, including a daring raid by British torpedo bombers that crippled the Italian fleet anchored at Taranto. On the morning of November 12, twenty-one obsolete aircraft, launched from the HMS *Illustrious,* caught the Italians napping. By the time the aircraft departed they had done what most naval analysts had previously considered impossible: struck capital ships riding at anchor in the shallow water of a defended port. Before the planes departed, half of Italy's battleships had sunk, reversing the entire naval picture in the Mediterranean—it was, once again, a British lake. Thousands of miles away, Japanese naval planners took careful note of the strike, while the Americans unfathomably did nothing to secure their equally vulnerable anchorage at Pearl Harbor.

Two days after the Taranto strike, the Greeks launched a major counterattack against invading Italian forces. By December, the Italians would be routed, barely able to hold on to Albania. (The Greeks would hold that line until German panzers smashed into the Balkans in early April 1941.)

In their first major offensive in North Africa—Operation Compass— the British, in ten weeks, annihilated the Italian Tenth Army, capturing 130,000 prisoners and destroying over 400 tanks and nearly 1,300 artillery pieces. It was by any measure a great victory, but one that also brought General Erwin Rommel and the Wehrmacht into North Africa.

The tide of the air war was also changing, although in the brutal battle of attrition that was far from apparent. Since July the Luftwaffe had relentlessly pounded Fighter Command's air bases. German losses were horrific, and the Royal Air Force remained resilient and effective, although its pilots were nearing utter exhaustion. With the outcome undecided, Hitler gave the RAF a desperately needed respite on September 4, declaring: "We will erase their cities." Three days later the Luftwaffe launched its first massive assault on London, the start of the fearsome "Blitz" that pounded Britain's cities until May 1941, killing over forty thousand civilians and injuring more than three times that number. Despite the damage and the losses, Hitler's decision to switch to terror bombing allowed the spent RAF to recover its equilibrium.

The Luftwaffe maintained the Blitz for almost half a year after the U.S. elections. But by early November, the assault was ebbing, and it appeared to Fighter Command that the Luftwaffe might have punched itself out. Churchill, after looking over the numbers, declared: "That man's effort is flagging." That was only partly true, since the Luftwaffe's redeployment for operations against the Soviet Union had much to do with its reduced assaults on British cities; and as 1940 drew to a close, though temporarily stymied, it remained a powerful force that might still succeed in breaking the morale of the British people. But as the bombs fell, American sympathy for Britain's plight escalated. Night after night broadcasters such as Edward R. Murrow brought the full horror of Germany's terror campaign into American homes. At the same time Hollywood, ignoring Joseph Kennedy's warning not to make films that might upset Hitler, turned out one pro-British film after another. Even as Americans went to the polls, *London Can Take It*, a blatant propaganda film, was playing in twelve thousand theaters across the United States. Churchill was counting on this growing popular support to convince Roosevelt that the time for decisive action had arrived, if not by an outright declaration of war, then through substantially increased assistance.

Still, Roosevelt continued to disappoint those who expected prompt action in support of Britain in the days and weeks after the election. Historians have long puzzled over his apparent aimlessness during this interval, the most likely presumption being that he was physically and emotionally exhausted. He consulted assiduously on the problems besetting the nation and the world, but was listless when it came time to move forward on any of them.

When an excursion on the presidential yacht was cut short due to poor weather, FDR slipped into what could only be called a funk. Looking for a bit of peace, he escaped to Hyde Park for Thanksgiving.

Trouble, in the form of Joseph Kennedy, followed him there. Before the election, Kennedy, upset at perceived slights from Washington, returned from the Court of St. James's, reportedly planning to resign his post and publicly support Willkie for president. Well aware that Kennedy's defection could cost him millions of Catholic voters in crucial states, Roosevelt invited him to the White House and launched one of the greatest charm offensives of his long political career. When it was over, Kennedy not only remained at his post, but also agreed to endorse Roosevelt in a nationwide radio address that he paid for out of his own pocket.

Joseph Kennedy, chairman of the U.S. Maritime Commission.

But now he was back to his old tricks. As soon as the election was decided, Kennedy lashed out on his favorite topics: Britain was as good as beaten; the United States should consider adopting a fascist government for itself; and, finally, the United States had to stay out of the war even if it meant making an accommodation with Hitler. Believing another burst of his radiant charm would bring Kennedy back into line, Roosevelt invited him to Hyde Park. Eleanor picked him up at the train station and dropped him off with the president. She had just returned to her own cottage, a couple of miles away, when she was summoned back. Hurrying to Roosevelt's study, she found her husband alone and in a cold rage. In a voice shaking with fury, Roosevelt said: "I never want to see that son of a bitch again as long as I live. Take his resignation and get him out of here!"

Eleanor reminded him that he had invited Kennedy for the weekend, and, besides, the train did not leave for several more hours. "Then you drive him around Hyde Park, give him a sandwich, and put him on that train," Roosevelt snapped. Eleanor called her subsequent interval with Kennedy "the most dreadful four hours of my life."

One might think that such an encounter presaged a final break between the two men. But Roosevelt, when he had time to reflect, decided that it was unwise to keep Kennedy—with his Irish Catholic contingent—in the doghouse forever. As for Kennedy, remarkably, he still hoped for further jobs in the Roosevelt administration. Within weeks, the two had patched things up enough that Kennedy found himself back on the radio supporting Roosevelt's proposals to aid Britain.

Unfortunately, the still overtired Roosevelt appeared incapable of making any firm decisions and problems continued to mount. In the absence of presidential guidance cabinet officers and the military chiefs struck out on their own, and in a remarkable series of meetings on December 3, 1940, Stimson, Knox, Hull, and Morgenthau began moving things along. First, Stimson and Knox met with Hull in his State Department offices, where they reviewed the current war situation, staggering Hull who for the first time learned the extent of British shipping losses. All three agreed that Britain would lose the war unless the United States supplied Britain with substantially more aircraft and assigned American warships to escort British convoys.

Marshall, Stimson, Knox, Jones, Knudsen, and several of their deputies then met with Morgenthau in his offices, reviewed British finances, and quickly came to the consensus that the almost insolvent nation would soon be unable to purchase American war matériel. They discussed the possibility of the United States picking up the British tab, but the assembly broke up when Jones and Stimson insisted that such a measure would require congressional approval.

Only Roosevelt could move Congress, and Stimson, Hull, and Morgenthau resolved to move Roosevelt before Britain went under. Just as they were preparing to storm the White House, however, they were stunned to learn that their quarry had slipped away from Washington for a ten-day cruise on the Navy cruiser USS *Tuscaloosa,* accompanied only by his gate-keeper, Pa Watson; his personal physician, Dr. McIntire; his naval aide; and Harry Hopkins. His announced intention was to conduct an inspection tour of the bases Britain had turned over in return for the old destroyers. His actual goal was to get the rest that had so far eluded him. His waking hours were devoted to fishing during the day—with advice on the best spots via wireless from Ernest Hemingway—and poker and movies at night.

Roosevelt had been at sea only a couple of days when on December 9, a seaplane landed alongside with official mail. Among the letters was one from the British prime minister—a four-thousand-word Churchillian masterpiece. Churchill, who had called the British ambassador, Lord Lothian, home to help him work on it, considered the letter "the most important of his life." In it he traced out the course of the war, the current strategic situation, and what America must do if Britain was to avoid defeat. Churchill's shopping list was extensive: two thousand aircraft a month and millions of tons of shipping—war matériel and foodstuffs. He saved his most pressing concern until the end: "The moment approaches when we shall no longer be able to pay cash for shipping and other supplies." Churchill sank the hook by questioning the morality of America stripping Britain to its financial bone when it was paying in blood to save civilization and buy the United States time to prepare.

Roosevelt was deeply moved. For several days, he sat in his chair reading and rereading the letter, but for the moment discussing it with no one. Hopkins later admitted that he had no idea what Roosevelt was thinking, "if anything," but he thought it unwise to press the issue. Then, a few evenings after the letter arrived, Roosevelt called Hopkins to his side and poured forth the entire program that would become Lend-Lease. As Hopkins remembered: "He didn't seem to have any clear idea how it could be done legally. But there was no doubt in his mind that he'd find a way to do it."

Roosevelt had his plan, but he did not return to the White House until December 16, after spending a full day with fellow polio victims at Warm Springs, Georgia. The next day, tanned and visibly relaxed, Roosevelt greeted the press, prepared to make the case for Lend-Lease. Typically, he began by announcing that he had little of interest for them, then offered a short history lesson, asserting that no major war had ever been lost due to

Edwin "Pa" Watson (right), U.S. Army major general and
senior aide to President Franklin D. Roosevelt.

lack of money—a patently false statement, as most major conflicts were
lost for exactly that reason. But facts, if they got in the way of a larger point,
were little valued by Roosevelt. After laying out some strawman options
that no one was considering—make a large loan to Britain, or give them
war matériel as a gift—Roosevelt got to the point: "What I am trying to do
is eliminate the dollar sign."

The president then followed with a folksy bromide about a hypothetical
fire in a neighbor's home, asking the assembled scribes whether, if they had
a nearby hose, they would charge the homeowner the cost of the hose before letting him use it to fight the fire, and supplying the sensible response:
"Of course not, I only want my garden hose back after the fire is over." The
United States would purchase what Britain required and then lend it to
them.

There was no British representative to alert Churchill of Roosevelt's momentous proposal, Lord Lothian having suddenly died, and it was a few
days before the equivalent of a diplomatic thank-you note was forwarded
to Washington. Churchill did his best to make amends by announcing in

front of Parliament that the plan was the "most unsordid act in the history of any nation."

Setting forth a proposal was one thing. Getting it through Congress was far from assured. Passage was not, however, as unlikely as it would have been a few months earlier. The national mood had hugely changed since the start of the Blitz, with a significant majority of Americans viewing Britain's fight, if not exactly as theirs, at least as the first line of defense protecting their own country. Just as important, Roosevelt had learned a few crucial lessons from the political defeats of his prior term. For one, with Congress out of session, Roosevelt put aside two of his favored predilections—subterfuge and backroom dealing—in favor of making a direct appeal to the American people. On December 29, he gave what may have been his most important fireside address. With Clark Gable and his wife, Carole Lombard, joining him and Eleanor in the White House, Roosevelt told the American people: "The people of Europe who are defending themselves do not ask us to do their fighting. They ask us for the implements of war, the planes, the tanks, the guns . . . We must be the great arsenal of democracy. For us this is an emergency as serious as war itself. We must apply ourselves to our task with the same resolution, the same sense of urgency, the same spirit of patriotism and sacrifice as we would show were we at war."

This "Arsenal of Democracy" speech significantly moved an electorate that was already polling strongly in favor of giving Britain all aid short of war. Roosevelt moved the polls further with his State of the Union address on January 6, forever known as the "Four Freedoms" speech, which laid out America's grand strategy as clearly as any laboriously crafted policy document:

> In future days, which we may seek to secure, we look forward to a world founded upon four essential human freedoms.
>
> The first freedom is freedom of speech and expression—everywhere in the world.
>
> The second freedom is that every person worship God in his own way—everywhere in the world.
>
> The third is the freedom from want . . .
>
> The fourth is the freedom from fear . . .

Roosevelt, striking while the iron was hot, put his well-practiced legal team to work crafting a bill for Congress's consideration, placing Felix Frankfurter, though sitting on the Supreme Court, in charge of the team preparing the bill. On January 10, 1941, the bill, aptly named HR 1776, was submitted to both houses of Congress, setting the stage for a battle royal. Despite the shifting public mood, the isolationists were far from ready to throw in the towel, and in early January, Senate Republicans lined up behind Senator Burton Wheeler when he declared on national radio that Lend-Lease would "plow under every fourth American boy." Roosevelt, ever alert to an opponent's misstep, pounced. At a press conference the next morning he told reporters that Wheeler's statement was "the most untruthful, the most dastardly, unpatriotic thing that has ever been said. Quote me on that."

As the battle raged in Washington and across the nation, Roosevelt played his ace in the hole. Planning to remain in the background himself, FDR asked Jimmy Byrnes to floor-manage the bill through the Senate. Byrnes gladly accepted the task and went right to work. By mid-January, Byrnes was sure he had the votes for passage but told Roosevelt to hold off, as he wanted to redouble his efforts in pursuit of an overwhelming majority. Roosevelt remained worried, asking Byrnes about the chances of the still-numerous and vocal opposition groups undercutting support for the bill. Byrnes calmed him with assurances that despite the howling he would deliver ten or more Republicans along with almost all the Democrats. He advised Roosevelt to stop worrying and "let the heathens rage."

As for the Republicans Byrnes was counting on, their path to a yes vote was greatly eased by Wendell Willkie, who had come out in favor of Lend-Lease but had not truly entered the political fray. On January 19, 1941, Willkie, who was about to depart on a well-publicized trip to Britain, met with Roosevelt at the White House. As Willkie waited in Pa Watson's anteroom, Roosevelt had his staff litter his desk with papers so as to appear busy but more than willing to be interrupted for a vital meeting. The discussion was cordial, and before Willkie left, Roosevelt penned a handwritten note to Churchill telling him that Willkie was "truly working to keep politics out over here, ending with a flourish from Longfellow:

> *Though, too, sail on, O Ship of State!*
> *Sail on, O Union, strong and great!*

Humanity with all its fears
With all the hope of future years
Is hanging breathless on thy fate.

Willkie's trip was so successful that Cordell Hull cabled, begging him to cut it short and return to Washington to testify before the Senate Foreign Relations Committee. Willkie returned from Britain on February 11, landing just hours before the hearing. He appeared before the committee, unkempt, tired, but as amiable as ever, and wholly committed to helping that hard-pressed island. He opened by announcing his strong and unalterable support of Lend-Lease, to competing cheers and boos from the spectators packing the chambers. For the next two days, his fellow Republicans hammered him. When asked about his previous comments about not wishing to help Britain, Willkie simply replied: "I struggled as hard as I could to defeat Roosevelt . . . and didn't pull any of my punches. He was elected President. He is my President now." When arch-isolationist Senator Nye asked him if he still believed that Roosevelt would lead the nation into war by April, Willkie hit just the right note, shrugging his shoulders and replying with a broad grin: "It was a bit of campaign oratory." As laughter swept the chamber, the Republicans realized they had nothing left to gain from interrogating their erstwhile candidate. Their last hope of stopping Lend-Lease died when Willkie departed the chamber.

As the "heathens raged," Roosevelt still had one nagging doubt to settle in his own mind. Like nearly every American, he was impressed with Churchill's speeches, but rhetoric would not win the war. Roosevelt needed to know how deeply Churchill was committed to his own words, and if Britons were overwhelmingly behind him. More critically, did Parliament stand behind him, and, not least, did the generals and admirals share Churchill's resolve? Roosevelt was also bothered by the constant stream of stories about the volume of Churchill's alcohol intake. Moreover, despite the prime minister's constant protestations of support for Roosevelt, the president knew he was an old conservative with no love for New Deal policies, or possibly for Roosevelt himself. What Roosevelt truly wanted was a face-to-face meeting with Churchill. For the moment, however, that was a political impossibility.

Hopkins offered himself as a go-between, and after initially demurring, Roosevelt concurred. Hopkins did not give him a chance to reconsider and immediately booked a flight on the Pan Am Clipper. Before leaving, Hopkins consulted with Jean Monnet, now running the British Purchasing Commission in Washington, who warned him not to waste time on anyone in Britain except Churchill, noting that "Churchill is the British War Cabinet, and no one else matters." Hopkins, who remained unconvinced of Churchill's true worth and was tiring of the endless accolades heaped on the prime minister from every quarter, snapped, "I suppose Churchill is convinced that he's the greatest man in the world." Of course, Hopkins had his own candidate for that position—Franklin Roosevelt, whom he believed Churchill held in low regard. Frankfurter, who had arranged the meeting with Monnet and was present, admonished him. "Harry, if you are going to London with that chip on your shoulder, like a dammed [*sic*] little small-town chauvinist, you may as well cancel your passage now."

When first told of Hopkins's upcoming visit, Churchill asked, "Who?" It was Brendan Bracken, a close Churchill intimate—sometimes referred to as Churchill's Hopkins—and soon to be Britain's information minister, who explained Hopkins's importance to Roosevelt. Churchill received further intelligence from a more unusual source. Frankfurter, alarmed by Hopkins's anti-Churchill attitude, contacted his friend Richard Casey, the first Australian ambassador to the United States, noting that Hopkins hated the Nazis and strongly supported Britain, but also warning that Hopkins idolized Roosevelt and reacted viscerally to any perceived slight of the president. Casey duly passed this intelligence on to London, where Churchill was already laying on the VIP treatment, and rehearsing lines of effusive "spontaneous" praise for Roosevelt.

When Hopkins landed at Poole Airport in southern London, Bracken was on hand to escort him to the first-class train car Churchill had sent to take him to London. Claiming exhaustion, Hopkins refused Churchill's dinner invitation for the first night he was in London. Instead, he stayed up late into the night with the American chargé d'affaires, Herschel V. Johnson, and the embassy's military attaché, General Raymond E. Lee. At dinner that evening, Hopkins learned of comments Churchill had made that day, as he dispatched his new ambassador, Lord Halifax, to the United States. Expecting that Hopkins would receive a full report on the speech, Churchill had larded it full of fulsome praise for Roosevelt.

Harry Hopkins departing for the United Kingdom from Lisbon, Portugal, 1941.

The next morning, Hopkins met with CBS broadcaster Edward R. Murrow, whose broadcasts throughout the Blitz had done so much to sway American opinion toward support of a beleaguered Britain. After peppering Murrow with questions about Britain's leading political figures and British morale, Hopkins finally allowed the correspondent to ask one of his own, namely Hopkins's purpose in coming to Britain. Warning Murrow that his reply was off the record, Hopkins said, "I guess you could say that I've come to find a way to be the catalytic agent between two prima donnas."

After meeting with Foreign Secretary Anthony Eden—who failed to impress—Hopkins made his way to 10 Downing Street to meet Winston Churchill. His first impression was that the prime minister's official residence was a bit "down at the heels," but he chalked it up to the many bombs that had dropped nearby. He was, once again, met by Bracken, who escorted him to a basement dining room, and then departed, but not before leaving Hopkins with a glass of sherry. In due time, Churchill strolled in:

"rotund, smiling—red faced, he extended a fat but none the less convinc-ing hand" welcoming Hopkins to London. Over lunch, Hopkins got right to the heart of matters, telling Churchill that there were those in the United States who believed Churchill disliked America, Americans, and Roosevelt. Churchill forcefully denied the charge, and placed the blame for this mis-understanding on the maliciousness of former ambassador Joseph Ken-nedy. As British intelligence had been listening to Kennedy's phone calls for years, Churchill was superbly briefed on the damage Kennedy had done to Anglo-American cooperation.

After letting Churchill vent for a bit, Hopkins told him the official rea-son for his visit: to get a handle on British needs. The pleased prime min-ister assured Hopkins he would not depart the island without a firm knowledge of Britain's requirements and how each would help win the war. Churchill then went into one of his prolonged but masterful assess-ments of the war to date. The Germans would not invade . . . If they did land, they would be thrown into the sea; Greece was lost, but Britain would make up the loss in North Africa . . . And so it went. The official day ended with a press conference, where Hopkins displayed a talent for sounding optimistic without making any solid commitments.

The next day Hopkins joined Churchill in the countryside for the week-end. Normally, Churchill spent his weekends at his official country home, Chequers, but as a full moon made that home too easy a target, the prime minister took Hopkins to his alternate residence—Ditchley. Briefed on Hopkins's past as a social worker, Churchill tried ingratiating himself with his guest by regaling him with postwar plans to improve the lives of the underprivileged. Churchill was just building up to rhetorical crescendo when Hopkins interrupted: "Neither the President or myself care about any of that. We're only interested in seeing that goddam sonofabitch in Berlin beaten." Not for nothing did Churchill give Hopkins the nickname "Lord Root of the Matter." Churchill gave up discussing social policy and switched to pressing war concerns, both impressing and exhausting his audience of one. Before departing with Churchill for a tour of military fa-cilities in Scotland, Hopkins cabled his impressions to Roosevelt:

> The people here are amazing from Churchill down and if courage alone can win—the result will be inevitable . . . Churchill is the gov't in every sense of the word—he controls the grand strategy and often the

details . . . I cannot emphasize too strongly that he is the one and only person you need to have a full meeting of minds. . . . I cannot believe that it is true that Churchill dislikes either you or America.

In Scotland, Hopkins attended an official dinner given by the secretary of state for Scotland. When asked to give a few words, he let his growing emotional attachment for the British people and their cause to carry him away: "Whither thou goest, I will go; and where thou lodgest, I will lodge; thy people shall be my people, and thy God my God." And then after a long pause he added, "Even to the end." Anyone who heard Hopkins's comments could be forgiven for thinking America's entry into the war was only days away. Churchill had tears running down his face.

Hopkins spent another month in Britain, including three weekends with Churchill at Chequers, which he considered one of the most miserable places on earth, and one weekend at Lord Beaverbrook's country residence. During the war, Beaverbrook—an old friend of Churchill's and currently running British war production—and Hopkins would become fast friends. But their first meeting was far from auspicious, as each man walked away singularly unimpressed by the other. In between these working weekends Hopkins toured various military sites with the tireless Churchill and held innumerable meetings with those he considered capable of getting things done. Churchill's old nemesis, Lady Astor, spent considerable time trying to get Hopkins to meet with society's "better people," but he considered her social set synonymous with the appeasers who had led Joe Kennedy down the wrong track, and rebuffed her entreaties.

It was, however, an open secret that Hopkins was staying at Claridge's, where he was bombarded by a steady stream of visitors and messages. Hopkins turned away most visitors and ignored those messages in which someone tried to explain England's true condition—he was seeing that for himself. The letters that touched him, and the ones he took back to the United States, were almost all from young parents: "My husband is fighting in North Africa . . . can you help get my five month old twins to America?" or "I am a proud working class woman who will fight here to the end, but can you please take my 12-year-old son to America." What struck him was that none of the many missives of this nature he received ever asked for something for the letter writers themselves. The requests were always imploring him to help someone else, and almost always one or more children.

Lord Beaverbrook and William Knudsen at the
OPM offices in Washington, D.C., 1941.

By the beginning of February, Hopkins had all the information he needed, and on February 8 he went to Chequers to say his final goodbyes. That night Hopkins, accompanied by Brendan Bracken, boarded a special train to Bournemouth, where he caught a plane back to America. He was met at New York's La Guardia Marine Terminal by Averell Harriman and the just-announced U.S. ambassador to Britain, John G. Winant. As Hopkins stepped off the plane, Winant yelled out: "Are they going to hold out?" Hopkins, noting the nearby crowd of reporters, shouted back, "Of course they are."

Hopkins, who now knew Britain's needs better than anyone else, was not as certain as he appeared in public, and this uncertainty is what he reported to the president, driving home the crucial importance of Lend-Lease. Hopkins's greatest accomplishment, though, was not in what he learned about Britain's military capacity; rather it was in forging a strong personal bond with Churchill. For much of the remainder of the war he would be on hand to explain Roosevelt and Churchill to each other and smooth out the inevitable rough spots in their wartime partnership. If Hopkins still accorded Roosevelt top standing as the greatest man in the world, he was now willing to accede to Churchill's occupying the next slot in that hierarchy.

Not everyone, however, was impressed with Hopkins's accomplishment. The always sour Harold Ickes observed: "Apparently the first thing that Churchill asks for when he gets awake in the morning is Harry Hopkins, and Harry is the last one whom he sees at night . . . Probably a good deal of this is true and the attachment of Churchill to Harry Hopkins may be entirely genuine. However, I suspect that if, as his personal representative, the President should send to London a man with the bubonic plague, Churchill would, nevertheless, see a great deal of him."

The opponents of Lend-Lease had managed to hold up its passage until March with a series of delaying tactics, but from mid-January the end was never in doubt. This in large measure was due to Jimmy Byrnes, as the *Washington Star* reported: "It was Byrnes who made the voting checks, talked to the waverers, soothed the grumblers, and shepherded the doubters into line." The final vote, on March 9, was 60 to 31. Byrnes declared himself satisfied, as was Roosevelt, who rewarded the senator with a seat on the Supreme Court that June. Byrnes's court nomination was unanimously approved by the Senate eight minutes after it received formal notice of the nomination.

The day after Lend-Lease was signed into law Roosevelt sent Congress a request for $7 billion to pay for war matériel for Britain.

16

Colors Become Rainbows

Amid the battle over Lend-Lease, and even as Hopkins was dining with Churchill, the U.S. military was taking a hard look at its strategic plans. Few doubted they needed an overhaul, as they remained rooted in the "color plans" of the 1920s. These plans, produced by the Joint Army and Navy Board, were color-coded depending on what nation the United States was going to war with. Plan Orange, for example, was the plan for war with Japan, while Black was for Germany, and remarkably, as late as 1938 there was an updated Plan Red for a war with Britain and Canada. By 1940, all of the color plans had been partially jettisoned as a result of events in Europe. In their place the Joint Planning Board established a series of "rainbow" plans designed to fight a war against two enemies at the same time.

Rainbow 1—Focused on defending the Western Hemisphere with
    no allies
Rainbow 2—Identical to Rainbow 1, but we were allied with
    France and Britain
Rainbow 3—Identical to Plan Orange (an assault on Japan), but
    that would only be undertaken after the objectives of Rainbow
    1 were completed.
Rainbow 4—Identical to Rainbow 1, but included more of South
    America.
Rainbow 5—Defend the Western Hemisphere, but in concert with

allies the United States would project forces to defeat Germany, Italy, or both.

It is also worth noting that during the war, Plan Orange (war with Japan) was, to a large degree, substantially implemented as it was originally envisioned (only with carriers instead of battleships as the main deliverer of victory), but as part of the bigger Rainbow 5 plan.

Through the first half of 1940, American planners favored Rainbow 2, counting on Britain and France to hold or defeat Germany, while America, with some Allied help, took on Japan. Rainbow 2 was a Navy favorite, as it did not involve America contributing to a war in Europe. As far as Marshall was concerned, France's collapse eliminated Rainbow 2. In his view, the German threat now far outweighed any action he considered Japan capable of launching. Believing Germany had designs on South America, Marshall directed Army planners to raise Rainbow 4—the protection of the Western Hemisphere—from the lowest priority to the top. This was the attitude Grenville Clark had ferociously attacked when he met with Marshall to gain his support for Selective Service legislation. Nevertheless, Marshall persisted, and submitted a joint recommendation with Admiral Stark that the United States cease sending war matériel to Britain and focus on hemispheric defense. The president, who consistently demonstrated more faith in Britain's capacity to hold out than his military chiefs did, roundly rejected such proposals.

By early November 1940 it was apparent, even to Marshall, that Britain would stay in the war far longer than he originally imagined. Consequently, he lifted his strategic focus away from defending the hemisphere against a German assault that was clearly impossible. Brigadier General Lawrence Guyer, in his unpublished history of the Joint Staff, claims that Marshall during a June 1940 conference with his senior staff posed a question about grand strategy: How would the United States meet simultaneous threats in both the Atlantic and the Pacific? He then answered his own question: "Are we not forced into reframing our naval policy, into one that is purely defensive in the Pacific, with the main effort in the Atlantic?" Despite this prescient conclusion, Marshall never ordered a policy review or any changes to the nation's basic military strategy, which maintained Japan as the country's most dangerous threat.

Changing the military's strategic direction was left to the chief of naval operations, Admiral Stark, who was becoming progressively more uneasy about the current direction of American strategy. In mid-October Stark, starting early on a Saturday morning, drew up a twelve-page estimate of the global situation America faced, as well as some ideas for meeting the onrushing challenges. Finishing well after midnight, he took his rough notes to the office the following day. There, he and his staff went at it "day and night for ten consecutive days," trying to come up with a new strategic framework for the situation America now confronted. By November 2, 1940, he was happy enough with the concept to produce a draft memorandum, which was forwarded to Marshall for review and concurrence, before it was presented to the secretary of the navy.

Stark's key assertion was that if Germany was decisively defeated the Allies could win everywhere, but if Germany was not beaten the problems confronting the Allies would lead to a situation where although "we might not *lose everywhere,* we might, possibly, not *win* anywhere." Stark's assessment closely coincided with Marshall's strategic formulations, and Marshall was glad to have the Navy carry his water. Most significantly, Stark considered that the consequences of a British defeat were so serious for the United States that he declared Britain must be assisted in every way possible. America's military chiefs had finally ended their bitter resistance to a position Roosevelt had been espousing for over a year.

As for Japan, Stark, breaking with long naval tradition, placed it on the second tier of enemies. Previously the Navy had been all-in for Plan Orange, aimed at the economic starvation of Japan followed by the destruction of her military power. But Plan Orange assumed that any such victory would take several years and absorb the full military and economic energy of the American people. Given events in Europe, Stark no longer considered this feasible. As he saw it, victory now required an all-out effort in the Atlantic, while standing on the defensive in the Pacific. Accordingly, Stark's memo set out possible options:

(A) Shall our principal military effort be directed toward hemisphere defense, and include chiefly those activities within the Western Hemisphere which contribute directly to security against attack in either or both oceans?

(B) Shall we prepare for a full offensive against Japan, premised on assistance from the British and Dutch forces in the Far East, and remain on the strict defensive in the Atlantic?

(C) Shall we plan for sending the strongest possible military assistance both to the British in Europe, and to the British, Dutch and Chinese in the Far East?

(D) Shall we direct our efforts toward an eventual strong offensive in the Atlantic as an ally of the British, and a defensive in the Pacific?

Though Stark's assessment laid out four options, he considered only the last—Option D, or "Dog" in military parlance—viable. He further argued that maintaining the existence of the British Empire, combined with building up America's defensive capabilities, was the best way to ensure the defense of the Western Hemisphere, and to promote crucial U.S. national interests. On November 12, 1940, with Marshall's concurrence, he forwarded his plan to Frank Knox, secretary of the navy, who in turn forwarded it to the White House. The next day Marshall ordered the Joint Planning Staff to initiate a study as a first step toward a joint plan implementing the "Plan Dog memorandum."

Although Roosevelt never officially commented on the Plan Dog memo, he also never disapproved it. As far as Stark and Marshall were concerned, silence was the same as approval, as they understood Roosevelt, having just won an election by promising to stay out of the war, needed to be able to disown the plan if it was ever leaked to the press. With the president's tacit approval and the full approval of Secretaries Stimson and Knox, the Joint Board began redefining Rainbow 5 to reflect America's new Germany-first strategy.

Notably, the Joint Board report made mention of two items that were to plague Anglo-American military relations for the next four years. The first was the board's insistence that American naval power could not turn the tide in Europe, and even the addition of massive amounts of airpower was unlikely to gain a victory. Accordingly, the board stated that the only certain path to victory was what would become the American, and particularly Marshall's, preoccupation—launching an invasion of northern Europe at the earliest possible date. For the British, with the nightmare of the Somme battlefields still playing on their minds, such an invasion was the ultimate nightmare scenario.

The Joint Board report also included the first official comment on the opinion American officers held of their British counterparts: "British leadership has not had the competence in any sphere that would justify our entrusting to it the future security of the United States." Both Stark and Marshall read and signed the document, indicating that they shared this low opinion of their future colleagues. This mindset caused problems right from the start, as the British, who had been at war for two years before America's entry, naturally assumed the American chiefs would make use of their experience and follow their lead. On the contrary, American officers looked at the British record and saw nothing but a long string of defeats. As far as they were concerned, the British had little to teach them about how to win a battle, never mind the war. Who's right? Perhaps the comments of the chief of the Imperial General Staff for most of the war—Field Marshal Lord Alan Brooke—are most telling. In his diary on March 31, 1942, Brooke lamented: "Half of our Corps and Divisional Commanders are totally unfit for their appointments, and yet if I were to sack them I could find no better! They lack character, imagination, drive, and power of leadership. The reason for this state of affairs is to be found in the losses we sustained in the last war of all of our best officers, who should now be our senior commanders." Brooke apparently never asked himself if this dangerous state of affairs was more a result of British training and officer education than of losses in the Great War. After all, the Germans rarely had trouble finding superior operational commanders despite having suffered even greater losses than the British.

The final Joint Board memo was sent to Roosevelt on December 21. Once again, Roosevelt failed to officially approve the Joint Board report, though Stark and Marshall assumed the new plan had his support, as he did approve covert Washington meetings between the American and British military planning staffs, with the report as their basis. Two weeks before those conferences took place, FDR assembled his military chiefs and secretaries to review the American position, and to make sure everyone knew the strict limits he was placing upon how much of the nation's treasure and resources they could commit: very little. During this conversation, Roosevelt also demonstrated his thorough knowledge of the Joint Board report and verbally accepted the proposition of putting Germany first and standing on the defensive in the Pacific. He also returned to Marshall a proposed conference agenda that he had heavily edited. As he did so, Roosevelt mentioned that he shared the planners' concerns about not allowing the British to unduly influence America's strategic ideas and launched into a pessimistic discourse about recent British reverses, blaming them on poor political and military leadership. He closed with a warning that the United States could not "afford nor do we need to entrust our national future to British direction."

The British arrived on January 29, 1941, for the first of what were termed the American-British Conversations (ABC). Hoping to avoid press notice, the British had sent relatively junior officers. Roosevelt, also anxious to avoid press leaks, did not meet with them and told his cabinet secretaries to keep their distance. In fact, after the British received an initial welcome from Marshall and Stark, no American military chief took part in the discussions, although they paid close attention to what was discussed. Once the meetings commenced, both sides found much to agree on. The British were particularly cheered by American plans emphasizing winning in the Atlantic first, as this accorded with the first two of the three priorities Churchill had given the British representatives: stress the vital importance of the European theater, and place a priority on defeating Germany and Italy.

It was Churchill's third priority, the defense of Singapore, that caused the Americans to balk. For the British, Singapore was the linchpin of its empire in the Pacific and Indian Oceans. If it fell, there was a probability that much of the eastern British Empire would be lost. The Americans, on the other hand, could not have cared less. As far as they were concerned, the maintenance of the British Empire was a political concern and not one with which they much wanted to bother. They agreed that losing Singapore might endanger the empire, but failed to comprehend what that had to do with winning the war. These opposing viewpoints would haunt Anglo-American councils for the remainder of the war, as British strategic conceptions were always put forth with an eye on ensuring Britain's hold on the empire in the postwar years, while American leaders preferred a postwar world in which the British Empire no longer existed. If Britain wanted to hold Singapore, they would have to do it on their own; America would expend no resources on doing so. The British were receiving an early and unwelcome primer on how American planners conceived of a war-winning strategy. The American path was very simple: what helps us win the war is good, politics be damned. It was, of course, a shortsighted attitude, and one American policymakers would later regret, as the purpose of any war must always be aimed at a just political settlement.

The American planners were also determined to avoid British plans to scatter American troops throughout the empire or regions the British thought vital to the empire's security, such as North Africa, Greece, and India. All such British attempts were viewed through the prism of the last war; senior American officers still vividly remembered ceaseless British attempts to use American soldiers as replacements within their own units, and so ensuring that the United States never formed an independent American army in France. This so-called "amalgamation controversy" had cast a long shadow on Allied relations during the last year of the Great War, and the Americans were keen on blocking any drift in that direction from the outset of the current relationship. As American planners saw it, their country's army was destined for only one thing: the invasion of northern Europe. Throughout the war, any British proposal that diverged from this one guiding principle met with sharp resistance from Marshall, and the coterie of like-minded officers gathered around him. As for the British, haunted by the Great War's carnage, they held on to the hope that they could avoid such an invasion until well into 1944, the very eve of D-Day. As Churchill told Hopkins while the ABC talks were in progress: "This war will never see great forces massed against each other." Still, this difference of viewpoints did not get in the way of a final understanding; such a collision was still a hypothetical for a later year. In the meantime, the Americans saw nothing wrong with the British plan of weakening Germany by all possible means, including an air offensive and economic pressure, and even by "nibbling away at the fringes of German power."

Notwithstanding the minor disagreements, the meetings were a great success. Stark's "Plan Dog," as restated by the Joint Board, proved a sufficient basis for agreement on the single most important strategic issue: Germany first, which was essentially restated as ABC 1. This agreement was later integrated into the Rainbow 5 plan and became the foundation for all subsequent discussions about strategy throughout the war. As the meetings ended, and despite the passage of Lend-Lease, which should have heralded the dwindling political potency of the isolationist movement, Roosevelt still moved cautiously, refusing to officially sign off on either ABC 1 or Rainbow 5. He did, however, order them returned to him for signature in the event of war.

Roosevelt's hesitation stymied the military. If they were going to meet the commitments outlined in ABC 1, they needed to begin detailed planning and preparation immediately. But without presidential approval no one was sure if they were permitted to do so. The matter was resolved by Marshall in a meeting of what was called the "war council"—Hull, Stimson, Knox, Marshall, and Stark—on June 10. Marshall told the assembled group that Roosevelt had been presented with two options, either approve or disapprove the plans. There was no middle way. As he did not disapprove them, Marshall claimed that they were approved by default, reasoning that as FDR asked for their return in the event of war, he must have approved them. Stimson, Knox, and Stark were easily convinced, and after a few moments the always cautious Hull joined the cabal. It was full steam ahead.

17

HAMLET FINDS AN ADMIRAL

ROOSEVELT'S RENEWED PHYSICAL STRENGTH SOON EBBED. FOR
the next few months he fought off a cold that never seemed to diminish, taking to his bed for days at a time. Even when he was up and about,
visitors often found him listless and distracted. All of this was likely symp-
tomatic of the heart disease that went undiagnosed by the incompetent
White House doctor, Admiral Ross T. McIntire, for several years. Illness
alone, including a persistent fever for much of May 1941, explains a good
part of Roosevelt's failure to lead during this bleak and crucial phase of the
war. But it is not the complete story.

The president's actions supporting Britain garnered record approval
ratings in the polls, but the nation was still divided over how much further
to go, with 70 percent feeling the country was already doing more than
enough. The debate over whether the U.S. Navy should escort merchant
ships across the Atlantic was particularly thorny: Although there was growing support for such missions, even at the risk of war, most Americans still
insisted that the country stay out of the conflict.

For the all-outers within the administration, Roosevelt was moving too
slowly on the matter and when he did move he was not going far enough.
They pushed him to order the Navy to commence convoy escort duty
across the Atlantic, arguing that Lend-Lease was pointless if the war matériel was sunk in transit. The most they could get was an order to move the
U.S. patrol zone out a bit further to the 25th meridian, generally bisecting
the distance between South America and Africa and running up past

Cordell Hull; Henry Morgenthau, secretary of the treasury;
First Lady Eleanor Roosevelt; and President Franklin D. Roosevelt.

Greenland. The president also agreed to allow any American warship spotting a U-boat to alert the British to its presence.

This was far from sufficient for Roosevelt's cabinet, now full of men lobbying for faster action. On April 25, these all-outers used a scheduled cabinet meeting to try to force the issue, pressing hard for the president to
authorize escorts all the way from U.S. ports to Britain. Roosevelt, unac-
customed to being on the defensive, repeatedly mentioned the extended
patrolling he had already approved and said, "Well, it's a step forward."
Stimson replied, "Well, I hope you will keep walking, Mr. President. Keep
walking." The cabinet burst into a roar of laughter, joined by Roosevelt.

Roosevelt, however, understood that the all-outers would only be satisfied with America's entry into the war, an ultimate step he refused to take.
In contemplating his reluctance, it might be sufficient to consider what was
being asked of him: to lead a great nation into what was certain to be a
long, costly, and bloody war. Certainly, Roosevelt was a man of strong
moral and physical courage. But who would not quake before so awesome
a responsibility? His advisers could push, plead, and cajole, but the responsibility for hundreds of thousands, possibly millions, of dead, maimed, and

psychologically shattered young men did not fall on their shoulders. That responsibility fell squarely upon the president. Roosevelt well remembered how the nation's attitude about World War I quickly changed when the full costs of that conflict were revealed. In 1917 Wilson had done much to lead a reluctant nation into war. After war was declared, America rallied behind him and remained supportive until Germany's surrender. But in that war Americans were only involved in major fighting during the last months of the cataclysm. When, after the fighting ended, they learned of the butcher's bill paid in the Meuse-Argonne, they turned passionately against the war. Roosevelt must have wondered how long the polls would show support for waging war once the casualty list lengthened in the second, third, or fourth year of a bloody global conflagration.

While Roosevelt played Hamlet and Anglo-American staff officers debated grand strategy, British forces were on the march. In North Africa, a brilliantly conducted assault had crushed the Italian army, netting the British over 130,000 prisoners. A second campaign in Somaliland and Ethiopia bagged 200,000 more Italian prisoners, and placed Haile Selassie back on his throne.

It was not to last. Snatching defeat from the jaws of victory, Churchill convinced the cabinet to move divisions from North Africa for service in Greece against the invading Italians. In some of the worst timing of the war the British divisions were withdrawn from North Africa just as General Erwin Rommel began assembling the Afrika Korps in western Libya to come to Italy's aid.

German intervention in the Balkans was certain from the moment British troops landed in Greece, since Hitler could not tolerate an enemy lodgment so close to the crucial Romanian oil fields. On March 27, a coup in Yugoslavia accelerated events when the anti-German seventeen-year-old Prince Peter was placed on the throne and promptly repudiated his nation's alliance with Germany. He did not have to wait long for the German reaction. On April 6, twenty-five Wehrmacht divisions marched into Yugoslavia. Belgrade fell a week later, and on the 17th Yugoslavia surrendered. The German assault on Greece, coming across the Bulgarian border, also began on April 6. Progress was initially slow, but gathered speed, particularly after Yugoslavia's surrender freed German troops for fighting in

Greece. By April 24 the British Army was again boarding transports. This time, however, they were evacuating Greece and heading for Crete.

The Germans were close on their heels, launching the largest airborne assault in history on May 20, 1941. General Kurt Student, commander of the German airborne troops, horrified at the losses his men had taken, dubbed the island "the graveyard of the German paratroopers." The Germans' losses were indeed heavy, but they took the island. Over four nights, from May 28 to 31, the British conducted a miniature Dunkirk evacuation, but this time they were forced to leave nine thousand troops behind. Moreover, the Royal Navy suffered grievous losses during the operation. At one point, British admiral Andrew Cunningham's staff advised him to halt the operation early. Determined not to let the army down, Cunningham replied that the Royal Navy had always stood ready to help the army in its hour of need, and concluded: "It takes three years to build a ship. It will take three hundred years to build a new tradition."

Elsewhere, the war was going little better. Rommel's counterattack had sent the weakened British forces reeling. By April 11, an entire Australian division was besieged in Tobruk, where they would still be holding the line months later. In the meantime, the Afrika Korps entered Egypt, where it threatened Alexandria and the Suez Canal.

As the battles in North Africa raged, U-boats were making their presence felt, having sunk 818,000 tons of shipping in the previous three months. Britain was losing the Battle of the Atlantic, as shipping losses exceeded replacements and German submarine construction outpaced Britain's capacity to build ships for antisubmarine warfare. Making matters worse was the threat that German battle cruisers and battleships, led by the mighty *Bismarck*, would break out and wreak havoc in the North Sea shipping lanes. This last concern was somewhat alleviated when the *Bismarck* was run down and sunk on May 27, but not before she had blown the mighty HMS *Hood* into oblivion. The following week a German wolf pack sank ten merchant ships just south of Iceland, causing Roosevelt to implement Hemisphere Defense Plan No. 1, which moved three battleships, a carrier, four light cruisers, and two squadrons of destroyers from the Pacific to the Atlantic.

Roosevelt—prodded by the news that the *Bismarck* was loose—ended his May 27 fireside chat with a declaration of a "state of unlimited emergency," upping the nation from the "limited" state of emergency it had been in since the invasion of Poland. The cheered all-outers, who expected a flurry of executive orders moving the nation to a war footing, were cast down again the next morning when Roosevelt told the press that it was all just a technical thing and did not presage any change in policy.

Stimson, Knox, and Morgenthau wanted Roosevelt to base his decisions on deep principles. As they saw it, the world was divided into two camps, one of which was evil, the other led by Roosevelt. Based on this Man-ichaean outlook, the all-outers were concerned about Roosevelt's refusal to move toward war when it was manifestly the right thing to do when con-fronted by evil. Most of the cabinet believed the president was waiting for some incident that he could use to rally a unified America. As Stimson wrote, Roosevelt was "waiting for the accidental shot of some irresponsible captain . . . to be the occasion for war," rather than forthrightly leading the crusade the all-outers wished him to. It was, in the end, left to the great war horse of the establishment, Henry Stimson, to confront Roosevelt on this point and to place the ethical choices before him: "The people must not be brought to combat evil through some accident or mistake, but through his [Roosevelt's] moral leadership." Roosevelt was unmoved, and later told Morgenthau that he was "waiting to be pushed into a situation."

On June 9, they learned that even a provocative incident was not going to be sufficient. On that day Roosevelt learned that the Germans had sunk a clearly marked American freighter, the *Robin Moor*, and then callously set the crew adrift with minimal food and water, and without radioing their location to potential rescuers. This followed an incident in April where a destroyer, the USS *Niblack*, had been fired on by a U-boat, and then en-gaged with torpedoes. Though Hopkins wrote a strong memo to Roo-sevelt, asking him to let the Navy establish the right to freedom of the seas by whatever means necessary, the president refused to act.

Roosevelt was not waiting for an "accident," as Stimson thought. He was waiting for a major explosion that would in and of itself lead America into war.

When that explosion came, he would have an admiral in place who could more than hold his own with Marshall and Arnold.

In April 1941, Roosevelt had declared Greenland worthy of American pro-tection under the Monroe Doctrine, shortly followed by Iceland in June, backed up by four thousand marines to make his point. Eager to exploit this spark of presidential aggressiveness, in May 1941 Hull, Morgenthau, Knox, Stimson, Arnold, and Marshall met with Roosevelt and Hopkins in the White House library, again urging the president toward more decisive action, again to no avail. Stimson claimed the only benefit of the meeting was that Roosevelt was so impressed by Arnold's briefing on the condition of the Royal Air Force that he gave up his lingering animus toward the air chief. But Stimson's pleasure at Arnold's rehabilitation was tempered by his annoyance at Admiral Stark's backtracking on the previously settled agreement to move three capital ships from the Pacific to the Atlantic, joined by Hull who expressed unease about Japan. A sullen Stimson confided to his diary: "He [Stark] is a timid and ineffective man to be in the post he holds." Stark's days as chief of naval operations were clearly numbered, as Secretary of the Navy Knox was already looking for a more decisive admiral, and his gaze had settled on the man running the Atlantic Fleet's expansion: Admiral Ernest King.

On his best day, Admiral King was a difficult man to get along with. Undoubtedly brilliant and hardworking, he was also abrasive and often abusive. One of his daughters commented that "my father was the most even-tempered in the Navy. He was always in a rage." Roosevelt once said that King "shaved with a blow torch." Naval historian Samuel Eliot Morison described him thus: "Endowed with a superior intellect himself, he had no toleration of fools or weaklings; everyone in the Navy respected him, but [he] was more feared than loved." According to historian Robert Love, King was "meaner than hell . . . a man who did not go out of his way to make friends with people." Handsome and, when he wished, charming, King had two other serious weaknesses: he enjoyed the company of beautiful women, particularly married women, and he often drank to excess. Though he claimed to have given up drinking for the duration of the war, there is voluminous evidence to the contrary. King, however, had two strengths that he expected everyone to recognize: he was a supremely competent sailor, and he could make the hard decisions when needed.

King was the firstborn child of a comfortable but lower-middle-class family in Lorain, Ohio. He gained admission to the Naval Academy in 1897, and he was still an Annapolis midshipman when the Spanish-American War erupted. Released for the summer, King, along with several other midshipmen, wrangled orders to go to sea aboard the USS *San Fran-*

cisco. During the conflict, the *San Francisco* took part in blockading Havana, where he had his first experience of hostile fire.

Upon graduation, even his friends considered King intellectually arrogant, and King himself thought few men his equal in intelligence. As one biographer says of him: "Once convinced he had the right answer, he was unyielding toward any suggestion that he might possibly be wrong. Unyielding may be too mild an adjective. [He was] stubborn. Adamant. Tenacious. And armed with a violent temper."

For the first five years after graduation there was little remarkable about King's career. He served on several ships, and spent well over two years on the cruiser USS *Cincinnati.* It was aboard the *Cincinnati* that his weaker character traits came close to wrecking his career. On at least three occasions King was confined to his quarters for drunkenness and insubordination. But even when he was not drunk King was troublesome, often challenging far senior officers so vehemently that it was impossible for them to retreat even if they were wrong. By the time King returned to the United States in 1905, he had resolved to rein in his temper and be more circumspect in his carousing. He often failed at both, but he got much smarter about not letting his temper or drinking affect his duty performance.

With the outbreak of World War I, King got a firsthand look at how unready the Navy was for war. It was not a pretty sight, and the confusion, delays, and disorganization had a lasting impact on him. Never a great admirer of the British, King also twice traveled to Britain, where he sat in on war councils at the highest levels and was not won over by anything he witnessed. If anything, his Anglophobia increased, and never truly diminished. Such an outlook would color much of his attitude toward the British during the fight to come.

King first came to national attention when in 1925 and 1927 he was given the job of raising recently sunk submarines (*S-51* and *S-4*), an undertaking the Navy had already announced publicly had little chance of success. After King succeeded, under the most arduous conditions, he basked in an avalanche of nationwide publicity that propelled his star far ahead of his fellow captains. He was rapidly making a name for himself as an officer who accomplished the impossible.

It still took almost a decade before King was elevated to vice admiral and took command of the Aircraft Battle Force, initially consisting of three car-

Admiral Ernest King (left), commander in chief, U.S. Fleet, and chief
of naval operations, and Vice Admiral Emory Land.

riers: *Saratoga, Lexington,* and *Ranger*—and later the *Yorktown*. In March
1938, King received permission to test his developing carrier theories during Fleet Problem XIX. Admiral Stark was aboard as an invited guest, and
the two men watched the *Saratoga* launch its aircraft toward Pearl Harbor.
In an action eerily prescient of the assault the Japanese would launch only
a few years later, the attacking aircraft achieved total surprise, although the
defenders were aware that a carrier was closing on them. Unfortunately,
King's demonstration of just how vulnerable Pearl Harbor was to a carrier
strike went unheeded by his superiors. King once again proved the value of
naval aviation in Fleet Problem XX, held mostly in the Caribbean, in which
his carriers performed credibly in an exercise heavily rigged in favor of the
traditional surface combatants.

Still, however respected he was for his abilities, King had accumulated too many enemies, many of whom were now admirals, and he was never truly in the running for the Navy's top job—chief of naval operations (CNO). In fact, his name was not even on the short list of candidates that the then CNO, Admiral William Leahy, forwarded to the president. In July 1939 King was sidelined to the Naval Board, where he could sit out a quiet few years until retirement.

World War II would start in less than two months. And as events accelerated, King's old friend Harold Stark recognized the need for a brilliant "sonofabitch" in the front ranks, bringing him back from oblivion to the key command of the Atlantic fleet.

In that capacity, King was summoned to Hyde Park in April to meet with Roosevelt, who informed him that the long-anticipated face-to-face meeting between the president and Churchill would take place at sea in the coming months. Sworn to secrecy and warned not to discuss the matter even with Knox or Stark, King was given a code word he would receive in the days prior to the meeting, so the required ships could be moved into position for the conference, likely off the coast of Canada.

18

DRANG NACH OSTEN

BEFORE DAWN, ON JUNE 22, 1941, THOUSANDS OF GUNS, STRETCH-ing from the Baltic to the Black Sea, belched flame and steel, heralding the latest installment of the German *Drang nach Osten*—Drive to the East. The Wehrmacht was on the march again, and this time its target was the Soviet Union. Despite abundant warning, the Russians were caught unprepared for the onslaught. On the first day alone the Germans destroyed over 1,800 Soviet aircraft, the overwhelming number of them blown apart on the ground. By the end of the week that number had more than doubled. Beneath this overwhelming German air armada, the panzers rapidly penetrated Russia's defensive perimeter and began driving deep into Soviet territory. Before them huge Soviet armies, stripped of air cover and lacking competent leadership, dissolved.

As Hitler predicted, the world held its breath.

American military leaders were just as surprised by the new German blitzkrieg as were the Soviets. Having seen what Germany did to the French Army—which until May 1940 had been considered the best in the world—Marshall advised Roosevelt that the Soviet Union might not last a month. British strategists agreed, but were grateful for even a couple of months respite from the threat of invasion and were hopeful that the distraction would open up possibilities in North Africa. Stimson was also looking at the German assault as an opportunity for the United States to further involve itself in the war, sending a note to Roosevelt the day after the invasion that held out little hope for the Soviet Union's survival but added: ". . . This precious and unforeseen period of respite should be used to push with utmost vigor our movements in the Atlantic theater of operations."

Roosevelt wanted to help, but beyond the politics of helping the officially atheist, communist Soviet Union, he needed answers to three questions: What were Russia's military needs, how would such matériel be delivered, and would Russia hold out? This last was crucial, for the chiefs were justifiably reluctant to send their precious war stocks to the Soviet Union only to see them end up in German hands. But in addition to the projections of his military advisers, Roosevelt was listening to others, including former ambassador to the Soviet Union Joseph Davies, who had publicly stated that ". . . the resistance of the Red Army will surprise and amaze the world." On July 8, Davies was in the White House to witness Jimmy Byrnes's swearing-in to the Supreme Court. Afterward, he accompanied Hopkins to his room, where he made the case for the Soviets outlasting the Germans, if only they could get material help from the United States. On July 10 Roosevelt and Hopkins met with the Soviet ambassador, Constantine Oumansky, promising him that the United States would meet the Soviets' most vital needs. Soon thereafter, the Russians delivered a list totaling nearly $2 billion.

The next evening, July 11, Roosevelt and Hopkins discussed the problem of moving supplies to Russia well into the night. If supplies were to get to the Soviet Union, the bulk of them would have to go past northern Norway on their way to the port of Murmansk. Along the route, they would be vulnerable to submarines, mines, surface raiders sortieing out of Norway's fjords, and air attack. It would only be possible if Britain employed much of its limited resources to cover the route. To help Britain shift assets Roosevelt ordered American warships to start escorting convoys to and from the United Kingdom as far out as Iceland, tearing a map out of *National Geographic* magazine and drawing a thick line from Iceland and through the Azores to mark the hand-off point. Even this expansion of American naval activity left the all-outers frustrated, as only U.S.-flagged merchant ships were permitted in these convoys, and they had hoped Roosevelt would draw the line well to the east of Iceland. Before the meeting was over, Roosevelt told Hopkins to pack his bags again. Someone had to coordinate these initiatives with Churchill and, at the same time, clear up the problems already besetting Lend-Lease. Roosevelt also gave Hopkins instructions to finalize the details of the upcoming meeting with Churchill and to alert Churchill to the fact that Averell Harriman, posted to Britain earlier, was there only to handle Lend-Lease's technical matters and had no policy role. Hopkins was expressly not told to discuss the United States entering the war, nor was he to make any deals.

Hopkins's initial meetings with Churchill were generally uneventful, as were his discussions with other British officials and the many Americans in London as "observers" helping to coordinate Lend-Lease activities. Things took an unexpected turn when, while staying with Churchill at Chequers, Hopkins met Adam Maisky, Soviet ambassador to Britain, who had come to deliver the first of Stalin's many demands that Britain immediately open a second front—quite a demand given that Stalin had been supplying Hitler with many of the raw materials used to bomb Britain for the past year. A few days later, on July 22, Hopkins and the American ambassador, John Gilbert Winant, had lunch with Maisky. Noting Hopkins's visible irritation over his incomplete answers for information beyond the Soviets' initial requests for supplies, Maisky suggested that Hopkins go to Moscow and get the answers from Stalin himself.

Hopkins's message asking Roosevelt for permission to head to Moscow as the president's personal representative arrived as Roosevelt was meeting with the Japanese ambassador, Admiral Kichisaburo Nomura, over Japan's aggressive move into southern Indochina. Roosevelt cabled his approval within hours of receiving Hopkins's request and followed with a direct message to Stalin asking him to "treat Mr. Hopkins with the identical confidence you would expect if you were directly talking to me." Hopkins immediately made his way to Scotland and then by PBY Catalina to Archangel, in the Soviet Union's Arctic north, during which trip Hopkins spent hours in the rear gun turret scanning the sky for German fighters as the unheated plane flew past Norway.

After some rest and a full day of sightseeing with American ambassador Laurence A. Steinhardt, who had been denied any information about the war by the secretive Russians, Hopkins wondered if his own mission was a waste of time. But later that evening when he was shown into Stalin's office, the Soviet premier got right to the heart of the matter. For the next four hours Stalin, aided by only a few slips of paper, detailed the information and data Hopkins had come for. Not an empty diplomatic word passed between them, and Hopkins departed with "facts and figures as cold, as

Harry Hopkins (left)
and Joseph Stalin (right).

informative, as colorless, and as barren of romance as the reports" that crossed his desk as secretary of commerce. During this first meeting Stalin laid out his immediate needs—antiaircraft guns, rifles, machine guns, and millions of rounds of ammunition—and mentioned that his most pressing long-term need was for high-octane fuel for the Soviet air force.

The next day Hopkins wasted his time meeting with Soviet officials and generals who, whenever a substantive issue was broached, halted the conversation. No Soviet official or officer would risk getting ahead of Stalin on any matter he was not given explicit permission to discuss. Time and again, Hopkins heard versions of "I am not empowered to say if we need tanks," or "That is something that must be taken up with Comrade Stalin." Giving up, Hopkins waited for his next meeting with Stalin that evening.

Stalin remained a font of crucial information, going on for hours with detailed descriptions of the fighting to date, and his plans. His optimism and determination went far toward convincing Hopkins that the Soviet Union would stem and then reverse the German tide—an opinion directly contrary to that held by every American and British general. But Stalin himself might not have been entirely confident of his ultimate victory, given that in almost the next breath he practically begged Hopkins to induce Roosevelt to lead America into the war, and even conceding that he would not mind having an American army fighting in the Soviet Union completely under American command. Stalin had every reason to worry. Just that week German panzers had trapped three Soviet armies at Smolensk, only 225 miles from Moscow. Hopkins was forced to explain that he was there only to discuss supplies, and the United States would enter the war only if it was directly attacked.

The Soviet leader also freely admitted that his army had been surprised and that many divisions were out of place at the start of the campaign. Russia, according to Stalin, had paid a massive price for this, but he was convinced that the front was stabilizing. He confided that the Soviet Union was mobilizing new divisions faster than the Germans could replace their losses, and was keen to get his new divisions into the fight, telling Hopkins that only in combat can the troops "learn the Germans can be killed and they are not supermen . . . nothing in warfare can take the place of combat, and I will need seasoned divisions for my spring offensives."

On his return to the United States, Hopkins would lay out a convincing case in support of much of Stalin's long-term optimism. At the end of his report to the president, Hopkins penciled in: "Mr. Stalin expressed repeatedly his confidence that the Russian lines would hold." Hopkins was convinced. Whether he would be able to convince Roosevelt, Stimson, and Marshall remained an open question.

First, Hopkins had to catch a cross-Atlantic ship ride with Churchill for the prime minister's first wartime meeting with Roosevelt, which had been set for early August, off the coast of Newfoundland. His return trip to Britain was even worse than the outbound journey, compounded by having left his medicines in Moscow. By the time Hopkins boarded the *Prince of Wales* he was a very sick man. The commander in chief of the Home Fleet, Admiral Sir John Tovey, ordered him to bed as soon as he set eyes upon him. Fearing his guest might not even survive the night he called for the doctors. Hopkins insisted on dinner, but he soon waned and was sent to his cabin, from which he only emerged eighteen hours later, before rapidly returning for another full night of rest. Churchill arrived the next day, and together they departed for the Atlantic Conference.

Toward mid-July Roosevelt seemed to have returned to his old self and started taking a much more active role in affairs. And although he was looking forward to weighing anchor and joining Churchill off the Canadian shore there were several important domestic matters in need of resolution. First on his agenda was an internal squabble regarding getting matériel to Russia. Having just received Hopkins's initial dispatches from the Soviet Union, during an early August cabinet meeting, Roosevelt declared himself unsatisfied with the pace at which the initial tranche of supplies was heading to the Soviets. He proceeded to give Stimson a harsh dressing-down, accusing the War Department of "dragging its feet." Growing visibly angrier as he spoke, Roosevelt demanded they get moving. Embarrassed in front of other cabinet members, Stimson rose to the bait, claiming that he had never seen any of the Russian requests, except for planes, which had been addressed immediately. This was at best only a half truth. Even if Stimson had not personally seen the Soviet requests, his numerous diary entries on the topic during the prior month leave no room for doubt that he and his staff knew all about them. In fact, Ambassador Oumansky and the head of the Soviet military mission to the United States, General Filipp Ivanovich Golikov, had spent several hours with Stimson only the day before.

In truth, Stimson and Marshall *were* dragging their feet. Both men were trying to build an effective army and an air force that was lacking everything a modern military requires. From their perspective, every truck, plane, and tank sent to the Soviet Union, or for that matter to Great Britain, delayed the day when the U.S. Army would be ready for war. Neither Stimson nor Marshall was rushing to fill Soviet orders, as they both remained certain the Germans would enter Moscow in a few more weeks. Roosevelt was having none of it: "I am sick and tired," he shouted, "of hearing that they are going to get this and they are going to get that. The only answer I want to hear is that it is under way." Stimson, realizing that further debate was useless, remained silent. That evening he recorded in his diary: "I didn't get half a chance with him. He really was in a hoity-toity humor and wouldn't listen to argument." The next day Roosevelt told one of his able assistants, the hyperefficient Wayne Coy, to take charge of getting Russia everything it needed and gave him written instructions to use Roosevelt's full authority and a heavy hand, but at all costs to get things moving.

Next on Roosevelt's agenda, and by far the most consequential item, was the fact that in just two months most of the U.S. Army was going to be gutted. The Selective Service bill had been limited to a single year and was near expiring, at which point most of the Army's 1.5 million trained soldiers would have to be discharged, the Army effectively disbanded. Army morale was running on empty, and the graffiti slogan OHIO (Over the Hill In October) was ubiquitous on military posts throughout the country. Congress, aware of the rank and file's dissatisfaction and the toxicity of the draft for the isolationist movement, wanted no part of a bill that would both extend the terms of those first drafted and institute a new draft call for later that year.

Stimson and Marshall spent much of the spring unsuccessfully trying to get Roosevelt to focus on the issue. When he finally did, in early June, he was only lukewarm about it, having been warned by Speaker Sam Rayburn that the Democrats might lose the House if they were forced to support a service extension. Polls showed that Americans favored the extension by a slim majority, which was not enough to make anyone on Capitol Hill feel secure. Understanding that he still did not have the clout on the Hill to move an unpopular bill, Roosevelt tasked Marshall with ensuring the bill's safe passage.

When Marshall learned that Republicans, seeing an opportunity to embarrass Roosevelt and regain their majority, were going to make opposition to the bill a test of party loyalty, he became desperate. He convinced James Wadsworth, one of the bill's original sponsors, to gather forty Republicans he thought might be persuadable for a private meeting at the Army and Navy Club. Marshall went at them for five hours, not finishing until well after 2:00 A.M. One congressman stated: "You put your case very well, but I'll be damned if I am going to go along with Roosevelt." By then, the lobbying had taken its toll on Marshall, who angrily responded: "You are going to let plain hatred of the personality dictate to you to do something that you realize is very harmful to the interests of the country." The vote remained uncertain until the closing moment when it seemed to pass by two votes. Then New York Democrat Andrew Somers, without warning, changed his vote. Before another wavering soul could reverse the slim victory, Speaker Rayburn slammed down his gavel and declared the vote closed. Marshall had saved his army, but only just.

19

RENDEZVOUS AT SEA

THROUGHOUT THE SELECTIVE SERVICE DEBATE ROOSEVELT HAD, perhaps wisely, kept his distance, limiting himself to a single but highly influential radio address on the topic. This was both shrewd political calculation and an indication that his attention had shifted to what he referred to as his "great adventure": the clandestine meeting with Winston Churchill. On Sunday, August 3, Washington was suffering under a brutal heat wave that made work almost impossible. Roosevelt announced he was going to take a short fishing excursion to escape the heat, his first since he had come up with the idea for Lend-Lease months before.

His train, rattling slowly north, reached New London, Connecticut, late in the day. As soon as the president boarded the waiting presidential yacht, *Potomac*, it left shore for a week of fishing in Long Island Sound. The next morning, in full view of hundreds of onlookers, the *Potomac* took aboard Norway's Princess Martha, her two daughters, and Prince Karl of Sweden, at South Dartmouth, Massachusetts. After a full day of fishing Roosevelt's guests went ashore, and late that evening the *Potomac* put back out to sea. The next morning the yacht went through the Cape Cod Canal, where many went to view the president and his cronies kibitzing on the afterdeck. They were looking at imposters. Roosevelt had already departed the *Potomac* and boarded the darkened USS *Augusta* on its way north toward Canada.

Following up on their initial meeting in April, Admiral King had been again summoned to meet Roosevelt on July 25 and given a firm meeting location and date. King tasked the *Augusta* with the mission, with the *Tus-*

caloosa kept nearby, in case the *Augusta* was torpedoed or hit a mine. Neither ship's captain was told the nature of their mission, although the *Augusta*'s captain must have suspected what was afoot when he was ordered into New York Harbor to have ramps installed and to pick up several VIPs. The VIPs turned out to be Admiral Stark, General Marshall (General Arnold traveled on the *Tuscaloosa*), and several key staff members, none of whom had any idea why they were there, or where they were heading, except that they were told to bring warm clothing. The only hiccup was a typical King explosion, over the Army's lack of understanding of Navy protocol: General Arnold had had the temerity to visit King without first announcing his visit.

As the American flotilla sailed north, Churchill, his entire military staff, and Harry Hopkins were proceeding west aboard the *Prince of Wales*. Churchill had one great aim and several minor ones. Foremost, he unreasonably hoped to get Roosevelt's agreement to enter the war. If that could be accomplished, Churchill wanted to make sure that the American war plans were fully in accord with his own vision, and he continuously met with his military chiefs to make sure they understood his vision. When he had downtime he spent it with Hopkins, playing backgammon (not well), watching movies, and constantly peppering Hopkins with questions about Roosevelt's likes and dislikes. Such preparation stands in marked contrast to what was happening or not happening on the American side. Roosevelt was never happier than when he could surprise his staff, and on this occasion, he had done so in spades. The American chiefs were unable to prepare, as they were not told where they were going or who they were meeting until the *Augusta* and *Tuscaloosa* were en route to the rendezvous. One may, however, doubt if they were taken as completely unaware as they pretended, as Stimson the day before they left New York recorded in his diary: "There is a wild rumor going around the town tonight to the effect that the President is going to meet Churchill somewhere up near Canada. Churchill will have with him Harry Hopkins according to the rumor, and the President will have with him George Marshall, Stark, possibly Knox, and Arnold. All of these men happen to be out of town and nobody knows where they went, and the newspaper men have ferreted this out and are having a beautiful time with a novel story."

On August 7 the *Augusta* entered Newfoundland's Argentia Harbor, one of the new facilities made available in the destroyers-for-bases deal. Two days later the *Prince of Wales* appeared on the edge of a low-hanging morning fog, flanked by American destroyers that had linked up with her the previous day. Honors were given by both ships, and the *Prince of Wales* settled astern of the *Augusta*. At 11:00 A.M. Churchill came aboard the American vessel. He found Roosevelt, in leg braces and assisted by his son Elliott, insisting on standing for their first meeting. The American band played "God Save the King" followed by "The Star-Spangled Banner." Everyone stood at attention in the cool breeze as a Marine Corps guard rendered an impeccable salute. The formalities completed, Churchill stepped forward, bowed, and presented Roosevelt a letter from the king.

"At last we have gotten together," Roosevelt said.

Extending his hand, Churchill replied, "Yes, we have."

In that simple moment the partnership that won World War II was born.

Roosevelt and Churchill went off to a private lunch, at the end of which they were calling each other Winston and Franklin. In the meantime, Marshall and Stark decamped with the British chiefs for their own working

Back row, from left: Admiral Ernest King, General George Marshall, and Marshal John Dill. Front row, from left: President Franklin D. Roosevelt and Prime Minister Winston Churchill.

lunch. Admiral King was present for these meetings, but as he was not yet one of America's military chiefs and had not been a party to the earlier ABC 1 discussions, he limited himself to just listening. The conversations were friendly but fruitless, as Roosevelt had forbidden his chiefs to have substantive discussions, ordering them not to commit America to any future plan. Always sensitive to the charge that he was planning America's entry into the war, Roosevelt hoped to circumvent such accusations by making sure his military chiefs were both unprepared and silent. Churchill's high hopes were, therefore, doomed from the start. He wanted an American commitment to enter the war, while Roosevelt was aiming for much less: to meet Churchill, and get his agreement to a high-minded statement of Allied postwar intentions.

Still, Churchill gave it his best effort. After dinner that first night he held forth with all his celebrated eloquence surveying each theater of the war in exhaustive detail, always putting British strategy and actions in the best possible light. Although he never directly addressed American entry into the war, his desire for just that was implied with every sentence.

The next morning, Churchill carefully choreographed religious services to create a moment of high emotion, while also providing a superb opportunity for photographers. He vetted the hymns, selected the Bible lesson, and even chose the prayers, having them all read to him the night before while he lay naked in his bath. The symbolism of the event was not lost on anyone present: two national flags, two nations' chaplains, everyone praying and singing in a common language and sharing the same prayer books. To cap it all off, here were two national leaders sitting side by side, with their military chiefs arrayed behind them in their dress uniforms. As Churchill remembered it, "Every word seemed to stir the heart. It was a great hour to live."

Almost immediately after services concluded, Churchill was again on the verbal offensive. This time he switched tacks—if he could not get Roosevelt to agree to further commitments in the Atlantic or Europe, he would try the Pacific. His first gambit was to try to persuade Roosevelt to agree to a joint statement—in effect, an ultimatum—to Japan to cease and desist from its adventurism or face the consequences, even if that meant war. Fearing a Pacific showdown at a time when his nation's resources were straining to meet the German threat, Churchill also still hoped for an American commitment to defend Singapore, and possibly even the movement of capital ships from Pearl Harbor to East Asia. Churchill got nowhere with either line of argument. For Roosevelt this was the "wrong war, in the wrong ocean, at the wrong time."

The major public outcome of the conference was the joint approval of the Atlantic Charter. After much debate and several rewrites Roosevelt and Churchill agreed on a common set of principles and war aims: no territorial aggrandizement; respect for the rights of all people to choose the form of government under which they would live; for all states to trade on equal access and equal terms; improving the global standard of living; and freedom of the seas. It was far from what Churchill had wanted or expected, but an agreement on war aims was something. Moreover, as both men must have realized, if America wanted any say in this postwar world it would, sooner or later, have to put its young men in harm's way.

Getting to a final agreement on the Atlantic Charter had not been as straightforward as either leader had hoped, and the debates that began aboard the *Augusta* plagued the Allied relationship throughout the war. The British, for instance, did not mean that the right of all people to choose their own form of government had any bearing on their empire, particularly India. Moreover, they had no intention of letting a commitment to free trade impact their system of imperial preferences, which the Americans, from the very start of their relationship, planned to eradicate.

There were, however, other things, less tangible but no less important, that came out of this meeting. By far the most important was that Churchill and Roosevelt enjoyed each other's company. One may even go so far as to say they were fond of each other, or as fond of each other as two men who never forgot they led two of the world's great powers would or could allow themselves to become. Unfortunately for Churchill, he had yet to learn that Roosevelt was only capable of friendship on a relatively shallow level. As FDR's long-serving personal secretary, Missy LeHand, once admitted: "He was really incapable of a personal friendship with anyone." Eleanor went further when she spoke about the men who got closest to Roosevelt, including Hopkins: "Each imagines that he is indispensable to the President. All would be surprised at their dispensability. The President uses those who suit his purposes. He makes up his own mind and discards people when they no longer fulfill a purpose of his."

There was one friendship that developed during this meeting that was longer lasting, and second in its impact on the war only to that of Churchill and Roosevelt. That was the relationship that developed between Marshall and Field Marshal Sir John Dill, chief of the Imperial General Staff. Soon after the Atlantic Conference ended, Dill wrote to Marshall: "I sincerely hope we shall meet again before long. In the meantime, we must keep each other in touch in the frank manner upon which we agreed." Marshall replied in kind: "I propose writing to you personally and very frankly whenever any matters arise which I think merit such attention."

The Atlantic Conference also revealed how Roosevelt intended to run the war. By giving the chiefs almost no time to prepare and then forcefully restricting the topics they could discuss with their British counterparts, Roosevelt was, in no uncertain terms, establishing his position as commander in chief. Moreover, it is notable that neither Frank Knox nor Henry Stimson was invited. As the war progressed and Roosevelt became more certain of his own footing, he would increasingly deal directly with his military commanders, bypassing the secretaries of war and the navy. He had long ago become his own secretary of state, so it is little wonder that Secretary Hull was not present. Instead, Roosevelt further increased animosity within the State Department by taking his favorite, Sumner Welles, along. Even so, Welles did not participate in any substantial discussions, spending most of his time debating the exact wording of the Atlantic Charter with his British counterparts.

At 3:15 P.M. on August 12, Churchill took his leave of Roosevelt and boarded the *Prince of Wales,* which steamed away a few hours later. As it sped toward the horizon the battleship, at Churchill's behest, signaled "God bless the president and the people of the United States." Just ten minutes later the *Augusta* cleared port. When Churchill arrived back in Britain, he told colleagues that Roosevelt did not plan to declare war. Rather Churchill believed he planned to wage war in a series of increasingly provocative incidents, until Germany attacked in such a fashion that the American people would demand a declaration of war.

As far as it goes, Churchill's account is likely an accurate reflection of what he considered Roosevelt to have said. What is missing are the nuances and qualifications in which Roosevelt habitually clothed every major pronouncement. Churchill was far from the first, nor would he be the last, who had heard Roosevelt say what he had hoped to hear, and had then dismissed the equivocations Roosevelt was famous for. Moreover, Roosevelt was not beyond, to put a fine point on it, dissembling when it suited his purpose, something that Churchill could never fathom. Churchill's basic honesty put him at a tremendous disadvantage later in the war, when he was forced to pit himself against two great masters of political deception, Roosevelt and Stalin—one basically a good man, the other evil, but both political chameleons.

20

PRODUCTION BATTLES

During the summer of 1941, as the Soviet Union and Britain struggled to survive, Americans were more interested in baseball than the war. Joe DiMaggio was in the middle of his fifty-six-game hitting streak, and Ted Williams was on track to hit over .400. Few Americans concerned themselves with the fact that production of war matériel was collapsing just as the military's requirements were achieving exponential growth. In July, former New Dealer and now all-outer Leon Henderson penned an article in *Fortune* magazine, reminding Americans that war was on their doorstep and that Germany had prepared for five years before launching its armies into Poland. America, he claimed, would have only months to prepare for a significantly greater challenge.

The challenge was indeed great—and the administrative system put in place to meet it was faltering. The Office of Production Management (OPM) was in a hopeless state, and Roosevelt refused to prod it into action. Structurally there were two major problems and a host of minor ones. The first of the majors was that OPM, like NDAC before it, had few powers to compel. Worse, OPM's senior management, Knudsen and Nelson, were hesitant to use those they did have. Matters were not helped by a poor organizational structure that divided OPM into three fiefs—production, purchasing, and priorities—each of which functioned as its own petty kingdom, rarely bothering to coordinate with the others. Any businessman looking for government orders soon found himself on a merry-go-round of office visits that more often than not failed to resolve anything. The single point of coordination, where internal problems could be resolved, was Knudsen's regular staff conference. Unfortunately, these were dominated by charts covered in production statistics—Knudsen's comfort zone—and never delved into the crucial matter of building a comprehensive national strategy for production. With no firm hand on the rudder, the inevitable intramural disputes became bitter and drifted along for months without resolution.

Internal management problems were hugely compounded by the fact that none of the major participants in the system—OPM, the military, and business—understood, liked, or trusted the others. OPM staff, particularly the all-outers, viewed themselves as on the side of the angels, while sharing a conviction that businessmen were motivated only by filthy lucre. They reserved a particular distaste for the dollar-a-year men who had flooded into Washington in recent months. These men billed themselves as coming to Washington to assist during the national emergency. Much was made of the fact that they took only a dollar a year for their services, but rarely was it said that many of them were still drawing a paycheck from their parent firm and were expected to steer contracts back to their own organizations. Were they patriots or infiltrators? In truth, they were something in the middle, but all too often the all-outers' view of them was the correct one. No doubt the dollar-a-year men saw themselves as doing a public service, but if they could do that while also sending contracts back to their own firm, well, who loses? That, of course, depended on the terms of the contract.

Roosevelt was not so much bothered by the dollar-a-year men looking out for their firms as he was by the fact that they were all Republicans. He once asked Knudsen if it was possible to find a Democrat to put on the dollar-a-year list. Knudsen's reply left the president chuckling: "I have searched the whole country over. There is no Democrat rich enough to take a job for a dollar a year." In a later press conference Roosevelt was asked if Hopkins was going to work for him for a dollar a year, or would he get paid? Roosevelt replied that he would get paid: "He's a Democrat! What a foolish question."

Businessmen, on the other hand, viewed the OPM staff as nothing but troublesome bureaucrats who had no inkling of how business worked. They greatly resented having to take instructions from academics who dwelt in the land of theory and had never seen an actual production line, never mind organized one and put it into operation.

In the middle of this was the military planning apparatus wishing a pox on both their houses. As far as the military was concerned, *their* needs trumped all else, and almost to the war's end they never stopped angling to take over the nation's entire industrial base. The military wanted to set priorities and make all the allocation decisions. As they saw it, only after all military demands were sated would civilian needs be given any consideration. The fact that they had no idea of the industrial base's capacity, or what it was capable of when it turned to full production for war, was never permitted to interfere with their absolute certainty that *they* knew best.

For his part, Knudsen's desire to push for more war production was often hobbled by his affinity for the auto industry, and his sympathy for their plight. In mid-May Stimson went to see Knudsen to plead for a cut in auto production, but Knudsen refused. That night Stimson recorded in his diary, "I was rather discouraged by his attitude . . . We will have a showdown pretty soon on this subject, as I am afraid that Knudsen is too soft and slow." Similarly, Knudsen's co-head at OPM, Sidney Hillman, despised the idea of depriving his labor constituency of the fruits of their labors, just as the economy was starting to improve. Both men understood that the auto industry needed to cut back to make room for more war production, but they were moving with glacial slowness. Still, not everyone at OPM was willing to wait upon developments. Leon Henderson, for one, was pushing his colleagues to curtail automobile production by as much as half, and that was only his opening position.

For Henderson, the choice was no longer about guns *and* butter . . . something had to give. As the immense requirements of a rearming American military were added to the British and Russian orders, a production emergency blossomed. Critical shortages in basic raw materials and production equipment were forcing hard choices that soon had the all-outers, along with their military supporters, casting covetous glances upon the 20 percent of steel production and 80 percent of rubber production the auto industry consumed. Harry Hopkins, after examining statistical projections put together by an economist working in OPM's Statistical Research Bureau, Stacy May, convinced Roosevelt that curtailing consumer production was a necessity. May had totaled the combined demands of the U.S. military, the Maritime Commission, and the British (the Russians were not yet making demands), and came up with a total of nearly $50 billion, or fully two-thirds of the nation's total GDP. Considering that the United States in

2016 spent approximately 3 percent of GDP on its military, one can easily see how astronomical the military's requirements had already become. And these initial orders were a small fraction of what the nation needed to actually fight a war.

Hopkins and Roosevelt may have been convinced by the numbers, but their pleas to rapidly curtail consumer production fell on deaf ears. Knudsen, possessed by an emotional faith in America's productive genius to rise to the occasion, was beyond swaying with something as meaningless as statistics that said otherwise. Certain that a *gradual* curtailment of consumer goods was the right answer, he left the steel-devouring auto industry mostly untouched. Throughout the summer the battle of the bureaucrats raged, until Knudsen made a fatal error: he allowed Hopkins, through an executive order from Roosevelt, to establish the Office of Price Administration and Civilian Supply (OPA) outside of his direct control. He then compounded his mistake by allowing a man beyond anyone's power to control—Leon Henderson—to take charge of the new organization.

Congress had given the administration permission to determine priority allocations for both the military and civilian sectors, and both Henderson and Knudsen claimed the new authority for themselves. But while Knudsen dithered, Henderson pounced. Fed up with the leadership's inaction, Henderson, in his capacity as OPA administrator, unilaterally ordered cuts in automobile production for the next model year. To help enforce this, he assumed, through the force of his own will, control of OPM's priorities division, planning to lower the priorities consumer producers had on raw materials. Henderson's next move was sheer bureaucratic brilliance. He fenced off a large portion of the civilian economy as his private domain, upon which he would brook no intrusions, but excluded most large consumer durables (such as automobiles). This effectively put a big "THIS IS FOR THE TAKING" sign out on all segments of the economy he did not take under his wing. In effect, it was as if a farmer had fenced off half of his sheep and told circling wolves they were welcome to the rest. Henderson had put a target on the back of those industries that were not under his protection, and then told the circling military and all-outers—the wolves—that they were welcome to convert them to war production.

When Knudsen, still moving cautiously, announced that he had persuaded the auto industry to voluntarily reduce auto production by 20 percent, an unimpressed Henderson struck again. He sent his deputy around to key auto executives to alert them to certain facts: that he was unhappy, that he did not need their goodwill, and that he was demanding further cuts. Not yet knowing much about Henderson, the auto executives opted to ignore him—a fatal error. Henderson promptly ordered all auto price increases rolled back to what they had been at the start of the year, and unilaterally ordered an immediate production cut of 50 percent. The auto industry howled, and Knudsen objected to the White House, but Roosevelt, at Hopkins's urging, backed Henderson. A compromise was then quickly brokered, cutting auto production by 40 percent.

By early August, OPM's internecine warfare was too destructive and, more crucially, too public for Roosevelt to ignore. Calling on his lawyer, sometime speechwriter, and friend Sam Rosenman, the president ordered him to find a solution. Expecting Rosenman to have an answer when he returned, Roosevelt departed for his meeting with Churchill off Newfoundland.

Rosenman's solution was very Rooseveltian. Without ever getting rid of OPM, he recommended the creation of another board, the Supply Priorities and Allocation Board (SPAB), which would sit alongside OPM and try to do a better job at controlling industry. It was a makeshift effort at best, and even Roosevelt supporters damned it with faint praise. World War I industrial czar Bernard Baruch, who had been offering Roosevelt advice on a weekly basis, stood on the White House steps referring to SPAB as a "faltering step forward." Roosevelt took offense at the phrasing, not to mention Baruch's choice of backdrop, and had him struck off White House access and invitation lists for several months.

Roosevelt was still not ready to place one man in charge of all production activities. What he, and particularly Hopkins, were looking for was a man tough enough to get the job done, but pliant enough to bend to presidential, as well as Hopkins's, dictates and whims. Strong weaklings being a rare commodity, Roosevelt instead created SPAB as just another of his weak "alphabet agencies." By 1942 so many of these agencies had been birthed—WPB, OPA, BEW, NWLB, etc.—that no one had any idea of what all the acronyms stood for, or for that matter what they all did. At one point, Harold Ickes answered a reporter: "I can't speak for the OPC." For a moment, the journalists surrounding Ickes stood in confused silence, until an aide whispered in Ickes's ear that he was the *director* of the OPC (Office of Petroleum Coordination). Ickes then complained about being "all balled up on all of these initials" before rapidly concluding the press conference.

At Hopkins's urging, Roosevelt placed Donald Nelson in nominative charge of SPAB, and put the entire apparatus on top of OPM. It was another all-too-typical organizational expedient, doomed to fail from the start, not least because of its tortuous organizational structure. Within SPAB, Donald Nelson was in charge and oversaw the work of Knudsen's OPM, but within OPM, Nelson still worked for Knudsen. Henderson's position was even more convoluted. He sat on the board of SPAB, was his own boss at the Office of Price Administration, and worked for Knudsen at OPM.

The first meeting of the Supply Priorities and Allocation Board in Washington, D.C., 1941. Seated, from left: Harry Hopkins, William Knudsen, Henry Wallace, Donald Nelson. Standing, from left: James Forrestal, Robert Patterson, Leon Henderson, Sidney Hillman.

Nelson compounded this muddle by declaring that SPAB would work through and report on most matters to OPM, thereby making SPAB subordinate to the organization it was created to oversee. Organizationally this was akin to parents leaving a babysitter in charge, but having the sitter run every decision past the child for approval. Moreover, although Nelson was the head of SPAB, Roosevelt had also placed two individuals well beyond Nelson's control—Vice President Wallace and Harry Hopkins—on the board. When push came to shove few doubted where the real power was. Throughout SPAB's existence, Nelson was constantly second-guessed by those he was supposed to control, and when Nelson tried to hold his ground his subordinates ran to Hopkins. Too often Hopkins obliged them, undercutting Nelson's authority at almost every turn. That, of course, was one of the reasons Hopkins liked having Nelson around; he was a reasonably competent bureaucrat who could be easily bulldozed by his politically minded betters, just the right kind of man whom Hopkins judged ready for even greater *nominal* authority in the future.

SPAB's creation sheds light on how Roosevelt's thinking about the war was evolving. He was no longer looking to merely boost production to give the Allies all "aid short of war." Rather, he wanted the system overhauled so that there was sufficient capacity to also supply the American military's vast matériel needs. The creation of SPAB was meant to increase military production, even if that meant a substantial reduction in the production of consumer goods. Just as Americans finally had spare cash in their pockets, Roosevelt was arriving at the party only to take away the punch bowl. A politician as savvy as Roosevelt does not tell millions of Americans they cannot buy a new car unless he has made a momentous decision about the nation's future. He may not have said it aloud, but Roosevelt was clearly readying the nation for entry into the war. If further evidence is needed, one need only look at the SPAB leadership. Roosevelt had filled its top spots with all-outers—Wallace, Hopkins, Henderson, Hillman, Nelson— expecting them to run roughshod over more timid souls, such as Knudsen. Moreover, Roosevelt directed the removal from OPM of many of Knudsen's business supporters. One of them, Edward Stettinius, was just too nicely pliable to send back to the business world, so Hopkins convinced the president to elevate him to administrative head of growing Lend-Lease operations.

By the middle of 1941 the nation's spare industrial capacity had vanished, and raw material shortages were cropping up everywhere. OPM and SPAB were doing their best to plan for future requirements but were stymied by a lack of data. No one had any idea what the Army needed to equip millions of soldiers or what the British could make for themselves and what they needed from the United States. Moreover, there was no agreement as to how far civilian consumption could be cut or how fast it could be done. On top of all of this there was no one who could even hazard a guess as to total Soviet needs, but everyone recognized they would be massive, assuming the Red Army was still in the field in the new year.

Into this morass stepped three of the war's most unlikely heroes: Simon Kuznets, Robert Nathan, and Stacy May. Each of these men had begun the crucial work of mapping America's industrial capacity years before. Kuznets and Nathan had worked together in the Department of Commerce designing the first set of national accounts, what is commonly referred to as Gross Domestic Product—GDP. Stacy May was a recent transplant to Washington, having been seconded there by the Rockefeller Foundation. Upon his arrival at OPM, May met and took up the cause of Jean Monnet. As France fell, Monnet's last official act as a member of the French purchasing commission had been to send a cable to the United States ordering that all war munitions on order by France instead be sent to Britain. He then crossed the Channel and offered his services to Churchill.

In Britain, Monnet became obsessed with forcing the British to link their war plans to American production lines, telling all who listened that "the whole industrial might of the United States should it be directed toward war-making, would constitute a power never dreamed of before in the history of Armageddon." He was so persistent and annoying that Churchill eventually got him out of the way by placing him on the British Supply and Munitions Board and sending him to the United States. If Churchill expected that Monnet would become less of a pest, he had misjudged his man. Monnet was indefatigable, preaching his gospel of a unified Anglo-American production system at his every stop. Robert Nathan later said of him: "He was a master operator at a critical time, when his rare talents were desperately needed. Monnet's operating and maneuvering were unbelievably creative, persistent, and ultimately effective." As an example, Monnet would often write cables for Roosevelt to send to Churchill, and then forward a note to Churchill on how best to respond to "Roosevelt's" missive. Monnet also had a rare talent for sniffing out Washington's true power brokers and getting close to them. To influence Stimson,

Stacy May, chief, Bureau of
Research and Statistics, OPM.

he worked very closely with Stimson's most able assistants, Assistant Secretaries of War Robert Patterson and Jack McCloy. To influence Roosevelt, he
befriended Justice Felix Frankfurter, who as a professional manipulator
himself must have appreciated Monnet's rare talents.

Together Monnet and May became the twin disciples coordinating
Anglo-American production. As a first step, with Monnet's encouragement, Stacy May began building a book that eventually detailed everything
that was known about American industry and raw material output, as well
as the specific requirements for building every major item in the U.S. military inventory. May's book not only laid out what America could do in
mid-1941, it also made stunningly accurate estimates about the nation's
future potential. Completing the task, however, required similar information from the British, which, as they considered such data a military secret,
they were unwilling to share. May kept asking, but the best answer he could
get was "We want as much as we can get of everything." Frustrated, May
would repeat his mantra: "We know you want all you can get of everything,
but what order do you want it in, how much do you want immediately, and
what can you do for yourself?" The British remained silent.

Only the direct intervention of Stimson and months of incessant
prodding by his assistant Jack McCloy got the British to open up. In late

summer, May flew to London with his production tables detailing U.S. production capacity. During the next two months he and a small team of assistants laboriously filled in what became known as the "Consolidated Balance Sheet" with British production data. When it was done, it weighed an astounding thirty-five pounds and contained a listing of every resource both nations would need to supply their home front and simultaneously wage global war. In short, May had produced a how-to guide for turning the entire American economy toward war. When it was complete it was the single most important document in the world; for within it was the essence of the Victory Program—a blueprint of how the United States would become the "Arsenal of Democracy."

Remarkably, when it came time to take his product home, May, traveling alone, boarded a plane in Manchester. A few minutes into the flight, weather forced the plane to land in Dublin, where German spies were thick on the ground. Nelson later marveled that this "plumpish, fortyish, dignified, preoccupied American statistician" carrying the "most important papers in the world" boarded a taxi from Dublin to Foynes, found space on a British aircraft, flew to Baltimore, and hailed a taxi to Washington, where he deposited his papers at the War Department. No one at any point thought to provide him with an armed escort.

The stark figures in May's Consolidated Balance Sheet told a harsh story. American factories possessed several times Britain's war production potential, but they were severely underperforming. If America was going to become the "Arsenal of Democracy," a rapid acceleration of plant conversions from consumer goods to military munitions had to start immediately. But even an immediate conversion of existing American industries would be insufficient to meet American as well as British and Soviet needs. That could only be done if America spent billions building new plants throughout the nation. Moreover, the Consolidated Balance Sheet failed to answer a crucial question. While it laid out in excruciating detail what was required to build a two-, four-, or eight-million-man army, it gave no clues as to how quickly this could be accomplished. Moreover, in mid-1941 no one knew how much force the military needed to win or when they would need it. Without an answer to both questions the production experts had no idea how fast they needed to establish new production lines or expand raw material production.

Unfortunately, neither Marshall nor anyone else in the War Department was prepared to give SPAB the answers it needed. On July 9, 1941, their failure to do so prompted Roosevelt to action. He ordered Stimson and Knox to provide him a detailed accounting of everything they required to defeat all potential enemies. For the first time, Roosevelt asked for more than just an estimate of what it would take to defend the United States. Instead, he wanted assumptions based on an all-out effort to win a global war. The joint Army-Navy response, delivered to the White House on September 11, 1941, left a lot to be desired. The Navy just handed over a list of the capital ships already in the pipeline, as Congress had approved a massive shipbuilding program a year earlier, and the Navy considered that it needed little else. It was these vessels—mostly a collection of unfinished keels in mid-1941—that began joining the fleet in 1943, and by 1944 would present the Japanese with a threat so enormous that it could scarcely have been imagined just two years before. The Army's hurriedly put together estimate was so absurd that it was soon forgotten.

The production experts at OPM-SPAB were astounded at the inadequacy of the Army's estimates. As far as they could tell, those running the Army's procurement programs did not know their jobs, leading Leon Henderson to tell his diary that "they are fine and sincere, but naïve." Just a week after the Army delivered what it believed were its final estimates, Nelson had to go back to the War Department with a simple request: Can you at least try and think about the realities of the problem? Robert Nathan, who was doing most of the begging for realistic estimates, later recounted his frustration:

> When I asked them about military requirements, they asked "are we preparing for a land war, a sea war, or an air war, a defensive war on the U.S. continent?" I was not in any more of a position to tell them what kind of war to prepare for than I was to tell them how to build a bomber or a tank. There seemed to be no way to get those requirements because they indicated that such numbers did not exist.
>
> I remember asking them: "What are your varying assumptions about defense? You must have some assumptions and some lists of quantities of weapons and planes and ships needed under varied assumptions." They said, "We have no estimates of requirements under varying assumptions." I then said, "Give us the requirements for a one-million-man, and a five-million-man, and a ten-million-man Army."

Their reply was: "We are not going to do all of that work unless we have some indication of what kind of prospective hostilities we will face."

Undeterred by the inadequacy of the military's estimates, Nathan, Kuznets, and May created their own estimates, substituting their own judgment for what the War Department refused to provide. While May tried to uncover how much factory capacity was required, Nathan and Kuznets worked tirelessly on trying to determine if such a program was even feasible. What they discovered astonished even them. To meet the requirements necessitated by a global war, the entire defense program would have to be doubled, and it would have to be done within months, not years. As they said in their report, the nation's GDP would have to increase to $150 billion in the following year (an almost 50 percent increase) and over half of the nation's total GDP would have to be dedicated to the war effort. By any measure these were stupendous totals. When asked if it could be done, their answer was a qualified yes. But such a feat was only possible if America centralized its economy for the duration and shifted to a full war economy immediately. Fortunately, the final report—the foundation of the nation's "Victory Program"—delivered to the White House (care of Harry Hopkins) laid out exactly how this could be done. It was delivered on December 4, 1941 . . . only seventy-two hours before the Japanese attack on Pearl Harbor.

21

WAR IN THE PACIFIC

As ROOSEVELT AND THE ALL-OUTERS PLOTTED AMERICA'S ENTRY into the war against Germany, a more immediate enemy was on the march in the Pacific. In 1937, Japan used a minor incident outside Beijing as an excuse to launch an invasion of China. Expecting an easy victory, the Japanese instead found themselves locked in a war that lasted over eight years and strained Japanese resources to the breaking point. It was not long before an invasion undertaken to create an exclusive economic trading zone was draining more from the Japanese economy than it was adding. Each operational success further overextended Japanese forces and hugely increased the cost of occupation. Extensive and never-ending military operations were consuming all newly acquired resources and then some. But there was nothing to be done for it. Japan had entered a vicious cycle where a politically dominant military, impervious to the damage their expansionist policies were inflicting on the nation's economic underpinnings, had no interest in ending such policies. Expansion's costs were fueling a never-ending quest for additional resources, launching Japan on a slippery slope from Korea to Manchuria to China to Indochina. And finally to Pearl Harbor.

By mid-1941, Japan had reached a point of no return. Its resource shortages were becoming critical, and it either had to go north and fight the Soviet Union, or south and risk war with the United States. Roosevelt himself appears to have had little doubt which route Japan would take, as he reportedly said at about this time: "They hate us. They come to me and they hiss between their teeth and they say, 'Mr President, we are your friends. Japan wants nothing but friendship with America,' and they hiss through their teeth again, and I know they are lying. Oh, they hate us, and sooner or later they'll come for us."

Japan had already taken advantage of Germany's 1940 victories by joining the Axis powers in the Tripartite Pact, and persuading Germany to pressure Vichy France to allow a Japanese occupation of northern Indochina. Earlier Japanese aggressions had already led to U.S. embargoes of such items as iron and steel scrap, but the political force of these acts was undercut when Washington announced that the embargo was not a sanction but a necessity to reserve the metals to boost America's own production. Japan remained unmoved by American ire.

On July 1, 1941, in the wake of Germany's invasion of Russia, the officers of the Imperial General headquarters met to discuss military options. While attacking a distracted Russia was tempting, Japanese army officers still remembered the severe drubbing the Soviets, led by General Zhukov, had handed their Kwantung Army at Khalkhin Gol in 1939. With the northern attack option unenticing, the fateful decision was made for an advance into southern Indochina. On July 28 the Japanese army moved south. Roosevelt was forewarned, the United States having broken several of the Japanese codes, and immediately froze all Japanese assets in the United States and ordered an oil embargo. This was a crippling blow, given that Japan obtained 80 percent of its oil from the United States. Hull, with the president's full support, had left oil off the first set of sanctions, believing that if oil was included it would lead Japan to launch a Pacific war sooner rather than later. Marshall and Stark concurred; they unequivocally stated the United States was not ready for war with Japan. As late as July 21, 1941, the Navy's War Plans Division had warned that any oil cutoff would lead to an early Japanese assault on Malaya and the Dutch East Indies. At a time when Roosevelt was preoccupied with the Atlantic, he could ill afford any diversions. In a letter to Ickes, written as the Japanese were debating a southern or northern advance, Roosevelt demonstrated his awareness of Japanese decision-making and America's woeful unpreparedness for a Pacific war:

> ... the Japs are having a real drag down and knock-out fight amongst
> themselves ... trying to decide which way they are going to jump—
> attack Russia, attack the South Seas, or they will sit on the fence and be

more friendly to us. No one knows what the decision will be but, as you know, it is terribly important for the control of the Atlantic for us to help keep the peace in the Pacific. *I simply have not got enough Navy to go around—and every little episode in the Pacific means fewer ships in the Atlantic.*

After the Japanese moved into southern Indochina, the clamor from the all-outers within the cabinet to cut off Japan's oil rose to a crescendo. Still, Roosevelt resisted. Instead of a complete oil embargo he ordered a complex system of graduated cutbacks where some oil would be sent to Japan and some would be withheld. What Roosevelt envisioned was a system in which he could punish or reward Japan in direct relation to their acquiescence to his demands. Once again, the president pulled back from the ultimate act, one that could not fail to start a Pacific war.

His reticence was driving the all-outers to distraction. As Ickes recorded in his diary: "The president on Thursday was unwilling to draw the noose tight. He thought it might be better to slip the noose around Japan's throat and give it a jerk now and then." Either because of a huge bureaucratic mistake or, more likely, the willful thwarting of the president's will by underlings, Roosevelt's graduated response did not come off as he intended. As Roosevelt rushed off to meet Churchill, Dean Acheson, now working for Welles at State, put his own interpretation on the president's order.

Welles, before departing as part of Roosevelt's entourage for the Atlantic Conference, advised Acheson that he thought the best course for the next couple of weeks was to take no action on any Japanese oil applications. On August 1, 1941, Acheson ordered the Foreign Funds Control Committee to cancel all Japanese oil export licenses. Through this and other means Acheson oversaw the start of a near-absolute oil embargo on Japan. Apparently, Roosevelt did not learn what Acheson had done until Welles informed him during a White House meeting on August 29. Another week passed before Hull, during a lunch meeting, gave the president a formal briefing. Roosevelt, however, failed to issue an order reversing what was already being done, apparently fearing that he or the country would appear weak if he bent to Japanese pressure to reopen the oil spigot.

At the end of July, Japanese navy chief of staff Osami Nagano informed the emperor that Japan had less than two years of oil stockpiled, and after that the nation's economy would collapse. Prime Minister Fumimaro Konoe, who still maintained hopes of lasting peace with the United States, had, up to then, counted on the navy leadership to help restrain the army's radicals. But the oil embargo changed the political dynamic within Japan, and Admiral Nagano was now arguing alongside the army leadership that if war was inevitable it should come soon.

Throughout these events, Hull continued talks with the Japanese ambassador, which had begun in March 1941. Hull, with Roosevelt's support, insisted on Japanese compliance on a number of points: evacuating their army from China, leaving the Axis alliance, and withdrawing from Indochina. As no Japanese government could survive such a face-losing retreat, the proposals were never seriously entertained in Japan. Still, the Japanese ambassador, retired admiral Kichisaburo Nomura, continued the talks. Nomura was almost deaf, had a glass eye, and possessed only a passing knowledge of the English language, leaving Hull to wonder if Nomura even understood his own government's position. Still, Roosevelt agreed to meet with him. When the president asked for his proposals, Nomura took a document from his pocket and announced that Prime Minister Konoe desired a face-to-face meeting with Roosevelt somewhere in the mid-Pacific. Roosevelt was sorely tempted to accept. It was just the kind of high-stakes personal diplomacy he relished. Moreover, he was supremely confident of his ability to win over anyone through the application of his personal charm.

Hull was aghast. He had learned to fear Roosevelt's personal diplomacy as a threat to the patient methods he and his department employed. He could think of little good that could come out of such a meeting. He was also concerned that Roosevelt would leave him behind, as he did when he departed for the Atlantic Conference with Churchill. That was small potatoes compared to the damage Hull thought the president and Welles would do if left to their own devices thousands of miles from his own steadying influence.

Hull marshaled the full resources of the State Department to create a barrage of material that spelled out why a Pacific summit meeting would be a bad idea. Roosevelt was unconvinced, but decided to do what he did best in such situations: play for time. And here is the crucial difference between how the Japanese, in the weeks and months after the oil embargo, viewed the negotiations and how the president saw them. Roosevelt did not want a conflict with Japan distracting him and the nation from the main effort: Germany. His policy was one of delay, to allow America to gather her strength and prepare for a final showdown. Maybe, after the Philippines had been further reinforced and fortified, and when the Navy's strength reached its apogee, he could push harder. In the meantime, Roosevelt would push but never hard enough, in his own estimation, to provoke a Japanese-American war. Roosevelt was certain such a war would eventually come, but that was a problem for a later date. What he failed to comprehend was that for the Japanese the American oil embargo had made an early war inevitable. When Roosevelt told Nomura that he would not meet Konoe, he considered it just another diplomatic delay. But the Japanese could no longer be delayed; they were on a fixed timetable.

On September 3, Admiral Nagano told his other military chiefs and the cabinet that Japan was growing weaker and the enemy stronger. At an imperial conference three days later, he demanded that a time limit be set on diplomacy. At that, the politicians in attendance were pushed aside, and the military technocrats got to work on initial requirements for a decisive first strike. Diplomacy did continue, but on September 6, Japan's military leaders, with the politicians in tow, decided to begin war preparations with a completion date in October. If substantial progress had not been made in the peace talks with the United States by then, they would make the decision for war. In mid-October the pace of events picked up. Army Minister Hideki Tojo informed the cabinet that negotiations had failed, and three days later Konoe's government fell and he was replaced by Tojo. On November 5, Tojo presented the political and military consensus to the emperor: If the matter was not settled through diplomacy by December 1, Japan would go to war. The emperor remained silent, signaling his acquiescence, if not his wholehearted support.

As the Japanese military pushed their agenda forward, Roosevelt continued talking to Nomura and a special ambassador recently arrived from Japan, Saburo Kurusu. During a White House meeting on November 17, Roosevelt pressed for a Japanese withdrawal from China, but Kurusu did not give an inch. As James MacGregor Burns points out, "There were few misunderstandings between the two countries, only differences." That did not stop Roosevelt, without consulting Hull, from putting together his own peace proposal. Reflecting that his primary concerns remained in the Atlantic, Roosevelt wanted Japan's pledge that it would not come to Germany's aid if the United States entered the European war. In return the United States would resume economic relations (including oil shipments) if Japan agreed not to reinforce their positions in southern Indochina, and if it began talks with China aimed at a later withdrawal of Japanese troops. Given the state of negotiations prior to this, Roosevelt's planned offer was remarkably generous.

The offer was never delivered. On the morning of November 26 it all blew up when Stimson, during a telephone call with Roosevelt, asked almost in passing if the president had found time to read a paper he had sent to the White House the day before. When Stimson told him it contained reports of a major Japanese expedition leaving Shanghai heading south, Roosevelt exploded, shouting that the whole situation was changed by bad faith on the part of the Japanese, who while negotiating for a truce were sending out a military expedition. Roosevelt was now certain that an expanded Pacific war was imminent. What he was unsure of was where the Japanese would strike, but he counted Malaya, Burma, and possibly the Philippines as the most likely possibilities. American intelligence had failed to detect the Japanese fleet that had departed from the Kuril Islands the day before—heading for Pearl Harbor.

The first wave of Japanese aircraft swept over Pearl Harbor at 7:48 A.M. Ninety minutes later, their mission complete, the Japanese carriers turned for home. In their wake, two waves of attacking aircraft had left a decimated American Pacific fleet. By any measure Japan had inflicted terrible human and material losses, leaving 3,500 Americans dead or wounded. Eighteen ships were sunk, severely damaged, or run aground, including what many in 1941 considered the backbone of American Pacific power, five battleships. But despite winning what appeared to be a major tactical victory and inflicting horrendous losses, Japan's Pearl Harbor attack was a strategic mistake of epic proportions, as it brought a fully committed United States into the war. When most Americans woke up on December 7, 1941, they were at best lukewarm toward the prospect of war, but by the end of that momentous day most sympathized with Admiral William F. Halsey, who upon arriving at Pearl Harbor aboard the carrier USS *Enterprise* angrily said, "Before we're finished with them the Japanese language will be spoken only in hell."

Though it was not apparent in the immediate aftermath of the attack, it was soon clear that the attack also proved to be a tactical failure. Although ship losses were indeed great, the damage to America's long-term prospects was slight. In a pattern that repeated itself throughout the war, the Japanese, after conceiving and executing a bold strike, shied away from the audacious coup de grâce. In this case, running short of fuel, concerned by the losses suffered by his second wave of attackers, and fearing a counterstrike, the Japanese commander, Admiral Chuichi Nagumo, decided against a third wave and turned for home. This fateful decision left Pearl's repair dockyards and fuel storage depots untouched. If they had been lost, the U.S. Pacific Fleet would likely have had to retreat to ports on America's West Coast. In fact, Admiral Chester Nimitz, the man who would soon command the Pacific Fleet, estimated that the loss of these crucial repair and resupply assets would have lengthened the war by at least a year. Just as crucially, when the Japanese struck, America's three aircraft carriers in the Pacific were all at sea. As a result, the true backbone of American naval power survived to fight another day.

It was already Sunday afternoon (Eastern Time) when word of Japan's attack began spreading among senior officials and military officers. At first, the news was greeted with disbelief, followed soon thereafter by consternation and white-hot anger. Roosevelt and Harry Hopkins had just finished lunch when Secretary of the Navy Frank Knox called to inform the president that a radio message was reporting that Pearl Harbor was under attack. Although Hopkins told FDR that he did not believe the report, Roosevelt, after a moment's reflection, replied that this "was just the kind of thing the Japanese would do, talking about peace as they planned its overthrow."

Calling Secretary of State Cordell Hull, who was about to meet with Japanese diplomats, Roosevelt ordered him not to let on he knew of the attack, and to remain cool and formal. Hopkins later reported that Hull, ignoring FDR's instructions, lost his temper with the ambassadors and used some Tennessee mountain language on them. Hull denied this, and claimed that after calling the Japanese liars, he silenced them with a mere hand motion and a nod toward the door. As he saw it, "no cussing out could have been stronger."

By 2:30 the president was still without details, but Admiral Stark had called to inform him that losses were severe. Roosevelt, growing increasingly frustrated, although outwardly almost surreally calm, ordered his key advisers Cordell Hull, Henry Stimson, Frank Knox, Harold Stark, and George Marshall to come to the White House. By 3:00 P.M. they were beginning to join the president and Hopkins in FDR's office. Throughout the meeting Roosevelt personally handled the numerous phone calls from harried officers trying to forward the latest updates. According to reports, the meeting was calm and for the most part focused on the big picture: it would be a long war and, rather remarkably, everyone still agreed that Germany remained the primary enemy. All present had for a long time been certain that America would eventually enter the war, and they were simultaneously appalled and elated "that Japan had given us the opportunity."

In the midst of the meeting FDR accepted a phone call from Britain. Churchill was dining with several guests, including Averell Harriman and Ambassador Winant. According to Harriman, Churchill seemed listless and depressed, but on hearing of the Pearl Harbor attack over the radio the prime minister jumped from his seat, exclaiming that he would declare war on Japan within the hour. Before he could do anything rash and irrevocable, Winant advised that he get official confirmation from his own military. This sage advice caused Churchill to pause just long enough to take a call from the Admiralty confirming the attack. Two minutes later he was speaking to Roosevelt.

"Mr. President, what's this about Japan?"

"It's quite true," Roosevelt replied. "They have attacked us at Pearl Harbor. We are all in the same boat now."

Churchill soon signed off, and after handling some immediate duties he went to bed pondering the fact that America was "in it to the death" before sleeping "the sleep of the saved and thankful."

The president turned back to his meeting and issued a series of immediate instructions before releasing most of the attendees back to their duties. As soon as they left, Roosevelt called in his dedicated secretary, Grace Tully, and dictated the first draft of his message to Congress.

Across the country, Americans were learning of the attack at approximately the same time as Churchill. In the White House, an aide to press secretary Stephen Early—Ruthjane Rumelt—was handing out tidbits to reporters as they became available. At Griffith Stadium the Philadelphia

Eagles continued a losing struggle (20–14) in the last game of the season, despite loudspeakers continuously interrupting with orders for various admirals and generals to report to their offices immediately. Stadium management refused to announce why, claiming they did not wish to contribute to any hysteria. One wife, driven frantic by the calls from her husband's newspaper office, sent a telegram addressed to *Section P, Top Row, Seat 27, opposite 25-yard line, East side, Griffith Stadium*. It read: "War with Japan. Get to office." Most Americans, however, got the news via the forty-five million radios in people's homes. In that shocking moment a seemingly distant conflict changed from Britain's war to "our war."

By early evening thousands of Washingtonians had converged for a silent vigil around the White House. There they saw first Roosevelt's cabinet and then the barons of Capitol Hill arriving for a series of meetings the president had called for the evening. At 8:30 the full cabinet sat silent and shocked as FDR briefed them on the extent of destruction relayed in the early reports from Pearl Harbor. Secretary of Labor Frances Perkins later remembered: "He [FDR] did not speak to anyone who came in that night. He was living in another area . . . he was very serious. His face and lips were pulled down, looking quite grey." According to Perkins, Roosevelt could hardly bring himself to describe the devastation. Twice he turned to Knox and demanded, "For God's sake why were the ships tied up in rows?"

Roosevelt read them the message he intended to deliver to Congress the next day. The only dissenting note came from Hull, who wanted a much longer message, detailing the entire history of the American-Japanese relationship. Roosevelt refused to consider it. He wanted the message short, crisp, and to the point.

At about 10:00 P.M., the cabinet was joined by the congressmen and senators who had been assembling in the hallway and Roosevelt briefed them on what he knew. He concluded by telling them that most of the air force had been caught on the ground parked wingtip to wingtip, before groaning, "On the ground, by God, on the ground." According to Stimson, the congressional leaders "sat in dead silence, and even after the recital was over they had very few words." Finally, Senator Thomas Connally, his face purple and his fist slamming the desk, shouted what they were all thinking: "How did it happen that our warships were caught like lame ducks in Pearl Harbor? How did they catch us with our pants down? Where were our patrols?" All Roosevelt could reply was, "I don't know, Tom, I just don't know." Despite their appeals, Roosevelt refused to tell them what he was going to say the next day, even refraining from letting them know if he was going to ask for a declaration of war, although they all assumed he would. The meeting ended when Roosevelt was told that Congress would be ready to welcome him on Capitol Hill at 1:30 P.M. the next day.

With the obligatory meetings out of the way, Roosevelt and Hopkins stayed up talking and reviewing new messages from Hawaii until a little after midnight, when FDR took his last meeting of the day. Edward R. Murrow, probably America's most famous reporter in 1941, and his wife had been invited to the White House as the Roosevelts' dinner guest. Eleanor, who had personally prepared her specialty meal—scrambled eggs and sausage—and was eager to meet Murrow, insisted the dinner go forward, regardless of whether the president could attend. During the dinner, White House usher Howell Crim asked Murrow to remain for a late-night meeting with FDR. What was said at the meeting has never been reported, as Murrow refused to file a story. His wife, however, later said that he was deeply troubled by what he heard and paced their hotel room chain-smoking all night.

As the president went to bed, thousands of Americans who had assembled outside along the fences remained. They were mostly silent, but from time to time they would sing "God Bless America" or "America the Beautiful." FDR's sleep was not disturbed.

The next day Roosevelt rode in an open car to the Hill. As he slowly and painfully made his way down the aisle, assisted by his son James, he was greeted by sustained, thunderous applause. His speech was short—only twenty-five sentences—and impeccably delivered in under ten minutes.

> Yesterday, December 7, 1941—a date which will live in infamy—the United States of America was suddenly and deliberately attacked by naval and air forces of the Empire of Japan . . .
>
> No matter how long it may take us to overcome this premeditated invasion, the American people in their righteous might will win through to absolute victory . . .

With confidence in our armed forces—with the unbounding determination of our people—we will gain the inevitable triumph—so help us God.

I ask that the Congress declare that since the unprovoked and dastardly attack by Japan on Sunday, December 7, 1941, a state of war has existed between the United States and the Japanese Empire.

By bringing the nation together behind one guiding principle—righteous revenge—Roosevelt's words did exactly what he desired.

Before the Senate could vote on the war declaration, arch-isolationist Senator Vandenberg rose to speak. Senator Connally, who had just introduced the joint resolution declaring war, tried to fend him off, but Vandenberg persisted. Finally, Connally relented: "Of course the Senator has the right to speak if he insists." A hush came over the entire Senate as members leaned forward to hear what Vandenberg had to say. Shocked by the destruction at Pearl Harbor, the senator was brief: "I have fought every trend which I thought would lead to a useless war; but when war comes to us—particularly when it comes like a thug in the night—I stand with my Commander in Chief for the swiftest and most invincible reply which our total strength may be capable."

The declaration of war passed 82–0 in the Senate, and 388–1 in the House. The lone no vote came from a dedicated pacifist, Jeannette Rankin of Montana. She had also voted against going to war with Germany in 1917 (and at the end of her life was a vocal opponent of the Vietnam War). That day she cast her vote and then ran off to an anteroom, where she sat in a phone booth crying until police arrived to escort her home. The escort was considered necessary for her own safety.

Two questions have dogged historians: Did Roosevelt know the attack was coming and hide that knowledge from military commanders in Hawaii as well as from the American people? And second, if he did not know, given all the warnings, how could he and America have been so easily surprised?

There is absolutely no evidence that FDR knew the Japanese were going to strike at Pearl Harbor. On the other hand, there is also no doubt that Roosevelt knew the Japanese military was moving substantial assets and that they were going to strike somewhere. Moreover, thanks to the codebreakers, who told Roosevelt that the Japanese ambassador had been ordered to deliver his final message by 1:00 P.M., he also knew the time of the attack. Reacting to all this intelligence, in the days leading up to the Pearl Harbor attack, a series of warnings had already been issued to American commanders in the Pacific.

In fact, at 10:30 on the morning of the attack, Stimson brought Hull and Knox together in the Munitions Building for a meeting. As he wrote in his diary: "Hull is certain the Japs are planning some devilry. But deducing what that devilry was has left him confounded." Stimson, after listening to the others' opinions, asked them to dictate what they thought was going on and how the United States should react. What becomes abundantly clear as one reads through this contemporaneous record is that none of the three men had an inkling that Pearl Harbor was a target. In fact, neither of them discussed any American possession or base as a possible target. Rather, they assumed that the Japanese would strike in the southern Pacific—at British and Dutch targets. At noon, the meeting broke up, as Hull had to return to the State Department for a 1:00 P.M. meeting with the Japanese envoys. Knox returned to the Navy Department, and Stimson went home to have lunch. All three men were keenly aware war was imminent. What they remained unsure of was where the first blow would strike, or if it would even hit American forces.

As the three cabinet members were meeting, Admiral Stark was in his office examining alternatives for moving ships from the quiet Pacific to the heating-up Atlantic conflict.

Marshall had been out on his regular morning horseback ride. Only on his return from nearly an hour of cantering along back trails did he learn that the full text of Japan's latest diplomatic cable was waiting for him at his office. When he arrived, his staff failed to direct Marshall to the last, key section of the cable, which specified the time the document must be delivered. After laboriously reading through all fourteen parts of the message, when Marshall got to the end, he asked a staff officer, Colonel Rufus Bratton, "What is the significance of a one o'clock delivery time?" Bratton explained that he and the rest of the staff thought it was linked to a Japanese attack somewhere in the Pacific. Marshall quickly penned a warning to Army commands in the Pacific alerting them to the one o'clock deadline and telling them to "be on the alert accordingly." He then called Admiral Stark and asked if he wanted the Navy's Pacific commands alerted as well. Stark told him that he considered the previous war warning (November

27) sufficient, but then called back moments later asking Marshall to add Navy commands to the recipient list. He even offered to let Marshall use the Navy's communications systems, which Marshall declined. That was a mistake. Unknown to Marshall the Army signal system to Hawaii was broken, forcing the signal staff to use a commercial telegraph company to send the message. Given a low priority by communications personnel, uninformed as to the urgency of the message, Marshall's warning was finally heading to General Walter Short's residence just as the first bombs rained down on Pearl Harbor. In fact, Marshall was talking to Short on the telephone before the message arrived.

But how could America have been so surprised? After all, U.S. intelligence had been reading the Japanese diplomatic codes—Operation MAGIC—since September 1940, and knew an ultimatum was on its way even before Japanese diplomats were aware of it. Moreover, the United States Navy was tracking what they assumed was a Japanese invasion force heading toward the southern Pacific. What they did not see, because they were not looking, was the Japanese strike fleet heading toward Pearl Harbor. The simplest and likely most accurate explanation for this failure is institutional racism, which viewed Asians as mentally and even physically inferior to the white race. For everyone knew that Pearl Harbor was vulnerable. Admiral King himself had proven as much in his mock carrier strike on Pearl Harbor during the 1936 war games, which was assessed to have caused severe damage. If a war game was not sufficient evidence of vulnerability, the Navy had only to look at the November 1940 Battle of Taranto, where a British carrier strike, using obsolescent biplanes, knocked out fully half of Italy's capital ships. Despite the British success in attacking a strongly defended harbor, no one in the American military believed Japan was capable of replicating such a daring and precise assault. Such blithe underestimation of the foe was behind the refusal of Pearl Harbor's naval commander—Admiral Husband Kimmel—to take the elementary step of having torpedo nets placed in the harbor, as they might impede the fleet from conducting a rapid sortie.

In the final analysis, FDR, his cabinet, and the senior military leaders all suffered from a failure of imagination in believing the Japanese incapable of striking Pearl Harbor. It was a serious miscalculation that cost the Pacific fleet dearly. Still, as grievous as the damage was, it was not devastating. The carriers had survived, and a great wartime battle fleet was already more than halfway completed in the many dry docks now littering the Pacific, Atlantic, and Gulf coasts. Moreover, a terrible lesson had been learned. America would never again underestimate the Japanese. When in 1944 the Army and Marines began their final island-hopping blitzkrieg across the Pacific, they were escorted by the most powerful naval armada in the history of the world. No one was taking any chances on any further Japanese surprises.

PART THREE

THE BEGINNING

We are determined that before the sun sets on this terrible struggle our flag will be recognized throughout the world as a symbol of freedom on the one hand and of overwhelming force on the other.

General George C. Marshall,
West Point commencement address, 1942

22

A CITY AT WAR

THE JAPANESE ATTACK LEFT ROOSEVELT WITH A MAJOR DILEMMA. He had been looking for a war against Hitler in Europe. Instead, he had one against Japan. When he went before Congress to ask for a declaration of war, he had, despite strong protests from Stimson, pointedly not asked for a joint declaration against Germany and Italy. Worried about sparking a debate at a time when he wanted complete national unity, Roosevelt waited to see what Germany would do. He did not have long to wait. On December 11, 1941, Hitler, having just rushed back from East Prussia, where he had been monitoring the disastrous German defeat at the gates of Moscow, went before the Reichstag and committed arguably the single greatest strategic mistake of the war. With the Wehrmacht collapsing in the East and Britain unbowed, Hitler, in an act of allied solidarity, declared war on the greatest industrial power on earth.

Hitler was convinced that a Japanese onslaught in the Pacific would help enfeeble Britain, and possibly deprive her of her great colonial prize: India. Based on this, Hitler had hoped to lure Japan into his war with Russia by promising to declare war on the United States if Japan attacked. In fact, a treaty was proposed to that effect on December 4, 1941, but there had been insufficient time to sign it before the Pearl Harbor attack. Moreover, Hitler and his advisers, despite having the experience of World War I to reflect upon, underestimated America's capacity to mobilize for war. Convinced that the United States was only good at producing consumer goods, the Führer had often declared that America would take years to mobilize for war. He was just as certain that most of what America did mobilize would be sent to face the Japanese, and it would be many years before that country would pose a threat to Germany. Too, Hitler had seethed as America expanded its undeclared naval war in the Atlantic and sent, free of charge, the food and munitions that kept Britain and the USSR in the war. A German declaration of war freed Admiral Karl Dönitz's U-boats to wage an unrestricted assault on U.S. shipping, which Hitler believed would reduce Lend-Lease supplies to Britain and Russia to a trickle—in effect, declaring war on America would so weaken Britain and Russia that Germany would win the war in Europe long before America could make its weight felt. All these mental constellations aligned with the Pearl Harbor attack, and Hitler never hesitated before declaring war on America.

Germany was now simultaneously at war with Britain, the Soviet Union, and the United States. Some in Germany were aware that their Führer had made a colossal blunder, one only matched by Japan's initial attack on Pearl Harbor. The correlation of forces, economic as well as military, now turned decisively against the Axis. Unless major victories could be won quickly and at little cost, the Axis was doomed to a slow grinding down, and eventual ruin.

Still, one man was worried. Churchill had read the tea leaves and made his own judgments about American popular opinion. Despite Hitler's declaration of war, and America's previous commitment to a Germany-first strategy, America had been attacked by Japan, not Germany, and demands for vengeance were reverberating across the nation. Churchill, uncertain about America's commitment to defeating Germany, and wanting to be assured that America did not take its eye off the ball, pressed Roosevelt to meet as early as possible. Two days after the Pearl Harbor attack, he cabled a request for a meeting in Washington. Roosevelt was initially reluctant, but after talking to Churchill on the phone he cabled: "Delighted to have you here at the White House" and concluded with his essential optimism: "The news is bad but will be better."

Churchill would be coming to a new Washington. What, to many, had been a sleepy southern town was rapidly completing its transformation into the hub of a nation at war. When Eleanor returned to Washington on December 15, she noted, "It seemed like a completely changed world." But it was a transformation that had been under way for a long time, now just given new impetus by the war. When Lincoln had first arrived in Washington pigs still roamed muddy streets, intermingling with the great men of politics and war as they crossed paths going from one imposing government structure to the next. In the intervening years, the city grew up, its population increasing in tandem with the expansion of the federal government. The Great Depression had almost completed the process, as government became America's only growth industry. If Washingtonians took time to look around they saw a city that prospered while most of America suffered. By the start of World War II, the sleepy provincial capital had vanished, and if not yet a metropolis, its one million inhabitants had transformed the "village on the Potomac" into a city that pulsed with activity.

Its parks were splendid, fountains and statues abounded, and the number of hotels had not only multiplied, they were ornate enough to rival those of Paris or London. Despite the leap in rooms for let, there were never anywhere near enough to handle the massive influx of people flooding the city throughout the war, although the temporarily homeless could find some solace in the hundreds of post-Prohibition bars that dotted the city.

The business of Washington was government, and so it avoided the layers of grime that coated the exteriors of the nation's great industrial cities. Working hours were short, but the required social events, particularly for the powerful, those that hoped to be powerful, and those who courted the powerful, were long. Women, over half of them working (a far higher percentage than in any other city), outnumbered men by a fair margin. It was a wealthy city, but most of the wealth was imported, as men, and sometimes women, made their money elsewhere and came to Washington to build grand homes on one of the city's stately streets. Behind these estates, on the side streets and alleys, lived the poor, mostly black population, sleeping as many as a dozen to a room, in conditions that bred tuberculosis.

At the center of power was the White House. At the time, the White House was run on a budget of $450,000, or nearly 150 times the salary of the average worker, notwithstanding the president's salary of $75,000. The gardeners, workmen, chauffeurs, and staff were all paid out of the public purse. The cost of food, however, was split. A tab was kept for food that was consumed by the family, and this was taken out of Roosevelt's salary, while the government picked up the bill for food used in connection with public functions. In 1942 the White House used $3,000 for fuel; and, despite having only a few air-conditioned rooms (Roosevelt complained that air-conditioning worsened his nasal problems), spent nearly $13,000 on electricity, four times an average worker's annual salary.

White House salaries were good. Roosevelt's personal secretaries received $10,000 each, more than three times the average wage, as did each of Roosevelt's six administrative assistants. Interestingly, Harry Hopkins, after much back-and-forth between himself, Roosevelt, and Budget Director Harold Smith, received only $15,000. There were twenty-nine White House staffers who were paid more than $3,000 a year, with personal secretaries to White House officials receiving $5,000 and private secretaries $2,600, slightly below the average for the city.

The White House housekeeper, Henrietta Nesbitt, oversaw the preparation of all food. By general agreement she served the worst meals in Washington society, leaving Roosevelt constantly begging for more variety, better quality, and decent preparation. His pleas fell on deaf ears, as for "twelve years, Mrs. Nesbitt turned out meals so gray, so drooping, and so spectacularly inept that they became a Washington legend. They also irritated an epicurean President three times a day—an outcome that may or may not have figured in Eleanor's calculations." Why did Roosevelt tolerate this? Primarily because in his complicated relationship with Eleanor she was given full control of the home. As such, she appreciated the fierce loyalty Nesbitt had for her personally, a loyalty that Eleanor fully reciprocated. Luckily, Roosevelt's favorite dish was simple scrambled eggs, of which he never seemed to tire and which were often served as Sunday dinner, with Eleanor doing the cooking.

The rest of Washington's power centers were arranged around the White House. The Army's nerve center was housed in three buildings. The most crucial building in 1942 was the Munitions Building, a long, squat, three-story edifice on Constitution Avenue within sight of the Lincoln Memorial. It was here that Stimson and Marshall worked. Although the two moved to new quarters during the war, their offices were always side by side, and shared an adjoining door, allowing each easy and unrestrained access to the other. Reportedly, for as long as Stimson and Marshall were in those jobs, the door was never closed. This single building had sufficed during the last war, but its miles of corridors and hundreds of offices were insufficient for the needs of the current conflict. A second building erected on Virginia Avenue was also soon outgrown, and turned over to the State

Department after the Pentagon's construction was completed, on land that once was part of Robert E. Lee's estate.

The main Navy Building was next door to the Army's Munitions Building. It was expanded early in the war by adding a floor and an additional wing. Even after the Pentagon was completed, there was insufficient office space for the Navy's needs, so a huge naval annex was constructed a few hundred yards from the Pentagon. By the time the war ended, the Navy occupied more than twenty-five buildings or groups of buildings scattered about Washington, Virginia, and Maryland.

The relations of the two men at the Navy's top were not nearly as cordial as those of their Army counterparts. Although Navy Secretary Frank Knox, more than any other person, was responsible for Admiral King's elevation to chief of naval operations, their relations, over time, became strained. King, always suspicious of civilians and viewing most of those he worked with as his intellectual inferiors, began bypassing Knox whenever possible, and had no time whatsoever for Knox's undersecretaries. There was never an open door between Knox's and King's offices, which were on different floors, and both maintained a battery of underlings outside their offices specifically to keep others away. At one point, King demonstrated his contempt for higher authority by purposely absenting himself from a meeting Knox had called. Knox waited a few minutes and then sent a message to King, informing him that he was about to issue orders to substantial segments of King's fleets. King never missed another meeting.

Secretary of State Cordell Hull occupied Room 208, at the center of an extensive suite on the south wing of State's headquarters at Foggy Bottom. Hull's great desk and high-back blue leather chair sat in front of huge windows, from which he could gaze upon the Washington Monument and the newly completed Jefferson Memorial. Bookcases and inviting chairs lined the walls, and in a far corner sat the desk at which John Quincy Adams had drafted the Monroe Doctrine. The office had fifteen-foot-high ceilings and several fireplaces, and the floors were covered with dark blue rugs. Visitors waited in a small conference room and had to walk through an office with three secretaries and a small anteroom before being ushered into the secretary's presence. It was all very grand, and hid the fact that throughout the war Hull and his department handled only the most routine business. Important international matters were handled directly by the president or by special representatives he appointed for specific assignments.

For the powerful and those on the edge of power, Washington was a social whirl. If the war had changed anything it was only on the margins. White-tie-and-tails gave way to the slightly less formal black-tie-and-tuxedo. And while the number of opulent galas was somewhat reduced, this was compensated for by a vast quantity of smaller social events. Only the White House, in the fall of 1941, had cancelled its formal social schedule, although a schedule of less formal events was maintained throughout the war. In fact, an invitation to a White House gathering trumped all other events, and most experienced hostesses waited until the first lady issued her schedule before announcing their own events. Most of the grander parties during the war were held at the over fifty embassies that dotted Washington. During Prohibition embassy parties overflowed with invited and uninvited guests, as they were the only place to get a legal drink. Prohibition's repeal had opened them up to competition, but even during the war years ambassadors, who usually had a long list of persons they wanted to influence, had the budgets to throw the most lavish affairs. Though the richest of Washington's society could compete dollar for dollar with the wealthiest Americans elsewhere, it was considered unseemly for a private citizen to hold an overly sumptuous affair when the nation was at war.

In official Washington, few congressmen or senators hit the social circuit. As they mostly lived on their salaries ($10,000 a year) and had to maintain themselves in both Washington and their home states, most were just too poor to keep up. Moreover, many of them were far from urbane, and the generally uncouth New Dealers were rarely made welcome by Washington society. In any event, most of them were of little importance as they almost always voted as their party leaders instructed them to. It was, therefore, the grand old men of the party, particularly those who were chairmen of important committees, who got the lion's share of the invitations that came to Capitol Hill.

Washington's social set was especially pleased with the new vice president and his wife. The Garners had disdained social events, and it was said they were in bed every night before the chickens. The Wallaces, on the other hand, enjoyed society and were often seen at various events. Many marveled at the social transformation of Mrs. Wallace, who came from Iowa in a frumpy dress, large eyeglasses, and unkempt hair. Within a year she had remade herself and was officially named Washington's best-dressed woman. Before and during the war, Washington's foremost social hermits were the Hulls. The secretary of state and his wife accepted no invitations that could be avoided, and for those diplomatic events that were unavoidable, Mrs. Hull was usually sent in place of her sleeping, or more often working, husband.

For those who could not get invitations to the best parties, Washington had many clubs where one could socialize with the "right" people. The Sulgrave Club on Dupont Circle was one of the swankiest. In attendance one could always find just the right mix of wealthy individuals, with diplomats and a few congressmen sprinkled among them. During the summer, though, most of the "best" people deserted the Sulgrave Club in favor of the Chevy Chase Club, out in the somewhat cooler suburbs. Of all the clubs in the suburbs, the Chevy Chase was the only one that was considered socially acceptable, and some of Washington's best-known socialites waited years for an invitation to join. It also boasted the best golf course in the Washington area, and was friendly to those who just wanted to lounge in the shade being served a never-ending supply of mint juleps.

In all societies and in every era the rich and well-connected have always been able to find expensive ways to entertain themselves. But what of the average person; what occupied them outside of the office? For many, evenings were spent consuming hard liquor, and Washington's per capita alcohol consumption far outstripped the rest of the nation's. In fact, Washington annually consumed about as much liquor (twenty gallons per person) as states with several times its population. As there was a relative paucity of nightclubs and because stand-up bars were illegal, most of this hard drinking took place in people's homes and in hotels. When not drinking, or as they imbibed, Washingtonians loved to gamble. Bookmaking, particularly betting on the horses, and several established numbers rackets were big earners for local criminal organizations. On any particular day, an estimated several hundred thousand Washingtonians (half the population) were carrying around a number slip, with a 1-in-999 chance of winning.

Prostitutes did a booming business before the war, and business became even more brisk as tens of thousands of men transplanted themselves to Washington during the war. There is, however, no evidence the actual number of prostitutes increased much. As there were no public areas in Washington where prostitutes gathered, most of this business was conducted in houses or, for freelancers, in apartments. Along with this growing prostitution business came a correspondingly enormous growth in the number of STD cases in the city. By mid-1942 the director of the city's venereal disease bureau was complaining that there were fifteen thousand more new cases than there were seats in Griffith Stadium (thirty thousand). Worried that his formerly sleepy city was becoming notorious for its burgeoning "sin" industry, the mayor ordered raids on the most infamous houses of prostitution. So many important politicians, senior military officers, and high-ranking government officials were rounded up that the raids were soon discontinued, and no charges were pressed. In any case, the police had more important concerns, as during the war Washington became the murder capital of the United States, with a homicide rate more than twice New York's.

For those wanting to raise their libidos through legal means there were the burlesque shows. Burlesque had once thrived in Washington, but by the time the war started only one theater remained—the Gayety on Ninth Street—which featured some of the most famous strippers of the day: Ann Corio, Margie Hart, Georgia Sothern, and Hinda Wausau. As reputations were not tarnished by visiting a burlesque theater many well-known public men were often seen in the galleries.

For significantly tamer entertainment, few options presented themselves: the theater, sports, or a movie. Unfortunately for those who craved variety, the National Theater was the only game in town. But every producer wanted to put on a show at the National, for the always packed theater allowed long runs. For the movie-loving public there was a line of theaters downtown that were filled every night. But with nothing to do afterward, most moviegoers headed for home after the show.

During the summer there was baseball, which meant watching those perennial cellar-dwellers, the Washington Senators, lose. Still, the games were always packed, and Washingtonians took an odd pride in the supposed complaint "First in war, first in peace, last in the American League." In the fall there were George Preston Marshall's Redskins, bought from the profits of his laundry empire. Fans usually got to see a winning team, listen to one of the few marching bands in pro football, and scream out the team's fight song, "Hail to the Redskins."

All of this was backdrop to a city much changed by war, now moving at a speed more familiar to those coming from New York. It is also worth noting that all of Washington's entertainments could only cater to a tiny fraction of the tens of thousands of civilians and military personnel who came to the city to do a job. For every person unwinding or blowing off steam in one or another of Washington's social venues there were always dozens working long into the night coordinating the administrative and logistical minutiae that kept huge military forces moving and supplied during a global war. And while the city's prostitutes were doing a booming business, the city's churches were often packed to capacity at all hours of the day. When Roosevelt came on the radio to announce the start of a new offensive, it was not the bars that filled up, it was the churches.

23

CHURCHILL COMES TO TOWN—

ARCADIA CONFERENCE

JUST THREE DAYS BEFORE CHRISTMAS 1941, WINSTON CHURCHILL, his entourage, and the British war chiefs arrived in Hampton Roads aboard the battleship *Duke of York*. To say that the American military chiefs, as well as most of FDR's senior civilian advisers, would have preferred to postpone Churchill's visit is an understatement. In the hectic days after Pearl Harbor everyone with a role in running the war was too busy reacting to the rush of events to pay much attention to long-term strategy. With the Japanese onslaught showing no signs of slowing, and increasing fears among those living on the West Coast that the Japanese would appear on their doorsteps at any moment, every available resource was heading west. For Churchill this was a disaster in the making. For if America, in all its righteous wrath, turned its full might on Japan, little would be left over for the war in Europe.

Churchill did not long delay at Hampton Roads. Boarding a waiting aircraft, he departed for Washington, where the president met him at the airport. After the obligatory round of pictures—Roosevelt, held up by braces, stood almost a foot taller than the prime minister—they moved on to the White House. Churchill was given the Lincoln Bedroom, but after declaring the bed "not right" he prowled the second floor for a proper bed, finally choosing a room directly across the hall from where Harry Hopkins slept. After a bit more exploration, Churchill settled on Eleanor's press room—the Monroe Room—for his traveling war room. By the end of the day, the Monroe Room had been transformed into the nerve center of the far-flung British Empire, adorned with maps and stuffed with the administrative paperwork Churchill needed to direct a global war. Roosevelt, impressed by Churchill's ability to monitor and direct the entire war from a single office, ordered a similar room for himself established in the White House basement. But before Churchill could fully settle in, the proper arrangements had to be made between himself and Alonzo Fields, the White House butler. Churchill, wearing just his long underwear, confronted Fields to inform him that "I must have a tumbler of sherry in my room before breakfast, a couple of glasses of scotch and soda before lunch and French champagne and 90-year-old brandy before I go to sleep at night."

For the next few days FDR and the prime minister relaxed in each other's company. Their conversations, almost always including Hopkins, went on long into the night, leaving Roosevelt exhausted. These free-flowing discussions covered every aspect of the war, including lengthy diversions into historical background. As Churchill may possibly have been the only person FDR enjoyed listening to, the prime minister's rambling discourses often went uninterrupted for long periods. After Roosevelt went to sleep, Churchill and Hopkins continued on in one or the other's bedroom until exhaustion took over, only to restart early the next morning.

At one point, FDR, not able to wait for the formal talks to begin in the morning, had himself wheeled into Churchill's room. As he entered, Churchill emerged from the shower, stark naked and his skin a glowing pink. Embarrassed, Roosevelt tried to take his leave, only to have Churchill protest: "The Prime Minister of Britain has nothing to conceal from the President of the United States."

Christmas passed relatively quietly. Churchill joined the president in the official tree-lighting ceremony, where they both broadcast uplifting messages. But their outward calm hid bitter reality: America was quickly losing the war. After MacArthur's inept preparations to fend off an invasion of the Philippines failed, he ordered Manila declared an open city, and American forces began the long retreat to the Bataan Peninsula. Once there they discovered that little had been done to ready Bataan for a last stand, and that they would be on a near-starvation diet from the start. Still, MacArthur's exhausted force grimly dug in for a long desperate siege. On the same day, December 23, the marines ended their heroic defense of Wake Island, but not before launching one final counterattack, which killed over a hundred Japanese soldiers at a cost of eleven marines.

Possibly reflecting on these events and the long struggle ahead, Churchill concluded his Christmas message: "Let the children have their night of fun and laughter . . . before we turn again to the stern tasks and formidable years that lie before us, resolved that by our sacrifice and daring, these same children will not be robbed of their inheritance or denied the right to live in a free and decent world." It was a somber reflection, but when asked by a journalist if he doubted the Allies' ultimate victory, Churchill replied: "I have no doubt whatever."

On Christmas Day, Roosevelt escorted his guest to the Foundry Methodist Church, where Churchill was introduced to the charming carol "O Little Town of Bethlehem." But it was the next day, while speaking to a joint session of Congress, that Churchill made his greatest impression on Americans desperate to get the measure of their wartime ally. In a speech broadcast around the world, Churchill tackled a difficult audience head-on. Even Hopkins had voiced some reservations about the prime minister's reception in a Congress set on punishing Japan, with the war in Europe as an afterthought. He was put at ease upon hearing congressional murmurs of approval after Churchill lamented that his American mother had not lived long enough to witness this moment. Murmuring turned to laughter and then cheers when Churchill quipped: "I cannot help reflecting that if my father had been an American and my mother British, instead of the other way around, I would have got here on my own." But Churchill's loudest and most sustained applause came when he addressed the war against Japan: "What kind of people do they think we are? Is it possible they do not recognize that we shall never cease to persevere against them until they have been taught a lesson which they and the world will never forget?" The lasting ovation greeting this comment brought home to Churchill the vital importance of this visit. The Americans might intellectually accept the principle of "Germany first," but in their hearts they wanted, above all things, to see Japan torn asunder. For the moment, though, Churchill had won them over, and that was a crucial first step toward achieving his goals. It was a bravura performance, one that was repeated four days later in Ottawa.

In the Canadian Parliament, Churchill took the measure of his audience and told the story of his travels to France just as her armies were collapsing before the German onslaught. During that visit Churchill had told the French leaders that Britain would fight on even if they chose to surrender. He then related the French commander General Maxime Weygand's prediction that in three weeks England would have its neck wrung like a chicken. Churchill, warming to his crowd, thundered, "Some chicken . . . some neck." Roosevelt, who had a vested political interest in Churchill's public performances, was greatly pleased.

The visit was to last only a week, but halfway through it Churchill decided to extend his trip. He remained three weeks, which would have completely exhausted Roosevelt had he not toward the end of the conference been able to send his guest to Florida for a five-day vacation. Churchill, as much in need of some respite as Roosevelt, took his physician, Dr. Charles McMoran Wilson—later Lord Moran—with him. Moran was worried, with good cause, as Churchill, while trying to open a stuck window the day after Christmas, had strained his heart. Moran had diagnosed a mild cardiac episode. But given the patient's well-known hypochondriac nature he and the prime minister's closest advisers decided that Churchill could do without knowing his condition. Still, they missed few opportunities to encourage him to get some rest. In the end, Churchill relented, and his nude frolicking in the waters outside Lend-Lease administrator Edward Stettinius's Florida home proved the perfect tonic.

Despite the break, and the prime minister's short excursion to Canada, the two warlords still managed fourteen days of substantive discussions between themselves and their combined military chiefs. Each of these meetings was preceded by lengthy discussions among the chiefs, designed to forge a unified military position before they had to face their political masters. Throughout history, developing a unified strategy among allies with differing experiences and objectives has always been difficult. It would be no different for America and Britain.

No matter how famously FDR and Churchill got along, the same was not true of their military chiefs. At the core of this animosity were two issues: The American chiefs did not trust and in some cases did not like the British, and the British chiefs considered the Americans a bunch of bumbling amateurs. Of course, there were many other concerns that hindered negotiations, but almost all of them had one or both factors at their root. Fundamentally, the Americans were convinced that the British were not overly concerned with winning the war as rapidly as possible. Rather, they thought the British wanted to make certain that the war was won in such a manner that it strengthened and extended the life of the British Empire, no matter how long it took. The Americans, on the other hand, starting with Roosevelt, gave no thought or concern to the longevity of the empire. In fact, they were actively, and often publicly, rooting for its quick demise. As for the British chiefs, they were confounded by the American chiefs' keenness for assaulting the coast of northern Europe as soon as possible. They could not fathom such bloody-minded determination to see tens of thousands of raw recruits slaughtered in the waves by German veterans. In the final analysis, the British had welcomed American participation in *their* war on the assumption the Americans would help carry through British plans. They were dismayed to discover the American chiefs had their own ideas on prosecuting the war.

Unfortunately, it takes a great deal of serious detective work to uncover even portions of these debates. This is partly a result of the chiefs emptying their conference rooms as soon as things began to heat up. Often aides, stenographers, and other note-takers were left outside the doors where they could hear the shouting but not make out the exact words. Worse, even when minutes were taken they are often unreliable. For instance, the official notes for the Washington conference run for many hundreds of pages, but we have no idea if they represent what was actually said. Why? Because the two persons responsible for keeping the official record— American brigadier Walter Bedell Smith and British brigadier Vivian Dykes—took what one historian called a "degree of secretarial license."

> Bedell Smith (after reading Dykes's draft of a meeting):
>   "That sounds fine; it's wonderful. There isn't but one thing
>   wrong with it."
> Dykes: "What's that?"
> Bedell Smith: "Hell, that isn't what they said."
> Dykes: "I know damn well it isn't, but it's what they should
>   have said."

Besides their problematic relations with British commanders, the American chiefs had two much bigger problems closer to home. For one, the war was only two weeks old and their relationship with FDR was un-

tested. Often the only way for the chiefs to get anything in front of the
president was through the good graces of Harry Hopkins. As always, if one
could sell Hopkins on a proposal, he would sell the president. But Hopkins
was never an easy sale. In time, FDR would come to know, understand,
and, to a point, trust his chiefs. But that day, though not far off, had not yet
arrived. It was, however, the second problem that truly plagued the U.S.
chiefs, and would do so throughout the war. They each had a very different
idea as to how the war should be fought and how to win it.

Although the American chiefs publicly agreed that the European war
took precedence over the Pacific conflict, Admiral King never believed it.

Admiral Ernest King and General George Marshall.

For King, Japan was always the primary enemy, as it was for most Americans. As he saw it, the only reason to support a Germany-first strategy was
to get the war in Europe over with as rapidly as possible, so that all of
America's war fighting potential could concentrate on battering Japan. Despite his reluctant agreement to "Germany first" he never stopped trying to
siphon off as much war matériel for the Pacific as he thought he could get
away with. Marshall, on the other hand, was raised in a tradition where the

primary job of a commander was to select the main effort and then support it with every available resource. As such, he viewed every diversion of matériel, even to fight Japan, as at best a necessary evil and at worst strategic malfeasance. And finally there was Arnold, who could usually be counted on to support Marshall, but apparently had no firm convictions in either direction. For Arnold, whatever enemy his Air Force was pointed at mattered little, as long as everyone realized that the war was going to be won by strategic bombing. In his view, soldiers and sailors had one primary function: to seize and secure bases that would place Germany and Japan within range of his bombers.

This internal division mattered greatly, because when the British appeared at a meeting they always spoke as one voice. Moreover, they were always probing for seams in the American position that they could exploit. Over time, this situation was somewhat alleviated by Marshall's rise to first among equals in the American hierarchy. As Marshall's stature grew, so did the military power of the United States. By late 1943, America's mounting military preponderance allowed Roosevelt and Marshall to increasingly direct rather than cajole their British colleagues. For the time being, though, the British were the dominant partner, and there was little the American military could accomplish, particularly in the Atlantic theater, without their ally's support.

One can hardly begin examining this first of the war's many great conferences without being astonished at how the petty took precedence over the crucial, or how much the Allies' distrust of one another's motives influenced policy. One such incident occurred on Christmas Eve when a small Free French naval force, under orders from Charles de Gaulle, seized the small islands of St. Pierre and Miquelon just off the Canadian coast. Vichy France owned these islands—the last remnant of France's once vast North American colonial empire—and had unwisely allowed a powerful radio transmitter to broadcast Nazi propaganda into French-speaking Quebec. The British had long planned to seize the islands, but the Canadians had indicated they wanted to do it themselves. All concerned had hesitated because the Americans had made it known that, for the moment, they did not want anything done that might unduly upset Vichy. But after getting a nod from the British secretary of state for war, Anthony Eden, de Gaulle ordered his forces to attack.

Secretary of State Hull was appalled. Returning early from his Christmas vacation, he spent most of Christmas trying to browbeat Canadian prime minister W. L. Mackenzie King into using the Canadian military to expel what he referred to as the "so-called" Free French. Despite a media explosion supporting the Free French action, Hull, for reasons as unfathomable then as they are now, persisted in labeling the attacks a criminal action and demanding they be overturned. He persisted in these verbal broadsides, to the exclusion of all else, long past the point where anyone else cared. As Churchill later noted: "I was struck by the fact that, amid gigantic movements, one small incident seemed to dominate his mind." As for Roosevelt, the incident confirmed his belief that Hull did not possess the intellectually supple temperament necessary for managing an international coalition in a global war. Hull's diminished role did not go unnoticed by Churchill, who commented of Hull that "he did not seem to have full access at the moment to the President." All concerned would have preferred Hull to have remained on vacation.

Christmas Day was further marred by the American chiefs' wariness that the British were converting Roosevelt to their agenda. Highly agitated by a memo produced by Churchill's staff stating that FDR favored handing reinforcements already earmarked for MacArthur over to the British, Marshall, Arnold, and Eisenhower stormed into Stimson's office. Stimson read the memo and called Hopkins. Boiling over in anger, Stimson announced that if the president persisted in such a course he "would have to take my resignation." Roosevelt hastily called a meeting with his chiefs and Stimson, where he threw out the casual aside "that a paper had been going around which was nonsense and which entirely misrepresented a conference between him and Churchill." Neither Stimson nor Marshall believed a word of it, but thankful that FDR had backed away from the proposal, they refrained from comment. But a lesson had been learned: it was very dangerous to leave the president alone with Churchill, where for much of the next year he proved all too susceptible to the prime minister's siren songs and soaring oratory.

A much more dangerous division took place later Christmas Day, over a point Marshall and the other American chiefs considered crucial to the future smooth running of the war: unified command. After first recounting the Allied experiences from World War I, where lack of a unified command brought the Allies close to defeat in 1918, Marshall broached the topic in the combined chiefs' conference. Stating that in battle it was not enough to manage through cooperation, Marshall pushed for the establishment of unified commands in whatever theater the forces of multiple nations were fighting. Nowhere was that need more pressing than in the newly created ABDA theater in Southeast Asia. The theater's acronym, standing for American, British, Dutch, Australian, neatly encapsulated the problem: too many national forces with no leadership to coordinate and direct their combined activities. With Japanese forces rapidly bearing down on the ABDA area, Marshall considered the immediate establishment of a unified ABDA command an absolute necessity. Churchill, however, resisted, claiming that over the kind of distances one dealt with in the Pacific it was best that each Allied force report to its national commander, and for that commander to then report directly to Washington and London. Evidently many U.S. Navy admirals were also against Marshall's proposal, bristling at the possibility that naval forces could come under Army command. King, however, strongly supported the plan, and crushed all naval resistance. An impressed Stimson later said of that particular debate that some stubborn admirals had "some dark days" ahead of them, as King had little tolerance for dissent once his mind was made up.

Bringing Churchill and the British chiefs over to the idea was more problematic. As the discussions dragged on, Lord Beaverbrook, Churchill intimate and head of British war production, passed Hopkins a note: "You should work on Churchill. He is being advised. He is open-minded and needs discussion." Hopkins wasted no time arranging a private meeting between Churchill and Marshall, where the prime minister was gradually brought to see the soundness of the proposal. To help bring Churchill's military advisers into line the Americans thought it wise to offer the first unified command to the British, in the person of General Archibald Wavell. Although there was much to recommend Wavell's selection, not least that he was already in the region and familiar with the developing situation, the British chiefs smelled a rat. Convinced that this was a Roosevelt trick to saddle a British commander with responsibility for what was clearly developing into yet another Allied military disaster, the British chiefs implored Churchill to resist the appointment of any Briton to the ABDA command. Churchill exploded, saying that he would not stand for suspicions that impugned the motives of the president. All futher discussion ended.

In the end, this was a matter of principle, as the selection of an ABDA commander was of little import. For the primary mission of the command—to hold the Malay Barrier—was overcome by events before Wavell could even gather sufficient forces to defend it. Before the Christmas season was over, Hong Kong had fallen, and Japanese forces were already pushing down the Malay Peninsula toward the great fortress of Singapore even as other Japanese forces were overrunning British defenses in Borneo. Within two weeks the Japanese had also entered Burma, and in a series of brilliant maneuvers pushed British forces back into India. Adding insult to injury, while Churchill was resting in Florida, his first vacation since the start of the war, he was informed that daring Italian commandos had steered torpedoes into Alexandria harbor, damaging the battleships *Queen Elizabeth* and *Valiant*. Both ships were out of commission for several months.

The rapid collapse of the Philippine defenses, added to by the fall of Singapore on February 15, effectively shattered the Malay Barrier. Ten days later, on February 25, Wavell resigned from his short-lived ABDA command. Within seventy-two hours what little hope remained of halting the Japanese advance vanished when an ABDA naval strike force was annihilated in a series of encounters in the Java Sea. Ten ships and over two thousand sailors were lost in engagements that delayed the Japanese invasion of Java for only a single day. Among the lost ships was the heavy cruiser USS *Houston,* which had often carried Franklin Roosevelt on his oceanic retreats.

Still, just a few weeks after the attack on Pearl Harbor, it was not all gloom. After almost six months of retreats, and horrific losses, the Russian army was counterattacking in front of Moscow. By Christmas, the Germans were reeling and, for a time, their entire position verged on complete collapse. Moreover, the British lion was on the offensive in North Africa. Eventually, the Germans stabilized both their Russian and North African fronts, and once again moved to the attack. But both Allied offensives revealed glimmers of hope for the future, as they exposed Axis vulnerabilities that the Allies would ruthlessly exploit before the end of 1942.

In the Pacific, although such glimmers were harder to discern, on the fringes of the onrushing Japanese there were small developments that were soon to turn the tide. First, and probably foremost, the leadership team that would fight the Pacific war was already forming. Most significantly, Admiral Chester Nimitz arrived at Pearl Harbor on Christmas Day, and officially took command of the U.S. Navy Pacific Fleet on New Year's Eve. The next day, at King's order, Nimitz began planning raids on the Gilbert and Marshall Islands, aiming to snatch away Japan's offensive momentum. The carrier *Yorktown* arrived in the Pacific, where it was soon escorting six thousand marines tasked to hold American Samoa. Even in the dark days immediately after Pearl Harbor, America was moving rapidly to defend what it still held and, more remarkably, preparing to go on the offensive.

There were other things unfolding, many of them of seemingly minor consequence at the time, but which would loom large in the years to come. Even as Wake Island fell, aircraft sent to support the beleaguered island— Marine Squadron 221—were diverted to Midway Island. They would still be there in June, when the unit was virtually annihilated defending Midway, but not before playing a pivotal role in the battle that effectively broke Japan's offensive naval power. As Squadron 221 began making Midway its new home, an obscure Navy admiral, Ben Moreell, the U.S. Navy's chief of bureau for yards and docks, was successfully selling the idea of recruiting naval construction battalions. Later made famous as the "Fighting Seabees," these construction battalions landed on Pacific islands, even as the fighting raged, to carve out the airfields that moved U.S. airpower one leap at a time to Japan's doorstep. Thus, the Japanese were forced to confront American airpower over their home islands far sooner than their prewar planning thought possible. An early taste of the massive air armadas to come was also in the works. On the second day of the New Year, Colonel Jimmy Doolittle began planning the first air raid—this one off carriers—on the Japanese home islands. Harvesting the fruits of these apparently minor developments still lay in the future, as did something more pivotal yet still invisible to most: as the war leaders of America and Britain talked, an economic behemoth awakened from a long slumber, and turned its pitiless factories toward war.

Upon Churchill's return from his five-day sojourn in Florida the conference participants picked up the pace, as everyone tried to put the many lingering disputes in the rearview mirror, to better focus on where there was agreement. Many of these agreements were routine and of minor consequence, such as replacing British divisions with Americans in Northern Ireland. Others were major and set the future direction of the war. Foremost among these was confirmation of the ABC 1 agreement that placed a strategic priority on winning the war against Germany first. As this had been Churchill's primary goal in rushing over to America, the British departed America's shores satisfied that they had achieved their chief objective. If they could have foreseen how much of America's military might would head toward the Pacific in 1942—to shore up a crumbling strategic position—it would have greatly diminished their buoyancy on the matter. Nor, at the time, could they have known just how clever and determined an advocate Admiral King would prove, as he constantly angled for additional combat power in the Pacific.

The other crucial decision made during the conference dealt with how to run the war, and more importantly where it would be run. The British favored the establishment of two command posts, one in London and the other in Washington. Roosevelt and Marshall, however, wanted a single command structure and they wanted it in Washington. In their view, two command centers that would only "liaise" with each other was too slow and cumbersome. Marshall proffered the perfect example to support his contention that such an arrangement could, and likely would, lead to disaster. At Pearl Harbor, Admiral Kimmel and General Short, the respective Army and Navy commanders, had also been told to liaise with each other. Marshall pointed out that if two commanders within walking distance of each other could not coordinate the joint defense of a single location, how much more difficult it would be to run a global war from two sides of the Atlantic. For Marshall, what made sense in a theater—the British had already conceded the point of unified supreme commands within theaters— also made sense for running the entire war. Marshall made two further arguments, neither of which the British were happy to hear. One was that the United States' geographical position between the two major war theaters made it the appropriate location for establishing the joint command. The second was even harder for the proud British chiefs to accept. After Britain had borne the brunt of the war for two hard years, the United States was already claiming right of place, because going forward, America would provide most of the manpower and resources for the Anglo-American war effort.

After what Hopkins called a "hell of a row," the British capitulated. The final organization was known as the Combined Chiefs of Staff and was headquartered in Washington. To represent the United Kingdom on a permanent basis, Churchill selected Field Marshal Sir John Dill, former chief of the British Imperial General Staff. Dill, who had been cited in dispatches eight times during World War I, had by the war's end progressively moved through the ranks from major to brigadier general. At the start of World War II, he was commanding I Corps in France, but was soon promoted to full general and appointed as vice chief of the Imperial General Staff, under Field Marshal William Edmund Ironside. When Churchill replaced Chamberlain as prime minister, Dill replaced Ironside. In mid-November, Dill was promoted to field marshal, but it was already obvious that he was a marked man, as he and Churchill could not get along. Dill was already on the outs with Churchill before Pearl Harbor, and their relationship has been described by Dill's biographer as ". . . an association strikingly lacking in empathy or understanding, etched in fundamental disagreement, and scarred by mutual disaffection, welling up at times into personal distaste." Dill had assumed his new role at the low point in the war effort, the collapse of the Allied armies in France, and had little patience for Churchill's methods or imperious hectoring. He was also, at the time, mourning the loss of a very much beloved wife.

Desperate to get him out of London, Churchill had planned to make Dill governor of Bombay: "A position of great honor, luxurious, remote, and inconsequential." Dill was saved from this professional oblivion through the friendship he had formed with Marshall during the Atlantic Conference. Employing his growing influence, Marshall insisted that Dill was the best man for the position of chief of the British mission to the United States. Churchill's acquiescence gave birth to one of the most unlikely and successful wartime collaborations in history. In his new role Dill sat within the locus of power, rather than being far removed from it as Churchill intended. Here he did yeoman service until his premature death in 1944, often being the only person who could explain the American chiefs to the British, and vice versa. Moreover, as a widower, he was much in demand on the tea circuit. One society matron commented that he was "the handsomest man in town." Marshall, unlikely to have noted his attractiveness, valued him more for his advice and his many useful services, particularly when Dill forwarded to Marshall copies of messages that Roosevelt had sent to Churchill without informing the Joint Chiefs. Churchill always shared these correspondences with *his* senior military commanders, while Roosevelt took great glee in keeping his chiefs in the dark as much as possible. He even went so far as to have one service encode outgoing presidential messages, while another decoded incoming messages, so as to keep

From left: General H. H. "Hap" Arnold, chief of staff of the Army Air Forces, and Field Marshal Sir John Dill.

any one service chief from being able to piece together an entire conversation. It was one of Roosevelt's many personality quirks that drove Marshall and the other chiefs to distraction.

Throughout the crucial early years of the war Dill played a unique and valuable role. He had the confidence of all the British chiefs, and in time he earned the respect and admiration of the American chiefs as well. Within weeks he was calling Arnold by his nickname, "Hap," and even got along well with Admiral King—no mean feat. But it was with Marshall that Dill built a special relationship. In fact, many considered Dill Marshall's best friend on the Combined Chiefs. When he died in November 1944, Dill was awarded the Distinguished Service Medal and buried in Arlington Cemetery, the only foreign soldier so honored.

Dill's move into his new role as the head of the British Joint Staff mission, as well as his earlier quiet acceptance of being moved aside and sent to Bombay, struck a chord with Marshall, who was pushing the idea of selfless service throughout the emergencies of the war's early months. With each new disaster or dramatic change of events Marshall needed men who would go where they were told, do the hard job, and not worry about recognition and glory. Such men were harder to find than one might imagine, even at the highest ranks of the Army. One example, sadly, involved one of his longest professional associations. It must have been doubly painful as the episode in question took place at precisely the time Field Marshal Dill was presenting a sterling example of doing as he was asked for the greater good of the war effort.

Breaking away from the great discussions of grand strategy, Stimson, Marshall, and Eisenhower huddled in Stimson's office to discuss how best to aid the Chinese war effort. But before they made a plan they had to have "the man"—someone senior enough to show Chiang Kai-shek the Allies were serious about helping him, while also encouraging the Chinese to pick up the pace of their combat operations. Stimson suggested the current First Army commander, General Hugh Drum. Marshall approved, and Drum was sent for.

Drum, who had been in the running for Marshall's job as chief of staff, was one of the few senior officers in the U.S. Army who had extensive experience managing large military formations during World War I. In fact, for several months during that war he was Marshall's boss. As such, he assumed he was being called to Washington to lead a major enterprise, probably command of the American forces heading for Europe. After learning that he was slated to take command in China, Drum balked, telling Marshall that "this assignment virtually closed his career so far as opportunity was concerned . . . [and] the future service he could render was of too great importance to send him out of the country in the matter proposed." Marshall did not take it well. After telling Drum that in the present emergency "the services of everyone would have to be given without regard to personal ambition," Marshall informed him that his services were no longer required in China. Drum appealed to Stimson, making the same point, that "the role in China was not big enough for his capabilities." Stimson was unsympathetic. Marshall, who had no time for any soldier who put himself above the immediate needs of the service, sent Drum back to the nearly meaningless Eastern Defense Command. Drum was never forgiven, and retired in September 1943, after waiting over a year and a half for the call that never came. Eisenhower summed up the entire situation in his diary: "Still working the China problem. Looks like Drum runs out of it. He wants none of it because he does not like the looks of the thing. He seemingly cannot understand that we have to do the best we can with what we've got."

Interestingly, sometime later Marshall called Eisenhower, then his chief war planner, into his office and told him: "I want you to know that in this war the commanders are going to be promoted and not the staff officers . . . Eisenhower, you are not going to get any promotion. You are going to stay right here on this job and you'll probably never move." Eisenhower, whose famous temper nearly broke loose, replied, "General, I don't give a damn about your promotion. I was brought in here to do my duty. I am doing that to the best of my ability and I am just trying to do my part in winning the war." As he headed for the door, Eisenhower, realizing he had made an ass of himself, turned back and saw a trace of a smile on Marshall's face. Within two weeks Marshall promoted Eisenhower to two stars and started him on his meteoric rise to supreme command of Allied forces in Europe.

Even as these mini-dramas played out in the background, the Arcadia Conference plowed forward with accords, both large and small, coming at an increasing pace. One Arcadia agreement that had little practical effect but much symbolic meaning was the joint Declaration of the United Nations. Twenty-six nations had signed the declaration, promising to adhere to the principles of the Atlantic Charter, to never make a separate peace, and to dedicate their full resources to defeating the Axis. The final document was signed on January 1, 1942, in the president's study. Roosevelt signed first, and asked if he should use the title commander in chief. Hopkins, with no inflection in his voice, replied, "President ought to do." Churchill signed, Maxim Litvinov signed for the Soviet Union, and Chinese ambassador T. V Soong signed for China. When all the signatures were affixed, Churchill noted that they represented four-fifths of the human race. Joseph Lash, a close friend of Eleanor Roosevelt, recorded, "There was a sense of Hitler's doom being sealed."

There was, however, one decision that was not made, and putting it off would later have monumental consequences. The British had arrived with a plan they called GYMNAST. Later it would be called SUPER-GYMNAST and after that TORCH. It outlined an operation that employed the fledgling American army for immediate effect in North Africa, where much of the British Army was committed against Rommel. To help entice the U.S. chiefs, Churchill and his accompanying generals announced that they had fifty-five thousand troops ready to embark immediately in support of the American effort. Marshall, wary of any diversion of resources from what he considered the main effort—northern Europe—was aghast. Unable to kill the idea outright, with the support of the other American chiefs, he managed to get the idea shelved for further study. But the damage to the American chiefs' position was done. The idea was now firmly fixed in Roosevelt's mind, where it lay dormant for months, before emerging in the spring to propel the chiefs into a North Africa invasion none of them supported.

Having accomplished much, if not all, of what he set out to do, Churchill and his entourage finally departed on January 15, 1942. When he arrived back in London a message from FDR awaited him: "It is fun to be in the same decade with you." It may have been fun, but it was also exhausting, particularly for Harry Hopkins, whose frail constitution was pushed to the limit. The day after Churchill departed, Hopkins checked himself into the nearby Naval Hospital. He had, in fact, intended to check in a day earlier, but there was one important task left before he did so. Postponing medical treatment, Hopkins stayed for a lunch between the president and William Knudsen in which war production dominated the agenda.

24

BUREAUCRATIC ROADKILL

A S SOON AS CHURCHILL DEPARTED, ROOSEVELT TURNED HIS FULL attention to war production. He expected a lot from American industry and, to date, deliveries had been disappointing. His growing pique achieved new heights when British production czar Lord Beaverbrook announced that "as America was four times Britain's size it should produce four times as much." Beaverbrook made his deliberatively provocative statement after meeting with American production experts who had repeatedly told him that his targets for American plane and tank production were absurd.

Roosevelt did not think they were absurd. Over the objections of both Hopkins and his production advisers, he included them in his January 6 State of the Union Address. After denouncing the Japanese and German governments and issuing a few platitudes about victory and freedom, Roosevelt became quite specific as to how America was going to win the war. To thunderous applause, greater than in any previous speech before Congress, Roosevelt, the master orator, laid out his plan: "The superiority of the United Nations in munitions and ships must be so overwhelming that the Axis Nations can never hope to catch up with it." Then, warming to his audience, FDR laid out his definition of the word "overwhelming." In just 1942 he called on the nation to build 60,000 planes, followed by 125,000 more in 1943. These were stupendous numbers for a country that, before the war, produced under 3,000 aircraft a year. But Roosevelt was just getting started. He also wanted 45,000 tanks that year and 75,000 the year after. Finally, he told an astounded but still wildly applauding Congress that American dockyards, which had produced just over a million dead-weight tons the year before, would produce six million in 1942, and ten million in 1943, an order of magnitude increase that would in a single year double the size of the nation's merchant marine.

If there were skeptics, Roosevelt silenced them with a thundering rally-ing cry: "Let no man say it cannot be done. It must be done—and we have undertaken to do it."

Unfortunately, it could not be done. Stacy May's report, delivered to the White House only three days before Pearl Harbor, revealed all too clearly the stark truth of U.S. war production. May had laid out a path for dou-bling the country's production in 1942, but that was not nearly enough to meet Roosevelt's demands for his "must items." In mid-January, however, Roosevelt was not concerned about whether a doubling of the American economy was enough. He was worried that industry might not even achieve the lower targets that May's Victory Program said were certainly achievable.

Belatedly, Roosevelt had arrived at a conclusion many of his advisers had come to months before: the agencies he had established to manage the nation's war economy were flailing. FDR's solution was always the same: if one organization was failing, replace it with another. Such an organization, in Roosevelt's estimate, also required new leadership. The president had long ago recognized that Knudsen was not up to the job, but he had not acted even as others argued that Knudsen be jettisoned. As early as a May 1941 cabinet meeting the knives had come out. As Stimson reported: "Ickes was dissatisfied with Knudsen, and claims there is general dissatisfaction with his performance. Knox agrees with Ickes." Stimson supported Knud-sen at the time, but he too was soon having his doubts, telling his diary that "Knudsen was slow and lacked initiative, but that he was the best man available at the time that OPM was created."

In private discussions with Hopkins, held as the Arcadia Conference was ongoing, Roosevelt mentioned placing a three-man board in charge of production: Vice President Wallace, Supreme Court justice William O. Douglas, and the former Sears, Roebuck executive Donald Nelson. But Hopkins reminded him of his dissatisfaction with the SPAB and OPM boards, and convinced him that he needed one man at the top. Roosevelt selected Douglas and called him to the White House, telling him that "whoever takes this job and does it as you can do it will have first call on the

William Knudsen.

Democratic nomination for President in 1944." Douglas accepted the position, but was not fooled by FDR's dangling the White House before him,
replying, "You will run again."

Hopkins, knowing Douglas was an able administrator, a strong personality, and a close confidant of the president, recognized him as someone
beyond his control, as well as a threat to his own unique position with the
president, and went into overdrive to get the decision reversed. Wallace
would likely have been Hopkins's preferred candidate, as he was no threat
to Hopkins's position. But his incompetence as chairman of SPAB and as a
board member of OPM was already part of Washington lore. Even Wallace's own staff had stopped asking him for quick decisions when it became known that he was seeking advice from mystics and astrologers.
Many took to calling him "the Prisoner of Zenda"—the name of a popular
Washington astrologer. Others in the SPAB leadership loudly complained
that his continual giggling and mystical digressions made him impossible
to work with. Assessing Donald Nelson as both competent and, more importantly, malleable, Hopkins campaigned to get Roosevelt to backtrack
on Douglas and confirm Nelson as the new production czar.

In his almost ten years at or near the top of Washington's power elite
Hopkins had learned to play politics with a ruthless intensity, often eviscerating enemies and potential enemies before they even knew they were in
his crosshairs. Moreover, he left few traces in his wake, leaving his targets
unsure of who was behind their political demise. According to journalist

and close observer of behind-the-scenes Washington Eliot Janeway, Hopkins enlisted British support in the persons of Churchill and Beaverbrook, as well as presenting his own arguments against Douglas: he was a New Dealer who would find it hard to work with businessmen, and he had no production experience. Finally, he reminded Roosevelt that he was vesting the holder of this position with the powers of an assistant president, who might contest him for political control at some later date. Roosevelt, always alert to rivals for power, came around to Hopkins's view and appointed Donald Nelson as head of the new War Production Department.

When the decision was made, Nelson was in a war production meeting with Vice President Wallace and the current production czar, William Knudsen. As the meeting was winding up Nelson and Wallace were summoned to the White House, where both were informed a new production organization was being created and it needed a chairman. As Roosevelt knew that Wallace desperately wanted the chairman's job, it was almost cruel to have him present when Nelson had already been chosen for the position. When the offer came, Nelson pronounced himself stunned, but took only a moment to accept. He and Wallace left the White House together and drove back to Nelson's office in the Social Security Building. Vice President Wallace, well understanding he was being pushed aside, remained silent during the ride. For the remainder of Roosevelt's third term the vice president remained a faint, but sometimes troublesome, presence in the corridors of power. Nelson was met at the elevators by his top aides, including the future Civil War historian Bruce Catton, who congratulated him on his promotion. The announcement had come over the news ticker minutes before.

Knudsen's office also had a news ticker. An hour after Nelson left for the White House, Knudsen emerged from his office and handed a scrap of ticker paper to John Lord O'Brian, a former federal judge and his current general counsel. "Look here, judge," he announced, "I've been fired." O'Brian, although taken aback at the president's callousness, was not surprised. For months, press attacks on Knudsen's management had been building toward a crescendo, fanned by unnamed officials in the War Department. O'Brian had pressed his boss to defend himself, but Knudsen had refused to play politics. To paraphrase Trotsky: Knudsen may not have had an interest in politics, but politics surely had an interest in him. Crushed, Knudsen announced he was going to call the president and demand an explanation. O'Brian, fearing he would not be put through, talked him out of it, and Knudsen then called it quits and headed for home.

With Nelson's appointment, Knudsen became superfluous, and Roosevelt, as he was prone to do, discarded and forgot him. Hopkins, believing that Knudsen could still greatly assist the war effort, and a bit worried that an embittered Knudsen might cause political problems, went to work salvaging the situation. He called Jesse Jones, the secretary of commerce, asking him to get hold of Knudsen and tell him not to make any statements or leave Washington, as Roosevelt had an important role for him. Jones went to Knudsen's home, where he found the dejected production czar disconsolately tapping on a piano. Staying until midnight, Jones convinced Knudsen to wait until he heard from the president before he made any decisions.

Hopkins next called Stimson's deputy for production, Robert Patterson, and asked him what he thought of taking on Knudsen as a deputy in charge of production. Patterson was in favor of the idea, but had a hard time getting it past Stimson, who had endured one run-in too many with Knudsen and considered him "soft and slow." Stimson had to be persuaded of Knudsen's worth, but was eventually brought around. Roosevelt, after being convinced that Knudsen's failures did not reflect any disagreement about administration priorities, agreed to have Knudsen to the White House for lunch.

During lunch, the president put on a bravura performance and in one of those gestures he was famous for informed Knudsen that he wanted to make him a lieutenant general (three stars). When Knudsen demurred, telling FDR that three stars were too many, Roosevelt explained that he would meet a lot of one and two stars during his trips who would try and pull rank on him, but they "can't do that now because you will be over them." Roosevelt clinched the deal by simply stating: "I want you to accept for another reason, too. I will feel better if you do."

Knudsen overcame his brutal dismissal and went on to do great service for his country, but as Jesse Jones later wrote: "He never got over the blow. He was never happy again."

It was now up to Nelson to take the reins of the new War Production Board (WPB) and accomplish the tremendous job of turning Roosevelt's vision and May's Victory Program into reality. May believed there was room to double military orders in 1942, and increase them further in 1943. That meant increasing America's gross domestic product to $165 billion, more than 50 percent higher than it currently was, and tripling the size of the economy at the time Roosevelt took office. Stupendous numbers by any measure. So astronomical, in fact, that May asked a crucial question: Were they feasible? Robert Nathan, and Simon Kuznets, in a separate report, answered yes, but only if the economy was under strict central control. That left a single question: Was Nelson the man to do it?

Nelson's ultimate failure cannot be blamed on Roosevelt's reluctance to confer real power upon him, as was the case with the previous production agencies and commissions. In comparison with these organizations' charters, the executive order bringing the WPB into existence was an almost perfect instrument, allowing Nelson to wield power almost as great as the president himself. Rising to the level of the crisis, Roosevelt did what he had never done before—shared real and extensive amounts of power: "The Chairman's . . . *decisions shall be final.*"

Unfortunately, Nelson wasted no time demonstrating a personal weakness already noted by many, and despised by a few: given unlimited powers he proved mortally afraid to use them. Before the ink had dried on the executive order giving him the power to control all Army and Navy procurement activities, Nelson issued his first executive decision handing that power back to the military, with ultimately disastrous results. In a city where the main sport was the accumulation and wielding of power, Nelson had from his first moments in charge presented himself as a patsy. There was no shortage of people ready to take him.

Foremost among these was General Brehon Somervell, the new chief of the Army's Service of Supply (later renamed the Army Service Forces). Somervell's rapid rise in the Army hierarchy was a result of his being held in high esteem by the two men who mattered most: George Marshall and Harry Hopkins. His job, supplying millions of men fighting on multiple continents, was certain to be a logistical challenge far beyond anything ever faced by any army in history. Meeting it would take a man of unusual drive and energy. Marshall went looking for a man who would not hesitate to crush anything or anyone that got in the way of providing combat commanders with what they wanted when they wanted it—Somervell fit the bill perfectly. As *Time* described him: "Somervell is quietly hot-tempered, and moves in on what he wants with a sophistication belying his contention that he is 'just a country boy from Arkansas trying to get along in the big city.'" His biographer said of him: "He was an instrument, not a maker of high policy, and he was not a deep thinker. But he had ideas on logistics, and he fought for those ideas with vigor and conviction." Distinguished by ambition, energy, and managerial brilliance, Somervell was a formidable figure who reveled in big tasks and was enough of an SOB to get them done.

Hopkins, who also possessed a keen understanding of the kind of man needed for the task at hand, thought Somervell an inspired choice. During the Depression, Somervell had worked for Hopkins, running the WPA in New York, where for almost two years he was in almost daily contact with Hopkins. They had become friends, and each had a deep respect for the other's professional abilities. Moreover, Somervell always moved quickly on Hopkins's priorities, which meant he had the qualities Hopkins prized most: he was highly competent, and he was manageable. Somervell, for his part, was never shy about employing Hopkins's clout in his many squabbles with official Washington. Only in his dealings with Marshall did Somervell keep his "Hopkins card" in his pocket, as Somervell, in company with almost every other senior officer in World War II, held Marshall in awe, tinged with a liberal dose of professional fear.

Somervell, however, loathed Nelson, and by extension his newly formed WPB planning team—Nathan, May, and Kuznets. There was never any hope that the Army and the civilian production agencies would peacefully coexist as equal partners, as the vastness of their dual enterprise guaranteed conflict. But disputes did not have to turn into all-out bureaucratic warfare. That they reached a point where the nation's entire production engine almost seized up was attributable to Somervell's and Nelson's contrasting personalities. Nelson liked to persuade people, and always assumed others were looking for ways to cooperate with him. Somervell thought that malleable people were the bureaucratic equivalent of roadkill and he was the truck driver. Remarkably, Leon Henderson, who would belatedly but decisively involve himself in the Nelson-Somervell dispute, liked Nelson, but he also considered him a "poor manager" and a "weak man who was always fearful of a contest."

Robert Nathan, who became fond of Nelson during their association, blamed the conflict on Somervell, who, he claimed, never ceased trying to

Donald Nelson.

undermine Nelson's authority. But he too recognized that Nelson was not tough enough to stand up to Somervell. According to Nathan, Somervell believed he was facing two enemies. One was the Axis powers. The other, whom he considered just as dangerous to his goals, was the American people. Somervell believed Americans were being coddled, and was continuously pushing to cut all nonmilitary production to the bone. Nelson agreed that the military had first priority on almost everything, but he also recognized the necessity of maintaining civilian and business consumption at a reasonable level, lest the entire industrial edifice collapse. In the titanic battles that followed, Nathan provides a description of the approach the two men took in their dealings. "Somervell would come into a meeting with a knife in his hand, which he would stick into Donald Nelson's back; Nelson would pull it out and say, 'pardon me General; isn't this yours?' and Somervell would reply, 'Yes, Don, thank you.' Immediately Somervell would place it in his other hand and stick it into the other side of Nelson's back. And Nelson would repeat the same response."

In no small measure this dispute contributed to continuously lagging production schedules for much of 1942. In fact, as the military first doubled its orders, in line with what Stacy May had recommended, and then tripled and quadrupled them, they threatened to seize up the entire production system. By the middle of 1942 the escalating production goals were no longer feasible. Moreover, because Nelson had abrogated WPB's responsibility for placing industrial orders and setting priorities to the military, avoidable bottlenecks were popping up everywhere. The system was collapsing and Somervell, rather than reduce demands and rationalize the flow of orders, just kept piling on more burdens. As far as he was concerned shortfalls were all the fault of poor WPB management, and he placed the blame squarely on Nelson.

Nelson was too weak to resist Somervell's onslaught, particularly as the general had Stimson's, Marshall's, and Assistant Secretary of War Robert Patterson's full support. After months of bureaucratic beatings Nelson took on all the characteristics of "battered executive syndrome," where he lethargically would go about his routine, but shy away from the fight his staff knew had to come.

With each passing month production fell further behind goals and requirements. By midsummer it was clear that American industry would not only fail to meet Somervell's outsized demands, but it would also miss the goals that Stacy May had declared feasible. Fortunately, for the sake of maintaining the nation's production miracle, Robert Nathan stepped up to the task of taking on Somervell. Throughout the winter and spring of 1942 he did what he could to prop up Nelson's courage, while having Kuznets and May prepare a report that spelled out the true state of the Victory Program and how to salvage it. While Kuznets and May toiled, Nathan made

Robert Nathan, assistant director of progress reports, War Production Board.

the rounds among Washington's power brokers explaining his team's analytical methods and gathering allies for the final showdown. He found his most powerful supporter in Leon Henderson, who as a trained economist could read the numbers as well as Nathan and saw the same looming disaster Nathan's team had spotted. When the final fight came, Nelson would be in the room, but Somervell's true antagonist was Nathan, with Henderson lurking in the wings waiting to be tapped in.

Having easily run over Nelson, Somervell was unprepared for the infinitely more pugnacious Nathan. In what was considered a flattering portrayal, *The New Republic* wrote that Nathan, ". . . a huge hulk of a man with a kettledrum voice, is no dreamy braintruster. Rather, he is more like a wrestler than a thinker and talks more like a barker than a savant. Yet when faced with a thorny problem, his mind can slip to the solution with the ease of a rabbit slipping through briar . . . Details do not sidetrack him. He uses them instead, to fill the main structure of his thinking, and the end product is to the point and frequently blunt: 'The only trouble with that plant is the guy running it. Fire him.'" Nathan, a former boxer, who relished any fight, whether in the ring or the corridors of bureaucratic power, stepped up to take on Somervell and the Army when Nelson refused to do so. Although their ultimate confrontation was postponed to the fall, much rested on its outcome.

25

A BITTER SEASON

FOR THE ALLIES, THE DAYS AND WEEKS AND MONTHS FOLLOWING the Arcadia Conference were horrific. In Asia, military debacles followed one upon another as the Japanese continued their blitzkrieg across the great expanse of the Pacific. The day after Pearl Harbor, General Tomoyuki Yamashita led seventeen thousand soldiers ashore in Malaya. Almost without pause he and his men began a torturous march through jungles the British had considered impenetrable, to assault Fortress Singapore from the rear. Two months later, Yamashita accepted General Arthur Percival's surrender of eighty-five thousand British troops to a force half its size. Also lost in the fighting were the HMS *Prince of Wales* and HMS *Repulse*, pounced upon by successive swarms of attacking aircraft. Churchill said of the loss: "In all the war, I never received a more direct shock . . . As I turned over and twisted in bed the full horror of the news sank in upon me. There were no British or American ships in the Indian Ocean or the Pacific except the American survivors of Pearl Harbor . . . In all this vast expanse of waters Japan was supreme, and we everywhere were weak and naked."

It was far from the only defeat British arms suffered in those dark months. In Burma the British were in full retreat, and by summer the Japanese were poised to invade India, after already cutting China's logistical lifeline. American lieutenant general Joseph "Vinegar Joe" Stilwell, who was advising the Chinese, later said, "I think we got a hell of a beating. We got run out of Burma and it is as humiliating as hell." Thrilled at their own success, Japanese forces had already moved on to capture Borneo, Celebes, and Sumatra. Adding to the carnage, in April a huge Japanese fleet wrought havoc in the Indian Ocean from Ceylon to Madagascar.

Washington, however, found itself consumed with its own problems, foremost among them the Philippines. Marshall had placed a colonel in his office in charge of saving the Philippines, but when he suddenly died the recently arrived Eisenhower got the nod. Eisenhower had been called to Washington five days after Pearl Harbor. Before that, Marshall had never worked with Eisenhower. The chief was, however, well aware of Eisenhower's Army-wide reputation as the perfect staff officer, something he had personally confirmed when he observed him at work during the Army's huge Louisiana Maneuvers the previous September.

At Marshall's behest, Eisenhower arrived at Union Station on December 14, a week before Churchill's arrival for the Arcadia Conference. His brother met him at Union Station and took him directly to the Munitions Building. Marshall was waiting and saw him within a minute of his arrival. With no preamble Marshall gave Eisenhower a succinct but detailed brief of the dire situation in the Pacific, focusing on MacArthur's plight in the Philippines. Eisenhower, who had spent years in the Philippines working closely with MacArthur, already knew the lay of the land. He was, however, as dumbfounded as Marshall when he learned that the Japanese had destroyed most of MacArthur's air force, including thirty-five new B-17 bombers sitting wingtip to wingtip on the ground eight hours after the attack on Pearl Harbor.

Marshall stopped talking and suddenly asked, "What should be our general line of action?" Surprised by the sudden request to present a plan on a topic he knew barely anything about, Eisenhower asked for a few hours to consider his reply. Marshall snapped his approval and returned to the paperwork on his desk. Eisenhower returned several hours later, handing Marshall a three-hundred-word paper that stated that the Philippines garrison was doomed. Eisenhower then reminded his boss that the people of Asia were watching. As he saw it, they would excuse failure, but not abandonment. Marshall, agreeing that the Philippines and its defenders were lost, but heeding Eisenhower's warning, ordered his staff to do their best to save them.

MacArthur, trapped and desperate, sent an unending series of cables to Washington demanding a major offensive to stem the Japanese tide and save his army. It fell to Eisenhower to answer these missives and encourage

MacArthur to keep fighting. By mid-January, Eisenhower, who had long experience with MacArthur, was complaining that his former boss was as big a baby as ever. By the end of the month Eisenhower was concerned that MacArthur was losing touch with reality and confided to his diary that it "looks like MacArthur is losing his nerve. I am hoping that his yelps are just his way of spurring us on, but he is always an uncertain factor."

Just how uncertain became clear in early February. Manuel L. Quezon, president of the Philippines, was with MacArthur on the fortress island of Corregidor. Discouraged by incessant Japanese air attacks, Quezon sent a message to Washington, asking for immediate independence and a withdrawal of all American troops from the Philippines. He then planned to disarm his own forces, declare Philippine neutrality, and ask the Japanese to depart. Such a break with reality might be excused from an old and sickly man who had seen his country overrun by invaders, but what shocked Stimson, Marshall, and Eisenhower was MacArthur's supporting cable: ". . . the plan of President Quezon might offer the best possible solution of what is about to be a disastrous debacle."

Stimson and Marshall—the first to see the telegrams—were dismayed. They understood that the dying Quezon was at the end of his rope, but they had expected more from MacArthur. Considering the combined messages "ghastly in their responsibility and significance," Stimson set Marshall to work on a reply. With their reply in hand, Marshall and Stimson went to the White House. Roosevelt met them in his study with Sumner Welles in attendance. Both Stimson and Marshall were a bit apprehensive. For more than a year they had worked with a president who was unwilling to lead if he thought the public would not support him. Consequently, Roosevelt had shied away from making the hard decisions both men thought necessary. Neither had yet realized how the war had liberated Roosevelt. Prior to Pearl Harbor, Roosevelt feared taking the lead only to later find that America was not behind him. Post Pearl Harbor, America was resolved for war, and Roosevelt, whose natural inclination was always to take the initiative, was ready to make the hard decisions.

After hearing out Stimson's appraisal of MacArthur's telegram, Roosevelt replied, "We can't do this at all," assuring both Stimson and Marshall that he would not agree to Quezon's proposal. Marshall later told his biographer, "I immediately discarded everything in my mind I had held to his discredit . . . I decided he was a great man." After a brief discussion of the

Philippine situation, Stimson and Marshall departed to work on a new message to MacArthur. Both men, joined by Admirals King and Stark, returned to the White House that afternoon. FDR joined them in redrafting a message authorizing MacArthur to facilitate the surrender of the Philippine army, but ordered the American forces to continue the fight. That night a weary Stimson wrote in his diary: "It was a pretty hard day, for taking the decision which we reached was a difficult one, as it ordered a brave garrison to a fight to the finish."

There was no doubt that Roosevelt knew what he was asking, as his message to MacArthur concluded: "I therefore give you this most difficult mission in full understanding of the desperate situation to which you may shortly be reduced." Roosevelt no longer wanted to hear MacArthur's plans on grand strategy or war-winning combinations. What he wanted was for his commander in the Philippines to focus on the situation at hand, and prepare a dogged defense that would buy as much time as possible for the U.S. military to regroup.

Although the president was clearly facing up to the fact that the U.S. force in the Philippines was lost, he was not prepared to sacrifice its commander. MacArthur, already a household name, was ordered to leave the Philippines and make his way to Australia. His departure was not without controversy. Before President Quezon, who was also leaving for safer environs, was permitted to depart, MacArthur demanded a backdated payment of $500,000 (approximately $7.5 million in today's money) for past services, and lesser amounts for his key staff. Only after the payment, through a New York bank, was confirmed did MacArthur authorize Quezon's departure from Corregidor. This transaction is still shrouded in mystery, and MacArthur never mentioned it in any of his later writings. Though debates over the transaction's legality continue, at the time neither Roosevelt nor Stimson objected to it. Whether or not it was illegal, it surely lacked probity, and has been a major stain on MacArthur's reputation ever since.

MacArthur departed for Australia on March 10, 1942. Even he probably did not believe that the exhausted, starving, and massively outgunned Americans trapped on the Bataan Peninsula could hang on much longer. But, exhibiting near superhuman endurance, they continued the fight for another month, before finally capitulating on April 9. Even after Bataan fell, MacArthur's successor, Lieutenant General Jonathan Wainwright, and a skeleton force held Corregidor—the Pacific Gibraltar—until May 6, when Wainwright radioed: "There is a limit to human endurance, and that point has long passed," before surrendering his command.

As defeats piled up in the Pacific, things were little better in the Atlantic theater. All America had by way of an agreed war plan was the big concept of "Germany first" and holding the line in the Pacific. As a slogan it was peerless, but as a war strategy in the early months of 1942 it was useless. For the Japanese could not be held, and the Americans would have no way of getting at the Germans for many months yet. That, however, did not mean that the Germans had no way to get at America. German U-boats were having their best months of the war in both the North Atlantic and their new happy hunting grounds off the U.S. East Coast.

In mid-January the U-boats appeared along the Atlantic coast and soon thereafter in the Gulf of Mexico. Operation DRUMBEAT was beginning. Caught unprepared by Hitler's declaration of war on America, the German submarine chief, Admiral Karl Dönitz, had only six U-boats ready to send into the western Atlantic, but they were crewed by his best men and captains. Commander Rodger Winn's London-based Submarine Tracking Room marked their passage. As Winn tracked the submarines across the Atlantic he sent a detailed message to Admiral King informing him of the looming threat. King alerted area commanders, but did nothing else.

For the Germans, DRUMBEAT was a second "Happy Time," as they sank 48 ships in January, 73 ships in February, and 95 in March. In just three months the Allies lost well over a million tons of shipping, many of them precious oil tankers. Worse, the American Navy did not sink its first U-boat until well into April. It was a naval catastrophe far worse than Pearl Harbor, and if it continued the war was lost. The blame for this unprecedented disaster falls squarely on King's shoulders, as he allowed his deep-seated distrust for the British to color his military judgment. Though the British gave the Americans their best advice, based on over two years of experience fighting U-boats in the North Atlantic, King refused to listen. Thus, basic measures such as instituting a convoy system along the coast were not implemented. Worse, in what amounts to nearly criminal neglect, the lights along the Eastern Seaboard were not extinguished until mid-April 1942, allowing U-boat commanders to lie well offshore and pick off targets silhouetted against city lights. Miami alone threw up a six-mile glow, creating a deadly gauntlet for ships navigating around the Gulf Stream. This murderous situation continued because local communities from Atlantic City to Florida raised hell about having their tourist seasons ruined. Over 250 ships were lost before the Navy acted to turn off the lights.

In dire need, King asked Marshall for help. Marshall reacted instantly. On March 26, he ordered all Army commands possessing aircraft capable of searching over the Atlantic's open seas to turn their full attention to looking for U-boats. He even went so far as to temporarily turn operational control of these aircraft over to the Navy. Even this doubling of the number of aircraft available for hunting U-boats was almost wasted because King refused to accept British advice on how to organize and integrate search units.

Appalled at their ally's catastrophic losses, the Admiralty put Commander Winn on a plane and flew him to Washington. Told by King's chief of staff, Rear Admiral R. S. Edwards, that the "Americans wished to learn their own lessons and had plenty of ships with which to do so," Winn exploded: "The trouble, Admiral, is it's not only your bloody ships you are losing; a lot of them are ours." The upshot of Winn's withering criticisms was that King finally ordered the creation of a "tracking room" to integrate all intelligence, ship locations, and anti-U-boat operations.

Realizing that his Army Air Forces pilots were not sufficiently trained for hunting U-boats, General Arnold established a training and research site for anti-submarine warfare at Langley Field, Virginia. He then offered to establish a Coastal Air Command, run by the Army Air Forces, to help search for U-boats. In making his offer, Arnold was adopting the British model where the RAF, in close cooperation with the Royal Navy, controlled all land-based aircraft assigned to submarine duty. He told King that the Army would handle the specialized training, run the airfields, and handle all the logistic and maintenance chores, but would take all of its orders from the Navy. This was not good enough for King, who was already anticipating the day when the Army Air Forces would gain its independence and feared the Navy would be stripped of its aviation. Consequently, King replied that if he did not own the whole thing he wanted none of it. The battle between Arnold and King was still raging in May, when Arnold threw up his hands and dumped the problem in Marshall's lap. In the meantime, ships were sinking, thousands of tons of precious cargo were lost, and hundreds of men drowned.

Marshall did not turn his full attention to the problem until mid-June. When he did, he was flabbergasted at the pettiness of the argument and the profound effects the resulting delay was having on the war effort. In a pointed letter to King, Marshall stated: "The loss by submarines off the Atlantic seaboard and the Caribbean now threaten the entire war effort . . . of the 74 ships allocated to the Army by the War Shipping Administration, 17 have already been sunk . . . I am fearful that another month or two of this will so cripple our means of transport that we will be unable to bring sufficient men and planes to bear against the enemy in critical theaters . . ." King remained unmoved.

Marshall swallowed hard and told Arnold to turn the entire operation over to the Navy. More months passed as the Navy put its own administrative backbone in place, replicating an infrastructure the Army had already built. Without a doubt, King was the man to snap the Navy out of its post–Pearl Harbor shock. Still there is little in this affair that accrues to his credit. In fact, his main biographer, Thomas B. Buell, never mentions these events. Because he disliked the British, and over a point of internal politics rising out of his fear of an event—an independent air force—still years in the future, King made a very bad situation inestimably worse.

Even as the U-boats wreaked havoc along the Atlantic coast, official Washington was dealing with many other crises. Among them was the defense of the West Coast, where an estimated 110,000 Japanese, 70,000 of them citizens, lived. In the immediate aftermath of Pearl Harbor few concerned themselves with the Japanese living in their midst. But as the Japanese onslaught raced across the Pacific, minds began to change. Suspicion was further driven by the intelligence section of the Fourth Army (responsible for the defense of the West Coast), which reported every rumor as fact, keeping everyone on edge with reports of bombers over San Francisco, and dozens of ships of the Japanese Imperial Navy (they were American fishing trawlers) cruising just off the coast.

The local press, eventually joined by the nation's most influential columnist, Walter Lippmann, gleefully published these reports along with hundreds of other fifth column and sabotage rumors. General Stilwell, then commanding the southern zone of the Fourth Army area, declared the reports as "wild, farcical, and fantastic stuff," labeling the latest report from Fourth Army intelligence "a two-pound bundle of crap." Despite the fact that no act of sabotage was ever proven, or any fifth column activity ever confirmed, the public overwhelmingly believed every report and rumor. Driven by fear, racism, and growing claims of military necessity—80 percent of the aircraft industry was on the coast and within range of Japanese warships—a growing chorus called for the forcible removal of all Japanese Americans to internment camps. When the Roberts Commission, which was examining the Pearl Harbor attack, announced that spies and fifth columnists had assisted the Japanese strike, resistance to interning America's Japanese population evaporated.

As for Roosevelt, he accepted the military necessity of a forced evacuation at face value. The matter was never discussed during cabinet meetings, and the only opposition to internment came from Attorney General Francis Biddle, supported by FBI director J. Edgar Hoover, who did not want to see the FBI's reputation besmirched by what he considered a dirty business. Hoover did have a list of over seven hundred Japanese he wanted interrogated, but thought the rest should be left alone. Biddle, unfortunately, was new in the job and was never a power within the Rooseveltian universe. In fact, once the decision to intern Japanese Americans was made he meekly moved aside, noting that Roosevelt was only interested in winning the war and that anything that threatened that prospect was dealt with boldly and harshly.

Roosevelt, with the many needs of the war pressing on him, pushed the job over to Stimson. During their first conversation on the topic, on February 11, Stimson was surprised to find the president was "vigorous about it," telling him to "go ahead on the line I myself thought best." Stimson probably realized that Roosevelt was avoiding making a formal presidential decision on the matter, but he let it pass. Stimson himself had qualms about the constitutionality of interning the Japanese, writing in his diary: "General DeWitt [Fourth Army commander] is anxious to have the Japanese evacuated from large areas. It is a difficult proposition for the most dangerous elements are not the aliens, but the second generation citizens. The second generation Japanese can only be evacuated either as a part of a total evacuation . . . or by frankly trying to put them out on the ground that their racial characteristics are such that we cannot understand or trust even citizen Japanese. . . . I am afraid this will make a tremendous hole in our constitutional system." Nevertheless, he handed the entire project over to John McCloy, his top assistant. McCloy, who had been pushing Stimson to get presidential direction one way or another, now had his orders. He immediately called the Fourth Army commander to inform him that "we have carte blanche to do what we want as far as the President is concerned . . . [but] be as reasonable as you can."

Prior to the war McCloy had made his reputation pursuing reparations for the 1916 German sabotage of munitions awaiting shipment in New York Harbor—the infamous Black Tom Case. His years working on this case gave him a wide knowledge of intelligence matters, and an acute sensitivity toward potential acts of sabotage. McCloy was also on the list to see MAGIC intercepts, and one in particular had caught his attention. On May 9, 1941, a Japanese government official assigned to the consulate in Los Angeles sent a message to Tokyo outlining ongoing spying activities. In it he stated: "We shall maintain our connection with our second generation, who are at present in the U.S. Army, to keep us informed of various developments in the Army. We also have connections with our second generation working in airplane plants for intelligence purposes."

For McCloy this was evidence that no Japanese could be trusted, and he immediately started work on his odious task. When Biddle's aides questioned the constitutionality of the act, McCloy, anticipating Justice Robert H. Jackson's concern that the Constitution might be converted into a "suicide pact," replied: "If it is a question of the safety of the country or the Constitution of the United States, why the Constitution is just a scrap of paper to me." McCloy was actually much more introspective than his comment makes him appear, recording in his diary: "I am afraid of no easy solution or one which will not be criticized whatever move we make." Working with Biddle, who was now resigned to the inevitable, he prepared Executive Order 9066 for Roosevelt's signature. On February 19, Roosevelt signed the order authorizing the War Department (Fourth Army) to establish restricted areas from which persons may be excluded. The order made no mention of the Japanese, nor did it have to.

Almost immediately the movement of the Japanese to internment camps began, without regard to their civil rights or their property, most of which they were forced to sell off at fire-sale prices. These camps were never as bad as those established by the Nazis or Stalin, and there were no recorded instances of abuse. Despite this, the act remains a stain on our national honor, as over a hundred thousand Americans were imprisoned with no evidence of wrongdoing and without any recourse to the nation's legal system.

Because he received conflicting advice and was afraid he would be blamed if there was an act of sabotage had he not acted, Roosevelt's support for the movement is somewhat understandable, if unwise. What is rather remarkable is that the great voices of liberalism were either silent or fully supportive. Harry Hopkins, for instance, asked Roosevelt to promote WPA director Howard Hunter for how he managed the internment camps. Throughout the war Hopkins remained tremendously proud of how his former organization, the WPA, handled this new responsibility. As for Roosevelt's in-house conscience, Eleanor, she penned an article for *Collier's* magazine in which she gave full-throated support for the internment policy.

Biddle, writing twenty years later, related: "If Stimson had insisted, had stood firm, as he apparently suspected that this wholesale evacuation was needless, the president would have followed his advice. And if . . . I had urged the Secretary to resist the pressure of his subordinates, the result might have been different. But I was new to the cabinet and disinclined to insist on my view to an elder statesman." Upon such moments of moral weakness great evils flourish.

26

JOINT CHIEFS

B Y THE END OF MAY, THE RUSSIAN SPRING OFFENSIVE, BEGUN WITH great optimism, had turned into another debacle. On June 28, the Germans began their own offensive (Case Blue) and the panzers were soon sweeping across the steppes, as the Red Army withered under the Wehrmacht's hammer blows. In North Africa, too, in late May and early June, General Erwin Rommel dealt Major General Neil Ritchie's British Army a devastating blow. By the end of June, German panzers were on Alexandria's doorstep and threatening the Suez Canal.

In Washington, the unending disasters were fraying nerves and testing both people and systems. As Hopkins wrote at the time: "This war can't be won with men . . . who won't take great and bold risks and Roosevelt has got a whole hatful of them in the Army and Navy that will have to be liquidated before we really get on with our fighting. Fortunately he has got in King, Marshall, and Arnold three people who really like to fight." Roosevelt had certainly done astoundingly well in selecting his most senior commanders (the Joint Chiefs), but a single point of personnel contention remained unresolved. Having two persons in charge of the Navy—Stark as chief of naval operations (CNO) and King as the newly appointed Commander in Chief, United States Fleet (COMINCH)—was proving unworkable. As CNO, Stark was responsible for the Navy's strategic direction and advising the president. King, in his lesser role as fleet commander, was expected to carry out the tasks Stark set out for him, nothing more and nothing less, despite his commanding fleets in almost every corner of the globe.

But King, probably already looking toward his own personal future, had gotten Roosevelt to agree to several demands before he accepted the fleet commander position. Some of these were trivial, such as King's desire to avoid speaking with the press and Congress, neither of which he was very good at. As Roosevelt did not want King talking to the press or Congress either, this was an easy one. King also got permission to keep his headquarters in Washington, where he could influence policy, rather than aboard ship with one of the fleets. It was, however, his seemingly easiest request, changing his job title from CINCUS ("sink us") to Commander in Chief, United States Fleet, that caused Roosevelt to momentarily balk, as FDR was the commander in chief and did not welcome someone else holding that title. But King's final request was huge and led to the current imbroglio. King insisted that he report only to the president and not have to go through Stark. Roosevelt, who always liked the idea of competing underlings, readily agreed, thereby giving the Navy two bosses—an intolerable situation.

The one thing Roosevelt did not grant King was the power to reorganize the Navy and crush the power of its various bureaus. Roosevelt, who had his own problems with the bureau chiefs when he was assistant secretary of the navy, clearly understood that these parochial fiefdoms could stifle any initiative they did not favor. King assumed he could clean out this viper's nest as Roosevelt had not interfered when Marshall reorganized the Army, neutering the Army bureau (branch) chiefs and slimming down the organization for war. But the Navy was different. It was Roosevelt's baby. As he often did within his own administration, Roosevelt allowed the bureaus to remain untouched, likely assuming that when problems arose he would provide the deciding vote. The only concession FDR offered was to fire any bureau chief with whom King could not work. King never stopped trying to reorganize the Navy, but each time he moved in that direction Roosevelt brought him up short. In the end, it did not matter much, as King bent the bureaus to his will through the same methods that had always worked for him in the past: he raged, yelled, destroyed careers, and demanded obedience. It was the rare man who stood up to King's wrath.

After Pearl Harbor the local commanders, Admiral Kimmel and General Short, were relieved of command. They were, however, insufficient sacrifice for a disaster of such magnitude. When Knox informed Roosevelt that the Navy's command relationship was not working, FDR took the opportunity to push Stark out. Stark, for his part, understood that after Pearl Harbor he could not long remain in the CNO job. He also knew that if he left on his own terms he could possibly still maneuver himself into a position to contribute to the war effort. After signaling Roosevelt that he would quietly accept whatever fate the president had in store for him, Stark, in March 1942, was ordered to London as commander of U.S. Naval Forces, Europe. Here, Stark provided important services throughout the war, but was far removed from strategic decision-making. The same order relieving Stark also promoted King to CNO. Both the CNO and COMINCH positions continued as separate and distinct entities with their own offices and staffs, united only in that the same man—King—headed both.

Even before Stark's removal, Marshall realized there was an imbalance within the Joint Chiefs that was bound to cause friction. With two Army members (Marshall and Arnold) and only one Navy member, the ever-suspicious King would view every disagreement as "we-they" and continually get his back up defending the Navy's turf. As Marshall well understood, each instance of such friction presented an opening for Roosevelt to interfere in the chiefs' deliberations. To correct the imbalance Marshall, thinking that King could not possibly object, proffered the idea of having Admiral William D. Leahy appointed as chairman of the Joint Chiefs of Staff. Marshall knew Leahy, but not well. He did, however, know enough about him to believe he would not make decisions based on parochial Navy interests. Marshall also knew that Roosevelt and Leahy had a long and close relationship dating from the president's days as assistant secretary of the navy, when Roosevelt, who loved to be at sea, often found excuses to sail with the Navy dispatch ship—the USS *Dolphin,* commanded by then-captain Leahy. During the interwar years Leahy carefully nurtured his relationship with Roosevelt, even visiting him several times at Hyde Park and Campobello. As president, FDR had appointed Leahy to the Navy's top job as chief of naval operations, where he began the naval buildup that would hit full stride in midwar. After Leahy's retirement, Roosevelt had first made him governor of Puerto Rico and then America's ambassador to Vichy France. He was still doing tremendous service in this crucial position when Marshall began considering him for the Joint Chiefs.

At first the president balked, telling Marshall, "But you are the chief of staff." Marshall replied, "But there is no chief of staff of all the military services."

"Well," Roosevelt said, "I'm the chief of staff. I'm the commander-in-chief."

Marshall patiently explained to the president that it was impossible for him, with all his presidential duties, to also oversee a myriad of military details. Marshall ended by telling the president that doing both jobs himself would be beyond the powers of a superman, but Roosevelt was unmoved.

Exiting a meeting of the Senate Foreign Relations Committee, 1939.
From left: Admiral William Leahy, chief of naval operations, and
Sumner Welles, undersecretary of state.

In early April 1942 a change of government in Vichy France precipitated a diplomatic crisis that forced Roosevelt to recall Leahy. Before he departed, however, his wife, Louise, had to have a hysterectomy, which could not be postponed until they returned to the United States. Two days after the operation (April 21), she suffered an embolism and died with her husband at her side. For unknown reasons, Roosevelt had by this time changed his mind and agreed to appoint Leahy as chairman of the Joint Chiefs. Though he offered him the job, Roosevelt neglected to inform Leahy of what he expected of him, what his role was, or even where his office was. Bewildered, Leahy went to see Marshall.

Marshall took him over to the Public Health Building where the chiefs of staff met and where the British had their offices. Marshall had already placed a desk in the office and introduced the new chairman of the Joint Chiefs to his secretary. After Marshall explained what he considered the chairman's role, Leahy was unsure if that was what the president intended, or how he would go about claiming such a position. As Marshall explained, "I took him in the room where the chiefs of staff met and showed him the chair where he should sit, which was unoccupied at the time because it was at the end of the table . . . I proposed to him when the next meeting came, he just calmly sit down in that chair."

King was not happy with this fait accompli, but there was little he could do about it. Leahy did not, however, stay long in the office Marshall set aside for him. Within a short time, he began functioning as Roosevelt's personal chief of staff, and moved his office into the White House. He still presided over the meetings of the Joint Chiefs, but in addition to translating the chiefs' deliberations to the president he began taking on an increasing number of political and diplomatic duties. Despite this, Marshall always considered Leahy the crucial piece of the Joint Chiefs machinery that kept everything else running smoothly. Later he said: "It would never have done to have tried to have gone right straight through the struggle with Admiral King in a secondary position and me as the senior, where I was also the senior of the air. And it was quite essential that we have a neutral agency at the top."

Throughout the war Marshall paid considerable attention to his relationship with King. It is doubtful that anyone else could have managed the volatile admiral. Even Eisenhower, another general with a unique capacity for handling prima donnas, found himself at his wits' end in dealing with King, recording in his diary: "One thing that might help us win this war is to get someone to shoot King. He's the antithesis of cooperation, a deliberately rude person, which means he is a mental bully." Eisenhower also recorded that "King . . . is an arbitrary, stubborn type, with not too much brains and a tendency toward bullying his juniors," but tempered that judgment with what he believed the crucial point: "But I think he wants to fight, which is vastly encouraging."

Marshall develops the picture better in his account of an incident from early in the war:

Admiral King came to see me without my knowing he was coming, and was received by this young woman in the reception room ... [I] was with the foreign minister of Australia who was a very difficult man to deal with. Admiral King was left waiting in the reception room. I couldn't even give a pause in the conversation to send word out or have them interrupt me to tell me Admiral King was there.

Whatever it was when I got rid of him—the Australian—and went over to greet King, I found he had left in a huff and had gone back to his office at the other end of the Munitions Building. So I went right over personally and was shown with military formality into King's office. I don't know—remember—just what his attitude was when he greeted me. But I said, "Now I've come over to talk to you right away and explain what was happening." And I did explain it. "Now," I said, "I think this is very important, because if you and I began fighting at the very start of the war, what in the world will the public have to say about us?" I said, "They won't accept it for a minute. So we just take our tickets and walk out. We can't afford to fight. So we ought to find a way to get along together." King listened to this and sat silent for a minute or two and turned to me and said, "Well, you have been very magnanimous in coming over here the way you have. And we will see if we can get along, and I think we can." And we did get along. We had one or two pretty mean fights, but anyone has that.

Their personal differences aside, Roosevelt now had in place the military team with which he would win the war. It had taken Lincoln three bloody years to find a general capable of leading Northern armies to victory. Many in Washington fully expected that Roosevelt would encounter many of the same problems Lincoln had, and their one hope was that FDR would not take three years to get it right. That Roosevelt and America could so easily find the right men to fill the Joint Chiefs positions as well as other senior leaders is extraordinary when one considers how small a manpower pool there was to work with. When General George C. Marshall became chief of staff, the U.S. Army ranked nineteenth in the world, cozily snuggled in between Bulgaria and Portugal. Its 174,000 men were poorly trained and scattered all over the country. From that meager beginning, in just a few years, the Army alone grew to over seven million men. Churchill, clearly astounded at the time, said of this expansion, "It remains to me a mystery as yet unexplained how the very small staffs which the United States kept during the years of peace were able not only to build up the armies . . . but also to find the leaders [to guide] those armies on a scale incomparably greater than anything that was prepared for or even dreamed of." Moreover, although the Navy was larger and in slightly better shape than the Army, it was still a mere fraction of the colossus that closed in on Japan in late 1944.

Churchill's mystification notwithstanding, the success of the huge expansion of American military power was no accident. It was the clear result of the lifelong preparations of the three men who eventually rose to the top of their respective services, and who collectively formed the Joint Chiefs of Staff. Over the years a myth has arisen that the United States was lucky that the system placed precisely the right persons at or near the top of their respective services, just when the nation needed them most. In this telling, the Joint Chiefs were selfless servants who happened to be there when the call came. The reality is a bit more prosaic, as all these men courted advancement and power with a singularly myopic focus. Interestingly, the cult of the selfless officer going without complaint to wherever he is sent has centered itself on Marshall. But the historical record is clear, and it does not correspond with the myth. Throughout his career, no one more assiduously pushed himself forward than Marshall, always with one goal: pinning on general's stars as a stepping-stone to being named Army chief of staff.

It was not that he made a spectacle of pushing himself forward, as that would have been self-defeating, as his many rivals discovered. Rather, Marshall understood how to exploit certain positions to ensure the right people took note. Moreover, he understood that there were but a few crucial levers of power that one needed to push and he had a knack for spotting these levers—persons of true influence—and then ruthlessly exploiting them. That Marshall became the postwar paragon of selfless service is a result of a single moment: when FDR asked him whether he wanted to command the invasion of northern Europe (D-Day), Marshall, despite a deep yearning for the job, told the president that he wanted him to "feel free to act in whatever way he felt was to the best interest of the country and to his satisfaction and not in any way consider my feelings. I would cheerfully go whatever way he wanted me to go." He was probably surprised when Roosevelt took him at his word and handed Eisenhower the command. After all, he had made his true desires plain to the two men most responsible for making him chief of staff: Harry Hopkins and Jimmy Byrnes. The difference this time was that both men now thought it best to keep Marshall on the Joint Chiefs.

That Marshall, King, and Arnold had done whatever was necessary to advance themselves does not weigh against their character. No officer rises to become a general or admiral without a large dose of personal ambition from the outset. This rarely means they are willing to be toadies to their superiors, and in the cases of the war's Joint Chiefs nothing could be further from the truth. Nor were they averse to risk. In fact, all of them often took positions on crucial issues and accepted assignments that could easily have ended their careers at an early stage. While career advancement was never far from their minds, and each of them assiduously tended to their future prospects, none was ever reluctant to speak truth to power, or anyone else who they deemed needed a good dose of candor.

All three men had another trait in common, one that was clearly visible early in their military careers, but became more pronounced as they reached the pinnacles of power: they were ruthless in pursuit of a goal. Fighting a war in which each of them truly believed the very fabric of civilization was at risk brought this trait to the fore. Although they often exhibited kindness and warmth in private settings, in their professional capacity this softer side was seldom in evidence. Instead, all three appeared to revel in being known as hard and demanding taskmasters. In a famous but apocryphal story, King, when asked why he was saved from retirement to command the U.S. Navy, supposedly replied, "When they get in trouble they send for the sons-of-bitches." He later denied saying this, but added that he would have if he had thought of it. As for Marshall, when asked about how he was going to select officers for high command, he replied, "I am going to put these men to the severest tests which I can devise . . . I am going to ask them more than human beings should be required to deliver . . . Those that stand up to the punishment will be pushed ahead. Those who fail are out at the first sign of faltering." And finally there was Arnold, of whom it was often said, "No one ever stayed around to disappoint him twice."

* * *

The Joint Chiefs were formed, but that was only a first step toward winning a war the Allies were currently losing. Marshall got to the root of America's problem in a single observation: "The Army used to have all the time in the world and no money; now we've got all the money and no time." America was not quite beginning the war from a standing start, but it was not far removed. Axis armies were on the march and there was not much the United States could do to stop them.

27

STRIKING BACK

O UT OF THE DESPAIR AND DARKNESS CAME A SINGLE BEAM OF light that would have consequences far beyond what anyone imagined at the time. Soon after Pearl Harbor, Roosevelt, realizing the American people needed a morale boost, asked his military chiefs if there was some way to strike back at Japan. Arnold and King immediately put their staffs to work on the problem. Captain F. S. Low, working on the Navy's operations staff, suggested a strike with the Air Force's B-25 bombers, though no one was certain they could take off from a carrier flight deck. When King brought the question to Arnold, he answered with an enthusiastic yes, and said he would begin training the flight crews immediately. Though Roosevelt was kept abreast of the planning, he was not given the operational details as to exactly when the strike would take place.

On April 1, 1942, sixteen B-25s were loaded onto the carrier *Hornet* at Alameda, California, which then sailed out to join the waiting Task Force 16, commanded by Admiral William Halsey. The strike, considered suicidal by many, was led by Lieutenant Colonel Jimmy Doolittle. Arnold considered him a natural choice. He was a fearless airman and a scholar, who would finish the war commanding the Eighth Air Force in Britain. After Task Force 16 was sighted by a Japanese fishing vessel, Halsey ordered an immediate takeoff, while the *Hornet* was still 650 miles from Tokyo.

Doolittle headed for Japan, as the fleet turned for home. His plane struck at approximately noon, with succeeding aircraft arriving a few minutes later. Their attack was almost uncontested, and the planes flew on to China, with foul weather and distance working against them. None of the aircraft made it to an airfield. Out of the eighty participants, sixty-nine escaped death or capture by the Japanese, three were killed in plane crashes, and eight were captured—three of whom were executed and one died in captivity. Doolittle, knowing that he had lost every aircraft in his command, believed he had failed and expected a court-martial when he returned to the United States. His country, delighted that they had finally struck at Japan, saw it differently and awarded him the Congressional Medal of Honor.

Roosevelt, while working with Sam Rosenman and his secretary, Grace Tully, on a fireside chat at Hyde Park, was called to the phone to hear the news. Grinning, Roosevelt told his two assistants that a radio message had been intercepted saying that Japan had been bombed. Rosenman wanted to know how that was possible, but Roosevelt demurred for a time. Explaining that the press would soon be asking the same question, Rosenman suggested telling them that the planes had come from Shangri-La—the mythical Tibetan land depicted in James Hilton's *Lost Horizon*. Roosevelt liked the idea and called his press secretary, Steve Early, to tell him what he would tell the journalists.

The raid had caused little physical damage, but its psychological effects were profound. In America, news of the raid gave the nation's morale—sagging under the unrelenting bad news out of the Pacific—a huge and much needed boost. But its effect on the Japanese high command changed the course of the war. Embarrassed by an attack they had promised the emperor could never happen, the Japanese military reacted furiously. In China, it is estimated that 250,000 persons in the areas that helped American fliers were killed. In Japan, General Sugiyama, who had personally made the promise to the emperor, in a cold fury threatened to have every air defense commander court-martialed. Most crucially, after the Doolittle Raid, the Imperial General Staff approved a plan—one that previously had only their lukewarm support—to attack Midway Island. As one Japanese naval officer later stated: "So far as Combined Fleet was concerned, the [Doolittle] raid steeled its determination to press for early execution of the [Midway] operations." The battle of Midway was still almost two months distant, but because of the Doolittle Raid the Japanese committed themselves to an operation that turned the tide of the Pacific war.

* * *

In Washington, however, other concerns dominated, and the Doolittle Raid was soon in the rearview mirror. Despite the constant requirement to rush all available forces to the Pacific in hopes of stemming the Japanese tide, Germany remained the priority. How best to get at Germany became the most crucial strategic debate of 1942. Although Marshall and King both hated the idea of invading North Africa, both had promised they would examine the potential for such an operation. With no other operations on the table, their staffs went at it with a vengeance. For approximately two months after Arcadia, the Joint Chiefs' planning staffs were consumed with planning for Operation GYMNAST (now often referred to as SUPER-GYMNAST): the invasion of North Africa. Marshall was originally informed that the earliest possible D-Day for a North African invasion was February 4, 1942 (D-Day at this time meant the day the transports would be loaded in the United States, and not the actual day of the invasion). As increasing amounts of shipping were diverted to the Pacific, the date slipped to April 1, and then to May 25. Further studies, after the British Eighth Army had suffered another reverse, convinced the planners that GYMNAST was impractical for 1942. The newly formed Combined Chiefs staff section agreed with this finding, as did Marshall and King. What they could not figure out was how to present their unwelcome conclusion to Roosevelt and Churchill. On March 3, Marshall and King decided to defer any action until they could consider how best to inform the president, who was looking to show the public American troops on the offensive and consequently was becoming increasingly fond of Churchill's North African proposal.

But Roosevelt and Churchill were already moving ahead of the Combined Chiefs. On March 4, Churchill cabled Roosevelt with his assessment of the shipping situation, and stated: "I think we must agree to recognize that GYMNAST is out of the question for several months." The following day Churchill cabled again: "I am entirely with you about the need for GYMNAST, but the check that Auchinleck [commanding the British forces facing Rommel] has received and the shipping stringency seem to impose obstinate and long delays." Roosevelt, in two long messages summarizing his commanders' views of the war situation and immediate future developments, agreed that GYMNAST must be postponed.

This, however, did not let the chiefs off the hook. If GYMNAST was out, they needed a substitute operation, as telling Roosevelt that 1942 was a buildup year, with the possibility of major action in 1943, was unpalatable. Eisenhower's Operations Division thought they had the answer. Writing in his diary in late January Eisenhower complained: "We've got to go to Europe and fight, and we've got to quit wasting resources all over the world, and still worse, wasting time . . . We've got to begin slugging with air in the West followed by a land attack as soon as possible." As early as February, Eisenhower had forwarded a written study to Marshall stating the need to develop a definite Anglo-American plan for operations against northwest Europe. On March 25, Eisenhower handed Marshall a memorandum, outlining the necessity of an invasion of northwest Europe at the earliest possible date, and urging the chief of staff to push the president and the British chiefs toward such a decision. Marshall needed little convincing.

That very afternoon, Hopkins, Stimson, Knox, Marshall, and King met with Roosevelt, where Marshall hoped to convince the president that the 1942 priority be directed toward operations in northern Europe. Stimson was onboard, writing in his diary over a month earlier: "In my talks with McCloy I have come to the conclusion that it would be a good thing psychologically if we could press hard enough on the expeditionary force through Great Britain to make the Germans keep looking over their shoulder in their fight with Russia." He had even said as much to the president several times. This view was seconded by Hopkins, who wrote to Roosevelt on March 14: "I doubt any single thing is as important this summer as getting some sort of front against Germany." Roosevelt had himself sent a cable to Churchill outlining the advantages of a cross-Channel invasion, asking the prime minister to "think about it." The one uncertain element was King, who despite giving lip service to "Europe first" was already telling naval planners that protecting the lines of communications to Australia required the seizure of South Pacific islands that could later be used as springboards for further offensives. In other words, if Marshall had no immediate plans to use his divisions, then King wanted them. In fact, he wanted those divisions even if Marshall did have plans for them.

Stimson and Marshall, believing Roosevelt was primed to listen to plans for operations in Europe, were staggered when the president launched into a brief of the world situation that indicated he planned to send military forces on the "wildest kind of dispersion debauch." But after he spoke at length about future Mediterranean operations, an idea Stimson considered him "much charmed with," Marshall managed to edge into the discussion. He gave what Stimson thought a "fine presentation," which apparently convinced Roosevelt to support a priority on operations in northern Europe. Toward the end of the meeting, Roosevelt even suggested that Marshall turn the whole matter over to the Combined Chiefs of Staff planners to refine the idea. Hopkins quickly interceded, telling Roosevelt that the combined staffs would "pull it to pieces and emasculate it." Instead he recommended that the American Joint Staff perfect the idea and that Marshall take it directly to England and present it to Churchill and his military chiefs. Roosevelt agreed.

When the plan—now called the Marshall Memorandum—was completed, Marshall took it to the White House. Joining him, for an afternoon meeting, were Stimson, Knox, King, and Arnold. After making his case as to why northern Europe should be the focus of all American operations, Marshall laid out his proposal for the invasion. In simplified terms the plan was broken into three parts: The first, Operation BOLERO, consisted of the buildup of at least thirty American divisions in Britain. The second part was Operation ROUNDUP (later named OVERLORD), which was the actual invasion of northern France and was scheduled for the spring of 1943. A third operation, SLEDGEHAMMER, was a smaller version of ROUNDUP, which could be launched with as few as a half-dozen divisions. This last operation was originally supposed to be carried out only if an imminent Soviet collapse necessitated a sacrifice to relieve pressure on the Russian front. Marshall had no confidence these troops would last long, but he hoped they could distract the Germans enough to allow the Russians to stabilize their front. Despite this sentiment, as presidential pressure to launch an offensive somewhere or anywhere before the end of 1942 grew, Marshall began viewing SLEDGEHAMMER as a viable alternative to invading North Africa (TORCH).

Roosevelt accepted the plan and told both Marshall and Hopkins to leave for London as soon as possible. Roosevelt then sent a short note to Churchill warning him that he was sending his emissaries. Hopkins also cabled Churchill begging him to "please start the fire" at Chequers, in the hope that he could avoid having to wear a coat indoors, as he had during his previous visit.

* * *

Hopkins, Marshall, and two aides left for Britain on April 4. They were joined by a Navy doctor Roosevelt sent along to ensure Hopkins's good health. The five of them had the huge Pan Am Clipper to themselves, so the journey was a leisurely one. Upon arrival, Hopkins and Marshall met with Churchill at 10 Downing Street, where Marshall laid out his plan in broad outlines. At dinner that evening Marshall presented more details, this time with the new head of the British Imperial Staff, General Alan Brooke, in attendance. Brooke was unimpressed by either the plan or Marshall, recording in his diary: "I liked what I saw of Marshall, a pleasant and easy man to get on with, rather over-filled with his own importance, but I should not put him down as a great man." Marshall was equally unimpressed, telling Hopkins that Brooke might be a good fighting man but he "lacked Dill's brains." Historians have often related that during the war each man changed his professional opinion of the other for the better. If this is true, there is scant evidence of it in the contemporary documents. Rather, the documentary record clearly shows that the impressions each made upon the other in April 1942 lasted throughout the war.

The next day, Hopkins conferred with Churchill while Marshall spent the day with the British chiefs of staff. Hopkins had the more unpleasant day. Churchill was furious over what he perceived as increasing American meddling in India. As Churchill was fighting to preserve the empire and one of Roosevelt's stated war aims was ending all colonial empires, this was a constant sore spot in the two men's relationship. Whenever the topic arose Churchill became incensed. Thankfully, Roosevelt was always wise enough to retreat before the fissures in their relationship ruptured. Hopkins, once again, smoothed matters over and spent much of the rest of the day convincing Churchill of the seriousness of Marshall's proposals. In doing so he related Roosevelt's qualms over the United States placing a vast army in Britain, only for it to sit idle for over a year. He also constantly harped on America's willingness to run great risks to help the Soviet Union. Churchill, convinced that the Americans were serious about a possible invasion of northern France as early as September 1942, decided to play along for now. As he saw it, the Americans could be forced to see strategic sense later. In the meantime, Churchill, afraid that any objection from him might cause the Americans to take a renewed interest in the Pacific, told Hopkins and Marshall what they wanted to hear.

While Hopkins worked on Churchill, Marshall did the same with Brooke and the rest of the British chiefs of staff. After masterfully outlining the basics of his memorandum, Marshall thought he was making progress in swaying his British counterparts toward a 1943 invasion, and quite possibly one in 1942. Brooke, however, was adamant that a 1942 invasion would turn into a slaughter, one involving mostly British troops because few Americans would be in Britain before the end of the year. He was backed by Lord Mountbatten, recently made a vice admiral, a lieutenant general, and an air marshal by a prime minister eager to ensure that no branch of the service could snub him. Mountbatten spent most of his time pointing out the logistical impossibility of supporting several divisions across the Channel. But only when Chief of Air Staff Charles Portal said he had strong reservations as to whether the RAF could maintain air cover over the invasion beaches did Marshall comprehend the depth of British distaste for such an adventure. As Churchill's personal physician, Lord Moran, explained to Marshall in confidence, he was not just fighting this war, he was also "fighting against the 'ghosts of the Somme.'" In short, Marshall had failed to convince the British chiefs, although they still gave every appearance of being open to a 1943 invasion.

At Chequers that weekend, the prime minister seemed much more disposed to Marshall's ideas than had his chiefs. Churchill, by this time, had also beaten his own chiefs into submission, getting them to officially give their full agreement to Marshall's memorandum, but withholding a final decision for a 1942 invasion until they saw how developments played out in the Soviet Union. Overjoyed by the support, Marshall immediately phoned his deputy chief of staff, General Thomas Handy, to tell him that the British had "virtually accepted the proposals I submitted to him." He had no idea that Churchill was merely playing for time and making agreements he had no intention of following through on.

At the evening's dinner Churchill continued the charade. Surrounded by his military advisers, he announced that he had no hesitation about Marshall's plan. He did, however, ask for whatever support the Americans could give him in the Indian Ocean, where the Japanese had practically wiped out Britain's naval presence. As Churchill announced his and his chiefs' complete unanimity toward plans for 1943, Marshall detected none of the reservations voiced in previous discussions. The next day he cabled Stimson that the prime minister was "solidly behind us." Unfortunately for later Allied relations, neither Churchill nor Brooke meant a single word of what they were telling Marshall.

General Hastings "Pug" Ismay, secretary of the Chiefs of Staff Committee, later said, "Our American friends went happily homeward under the mistaken impression we had committed ourselves to both Roundup and Sledgehammer." Ismay believed that Churchill and the British chiefs should have "come clean much sooner than we did . . . and told Marshall that an invasion could be undertaken only when there was a cast iron certainty of success." Brooke, who never displayed any qualms about lying to the Americans, recorded in his diary: "He [Marshall] I should think is a good general at raising armies and providing the necessary links between the military and the political worlds. But his strategic ability does not impress me at all! In fact, in many ways he is a very dangerous man whilst being a very charming one!" After further discussions with Marshall, Brooke recorded:

> I discovered that he had not studied any of the strategic implications of a cross Channel invasion. . . . I asked him to imagine that his landing had been safely carried out and asked him what his plans would then be. Would he move east towards Germany exposing his southern flank? Would he move south to liberate France and expose his left flank? Would he move east to secure some lodgment? I found that he had not begun to consider any form of plan of action, and had not even begun to visualize the problems that would face an army after landing.

Brooke never changed his opinion, stating that throughout the war he "appreciated that his [Marshall's] strategic ability was of the poorest. A great man, a great gentleman and great organizer, but definitely not a strategist."

Over seven decades later, what are we to make of this? Even today army officers are raised in a tradition that reveres Marshall as the epitome of the "soldier-statesman" and the great architect of victory. It is true that Marshall deserves most of the accolades that have been heaped upon him. But it is equally true that Brooke's criticisms are, on the whole, correct. For all his great qualities, Marshall was not a great strategist, or even a mediocre one. His fixation on invading northern Europe as soon as possible is an egregious example of his lack of capacity in this regard. Judging from the dismal early performance of American combat forces in North Africa, there is little doubt that if America's barely trained and combat-inexperienced divisions had been thrown into France in 1942, rather than North Africa, they would have been slaughtered. Moreover, the veteran Wehrmacht troops already in France likely would have done so without any disruption of German efforts in Russia. The United States would have been able to send more and presumably better-trained divisions into France in 1943, but they still would have lacked battle experience. While the Wehrmacht might have had somewhat more trouble dealing with them, it is difficult to believe they would have lasted too much longer than a force sent a year earlier. Senior British officers may have been dissuaded by the "ghosts of the Somme," but, in this instance, those ghosts were giving wise counsel.

What Marshall never appears to have considered as he argued the necessity of "a sacrifice for the common good" is what such a sacrifice would have done to already fragile civilian morale. Even more crucially, a 1942 setback or even one in 1943 would have cost the American forces the best of their newly raised divisions, and exhausted the carefully husbanded reserves of the British Empire. If these forces had been lost it would certainly have been years before there was another Anglo-American force of sufficient size and quality to try again, assuming the stomach remained for such a perilous endeavor. In the meantime, Germany would have been free to send dozens of divisions east, where they could have turned the tide in their struggle with Russia. In that event, Stalin, facing a threat of increasing magnitude, and knowing there would not be a second front for years, if ever, would have had every reason to make a separate peace on the best terms available.

But did Marshall's inadequacies as a strategist matter? Probably not, for two reasons. The first was that America did not need a master strategist at the top. For one, Roosevelt was his own grand strategist. It was he who set the overall goals and the political direction of the war. As such, what he required from his senior military commanders was the capacity to organize, train, and equip the massive forces the nation was raising; in short, the nation needed a superb military technocrat. In this capacity, Marshall excelled. He also commanded the respect of every senior Army officer, as well as the firmness to keep these aggressive and highly opinionated men all pulling in the same direction. Finally, it is hard to imagine any other officer, either British or American, who could have managed his brethren on the Anglo-American Combined Chiefs with the success Marshall did.

Second, the American military had developed and continues to sustain a system that is extremely effective at warfare without requiring the rise of a strategic genius. Rather, it relies on a "system of genius" that prepares many hundreds of officers to operate at the strategic level. Here these officers can push their ideas into an open system of discussion and debate. The surviving plans and schemes flow up to senior commanders, where they are appraised and sometimes adopted. But even at the most senior levels every plan is fought over until eventually there is an optimal solution. This is what Marshall was doing in London, pushing his idea. For the moment, he had carried the day, but the debate, much to his chagrin, was far from over. Eventually Marshall would be forced to give up his plans for a 1942 invasion, and then a 1943 invasion. Other priorities arose to replace them, and in hindsight the Allies hugely benefited from the delays in conducting Marshall's scheme. Compare this to the closed system that by 1942 pervaded Nazi Germany, where one man made almost every military decision of consequence, and debate was either limited or completely stifled. History is replete with military geniuses who came to ruin. It is far better, in the long run, to have a system of genius that eventually gets to the right answer, than to wait for a military genius who will almost invariably lead his forces to destruction. In the final analysis, the qualities that the nation and its military needed to wage a modern global war were precisely those Marshall had in abundance.

28

DESERTING THE BEAR

O N APRIL 18, 1942, THE SAME DAY OF DOOLITTLE'S RAID ON TOKYO, Hopkins and Marshall arrived back in Washington. As soon as Hopkins finished briefing Roosevelt on all that had happened in London, the president called Churchill. He first congratulated the prime minister on his agreeing to Marshall's proposals and for corralling unanimity of opinion from his military chiefs. Churchill, not yet willing to upset the applecart, failed to mention his reservations. Roosevelt then shifted the discussion to a message he had received from Stalin alerting him that he was sending Russian foreign minister Molotov to both London and Washington for consultations. An ebullient Roosevelt was already becoming excited at the prospect of assuring Molotov that a second front in Europe would soon open. Thus, Churchill's deception of Marshall and Hopkins was about to be unknowingly extended through Roosevelt to Stalin, with grave consequences for Allied unity.

Molotov was coming to get an Allied commitment for the two things Stalin most wanted: more war matériel, and a second front. At the time, three routes were available for supplying Russia. The first, crossing the northern Pacific and Siberia, had been left unmolested by the Japanese in hopes of keeping Russia neutral in their war against America. Still, this was a slow route, as it meant moving supplies literally across the world. The second route was through Iran, but in early 1942 only a trickle of supplies was coming through that route. In 1943 this would become the preferred route, but that had to wait until the Mediterranean was secured, the port of Basra enlarged, and the rail infrastructure from Basra to the fighting front improved. In the meantime, the bulk of supplies traveling to Russia came through Murmansk or Archangel, on the edge of the Arctic Circle.

Getting to Murmansk, however, entailed a major British naval operation and was fraught with risk, not just from submarines but also from land-based German airpower and surface vessels operating out of Norway. Soon after Hopkins and Marshall returned from London, Roosevelt cabled Churchill asking him to make a greater effort to get supplies through to the USSR. Churchill replied that they were already making every effort, but losses were severe and he was not sure how much more the overextended Royal Navy could do. In any event, the British succeeded in pushing a major convoy (PQ 16) through to Murmansk and Archangel in late May 1942. But the cost was high: seven of the original thirty-five merchant ships were lost, most to air attacks. A second convoy (PQ 17), which left Iceland in July, was not even that fortunate. When incorrect intelligence reached the First Sea Lord, Admiral Dudley Pound, that the *Tirpitz* had left its moorings, he feared that the massive German battleship was bearing down on PQ 17. Pound summoned his staff and asked for their opinions. They almost unanimously advised the admiral to maintain the escort and not scatter the convoy. Pound ignored them, and ordered the escorts to abandon the merchantmen and for the convoy to scatter. At 8:00 A.M. the next day (July 5) the slaughter began. For three days, German aircraft and subs sought out and attacked their fleeing prey. When it was over only eleven of the original thirty-four merchant ships made it to the USSR, delivering a mere 70,000 tons of matériel out of the more than 200,000 tons the convoy had started with.

When news of the disaster reached Washington, King was enraged. He had previously started building Task Force 39 in Britain, around the carrier USS *Wasp* and the battleship USS *Washington*. He had planned to use this task force for escort duties in the Arctic. But now King believed Pound could not be trusted to properly employ it, and he ordered the task force withdrawn and sent to the Pacific. King's reaction was mild compared to that of Stalin, who refused to believe that two dozen ships from a single convoy could have been lost, and openly accused his allies of lying about the number of ships they were sending. Another seed of distrust was sown.

Supplies were important, but what Stalin wanted above all was a commitment for a second front as soon as possible. Molotov first tried to get such a pledge in London, but was given little besides assurances that planning was under way. Rather than promise an invasion, Churchill related how the simple threat of an assault was already tying down forty German divisions in the west. He went on to discuss the powerful air armadas that Britain and the United States were building, which would soon start laying waste to German cities. Churchill was ready to promise everything except a second front. Molotov left for Washington, hoping to do better there.

As Molotov departed, Churchill cabled the president, to tell him how careful he and Eden had been in avoiding a promise for a second front, apparently believing Roosevelt would welcome such information. He also informed FDR that his staff officers were ceaselessly working on plans for BOLERO, SLEDGEHAMMER, and ROUNDUP, but tamped down expectations by stating that "Dickie [Lord Mountbatten] will explain to you the difficulties of 1942 when he arrives." After mentioning the possibility of invading Norway, so as to ease resupply of the Russians, Churchill concluded with the idea he wanted Roosevelt focused on: "We must never let GYMNAST [North Africa] pass from our minds."

Churchill was not the only one pushing back against an early invasion of northern Europe. In Washington, a worried King was demanding that at least 215 more aircraft be sent to Australia, along with more combat troops. Even Roosevelt was asking if 25,000 more troops (one and a half combat divisions) could be sent to the Pacific. FDR backed off when Marshall told him that because of shipping distances, sending one and a half divisions to Australia meant delaying the departure of three divisions to Britain, making a 1942 invasion impossible and limiting the prospects for a 1943 invasion. King was still voicing his support for BOLERO (the buildup of American forces in Britain), stating: "There must be no undue delay in the deployment of the main effort." But in the next breath he declared that he did not believe the forces in the Pacific were sufficient to hold off a determined Japanese assault. He went on: "As urgent as the mounting of BOLERO may be, the Pacific problem is no less so, and it is certainly the most urgent—it must be faced now!"

Marshall countered that he saw no need to waste troops garrisoning every speck of land in the Pacific, where the soldiers would spend their days fending off flies without contributing to the war effort. After reminding Roosevelt that the British had agreed to BOLERO under the impression that it was going to be America's main effort, he said: "If such is not the case, the British should be formally notified that the recent London agreement must be cancelled." Replying in writing, on May 6, Roosevelt said that "he did not want BOLERO slowed down." FDR then stated that his principal military objective was helping the Russians who were "killing more Germans and destroying more Axis matériel than all the twenty-five united nations put together." As far as Roosevelt was concerned, the Atlantic would be the focus of offensive operations, and the Pacific would remain a "holding operation." He did, however, leave the door open for limited Pacific offensives to "hasten the attrition of Japanese arms." He concluded by declaring that "I regard it as essential that active operations be conducted in 1942 . . . the necessities of the case call for action in 1942—not 1943."

Even as Marshall was applying pressure to maintain BOLERO, as well as increasingly favoring an invasion of France in 1942, General Somervell, in a conversation with the president, voiced concern that there would not be enough landing ships in 1942 or possibly even 1943 to launch such an invasion. After hearing this, Roosevelt asked Somervell to prepare a study on "what we could do and not do by September 1942, as well as what we could do or not do by April of 1943." Roosevelt affirmed that he was not interested in any operation past April, telling Somervell that if a cross-Channel invasion was not possible before April of 1943, "it might be better to consider some other operation."

Such was the situation when Molotov arrived at the White House at 4:00 P.M. on May 29. As the president greeted him, a valet took his bag to his room, where upon opening it he was shocked to find a loaded pistol lying beside a loaf of bread. Molotov, already known as "Iron Pants" for his ability to outsit other negotiators, had apparently come prepared for a long siege. The Secret Service ordered the valet to leave the weapon alone and warned him to be careful that it was not used on him. The early meetings, where Hull was the main cabinet participant, were cordial and mostly given over to secondary concerns. But the next day Molotov met with Roosevelt, Hopkins, Marshall, and King. Notably, now that the minor business was finished, Secretary of State Hull was no longer invited. When it came to important matters, Roosevelt was already comfortable acting as his own secretary of state, but by excluding Knox and Stimson to deal directly with his military chiefs he was demonstrating an increasing willingness to take a direct hand in military operations.

Molotov got immediately down to business, asking point-blank when Russia could expect an Allied offensive that would draw off forty German divisions. After requesting a straight answer, Molotov urged Roosevelt to remember that the difficulties of such an invasion would not lessen in 1943 and that the chances of success were actually better at present while the Russians still had a solid front.

Roosevelt put the question to General Marshall, asking if developments were clear enough for him to promise Mr. Stalin a second front. Marshall with no hesitation replied, "Yes." A beaming Roosevelt then authorized Molotov to tell Stalin that there would be a second front that year. Unexpectedly, Marshall then began backing off, warning Roosevelt that a firm 1942 date had many factors—primarily a lack of landing craft—working against it. Both Marshall and Roosevelt then explored the possibility of reducing Lend-Lease supplies to the USSR, to rapidly build up forces in Britain for a second front. Molotov balked, explaining that a second front would be worthless if the first front (Russia) had already been shattered. After a bit more bristling, Molotov relented somewhat and said any aid reduction must be accompanied by Roosevelt's absolute promise that there would be a second front in 1942. Roosevelt hedged, telling Molotov that he fully "expected" to establish a second front in 1942, and that Lord Mountbatten was already on his way across the Atlantic to finalize planning for the invasion. Molotov almost certainly knew that Roosevelt's "expectation" of an invasion was a long way from an absolute promise, just as Roosevelt was aware that Mountbatten was not coming to help plan a second front in France. Rather, he was coming to kill it.

As the visit wound down Molotov was given a joint communiqué to read. He took objection to its failure to mention the president's promise, or, for that matter, even his expectation. Not to be put off, Molotov took it upon himself to make a change, writing that a "full understanding was reached with regard to the urgent tasks of creating a second front in 1942." Marshall objected and took his concerns to Hopkins. Though he still supported a 1942 invasion (SLEDGEHAMMER), he wanted all specific dates removed. Hopkins agreed and went to Roosevelt. But the president, looking to boost Russian morale, overrode the objections, allowing the communiqué to stay as Molotov desired.

With Roosevelt's promise in hand, Molotov returned to London, with a fresh demand: that Churchill also put in writing the promise of a second front. After once again listing everything the British were doing to tie down German divisions, and keep half of all German airpower occupied, Churchill caved and agreed to a communiqué with precisely the same promise as Roosevelt had made. Molotov might have thought he had two promises in hand for a 1942 invasion, but all he really had was Roosevelt's and Churchill's "understanding" that such an invasion was desirable, which meant precisely nothing. As if to underscore this deception, Churchill handed a departing Molotov an aide-mémoire for Stalin that stated his support for an immediate second front, but added the caveat that "all was conditional and nothing was guaranteed." When Molotov returned to Moscow, he found Stalin undeceived. The Soviet leader did not believe a word of his allies' promises. It was the beginning of a major rupture in Allied unity, far worse in its long-term effects than Churchill's earlier deception of Marshall about a 1942 invasion.

29

STOPPING THE TIDE

W**ITH THEIR SOUTHERN ADVANCE TEMPORARILY HALTED BY THE** Battle of the Coral Sea, and still humiliated by Doolittle's raid, the Japanese Imperial Headquarters gambled all on a final decisive battle in the mid-Pacific. In many ways, their plan was a mirror image of the U.S. Navy's prewar Plan Orange, which called for an American fleet to advance across the Pacific and force the Japanese into a winner-takes-all showdown. Now Yamamoto was betting that if he could seize Midway, the U.S. Navy would have to risk all attempting to retake it. He planned to greet the onrushing U.S. fleet with an annihilating ambush that would break the back of American naval power in the Pacific. As the Japanese fleet sailed, Yamamoto was unaware that American intelligence had cracked his codes and identified Midway as the point of attack. Instead of arriving at Midway and setting an ambush, Yamamoto walked into one of American making.

At Pearl Harbor, Admiral Nimitz was scraping up everything available for the climactic battle, including the severely damaged *Yorktown*. When the *Yorktown* returned to Pearl Harbor, after the Battle of the Coral Sea, experts estimated that repairs would take months. But repair crews went to work with a vengeance, and seventy-two hours after its arrival, the *Yorktown* steamed out of the harbor, with dozens of welding flares marking her passage. On June 4, a running battle commenced and did not end until the early morning hours of June 7. When it was over, four Japanese carriers— *Akagi, Sorya, Kaga,* and *Hiryu*—were at the bottom of the Pacific. The fact that these carriers were all part of the force that had struck Pearl Harbor only six months before added much to American satisfaction with the result. Yamamoto, with his carriers lost, along with one cruiser sunk and another damaged, ordered a retreat. Unfortunately for the Americans, the *Yorktown,* despite a valiant struggle, went down after enduring two air strikes and a submarine attack.

Defeat at Midway upended all of Japan's immediate strategic plans. The emperor still commanded a formidable fighting force, but its offensive power was broken. From this point on, the Japanese would be on the strategic defensive, with the American Navy deciding on the location and timing of almost every future major battle. For King, this presented a dilemma. His continuous clamoring for additional forces was based on stopping a Japanese juggernaut threatening to expel the Allies from the Pacific. When that threat suddenly vanished, so did King's rationale for more assets. It was quite clear that he had all the ground forces required to hold the line. Further, the Navy was still lacking in its own offensive power, as the great ships Congress ordered built before America's entry into the war would not start joining the fleet until 1943. In the meantime, Marshall wanted every available soldier sent to the Atlantic. As Stimson wrote in his diary: "We could reverse our rush of reinforcements to the West Coast and send back the forces that we had diverted from BOLERO." Unwilling to see this happen, King began talking about an "offensive-defensive" that, while staying on the strategic defensive, allowed for some offensive actions aimed at keeping the Japanese off balance and preventing them from creating an impenetrable island barrier across the Pacific. MacArthur joined the chorus, requesting permission to start planning for a drive north on Japan's major base in the region: Rabaul. Without authorization, he began planning for an offensive requiring a force so extravagant that it would certainly forbid operations in any other theater in 1943.

Into this maelstrom of new strategic thinking came Lord Mountbatten, sent by Churchill to start the long process of walking the United States back from plans for a 1942 and, if possible, also from a 1943 invasion of France. Arriving on June 3, Mountbatten—Churchill's protégé and the British king's cousin—began a series of technical meetings with the Joint Staff the next morning. Employing all of his considerable charm, Mountbatten assured the Americans that British planning was rushing forward. Luckily for him, no one asked him about British preparations—which were nonexistent—as opposed to planning. As talks progressed, it dawned on Marshall and his staff that although Mountbatten was politely listening to American proposals, he was doing so only to better offer detailed lists of problems for consideration. He never offered solutions, and he time and again returned to the problem of a lack of landing craft, which he considered insurmountable in the near term.

On June 9, Mountbatten met with Roosevelt. Given the president's susceptibility to British schemes, King and Marshall were rightly worried about not having been invited. But it was not until Field Marshall Dill handed Marshall a copy of Mountbatten's report to the British Chiefs that they discovered how much they really had to worry about. Marshall was shocked at how far the president had shifted toward the British position—using American troops in North Africa. Roosevelt, in his way, thought he had held the line, telling Mountbatten that he did not want a million American soldiers sitting in England to find that a Russian collapse had made an invasion impossible. The president also voiced displeasure over sending American troops to Britain only to see a corresponding number of British troops depart to far corners of the world to prop up a tottering empire. But what caught Marshall's eye as he read the memo were the words "Don't forget Egypt."

For over six hours, Mountbatten had steadily worked on Roosevelt, making sure he knew that SLEDGEHAMMER had only the minutest chance of success, and even as a sacrifice to help the Russians it would fail, as the Germans already had over two dozen divisions in France and would not have to move any troops out of the USSR to defeat the invasion. Eventually, Mountbatten got what he wanted. If SLEDGEHAMMER and an early ROUNDUP (by April 1, 1943) were out of the question, Roosevelt said he was inclined to push his chiefs toward North Africa (GYMNAST) even if they despised the idea. Mountbatten departed the next day to deliver his impressions to Churchill.

Churchill jumped at the opportunity to seal the deal for North Africa, which he now needed more than ever, as Rommel was once again on the offensive and British forces, after losing hundreds of tanks, were falling back to the Libyan-Egyptian border. All Churchill could do was plead with his commander on the spot, General Claude Auchinleck, to hold as best he could and not give up Tobruk. In 1941, Tobruk had held off besieging Axis forces for an epic seven months, the successful conclusion of which had done much to help British morale. Then, "Fortress Tobruk" acted as a thorn in the side of Rommel's further advance, a role Churchill once again demanded of Tobruk's defenders. Even if Auchinleck succeeded in holding Tobruk, Churchill was increasingly convinced that if the British were ever going to defeat Rommel, it was essential that an American army land in his rear to threaten his base of supply. So, on June 13, having learned from Hopkins that Roosevelt was willing to see him, Churchill once again invited himself to the White House, arriving with his chiefs in tow on June 20.

Forewarned by Roosevelt during a meeting of his unofficial war council that the prime minister would be arriving in a few days' time, both Marshall and Stimson viewed the visit with some trepidation. Roosevelt was already speaking warmly about the prospects for GYMNAST, and both men feared it would take but a little push from Churchill to get FDR to order an American assault on North Africa. An anxious Stimson recorded: "It looked like he [Roosevelt] was going to jump the traces over all we had been doing in regard to BOLERO and to imperil really our strategy of the whole situation." Warned by Dill that Churchill had detected the president's strategic wavering, Marshall came to the war council meeting with a prepared paper, listing the advantages of an early invasion of France and the disadvantages of GYMNAST. Marshall, playing on Roosevelt's reluctance to do much to prop up the postwar British Empire, reminded FDR that the British viewed holding North Africa as crucial to maintaining the empire after the war. To them Egypt and the Suez Canal were the lifeline to India and Persian Gulf oil. Marshall went on to tell Roosevelt that he did not consider the canal was in immediate danger, and then reiterated his point that the United States could not care less about the longevity of the British Empire. Roosevelt listened, but did not commit to any course of action.

Marshall's visceral reaction to anything that diverted forces from the main effort—northern Europe—was, unfortunately, not fully supported by the president's other military advisers. Knox refrained from the debate, while King also remained mostly on the sidelines. King's silence was not unusual as he habitually fell apart when in Roosevelt's presence. Stimson recorded: "King wobbled around in a way that made me rather sick with him. He is firm and brave outside of the White House but as soon as he gets in the presence of the President he crumbles up." Despite Marshall's and Stimson's protestations, Roosevelt ordered them to start planning for a North African invasion to "see if it could be done." Stimson thought it a "foolish exercise," but detailed planning for GYMNAST was begun.

When Churchill arrived in Washington, his military advisers were immediately sent to cajole their American counterparts, while he boarded a small aircraft to spend the weekend with Roosevelt and Hopkins at Hyde Park. Why Roosevelt was not in Washington to greet him has never been explained, but one can assume the president desired a series of private meetings before they jointly faced the Combined Chiefs. As they usually did, this renewal of the private diplomacy of the two nations' leaders increased Marshall's uneasiness. As he later stated: "We were largely trying to get the president to stand pat on what he had previously agreed to. The president shifted, particularly when Churchill got hold of him." This time Marshall received a strong assist from Stimson, who had spent the prior two days working on a personal brief defending BOLERO. When it was complete he walked it in to Marshall, who read it aloud to a group of officers already in his office, Arnold and Eisenhower among them. With their unanimous support Stimson forwarded his rousing defense of BOLERO and SLEDGEHAMMER to Hyde Park, in hopes of limiting the effect of Churchillian wiles.

But Churchill had brought a note of his own for the president. And although it laid out the continuing planning for an invasion of France in 1942, it went on to say that the British government "did not favor an operation that was certain to lead to disaster." The note concluded that "no responsible British military authority has so far been able to make a plan for September of 1942 that has any chance of success."

Faced with two such diametrically opposed opinions, and probably wondering how he could back out of commitments he had just made to Stalin, Roosevelt decided that he and Churchill could not possibly reach an accord alone. He therefore cut the weekend excursion short by a day, and before midnight Roosevelt, with Churchill and Hopkins in tow, boarded his private train to Washington. Word was sent ahead for Marshall to meet him in the Oval Office at 11:00 A.M. to discuss options in the event of a Russian collapse that summer. Knox, Stimson, and King were told to be ready for a conference that afternoon.

While Churchill worked on Roosevelt, Marshall was working on Brooke. As for invading France in 1942, the field marshal was unalterably opposed, but he did announce that he thought "the BOLERO plan sound" and that he was "strongly in favor of concentrating all possible efforts on carrying it through as agreed." Marshall was gratified to gain Brooke's support for continued preparations for a 1943 invasion, and with it the field marshal's offer to help counter Churchill's lobbying for a North African invasion. Brooke, however, may have been playing strategic chess, as he was dealing with a critical situation in North Africa and desperately needed to reinforce the reeling Eighth Army in Egypt. By delaying a combined North Africa invasion, Brooke likely hoped to avoid diverting British forces to support an American invasion in Algiers and Morocco. Moreover, by encouraging Marshall in the idea that he fully supported a 1943 invasion, he could keep the Americans firmly committed to their Germany-first strategy, while ensuring that Britain had a ready pool of American manpower for other operations.

Brooke, however, kept his options open, telling Marshall that if "a cross-channel invasion was impracticable, other alternatives should be considered." Among Brooke's alternatives was reviving GYMNAST at a later date. Here, Marshall finally got some help from King, who declared himself unalterably opposed to GYMNAST. King said that he was not impressed by the idea of opening what he called a "ninth front" and that the risks already being run in the Pacific to provide for BOLERO were making him sick with anxiety. King made it clear that he could not provide the support ships for GYMNAST without endangering America's hold on the Pacific. Marshall reiterated that opening another front would achieve nothing, and that the only "logical course was to concentrate on BOLERO."

With the Combined Chiefs in general, if shaky, agreement, they prepared, with some apprehension, to meet with their national leaders. Brooke was just as anxious as Marshall about what plans the prime minister and the president had concocted while they were separated from the tempered counsel of their military advisers. As Brooke told his diary: "We fear the worst and are certain that North Africa or North Norway plans for 1942 will loom large in their proposals, whilst we are convinced that they are not possible."

It was already sweltering when, on June 21, Marshall, Hopkins, Churchill, Brooke, and Ismay gathered in the un-air-conditioned presidential study. Neither the War nor the Navy secretary was invited, leaving an upset Stimson in his office all day "waiting to be called by the President." Churchill fired the opening barrage with a terrific attack on SLEDGEHAMMER. Roosevelt listened politely, but after being well briefed earlier that morning by Marshall, he did not appear convinced by the prime minister's argument. When Churchill paused, FDR reminded him that the British had previously committed to a 1942 invasion, and on that basis, he had made promises to Stalin. Roosevelt then invited Marshall to speak, and according to what Hopkins later told Stimson, Marshall made "a very powerful agreement" in favor of early operations "disposing of all the clouds that had been woven" during Mountbatten's visit. Stimson's diary entry was wrong, as Churchill was unmoved by Marshall's rhetoric. Haunted by visions of thousands of bodies floating in the surf and piled up on the beaches, Churchill remained determined to forestall what he and his generals considered American imbecility.

Soon after lunch, as Churchill and Brooke stood beside Roosevelt's desk conversing with the president, Marshall entered the room. He handed a slip of paper to the president, who after a quick glance handed the slip— announcing the fall of Tobruk and the capture of twenty-five thousand British and Dominion soldiers—to Churchill. Tobruk, which had held out for thirty-three weeks the year before, had fallen in a single day. A shaken Churchill's foremost concern was what this meant for the British military position in Libya and Egypt, but he was also worried about British morale, as well as what it would do to the reputation of the British Army. As he later wrote: "This was one of the heaviest blows I can recall during the war . . . Defeat was one thing; disgrace is another."

Roosevelt stood silent for a few moments, allowing Churchill to absorb the enormity of the blow. Finally, he asked a simple question, "What can I do to help?" Churchill's immediate reply was "Give us as many Sherman tanks as you can spare and ship them to the Middle East as quickly as possible." Marshall, momentarily nonplussed at having to give up Sherman tanks that had only recently been issued to an American armored division, remarked that it was "a terrible thing to take the weapons out of a soldier's hands" before quickly adding, "Nevertheless if the British need is so great they must have them." As Churchill later recounted it, Marshall immediately offered three hundred tanks and one hundred artillery pieces. In truth, Marshall had first decided to send an entire armored division to Egypt. As such, he sent for General George Patton and placed him at the

Army War College with a small staff to start planning the move, specifically ordering that the operation be kept small—no more than a single division and some support troops. When the next morning Patton said he would need a second division, Marshall promptly put him on a plane and returned him to the desert training center in California. Marshall reveled in the idea that he had "scared George" half to death, as it left Patton wondering if his impertinent request had cost him a future command. By this time, Marshall realized it would take months to finish training the Second Armored Division and transport it to Alexandria, forcing him to dispatch the three hundred tanks and one hundred artillery pieces without any American troops to man them. Despite the diversion Marshall was no nearer to approving a full-scale multidivision invasion of North Africa.

Churchill was grateful for the rapid American support, but he did not allow such emotions to influence his main purpose in coming to Washington. All that afternoon and evening he employed his forceful eloquence, but it was for naught, as Roosevelt and Marshall stood firm against the flood of Churchillian rhetoric. By the late evening of June 21, Churchill appeared to give in when he agreed that BOLERO and an early ROUNDUP must remain the primary focus of Allied efforts. In a draft agreement prepared by General Ismay and amended by the American chiefs, the Allies stated that "preparations for BOLERO on as large a scale as possible are to be pushed forward with all speed and energy." In the same paper both sides agreed that operations in France and the Low Countries in 1942 would show greater strategic gains than were possible in any other theater. Marshall and Stimson considered the battle won. Churchill, however, was focused on another section of the document, which stated that "possibilities for GYMNAST will be explored carefully and conscientiously, and plans will be completed in all detail as soon as possible."

Marshall was willing to undertake finishing such plans as a sop, as he was convinced they would never be enacted. Churchill, on the other hand, had purposely placed a final caveat in the agreement that, in his mind, made GYMNAST all but certain. After stating that all efforts must be made to overcome obvious dangers to launching either SLEDGEHAMMER or ROUNDUP, Churchill's insert read: "If, on the other hand, detailed examination shows that, despite all efforts, success is improbable, we must be ready with an alternative." Churchill approved the document in the utter assurance that the odds of success would be discovered to be "improbable." The British official historian relates that the British chiefs referred to the day the Americans agreed to this proposal as "the Day of the Dupes."

As the last late-night meeting concluded, Roosevelt asked Marshall to tarry behind. When the room was cleared, Roosevelt asked Marshall what he thought of the idea of throwing "a large American force to cover everything from Tehran to Alexandria." Marshall was aghast, telling Roosevelt that such an idea would "overthrow everything they had been planning for." Roosevelt did not immediately reply, and after a moment Marshall told him that he refused to discuss the topic at this late hour; the discussion soon concluded. Stimson learned of Roosevelt's new suggestion the next morning, only fifteen minutes before he was to meet with the president. News that Roosevelt was once again off the reservation confirmed him in his opinion that he needed to continue pressing for BOLERO and SLEDGEHAMMER that day and for many days thereafter.

During their meeting, Roosevelt, with Churchill in attendance, brought up a Joint Staff paper on GYMNAST, jolting Stimson into action. He once again laid out all the reasons why such an assault was both impractical and ill advised. But during the debate Stimson highlighted a revealing weakness in his position, saying that his views were "not based on political reasons." But Roosevelt, unlike Stimson, could never ignore the politics of the war. In this he, likely unknowingly, agreed with Clausewitz that war was an extension of politics. In fact, wars are always waged for some political objective, and thus the continuing popular support for wars remains, as it always has, a result of political theater. In this vein, Marshall later recounted that he had "failed to see that a leader in a democracy has to keep the people entertained." Though he later admitted that "entertained" was not the best word, it conveyed his meaning. What he truly meant was that Americans would grow impatient if they had to watch a million men languishing in England when they could be fighting elsewhere. Roosevelt appreciated from the start what Marshall and Stimson did not grasp until much later, that the people supporting the war would endure setbacks, but they had to see movement. The president understood something about war that Marshall did not comprehend: military idleness could easily kill the American spirit of victory.

After hearing out Stimson's arguments, Churchill repeated what he had already told the president, namely that he "hadn't found a responsible soldier on his Staff who thought it [an early invasion of northern Europe] could be done at this time. The Germans had spent all their time digging defenses on the northern coast and it was well-nigh impregnable." Seeing the ghosts of the Somme again, Churchill admitted that he "shrank from the image of sending troops to another Dunkirk." Stimson continued the fight, but gathered no hope from Roosevelt, who once again voiced his idea for sending a large force to protect the now-denuded Egyptian frontier. This time it was Churchill's turn to pull the president back, saying that British forces could hold the line and he would not ask that of the president. Stimson therefore continued his plea, but in the end he understood that he was not winning the argument. Convinced that ROUNDUP would not be made in 1943 and that Churchill and Roosevelt were endangering the war effort, it was a melancholy Stimson who returned to his War Department office. That night a distraught Stimson wrote that it was a most unhappy meeting and that he considered the president irresponsible, claiming that throughout their meeting Roosevelt "was talking of the most critical situations and in the presence of the head of another government with the frivolity and lack of responsibility of a child."

Though Churchill made time the next day to visit American troops training in the Carolinas, he was soon heading back to Britain to beat back a vote of censure in Parliament over his handling of the war. Behind him lay a dispirited Stimson, convinced that Churchill would never allow an invasion to take place. Marshall, however, still thought Roosevelt was firmly behind the idea. Stimson was not so sure, and neither was Hopkins, who understood that "right or wrong—for better or worse—Churchill's arguments always appealed to Roosevelt." Moreover, the circumstances of the war radically changed in early July 1942.

Rommel's offensive, using the supplies captured at Tobruk, continued and by July 2 the British were just barely holding at El Alamein—a mere seventy miles from the great port of Alexandria. On the eastern front, the siege of Sevastopol had ended, giving the Germans control of the entire Crimea. Moreover, a massive tank battle near Kharkov had crushed a Soviet offensive and blown a hole in the Russian lines that the Germans would exploit in their delayed summer offensive toward the Volga and Stalingrad. Things had also gone from bad to worse in the North Atlantic, where over 600,000 tons were sunk in both May and June and a further 400,000 tons were lost in a single week in July. As Churchill grimly noted in mid-July, the U-boats were sinking ships at twice the rate the Allies were building them. In the Pacific, Japanese forces were still conducting limited advances, and on July 3 they landed on Guadalcanal. By the middle of the month they were constructing an airbase capable of interdicting supply lines between Australia and the United States.

Under these circumstances Churchill, with the full concordance of the British Combined Chiefs, on July 8 forwarded a message to Roosevelt that met with a violent reaction from the American chiefs. In it Churchill repeated the line he had employed several times while in the United States: "No responsible British General, Admiral or Air Marshal is prepared to recommend SLEDGEHAMMER as a practicable operation in 1942." After presenting a list of reasons why this was so, Churchill recommended GYMNAST "as by far the best chance for effective relief of the Russian front in 1942." He sweetened his plea by giving Roosevelt credit for conceiving such a masterstroke, stating that "this has all along been in harmony with your ideas. In fact, it is your commanding idea." It fell to General Dill to deliver the British chiefs' official memorandum on the subject to his friend Marshall. Dill remained in the doorway while Marshall read the document and was thereby treated to a rare event: Marshall's temper exploding beyond the tight confines in which he worked to contain it.

30

ON TRACK

G YMNAST MIGHT HAVE APPEARED AS THE ONLY ALTERNATIVE FROM the British perspective, but that was not the case for the American chiefs. MacArthur was already screaming for more forces to conduct large-scale operations aimed at Rabaul, even as King and Nimitz pressed for more Army support to conduct operations capitalizing on the success at Midway. In fact, they were already preparing an assault on Guadalcanal, which was going forward on a shoestring. If the British insisted on GYM-NAST, Marshall informed Dill that then he would insist on the abrogation of the "Germany first" strategy in favor of concentrating on the Pacific. Dill was so taken aback by the vehemence in Marshall's tone that he sent a cable to his government, warning "that to press acceptance of GYMNAST at the expense of BOLERO would drive U. S. A. into saying we are finished off with West and will go out in Pacific."

As King was out of town, the Joint Chiefs could not meet until July 10. At that time, Marshall read the dispatch to his fellow chiefs. According to the minutes, Marshall read his own personal comments about the British attitude, the gist of which was that Operation GYMNAST would be expensive and ineffectual, and that it was impossible to carry out SLEDGEHAM-MER or ROUNDUP without full and aggressive British support. He then proposed that if the British position must be accepted, the United States should turn to the Pacific for decisive action against Japan. He added that this would help concentrate U.S. forces and that it would be highly popular throughout the United States, particularly on the West Coast. Marshall further claimed, without explaining how, that, except for BOLERO, operations against Japan would have the greatest effect on relieving pressure on Russia. King expressed himself as being completely in agreement with Marshall's proposal, stating that he never considered that "the British were in wholehearted agreement with operations on the Continent." Referring to GYMNAST, he said that "it was impossible to fulfill naval commitments in other theaters and at the same time provide the shipping and escorts which would be essential should that operation be undertaken." As a result, the Joint Chiefs forwarded a memorandum to the president, who was at Hyde Park, asking permission to, as Stimson put it, "turn our backs on them [the British] and take up our war with Japan." The memorandum pointed out that GYMNAST would be a heavy and indecisive drain on U.S. resources, which would jeopardize the American position in the Pacific while rendering no decisive support to any other theater of war. Marshall and King concluded by asking the president to send an ultimatum to Churchill warning him that "if the United States is to engage in any operations other than the forceful, unswerving adherence to full Bolero plans . . . we should turn to the Pacific."

At Hyde Park, Roosevelt, after carefully reading the memo, called Marshall and King's bluff. Telephoning the War Department, the president demanded that the Joint Chiefs dispatch to him "*at once, by airplane, a comprehensive and detailed outline of the plans for redirecting the major effort of the United States to the war against Japan*—including the effect of such a decision on the Soviet and Middle East fronts during the balance of 1942." Roosevelt also demanded definite plans for the remainder of 1942 and tentative ones for 1943. He concluded by emphasizing that "it is of highest importance that U.S. ground troops be brought into action against the enemy in 1942."

Inasmuch as no one had foreseen any possibility of such a change of strategy, there were no detailed plans to send the president. Stimson had Marshall called back from Leesburg, where he was enjoying his first day off in some time. Both men arrived at their adjoining offices at 3:00 P.M. and immediately got to work. General Thomas Handy, who had taken over the operations position after Eisenhower's departure for Britain in May 1942, had already produced a rough memorandum, which Marshall personally walked over to King at the Navy Department. After King had added a "little more punch to it" Stimson approved sending it to the president, commenting that he hoped it would force the British to give up on their "fatuous defeatist position." But he was not hopeful, writing in his diary: "The trouble is neither he [Churchill] nor the President has a methodical and careful mind. They do not implement their proposals with any careful study of the supporting facts upon which success of such expeditions must rest."

Henry Stimson and General George Marshall.

Roosevelt received the memo while still at Hyde Park. After discussing it with Hopkins, he rejected it out of hand and went to have lunch with Queen Wilhelmina of the Netherlands. Roosevelt soon passed his hosting duties on to Eleanor and went to meet with Wendell Willkie, who was requesting permission to visit Russia. Roosevelt, who apparently truly liked Willkie, readily agreed, and proposed he expand his trip to the Middle East, India, and China, explaining that it would demonstrate national unity for the head of the opposition party to conduct a worldwide tour as a presidential emissary.

* * *

There was one further distraction at Hyde Park that weekend: Hopkins's fiancée, Louise Macy. Hopkins and Macy had been introduced through a letter of recommendation when he was in the hospital the previous January. She needed a job, after her wholesale dress business failed, and Hopkins was a good man to go to for a job. He had been a widower since 1937, but retained an "eye for the pretty face." They met for lunch at the St. Regis Hotel in Manhattan, and began a whirlwind romance. Macy was thirty-six, a socialite, and known for her quick smile, charm, and vivacious wit and for radiating good spirits. The first to learn of Hopkins's engagement was Churchill, whom Hopkins told as the prime minister departed Washington in June. By mid-July it was an open secret, and the wedding date was set for the end of the month.

Roosevelt, like most men who entered Macy's orbit, was initially smitten by her and convinced the couple to live in the White House. FDR's attraction ended when, incensed about White House conversations being quoted in the *Washington Times-Herald,* he suspected Hopkins's wife as the source (she and the *Times-Herald* columnist were close friends) and had her followed by the FBI. The crucial point, as it relates to the summer of 1942, is that Hopkins, because of his romance, had far less time to spend with Roosevelt. From this point forward their relationship went into decline. Although Hopkins remained a close presidential confidant throughout the war, the cooling between Hopkins and Roosevelt opened the door for others to move into the president's circle.

Distractions, such as visiting royalty, meeting former electoral foes, and wedding announcements, could not long delay the inevitable clash between Roosevelt and his Joint Chiefs. With the passage of time it is easy to underestimate how crucial this moment was. All three of his chiefs (Marshall, King, and Arnold), fully supported by their respective secretaries (Stimson and Knox), had asked the president to send an ultimatum to the leader of an allied nation demanding he bend to U.S. strategic plans or see America abandon the Atlantic theater until the war against Japan was won. Unlike Churchill, Roosevelt never considered himself a military genius and, for the most part, left his carefully chosen military leaders to get on with running the war. In fact, when Brooke, who was with Churchill almost every day, learned that Marshall saw Roosevelt only every six weeks or so he was quite envious of their relationship. But now, just a half year into the war and before American ground forces had taken the offensive in any theater, Roosevelt was preparing to overrule *all* of his military advisers. It was surely not a step he took lightly, as the potential for a civil-military rupture was certainly present.

Upon his return to the White House on July 15, Roosevelt allowed Marshall and King to make their case. According to Robert Sherwood, Marshall, his patience exhausted by the off-again-on-again status of the second-front planning, strongly asserted that the United States forsake major operations in Europe in favor of an all-out offensive in the Pacific. Stimson, who had met with the president earlier that day, reported that Roosevelt told him that he was squarely behind BOLERO, but did not favor sending any memorandum (read: ultimatum) to the British, saying that the alliance could not sustain itself if every time we could not have our way "we would take up our dishes and go home." To all concerned he made it clear that he was very much against transferring the major effort to the Pacific, referring to the proposal as a "red herring," and went so far as to suggest that "the record should be altered so that it would not appear in later years that we proposed what amounted to the abandonment of the British." Despite this, both Marshall and Stimson thought they had "knocked out the President's lingering affections for GYMNAST."

Roosevelt, however, was not as solidly behind BOLERO as his military advisers supposed. By the end of what Stimson said was "a rough day," Roosevelt was sure of only two things: that American troops must fight somewhere in 1942 and that the decision as to where must be resolved soon. That evening, Roosevelt had a long talk with Hopkins during which he admitted that losing SLEDGEHAMMER was a blow, but that if "we cannot strike at SLEDGEHAMMER we must take the second best—and that is not the Pacific." As a result of the day's conversations Roosevelt ordered Hopkins, King, and Marshall to depart immediately for London for talks with Churchill and the British chiefs.

To make sure he got what he wanted, Roosevelt prepared a detailed letter of instruction for the three men. In it, he spelled out that he was unalterably opposed to an all-out effort in the Pacific against Japan, reminding all concerned that defeating Japan did nothing to help defeat Germany, while giving the Nazis time to complete their domination of Europe and Africa. Roosevelt also asked his representatives to keep three cardinal principles in mind: speed of decision on plans, unity of plans, and attack combined with defense but not defense alone. But it was the middle paragraph that ensured everyone knew what they had to come home with: "It is of the highest importance that U.S. ground troops be brought into action against the enemy in 1942." In short, if SLEDGEHAMMER was out, don't come home without a new plan.

The three men left as part of a small party on July 16. Hopkins's biographer noted that Hopkins, who always loved these kinds of trips, did not want to go on this one. Rather, he wanted to stay home with Louise and get married. When they arrived, Churchill requested that the party stay at Chequers for the week, but Marshall and King insisted on going straight to London to meet with Eisenhower and Stark, and then to start discussions with their British counterparts as soon as possible. No sooner had the party checked into Claridge's than Churchill was on the phone with Hopkins. It took some time for Hopkins to convince the prime minister that no insult was intended and the American chiefs were not being rude. Hopkins later told Roosevelt that Churchill had thrown the entire British constitution at him, but since it was unwritten no damage was done.

Marshall and King fought hard for SLEDGEHAMMER, even at one point changing it from a sacrifice to help the Russians to an all-out assault that would form a lodgment at Normandy or Brest and then dig in until reinforced by a larger ROUNDUP operation the following year. It was all useless. Churchill had sensed that the fight had gone out of Roosevelt, and that all the president wanted was American troops in the war, no matter where. Even Brooke realized he was facing a divided American party, writing in his diary on July 15: "It will be a queer party as Harry Hopkins is for operating in Africa, Marshall wants to operate in Europe, and King is determined to strike in the Pacific!" The Americans were hooked. All the British had to do was hold tight and wrestle them into the boat.

The arguments raged for five days, but by Tuesday night King and Marshall conceded that a 1942 invasion of northern Europe was not in the cards. After a bit more discussion the Americans caved and agreed to GYMNAST. But at the last moment, Marshall insisted that the British also agree that GYMNAST would not be permitted to delay ROUNDUP in 1943. As he and everyone else surely knew, an invasion of North Africa would consume such huge quantities of resources that a 1943 invasion was nigh impossible. Marshall's hope was that the British would balk, making it possible for him to tell Roosevelt that he would have to wait until 1943 for Americans to get into the ground war. The British, however, were more than happy to agree to Marshall's terms. They had what they wanted for 1942; they could argue about 1943 plans another day.

In a last grasp to salvage something, Marshall asked that September 15 be set as the final date to decide on an invasion. Hopkins, fearing that without a firm commitment to a start date there would be too much room for delays and procrastination, cabled Roosevelt. He strongly urged the president to set October 30 as the date for GYMNAST—now code-named TORCH—to begin. Roosevelt replied immediately, ordering that October 30 be set as the invasion day and that all planning and preparations start immediately. At the same time, he ordered Hopkins to start for home, so as not to miss his own wedding. Defeated, Marshall ordered Eisenhower to start planning Operation TORCH, and informed him that if he still had any influence with Roosevelt, he—Eisenhower—would command the invasion.

Despite having bowed to a presidential directive to get on with TORCH, Marshall remained convinced that the operation was fundamentally unsound, as he would have considered any operation that delayed the invasion of northern Europe. This was a conviction he shared with Stimson, who, after discussing it with Marshall, recorded that the more he reflected on it the "more evil the President's decision appears to be." As Stimson saw it the diagnosis for what was ailing the Allied cause was simple: "British leaders have lost their nerve." Together the two men spent much of the next few weeks covertly sabotaging the planning and preparation for the operation. Marshall, with King's support, told Leahy that since Roosevelt had not cancelled ROUNDUP for 1943, he was justified in maintaining BOLERO (the buildup in Britain) until Roosevelt cancelled the 1943 invasion. As there were not sufficient resources available to conduct TORCH and continue the BOLERO buildup, Marshall was clearly looking for loopholes that would allow him to postpone TORCH until it was no longer feasible in that year. Roosevelt put a quick end to this ploy when, during a meeting with the Joint Chiefs on July 30, he announced that he as commander in chief "had made the decision that TORCH would be undertaken at the earliest possible date. He considered that this operation was now the principal objective and the assembling of means to carry it out should take precedence over other operations as, for instance, BOLERO."

Inevitably the press picked up the split between Roosevelt and his military advisers, and began pounding the president about overriding the Joint

Chiefs on military strategy. Incensed by the charges, at an August 6 cabinet meeting Roosevelt pointedly denied that he had ever overruled the Joint Chiefs on a military matter and made it clear that any further leaks to the press on this matter would not bode well for those concerned. Stimson, upset by FDR's claims that he had not overruled his chiefs, told his diary: "The President has the happy faculty of fooling himself and this was one of the most extreme cases of that I have ever seen."

After further consultations with Marshall, Stimson prepared a memorandum to the president, intending to have it out once and for all. In the memo, Stimson detailed how Roosevelt had overridden all of his military advisers when he ordered the TORCH operation, in hopes the president would see the error of his ways. But when he showed the memo to Marshall on August 10, he found the chief of staff a changed man. He strongly advised Stimson to shelve the memo and let things play out. From that point on Marshall began energetically pushing all obstacles to TORCH aside, determined to get on with the mission.

What accounts for this sudden change of heart? Of course, Roosevelt's firm declarations that TORCH was his first priority had much to do with it. But equal measure must be accorded a personal note Marshall received from Sir John Dill, an officer he truly respected:

> I am just a little disturbed about TORCH. For good or ill it has been accepted and therefore I feel we should go at it with all possible enthusiasm and give it absolute priority. If we don't, it won't succeed.... Those playing a part in mounting the operation must be entirely whole-hearted about it, or they cannot give it all the help it should have and overcome all the difficulties that will arise.

The official Army historians declared that Marshall was unimpressed by his friend's note, but this clearly was not the case. Marshall lived by a code, and a big part of the code, drummed into him since he was a cadet at VMI, was that once a decision is made you do your best to make it a reality. The time for argument had passed, and the commander in chief had decided. Thus, the code Marshall lived by left him only two options: make the decision his own and see it through to the end, or resign. For several weeks, Marshall, with all the right intentions, had forgotten that code, and as a result endangered the success of TORCH. It took Dill's gentle reminder to snap him back to his duty. Stimson remained worried, and thought Marshall was taking his eye off the prize, but he bowed to his chief's desires.

Debates continued as to the scope of TORCH: how many beaches, would Algiers be included, would British troops participate in the landing? All of these concerns prompted what Eisenhower called a transatlantic essay-writing contest. But by September 5, all of the major moving pieces were agreed on, allowing Roosevelt to cable Churchill: "Hurrah." To which Churchill replied the following day: "Okay, full blast." Interestingly, as late as September 28 (just six weeks before the TORCH landings), Stimson recorded the following after a long discussion with Eisenhower's deputy, General Mark Clark: "I found that he fully agreed with me about the hazards and unwisdom of the whole movement. It is a superb tribute to our leaders to see the vigor and enthusiasm they are putting into a job of which they really disapprove."

All that remained was the delicate task of informing Stalin that the promised second front was no longer in the cards. That chore went to Churchill, who personally went to Moscow to deliver the news. En route, he made a quick stop in Cairo to place General Harold Alexander in charge of the Middle East and General Bernard Law Montgomery in charge of the Eighth Army in North Africa. It had taken several attempts, but Churchill had finally found a winning combination of commanders.

In Moscow, things initially did not go so well. Stalin, who was losing ten thousand men a day in combat, could not or would not understand the Anglo-Americans' apparent timidity. After hours of lambasting, Churchill erupted into what those with him (General Brooke and Averell Harriman) thought was one of his most brilliant statements ever. It was always difficult to get an interpreter who could translate Churchillian English into Russian. But it was all the more difficult that night, as Churchill continually punched his interpreter in the arm, demanding to know if Stalin had gotten his exact point. Stalin eventually took pity on the interpreter, intervening and with a broad smile declaring: "Your words are of no importance. What is important is your spirit." From that point things were better, allowing Churchill to cable Roosevelt from Cairo on August 18: "Now they know the worst, and having made their protest are entirely friendly . . . Moreover, Monsieur Stalin is entirely convinced of the great advantages of TORCH." Stalin was likely making the best of what he viewed as a bad situation. For it stretches credibility to believe that he considered seizing North

Africa as an equal substitute for driving armored divisions across France, especially as the Wehrmacht was at that moment driving on Stalingrad.

Even as the GYMNAST-TORCH debates raged, the Americans kicked off their first ground offensive in the Pacific. On August 7, 1942, the First Marine Division invaded Guadalcanal and seized some nearby smaller islands—all part of the Solomon Islands. The islands were easily taken, but disaster stuck forty-eight hours later, when part of the Japanese Eighth Fleet operating out of Rabaul struck a group of Allied cruisers and destroyers near Savo Island. One Australian and three American cruisers were lost and three other ships damaged. As Admiral Frank Jack Fletcher had already withdrawn the American aircraft carriers from the area, the transports and landing beaches lay bare to the Japanese fleet. But as at Pearl Harbor, the Japanese were unwilling to dare the final audacity and turned for home rather than come on to destroy the nearly defenseless American transports. As it was, the transports departed the next day (most of them only partially offloaded), stranding the marines, who began a prolonged slugging match short of nearly everything needed to conduct a battle.

Leaving his Joint Chiefs to work through the daily problems of fighting a global war, Roosevelt undertook a cross-country tour of defense plants. As he considered it unseemly to launch a partisan election campaign in the midst of war, Roosevelt banned any reporting of his trip. Still, campaigning was part of his DNA, so he took along some favored journalists, but forbade them to file any stories until he had returned to the White House, and then only after he had reviewed the copy, ostensibly for security reasons—but that line fooled no one.

31

THE GREAT FEASIBILITY DISPUTE

ROOSEVELT'S DEPARTURE LEFT MORE THAN HIS GENERALS BE-hind. He was also escaping a wartime administrative system nearing an abyss. Inflation was gathering steam and his chief inflation fighter, Leon Henderson, was under attack from all sides. Further, manpower shortages were turning up everywhere, and he was continuously refereeing squabbles between the military and the manpower commission. Most worrying, though, was that production of war matériel was falling well short of established goals, and in some areas targets were missed by alarming numbers. All of this led to unprecedented levels of interdepartmental bickering, of which Robert Sherwood later wrote: "In the Battle of Washington, as in most of the real fighting fronts, this was the lowest point of the war." Roosevelt could escape these battles for a two-week trip, but they raged in his absence and would be there upon his return.

Undoubtedly, the most worrisome problem on FDR's agenda was the failure of production to keep up with strategic plans. Grand plans were being made, great armies were stirring, and titanic clashes were on the near horizon. But, as so often in the past, plans were easily wrecked and armies defeated for want of the proverbial nail. In America's case, however, many millions of metaphorical nails were not finding their way to the combat forces. In short, the vaunted arsenal of democracy was seizing up, as new demands piled in upon already backlogged order books. With each passing day factories fell further behind on their ambitious schedules.

In such circumstances, there are only two options: adjust plans to meet economic reality, or adjust reality to meet necessity. For the Army, particularly General Somervell, the answer was easy: pile on more orders and let America's ingenious industrial managers and workers rise to the occasion. For the statisticians and economists within the War Production Board (WPB), Somervell's views were folly based on ignorance. As they saw it, American industry could produce a finite X amount of goods at any one time. Asking for more than X was not only foolhardy, it meant, in the long run, you would get far less than X. The attempt to resolve these two viewpoints led to the greatest military-civilian dispute of the war. How they were resolved determined the course of the war.

When Roosevelt appointed Donald Nelson to head the WPB, he also gave him unlimited authority to control every aspect of production. Nelson, however, promptly handed much of this power to the military, particularly as it related to procurement. As he later explained to the Truman Committee—established under Harry S. Truman to oversee war spending—he did not even consider setting up an independent buying organization as he knew "that would be just dead wrong." No one asked him why it would be dead wrong. One may assume that he thought the Army had a better idea of what it needed than his WPB staff did. In any event, as he organized the WPB he was "very careful not to take a bit of authority away from the Army or Navy." In fact, he boasted that he enhanced the military's power. In return, Nelson expected harmony between his agency and the military. Instead, he got all-out war.

It was just the kind of bureaucratic street fight that Nelson hated. By temperament he was a man who preferred slow advances, examining all sides of an argument, and then only going forward after he had a consensus. Somervell, on the other hand, believed the best way to move ahead was to decide quickly and then kick in the teeth of all who opposed him. As such, Nelson's participation in the great debates of 1942 was slight, and always from the sidelines. Taking his place in the fighting pit was Robert Nathan, ably supported by his two bookworm professors, Simon Kuznets and Stacy May.

By this time, Nathan was running the Planning Committee within WPB, and in a reversal of their earlier roles Kuznets as well as May worked for him. Nathan and his team had no duties except analyzing American production to forecast when the Victory Program goals would be met, without damaging the U.S. economy. Industry soon learned that there was no hid-ing from Stacy May. Every day, dozens of field teams forwarded volumes of information detailing deliveries of armaments versus assigned quotas for almost every company with a military contract. May fed all of these statistics to Kuznets, who was working on a plan to bring production objectives in line with the nation's capacity.

So far, Nathan and the Planning Committee were well within their writ. It is what they did next that caused a stir. Not limiting themselves to identifying problems and bottlenecks, Nathan and his team also took it upon themselves to offer specific solutions. Unfortunately, as these solutions centered on having the Army reduce its demands, Somervell found them decidedly unwelcome. Moreover, Nathan, a former boxer who had lost none of his youthful pugnaciousness, was never reluctant to tell everyone involved that production was going off the rails and he was the man with the solution. Nathan's constant prodding inevitably led to bouts of bloody bureaucratic warfare, or what the official history, *Industrial Mobilization for War*, referred to, in a passage larded with understatement, as "opposition by a few affected individuals."

From the start, Nathan's opponent, General Somervell, viewed the War Production Board as an enemy on par with the Axis powers. Somervell refused to accept that there were limits to what American industry could produce. But here were Nathan, Kuznets, and May using something they called the "Consolidated Balance Sheet" complete with statistical evidence to prove there actually were limits. Nathan told Somervell that based on current production infrastructure the U.S. GDP could grow maximally by 60 percent by mid-1943. This meant that the United States could spend $45 billion on the war in 1942 and $65 billion in 1943. Military orders, according to Nathan, could only rise above those numbers by severely damaging the civilian economy—the goose that was laying the golden eggs.

All of this was in the report May had delivered three days before Pearl Harbor. But, remarkably, there was much more in that report. The statisticians had peered into the future and determined, with truly remarkable precision, when all the elements of the Victory Program *could* be available. Their projections clearly stated that by 1943 there would be enough war matériel on hand for limited offensives throughout that year, but that any major offensive could not be supported until well into 1944. If anyone on the Joint Staff had paid attention to the report, and its subsequent updates,

they could have told Marshall that any substantial invasion of Europe before 1944 was just a fantasy unless he was willing to undertake it with a
partially equipped army.

But General Somervell ignored that part of the report, seizing instead
on the section stating that the military was requesting far less than American industry could deliver. In bold language, the Army was told to double
its orders if they were to have any hope of achieving 1943 goals. May's report also claimed that even after such an increase, consumer consumption
would remain high. Consumers might not be able to get cars or refrigerators for a while, but there would be plenty of the essentials. In fact, the idea
that American civilians sacrificed during the war is something of a myth,
as consumer spending went up throughout the war, even after accounting
for inflation. Reflecting on the war years the economist John Kenneth Galbraith said that "never in the long history of combat have so many talked
so much about sacrifice with so little deprivation."

By early 1942, the Army had already blown past May's recommended
doubling of orders, and was on course to triple them. This, when added to
Roosevelt's "must items"—60,000 planes in 1942, 125,000 planes in 1943,
120,000 tanks over two years, and 20,000 antiaircraft guns—soon brought
up the question of feasibility. The president and the military were asking
the impossible. Unfortunately, Roosevelt had in his State of the Union Address already told the American people his attitude toward naysayers: "Let
no man say it cannot be done. It must be done—and we have undertaken
to do it."

But Nathan *was* saying it could not be done, and was proposing an immediate cutback of 25 percent in military orders. Moreover, he wanted to
create an organization dominated by economists who would have oversight over the Joint Chiefs. When he briefed Somervell on this plan, he
might as well have just poked him with sharp sticks.

In mid-March, Kuznets handed Nathan more ammunition, in the shape
of a detailed report demonstrating production shortfalls far worse than
they thought. If the program was going to be salvaged, military orders
would need to be cut by 35 percent. On March 17, Nelson asked the Joint
Chiefs to send service representatives to discuss the problem. The Navy
ignored the request, but the Army sent Brigadier General Lucius Clay, who
agreed to make marginal cuts, but these barely moved the needle. Even
these were soon rescinded, as the Army refused to cut its requirements un-

less Roosevelt could be persuaded to cut his "must items." As the Army saw it, when the president demanded eighty thousand tanks, he was also ordering everything necessary to employ them in armored divisions, such as trucks, artillery, and ammunition.

At the end of March, Nathan prevailed on Nelson to send a letter to Roosevelt, informing him of major production shortfalls caused by an economy being asked to do the impossible. Nelson sent the note, but refrained from asking Roosevelt to do anything about it. As Nelson surely must have known by this time, if one allowed Roosevelt to postpone a decision, he would postpone it. It was standard Rooseveltian operating procedure to let underlings fight it out until he absolutely had to pick a side. As Roosevelt employed a great deal of his personal charm during the preliminaries of these fights, each side of an argument always left his presence convinced the president was with them. Consequently, each side dug in its heels awaiting presidential rescue. The end result of Roosevelt's management style was that many issues that could have been settled by an early nod from him festered until they turned into crises.

Unbeknownst to Nelson, General Marshall sent a letter to Roosevelt the next day, probably written by Somervell, stating that if Roosevelt replaced his "must" number for tanks with increases in armored cars and self-propelled artillery there would be no need to reduce production and all the needs for a balanced military force would be met.

After reading both letters Roosevelt decided that everything was fine, and could be even better with just a bit of tweaking. Well, tweaking was for functionaries, not presidents. So FDR did nothing. Without Roosevelt's full support, Nelson refused to use his powers to unilaterally reduce military orders, opting instead for good-faith negotiations. These made some gains, but by the end of April the military was still requesting significantly more matériel than the system could produce. Nathan was clearly losing the fight, and even within the WPB many turned against him, claiming that the military must decide what their requirements were and "our job is to get industry to fill those requirements." Many of these critics had worked in industry their entire lives, and firmly believed that production could always be increased by throwing additional labor and capital into the mix. That is how it had always worked and no trio of "longhairs" was going to persuade them otherwise. In line with Somervell's thinking, they held that if production was slowing it had nothing to do with the limits of feasibility and everything to do with poor administration and coddling of consumers. Using his personal connection with Hopkins, Somervell got Roosevelt to write Nelson confirming that neither the current military program nor the president's "must items" were negotiable.

Having lost the first battle, Nathan retreated until Kuznets could complete a more thorough analysis of the entire production program. While Kuznets toiled, and production schedules fell further behind, Nathan prepped the bureaucratic battlefield. For the remainder of the spring and summer he made the rounds explaining the concept of feasibility to senior WPB members and others within the government. His greatest convert was Leon Henderson, a trained economist himself, who easily saw what the numbers were saying.

On August 12, Kuznets delivered his 140-page report. It was damning and, for anyone who could understand the statistical tables, dismal reading. By Kuznets's estimate, the military requests were at least 30 percent too high. But because of the damage that such huge undeliverable orders would do to scheduling, the Army might get less than half of what it ordered in the years they expected it. Without going into all of the math, what Kuznets told the Army was that if they asked for the optimal amount for 1943, they would get all they asked for during that year. But if they persisted in asking for 30 percent more than was possible, at least half of what they expected in 1943 would not be delivered until well into 1945 (eighteen to twenty-four months later). But, in a remarkable piece of naïveté, Kuznets went on to recommend, as Nathan had earlier, a joint military-economist board to reconcile strategy with production capacity. How they thought the military would acquiesce to such a power grab beggars belief. To make matters worse, Kuznets only wanted representatives of the Joint Staff on his coordinating body, leaving Somervell out in the cold.

Sixty copies of the report were published. In a break with protocol, Nathan personally delivered a copy to Somervell and Harry Hopkins. Hopkins made no reply, but Somervell sent a point-by-point rebuttal. He was dismayed that the same economists, who only a few months previously had told him to double his orders, were now telling him to drastically cut them. Unable to resist twisting the knife, Somervell concluded with "To me this is an inchoate mass of words . . . I am not impressed with either the character or basis of the judgments expressed in the reports and recommend they be carefully hidden from the eyes of thoughtful men."

Confident in their analysis, Kuznets and Nathan replied with a full broadside: "In view of the gravity of the problems discussed in these documents, I hesitate to take your memorandum seriously." Nathan went on to tell Somervell that when they had previously asked for a doubling of military orders, they had not meant that orders be quadrupled, and it was well past time for Somervell to end his "ostrich-like behavior" on these crucial issues.

The cudgels were out and it was time to enter the lists.

Both sides of the production dispute knew they had gone too far, but the matter was finally out in the open now and it needed to be addressed. In fact, the press had gotten wind of the quarrel, and a concerned Roosevelt sent word that he wanted the matter resolved quickly. Nathan was called to the White House to explain his data and reasoning to Hopkins, who had his aide Isador Lubin, an expert statistician, at his side. When he had finished, Nathan made an appointment with Leon Henderson. After reviewing the report, Henderson voiced his complete agreement and became a valuable and forceful ally for Nathan's crusade. After clearing all other business off the calendar, Nathan scheduled the showdown for the WPB meeting on October 6, 1942. He then went to prepare his case.

Somervell arrived at the meeting with a letter from General Marshall, which concluded with "Lt. General Somervell is the designated representative of the War Department for the interpretation of strategy to the War Production Board." Before the meeting began Somervell proudly showed off this "magical charm" to everyone present. In addition to securing the letter, Somervell had also garnered the support of Undersecretary of War Patterson, who firmly believed that consumer coddling was damaging the war effort.

Nathan began the meeting with a summary of Kuznets's findings, without telling anyone anything new. When presidential assistant Wayne Coy asked if the Army could agree that their requests for the remainder of 1942 and the start of 1943 were too high, Somervell protested that the goals were achievable if "more effective controls were instituted" and "producers intensified their efforts." He emphasized that the needs of soldiers and sailors came first, and the nation needed to meet those needs, even if it meant cutting civilian production. Somervell concluded by stating that doing the recomputations necessary to reduce the Army's orders was not worth the work, and that besides, he had no faith in Nathan's interpretations of the economic statistics.

At this last point, Henderson, who had been slumped quietly in a corner, stirred a bit to defend the statistical methodology employed. He then slumped back into quiescence. Somervell, slightly irritated by the interruption and correction, went on to attack the idea of a "supreme war council" made up of Joint Staff representatives and economists. "We already have the Combined Chiefs, Joint Chiefs, the Combined Production and Resources Board, the Munitions Assignments Board, the Army and Navy Munitions Board, and the War Production Board. What good would be a board composed of an economist, a politician, and a soldier who does not know production?"

When Nathan interrupted to ask if any of these other organizations, particularly the Joint Chiefs, had even bothered to study the problem of feasibility, Somervell again showed off his letter from Marshall and informed the group that the Army's orders reflected the Joint Chiefs' agreed strategy and that really was all there was to it. As Somervell saw it, there was absolutely no need for the WPB to concern itself with any strategic questions. Undersecretary of War Patterson then entered the debate by stating his opposition to the creation of a new production-strategy board, but suggested that it would be helpful if certain WPB personnel met periodically with the Joint Chiefs "for an exchange of attitudes." This was the only conciliatory note voiced.

When Somervell relinquished the floor, the other meeting participants, whom Nathan had been prepping for months, launched a concerted attack on his position. Despite the barrage of criticism, it appeared as if Somervell was going to win by default. He was playing out the clock, for if he did not give in to Nathan's argument there was little the WPB could do about it.

As the meeting began winding down to an unsatisfactory conclusion, Henderson bestirred himself. Speaking in a low voice, as though speaking to himself, Henderson launched into a quasi-soliloquy. "The amount in question, 90 billion dollars, was interesting," said Henderson, "because it exceeded by far the value of our entire national product both for 1933 and 1934." Raising his voice, Henderson then twisted the knife: "Maybe if we can't wage a war on 90 billions, we ought to get rid of our present Joint Chiefs, and find some who can." Coming from a Roosevelt intimate, this was a threat that could not be taken lightly.

Stunned, the only reaction from those present was dead silence, allowing Henderson to turn the full force of his vitriol on Somervell. In what the other participants considered the most violent personal attack they had ever heard, Henderson lambasted Somervell for his arrogance and ineptitude. Almost screaming, Henderson declared himself disgusted with Somervell's obstinacy, overbearing manner, and ignorance of production problems. He flatly stated that he thought Somervell was padding his requirements, and that the general had no idea of the disastrous implications of infeasible goals. Having stated the pertinent points, Henderson went on at length, giving vent to every grievance he had accumulated throughout the first year of the war. Somervell, who likely had never been spoken to in this manner, sat silent throughout Henderson's tirade.

When it was over, William L. Batt, the WPB vice chairman, tried to calm the waters by pointing out that Somervell did not after all make the strategy; he was just trying, like all of them, to support it. Henderson, mustering all the sarcasm he was capable of, replied, "Ain't he got a letter?"

After the meeting adjourned, Stacy May suggested that the Planning Committee throw out the idea of "a supreme strategy coordinating body" that the military would never agree to. Kuznets then chimed in with the idea that the Planning Committee should just tell the Army it could have everything it wanted, but on a new date, an idea Somervell had proposed during their meeting. In effect this was the same as cancelling half of one year's orders and reordering them for the following year, but Kuznets had found a more palatable way of framing this. As Kuznets saw it: "If we say that the objectives in many areas are to be pushed forward—say to the middle of 1944 . . . we would perhaps encounter less opposition than if we insist on the reduction of the objectives proper."

Once the plan for a new board to oversee strategy and production was dropped, Somervell and Patterson accepted the new formulation for stretching out deliveries. To avoid being the bearers of bad news, Nelson was handed the task of informing the Joint Chiefs that much of what they wanted to fight the war in 1943 would not arrive until 1944, and to ask the chiefs to then decide precisely what to reschedule. The Joint Chiefs took up the matter on October 20, and after some discussion agreed to almost

$10 billion in cuts for 1943. It was not as much as Nathan and Kuznets had hoped to get, but they declared the new objective doable and closed the matter.

Nathan, Kuznets, and May had won a stunning bureaucratic victory, one that likely shortened the war by many months and saved countless lives. For without a reduction of Army goals the masses of armaments and munitions the Allies hurled upon the Continent in June 1944 would not have been available until well into the next year.

It was, however, a pyrrhic victory. When the WPB leadership later looked to mend fences with the military, the chief obstacle was Somervell's unrelenting hostility toward the Planning Committee's members. As such, the committee was demoted to a second-tier organization and soon dissolved. Kuznets and May returned to academia. Nathan, joined by Leon Henderson's top aide, David Ginsburg—stunned by an article in a Virginia newspaper claiming that thousands of Americans were dying while a couple of Jews (Nathan and Ginsburg) got paid for planning how to send Christian boys off to war—enlisted in the Army. When they arrived at boot camp, they were shocked to see a *Washington Post* article about their enlistment posted on a bulletin board, with "These sons-a-bitches arrive today" scrawled in grease pencil beside it. Later, when both men were cleaning out latrines, Ginsburg commented that the Army was not treating them very well, to which Nathan retorted, "About as well as or better than they treated us in Washington." There were still many production questions left unanswered, but as *Time* magazine wrote: "Into the Army as a private last week went a man [Nathan] who carried many of the answers in his big, black-thatched head."

Unfortunately, as crucial as resolving the feasibility dispute was, it did nothing to bring an end to the multitude of other disputes plaguing Washington. Throughout 1942 and well into the next year it seemed as if every one of the "alphabet" agencies was at the throat of the others. At the time, many considered that such petty bickering reflected a lack of patriotic sentiment or insufficient zeal to get the job done. That, however, was never the case. Rather, it was too much patriotism and zeal that was causing the problems. Hard-driving men, most of whom had already achieved great things in business and were accustomed to getting their way, were entrusted with important jobs to help the war effort. Rarely were any of them privy to the big picture, nor did many of them care. Each was given a specific job to do, and went about it the only way any of them knew how, by running over anything that stood in their way. Told to produce X quantity of anything, these titans of industry could not accept that some other agency had a priority on some crucial commodity they required. In such a situation, there could be only one solution: get that commodity at any cost. If some other agency failed because they never got the material they needed, so be it. In the Darwinian world these men inhabited, the answer to failure was to replace the losing agency's leader and restart the struggle.

When the WPB was established many thought that Nelson would take on the role of national referee between such warring parties. But, as we have seen, he gave away much of his power in the first hours he was on the job and was never able to retrieve it. In fact, throughout his tenure he continually either gave away power or allowed it to be usurped by a series of czars appointed to run specific sectors of the economy. Worse, early on, Nelson decided to operationalize WPB. That meant that rather than establishing himself and WPB as a small policy board that sat above every other organization, Nelson took on the job of running the economy. Instead of refereeing disputes, WPB often found itself in the middle of them. Where there was a chance in early 1942 for Nelson to grab the reins and make himself, in effect, an assistant president, he had opted to assume the role of just one more claimant for the presidential ear.

32

NO RUBBER, NO WAR

ALTHOUGH PROBLEMS AROSE AS EARLY AS 1940, AMERICA'S entry into the war had turned a series of manageable problems into crises. First up was an entirely predictable rubber crisis. Japan's rapid advance in the Far East had deprived the Allies of 90 percent of the world's naturally produced rubber, and stocks were woefully low. By the end of 1941 the nation had stockpiled 533,000 tons, and if you counted what was still making its way to American ports the country had a bit over 630,000 tons available. Even if the United States bought all of the production remaining outside of Axis control it possessed only a few months' supply. To meet civilian and growing war needs the United States had to conserve rubber, enhance natural supplies from other sources, and hugely increase production of synthetic rubber to 800,000 tons a year—a nearly thirtyfold increase.

Washington handled this in typical fashion: it created a bureaucratic maze. To help increase overseas purchases, overall policy was set by the State Department, while the Bureau of Economic Warfare was responsible for all matters concerning "business judgment" and the recently established Rubber Reserve Company was accountable for actual procurement. Many unfairly blamed the Rubber Reserve Company for not buying enough rubber, at a time when it was purchasing everything available on the global market. Jesse Jones, the head of the Reconstruction Finance Corporation, which ultimately controlled the Rubber Reserve Company, became the subject of increasingly personal attacks. Thin-skinned at the best of times, Jones was incensed when a *Washington Post* editorial claimed that "Jones fell down rather badly on the job . . . because of his boundless ambition for power." Jones fired off a cable to the paper's owner, Eugene Meyer, demanding a retraction. There was no reply, but, as luck would have it, the two men ran into each other in the ballroom of the Willard Hotel that very evening. Jones began by berating Meyer, and then grabbed him by his lapels and shoved him against a wall. Meyer wrenched free but his glasses fell to the floor and shattered. Not one to be pushed around, the sixty-six-year-old Meyer fired an uppercut to the jaw but missed. As Meyer tried to regain his balance, the sixty-eight-year-old Jones, making the most of his thirty-pound weight advantage, closed to grapple. It was only then that bystanders pulled the two men apart. The next day, Roosevelt joked with reporters that he hoped they would not ask him to referee a second round.

Jesse Jones (right).

In the meantime, administrative confusion was slowing construction of synthetic rubber plants to a crawl. To meet an expected need of 600,000 tons the WPB, in its infinite wisdom, thought it sufficient to build facilities capable of producing only about a quarter of what was needed. When Congress threatened to take an active hand in the situation, Roosevelt was finally moved to act. But by asking Bernard Baruch to conduct a study of the problem he only delayed finding a remedy for a couple of months. Baruch's report was delivered on September 1 and it was not happy reading: "We find the existing situation so dangerous that unless corrective measures are taken immediately the country will face both a military and civilian collapse." Baruch recommended the creation of a rubber czar, and on September 15, just before departing on a nationwide inspection tour,

Donald Nelson and William Jeffers.

Roosevelt finally took the plunge and appointed the president of the Union Pacific Railroad, William "Bill" Jeffers, to the position.

Jeffers stood just under six feet and weighed in at a muscular 220 pounds. He had worked his way up from the bottom of the railroading business by dint of his raw intelligence, capacity for hard work, and physical toughness. At Union Pacific he ruled through the time-tested methods of fear and intimidation. He was a man, as *Time* said, who "would take his coat off at the slightest provocation." More than one railroad debate had ended with Jeffers's antagonist out cold on the floor. When he arrived in Washington, he took a suite at the Mayflower Hotel, told Roosevelt he would have the bulk of the job done in a year, and then went to work. And work he did. Jeffers had no hobbies, no outside interests, and nothing to distract him from the task at hand. Technically the rubber czar's office was set up within

William Jeffers.

the WPB, meaning Jeffers worked for Nelson. But once again, when offered the opportunity to take power, Nelson balked, stating that Jeffers "would be vested with all of the authority of the Chairman of the War Production Board." In one sentence, Nelson had made Jeffers equal to himself within the WPB. It was not long before Jeffers's bellowing, threats, and physical domination had cowed all of his WPB colleagues.

Almost as soon as Jeffers began, he ran into problems. He had decided to use synthetic rayon for manufacturing tires, while senators from cotton states wanted him to use cotton, which had not yet been tested for such use. When South Carolina senator Ellison "Cotton Ed" Smith came close to presenting him with an ultimatum, Jeffers shouted his reply: "I do not intend to be influenced by anyone, anywhere, at any time. The whole thing has been muddled up for months, and I am going through or else." When Smith persisted, Jeffers stated: "The trouble with this whole situation is that it has been a muddle of men who were afraid that some Congressional committee or pressure group wouldn't like their decisions. I am going to make my decisions and I'll stand by them." Having disposed of Capitol Hill, Jeffers next took on the Army. Here he ran straight into the equally tough Patterson. This time the fight was over construction material that could go either to rubber plants or to refineries capable of producing the high-octane fuel that aircraft required. The dispute turned nasty when Jeffers, before a joint session of Congress, called the military's factory expediters "loafers" and accused them of making off with material he could put to better use. This fight only ended when one of the WPB's new directors, Ferdinand Eberstadt, called both Jeffers and Patterson to his home. After hours of discussion the two hard men could not be made to see eye to eye, but they did develop a mutual respect and agreed to lower the rhetoric. Patterson, though he left the meeting feeling kinder toward Jeffers, was more convinced than ever that if Nelson could not control a man like Jeffers he was too weak for the job. Jeffers, on the other hand, appreciated Nelson's weakness, as it allowed him to range and rage freely.

Jeffers left Washington in September 1943. By that time, the plants required to assure a steady supply of rubber were either already operating or nearing completion. At his departure Jeffers said, "The big job is done." As he saw it, the best way for him to continue contributing to the war effort was to retake the reins of the Union Pacific Railroad. His replacement, the equally tough-minded Bradley Dewey, resigned a year later pleading that the job was done. Between the two of them they had bulled through a project many thought had little chance of success and in the process made the United States the largest rubber producer in the world. Then they had done that rarest of all things in Washington: they closed their section of the bureaucracy and went home. Both men must qualify for the laurels of a "bureaucratic Cincinnatus."

During America's first year in the war, the rubber crisis interacted with a burgeoning oil crisis in ways that affected every American. Roosevelt had long recognized the crucial importance of oil to the war effort and America's vital role in supplying it. From Pearl Harbor until the end of the war, the Allies consumed seven billion barrels of oil, of which 80 percent was produced by the United States. To manage this massive flow, Roosevelt appointed Secretary of the Interior Harold Ickes as petroleum coordinator in early May 1941. At the time, he had done so through a personal letter, rather than an executive order, obviously intending to get Ickes involved but to limit his power.

Roosevelt wanted an amicable relationship with the oil industry. But if that failed he was putting the industry on notice that beneath his velvet glove he grasped a Harold Ickes ready to rampage through their corporate offices. Upon hearing that Ickes was in charge, one oilman said: "Ickes is

Leon Henderson.

now captain of our souls, my day is ruined." But oilmen discovered that they could work with Ickes. In fact, he often followed their lead and became their greatest supporter in Washington. Ickes even went so far as to take on the redoubtable Leon Henderson in a mostly losing battle to raise the price of gasoline.

Ickes's first major problem was supplying the East Coast. Almost all of the east's oil supplies moved by ship from the Gulf Coast and along the Eastern Seaboard. Just as Ickes took office, Roosevelt allotted fifty of these vessels (14 percent) to supplying British needs, immediately throwing the Eastern Seaboard into a crisis. To make up for the lost ships Ickes began using railcars, while lobbying for construction of pipelines from Texas to New York. The railroads rose to the challenge, but Ickes's pipeline proposals ran into a series of political firestorms in every district he wanted to build in. Moreover, the WPB mandarins twice turned down his requests for matériel, as they considered the pipelines a waste of precious steel. And though Ickes raged, progress came at a snail's pace.

The east's oil crisis worsened immeasurably after America entered the war. We have already seen the damage that U-boats did in the spring and summer of 1942, when many of the ships sunk were oil tankers. Only the railroads, which within weeks increased their daily oil shipments from

70,000 barrels to an impressive 640,000, kept the Eastern Seaboard moving at all. Still, this only met half of the eastern states' needs, and even doing this much was bankrupting the oil companies. Moving oil by rail nearly doubled the cost of a barrel of oil, and Henderson would only let the price of gasoline go up by 1.2 cents a gallon, less than half of what was needed to cover the oil companies' costs. In this atmosphere, the WPB relented and gave up the steel for two pipelines, while Jesse Jones came up with $150 million to fund them. Between 1943 and 1945, these pipelines moved 380 million barrels of oil to the East Coast, relieving most of the wartime pressure.

In the meantime, the only short-term solution was rationing. On April 22, 1942, Leon Henderson announced that gasoline rationing would commence for the eastern states on May 15, and that the average East Coast motorist could expect between 2.5 and 5 gallons a week. Strongly supported by Patterson, who likely thought the amount was overly generous, Henderson weathered a barrage of criticism from every corner. Horrible Harold, as many in the press referred to Ickes, said there had to be rationing but it would be nowhere near as stringent as Henderson stated. But Henderson stuck to his guns, telling the average motorist they would get three gallons per week, which was "a damned sight more than they were entitled to." The rationing, although far from foolproof, served its purpose. Driving was severely reduced and demand fell into line with supply.

But the WPB also saw gasoline rationing as the answer to much of its still ongoing rubber problem. Until the synthetic rubber plants were online, no one in the United States was going to get a new tire. That meant the tires currently on American cars and trucks required preservation, meaning Americans had to drive less. Initially the WPB proposed limiting vehicles to a certain number of miles, and enforcing it with weekly inspections of the odometer reading of every vehicle in the country. But just this one time, even the WPB considered such a system as too massive and intrusive to be workable. Instead, Nelson and Henderson pushed the president to order *nationwide* gasoline rationing, although gasoline was only in short supply on the East Coast.

Congress exploded, and with it so did a substantial portion of the American people. In areas where oil was plentiful, such as Texas and California, no one could understand why they could not drive. The alternative as they saw it was that the oil would just be burned off, as there were no storage facilities. Neither Congress nor the American people were stupid. Rather, they were being willfully obtuse. The connection of gasoline use to rubber conservation was easy to see, if one wanted to see it—but few did. Roosevelt, who in reaction to public sentiment could switch positions on a dime, spoke about overexcitement and told the public that rubber substitutes were on the way, and not to worry—knocking the rationale for rationing out from beneath the WPB planners.

On June 5, Nelson, Henderson, Ickes, Arthur Newhall (who had been head of rubber supply within WPB before Jeffers became czar), and Joseph Eastman (Office of Defense Transportation) trooped over to the White House. But the president was not willing to be convinced. Roosevelt opened the meeting by telling the group he did not believe the rubber situation was as dire as they believed—another example of what Stimson called his "happy faculty of fooling himself." Henderson then rattled off the facts supporting the case for conserving rubber by rationing gasoline, but Roosevelt waved him off. Ickes, who was more interested in keeping the oil market vibrant than in conserving rubber, suggested that a million tons of rubber could be had just by collecting scrap. Roosevelt seized on this, though no one else in the room believed there was anywhere that much usable scrap available. Three days later Roosevelt ordered the start of a campaign to collect scrap rubber.

It failed miserably. After gathering less than a quarter of what Ickes predicted, the drive was extended for a further ten days. An embarrassed Ickes took to stealing rubber mats from the White House and bizarrely accusing Americans of hoarding rubber. The press was courteous enough not to ask what these nefarious rubber hoarders planned to do with their useless scrap. Roosevelt was forced to accept that rationing was now the only solution. On the same day he agreed to Jeffers as rubber czar, he also surrendered on the issue of gasoline rationing. Roosevelt, however, left it to Jeffers to make the announcement, and hopefully take some of the political heat. Just before Thanksgiving twenty million motorists began lining up to get their "A" books, entitling them to sixteen gallons a month.

Roosevelt escaped the Washington bickering by embarking on a nation-spanning inspection trip. He returned on October 1, 1942, refreshed and buoyant, in a way that usually only happened after an extended trip at sea.

Unfortunately, Americans were not of similar good cheer. Without positive war news, and chafing at rubber shortages, gasoline rationing, and numerous other wartime regulations, the mood of the American voter was beginning to turn foul. As pervasive political squabbles and management ineptitude were increasingly splattered on the front pages of every newspaper in the country, many Americans were wondering if the visible lack of progress was due to the current political leadership not being up to the task.

Many pundits were already predicting Republicans would retake both the House and the Senate, and Roosevelt himself thought his party was on the verge of a historic rout. Despite his political misgivings, Roosevelt maintained his focus on the war. Throughout the month, he kept himself abreast of the planning for the preparations for the TORCH invasions without getting involved in the details. Roosevelt was always determined to avoid letting electoral politics influence battlefield preparation, but in early October he weakened, just slightly. During one of General Marshall's TORCH briefings, the president held his hands up as if in prayer and said, "Please make it before Election Day." According to Marshall, that was the only time the president allowed political concerns to enter into wartime planning. When Marshall later disappointed him with the news that the invasion could not possibly be launched before the election, Roosevelt did not utter a word of complaint. On the other hand, Steve Early, the president's press secretary, who was told about the invasion just one hour before the landings, exploded in hot anger over the delay that almost cost the Democrats their majorities on the Hill.

As Election Day neared Roosevelt did find time to meet with the commanders of the invasion force. On October 21 the Navy commander, Admiral Henry Kent Hewitt, and the Army commander, General George S. Patton, duly presented themselves. When Roosevelt airily asked what was on their minds, Hewitt began a long discourse on the plan, which seemed to bore Roosevelt. During a pause, Patton issued his own appreciably more succinct blast of bombast: "Sir, all I want to tell you is this—I will leave the beaches either a conqueror or a corpse." Roosevelt waved the comment off, and soon he and Hewitt were discussing the banalities of mooring ships and yachts. Sensing their time was almost up, Patton again interjected: "The Admiral and I feel that we must get ashore regardless of cost, as the fate of the war hinges on our success." Patton claimed his comment was meant to pressure Hewitt into landing no matter how difficult the seas, but Roosevelt did not know what to make of it. Finishing the meeting, Roosevelt simply replied: "Certainly you must." A disappointed Patton wrote in his diary that night: "A great politician is not of necessity a great military leader."

Election Day found Roosevelt at Hyde Park. He had reason for serious concern. Though the war news had started to turn up, the change had not been fully absorbed by the electorate. As he went to vote Roosevelt noted the low turnout at the Hyde Park polling station (nationwide the total vote was half that of the 1940 presidential election year) and understood it did not bode well for the Democrats. James Farley, until recently one of Roosevelt's closest confidants and now New York party chairman, spent the night glumly looking at a silent phone, understanding that when county chairmen had good news to relate, they do it fast, but when the news is bad no one wants to make the call. He was supposed to get a Democrat elected governor of New York. Instead the election went to Thomas E. Dewey, the young, brash, racket-busting prosecutor, whom Willkie had edged out for the Republican presidential nomination in 1940. He was the new boy wonder of politics, and everyone knew the election was only a stepping-stone to his challenging Roosevelt in 1944.

The results came close to a disaster for Roosevelt, but did not quite get there. The Republicans gained nine seats in the Senate and forty-seven in the House, but the Democrats held on to slim majorities in both chambers. The next day, Roosevelt appeared in high spirits and gave no indication of the gloom many expected would enshroud him. His only private comment on the elections was that if the Democrats wanted to win in the future they would have to put forward better candidates. His only public comment came a few days later when he told the press that he assumed "the new Congress . . . would be as much in favor of winning the war as the Chief Executive."

And by Election Day 1942, the Allies had turned the tide of the war, even if American voters failed to appreciate it. In late October, the Japanese made a final major effort to retake Guadalcanal, but by this time King had placed Admiral William "Bull" Halsey in charge of naval forces in the area, which had an immediate positive effect on the fighting spirit of the force. As a major Japanese land assault aimed at the island's airfield—Henderson Field—got under way, the Japanese navy simultaneously tried to sweep away protecting U.S. naval forces. In the resulting Battle of Santa Cruz, the United States lost the carrier *Hornet* and saw the *Enterprise* crippled, while the Japanese had two of their carriers severely damaged but had also lost many more almost irreplaceable veteran pilots. The result was a tactical loss for the United States. But just as at Coral Sea, it was a major strategic victory. The Japanese never again made a serious attempt to retake the island. Months of hard fighting remained before the island was fully secured, but from this point forward the Allies were unquestionably on the offensive in the Pacific. The loss of another carrier was, of course, temporarily crippling, as America now had only one carrier in the Pacific, and it was damaged. But help was on the way. In December the USS *Essex,* the first of the war's huge Essex-class carriers, was commissioned, with nearly two dozen more to follow before the war ended. Still for most Americans, the fact that the tide had turned in the Pacific was far from obvious, as all they saw was that the *Hornet* had gone to the bottom, and the marines were just barely maintaining their toehold on a speck of an island no one had ever heard of a few months before.

At the same time, when Americans went to the polls, the German offensive in southern Russia was still grinding forward. Few Americans could see that the Wehrmacht had reached its culminating point, as its exhausted formations were being pulverized into dust in Stalingrad's bloody streets. The Soviets, who had even less regard for the U.S. election calendar than American planners, launched Operation Uranus two weeks after the elections, trapping Germany's powerful Sixth Army and dooming it to complete destruction. In fact, the Soviets came within a whisker of collapsing the entire German front.

In Africa, General Bernard Law Montgomery on October 23 launched the three corps of the Eighth Army against Rommel's forces at El Alamein. Though the American public, in the days leading up to the election, followed the attack with near-breathless anticipation, Montgomery, despite horrendous losses, made little progress. The German line did not give until November 4, allowing Montgomery to finally get his pursuit fully under way, but too late to have any effect on the U.S. election.

PART FOUR

NEW FRONTS

We must not get soft. War must be destructive and to a certain extent ruthless and inhuman.

General Henry "Hap" Arnold,
memo to Secretary of War Stimson, March 1945

33

TORCH

B EFORE DAWN, ON NOVEMBER 8, 1942, ALLIED LANDING CRAFT began their slow bobbing crawl toward invasion beaches scattered along eight hundred miles of North Africa's coast. Awaiting them were sixty thousand Vichy French soldiers. What none of the approaching soldiers knew was whether the French would resist the landings or welcome the invading forces with open arms. Despite months of secret diplomacy and clandestine missions aimed at convincing the French to abandon Vichy and join the Allies, uncertainty lingered, even as the moment of decision arrived. That this was so was because the Allies had placed too much initial faith in the ability of General Henri Giraud to gain command of the Vichy force in North Africa. Giraud, who had escaped from German captivity both in 1914 and 1942, had assured the Americans that the Vichy French army in North Africa would follow his orders. When the time came, however, Eisenhower was chagrined to discover that Giraud was powerless, as most French officers had sworn oaths to Vichy and its leader, World War I hero Marshal Philippe Pétain. Few, if any, of the French military commanders in North Africa were disposed to follow Giraud's orders.

When the TORCH landings commenced, Roosevelt was at Shangri-La—his name for the presidential retreat now known as Camp David—with Hopkins and his new wife, along with a few other intimate friends. All evening he and Hopkins had been preoccupied and on edge, explaining to others that they were waiting for an important phone call. At last, the telephone rang and his secretary, Grace Tully, announced that the War Department was on the line. With trembling hands, Roosevelt grasped the phone and listened intently to the entire message and then burst out: "Thank God. Thank God. That sounds grand. Congratulations. Casualties are comparatively light—much below your predictions. Thank God." Roosevelt dropped the phone and announced to the group: "We have landed in North Africa; Casualties are below expectations. We are striking back."

The optimistic report delivered to Roosevelt belied what was happening on the invasion beaches, where green American troops, reinforced at points by British forces, were meeting ferocious resistance at many points. The Giraud gambit had failed, but by a stroke of luck, Admiral François Darlan was in North Africa visiting a son suffering from polio. Darlan was the number two man in France, and in effect ruled Vichy in place of the increasingly feeble Pétain. As commander of the entire Vichy military, and empowered to act in Pétain's name, he could order an immediate ceasefire and be obeyed. When informed by U.S. diplomat Robert Murphy that 500,000 American troops (Murphy felt free to exaggerate the size of the invasion) were at that moment storming beaches all across North Africa, Darlan was at first purple with rage. A few moments later, self-interest, always Darlan's driving motive, took over. The day after the invasion, under pressure from Eisenhower's deputy, General Mark Clark, Darlan ordered a ceasefire throughout French North Africa. But Eisenhower needed more. He not only wanted the French army to stop resisting, he wanted it to take an active part in future operations against the Germans. To get that, Eisenhower made an "expedient" deal with Darlan—the archcollaborator with the Nazi regime—that allowed Darlan to establish a French government in North Africa, with himself in charge. Giraud, displaying a humility rarely seen among senior French officers, understood his political impotence and agreed to serve under Darlan.

What seemed sensible on the fighting front caused a firestorm in Washington. Attacks came from every quarter. This was the United States' first major political-military venture of the war, and one of Hitler's stooges was placed in charge of the civilian government in North Africa. Churchill, who was trying to appease an irritated de Gaulle, leader of the Free French forces, was less than happy, while de Gaulle himself was near apoplectic, shouting: "What remains of the honor of France will stay intact in my hands . . . The United States can pay traitors but not with the honor of France." *Time* asked: "If Norway were invaded, would the U.S. thenceforth move to strengthen the hand of Vidkun Quisling?" Others asked if the United States invaded Germany would we make a similar deal with Goering or Goebbels? Seizing on the Quisling analogy, *The Nation* editor and publisher, Freda Kirchwey, penned an article—"America's First Quisling"—in which she reminded everyone of Darlan's status: "Prostitutes are used; they are seldom loved. Even less frequently are they honored."

Roosevelt, according to Sam Rosenman, was more affected by these attacks than any he had ever suffered before, particularly as they came from publications that had in the past always supported him. He must have been bewildered that he, the one U.S. leader who had recognized the inherent evils of the Nazis from the start and had led the nation in its growing opposition to fascism, was now accused of being in league with those he detested. Distressed, Roosevelt refused to talk about North Africa, and began reading aloud criticisms word for word. In North Africa, Eisenhower was equally stunned by the intensity of the criticism. Still a political neophyte, who would hereafter rapidly climb that particular learning curve, he was taken aback by the storm of condemnation, much of it aimed at him personally. He cabled a long explanation of the Darlan deal to the Joint Chiefs of Staff, reminding them that it was saving American lives and asking that they not do anything that would upset the fragile equilibrium he had created.

But attacks were not only coming from the press; many within the administration also harbored strong doubts about the deal's wisdom and morality. McCloy informed Stimson that those in "starry-eyed circles" were in a high state of excitement over the Darlan deal. Stimson asked him to gather a few of them at his mansion, Woodley, where he would see about calming them. When Stimson arrived home, he found Henry Morgenthau, Felix Frankfurter, and Archibald MacLeish (a Frankfurter acolyte, heavily involved in wartime propaganda and public affairs). Stimson thought that "Morgenthau was sunk" and "ready to give up the war which had lost all interest for him." Stimson went into a diatribe about how many lives were saved by Darlan's ceasefire order, and how the early termination of hostilities with the Vichy forces had helped keep Spain from seizing Gibraltar. After reading the group the entirety of Eisenhower's three-page cable, Stimson allowed that "this was just a temporary arrangement; and that the army could not make foreign policy." Throughout the discussion Frankfurter kept his own counsel, and Stimson thought MacLeish was mostly just puzzled. But Morgenthau was the main target of his argument, and after many "grunts and groans" Stimson believed he had gotten "Morgenthau into line" and had sent him home reconciled.

Henry Morgenthau.

Stimson was very much mistaken in that belief. The Morgenthau diaries tell a very different story of what took place that evening, claiming that Stimson lost his temper at several points and that there was a long discussion of a memo that the president had dictated on the entire situation. In the memo, Roosevelt sides with the military in favoring the Darlan deal as a matter of military expediency, but at the same time he remains noncommittal about how long Darlan would remain in power. MacLeish said that Roosevelt wanted the memo cleared with Hull and Marshall, but had told him he could skip Stimson; another indication of Roosevelt's mounting confidence that he could run the war without employing Stimson or Knox as intermediaries. At the time, Frankfurter considered it a "cruel thing for MacLeish to say" in Stimson's presence, while Morgenthau just considered it "crude."

After the memo discussion ended, Morgenthau made a passionate address about his true thoughts on Darlan:

> I said he was a most ruthless person who had sold many thousands of people into slavery, and that to use a man like that in these times, no matter what the price is, the price is too great. I went on to say that there is something else besides temporary military victories, and I said, "You can't tell me the whole campaign was set up with the expectation of using Darlan because the President told me that that wasn't so." Then I said, "There is a considerable group of rich people in this country who would make peace with Hitler tomorrow, and the only people who really want to fight are the working men and women, and if they once get the idea that we are going to sit back and favor these Fascists, these Hitlerites etc., not only in France but in Spain which is what we are doing every day because we are freezing Franco into his job, these people are going to have sit-down strikes; they are going to slow up production, and they are going to say 'What's the use of fighting just to put that kind of people back into power?'" I said, "If something isn't done about it and that idea once gets into the minds of the people, you will never be able to get it out."

Morgenthau said he could tell from MacLeish's face that he agreed that Darlan should be immediately dismissed, and wrote in his diary that Frankfurter said, "Yes, we agree with what Henry has said." When Stimson tried to find a middle ground, Morgenthau declared that "he had never been so disgusted in his life." The meeting broke up soon thereafter. Clearly, if Stimson thought he had convinced any of the "starry-eyed crowd," he was deluding himself. Frankfurter called Morgenthau later that night and offered him some suggestions on how to handle Stimson and what to say to the president. An angry Morgenthau recorded: "It was typical of Frankfurter. He didn't say anything while we were all together; yet as soon as he got home he wanted to become 'Mr. Fixer.'"

Though he had made little impression on Morgenthau, Stimson did do Roosevelt a great service in this debate. After his guests left, McCloy called to alert him that Willkie was planning to attack the president over the Darlan deal in a nationally broadcast speech that night. Stimson got to Willkie just before he departed for the forum and bluntly told him that if he attacked the Darlan deal now it would jeopardize the war effort and cost American lives. Willkie flew into "a terrific rage," calling Stimson a series of names and wanting to know if Stimson was "trying to control his freedom." Stimson, not easily cowed, stuck to his guns and read Willkie part of Eisenhower's cable. When he was done, Stimson told Willkie that he always respected him, but that would be gravely diminished if he attacked the Darlan deal as planned. Fearing that he had failed to move Willkie, Stimson went to bed without listening to the speech. At 11:00 P.M., Roosevelt called to tell Stimson that he had listened to Willkie and that the offending passages had been removed.

Roosevelt had accepted Eisenhower's arguments and was willing to just let the whole matter blow itself out. But rather than blow over, the storm intensified. As pressure mounted Hopkins prevailed on Roosevelt to issue a statement. In it, Roosevelt said that he accepted Eisenhower's political arrangements in North Africa, but then said that based on Darlan's having worked closely with the Nazis, no permanent arrangement could possibly be made with him. He then affirmed the principle that any future French government would be decided on by the French people, after the ultimate Allied victory. As for the present situation, Roosevelt stressed that it was a temporary expedient "justified solely by the stress of battle." In a personal message to Eisenhower, the president confirmed his full support for his on-the-spot decision, but warned him not to trust Darlan and not to keep him in power a moment longer than necessary. To Churchill, Roosevelt sent an old Orthodox church proverb: "My children it is permitted you in times of grave danger to walk with the devil until you have crossed the bridge." He released the same quote to the press, but the storm continued to blow unabated. There is no question that Darlan understood his position and likely fate, describing himself as "a lemon the Americans would drop once they had squeezed it dry."

As soon as Hitler learned of the Allied invasion of North Africa he ordered the execution of Case Anton—the military occupation of Vichy. What semblance of French freedom that remained was extinguished in less than a week, signaling that Darlan's usefulness was running out. One of Darlan's chief drawing cards had been his promise to deliver the still powerful French fleet, currently in Toulon, to the Allies. But, as the Germans were occupying Vichy, the naval commander at Toulon chose to scuttle the fleet rather than bring it into the war on either side. Moreover, the German invasion swept away the fiction that there was an independent Vichy France that had some claim on the loyalty of French soldiers, in effect neutering Darlan, who no longer had the authority to command French forces.

The immediate problem was how to dispose of the admiral now that his hour had passed. It was solved by twenty-year-old Fernand Bonnier de la Chapelle, a monarchist currently finding common cause with the Gaullists. On Christmas Eve, Bonnier, armed with a pistol, a false passport, and $2,000 ($30,000 in today's money), sneaked into Darlan's office and put two bullets in him. Bonnier was captured on the scene, severely beaten, and then executed less than forty-eight hours later. Who put him up to it remains one of the war's great riddles; as Bonnier went to his grave claiming he acted alone the mystery remained unsolved. Giraud had twelve alleged co-conspirators arrested in a "round up the usual suspects" move that was widely understood as the start of a new power struggle over the future of France. The arrests ensnared almost every element of French politics: conservatives, liberals, fascists, communists, Gaullists, republicans, and royalists. Many, however, credited either British intelligence or de Gaulle's organization with the assassination, but no firm evidence linking either has ever turned up. What is certain was the Allied leaders welcomed being let off the hook. As Churchill said, Darlan's death "relieved the Allies of their embarrassment for working with him and left them with all the advantages he had been able to bestow."

34

New Hands at the Helm

A S THE FIGHTING IN NORTH AFRICA INTENSIFIED, THE DUAL CRISES in oil and rubber were reaching their denouement. They did not magically end, but as 1942 closed both were clearly on the road to a permanent solution. There were, however, many other crises to take their place. The most dangerous of these was inflation, and many feared a repeat of World War I's out-of-control price increases. Because of how that war was financed, inflation galloped along at between 13 and 20 percent annually. By 1920 the dollar only bought half as much as it had in 1914. The worst of these increases was felt in just the short time the United States had been in the war: 1917–1918. As World War II began, both financiers and politicians were scared out of their wits that a worse inflation would take hold as the nation came to grips with paying for a much longer and immense war. The problem was easy to see, but there were huge divisions over the answer.

When it comes right down to it, there are only a few ways to finance a war. The first, plunder, favored by Alexander the Great, the Roman Republic, and many conquerors throughout history, was still being employed by Imperial Japan and Nazi Germany with decidedly mixed results. For the United States this was, of course, never an option. The other three approaches—printing money, higher taxes, and borrowing—all had pluses and minuses. Printing money is shorthand for a complex procedure by which the Federal Reserve creates new money. It is fast and reliable, but also brings on rapid inflation. If the memories of inflation during the last war did not suffice to warn Americans against this path, economists hoped the experience of other American wars would do the trick. In the 1940s, the phrase "not worth a continental" remained in fashion, and the collapse of the Confederacy's currency during the Civil War was still within living memory.

Higher taxes could pay for the war on a pay-as-you-go basis, and had the added benefit of taking the cash that stoked inflation out of people's pockets. Though there was a general agreement that taxes had to rise to pay for the war, questions such as by how much and whose taxes would go up were hotly disputed. Voters never liked higher taxes; thus, politicians rarely liked them either. The other alternative was to tax business, but there was a general awareness that business would just shift higher taxes onto consumers. Still, there was sympathy for an excess-profits tax, as no one wanted to see big business make outsized gains during the war. Eventually taxes on business did rise substantially, but Stimson's wisdom on the subject—let business make money out of the process or business won't work—was the rule.

That left debt. In the mid-twentieth century, many persons considered it immoral to saddle future generations with billions in debt to fight a war in the present. Others, however, countered that since the war was being fought so that future generations could live in freedom and prosperity it was only right that those yet unborn helped bear the burden. As printing money was a widely known evil and there were political limits to taxation, debt became the default mechanism for funding the war.

Actually, although the Federal Reserve claimed to have financed the first year of the war through taxation (25 percent) and debt (75 percent), that was not the unvarnished truth, as a huge proportion of that debt wound up back on the Federal Reserve's balance sheet, which in effect meant the Federal Reserve was printing money. At the same time, paychecks were getting larger, and there were many millions more Americans getting checks than ever before. All this money was available for consumer purchases, but there was only a limited number of goods available to buy. This established the very conditions—too much money chasing too few goods—necessary to ignite runaway inflation.

Trying to hold the line against inflation—which was already edging over 1 percent a month—stood a lonely Leon Henderson. Arrayed against him were the labor unions who wanted wages raised, farmers who wanted more money for their crops, businessmen who wanted to raise prices to keep up with additional costs, and every congressman and senator who wanted to

make his voters happy. Thus, Henderson became the target of vicious public abuse, as few other government officials have had to endure. Much of
this was brought on by Henderson himself. Loud, bellicose, and almost
always the smartest guy in the room, he was incapable of softening a blow,
compromising, suffering fools, or making allies. When a reporter asked
him why Congress hated him so much, Henderson guffawed his answer:
"My lack of politeness." More seriously he continued: "I belong to the
group [of people] with a low boiling point . . . and I've had plenty of flame
applied to me, too." When Henderson took the job, Bernard Baruch had
told him that he would become the most hated man in America, so it says
much about Henderson's self-awareness that he understood he brought
much of the opprobrium upon himself.

Despite Henderson's cussedness and never-ceasing efforts to hold the
line on inflation, he was fighting a losing battle. By mid-1942 there was a
third more cash in circulation than the year before, and almost triple the
level of 1929. Farm incomes had doubled in three years and paychecks for
daily laborers were on a similar trajectory. Though Americans, with strong
memories of the Depression, were saving large amounts for a rainy day, the
impulse to spend at least a portion of their bounty was growing. But even
as cash increased, the amount of goods on store shelves was falling. By
mid-1942 Americans had $84 billion in pent-up spending power, but there
was under $75 billion worth of goods available for purchase—a sure recipe
for inflation. Trying to hold the price line was further complicated by the
fact that Henderson was never able to attract top talent into the Office of
Price Administration. Who after all wanted to work in America's most
hated organization?

By Labor Day 1942, it was clear to all that the war against inflation was
going even worse than the war against the Axis powers, where only the
Battle of Midway stood out against the gloom of repeated setbacks and
defeats. Congress, looking to avoid voter fallout, urged Roosevelt to let
them off the hook and issue executive orders freezing wages and prices.
Roosevelt knew action had to be taken soon but was in no more of a hurry
than Congress to take the blame for freezing wages. He was also keenly
aware of the fact that if he did freeze wages he would be condemned by the
same congressmen privately urging him to do so, as they sought personal
political gain in an election year.

Roosevelt made his decision while at Shangri-La—Camp David. At the urging of Hopkins and Henderson, he ignored those advising immediate action and refused to issue an executive order his staff had already prepared. In a stern message to Congress, followed by a fireside chat on Labor Day, Roosevelt demanded that Congress do its job before October 1, or he would. In a stroke Roosevelt had denied Congress political cover and, in the event he was forced to act by dictate, he could point the finger at Congress for shirking its duty. Congress grumbled, debated, swore, and fought for the rest of September, but then gave Roosevelt everything he had asked for, including authority to set up a new office to manage the war against inflation. The very next morning Roosevelt created the Office of Economic Stabilization, took his old friend and political fixer Jimmy Byrnes off the Supreme Court, and handed him the reins of Washington's newest fiefdom.

Byrnes was now in the position of a super-umpire, with powers verging on those of Roosevelt himself. To make sure everyone knew that he spoke for the president, he moved his office into the White House. Moreover, although Roosevelt hated the term "assistant president," Byrnes employed it often. For the moment, his powers were a bit circumscribed by his statutory focus on inflation. But Byrnes wasted little time before acting in Roosevelt's name in many other areas. As Roosevelt told him when he took the job, "the office was important, but less so than the other duties I want you to perform for me by direct delegation." Moreover, Byrnes's official powers were set to vastly increase when he was placed in charge of the yet-to-be-created Office of War Mobilization.

The choice of the respected and well-connected Byrnes was almost universally applauded, although there were some grumblings from labor, particularly from the neglected Sidney Hillman. As Bruce Catton, then a WPB official and later a Civil War historian, observed, Byrnes was likable, suave, and gifted with the knack of persuading rivals to compromise. "Suppose," said Catton, "you and I had an argument . . . you claim two and two make four, while I claim two and two make six. We take it to Jimmy Byrnes for a decision. He is apt to get us both to agree that two and two make five."

The news of Byrnes's appointment staggered Donald Nelson. He learned of it the same way Knudsen had learned that Nelson was replacing him at the top of the heap: via the news ticker. He assumed that he was being fired, but relaxed somewhat when Roosevelt sent him a message, declaring that he was doing a great job and to keep it up. But Nelson, like everyone else, knew there was now someone between him and the president and that there now existed an office where WPB decisions could be appealed short of the president. Clearly, Washington's power structure had changed in a most unsubtle way.

Another person who was likely not pleased with this change of events was Harry Hopkins. For all his failings, Nelson was still Hopkins's creature. That was decidedly not true of Byrnes. When Hopkins visited Byrnes on his first day on the job, he intended to lay out his ideas for how Byrnes should resolve a certain issue. More important, he wanted to impress on Byrnes where he stood in the power structure around the president. Byrnes listened patiently and then said he had a suggestion of his own. Hopkins leaned in expectantly, noting that a sudden unnerving smile had come across Byrnes's face. "Harry," Byrnes said, "stay the hell out of my business."

Nelson may have been spared for the moment, but Henderson's days in official Washington were coming to an end. He was sick, battered, and tired. He was also hated by Congress and every lobbying organization in Washington. He had done his job and taken the abuse, but nothing could save him. On December 8, 1942, he resigned as head of the Office of Price Administration, stating that more attacks were on the way and he could best serve OPA by leaving it. The president, at first, refused his resignation. But when Henderson sent a note to Byrnes telling him to get FDR's approval or he would announce his resignation on the radio that night, Roosevelt accepted it.

Henderson spent the next several months in Mexico and California recovering his health and restoring his reputation as the best no-trump bridge player in the country. When he eventually went to New York, he established himself as the chairman of the Research Institute of America with a hefty salary of $75,000, compared to the $12,000 he was getting in government service. He would not return to government service until late in 1944, when he conducted a European inspection tour at Roosevelt's behest. He reported his findings to Roosevelt just days before the president's death.

Even as Byrnes was settling in, another crisis on the economic front was racing toward its denouement. When the feasibility dispute ended in October, it solved one major difficulty: getting production targets in line with what the nation could realistically produce. But this left two major problems—priorities and scheduling—unresolved. Nelson had first tried to fix the priorities problem with a convoluted Production Requirements Plan (PRP). It was an unmitigated disaster. The PRP called for almost every firm in the production chain to list its material needs for over two dozen commodities, for every purchase order it had, whether civilian or military. This information was consolidated within the War Production Board, which then undertook the job of coordinating deliveries. The system took tens of thousands of persons to administer and was always on the wrong side of administrative chaos. As firms could never be sure they would get the material they needed when they needed it, they had every incentive to stockpile needed commodities, leading to tons of material sitting unused for months at a time when there was an urgent need for that material elsewhere. By mid-1942, there were, to take one example, thousands of tank treads piling up without tanks to put them on, as the steel for the tanks was sitting in dockyards waiting for an order for a new ship to arrive.

The entire system was seizing up, and Secretary of War Stimson was becoming vocal in his complaints. In his eyes, the problem was Donald Nelson, who, he thought, had come to Washington "with a big reputation, which is apparently facetious." Nelson's incapacity for the job was compounded by what Stimson saw as an inefficient organization, and a "lot of weak men around him, none of whom is competent to face and handle the vital problem of allocation." This was a bit rich, as the War Department had run off the WPB's strongman—Nathan. At Stimson's direction, the Army, in the persons of Patterson and Ferdinand Eberstadt, began applying the heat to Nelson. Eberstadt, who was responsible for bringing Patterson and rubber czar Jeffers together, was currently head of the Army-Navy Munitions Board. The board, whose existence preceded the start of mobilization, had taken over many of the production duties that Nelson had abrogated. Adding to Nelson's troubles with the military were the increasing complaints coming from business as a result of the WPB's inability to handle scheduling.

On July 22, 1942, Stimson, Knox, Patterson, Forrestal, Admiral Samuel M. Robinson (King's representative on production matters), McCloy, and Somervell visited Nelson. Stimson, in his diary, said that this was a rather singular meeting as it was an indictment of Nelson's administration "by

Ferdinand Eberstadt.

men who were his friends" and men "who desired to help him rather than depose him." Sometimes men lie to themselves, even in their own diaries. Not one of the men in that room, including Stimson, would have shed a tear at Nelson's ouster. The entire first half of the meeting was dedicated to a round-robin discussion of Nelson's many failings, before the group turned to considering the names of men they thought might be able to pull Nelson's organization out of the mire. Nelson heeded the advice and, to ward off his own political demise, he brought Eberstadt and production expert Charles Wilson into the WPB as co–vice chairmen.

Eberstadt was a New York financier with a law degree. He had sold his partnership at Dillon Read for a fortune, and then made money all through the Depression by specializing in small stock issues that larger firms disdained. He was friends with both Patterson and Navy undersecretary James Forrestal, who jointly talked him into coming to Washington. When he took over at WPB, many complained that he was too close to the military. This he typically waved off by commenting that the entire rationale for the WPB was to service the military. During World War I, Eberstadt had temporarily left Columbia Law School to serve in France in the 304th Field Artillery. He was wounded, promoted to captain, and noted for commanding the best-drilled, best-disciplined battery in the command. Eberstadt, like the rubber czar, Jeffers, did little besides work. He stayed out of the limelight, rarely entertained, and worked seven days a week. He was once described as "a remarkably blunt and forceful character of scholarly attainment and penetrating intellect, and an administrator able to master endless detail and yet formulate comprehensive and workable over-all policy." Known as a protégé of Bernard Baruch, he often tried, while he was on the Army-Navy Munitions Board, to implement the methods Baruch had used in World War I. As such, he was always at loggerheads with the WPB, and often publicly proclaimed that the WPB could work if only it was run by better men. He was about to get a chance to prove his point. In Eberstadt, Nelson had someone who could begin mending fences with the military and had the intellect and decisiveness to take on and repair the shambles brought on by Nelson's Production Requirements Program (PRP).

Mr. Make-It, as Charlie Wilson, the other new WPB vice chairman, was nicknamed, brought literally a lifetime of manufacturing experience with him to Washington. He grew up in Manhattan's run-down ghettos on the Lower West Side, was left fatherless at three, and left school for work when he was twelve. Starting as an office boy for General Electric (GE), he made his way through the ranks as factory hand, clerk, and then accountant—a skill he picked up at night school. He was running a factory before his twenty-first birthday and eventually rose to take over GE's appliance business—a role that according to one source actually meant he was exec-

Charles E. Wilson.

utive vice president in charge of everything. When Gerard Swope retired from the top job at GE, Wilson replaced him. Swope was kind enough to go back to his old job while Wilson went to Washington for war work. Unlike Eberstadt, Wilson did enjoy a few leisure activities. He was known to enjoy deep-sea fishing and golf, and he rarely missed a big prizefight. He was even known to have gotten into the ring more than a few times himself. Once, while he was inspecting a factory, he was stopped at the gate by a guard who boasted he had once knocked Wilson out. Wilson paused and said, "Then you're Joe So-and-So. He's the only man who ever knocked me out." Wilson's true passion, though, was hard work, and most of his leisure pursuits were put on hold for the duration. But he was not without some negative traits, including insecurity, pettiness, and a predilection for surrounding himself with yes men.

Eberstadt's first assignment was to get PRP working. He did so by killing it. He replaced it with the brilliantly simple Controlled Materials Plan (CMP). Instead of tracking dozens of items and thousands of firms, Eberstadt decided that the WPB would control only three essential commodities: steel, aluminum, and copper. The CMP then listed seven top claimants (among them the Army, the Navy, and the Maritime Commission) responsible for making their needs known eighteen months in advance. The WPB would then divide up the total production of these three items among the seven groups. A requirements committee, headed by Eberstadt, would adjudicate disputes. Once each of the seven major claimants knew what they were getting, it was their job to divide it among their prime contractors, who in turn would divvy up their allocations among subcontractors. After some slight teething pains the new plan worked like a charm, silencing critics through its demonstrable efficiency and success. Journalist Eliot Janeway summed up the total effect: "CMP flooded the fighting fronts with firepower . . . the question: How soon will we have enough to fight with was transformed into the immeasurably less anxious question: How soon will our troops be able to fight with what they have."

While Eberstadt fixed the flow of materials, Wilson went to work on the scheduling problems. Eberstadt had made sure the right amount of matériel was getting to the manufacturers. It was left to Wilson to make sure everything arrived at the right time. If anything arrived too early it lay useless; if anything arrived late a production line would shut down. Wilson, through his experience at GE, was an expert at planning and executing incredibly complex industrial schedules. It was a job Knudsen would have performed just as well if he had not been cashiered many months before.

On November 11, Wilson announced to Nelson and the rest of WPB's leadership that he had his team in place and was ready to get the military out of the production scheduling business. He requested total control over all scheduling, and ten days later Nelson sent a memo prepared by Wilson to Patterson's office. In provocative language, Nelson "terminated the armed services power over production" and assigned that task to Wilson. Thus flared what Nelson called "the bitterest fight I ever had with the War Department people."

Wilson's supporters looked at production scheduling and saw that some outside agency had to resolve conflicts among the masses of orders coming in from the Army, Navy, Air Force, Maritime Commission, Lend-Lease, the civilian economy, and a lengthy list of other competitors for scarce factory space. But all the military saw was that the WPB was once again trying to preempt the Joint Chiefs on deciding the relative urgency of military munitions and matériel. As Patterson saw it, Nelson's proposal "would take from the Army and Navy the power to decide what weapons they need, how many they need, when they need them, and where they need them." Patterson was convinced that such a course would cripple the war effort. Stimson thought that "Nelson had apparently gone completely off his head."

Both Patterson and Stimson considered Nelson's sudden abrogation of their March 21, 1941, agreement, where Nelson had given much of his power to the military, as a dishonest power grab. It wasn't, but with nerves stall raw from the recent "feasibility dispute," Nelson, as he often did, mismanaged the politics. Clearly, he would have had a much easier time of it if he had spent a few weeks preparing the ground and gathering supporters, particularly within the White House. As it was, Stimson believed "he was crazy to try it" and Patterson told a meeting of senior Army personnel that Nelson was a liar whose word could not be trusted.

Nelson, who was on the receiving end of the Army's furor, ruefully lamented that the Army's purpose was to enforce its will on the enemy. He only wished that they had not picked him as their enemy. Stimson, in turn, was incensed at articles attacking his and Patterson's performance that he was certain were planted by WPB officials. Still, he was sure that the Army would win in the end, recording that Nelson "had made such a flop of his own work . . . how could he think that the President will turn over to him the work that the Army and Navy are doing pretty well." Stimson briefly talked the disagreement over with Roosevelt on the phone, concluding by saying that in public he "was keeping his mouth shut." Roosevelt told him that was a good idea.

On Thanksgiving Day, Nelson and Wilson visited with Stimson. The meeting did not go well. Stimson liked Wilson, but was stunned at Nelson's appearance and ill-informed answers: "He [Nelson] looked very badly—as if his troubles were upsetting him. And then he was not frank. He was not ingenuous; he wrung his hands and said he wished he could get out; that the job was very unhappy for him." After the meeting, Stimson recorded: "He is a weak man who can't face the troubled situation that he has."

After Stimson discussed the matter with Hopkins, the President decided that he had to step in. As Nelson remembered the meeting, Roosevelt mentioned that he heard that he was in another fight with the Army. Nelson confirmed this, telling Roosevelt that he was in a "life or death fight." Roosevelt replied that he would be glad to help, but Nelson told him he would prefer to fight it out alone. Roosevelt laughed and said, "Well. If you need me, come to Poppa." Soon thereafter the argument petered out in a series of back-and-forth conciliatory notes. When, during congressional testimony, Somervell was asked how the dispute ended, he was forced to admit, "I don't know exactly." But that was not the whole truth. Wilson had gotten what he wanted—control of all scheduling—and Nelson had been sidelined within his own organization. As Nelson retreated to lick his emotional wounds, real power within the WPB shifted to Eberstadt and Wilson.

Roosevelt too had had enough of Nelson, and he decided to act when it became apparent that Nelson could not control his two forceful subordinates. Both Wilson and Eberstadt were essentially coming at the same problem from two different directions, and soon discovered they had many overlapping responsibilities. As such, it was only a matter of time until they were at each other's throats. Behind Eberstadt stood the Army and the Navy. As he had come to the WPB from the Army-Navy Munitions Board and had close social ties to the undersecretaries of both services, he was correctly considered by many the military's man inside the WPB. In Wilson's corner stood the few remaining members of the New Deal's Palace

Guard, who were looking to halt any further encroachments of the military into the job of running the economy. In the past, they would have hated Wilson, seeing him as a stalking horse for big business. But for now, they viewed the military as the New Deal's Enemy #1, and Wilson received a temporary pass. New Dealers were soon putting it about Washington that Nelson would have to pick between "a production man who really knew production and a Wall Street banker who knew how to give orders." According to *Time*, among those supporting Wilson and plotting Eberstadt's overthrow were Simon Kuznets and Robert Nathan. The nation could not spare the service of either man, but as *Time* stated, "Nelson is not the man to harness such men together."

At a loss as to how to make the two men work in tandem, Nelson decided it was simpler to transfer a number of Eberstadt's responsibilities to Wilson. It was a horrendously stupid move, as it stirred up the just recently settled down Stimson and Patterson. Both men approached Roosevelt, who agreed that Nelson was causing unnecessary strife. In the meantime, Wilson decided that he was not getting sufficient support from Nelson and tendered his resignation—twice. The first time, Roosevelt refused it, and the second it was left to Byrnes to talk Wilson back from the cliff. Byrnes succeeded in securing a truce among all parties, but even he did not believe it would hold.

Pressure continued to mount. Patterson's attacks could be handled, but now the Truman Committee was also mounting attacks on Nelson. Worse, Senator Claude Pepper put forth a bill to wipe out the WPB entirely and start over. As the bill began to pick up backers, Roosevelt, always alert to any congressional action that might diminish his powers, spoke to Byrnes about replacing Nelson with Wilson. On February 5, 1943, Byrnes went to Roosevelt with a bold proposal; keep Wilson where he was and replace Nelson with Baruch. Byrnes made the case that putting Baruch in charge would appease the Truman Committee, stop Claude Pepper's bill in its tracks, and thrill many of the WPB's critics. Byrnes closed by reminding Roosevelt of the many services Baruch had performed for him, and of his continuing loyalty. This last point was crucial as, despite his personal liking for Baruch, Roosevelt had not forgotten that Baruch had financed the campaign that wrecked his plans to purge the party. Reluctantly, Roosevelt told Byrnes to prepare a letter offering Baruch the appointment.

Baruch and Byrnes rightfully suspected that Hopkins had done his best

Bernard Baruch.

to keep Baruch on the sidelines for much of the war, though that did not stop Baruch from throwing a sumptuous dinner party at the Carlton for Hopkins and his new bride. Hoping to present Hopkins with a fait accompli, Byrnes rushed to Baruch's hotel room and handed him Roosevelt's signed offer letter. Unexpectedly, and fatally for his chances of assuming the top role, Baruch balked. Despite Byrnes's pleading, Baruch left for New York, telling Byrnes he would have his answer the next day. But Baruch fell ill during the trip and was ordered to stay in bed for a week. By the time he returned to Washington, ready to take the job, much had changed.

Late on the night of February 16, Nelson was awakened by a call from Robert Nathan, who had been tipped off by a friend in Byrnes's office to what was afoot. Over breakfast Nathan told Nelson that Stimson and Patterson were meeting with Roosevelt that afternoon to demand his replacement, and that an offer had already been extended to Baruch to take the job. Nelson reacted with a speed he had never displayed in all of his time at the WPB.

Nelson first tried to call the president but was not put through. Calling Hopkins, he asked if he was going to be executed without a hearing. Telling him the president expected him to take things into his own hands, the

Machiavellian Hopkins then directed the clueless Nelson toward a solution. Pointing out that his problems were centered around Eberstadt, Hopkins said, "Do something about that and see if the boss doesn't invite you in for a chat." Hopkins, by now fully alerted to what was afoot, was doing his best to protect his investment in Nelson, and to prevent the uncontrollable Baruch from moving into the top job.

Nelson grabbed at the suggested lifeline and called a press conference to announce Eberstadt's resignation. Keeping with a now-established tradition, Eberstadt learned he had "been resigned" from the newswires. In a later press conference Nelson said that he was fighting for his job against a military cabal that wanted to take over American industry. Obviously feeling good about himself he went on: "I will fight to hold my job until a better man comes along—and I have not seen him yet." One observer punned that Nelson's problem was that "he wanted a rubberstadt and not a thermostadt."

Nelson's actions put Roosevelt in a quandary. He wanted to get rid of Nelson, but knew that would be seen as a reaction to Nelson's firing Eberstadt, who would likely have to be recalled, given his popularity with the armed services. But Roosevelt had taken a dislike to Eberstadt when he had the effrontery to ignore a presidential "suggestion" to fire someone early in his tenure. Roosevelt had an elephantine memory for such slights and had welcomed Eberstadt's departure. But bringing in Baruch now would make it appear as if he had caved to military demands. Besides, Nelson's move was widely applauded on Capitol Hill, particularly by Claude Pepper, who put his bill to create a new WPB on the shelf. Once told by Stimson and Hopkins that Wilson would quit if Baruch got the top job, Roosevelt decided to let Eberstadt's firing stand and keep Nelson on at WPB.

The only problem was that no one thought to tell Baruch. As soon as he was out of his sickbed he went to the White House to accept the job as head of the WPB. Sam Rosenman and Pa Watson intercepted him in the hall, but had time only to say that the president had changed his mind before Baruch was summoned into Roosevelt's office. Baruch knew that Roosevelt was going to withdraw the job offer, but still opened with "Mr. President, I am here to report for duty." Roosevelt ignored the greeting and said, "Let me tell you about Ibn Saud, Bernie." Roosevelt went into an uninterrupted discourse on the Middle East leader before suddenly announcing he had a cabinet meeting and rolling himself out of the room.

Neither man ever brought up the WPB chairmanship to the other—then or later.

Nelson had survived, but survival was costly. Within his own organization, he became a figurehead, as Wilson centralized all decision-making in his office. But dissension in the agency continued to grow, as did Nelson's paranoia. Within a few months Wilson, who was trying to mend fences with the Army, replaced Eberstadt in Nelson's mind as Public Enemy #1. Nelson continued in the chairmanship position for another eighteen months, but he was increasingly isolated and still under unremitting attack from Somervell, Patterson, and Stimson. As he became increasingly ineffectual, even Roosevelt was forced to concede the obvious and offered him a face-saving exit by sending him on an extended mission to China. In his place, he appointed the quiet and competent Julius Krug, who saw the agency through to the end of the war.

35

BYRNES CAST UPON
TROUBLED WATERS

THERE WAS A REASON NELSON SURVIVED AS LONG AS HE DID: Jimmy Byrnes. As the head of the Office of Economic Stabilization he progressively took on the role of mediating all disputes that did not have to do with the running of the war. As Roosevelt became increasingly more absorbed with the quickening pace of military operations he had increasingly less time to spend on the home front. Moreover, as Hopkins was absorbed in doing his boss's bidding in matters directly relating to combat operations, as well as managing the alliance with Britain, a large power vacuum developed at the top of the home front. Byrnes, never hesitant to accept power, quietly stepped into the vacuum. With Byrnes now making all the big decisions everyone felt free to ignore Nelson, who became the worst of all things in Washington power circles—irrelevant. The military and others would still attack him when opportunity presented itself, but he was no longer worth expending the political capital necessary to get him removed.

Initially, there were limits to Byrnes's power. His position was primarily responsible for wage and price stabilization, duties previously handled by Leon Henderson. Because he was more amicable and easier to get along with than Henderson, he was meeting with some successes. But as the weeks and months passed he found there were limits to how much inflation could be held back as the economy rapidly expanded. Byrnes also understood that the foundation of his power was his closeness to Roosevelt. But his usefulness to the president would abruptly end if he had to elevate every dispute to his boss. As he saw it, he needed the power to resolve disputes well short of going to FDR for resolution. The other source of Byrnes's power was that everyone liked and respected him. But he could feel that eroding as he was repeatedly forced to say no to friends on the Hill who came pleading for special favors. He was already well along the road Henderson had trod on his way to becoming the most hated man in America when he realized he had to get off the path.

Byrnes needed another way forward that would enhance his powers to oversee the entire home front. On May 14, he sent Roosevelt a letter stating that he had no political ambitions but felt that he could not assist the president in a post "that requires me to daily antagonize farmers and wage earners who want higher prices and higher wages, as well as their friends in Congress."

An answer was about to present itself. On May 6, the Truman Committee issued another blistering report on the numerous problems in war production, laying the blame squarely on the fact that there were too many independent czars. By this time czars were a dime a dozen: the U.S. had Economic Stabilization Czar James F. Byrnes, Production Czar Donald Nelson, Manpower Czar Paul McNutt, Food Czar Claude Wickard, and Rubber Czar William Jeffers, and these were just the tip of the iceberg. But as journalists repeatedly pointed out, they were more like grand dukes than czars: under their high-sounding titles, divided authority and lack of direction left them helplessly snarled in invisible red tape. According to Truman's report the principal problem was that the original broad powers given to the WPB and Nelson had been siphoned off and diluted by the creation of fiercely competing petty principalities. Truman insisted that all "discussion of the over-all legal authority of the WPB is mere pedantry. Although authority may exist, it has never been exercised." As Baruch complained after the last WPB reorganization, which had shown Eberstadt the door: "Tinkering, tinkering, always tinkering. Patching. They have no overall plan." When Roosevelt saw that Congress was once again preparing to act, he entered into intense talks with Byrnes on creating an organization that could run the home front while Roosevelt focused on the war.

* * *

On May 27, 1943, Roosevelt bowed to the inevitable, and acting on Jimmy Byrnes's recommendation, he created the Office of War Mobilization (OWM), with Byrnes in charge. Byrnes moved rapidly to establish his authority, first by making it clear that he considered himself Roosevelt's deputy for the home front, with his decisions carrying the same weight as the president's. Anyone wishing to buck him or bypass him on their way to the president did so only at immense peril to their prospects in Washington. Mindful of the politics of prestige, Byrnes forbade his staff to visit anyone's office, no matter how illustrious they were or thought they were. If anyone had business with Byrnes or his staff, *they* would come to OWM's cramped White House offices. But the wisest decision Byrnes made was to keep OWM small. This had several benefits. Foremost among them was that no one could cajole or otherwise ensnare OWM members into the technical details or the minutiae of day-to-day operations, as the staff was never large enough to handle this kind of detail. Byrnes continually warned his staff about getting involved in administrative work or detailed planning, as the day you started down that road "you became a competitor to the other agencies and trouble ensues." Because of OWM's small size it could never be operationalized and diminished as Nelson had allowed WPB to be. It never became involved in the details of any organization's administration or problems; rather, Byrnes kept OWM above the routine squabbles and focused on humbling unruly czars and bringing peace to troubled waters.

One man now stood at the top of the sprawling war production and administrative agencies. He had the full confidence of the president, had cowed the formidable Harry Hopkins into full retreat, and was so well respected by the Joint Chiefs that they often invited him to their regular luncheons. Moreover, Byrnes was still esteemed on Capitol Hill, where everyone knew if you wanted something done you went to see Jimmy. Byrnes had also been invested with exceptional powers to accomplish his huge undertaking. As *Time* noted: "Byrnes, unlike too many timid czars before him, really intended to use his powers." And to make sure he kept on the right track, he brought Baruch in as personal adviser. In that single stroke, he brought an often-uncontrollable critic inside the tent, where, as the Washington saying goes, "he could piss out, rather than stand outside pissing in."

Before Byrnes could get down to running the war on the home front, however, Roosevelt wanted him to solve a dispute between the only two men in Washington whom Byrnes lacked the power to control or intimidate. Vice President Wallace and Jesse Jones were at each other's throats and Roosevelt wanted it stopped, or at least out of the headlines.

In July 1941, Roosevelt, looking for important work for Vice President Wallace, created the Economic Defense Board, soon renamed the Board of Economic Warfare (BEW), and placed Wallace in charge. Roosevelt was probably hoping to keep some of the spotlight on the man he hoped would succeed him as president and torchbearer for the New Deal. The president tasked the BEW with managing the nation's overseas economic relationships and put most of the cabinet on the BEW board. The board's mission was to "advise" the president on matters of economic defense, but all the actual work fell to other agencies. To one and all, the BEW seemed a paper tiger, and as Dean Acheson said, "it bore all the earmarks of futility and early demise." But no one had counted on Milo Perkins—Wallace's first major hire.

Perkins was a stocky, slit-eyed, tweedy, hard-driving businessman and an ardent New Dealer who devoutly believed that no one in the world should ever go hungry. Acheson described him as one of the most able, adroit, and energetic administrators the war had brought to Washington. He also ordained himself as "priest-in-charge" of his own breakaway religious sect called the Liberal Catholic Church of the United States. He conducted services in his attic every Sunday, claimed his home (called the Church of Raphael the Ark [sic] Angel) as a religious building, and exempted himself from paying property taxes. He had come to Washington a nonentity, but after conceiving the idea of giving food stamps to the poor that they could exchange for surplus foodstuffs he became a Washington sensation.

By introducing a man like Perkins into the mix, Wallace had grossly violated the recognized rules of bureaucratic warfare. Rather than argue the big policy questions with cabinet officials, Wallace was determined to make the board an "action agency," one that could support his broader postwar agenda. As such, the BEW took on an operational role, issuing orders and sending out its own teams to conduct tasks already within the statutory purview of one or another agency. In doing so BEW followed the first rule of all bureaucracies: grow to the maximum possible extent, as fast as possible. Within months of its coming into existence the BEW had a hand-picked staff of 1,100, housed in a new office building on Q Street and busily justifying their $12 million in total salaries by getting in everyone else's way.

Wallace did not see any need to work with other agencies. Rather, Hopkins, Jones, Hull, and others were all merely "obstacles to his vision of coordinated economic defense." It even helped his cause that most of the cabinet members on the board thought he was a fool and soon stopped attending BEW meetings. Hull sent Dean Acheson to represent him, and Stimson refused to send anyone, commenting that each meeting meant sitting "through masses of philosophic unrealities," which Stimson identified as the primary reason serious people avoided Wallace whenever possible. Unfortunately for Wallace, when Roosevelt established the organization he did not get Congress to give BEW its own line of funding. Rather, he ordered Jesse Jones to provide whatever BEW wanted out of Reconstruction Finance Corporation (RFC) funds. And that is when the real trouble began, for much of what Wallace wanted the BEW to do was already being done by the RFC. This was particularly true when it came to purchasing commodities crucial to the war effort. Jones already had an RFC subsidiary doing this work, run by the extremely competent Will Clayton.

As Jones put it, though the president ordered him to fund BEW initiatives, he "did not have the same confidence in Henry [Wallace] that the

Henry Wallace.

President did." Whenever the BEW requested funding, Jones would start a process of inquiries to make sure the money was being well spent. Wallace accused Jones of obstructing his efforts, to which Jones retorted that the only thing he was obstructing was "throwing money away to no good purpose." Jones claimed that he promptly paid all BEW's "sensible bills" and only resisted those he considered had little to do with the war effort or BEW's job. Some of the projects dear to Wallace's and Perkins's hearts that Jones balked at included programs to teach Amazonian farmers how to grow vegetables they had no interest in eating, and spending hundreds of millions of dollars on nutrition programs throughout South America.

Wallace complained to Roosevelt that, although he had an executive order establishing his agency, he had no real power unless Roosevelt called Jones and Hull in and personally ordered them to obey BEW mandates. In early April 1942, Roosevelt had Wallace and Budget Director Smith put together another executive order (Order 9128) specifically giving the BEW authority to establish organizations parallel to what was already in the RFC, and to send missions abroad that duplicated much of the State Department's job. The order fell like a thunderclap on the State Department and pushed State into alliance with Jesse Jones. As Hull was out sick, Sumner Welles took up the cudgels, arguing to Roosevelt that it made no sense to deal with nations on a per topic basis, and that everything one wanted to do with any nation was integrated with everything else. He concluded by telling Roosevelt that if the order was not rescinded then the State Department might as well close up shop.

Roosevelt, looking for an easy way out, sent Hull to talk it over with Wallace personally. Wallace, working on Hull's well-known dislike for his subordinate, took the opportunity to blame everything on Welles. But Wallace then went too far by declaring he would not work with Welles on BEW matters, an edict that went to the heart of Hull's powers to appoint representatives as he saw fit. On April 23, FDR had everyone in to bang heads together. Roosevelt became visibly angry when he learned that Wallace had not cleared Executive Order 9128 with the State Department or the RFC before asking him to sign it. Glowering at Wallace, Roosevelt said, "I was always told that the State Department knew about this transfer of authority and agreed to it. Otherwise I would not have signed it." Sheepishly, Wallace replied, "We knew that if you knew that the State Department had not agreed to it you would not sign it." After two weeks of negotiations in which Wallace was purposely excluded, Roosevelt, in a press conference, with Hull at his side, reaffirmed that the State Department was in charge of all foreign relations and that his executive order would be modified to reflect this. Roosevelt wanted to amend his order through a joint memorandum signed by Hull and Wallace, but Hull refused and demanded a presidential order addressing the problem. Hull got his way on May 20, 1942, leaving Wallace to complain: "Everyone wants to kick us over the Potomac Bridge four times a day."

Wallace had been on the receiving end of a master class in Washington infighting. As *Time* commented on the dispute: "A Washington saying of the past decade is that the city is littered with the bones of men who have opposed Cordell Hull; that the old Tennessean feuder works quietly and cautiously but he always gets his man." Wallace had not only suffered a serious bureaucratic defeat, he had also greatly angered Roosevelt when he tried to get his way by deceiving the president. While Roosevelt was never angered by duplicity when subordinates were squabbling among themselves, misleading him was unforgivable. Wallace was never again able to build up the easy rapport he had previously enjoyed with Roosevelt, who never trusted him again. But, incapable of learning from this defeat, Wallace continued and even intensified his war with Jones and the RFC, leading to a more humiliating defeat and the destruction of the BEW.

Wallace fired the opening salvo by issuing Order No. 5, while Roosevelt was at the Casablanca Conference. Without consulting anyone, least of all Jones, Wallace issued what he considered an executive order usurping all of the RFC's powers to make overseas commercial deals. As these RFC responsibilities were established in law, Jones refused to comply. But after months of back-and-forth bickering Jones, in what he called an "exasperated final effort to get Wallace's long-haired, incompetent, meddlesome disciples" out of his hair, was ready to throw in the towel. In late May 1943, Jones took Clayton to meet with the vice president and proposed turning over the entire RFC apparatus currently engaged in preemptive buying all over the world to Wallace. But before that proposal could move forward, Wallace, disregarding the president's instruction to cease airing interagency differences in public, released to the press a plaintive twenty-eight-page letter he had sent to Virginia senator Carter Glass, charging the RFC with foot-dragging and hampering the war effort. He told Glass, "We are helpless when Jesse Jones, as our banker refuses to sign checks in accordance with our directives . . . it is bureaucracy at its worst; it is utterly inexcusable in a nation at war."

Jones, incapable of not rising to the bait, demanded a full congressional investigation of Wallace's charges. Here, Jones was on sure ground. He had been visiting Capitol Hill for months, whispering to his many friends and stoking rumors that the BEW was an irresponsible one-man show, more interested in giving away American money to build up postwar Russia and South America, and in supplying bathtubs to Amazonian tribes, than in winning the war. Moreover, whenever he visited congressional offices, Jones never lost an opportunity to remind one and all who it was who had been doling out checks in each of their districts for the past decade. His campaign was having the right effect, and Wallace was likely prompted to release his blistering letter after learning that the Senate was planning to cut BEW's travel funds and give Jones veto power over its foreign purchases. Still, Wallace had picked the wrong battleground for his new fight,

Jesse Jones.

one where Jesse Jones had many friends, whereas the aloof and often disdainful vice president had none.

For several days Jones raged. Calling friendly senators, he shouted: "That damned liar has called me a liar three times. I'm going to call him one ten times." To one senator he said: "I'm 69 now, but if I can't handle that little shit from Des Moines I'm older than I think and maybe I ought to go back to Houston." By week's end Jones had finished a thirty-page letter of rejoinder to Wallace's letter to Carter Glass. It opened with a broadside and got worse: "[Wallace's] tirade is so filled with malice, innuendo, half-truths and no truths at all, that considerations of self-respect and of common justice to my associates force me to expose his unscrupulous tactics." The only one of Wallace's charges that Jones pleaded guilty to was "safeguarding the taxpayer's money."

An incensed Roosevelt told Byrnes to smooth it all over. Byrnes had both men come to his office on June 30, 1943. Jones purposely arrived fifteen minutes late and refused to return Wallace's greeting when he walked through the door. For the first part of the conversation Jones just listened as Wallace listed his complaints, and Byrnes asked both men to consider the damage this public quarrel was doing to the administration. When they paused, Jones told Wallace "that when he said his prayers that night he should ask God to stop him from lying." Jones then left, claiming that it was plain that nothing could be accomplished. Byrnes claimed that he ended the meeting when he got worried that Jones was about to punch the vice president. He reported the meeting's results to the president, concluding with "They lived in peace but a short time."

When both men issued unhelpful statements within hours of the meeting's conclusion, Byrnes understood that a reconciliation was impossible. He advised Roosevelt to destroy the BEW and replace it with a new organization—the Office of Economic Warfare. Roosevelt agreed and stripped Jones's RFC of all the organizations that had anything to do with the purchasing of overseas commodities. These were then stuffed into the new Office of Economic Warfare with longtime Roosevelt troubleshooter Leo Crowley in charge. Jones still held the power of the purse strings, but this was never a problem as Jones and Crowley were friends of long standing. Crowley even kept an autographed picture of Jones behind his desk, and had done so for many years.

Wallace did not fare nearly so well. Everyone in Washington politics understood that he had been cast into the political wilderness. He would
never be elected president, and the odds of his remaining on the Roosevelt
ticket in 1944 were negligible. His top assistant, Milo Perkins, went down
fighting, telling the entire BEW staff that Wallace's attack on Jones had
been warranted, as Wallace "only did what any red-blooded American
would do when he turned over a rock and saw slimy things crawling." It
was a hollow rhetorical victory as Wallace for the remainder of his term as
vice president had but one task—to stand ready if the president died—
while Jones retained virtually all of his power and responsibilities.

Wallace did, however, make one last stab at victory. Although Roosevelt
eventually dumped him from the 1944 reelection ticket, he realized he still
needed Wallace on the stump rallying the New Dealers to the polls. Thus
he promised him any cabinet office he wanted after the election, except the
State Department. Wallace chose to take Jones's job as secretary of commerce, which had the extra benefit of taking over the RFC by default, as
Jones had placed it within Commerce's organizational structure. Wallace
was convinced that he had finally vanquished his great rival. But no sooner
was the nomination sent to the Senate than Jones's friends introduced a
bill stripping Commerce of the RFC and establishing it as a separate agency.
The measure passed 400–2 in the House and 74–12 in the Senate. Wallace
was confirmed as Commerce Secretary, but the power he craved continued
to elude him. Jones had won again.

In the aftermath of this all-too-public fight, Byrnes, looking to bring an
end to the "Washington war," prepared a memorandum for Roosevelt to
send to the head of every department and agency: ". . . If you have a disagreement with another agency . . . [and] you feel you should submit it to
the press, I ask that when you release the statement for publication you
send to me a letter of resignation." The last of the great fights over mobilization had ended. There would be many other disputes, but none that
Jimmy Byrnes was unable to handle. Wielding the full power of the presidency as if he held the office himself, Byrnes cajoled, swore, and when necessary crushed all who opposed him. Roosevelt, though he remained wary
of Byrnes's grip on power, later reflected that once Byrnes appeared on the
scene, "I finally had time to think." He would need every moment of that
thinking time, as the war had not paused to allow those executing America's industrial mobilization to sort themselves out. Long before the feasi-

bility dispute was over, the rubber shortage relieved, the WPB brought to heel, or Wallace neutered, American combat troops, after landing in North Africa, were finally taking the fight to the Germans. It was this that occupied almost all of Roosevelt's attention, while Jimmy Byrnes, assistant president for the home front, took care of the country.

36

A Non-United Front

A s the American invasion force wheeled to face Rommel's Afrika Korps, retreating back from El Alamein, Roosevelt was already looking ahead. On November 25, he had the Joint Chiefs over to the White House to discuss operations after North Africa was secured. Once again Roosevelt did not invite either Stimson or Knox. When Roosevelt opened the meeting by inquiring how long it would take to conclude current operations, Marshall optimistically said that Tunisia would fall within two weeks, but possibly a few weeks longer if another division or two were required. In actuality, and much to Marshall's chagrin, Tunisia was only declared secure on May 6, 1943, after almost six months of hard slogging. Marshall further stated that before any further operations were decided upon, he wanted "careful consideration of what it would cost to clear the Mediterranean . . . and whether or not the large air and ground forces required for such a project could be justified." Most of the remainder of the meeting was given over to matters of war production and allocation, concluding with Roosevelt alerting the Joint Chiefs that he and Churchill were discussing holding a meeting in North Africa at the earliest possible date. In fact, Roosevelt had cabled Churchill that morning with a suggestion for a conference of the big three (Roosevelt, Churchill, and Stalin) to be held in Cairo or Moscow in four to six weeks. The conference would take place in January—in Casablanca.

Marshall's meeting with the president had provided a perfect opportunity for him to divert Roosevelt's attention away from the Mediterranean and back toward an invasion of northern France. That is, if Marshall still held out a real hope for his precious Allied invasion of northern Europe in 1943, this was the time to forthrightly say so. Instead, Marshall pulled his punches and offered no ideas of what would come after North Africa. That he had reason to fear that the U.S. Army would find itself sucked into protracted Mediterranean operations was made clear during a JCS meeting held the week before the meeting with the president. At that time, Leahy told the other chiefs to start planning for further activities in the Mediterranean, which they could discuss with the British when the latter presented their own ideas on the subject. Rather than objecting to this switch of strategic emphasis Marshall suggested the matter be tabled and handed over to the Joint Strategic Survey Committee for further analysis. This committee, headed by retired general Stanley Embick, was formed in early November 1942. Consisting of a limited number of flag-rank officers, it was charged with conducting deep examinations and making recommendations on future strategy, free from the daily pressures of dealing with immediate operations. Marshall and Embick had a long association, and in matters of strategy, Embick had Marshall's complete confidence.

It remains notable that in the weeks after the North Africa invasion and the conclusion of the Casablanca Conference, whenever future Mediterranean operations were addressed, Marshall made no immediate objection. This was not the Marshall that had fought the invasion of North Africa every inch of the way, leaving one to wonder if he was having a change of heart, and if so what caused it. There is fragmentary evidence that Embick was already advising him as to the impossibility of such an invasion in 1943. Moreover, it was about this time that Marshall began to learn of the outcome of the feasibility dispute, and that he would not have all the forces he expected until well into 1944.

Such idle concerns could not, however, occupy him for long. On December 10, Roosevelt once again met with his Joint Chiefs. This time Marshall appeared back in form and explicitly stated he was opposed to dabbling in the Mediterranean in a wasteful way, and that "he considered it important to be ready in March or April to launch operations against the Brest Peninsula, or Boulogne." Given that American troops were entering Britain at an unimpressive 8,500 a month Marshall's stance was rather remarkable (in World War I the nation had sent 10,000 men into France every single day). As April was only four months off, one wonders how Marshall thought that the barely trained single division currently in Britain was going to make much of an impression on the Germans in northern France. Moreover, to date no serious planning had been accomplished, all the required transports were in the Mediterranean, and even if there was a rapid conclusion to the fighting in North Africa the divisions involved would need several months to refit. On this occasion, Marshall appears guilty of a lot more than just optimistic thinking.

Even so, his new proposal represented a markedly scaled-down invasion plan compared to what he had previously advocated. He was no longer calling for a full-blown invasion and breakout. Rather, he was recommending something much smaller: a lodgment in an isolated sector that was relatively easy to defend. Brest, in the upper northwest corner of France, was perfect for such a limited enterprise. He had originally raised the idea of seizing the Brest peninsula that summer as a face-saving operation to show that the Anglo-Americans were doing something to open a true second front. Now it was moving to the forefront of his thinking, as operations around Boulogne, in the teeth of the Wehrmacht's strongest defenses, only made sense if Germany was crumbling. With the Russians chewing up German divisions at Stalingrad, Marshall may have envisioned a glimmer of a chance that the German army would crack up, giving him an opening that could be exploited by a small number of American troops thrown onto the Continent. Failing that, even the preparations for such a thrust worked to his ultimate benefit, as troops and matériel would stop flowing to the Mediterranean and instead build up in Britain to await the ultimate final offensive.

On December 11, Embick's Joint Strategic Survey Committee forwarded its recommendations for 1943 to the Joint Chiefs. These were its main recommendations:

1.   After Tunisia was secured, to cease further operations, except for strategic bombing, in the Mediterranean.

2.   To concentrate all efforts on BOLERO for a decisive assault on northern Europe in 1943.

3.   To stay on the defensive in the Pacific, conducting only enough offensive operations to keep open communications with Australia, and to continue to limit operations in Burma.

These recommendations were discussed in a closed JCS session on December 15. Most of the discussion was dominated by King, who was greatly offended by the idea that the Navy would stay on the defensive just when its forces were being vastly augmented. King argued that any letup of pressure on the Japanese would greatly lengthen the war. Moreover, he considered operations in Burma as vital, as otherwise China could not be kept supplied and in the war. King still professed his support of a Germany-first strategy, but told the other Joint Chiefs he did not consider the Germans as the "primary enemy." As such, he said he remained unconvinced that Europe should be the primary effort for early 1943, given the critical situation in the Pacific. Following up on his rhetorical advantage, King claimed that the Pacific was only getting about 15 percent of the total forces and matériel produced for the war effort, and that to keep the Pacific offensives rolling would require 25–30 percent. This was a bit disingenuous on King's part, as he was surely aware that over half the divisions deployed so far in the war had gone to the Pacific, along with most of the new warships. Whether he was truly asking for a major increase in his share of the nation's resources, or setting a marker that would make it difficult to reduce what he already had, is difficult to tell. King, no doubt, thought he had a winning argument and reiterated it again at Casablanca the following month.

Marshall agreed that the report needed to be changed to reflect the requirement to maintain pressure on the Japanese. His main priority, however, was to change the report's emphasis on a rather slow buildup in Britain to a rapid massing of forces aimed at a spring 1943 invasion of the Brest peninsula. He concluded that conference by stating that every effort should be made to have sufficient forces "in England for some quick, decisive, continental action." Once the document was revised it was forwarded to the British chiefs, who in turn sent their own plans for 1943 to the Americans. As everyone expected, the respective U.S.-UK plans diverged dramatically, setting the stage for the next round of talks at the Casablanca Conference.

By this time, Churchill had cabled back his agreement to meet with Roosevelt and Stalin, but he wanted either the Joint Chiefs to come to London first or to have a preliminary meeting with Roosevelt. The president balked at both, claiming that he did not want to give Stalin any reason to think America and Britain were forming a common front in advance of negotiations, which, of course, was precisely what Churchill wanted. The point was made moot when it became clear that Stalin could not be coaxed out of the Kremlin at a time when his armies were engaged in the vast Stalingrad counterattack. Nor did the dictator volunteer Moscow as a meeting place, sparing Roosevelt a visit to the Russian capital in the midst of winter; cabling Churchill he said, "I prefer a comfortable oasis to the raft at Tilsit." Stalin, however, knew what he wanted out of the conference and in his cable declining the invitation wrote: "Allow me to express my confidence . . . about the opening of a second front in Europe . . . [which] will be actually opened by the joint forces of Britain and the United States of America in the spring of next year."

Churchill also wanted to bring his foreign secretary, Anthony Eden, with him. Again, Roosevelt balked. If Eden came, Roosevelt would have to bring Hull, which he decidedly did not want to do. Hull took this as a deliberate marginalization of his role. But it is just as likely Roosevelt wanted to keep the conference focused on war strategy, and he knew if Eden and Hull were there both men would insist on starting to plan for the postwar world. This was a topic Roosevelt had strong feelings on, but his specific ideas were still in the formative stage. At this point he was far more interested in getting closer to victory, so that he could get a better view of the postwar landscape before he decided how he wanted to rearrange it.

As 1943 dawned, the Allies, who only six months before had been reeling on every front, were now victorious in virtually every theater. The single exception was the brutal submarine battle in the North Atlantic, but even here the Germans were rapidly approaching their high-water mark. Hard fighting continued on Guadalcanal, as well as throughout MacArthur's theater, but King already had his Pacific commanders looking forward, as plans were laid for a blitzkrieg across the central Pacific. As far as King was concerned the mostly defensive phase of the war was over, and he could already envision the day when the rapidly growing U.S. fleet would sally forth to shatter Japan's remaining military power. In North Africa, Rommel's desperate stand had bogged down the Allied offensive toward Tunisia. Still, American and British troops, despite setbacks, continued to crawl forward, and few doubted that the Axis army in North Africa was doomed.

Most spectacularly, the Red Army still held almost two dozen divisions of the Wehrmacht's Sixth Army in a death grip within the Stalingrad pocket, after having held off determined relief attempts led by Germany's best operational commander, Erich von Manstein.

Against this backdrop the British and Americans began preparations to meet in Casablanca to decide the future strategic direction of the war. Roosevelt was well aware that the British would arrive with a well-rehearsed common position, and intended that he and the Joint Chiefs should do so as well. FDR was preparing for a battle between unbreakable phalanxes, in which the victor would be the side whose energy and resolve did not flag. As a preliminary in building that resolve, FDR on January 7, 1943, assembled the Joint Chiefs in the White House. He opened with a bombshell. After stating that Stalin might be suffering from "a feeling of loneliness" he announced that he was going to propose to Churchill that they inform Stalin that they would continue to prosecute the war until Berlin was captured, and that the only terms would be "unconditional surrender." In a rather surreal moment, no one questioned or even commented on Roosevelt's pronouncement, which in a single sentence established the war's strategic endgame. Rather, discussion immediately shifted to their immediate travel plans, and who would represent them while they were out of Washington, entirely neglecting Roosevelt's comment on unconditional surrender. The words would attract far more attention the next time Roosevelt uttered them at Casablanca.

After dispatching some rather routine matters Roosevelt asked: "Are we all agreed that we should meet the British united in advocating a cross-channel operation?" Remarkably, Marshall replied: "There is not a united front on that subject." After months of arguing and debate the American Joint Chiefs remained split. Marshall still wanted to focus on the buildup for invading northern France, although he now stated that could not take place until late summer. King, on the other hand, thought Sicily should be taken and Italy knocked out of the war to open the Mediterranean shipping lanes, thereby freeing up millions of tons of shipping for other duties. Arnold, as always, was agnostic, as long as airpower played a dominant role in whichever direction was chosen.

Marshall saw the whole question as a matter of logistics. He feared that any attack on Sicily or Sardinia would expose still scarce Allied transports to air attack and irreplaceable losses—estimated at 20 percent. He said he personally favored operations against the Brest peninsula, as "the losses there would be in men . . . to state it cruelly, we could replace troops, whereas a heavy loss of shipping . . . would destroy any opportunity for successful operations against the enemy in the near future." When Roosevelt asked what the estimated troop losses would be, Marshall could not give him an answer. When asked what difficulties could be expected in a Brest landing, Marshall rather nonchalantly answered that he expected the landings to be rather easy; "the difficulties would come later in fighting off the German armored units." It is apparent that Marshall, despite nearly three years of German operations to reflect upon, had no understanding of just how punishing a German armor counterstroke could be. That lesson was not hammered home until two months later, when Rommel's panzers delivered an embarrassing whipping to American forces defending Kasserine Pass. When Roosevelt eventually asked what Marshall proposed to do with the nearly 900,000 troops in North Africa, Marshall rather sheepishly replied that they and additional troops now in training could be used against Sardinia or Sicily. So, after first stating his objections to operations in Sardinia or Sicily, Marshall had, in the span of a single meeting, reversed himself and approved the very operations he had been fulminating against.

After standing alone in advocating an early invasion of northern Europe, Marshall was clearly changing his mind. Given his earlier fanatical insistence on the earliest possible invasion date, what was causing his change of mind? One can only speculate, but with the Red Army advancing over a 500-mile front no one was worried any longer about an imminent Soviet collapse. Moreover, a division-sized British raid on the Channel beaches around Dieppe in August 1942 had been a disaster, alerting everyone to the enormous practical difficulties of landing troops on a defended beach. Just as crucially, when the great "feasibility dispute" ended, Marshall was not immediately made aware of its impact on the Army, as Somervell had inexplicably lied to Marshall, telling him that the full operational requirements for a 7.5-million-man force would be met by the end of 1943. Because of Somervell's reluctance to give his boss bad news, a problem Marshall had to contend with throughout the war, only in early December did Marshall learn the truth from the JCS planners: the Army was delaying the organization of fourteen combat divisions Marshall was counting on for his European invasion. Even Marshall could not argue for an invasion employing forces that did not yet exist.

37

CASABLANCA

I F ROOSEVELT WAS DISPIRITED BY THE FAILURE OF HIS JOINT CHIEFS to unite behind a unified strategy to win the war, he made no indication of it. In fact, as the time of his departure for Casablanca neared he became visibly more buoyant. Trips were always good for presidential morale, and always recharged his personal batteries—this one more than most. He was about to become the first president to fly overseas, and the first to visit an active war zone since Abraham Lincoln. The more the dangers, ranging from German bombers to assassins, were explained to him the more eager he became. It was a nervous Secret Service detail that took Roosevelt to his train on January 9, 1943. Under a total security blackout, he and Hopkins were ostensibly heading to Hyde Park for a typical retreat, but in Baltimore the presidential train was turned around and proceeded to Florida, where a luxurious Boeing Clipper was waiting to take them to North Africa.

On the afternoon of January 14, Roosevelt's plane touched down at an airfield near Casablanca, from which he was immediately whisked away by the head of his Secret Service detail, Michael Reilly, to the conference location at the Anfa Hotel. The hotel had nice views of the Atlantic and fourteen associated two-story villas. The entire compound was surrounded by two massive lines of barbed wire and dozens of antiaircraft guns, and hundreds of infantrymen were on constant patrol. General Patton oversaw security, and the responsibility kept him in a state of constant agitation. Roosevelt was assigned Villa #2, "Dar es Saada," while Churchill was placed fifty yards away in Villa #3, "Mirador." Just moments after entering his room, Roosevelt sent Hopkins to get Churchill, who was at his door a minute later. Over cocktails the two men spent an hour conferring about General Montgomery's impending advance into Tunisia before heading to dinner with the Combined Chiefs.

When Roosevelt arrived in Casablanca, the American and British Combined Chiefs had already been going at it hammer and tongs for three days, with little to no progress. The British had come united behind both a plan and a method of achieving it. The plan, simply put, was to expand operations in the Mediterranean, and to keep the Americans from doing something as "foolhardy" as wrecking their newly raised and barely trained divisions in a premature assault on northern Europe. The method was explained to the British chiefs by Churchill: Let the Americans present their views, never argue, but instead allow for full discussion. In other words, wear the Americans down by incessant talking. To help them the British chiefs brought a huge contingent of staff planners, a staff study for nearly every conceivable topic, and a supporting signals ship that acted as a floating library. The American chiefs, in keeping with Roosevelt's desire to have as small a footprint as possible, brought a total of two planners. One of them, General Albert Wedemeyer, complained: "They swarmed down on us like locusts . . . with prepared plans . . . From a worm's eye's viewpoint, it was apparent that we were confronted by generations and generations of experience in committee work, in diplomacy, and in rationalizing points of view. They had us on the defensive practically all the time." The avalanche of papers caught the Joint Chiefs by surprise, leading King to complain that "the British had a paper ready for every subject raised for discussion."

To Marshall and the other chiefs, the first two days of discussion were a replay of the months of debate prior to the Americans giving in and conducting Operation TORCH. The British pushed to expand operations in the Mediterranean, while Marshall was looking to curtail such operations at the earliest possible date. King threw another spanner into the works when he demanded more assets in the Pacific, claiming that the progress already made must be sustained or the Japanese would consolidate their positions. As he did during the December 15 Joint Chiefs meeting, King demanded 30 percent of all resources for the Pacific. When he could give no strategic rationale for why, an irritated Brooke warned that this "was hardly a scientific way of approaching war strategy." That mattered little to King, who continued to reiterate his demand for the next few hours, before the matter was finally tabled and handed to the planners for further study.

Standing, from left: Harry Hopkins, General Hap Arnold,
General Brehon Somervell, and Averell Harriman. Seated, from left: General
George Marshall, President Franklin D. Roosevelt, and Admiral Ernest King.

Marshall and Brooke both worked overtime at keeping their fabled tempers in check, but the constant merry-go-round arguments were going nowhere, and relations began fraying. Brooke, frustrated at his inability to move Marshall, recorded in his diary: "The whole process is made more difficult by the fact that amongst Marshall's very high qualities he did not possess those of a strategist. It was almost impossible to make him grasp the true concepts of a strategic situation. . . . He preferred to hedge and defer decisions until such time as he had to consult his assistants. Unfortunately, his assistants were not of the required caliber." Discussions were further complicated by Roosevelt and Churchill's arrival. On their first night in Casablanca they hosted a dinner party where King, despite his pledge to forgo liquor for the duration of the war, became, as Brooke recorded, "nicely lit up." Brooke amused himself by watching a gesticulating drunk King argue with an equally inebriated Churchill.

General George Marshall and Field Marshal Alan Brooke.

The renewed camaraderie engendered by the candlelight social—electricity was cut off due to an air raid alert—did not last through the next morning, as both sides dug further into their entrenched positions. What was truly petrifying for the British chiefs was that the more they tried to make the Americans see the logic of continued Mediterranean operations, the more King insisted, with Marshall's and Arnold's growing support, that greater resources be sent to the Pacific. In fact, as the debates dragged on the Americans seemed to expand their plans in the Pacific, first for limited offensives to disrupt Japan's consolidation of its gains, then for major operations in Burma aimed at opening a supply line to China, and finally for operations in the Pacific intending to capture Japan's fortress island of Rabaul, as well as revving up a separate campaign across the central Pacific. To the British this all smacked of an abandonment of the "Germany first" strategy.

Brooke referred to the negotiations on January 17 as "a desperate day," one that ended with the two parties as far apart as ever. Worse, when he asked that the British chiefs at least be kept abreast of American plans for the Pacific, King in no uncertain terms told him that America's Pacific operations were none of Britain's business. When the meeting finally broke up, both Marshall and Brooke despaired of reaching common ground. In private, Air Marshal Portal counseled that Brooke remain patient, saying: "We are in the position of a testator who wished to leave the bulk of his fortune to his mistress. He must, however, leave something to his wife, and his problem is to decide how little he can in decency set apart for her."

The next day, Marshall, likely advised by Dill, eased off a bit, and forthrightly declared that America was committed to "Europe first." Continuing, he made a major concession, claiming that while he advocated an assault on northern Europe he was against immobilizing huge forces in Britain in the uncertain hope of a 1943 invasion that might be better employed in other theaters. As it was just as ludicrous to leave these forces idle in North Africa, Marshall had opened the door to future operations in the Mediterranean. King, however, immediately reiterated his demands for a doubling of Pacific resources, causing Brooke to lose hope and adjourn the meeting.

Once again, Dill rode to the rescue. Pulling Brooke aside he pleaded with him to go back in and find a compromise solution. An agitated Brooke replied, "It is no use; we shall never get an agreement with them!" Dill told him that to the contrary, Marshall had already come a long way toward the British position and that he believed they were all close to a settlement. Over lunch, Dill continued to work on Brooke, asking how far Brooke was ready to go to get an agreement. Brooke said, "Not a single inch."

"Oh yes you will," Dill replied. "You know that you must come to some agreement with the Americans and that you cannot bring the unresolved problem to the Prime Minister and the President. You know as well as I do what a mess they will make of it." Dill had with him a paper quickly written by one of Portal's aides that sketched out the basis of a compromise. Portal had already blessed it, and Brooke, mindful of Portal's admonition that the British had to give the Americans (the wife in Portal's phrasing) something, gave in on allowing an expansion of Pacific operations, as long as they did not greatly impact efforts in Europe. By this time, Marshall had already agreed, without any remonstrance from King, that the first phase of America's expanded Pacific operations could be accomplished with resources already available in the theater.

After getting Brooke's agreement to several other minor points, Dill went off to discuss them with Marshall. With Brooke and Marshall close to an agreement, only King was left to be brought aboard. At the start of the next combined meeting, Marshall pulled King aside and showed him the

British paper. When King saw that his key demand—expanding offensive operations in the Pacific—had been agreed to, he quickly assented. With that done the rest of the military strategy for 1943 fell quickly into place, for there were many areas of agreement between the Allies. Winning the battle of the Atlantic, keeping Russia in the war, and maintaining an unabated and powerful bomber offensive were givens. As such they led the list of strategic priorities for 1943. The debate had really been about what to do with each side's armies, and the priorities for landing craft. With Marshall's agreement that further Mediterranean operations were unavoidable, and King's signaling that he could expand Pacific operations without jeopardizing the Allies' capacity to defeat Germany if a favorable opportunity arose, the deal was set.

Marshall had given up on any chance for a 1943 invasion of Europe, but he had known he would have to do so, as well as agree to a further expansion of Mediterranean operations, before he left the United States. As for the rest of the Combined Chiefs, they had gotten almost everything they wanted. King would get to launch his precious Pacific offensives, and Arnold was assured that he would lead the Air Force in devastating bomber campaigns on multiple fronts. Brooke and the British had also gotten everything they wanted: expanded operations in the Mediterranean, a recommitment by America to the Germany-first policy, and, most crucially, an indefinite postponement of the invasion of northern Europe.

There was something else that King and Marshall took away from these meetings. To them the British had seemingly not wanted to give in on a single American position, particularly in the Pacific. They were, to use Portal's analogy, willing to leave everything to the mistress. But when faced with a united and unbreakable American front to expand Pacific operations, the British chiefs had caved. Further, they had gotten away with making the Pacific an American lake, in which the British would have no say in the conduct of future operations. These lessons were not lost on the American chiefs. In the future, as American men and matériel began to overtake British resources in every theater, the American chiefs would become progressively less tolerant of British proposals on how to run the war.

Over the intervening decades, a legend has grown that the Americans were outnegotiated at Casablanca. According to myth, this unhappy result was due to the Americans arriving with too small a staff and incomplete plans and position papers. This reflects Wedemeyer's already stated position that the British planners "swarmed down on us like locusts," or as he said after the war: "We came, we listened, we were conquered." Such an analysis severely distorts the reality of negotiations at the highest levels of the government or the military. The American staff might have been embarrassed by their lack of preparation, but it was irrelevant. Marshall, King, and Arnold were without question strong-willed men. They were not about to be moved off their positions because some staff officer had written a paper on the topic. While it may have been helpful to go tit-for-tat with position papers, as happened at subsequent conferences, there is no indication in the record of anyone ever changing his outlook based on a position paper. Both the British and the American chiefs were immersed in the war every moment of every day. They needed staff papers to inform them of certain technical details, not to guide them on strategic precepts. The American chiefs could have brought hundreds of planners and thousands of position papers and their arguments, as well as the conference's results, would not have changed a single iota.

The true reason why the British got almost everything they wanted at Casablanca was because the Americans agreed with them on all crucial points. The top menace remained the U-boats prowling the North Atlantic: they had to be destroyed. Strategic bombing was viewed by everyone as a potentially decisive weapon, so that remained on the priority list; as did supporting the Soviet Union, which was still killing ten times the number of Germans that the Anglo-Americans were. King got what he wanted in the Pacific—permission to conduct further offensive operations—because he was King, and the British finally gave up on wrestling in the mud with him over a theater in which they were barely involved. Of course, the debate of most significance revolved around whether 1943 would be dedicated to further operations in the Mediterranean, or would these be mostly shut down in favor of an invasion of northern Europe. And it is in this debate that the Americans supposedly got their clocks cleaned by the scheming and cunning British. But as we have seen, the Americans had surrendered to the British position before they arrived at Casablanca. Marshall's arguments for an invasion of northern Europe at the earliest possible date had nothing to do with a 1943 invasion and everything to do with making sure the date did not slip past 1944. In that regard, he also walked away from Casablanca a winner. As he later wrote, it was not until after Casablanca that he had a firm idea of what the strategy for the conduct of the war entailed.

Although the conference was specifically aimed at deciding military strategy for 1943, Roosevelt spent most of his time in Casablanca on other matters. First was the selection of the commander for the next phase of operations. Eisenhower had gotten off to a brilliant start with TORCH, but since then his offensive into Tunisia had bogged down. His neck was in a noose and he knew it. But Roosevelt had noted several crucial points. Foremost among them was that although Eisenhower's British subordinates outranked him, the general was able to control them, while at the same time gathering their fulsome praise. Roosevelt was particularly impressed by the praise coming from Britain's Admiral Cunningham, whom the president considered a true fighting admiral. Roosevelt was also impressed by the strong support Marshall continued to display for his protégé. But what likely tipped the balance in Eisenhower's favor was his reply when Roosevelt asked him why he had done the Darlan deal without checking with Washington. Understanding that if the deal blew up—as it did—after Washington (Roosevelt) gave its approval, it could do irreparable damage to the administration, Eisenhower told the president that "generals can make mistakes and be fired, but that governments could not." In effect, Eisenhower told Roosevelt that he went forward on his own so as to leave the president the option of firing him and blaming the entire episode on an overanxious general. In any event, Roosevelt had supported Eisenhower's decision, but a seasoned politician such as FDR could not help but be impressed by a general who not only made decisive moves but also thought to leave political running room for Roosevelt to maneuver in the event it all went wrong. As a result of his political abilities, which are always crucial at the highest levels of command, Eisenhower kept his job, received another star, and placed himself in good stead for appointment as supreme commander for the invasion of northern Europe.

The second problem Roosevelt was forced to resolve was bringing peace to internal French politics. Darlan's assassination had catapulted Giraud into the leading position in North Africa and put him on a collision course with de Gaulle, who was still in London. Giraud was ready to sign any kind of a deal that would allow him to concentrate on the army and the war, but de Gaulle was having none of it. At first, he even refused a written invitation from Churchill, delivered after the conference had begun, to come to Casablanca. In London, he had stayed aloof from the political fray in North Africa, remaining pure and unsullied by the compromises and gritty reality French leaders in North Africa had to make and deal with every day. Thus de Gaulle remained blameless, as he wrapped himself in the unstained cloak of French liberty and honor. Moreover, already angry about not being informed of the TORCH operation until it was under way, he was further incensed over not being informed about the Casablanca Conference—which would determine France's fate—until after it began. Only when Churchill threatened to bypass his organization and cut off his funding was de Gaulle induced to come to Casablanca.

De Gaulle remained obstinate even after his arrival. Rounds of shuttle diplomacy failed to convince him to meet with Giraud, or anyone who had been associated with Vichy. When he finally met with Churchill, de Gaulle's first comment was to complain about being surrounded on French territory by American bayonets. After a disastrous meeting, where he dismissed out of hand Churchill's proposal for a unified French National Committee with co-equal presidents and accused the prime minister of deliberately driving down the value of French currency, he then broke off the meeting and stalked off. Churchill, in angry temper, beckoned his doctor to the window to complain: "His country has given up fighting, he himself is a refugee, and if we have to run him down he's finished." Continuing as de Gaulle strode down the path away from the villa: "Look at him! He might be Stalin with 200 divisions behind his words." Roosevelt, equally irritated by de Gaulle's conceit, later told intimates that in one discussion de Gaulle said that he represented the spirit of Jeanne d'Arc, but the next day he claimed that in the present emergency he must play the role of Clemenceau. Roosevelt claimed, "I almost laughed in his face." When a de Gaulle aide later told both Roosevelt and Churchill that de Gaulle was most certainly the new Jeanne d'Arc, the prime minister replied: "I know it, but I can't get any of my bloody bishops to burn him."

Determined to make the best of it, Roosevelt invited de Gaulle to meet with him. The dour de Gaulle became more perturbed when he noted the room's floor-to-ceiling curtains were moving in unusual ways. He assumed that members of FDR's staff were eavesdropping on his supposedly private talk with the president. In reality, Mike Reilly, head of Roosevelt's Secret Service detail, had taken one look at the fuming de Gaulle and decided to hide himself behind a curtain with weapon drawn. Other Secret Service agents, armed with submachine guns, stood ready behind every door. After an hour of discussion and barely concealed threats, Roosevelt got de Gaulle to agree to sign a memorandum of unity. When de Gaulle asked that he be permitted to draft the missive, FDR relented, ending the meeting with the French leader again stalking out of the room.

By the next day de Gaulle had soured again. As they were preparing to go outside with Giraud, Churchill and the testy Frenchman got into another argument. Roosevelt, ever nimble and politically aware, pushed himself past Churchill and asked de Gaulle if he would do him the personal favor of having his picture taken with himself, the prime minister, and Giraud. De Gaulle agreed and allowed himself to be photographed shaking Giraud's hand, knowing he was playing a role in Roosevelt's political theater. It was, however, a deal without substance. Roosevelt had forced this shotgun marriage, but the bride and groom still lived apart. Their divorce became final when de Gaulle engineered Giraud's removal from the political scene in September 1943.

When the Frenchmen left, a buoyant Roosevelt released his bombshell. Talking amicably to the reporters who had gathered to witness Giraud and de Gaulle shake hands, he began to relate how General Ulysses S. Grant had gotten his nickname "Unconditional Surrender Grant." Without pause he went on to say that defeating the Axis powers would entail their unconditional surrender. Roosevelt later said that his comment was a spur-of-the-moment thought. But this is belied by the fact that it appears in the JCS minutes for January 7, 1943, and that he was speaking from notes that clearly included the term "unconditional surrender." Churchill, despite stating in his memoirs that he was astonished by the announcement, had discussed unconditional surrender during his meetings with Roosevelt. He may have been stunned by Roosevelt's timing of the announcement of a new grand strategic policy, but he recovered quickly and stuck by the pronouncement throughout the war. Ever since, historians have debated if the unconditional surrender policy lengthened the war and therefore caused more human and material loss than necessary. To believe this means accepting that the Nazi extremists were so worried about Roosevelt's rhetoric that they had no choice but to fight to the bitter end, as if having their crimes against humanity revealed at the war's end did not provide suffi-cient incentive. As Churchill wrote: "Negotiation with Hitler was impossi-ble. He was a maniac with supreme power to play his hand out to the end, which he did; and so did we."

The conference was not all work for Roosevelt, as he found quite a bit of time to relax. Both Roosevelt and Hopkins found time to visit with their sons, who were on active duty and serving in North Africa. Between work-ing meetings they also had plenty of time to socialize and enjoy some ex-quisite cuisine, something Roosevelt rarely enjoyed at the White House. The highlight of the trip, as far as Roosevelt was concerned, was when he left the Anfa Hotel compound to visit with the troops, where he ate his meal outdoors as soldiers shyly approached him for a quick hello. Such tours always raised his spirits, although he later said he almost cried talking to the members of one division, knowing they would be moving up to the front as soon as he departed. Before both national leaders departed, Churchill convinced Roosevelt to join him for a 150-mile drive to look at the snow-capped Atlas Mountains. It was an enjoyable drive with good conversation, but one that drove Patton and the president's security detail nuts. Throughout the trip dozens of American fighter planes circled over-head watching for German aircraft.

After a five-hour journey they arrived at a spectacular villa that had a tower standing six stories high. Churchill insisted that FDR see the view from the tower and Mike Reilly and another Secret Service agent dutifully carried the president to the top. The two leaders stayed looking at the mountain and easily conversing for a half hour. Churchill was in an ebul-lient mood, as he should have been. He and his nation were at the height of their power, and he had gotten what he wanted most: a postponement of the cross-Channel attack. For the moment, Churchill was the undisputed leader of the strongest military coalition ever assembled. It was not to last.

The next morning Roosevelt departed for home. Churchill, who had abided far too much and long into the night, almost missed his departure. Clad in his dressing gown and velvet slippers he rushed out of his villa to say a quick goodbye. As Roosevelt drove off, Churchill turned to American vice consul Kenneth Pender and said, "If anything happened to that man I couldn't stand it. He is the truest friend; he has the farthest vision; he is the greatest man I have ever known."

Upon his return to Washington on January 31, 1943, Roosevelt received news that the Battle of Stalingrad was over, and that Field Marshal Friedrich Paulus and what remained of the battered Sixth Army were in captivity. The destruction of the Sixth Army forever removed the fear of the Soviet Union's precipitate collapse from the list of concerns for Allied planners. That still did not relieve the Anglo-American allies of the necessity of keeping Stalin abreast of their plans, as well as of reassuring him that they remained every bit as committed to the war effort as he was. Roosevelt hoped that his call for an unconditional Axis surrender would make up with rhetoric for what the British and Americans were not yet prepared to do on the ground. This pronouncement was followed up with a joint cable from Churchill and Roosevelt to Stalin, explaining the details of what was agreed to at Casablanca and emphasizing their continuing commitment to a second front. Stalin was not impressed, and he waited a day before responding and asking for a concrete date for the invasion of northern Europe.

Over the next few weeks an exchange of cables ensued between the three leaders in which Churchill and Roosevelt laid out the difficulties that were slowing progress in North Africa, and promised an invasion of Sicily no later than July, with an invasion of northern Europe possibly ready to go in September. The September invasion scheme was loaded with so many caveats and hedges that Stalin instantly knew there was no possibility of it taking place. This transatlantic traffic came during a bad time for the Allies. Churchill had come down with pneumonia, and Roosevelt was running a persistent fever. Moreover, on the battlefronts, the Soviet onslaught had been blunted by a punch in the nose delivered by Field Marshal von Manstein's counterattack at Kharkov. By the end of March the front had stabilized, demonstrating to all concerned that the Germans still possessed a kick. Over the next few months Stalin anxiously watched the Germans build up two powerful armored fists aimed at a great bulge in his lines around the city of Kursk. In North Africa, the supposedly defeated Germans had rounded on the American II Corps and delivered a humiliating defeat. Afterward, Marshall and Eisenhower both refused British recommendations to pull U.S. combat units from the front lines for more training, opting instead to remove the hapless II Corps commander, General Lloyd Fredendall, and replace him with the fierce General Patton. Though the Americans had suffered a tactical defeat, it led to a later strategic victory. Hitler, convinced that Tunisia could be held, poured an additional

100,000 crack troops into North Africa. When the Germans and Italians finally surrendered on May 13, over 250,000 Axis soldiers were captured, an Allied victory almost as great as Stalingrad. In the North Atlantic, the Allies were suffering their worst monthly losses of the war, and there was consternation in both London and Washington. But this was the high-water mark for the U-boats, as increasing numbers of escorts, new technologies, and new sub-killing tactics turned the tide. In 1943 alone, Germany lost 258 submarines, and the North Atlantic became so dangerous that U-boats abandoned it in favor of safer, and less trafficked, hunting grounds. It helped that by this time almost all of the most aggressive U-boat commanders were dead. Those that remained rarely demonstrated the ruthless disregard of risk that had driven earlier commanders when pursuing their quarry.

Though the battles continued with unrelenting fury in both the Atlantic and Pacific theaters, in Washington there was something of a lull. The overriding direction of the war had been set and it was now up to the military planners to figure out how to get on with the next great moves. Fights were still raging over the administration of the economy and the many other concerns of the home front, but as we have seen, the hyperefficient Jimmy Byrnes was rapidly bringing the home front into his orbit and relieving the president of many of his concerns in this regard. All in all, Roosevelt considered that things were rolling along well enough for him to take an extended tour of the military camps in the southern United States.

38

MAN—AND WOMAN—POWER

THE BATTLE OVER PRODUCTION, AS WELL AS THE MOBILIZATION OF industry and capital, were finally brought from a boil to a simmer, just as the other side of the equation—labor—began causing almost as many problems. Of primary importance as the war raged on was solving the basic question of labor supply. Unfortunately, this is rarely just a matter of mathematics, where one could add military requirements to the economy's needs and arrive at a total quantity of required labor. Rather, it was an area fraught with interested parties and pressure groups—agriculture, labor organizations, industry, mothers, wives, and many others—all of them politically active. In general, each of these parties had one aim: to tell the military, particularly the Army, whom it could *not* draft. At the same time, military manpower requirements skyrocketed just as expanding war industries needed all the manpower they could lay their hands on.

At the start of the war, the lingering effects of the Great Depression meant that there was a huge surplus of available manpower. But by early 1943 this reserve was gone, forcing the Army to push down the draft age and start exploring how to get more men with families into uniform. At the same time, business was just as feverishly exploring new sources of labor, particularly women. Every one of these efforts aroused complaints and suspicion from one quarter or another. For instance, getting approval to draft eighteen-year-olds required repeated visits by Stimson to Congress to convince them that the "War Department was not planning some sort of infant slaughter."

Despite women entering the workforce in droves, labor shortages were manifesting themselves everywhere, particularly among skilled workers and craftsmen. In the period after Casablanca, draft calls were averaging 400,000 a month and the pool of single men under thirty was soon exhausted. Farm deferments had already taken two million men out of the draft pool, and industrial deferments accounted for another 1.5 million. By the middle of 1942, nearly 25,000 male retirees had voluntarily given up their Social Security benefits and gone back to work, while 700,000 more men over age sixty-five had deferred their pensions and stayed on the job.

The first signs of real trouble showed up in the statistics tracking the number of men quitting their jobs, mostly for better pay elsewhere. During the Depression quitting was almost unheard of as there was unlikely to be a new job to move on to. At first, the WPB and other agencies tried to stigmatize firms that hired away another firm's employees as "labor piracy." But faced with intense demands for skilled labor and first-line supervisors, few managers concerned themselves with being stigmatized. Roosevelt's first serious response to the problem was to create the Manpower Commission under Paul McNutt, a former governor of Indiana and most recently the head of the Federal Security Agency (which controlled a hodgepodge of other New Deal agencies, such as the Civilian Conservation Corps and Social Security). He was also a fraternity brother of Wendell Willkie, at a time when both men were still Democrats. McNutt had strong political ambitions and twice put himself forward as a candidate for the presidency. Roosevelt took the threat seriously enough to appoint him as high commissioner to the Philippines to keep him out of the political arena in the run-up to the 1940 election. He was a thick-skinned political opportunist, comfortable with machine politics, but he was also considered politically shrewd. Although disliked by most of the important New Dealers, McNutt still garnered their respect. He was a handsome man who was "conscious of his bodily grandeur," and reveled in being described as "the Adonis of American Politics." It was said that "he has got more out of a head of platinum hair than any other American, barring Jean Harlow."

In taking the job, McNutt made sure that he was independent of the WPB, in effect establishing another personal fiefdom that reported only to the president. There were other members of the Manpower Commission with whom he was obliged to consult, but he was under no requirement to follow their guidance. Thus, McNutt easily established himself as a dictator, whose powers only fell short of full control of his chosen domain due to the Selective Service apparatus remaining under the War Department.

Under pressure to get results in balancing the needs of the economy and the military against the total manpower supply, McNutt lobbied Roosevelt for control of Selective Service. Stimson liked the idea of putting one man in charge of everything to do with manpower. Unfortunately, he did not believe McNutt was the man for the job. Patterson thought Baruch should take the position, but Stimson was not sure of him either. Baruch, however,

Paul McNutt and his wife, Kathleen.

thought himself up to the job and likely lobbied for it when he advised Roosevelt to both place Selective Service under the purview of the Manpower Commission and find someone other than McNutt to run it. As they had done with Nelson, the War Department began a backroom campaign aimed at overthrowing McNutt. As he had been doing to Nelson for over a year, Patterson began publicly referring to McNutt as the "second team." Even Stimson got in on the act. Although he refrained from direct attacks on McNutt, he did not hesitate to attack his staff. Calling them "a lot of callow New Dealers with more ambition than brains" was among his more polite utterances. McNutt, under attack by the Army and also by Nelson's WPB, which wanted the Manpower Commission brought under its direct control, was getting his bureaucratic brains beaten in. It did not help that the commission's sixty administrative orders, aimed at stabilizing manpower, were routinely ignored by all concerned.

As the manpower crisis intensified, Roosevelt decided to replace McNutt. It was Budget Director Harold Smith who came to his rescue, reminding the president that McNutt had taken many public beatings for the administration and had always done so "like a gentleman." Smith was clearly exploiting Roosevelt's well-known reluctance to remove anyone who had demonstrated their personal loyalty to him, particularly when they had paid a cost for doing so. When Jimmy Byrnes proposed a grand bargain to move around several cabinet members, leaving Ickes in charge of Manpower but giving McNutt another major role in the government, the president accepted. But Ickes hesitated, and by the time he agreed to take the job Roosevelt had changed his mind and decided to keep McNutt.

Having decided to keep McNutt, Roosevelt moved to strengthen his position. Accepting presidential counselor Rosenman's advice to override Stimson's objections, Roosevelt took advantage of Stimson's taking a short vacation to give McNutt control of Selective Service. The change was announced at the next cabinet meeting, for which Stimson had returned. Roosevelt quipped: "Harry, I've been robbing your roost while you were away." Stimson snapped back: "I won't go away again." That night Stimson confided to his diary that Roosevelt had handled the issue "with a great lack of tact."

Stimson personally got along with McNutt, but he thought this preemptive move by the president unnecessarily put him in the position of smoothing over the inevitable bad blood that would arise between McNutt and the military. McNutt had entered the military's domain uninvited. In taking over the Selective Service apparatus he had won an initial victory but—and unless Stimson could cut it off early—his victory had painted a bull's-eye on his back at which Patterson and the War Department took aim. Stimson had little doubt that Patterson would redouble his campaign to subvert McNutt, in similar fashion to the war he had been waging to undermine Donald Nelson. McNutt, however, was blessed with much more sensitive political antennae than Nelson. Realizing he was in trouble, McNutt reacted as any good politician would: rather than dig in his heels, he became accommodating. After a long talk with Stimson, in which McNutt assured him that Selective Service would be run along the lines established by the War Department, the secretary put away the cudgels and told Patterson to move on to other targets. But, as increasing demands by both the military and industry for manpower went unfilled, demands for McNutt's head rose in tandem.

By the middle of 1943 the Army was getting worried, as it discovered that waging modern war on a global scale required far more personnel than anyone had imagined. Just keeping one fighting man on the front lines in Asia or Europe took more than a dozen support personnel to man the training base and provide logistical and other support activities. More- over, despite witnessing the massive bloodletting on the eastern front, the speed at which casualties, sickness, and exhaustion decimated combat di- visions, particularly the front-line forces, caught military planners by sur- prise. At the start of the war the Army had planned to mobilize 213 combat divisions. By early 1943 manpower shortages and delays in matériel pro- duction forced the Army to cut its planned number of divisions by more than half—to 100 divisions. By July that estimate had been further reduced to 88 divisions, then soon raised to 90 divisions. Given that 21 of these di- visions would fight in the Pacific, planners were certainly gambling that such a small number of divisions would prove sufficient to reenter the Eu- ropean continent and destroy an estimated 60 or more veteran German divisions.

Neither the Navy nor the Army Air Forces felt the same manpower pres- sure as the Army, but their total demand did put pressure on the number of persons available to maintain the economy. Desperate to feed the mili- tary's voracious manpower requirements, the Manpower Commission planned to induct men as old as forty-four, while those passed over for minor medical problems were made eligible for noncombat duty, freeing able-bodied men for the front. Patterson even forced the Army to open its doors to the over one million young men previously barred for being illit- erate, telling Stimson, "I had fine soldiers in my company in the last war who signed their name with an X."

Despite the urgent need for manpower, one group remained largely ex- cluded when it came to furnishing both soldiers and workers for the arms industry: African Americans. Over half of all job openings were barred to blacks as a matter of policy, and most of the rest as a matter of habit. By the end of 1942, blacks made up just over 4 percent of the total employment within war industries, though they were nearly 10 percent of the population. Through executive orders, and as a result of crushing need, this improved to over 8 percent by the end of the war.

In January 1943, the military and essential war jobs had emptied the cupboard of single men, and sights were reset on married men with families. McNutt issued a controversial "work or fight" order, giving everyone under the age of thirty-eight until April to move from a nonessential job to an essential one. Everyone between thirty-eight and forty-four got an additional month. After that, anyone not in a vital job would be drafted. The order caused an immediate uproar, and Congress soon neutered it with Public Law 197, which ordered that fathers, regardless of occupation, be drafted last. As the "work or fight" order was aimed at just such men, Congress effectively killed it.

As 1943 closed, both the War Department and business interests remained desperate for manpower. And though most business leaders hesitated to press for it, Stimson and Patterson increasingly turned to the idea of "compulsory national service." This idea was another brainchild of Grenville Clark, the father of the peacetime draft (Selective Service). Clark had opposed the "work or fight" order, sure that it would not solve the problem and because it positioned the Army as a penal colony. National service, however, put the Army and labor on the same footing. Every male, and possibly female, between the ages of eighteen and sixty-five would be registered and then made available to work as directed. In effect, it was a civilian draft. Though Britain had instituted state control of labor at the start of the war, for many Americans conscripted labor smacked of something done by dictatorial regimes. At first Clark's national service push made little progress, but as manpower shortages multiplied he was able to induce two members of Congress, Senator Warren R. Austin and Representative James Wadsworth, to introduce a national service bill in February 1943. The proposed legislation covered every male from eighteen to sixty-five and every female from eighteen to fifty. In short, it allowed local draft boards to conscript labor to fill vacancies in essential industries, just as they decided who was available for the military draft. As might be expected, Stimson and Patterson supported the bill, but Byrnes opposed it. Baruch went directly to Roosevelt and cautioned him that it was "unconstitutional to compel one man to work for another." Warming to his topic, he scolded the president, saying that conscripting labor was not only unjust but also impractical, for "unless we are prepared to resort to the lash," we could not force a drafted man to produce.

The bill was hotly debated, but debate was all Congress was willing to do. Once it stalled other recommendations came to the fore. One, first proposed by Representative Clare Boothe Luce, called for the army to draft men from Category IV (physically unfit for military service) and assign them to a special "labor corps" from which they could be assigned to essential industries facing manpower shortages. When this idea was crushed by a combination of Army disinterest and the Selective Service Agency's refusal to participate, Congress was at a loss as to how to proceed. Roosevelt then took his turn at the problem, appointing a board consisting of Baruch, Byrnes, Leahy, Rosenman, and Hopkins to study the problem. The board convened at the beginning of March, and within two weeks reported to Roosevelt that the problem could be solved by employing more women and through better administration within the Manpower Commission. In short, there was no pressing need for a national service law. With no support and waning interest, the Austin-Wadsworth bill died in committee.

As no real solutions were being offered, the manpower crisis worsened throughout 1943, particularly on the West Coast, where the aircraft industry could not find workers and was falling a thousand planes behind schedule every month. McNutt, convinced the shortfall was a result of poor management and not actual manpower shortages, refused to take action. Unable to move McNutt, an incensed Patterson went to Byrnes, who handed the matter to Baruch to do another study. Patterson, who had little faith in Baruch's impartiality, or possibly not wanting an impartial analysis, sponsored his own independent study. Patterson's team duly discovered that things were much worse than thought, and if the aircraft industry were not soon provided with additional manpower, it would fall tens of thousands of planes behind schedule. Baruch's analysis provided a simple answer, copying a plan enacted in Buffalo, New York, that forced unemployed men to take jobs "only" within essential industries, and forbade men in such industries from leaving without permission from their employer. Labor unions denounced the scheme as "labor servitude," but on September 4, 1943, Byrnes ordered the execution of the so-called "West

Coast Plan." As there were few unemployed men looking for work on the West Coast the new plan had no immediate effect.

One crucial, and overlooked, reason the aircraft industry remained undermanned was its generally low pay and the resulting poor labor relations. In 1935 the United Auto Workers had convinced four hundred Douglas plant workers to conduct a sit-in strike. After three days, masses of tommy-gun-toting police surrounded the workers and dragged them off to jail, where company president Donald Douglas kept dozens of what he called "industrial termites" in prison for weeks. Douglas was also notorious for handing the names of subpar workers—those who demanded an improvement in pay or working conditions—to the local draft board for immediate induction. When the brutal and often sadistic Los Angeles police chief James E. Davis, founder of the notorious LAPD "Red Squad" was finally fired, Douglas immediately hired him for "plant protection." Unfortunately for workers, Douglas was typical of the owners and management of most aircraft plants. But despite their strikebreaking efforts, by early 1941 strikes had cost the industry two million man-days, and the War Department was diverting infantry heading to the Pacific to break up further strikes, sometimes at the point of the bayonet.

Plant owners soon realized that intimidation might work on current workers, but if they were going to recruit the hundreds of thousands of workers they needed to meet military orders they would have to raise wages. Some of this was accomplished in direct violation of wage stability laws and regulations, which allowed raises of only twenty cents an hour within established firms. Plant managers got around this by farming out large amounts of work to newly forming firms that could pay wages beyond those allowed by the West Coast Plan. Through such measures the crisis was brought under control, as thousands of migrant workers departed areas of labor oversupply for the West Coast. Labor strife did not vanish, but it never again reached the point where infantry with bared bayonets were diverted away from the war zones.

Manpower shortages were far from the only labor-related problems to rear up during the war. Even more troubling, because of their abrupt and often spectacular effect, were strikes. Roosevelt had recognized this danger from the start, and immediately after Pearl Harbor he tried to inaugurate an era

John L. Lewis, president of
the United Mine Workers and the
Congress of Industrial Organizations
(CIO).

of labor peace. Only ten days after the attack the president brought together a dozen labor leaders, half from the AFL and half from the CIO, and
an equal number of representatives from large employers. The attendees
reached unanimous agreement on two policies, the most important being
a prohibition on strikes and lockouts for the duration of the war. The other
was an agreement to submit labor disputes to a government board for resolution. Together, these agreements seemingly assured a period of labor
peace and uninterrupted production for the war's duration. On January
12, 1942, Roosevelt created the National War Labor Board (NWLB), which
was responsible for mediating disputes and had the power to issue final
decisions as "directive orders." Late that same year, he extended the NWLB's
powers to cover all wage rate adjustments, which was codified into law in
June 1943 by the War Labor Disputes Act.

But as inflation galloped ahead, organized labor disregarded early war
agreements and began employing their entire bag of tricks to exploit, out-
flank, and shatter the wage stabilization program. Throughout 1943 the
number of strikes, big and small, mounted to the point that the White
House was forced to order employees back to work so often that it lost its
authority as a neutral arbiter of disputes. Most of these strikes were trou-

blesome but manageable. Only the challenges posed by the railroad and mine workers unions posed a true threat to the war effort.

It will be remembered that during the 1940 election, John L. Lewis swore to resign from the CIO if Roosevelt won. Though he tried to renege on his promise, Sidney Hillman forced him out. But Lewis took the United Mine Workers, which he still led, out of the organization with him. In 1943, Lewis, who had just lost his wife and was still nursing a passionate hatred for Roosevelt, demanded a two-dollar-a-day raise. The NWLB ordered Lewis to keep the miners at work until they had decided on their wage demands, but Lewis was having none of it. His goal was to destroy the NWLB, and, as he saw it, the quickest way to do so was to ignore its orders. In defiance of the NWLB he took the miners out on strike.

The government promptly seized the pits, and a furious Roosevelt took to the radio to blast the miners for stopping the coal supply and thereby gambling "with the lives of American soldiers and sailors and the future security of our whole people." It was a wasted speech, as Lewis, who only wanted to fire a shot across the NWLB's bow, had already ordered his men back to work. When in June the board rejected the miners' demands, Lewis once again led his men out. Byrnes told the NWLB to negotiate, but the board, convinced that would make them appear weak, refused. Byrnes kicked the matter up to Roosevelt, who first overruled Ickes's plan for an interim agreement with the miners, in favor of just ordering the miners back to work. Many of the miners complied, but not all, and trouble continued throughout the summer.

Lewis was lambasted in papers across the country, with the Army newspaper, *Stars and Stripes*, writing, ". . . Speaking for the American soldier, John L. Lewis damn your coal black soul." Roosevelt increased the pressure, and tried to intimidate the miners by threatening older miners with the draft and using the IRS to go after Lewis. Sensing an opportunity to weaken some key labor-protection planks of the New Deal, Republicans and their allies—southern Democrats—passed the Smith-Connally Act, restricting the right to strike. Roosevelt, who wanted the extra powers to break the miners but was wary of giving up any more of the New Deal, vetoed the bill. An unimpressed Congress overrode his veto in under four hours, demonstrating once again how weak a hand the president was playing when it came to any matters not directly relating to the war fronts.

Lewis bent under the pressure, but did not break. He ordered his miners

Harold Ickes.

back to work, but only until the end of October. When their repeated pay demands went unheeded through the summer and fall, the miners, rejecting an NWLB offer of $8.25 a day (they were demanding $8.50), once again walked away from the pits at the end of October. Every day that Lewis's 500,000 miners stayed home cost the nation two million tons of coal production. There were sufficient coal stocks to keep most of industry running, but civilian consumption, particularly on the East Coast, was plummeting. With millions of homes dark and cold, a worried Byrnes moved quickly to break the strike before it devastated American living standards and wrecked the economy. On November 1, he cabled Roosevelt at Hyde Park with a draft presidential order to seize the mines. Roosevelt signed the order immediately, but also authorized Ickes to enter into talks with the union in hopes that the "old curmudgeon" could force a deal before he had to send troops in.

So many people saw Ickes as their salvation that he felt it necessary to publicly announce "I am not god," a rare moment of humility for a man who often behaved with divinely inspired certainty. Ickes, who was no friend of Lewis, realized something Roosevelt and Byrnes overlooked: one could seize the mines, but not a union. Taking ownership of the mines was

Leon Henderson (left) and Donald Nelson (right).

a useless gesture if the workers refused to mine the coal. From the start, Ickes was ready to surrender, and Lewis was ready to let him. Through fiddling with the time allotted for lunch and increasing the payment miners got for the time it took them to get to the coal face, Ickes found a way to give the miners their requested $8.50, while making it appear no wage stabilization rules had been violated. It was a face-saving gesture for the government, which had in the end caved in to Lewis's demands. Byrnes was not pleased by the deal, but as it kept up the façade that his stabilization rules were still in effect he decided to let the matter rest.

The coal strikes, despite the fact that none of them lasted long enough to empty the nation's coal stocks, did considerable damage to the war effort. Over twenty million tons of coal were lost, which delayed the production of 100,000 tons of steel. If it had continued it would have brought U.S. war production to a grinding halt by cutting off two-thirds of the nation's electric power. Rather than run this risk, Byrnes and Roosevelt decided to live with the breaching of their Maginot Line against inflation.

Lewis stood between crossed American flags when he imperiously ordered his men back to work. He had gotten them their pay raise, reestablished himself as labor's most potent leader, successfully flouted the hated NWLB, and harassed and embarrassed his hated and formidable enemy—Franklin Roosevelt. For Lewis, it had been a good year.

Roosevelt had lost.

* * *

Unfortunately, dealing with the miners was not the only major labor problem plaguing the administration. Emboldened by the mine workers' gains and feeling jealous of war-plant workers who were earning more than skilled railroad men, the rail unions asked for a minimum three-dollar-a-day wage increase. After considering the case for months, a special Government Railroad Labor panel gave the workers four cents an hour—thirty-two cents a day. Economic stabilizer Fred M. Vinson, who had taken over the job of holding inflation in check after Byrnes had himself promoted to head the Office of War Mobilization, hurriedly approved the raise. Insulted, the unions refused the increase and prepared to strike.

Just before Christmas 1943, Roosevelt, having just returned from the Tehran Conference, met with the rail and union bosses in the White House. According to Byrnes, Roosevelt's opening gambit was to criticize the union leaders for threatening a strike during a war, telling them that he was disappointed that they were here fighting for increased pay when millions of soldiers were fighting for their country.

This was a potent argument that Roosevelt, Stimson, Byrnes, and Patterson rolled out whenever there was a hint of labor problems. What it overlooked was that as inexperienced workers flocked into dangerous war jobs, their dead and injured exceeded battlefront losses by many multiples through 1943. Moreover, even as their own government was belittling factory workers as draft dodgers, it was also putting up government-printed posters telling workers not to enlist as they could serve their nation best by working in war production until they were drafted.

While the publicity accorded the coal and rail strikes gave many Americans the impression that all unions were making demands that were hobbling the war effort, the truth is that between 1941 and 1945 time lost to strikes was only 0.1 percent of days worked. Still, the railways were different. They were not just an insular business concern, but the one "concern" that linked every other business and military endeavor throughout the nation. Coal could be stockpiled and reserve stocks could be prioritized to provide breathing room for negotiations, but a rail strike would paralyze the nation from its first moment. Though no agreements were reached, Roosevelt's intercession persuaded the unions to push the strike deadline off until the end of December. As the deadline approached, Roosevelt called Stimson to his office and "threw a bombshell of the largest possible size" at him. After claiming that he had offered generous wage hikes, which the rail unions had refused, he wanted a plan to take over the railroads. Stimson returned to his own office, where he and Marshall decided to hand the details of the takeover to General Somervell and Patterson. According to Stimson, Marshall had told him that a rail strike was a propaganda boon for Goebbels, and that it would likely lengthen the war by six months. Marshall was so upset at the entire state of affairs that he asked Byrnes if it was his duty to go on national radio, "give his opinion and then resign."

On December 27, Somervell brought his detailed plans for taking over the railroads to Stimson to review. Stimson approved, and with Somervell in tow he went to the White House to see Jimmy Byrnes. There he learned that Roosevelt had become increasingly indignant with the "stubborn and arrogant" union leaders' demands. Before he left, Byrnes told Stimson that Roosevelt was at his wit's end and the order seizing the railroads would be signed that evening. At 6: 40 P.M., Stimson, who had gone home to await a final decision, got Byrnes on the phone and learned Roosevelt had signed the order ten minutes before. Less than two hours later Somervell was at Stimson's home receiving his signed orders to have the Army take over all railroad operations. Later that evening Marshall gave one of his infrequent interviews to twenty newsmen. In a rare display of temper, he pounded a desk and exclaimed the strike was "the damnedest crime ever committed against America."

At 8:00 A.M. the next day a major and a lieutenant colonel, armed with a mimeograph of the presidential order directing the seizure of the railroads, walked into Union Pacific's Omaha headquarters. When they got to the twelfth-floor executive offices, Vice President G. F. Ashby grinned and took them to see the firm's president, Bill Jeffers—former rubber czar. Ashby announced that they have "come to take us over" and left the room. Jeffers shook the officers' hands and told them: "Anything you want, just let us know." He then had an assistant find them an office down the hall and thoughtfully presented them with a map of Union Pacific's rail network for them to get acquainted with their new responsibilities. At the New York Central, its president was given the rank of colonel and told to keep the eastern region operating. Six other railroad heads were also made colonels before the day was over, and as such continued to run their rail lines as they saw fit.

The takeover stopped the majority of the strikers—the union rank and file did not want to strike against the government—from walking out but did not resolve the underlying problems. The rail workers wanted their raises, and their leaders were muttering aloud about "revenge at the polls." Such threats had helped Roosevelt overlook pay raises for 500,000 miners, and they would do the same for the rail workers. The miners had stuck with Roosevelt in 1940, despite Lewis's calls for them to vote for Willkie. But without a pay raise, Roosevelt knew their votes would disappear in 1944. When the rail workers, with three times the numbers of the miners' union, threatened to take their votes to the Republicans, Roosevelt's highly sensitive political ear tuned in. For Roosevelt, crippling strikes in wartime were unthinkable, as was giving in to threats made when the bargainer was holding a pistol to the nation's head. Still, elections trumped all! So Roosevelt in January 1944 endorsed a new arrangement the rail unions had already accepted. Just as with the mine workers, the rail union got the raises they wanted, but, once again, they were dressed up to give the appearance that the wage stabilization rules were still in effect.

The Army handed the railroads back and for the most part labor peace held until war's end. Roosevelt had lost the fight, but he had secured two million reliable Democratic votes.

39

THE JEWISH QUESTION

FEW QUESTIONS ABOUT WORLD WAR II PROVOKE AS MUCH DEBATE as whether the United States and particularly the Roosevelt administration did enough to help European Jews avoid near extermination. The simple answer is no. But, given the context of the time, America did quite a lot to help the Jews. In fact, American actions and diplomacy saved directly or indirectly at least 200,000 Jews, and possibly double that number, from certain extermination. Many would also argue that the best way America could save European Jewry was through a single-minded focus on winning the war, eradicating Hitler's regime, and permanently closing the Nazis' vast killing apparatus as rapidly as possible. Still, there was more that could have been done, and should have been done. Why it was not done is one of the more unglamorous chapters of America's war effort.

From the start of his presidency, Roosevelt had always taken unpopular stands on the issue of Jewish immigration and refugees. As early as 1933 he supported Eleanor when she joined Albert Einstein in helping create the International Rescue Committee, which brought intellectuals, labor leaders, and political figures escaping Hitler to sanctuary in the United States. Throughout the 1930s Roosevelt also supported Labor Secretary Frances Perkins's constant attempts to loosen the highly restrictive rules established by President Hoover to reduce the flow of refugees during the Depression. Still, Roosevelt could not ignore the same national anti-Semite politics that had forced Hoover's hand. Moreover, his priority was always on getting New Deal legislation into place. Consequently, the president initially moved slowly on refugee issues. But after the 1936 election a more secure president ordered a looser interpretation of the immigrant rules, allowing over 200,000 refugees to enter the country over the next few years—double the combined total of the rest of the world. As historian Gerhard Weinberg has observed: ". . . Roosevelt acted in the face of strong and politically damaging criticism for what was generally considered a pro-Jewish attitude by him personally and his administration." In 1938 Roosevelt also convened a thirty-two-nation conference in Évian, France, on the shores of Lake Geneva. The conference's aim was to explore the possibility of settling large numbers of Jewish refugees in Africa, South America, or some other distant locale. After nine days of sympathetic speeches only the Dominican Republic stepped forward to accept a small number of refugees.

In the face of fierce domestic opposition to any immigration during a period of continuing unemployment, and already eyeing a third-term election race, there were limits to what Roosevelt was willing to do. Surely a desire not to alienate voters played a large role in his decision in late May 1940 not to allow the SS *St. Louis*—a German liner carrying nearly a thousand Jewish refugees—to enter any American port. The *St. Louis* was eventually forced to return to Europe, where Jewish organizations negotiated visas with four European nations. Many of these nations were overrun by German forces during the war, and 254 of the *St. Louis*'s passengers perished in the Holocaust. Election-year politics also had much to do with Roosevelt's unwillingness to expend any political capital on the Wagner Bill, which would have admitted twenty thousand Jewish children above the established quota. Without presidential support the bill died in committee, though it is not clear what Roosevelt, his political power on the wane after the failed court-packing scheme and the attempted purge of his own party, could have done to move the bill against entrenched opposition.

Little changed after the United States entered the war. But now the reasons for inaction were new. It must be remembered that Nazi propaganda was blaming the Jews for starting the war and for its continuance. Much more of this propaganda fell on fertile soil than most Americans and other Allied citizens are comfortable admitting. No Americans wanted to see the Jews exterminated, but neither did they want to fight a war in support of perceived Jewish interests. And while the dispute about when Allied leaders understood the full extent of the Nazis' huge extermination program continues (it was likely much earlier than is commonly conceded), the American public was generally in the dark, or disbelieving, until after the war. At the very least, Roosevelt was always concerned that even the hint that the United States was fighting a war for the Jews in Europe would place the "Germany first" strategy at significant peril.

A far more important consideration was that until the final months of 1942 the Allies were losing the war, and it was well into 1943 before they were certain of victory. For all of that time, the entire focus of the Allied leadership was absorbed with turning the tide of battle. All else were peripheral issues that could be put off to a later date. The sad truth was that with no army on the European continent there was nothing the United States could do to help the Jews. Even when the leaders of Germany's satellite states were inclined to protect their Jews it was difficult to stand up to unrelenting German pressure to turn them over, particularly when Allied armies remained distant and the Wehrmacht was a visible daily reality. Only a truly brave and strong-willed leader would dare defy Hitler in such circumstances. It was not until late 1944 that America was positioned to act. It was then that two issues, still much debated, came to the fore: saving the Jews still alive, and interfering with the operation of the extermination camps, particularly Auschwitz.

On August 8, 1942, Gerhart M. Riegner, a member of the World Jewish Congress in Geneva, sent a telegram to British and American diplomats with reliable information from an unimpeachable source—German industrialist Eduard Schulte—about Nazi plans for the mass extermination of the Jews:

> Received alarming report about plan being discussed and considered in Führer headquarters to exterminate at one fell swoop all Jews in German-controlled countries comprising three and a half to four million after deportation and concentration in the east thus solving Jewish question once and for all stop campaign planned for autumn methods being discussed including hydrocyanic acid.

The cable was sent with a notation from local U.S. diplomats that it had the "earmarks of a war rumor inspired by fear." Elbridge Durbrow, a member of State's European Division, advised Sumner Welles to file it without distributing it further. Welles concurred, but three weeks later the British delivered a copy of the cable to Rabbi Stephen Samuel Wise, chairman of the World Jewish Congress. After rushing to Washington, on September 2 Wise handed his copy to Sumner Welles, who advised him to wait a few days for him to check on the report. Welles's experts all considered the telegram a wild exaggeration and put forward the theory that the Jews being transported to the east were being resettled in work camps. It made no sense to them that the Nazis would willingly destroy so much valuable labor. Here we have an abject lesson of what happens when rational men come face-to-face with an irrational ideology. Welles accepted this expert opinion and on September 9 asked Wise not to publicize the cable until it was fully investigated.

Three months passed without action, but on November 24, Welles informed Wise that he was now in possession of irrefutable evidence that large numbers of Jews were being killed in death camps. Because of the nature of his sources Welles claimed he could not reveal this information to the press, but he encouraged Wise to do so on his own initiative. Wise immediately held a press conference and released everything he had. His bombshell—State Department confirmation that half of Europe's four million Jews had already been slain in extermination camps—blasted onto the front pages of many newspapers the next day. Many other newspapers, still dubious of such wild claims, buried it—it was on page 10 of *The New York Times*—and others failed to cover it at all.

Throughout this entire period, Roosevelt remained mum, and there is no evidence in the record that he was even briefed on the issue. It was not until December 8 that Roosevelt agreed to meet a small delegation of Jewish leaders. They met in the Oval Office for less than half an hour, and though Wise was pleased with the results—Roosevelt promised to make a statement—he departed without any concrete offers of help from the president. This was because, beyond making a statement, Roosevelt had precious little to offer. The Americans were in North Africa, and Roosevelt had abolished the Vichy government's Jewish laws there, but that was it. Without an Anglo-American army on the Continent there was nothing Roosevelt could do. It was the first and last time Roosevelt would meet with a delegation of Jews from outside his inner circle. On December 17, 1942, Roosevelt, joined by Churchill and Stalin, issued a statement that the Allies intended to try war criminals at the end of the war—the first mention of what would become the Nuremberg Tribunal. While this message was meant to include crimes against the Jews, their special plight was not elevated above that of any of the Nazis' many other victims. It was not much, but Wise still sent the president profuse thanks: "I do want you to know how very grateful I am and all American Jews will be for your message."

Soon after the president's comments another cable arrived from Geneva. This time Gerhart Riegner presented further details of the Nazi extermination apparatus, which he claimed was killing six thousand Jews a day. After that there was a long silence, as the State Department forbade its embassies to forward such cables in the future, on the specious grounds that neutrals would curtail sending the State Department official information. The order was signed by Sumner Welles, until now a lonely advocate for Jewish causes inside the State Department. It appears that Welles had no idea such an order had gone out under his name. He likely signed it as just one more page of the large stacks of paperwork he affixed his signature to every day. When he discovered the cutoff of information, he at once requested the backlog of data be forwarded immediately and ordered communications reopened. But three months had been lost.

It remains difficult to understand State's reluctance to act throughout this period. Some of State's inaction is somewhat explicable in terms of disbelief, as few in the department, particularly in the early war years, believed the Nazis were really set on exterminating an entire people. But this is only part of the story. At the foundation of State's resistance was an underlying anti-Semitism, which was widespread among the patrician class populating State's offices. If, however, one is looking for a specific individual to blame, then the spotlight falls squarely on Breckinridge Long, whom his biographer called the "American Eichmann." This may overstate the case in terms of intent, but not outcome. Long entered the State Department in 1917, after the slogan he originated—"He kept us out of war"—helped Wilson get reelected. He left in 1920 and twice ran for senator in his home state of Missouri. Electoral failure did not dent his support of the Democratic Party, and he was a major contributor to Roosevelt's 1932 campaign, having become friendly with FDR when the latter was assistant secretary of the navy. His support led to an ambassadorship to Italy. Upon his return, Roosevelt sent him a personal note: "I do not need to tell you how proud I am of the splendid record you made in Rome . . . You are a grand fellow . . . and you know my devotion to you." In 1940 Long was posted back in the State Department, where he crucially took over the de-

partment's Immigrant Visa Section. From here, Long lost no opportunity
to limit the number of Jews entering the United States.

For years historians have debated whether Long was an overt anti-
Semite or just indifferent to the plight of Europe's Jews. It is stunning that
this remains a matter of debate, since Long called *Mein Kampf* as "eloquent
in opposition to Jewry and to the Jews as exponents of Communism and
chaos." This attitude was evident long before America entered the war, as
Long had almost single-handedly directed obstructionist policies directed
at keeping Jews out of the country. As pressure built for the nation to admit
some refugees, Long sought to move the State Department out of the line
of fire by moving the locus of inaction overseas. To do so he sent a cable to
European embassies and consulates outlining effective methods for them
to obstruct the issuing of visas on a local basis: "We can delay and effectively stop for a temporary period of indefinite length the number of immigrants into the United States. We could do this by simply advising our
consuls to put every obstacle in the way and to require additional evidence
and to resort to various administrative devices which would postpone and
postpone and postpone the granting of the visas."

When, early in the war, there appeared to be a chance to save six thousand Jewish children in Vichy France, Long strongly opposed doing so. He

thought it would set a bad precedent and wrote in his diary: "They are derelicts. Their elders are being herded like cattle and deported to Poland or to German workshops." And despite writing that their "appeal for asylum is irresistible to any human instinct," he still managed to conclude that "we cannot receive them into our midst." Long, through lies and deceit, perpetuated such obstructionist programs for years. He was even able to garner a large amount of support from Roosevelt by claiming that Nazi spies and saboteurs were seeking entry among the mass of refugees. This being so, Long told the president, he had to move slowly through the vetting process. Whether a paranoid Long actually believed this convenient fiction is unknown; that the lie provided cover for callous inaction is indisputable.

In late July 1943, Felix Frankfurter asked Hopkins to arrange a meeting with a Polish partisan with an incredible story to tell. Jan Karski, an officer in the Polish underground, had snuck into the Warsaw Ghetto and a Nazi extermination camp. Armed with firsthand knowledge of Nazi atrocities, he had made the rounds of influential people in London and Washington. Roosevelt agreed to the meeting but still tried to avoid the one topic Karski had come to discuss with him. Sensing the meeting was coming to an end Karski became desperate to steer the conversation toward the plight of Poland's Jews. As he related in a postwar interview:

> I caught him in a trap . . . I realized that the meeting was coming to the end. So I got up and then said to him: "Mr. President, I am going back to Poland, everybody will know I saw President Roosevelt. Everybody will ask me, 'What did the President tell you?' Mr. President, what am I going to tell them?" You never forget this kind of a thing. He was smoking his cigarette and said, "You will tell your leaders that we shall win this war! You will tell them that the guilty ones will be punished for their crimes." Smoking, smoking. "Justice, freedom will prevail. You will tell your nation that they have a friend in this house." I was convinced that I heard the voice of almighty God. I settled all problems. I, Jan Karski, made the president a friend of my country. That was my impression. Only when I then walked to the car with the Polish ambassador who accompanied me he said, "Well, the president did not say much." He was clever. About the dead Jews, Roosevelt said nothing. So I was disappointed after all.

Typical of Roosevelt, he had told a visitor what he thought he wanted to hear, and then refused to take any immediate action. Roosevelt may have had reasons for continued presidential neglect, but it was not lack of knowledge. By this time in the war Roosevelt was receiving information on the Nazi death machine from many quarters, including the OSS, which delivered this message to the White House just prior to FDR's meeting with Karski:

> The new Nazi policy is to kill Jews on the spot rather than to deport them to Poland for extermination there. High officers of the SS reportedly have decided that Berlin shall be liberated of all Jews by mid-March. Accordingly, 15,000 Berlin Jews were arrested between January 26 and March 2. All closed trucks were requisitioned: several hundred children died; several hundred adults were shot. Extension of these methods to other parts of Germany is expected.

By now, Treasury Secretary Morgenthau had entered the debate. As a Jew, the plight of Europe's Jews was always of keen personal interest to him. Despite this, Morgenthau had stayed away from Jewish issues for years, often telling subordinates that he was the secretary of the treasury for all Americans and not just Jewish Americans. In the early years of the war he continued to maintain a delicate balance between his official responsibilities and his advocacy for Jewish causes. But as Morgenthau became increasingly aware of State's reluctance to act, he, by degrees and on his own authority, pushed the Treasury Department into the policy void.

In early August 1943, Morgenthau asked Hull to help facilitate moving 70,000 Romanian Jews out of Europe for the cost of $170,000. This money, mostly bribes, was to be placed in blocked accounts in Switzerland and not distributed until after the war, to ensure none of the funds went toward helping the Nazi war effort. After Hull received FDR's verbal approval, he offered his cooperation. Despite the secretary's expressed approval, a legion of lower-level State Department functionaries threw up a series of obstacles, until the opportunity was snuffed out. Only Welles had the clout, inclination, and energy to break the logjam, but by this time he had fallen victim to a vicious cabal set on forcing him out of the government. With Welles gone, Jewish organizations had lost their only advocate within the

State Department at a time when tens of thousands of Jews destined for hideous deaths could still have been saved.

On November 23, 1943, Morgenthau brought together those members of his staff actively working on refugee issues to plot their attack on the State Department. Morgenthau warned them against the idea that they "could nail anyone at the State Department" as they were up against "successive generations of people . . . who don't like to do this kind of thing [admit Jewish refugees]." Rather, he wanted to catalog State's obstructionist actions in minute detail, so that he could present their findings to Hull. Still, he was not optimistic, and he ended his pep talk on a low note: ". . . All I can do is put this thing in Cordell's hands and say, 'Now please do this thing.' Then it is up to him to get angry at his people."

In what was supposed to be a showdown meeting on December 20, 1943, Morgenthau, Hull, and Long met. During a lull in the discussion, Long took the treasury secretary aside and complained that all of these problems resulted from actions of people in both departments lower down the line. Morgenthau was having none of it: "Well Breck, as long as you raise the question we might as well be frank. The impression is all around that you, particularly, are anti-Semitic." Before Long replied, Morgenthau stepped closer and looking him right in the eye said, "I know that is so."

When, in the days following the meeting, no action was forthcoming, Morgenthau, on January 16, 1944, went to Roosevelt and demanded that responsibility for refugee issues be removed from the State Department's purview. To make his point, Morgenthau handed Roosevelt a copy of the extensive report written by his subordinates, originally titled "Report to the Secretary on the Acquiescence of the Government in the Murder of the Jews." In explicit detail the report spelled out how the State Department had deliberately suppressed information relating to the mass murder of Europe's Jews, concluding with a warning that if the United States failed to act soon it would share the responsibility for the mass slaughter. After listening to an oral summary of the report, Roosevelt, even at this late date, tried to protect his friend Breckinridge Long. According to a memorandum of the meeting the president remained disinclined to believe that Long wanted to stop effective action from being taken. In his friend's defense, Roosevelt claimed that Long had soured on the Jewish problem when Rabbi Wise got him to approve a long list of Jews to be brought into the country. As Roosevelt related it, Long had told him that many of these immigrants turned out to be bad people, though no evidence supporting this statement was produced. When Morgenthau reminded the president that, at a cabinet meeting, Attorney General Biddle had stated that only three Jewish immigrants out of thousands had committed any crimes upon entering the United States, Roosevelt went silent.

Despite his desire to defend Long, Roosevelt did not dispute any of the facts presented in the report, or its conclusion:

> This much is certain, however, the matter of rescuing the Jews from extermination is a trust too great to remain in the hands of men who are indifferent, callous, and perhaps even hostile. The task is filled with difficulties. Only a fervent will to accomplish, backed by persistent and untiring effort can succeed where time is so precious.

That night Morgenthau reviewed everything he had told the president with Judge Rosenman and Welles's replacement as assistant secretary of state, Edward Stettinius. Stettinius had no problem believing any of what Morgenthau said about Long, and informed the secretary that he was about to reorganize the department in a way that would strip Long of his responsibilities. Stettinius then examined Morgenthau's draft of an executive order establishing the War Refugee Board, and declared, "I think it's wonderful."

With Stettinius's endorsement, Roosevelt approved the creation of the War Refugee Board on January 22, 1944. Morgenthau was elated, but grieved over the opportunities lost over the past eighteen months. For him it had been a long and heartbreaking fight. At stake was the obliteration of the entire Jewish people, who he now hoped, in the meager months remaining in the war, could be saved from total annihilation by "crusaders, passionately persuaded of the need for speed of action."

The second great issue related to saving European Jewry was whether the extermination process itself could be disrupted. Many schemes were proposed, but by far the most serious debate revolved around destroying or at least interrupting the greatest extermination center of them all: Auschwitz. During the spring of 1944 the Allies began receiving much more detailed information about the mass murders being carried out at Auschwitz-Birkenau. By this time, most of the large concentrations of Jews in Europe had been eradicated. The only place Jews still existed in large numbers was Hungary, where 750,000 had escaped deportation to extermination camps. As the Wehrmacht retreated, German executioners began focusing on this last remnant of free European Jewry. It is interesting to note that for the first time during the war there was more than ideology at work here. Without large numbers of Jews and other undesirables to exterminate, the entire German killing apparatus was worthless and would soon have to be closed. By now the fighting fronts were consuming manpower at a frightful rate, and the only protection the exterminators had from being sent to the front lines was finding more "undesirables" to slaughter. By the summer of 1944, however, four of the five specialized death camps had already closed. Only Auschwitz remained, and it was waiting for the Hungarian Jews. Without them the murderers waiting at Auschwitz would soon find themselves at the front, pitted against the fearsome and vengeful Red Army.

Hungary's leader, Miklós Horthy, had allied his nation with the Axis in 1938. He was no friend of the Jews, having instituted his first anti-Semite laws as early as 1920. Still, for most of the war, he had resisted Hitler's most strident demands. He finally succumbed in mid-March 1944, when Hitler summoned him to Schloss Klessheim, near Salzburg, and threatened an immediate invasion and overthrow of his government if he did not at once agree to start transporting Hungarian Jews to Auschwitz. Sonderkommando Eichmann, a special group of SS soldiers under the command of Adolf Eichmann, had already been activated a week earlier for the specific purpose of deporting Hungarian Jews. Horthy returned on March 19 to discover that the Germans had already taken over the government and were in the process of occupying the country. In early April the deportation of the Jews began.

It was at this time that Jacob Rosenheim, a New York Jew, made the first of several requests of the newly formed War Refugee Board to bomb the rail lines leading to Auschwitz. Other Jews opposed such an attack as it would kill Jewish prisoners and provide fodder for Nazi propaganda that could be used to disguise their own atrocities. On June 28, the War Refugee Board heard proposals to insert commandos into Silesia for an attack on the camp's installations. It was considered so unrealistic that it was never forwarded to the War Department. But on June 21, the board sent a formal request to the War Department to bomb the railways.

On June 24, John W. Pehle, formerly assistant secretary of the treasury and now the board's executive director, personally spoke to Assistant Secretary of War McCloy and asked him to examine the possibility. McCloy did not offer a lot of hope, telling Pehle that he doubted the lines could be damaged sufficiently or for a long enough period to do any good. The Army's Operations Division, dealing with repeated crises in the month after D-Day, turned the request down flat, saying that it would divert considerable "air support essential to the success of our forces now engaged in decisive operations." General Thomas Handy replied to McCloy: "The most effective relief to victims of enemy persecution is the early defeat of the Axis, an undertaking to which we must devote every resource at our disposal." On July 4, McCloy delivered the bad news to Pehle, adding that the War Department considered that the attack was of such "doubtful efficacy that it would not amount to a practical project."

Here we have the two standard arguments the War Department was to deploy throughout the remainder of the year: it would divert resources from the winning of the war; and the Jews' best chance of salvation was a rapid Allied victory. Then and now many have also mentioned that such an attack was not feasible given the distances involved. As the Allies bombed industrial targets just five miles from the camp, this line of argument can be safely discarded, as there remains little doubt that the Allies could have bombed Auschwitz and the nearby rail lines with units out of the Fifteenth Air Force in Foggia, Italy.

On June 29, 1944, the War Refugee Board considered a recommendation from the World Jewish Congress to bomb Auschwitz. The case for bombing was presented by board member Benjamin Akzin, who concluded with the observation that "presumably, a large number of Jews in these camps may be killed . . . But such Jews are doomed to death anyhow. The destruction of the camps would not change their fate, but it would serve as visible retribution on their murderers and it might save the lives of future victims." Two months later the World Jewish Congress's Rescue Department seconded the board and pleaded with McCloy to once again ask that Auschwitz be bombed. Finally in November Pehle forwarded a version of the Vrba-Wetzler report to McCloy. The forty-page report contained the testimony of two Jews who had escaped Auschwitz—Rudolf Vrba and Alfréd Wetzler—and presented gruesome details of the inner workings of the Nazis' killing apparatus. Despite this new evidence of the Nazi horrors,

McCloy turned down every request to bomb Auschwitz. His counterargument was always the same: "At the present critical stage of the war in Europe, our strategic air forces are engaged in the destruction of industrial target systems vital to the dwindling war potential of the enemy, from which they should not be diverted. The positive solution to this problem is the earliest possible victory over Germany, to which end we should exert our entire means."

Thus ended attempts to get the War Department to bomb Auschwitz. There is no archival evidence that Roosevelt was kept informed of these deliberations or decisions. Much later, McCloy, under intense pressure to defend these decisions, claimed that Hopkins and Rosenman had inquired into bombing Auschwitz and told him that the president had rejected all such proposals out of hand. A page-by-page review of Rosenman's and Hopkins's papers revealed nothing to corroborate this account. Interestingly, it does not even appear that McCloy consulted his direct superior—Henry Stimson—as a review of each of the thousands of pages of Stimson's wartime diaries fails to reveal a single reference to his and McCloy's discussing bombing Auschwitz. There is but one single conclusion: that McCloy accepted the Army Operations Division's reasons for not bombing Auschwitz and then took it upon himself to establish War Department policy in this area.

Why? Unlike Breckinridge Long, McCloy was not consumed by prejudice. Rather, he shared with many of his class and social station an anti-Semitism that accepted most Jewish stereotypes without ever desiring to do Jews harm. He may have belonged to clubs that refused Jews admittance, but he took enough offense at Morgenthau calling him an "oppressor of the Jews" to go directly to Morgenthau's home and confront him about the slight. All of the evidence suggests that even into late 1944 McCloy doubted the veracity of the reports of the mass extermination of the Jews, particularly because the sources for the most damning evidence were all Jews. Even if he did believe them in their entirety, the possibility remains that he may still not have acted, for he truly believed that the best way to save the Jews was by winning the war as soon as possible. As such, he was never prepared to countenance diversions from that priority.

History is left with one burning question: Would the bombing have helped? Ambassador William J. vanden Heuvel commented that Hitler's "central obsession, the life's mission of this deranged, monomaniacal psychopath, was to kill as many Jews as he could. Nothing diminished this mission—not the defeat of his armies, not the destruction of his country. As Germany lay in ruins . . . his Nazi acolytes continued his mission above all else, diverting even urgently needed reinforcements for his retreating armies to complete the assignment of the Final Solution." Two million Jews had been killed before Auschwitz opened, and hundreds of thousands more were killed after it was closed. Given such ruthless determination to murder every Jew in Europe, one doubts how long a few destroyed rail lines would have delayed the slaughter of Hungary's Jews. By this time in the war, the Germans were well practiced in the art of repairing bomb damage and would likely have had the death trains rolling again within days, and perhaps hours. Furthermore, even the utter destruction of Auschwitz-Birkenau could hardly be expected to save even a small number of Jewish lives. As Professor Weinberg has stated: "The idea that men dedicated to the killing program . . . were likely to be halted by a few cuts of railway lines or the bombing of the gas chambers is preposterous. By 1944, these people had managed by one means or another to kill four million, and quite probably five million, Jews; the notion that they lacked the persistence, ingenuity, and means to kill the majority of Hungary's 700,000 Jews defies all reason."

But should the Allies have bombed Auschwitz, even if it was only a symbolic gesture? One must first take note of the speed at which the Germans were killing Jews and other undesirables in the last months of the war, and then add to that the destruction of life taking place on the fighting front. It is unknowable if or for how long a diversion of the Fifteenth Air Force's heavy bombers to strike at Auschwitz would have extended the war. What if it had added a week, or even as little as a day—how many lives would have been lost? It is only a mental game, but one could easily make the case that such a diversion would have saved no Jewish lives, while adding tens of thousands of other innocents and soldiers to the death rolls. That is a high price to pay for symbolism. On the other hand, a symbolic attack would have declared to humanity, then and in the future, that there are some lines so horrible they can never be crossed without just retribution. Moreover, it would have given tens of thousands of camp inmates hope, and possibly have given some non-Jewish Europeans the courage to help the few survivors still wandering the European landscape.

Today, it has become increasingly common to cast blame on Roosevelt for not pushing his subordinates to do more to relieve the plight of the Jews, or to condemn him for not speaking out more often and with more passion. But as Ambassador vanden Heuvel points out:

> How ironic that our greatest president of this century—the man Hitler hated most, the leader constantly derided by the anti-Semites, vilified by Goebbels as a "mentally ill cripple" and as "that Jew Rosenfeld," violently attacked by the isolationist press—how ironic that he should be faulted for being indifferent to the genocide. For all of us, the shadow of doubt that enough was not done will always remain, even if there was little more that could have been done. But it is the killers who bear the responsibility for their deeds. To say that "we are all guilty" allows the truly guilty to avoid that responsibility. We must remember for all the days of our lives that it was Hitler who imagined the Holocaust and the Nazis who carried it out. We were not their accomplices. We destroyed them.

All wars are indeed terrible, but in this instance, even if in no other, the United States fought on the side of the angels. Undoubtedly this nation, Britain, the Soviet Union, and the rest of the Allied nations saved much of humanity from an unimaginable evil. That something more could have been done must never obscure the fact that if the Allies had failed in the great endeavors they did undertake, all of humanity would have been yoked to history's most evil regime.

In the final analysis history provides no answer. Each of us must seek out such answers on our own. Still, it is worth noting Holocaust survivor and Nobel laureate Elie Wiesel's reflection on the power a single bombing raid near Auschwitz had to give hope to thousands of the condemned:

> To see the whole works go up in fire—what revenge! . . . We were not afraid. And yet, if a bomb had fallen on the blocks, it alone would have claimed hundreds of lives on the spot. We were no longer afraid of death; at any rate, not of that death. Every bomb filled us with joy and gave us new confidence in life.

40

AULD LANG SYNE

B Y THE MIDDLE OF 1943, ROOSEVELT WAS AN INCREASINGLY SOL-
itary figure. All of those who had helped him originally gain the White
House and were swept into office with him were long gone. His political
guru, Louis Howe, the only man who could berate Roosevelt and yet remain in his good graces, was long dead. His replacement in the political
sphere, James Farley, had quarreled with the president over a third term,
and the breach had never mended. For most of his presidency he had
leaned heavily on the presidential secretary, Marguerite "Missy" LeHand,
who had not only taken an immense burden of work off Roosevelt, but
had acted as a substitute wife. Missy had a natural understanding of Roosevelt. She knew when to be lively and engage with him, and she knew
when to sit quietly and let him work on his beloved stamp collection. No
one doubted Missy was in love with Roosevelt, but his own feelings were
more ambiguous. But Missy was also gone now, still trying to recover from
a stroke she had suffered in mid-1941. From then until her death in July
1944, Roosevelt never called or wrote to her, but in his will he left the in-
come from half of his entire estate to care for her. Grace Tully had ably
stepped in to take over Missy's workload, but she never developed the intimacy her predecessor had had with the president.

After his marriage even Hopkins, who had been a constant presence
during Roosevelt's waking hours, had less time to spend with the president. His slow departure from Roosevelt's intimacy was completed in December of 1943, when, at Louise's insistence, the couple moved out of the
White House. Hopkins continued to proffer valued advice, but from the

day he moved out until Roosevelt's death, his relationship with FDR was no closer than that of Byrnes, Smith, Rosenman, or Sherwood. Many men over the years had considered themselves indispensable to Roosevelt, but Hopkins like all the rest learned the truth that lay in Eleanor's observation that FDR quickly discards people who no longer suit his purposes.

In 1944, Roosevelt filled part of whatever void he felt for human intimacy by having his daughter, Anna, come live in the White House while her husband was serving overseas. Once back in the White House, Anna took over the role of presidential guardian, caregiver, and companion. After renting out her Seattle home for $350 a month, she moved into the spacious Lincoln Room, recently vacated by Hopkins and his wife. Anna was beautiful, vivacious, witty, and charming, and she loved to laugh. Roosevelt adored her, and she for the remainder of his presidency replaced all those who had departed from his inner circle. But with his health failing, Roosevelt had few outlets for relaxation in the war's final two years, and most of his dwindling energy was consumed by the war; such concerns likely hastened his death. Roosevelt would likely have collapsed under the strain sooner if others had not stepped forward to shoulder many of his previous burdens. Jimmy Byrnes, for instance, was ably running domestic affairs, and under his firm hand the various agencies were mostly operating in the kind of harmony Roosevelt had been reluctant to enforce. Disputes still cropped up, but Byrnes, the master politician, could always smooth them over or, failing that, destroy one or both miscreants.

After the Quebec Conference in August 1943, the strategic direction of the rest of the war was firmly established. Roosevelt recognized that with the strategy set, the actual conduct of military operations was best handled by superb technocrats and specialists in violence—the Joint Chiefs. Thus Roosevelt rarely saw much reason to interfere with his Joint Chiefs and their subordinate commanders in the execution of campaigns, now that they had been decided upon. But in his roles as arbiter in chief, strategic direction setter, and bender of Churchill and (on those rare occasions when it became necessary) the Joint Chiefs to his own strategic will, Roosevelt still found much to keep him busy.

With the tremendous military forces America was gathering firmly set on the road to victory, Roosevelt began devoting substantial time to forcing a consensus as to what kind of world the victors wanted to live in at the end of hostilities. Until now he had allowed other agencies to begin planning alternatives and establishing the groundwork for his still-forming vision. As Roosevelt saw it, there were two major elements to this plan: the establishment of a global economic order that would prevent a return to the Great Depression, as well as ensure an age of global growth and prosperity; and the creation of a new global political order that would secure a lasting peace. For the first, Roosevelt counted on Morgenthau and his hyperactive staff to establish the technical framework. For the second, FDR had counted on Sumner Welles to drag a hidebound State Department into line behind his vision.

Unfortunately, in one of the Washington war's more sordid episodes, Welles was driven out of government in July 1943 as a result of earlier personal indiscretions. This was a major blow to Roosevelt, who had never conceived of Secretary of State Hull as the man to help him build a new international order. Welles's dismissal was accomplished through the unholy alliance of Cordell Hull and William Bullitt, the ambassador to France who had awakened Roosevelt with the news of the German assault on Poland.

Cordell Hull and Sumner Welles.

In the years before the war, Bullitt was perceived by many, including himself, as being as close to Roosevelt as Welles was. He had free access to the White House and the president, which had as much to do with his brief romance with Missy LeHand as with his relationship with FDR. Roosevelt thought enough of him to give him the plum assignment as ambassador to France, where Bullitt became his eyes and ears on the Continent. As he was often in direct phone conversation with Roosevelt, many assumed he was also his spokesman on all European affairs. Even Bullitt assumed as much. However, when Roosevelt sent Welles on his peace tour of the European capitals in 1940, he created a permanent antagonism between the two men. Bullitt was initially upset by Roosevelt's having kept him in the dark about the trip—another instance of the president's love for secrets damaging relationships he would have been better served maintaining. But that minor slight was nothing compared to the rage Bullitt felt when he learned that Welles was undertaking a mission he thought was rightfully his. As Bullitt could not attack the president, Welles became the focus of his enmity.

After France's fall, Bullitt returned to the United States and began prowling the halls of the State Department as he waited for Roosevelt to reassign him. It was an open secret that Bullitt wanted to be the next secretary of state, or, failing that, he wanted Welles's job as assistant secretary, as a stepping-stone to the top job. In the meantime, he was growing restless and was very sensitive to the fact that he had no official position and important people were becoming less and less available to see him when he made the rounds. In early October, at Bullitt's instigation, Ickes took the matter up with the president. Roosevelt was planning cabinet-level changes and told Ickes that he knew Bullitt wanted to be secretary of state, but because "Bill talked too much" the president was not going to give it to him. Bullitt was left in limbo until December 1941, when Roosevelt posted him to the unpromising position of presidential observer in the Middle East and North Africa. The job did not agree with Bullitt and he was soon back in Washington, where he lingered in semi-obscurity.

Unable to secure a position suitable for his high opinion of himself, Bullitt began looking for whoever must be responsible for his fall from grace. He seized on Welles, certain that the presidential favorite and toady was working against his interests. He had, in April 1941, tried once before to have Welles pushed aside, but failed. That time, he went straight to Roosevelt with confidential information about Welles's personal indiscretions.

He presented evidence that Welles, while returning home from House Speaker William Bankhead's funeral in September 1940, drank heavily, and continued drinking long after everyone else had gone to sleep. Toward morning he rang for coffee, and when the black Pullman porter delivered it, Welles sexually propositioned him. The porter reported the incident, but after a short Secret Service investigation the story was hushed up. But in official Washington there were few secrets, and Welles's indiscretion made the rounds. After having J. Edgar Hoover's FBI confirm the veracity of the story, Roosevelt, at Hoover's suggestion, gave Welles a permanent bodyguard, tasked to protect the assistant secretary and to make sure there were no further indiscretions. Bullitt was not assuaged, asking Roosevelt "how he could call upon Americans to die in a crusade for all that was decent in human life, when he had among the leaders of the crusade a criminal like Welles." Visibly upset at his visitor's impertinence, Roosevelt dismissed Bullitt and cancelled the remainder of his appointments for the day.

Unable to get at Welles through the president, Bullitt took his story to the press, and then later, with Hull's connivance, he leaked it to senators unfriendly to the administration. Roosevelt got word of what Bullitt was doing and became progressively more incensed. Once, while talking to Vice President Wallace on other issues, FDR suddenly started talking about Bullitt, calling him a "terrible person." When Wallace asked why, Roosevelt replied: "Because of the awful story he spread all over town about Sumner Welles." Roosevelt concluded by saying, "Bill ought to go to hell for that."

Throughout this period, Secretary Hull's resentment of Welles's setting State Department policy without consulting him, as well as his close ties to the president, became increasingly more obsessive. Starting early in 1942 he began to undermine his assistant secretary at every opportunity, and welcomed the juicy scandal Bullitt brought to his attention. In September 1942 Hull discussed the accusations with Breckinridge Long, who warned that just the hint of such a scandal, if it found its way into print, would damage the department and rock the administration. Ignoring this wise counsel, Hull gathered information and sought allies on Capitol Hill. Risking Roosevelt's wrath, Hull summoned his courage and mentioned it to Roosevelt, just before the Casablanca Conference. Roosevelt, realizing one of his favorites was under attack from a new quarter, "looked miserably at the ceiling" but refused to give Hull a definitive answer as to how he would proceed. Over the next few months Hull brooded as Bullitt continued to prod him to action. In June 1943, Hull broached the subject one more time, informing Roosevelt that Welles's indiscretion was known throughout the Senate, and that it was only a matter of time before the scandal broke in the press.

As the pressure mounted, Welles vacated the field to his enemies and took an extended vacation. Bullitt seized the opportunity to confront the president again. On July 27, he brought his charges to the Oval Office. Roosevelt had had enough. Fuming with anger he called Bullitt unchristian and accused him of leaking the story to that "bitch friend of yours"—journalist Cissy Patterson, publisher of the *Washington Times-Herald*—for whom Roosevelt nursed a passionate hatred, and who had previously been romantically linked to Bullitt. Roosevelt ordered Bullitt out of his office, declaring that he needed Welles, who was "younger and more intelligent than that old fool Hull."

But the "old fool" had been busy. On August 4, *The New York Times* published a front-page story stating that "conflicting personalities, and lack of cohesive policy are resulting in the impairment of the efficiency of the State Department." Almost identical stories appeared in other newspapers that were friendly to Hull, but not necessarily to the president. Two days later the *New York Times* star columnist and close friend of Secretary Hull, Arthur Krock, used his "In the Nation" column to place the blame for the ongoing bureaucratic war within the State Department squarely on Roosevelt's shoulders, concluding that ". . . the State Department will function smoothly when the President permits the Secretary to be the real, undisputed head of a loyal staff."

Roosevelt had been away fishing when these articles exploded onto the Washington firmament. Upon his return, he met with Hull two days in succession. Stalin had just agreed to a meeting with Roosevelt and Churchill in October, and this provided Hull with his long-awaited opening; Roosevelt could choose between him or Welles. Hull had chosen his moment well, as Roosevelt was set to go that day to Hyde Park to meet with Churchill. Hull's sudden resignation would be a political bombshell that would have focused attention on a scandal rather than where Roosevelt wanted it: his discussions with world leaders. Moreover, Roosevelt had already decided to run for a fourth term, and he needed to put this brewing scandal behind him before the Republicans opened a senatorial inquiry. When Hull departed, Roosevelt consulted with Byrnes, who had been well prepped by Hull. Feigning reluctance to get between old friends, Byrnes nevertheless took the opportunity to offer Edward R. Stettinius—a mere cipher with few ideas of his own—as Welles's replacement. Byrnes, while claiming "disinterest" in the result, showed himself to be as prone as Hopkins to use any opportunity to replace anyone with an independent power base with someone of his own choosing. Byrnes often decried the Washington war, but never when he was winning it.

On August 11, 1943, Roosevelt, awakening to the fact that he was cornered, called Welles to his office and explained the fix he was in. Stunned at the abrupt turn of events, Welles went home and had a heart attack. But a few days later he was well enough to dictate his letter of resignation. Welles continued to play a bit role at the fringes of power in Washington, but from then until his death in 1961 he was never again a major player in Washington power circles. But Hull was also finished, as many, including the liberal press, blamed him for the chaos at State and for the dismissal of one of their favorites. Hull, his friendship with the president irredeemably broken and his power to affect events nil, lingered at State until November of 1944, when, pleading ill health, he resigned.

As for Bullitt, soon after Welles's resignation he had reason to visit the White House, where a still livid president spotted him. "William Bullitt, stand where you are," Roosevelt thundered. In a terrible rage, Roosevelt shouted: "Saint Peter is at the gate. Along comes Sumner Welles who admits to human error. St. Peter grants him entrance. Then comes William Bullitt. St. Peter says: 'William Bullitt, you have betrayed a fellow human being. *You can go down there.*'" Roosevelt then ordered Bullitt out of the White House, telling him he never wanted to see him again. The president's stenographer, Dorothy Brady, who was with Roosevelt, remembered that the president was "raving" at the time and went on raving long after Bullitt departed, repeatedly saying that Bullitt would be sent to hell.

To get him out of Washington, Roosevelt employed go-betweens to suggest he might run for mayor in his home city of Philadelphia. Unbelievably, Bullitt thought he had Roosevelt's support and leapt at the opportunity. Only too late did he learn that Roosevelt had secretly ordered local party bosses to "cut his throat." Finally realizing he would never get a major job in Washington, Bullitt went overseas and joined de Gaulle's Free French forces. It was probably as close as he could come to running away and joining the French Foreign Legion.

Welles, one of Roosevelt's few remaining intimates, had departed from his close personal circle. But to Roosevelt, such departures were mere distractions to his all-consuming twin passions—winning the war and establishing a new world order. Though there would still be moments of conviviality with old or former friends who remained in his orbit, from mid-1943 until his death in 1945 Franklin Delano Roosevelt was a different man. Whether this was because of his failing health or the natural result of being responsible for waging a murderous global war cannot be determined—likely some combination of both is to blame. Roosevelt must also have known that his time was running out. And although he always displayed a large degree of nonchalance about his health, to the point of not even asking for the results of his examinations, he surely felt his energy ebbing. Though his doctors kept the true extent of his deterioration from him as well as the public, Roosevelt was a gravely ill man. By mid-1944 he was only able to work a greatly reduced schedule and spent more and more time in bed. Those around him could see he was dying. But for almost another full year he summoned just enough of the old Roosevelt to put his indelible stamp on every action that mattered.

41

STORM CLOUDS OVER

THE ALLIANCE

B Y THE END OF MAY 1943, NORTH AFRICA WAS SECURE AND THE invasion of Sicily was less than six weeks away. But what came after that? King might bluster that he needed more of everything to maintain his Pacific offensives in 1943, but the reality was that his needs were not pressing. Without a complete "fleet train" capable of supplying huge invasion task forces over tremendous distances, or sufficient carriers to protect them, the Navy was not going far in 1943. Guadalcanal was finally secured early in the year, but for most of 1943 Nimitz's forces limited themselves to securing the rest of the Solomons—first New Georgia, followed by Bougainville. Meanwhile, MacArthur might stare longingly at maps of the Philippines, but for the rest of the year he would be stuck fighting for New Guinea. Forces were scraped up to retake two Aleutian Islands the Japanese had seized during the Midway campaign, but this was done as a matter of national honor, rather than military necessity. Only as the year was closing did Nimitz find sufficient strength to strike out into the central Pacific, seizing Tarawa and Makin in the Gilbert Islands. It was the first step, but only the first, of a blitzkrieg across the Pacific that brought American power to Japan's doorstep and signaled to Japan's military leadership that the end was at hand, as American industrial might was now rolling out a fleet of unprecedented and unrivaled power.

To maintain the Allies' momentum everyone's eyes turned back to the Atlantic. The invasion of Sicily was settled, but nothing else. At Casablanca, there had been general agreement that northern Europe was the next priority, but no date was set, nor did anyone discuss whether further operations in other locations were permissible in the months leading up to the big show. Churchill wanted to stay focused on the Mediterranean, while the Joint Chiefs were just as determined to close up shop on that front and reorient every available asset to the BOLERO buildup. The decision rested with Roosevelt, and as Axis forces collapsed in Tunisia, Churchill was steaming across the Atlantic in the lice-infested *Queen Mary* to pry the answer loose.

Before he arrived, official Washington entertained two other guests. One was the beguiling American-educated wife of China's leader, Chiang Kai-shek—Soong Mei-ling, or Madame Chiang. She and her brother, the Chinese ambassador to the United States, T. V. Soong, were forceful advocates for China's needs, of which there were many. Foremost among them was getting an American commitment for a Burmese offensive to reopen China's vital supply lines. Roosevelt was sympathetic, but with Britain claiming it lacked the resources for a major offensive in Asia and his own predisposition for a Germany-first strategy, he had little to offer her. The Joint Chiefs, fearful that China might make a separate peace that would free millions of Japanese soldiers for other duties, were more interested in helping. But, lacking resources to open up another major front, they could offer only plans for an offensive at some undefined time in the future.

A disappointed Madame Chiang took her message on the road, where she wowed large crowds with her stunning beauty and Georgia-accented English. She had just sold out the Hollywood Bowl for the first time since Pearl Harbor when on April 6 Roosevelt met with his Joint Chiefs to discuss the possibility of operations in Burma (the proposed operation was given the code name Anakim) aimed at opening the Burma Road into China. FDR appeared only lukewarm about the idea of continued American operations in the theater. Further, he informed the JCS that Churchill was souring on the operation, and that he personally feared there was insufficient shipping to make it a feasible option before the winter of 1943. General Arnold, who hoped to launch bombing raids on Japan from Chinese bases, made a strong plea in support of the operation, reminding everyone that they had promised Generalissimo Chiang Kai-shek that they would conduct operations aimed at clearing Burma of Japanese troops. Roosevelt was unconvinced, but after more debate he said he might consider operations limited to northern Burma, but he wanted the Chinese army to carry most of the burden, stating that he "disliked having white troops engaged in that theater."

Returning to Washington, in hopes that it would show her more kindness, Madame Chiang went before a joint session of Congress. As *Time* related: "Madame Chiang stepped to the rostrum . . . , shot a smile at the Senators, and then, after apologizing for not having a set speech, knocked their silvery blocks off extemporaneously." She began with some deft compliments, which always went down well with a compliment-starved Congress, and then said some nice words about American troops serving in China, before going on to make her country's case. Careful to avoid the appearance of begging, she pulled at her audience's heartstrings, reminding them that her country had been killing the hated Japanese for years. In the end, she added greatly to the sympathy Congress and Americans generally felt for the Chinese, but with little practical effect. For Congress, while willing to make its power felt in many spheres, generally left directing the war in the hands of Roosevelt and the Joint Chiefs.

The second visitor was Churchill's number two, Anthony Eden, who had come to sound out Roosevelt on his thoughts for the future of the world. In their hours of conversation, the two men traversed the globe. Eden found the discourse fascinating, but he became alarmed at "the cheerful fecklessness with which the President seemed to dispose of the fate of whole countries." Interestingly the Joint Chiefs were never present for these meetings, as Roosevelt did not consider the postwar political settlement their concern. Moreover, though Hull and the national ambassadors—Halifax for Britain and Winant for the United States—were sometimes present, most of the sessions included just Roosevelt, Eden, and Hopkins.

It was, however, during these conversations that we catch a first glimpse of the negotiating positions Roosevelt would employ at the Yalta Conference in early 1945. Revealing a pragmatism that Eden found shocking, Roosevelt declared the Baltic states as lost. As he saw it, Russia had owned them for two hundred years and needed just recompense for its wartime sacrifices. He was, however, in favor of conducting a fig-leaf plebiscite to give the appearance of legitimacy. He also hoped that by handing over the

From left: Edward Stettinius, Anthony Eden, Vladimir Pavlov (Stalin's translator),
Joseph Stalin, President Franklin D. Roosevelt, Winston Churchill,
and Vyacheslav Molotov.

Baltic states—and Finland, where Russia should at least be entitled to what it had gained by conquest in 1940—he could get Stalin to bargain on the fate of Poland. FDR announced that he was fine with the Curzon Line, which moved Poland's eastern border on average 160 miles west, in return for Poland gaining East Prussia as part of its territory. So the discussion went, as Roosevelt roamed the far corners of the earth giving vent to his ideas for a new world order. For Eden, it was a tour de force, and he later noted that Roosevelt "felt so sure of himself disposing of the fate of many lands; allied no less than enemy. He did this with so much grace that it was not easy to dissent. Yet it was too like the conjuror, skillfully juggling with balls of dynamite, whose nature he failed to understand." But Roosevelt was not naïve, being among the first to realize that at the war's end Russia's writ would extend to wherever the Red Army's advance ended. As such he was already dispensing with fantasies and giving himself over to realpolitik in a search for the best possible deal. So, despite the Allies' having gone to war in 1939 to defend Poland's integrity, Roosevelt's main concerns in re-gard to Poland were already centered on what concessions he could draw from Stalin that would appease the seven million Polish American voters who would desert the Democratic Party in droves if he was seen to throw over Poland's independence.

Roosevelt also discussed the fate of Germany, which he envisioned partitioned into harmless proto-states incapable of ever again threatening the peace of Europe. But the major point of presidential concern centered on the creation of a postwar world organization. Following Welles's lead, Roosevelt was emphatically against the United States participating in small regional organizations. This was an idea favored by both Churchill and Hull, on the assumption that the states most impacted by local disputes would have much greater interest in solving them. Rather, Roosevelt wanted a global organization consisting of all states, advised (read: controlled and policed) by the Big Four—the United States, the USSR, Britain, and China. The details were still nebulous, but from this point forward the idea of a United Nations became Roosevelt's primary postwar vision and goal. Though Roosevelt had included Britain in his Big Four, he could already see that the tiny island nation had exhausted itself in two great wars. In a world ruled by realpolitik FDR was convinced that Britain would be of limited consequence, while Russia, despite requiring years of economic rehabilitation, would stand like a colossus over much of Eurasia. Achieving his postwar vision, therefore, rested on aligning Stalin's postwar designs with his own. As such, Roosevelt increasingly distanced himself from Churchill in favor of building a relationship with Stalin, the one man who could thwart Roosevelt's postwar ambitions.

Yet the priority remained winning the war, and doing so in such a way that American forces were deep within continental Europe when it ended. Just as Roosevelt understood that Russian authority would run as far as the Red Army advanced, he knew that America's power to influence the European postwar settlement rested on having a large American army deep within Europe. This dawning understanding of geopolitical reality finally aligned his long-term political interests with the shorter-term goals of his Joint Chiefs. As such, Roosevelt was now ready to support the earliest possible date for a cross-Channel invasion, with as few diversions as possible. Although his chiefs remained worried about his susceptibility to Churchillian siren calls for quick victories in distant locales, Roosevelt was now immune. Likely he always had been, as he tended to follow Churchill's suggestions only when they corresponded to his own developing ideas. But even if he had been Churchill's pawn in the war's early days, that time had passed. FDR now analyzed every plan and scheme through the prism of how they impacted the invasion of northern Europe, awakened to the fact that creating a working partnership with Stalin required that American troops meet the Red Army somewhere in Germany. It was, therefore, a new and determined Roosevelt who awaited Churchill's next visit to Washington in May 1943—the Second Washington Conference (code-named Trident).

As the prime minister and his Combined Chiefs made their crossing, Churchill drilled them on the issues he expected to confront. As always, he wanted to be sure that his entire team presented a united front to their allies. But this time the British found themselves facing a unified American team, supported by staff officers ready to meet the British staff paper for staff paper. In the past, the Americans had been buried under a mountain of British paper, which they credited to three causes: British planners did not attend the meetings of the Combined Chiefs, so they could dedicate all of their time to planning and writing; the British had two hundred years' more practice in interweaving diplomacy and military strategy; and British planners typically outnumbered the American planners ten to one. This time the Americans would be playing on their home turf, with literally thousands of staff planners, stenographers, and typists standing by throughout the conference. To make sure they were ready, the JCS ordered the preparation of plans for every reasonable course of action following Operation HUSKY (the invasion of Sicily), and made it clear that "reasonable" was to be given a liberal definition. Admiral Charles M. Cooke, who often represented King at JCS meetings, told the planners to also complete data-filled studies for every plan they put together, as well as every plan the British might present. The Joint Chiefs wanted to be ready for every contingency, but they were particularly aroused by recent British cables that seemed to state that "Husky was a means to an end" and that end was the invasion of Italy.

The JCS, however, were adamant that "Husky was an end in itself," and that once it was completed every available soldier would depart the Mediterranean for Britain. Italy, according to Arnold, would be knocked out of the war by air bombardment from Sicilian airfields. To make sure the British chiefs were unprepared for this line of attack, the Joint Chiefs ordered that all plans and studies be concealed from the British; as Marshall stated,

"We will do well avoiding preliminary skirmishes that would weaken our position during the conference." Still, Marshall was worried, telling Stimson the day before the British arrived: "I fear it will be the same old story over again. The man from London will arrive and will have his way with our Chief [Roosevelt], and the careful and deliberate plans of our staff will be overridden." Marshall was also bothered that one of his strongest supporters in arguments with the British, Hap Arnold, had gone into the hospital the night before after suffering a severe heart attack. Stimson too was worried about the loss of Arnold: "We all know Arnold would be a great help. He is brilliant in his presentations and fearless and undiplomatic which is very necessary as a good counterpoise to Marshall who is a little over-diplomatic."

On May 11, Hopkins was at the pier on New York's Staten Island when the *Queen Mary* berthed. He escorted Churchill, with his hundred-person staff, including over a dozen Wrens (members of the Women's Royal Naval Service) that Churchill insisted accompany the party, to a waiting train for the trip to Washington. The Trident Conference started the next day in a jubilant mood. As Stimson recorded: "Today is a great day of victory for Allied arms in Tunisia. All day news has been coming in of the Germans crumbling and surrendering in masses." Many remembered the last time they had been gathered in the same room, less than a year before, dealing with the bombshell news that the British had surrendered Tobruk.

The mood shifted when the conferees got to work. As expected, Churchill struck first, aiming his rhetoric right at his main objective. After a short discourse on the state of the war since Casablanca, he declared that he was not going to discuss the Battle of the Atlantic or the strategic bombing campaign, as the differences between the Allies were too minute to mention. As Churchill saw it the first objective was to be the Mediterranean and the "great prize was Italy." Warming to his topic he declared: "The collapse of Italy would cause a chill of loneliness over the German people and might be the beginning of the end." And even if it did not lead to Germany's immediate demise, Churchill believed it would surely help bring Turkey into the war. Churchill went on: "Twenty-five Italian Divisions would leave the Balkans, the Italian fleet would be neutralized, and British ships would be freed to join the fight against Japan." Churchill at this point had no idea that King loathed the idea of a British fleet in the Pacific, and that it would take a presidential order for him to accept British help during the 1945 invasion of Okinawa. The prime minister concluded by observing that many months would pass between the conquest of Sicily and the invasion of France, and that Anglo-American troops could not stand idle, leaving the Russian armies to face 195 divisions alone. As he saw it, since there was no immediate prospect of using these troops in northern Europe, they should be employed on the Italian mainland.

Roosevelt declared himself a firm believer in attrition as an effective weapon, and pointed out that as the Allies were now far outstripping German and Japanese production, "we only need to break even in our losses to forge ahead." He then sent the Joint Chiefs into quiet apoplexy by stating, "Given the large armies and naval force available to the United Nations [the Allies] every effort must be made to keep them engaged with the enemy . . . the United Nations was losing ground if our forces remained idle." Only a few minutes had passed since the opening of the conference and Roosevelt had seemingly gone more than halfway toward the British position. But then he said, "Where do we go from Husky?" Before anyone could answer, he said that he had always shrunk from the idea of putting large armies in Italy. He went on to declare that he was wary that such an invasion would saddle the Allies with the burden of feeding millions of destitute Italians. Roosevelt then drove a stake through Churchill's rhetorical heart by telling him he wanted any surplus forces in the Mediterranean sent to England. "We have talked about ROUNDUP and SLEDGE-HAMMER for two years without accepting a concrete plan or timetable," Roosevelt said, and then with some vehemence he affirmed that he wanted "ROUNDUP or SLEDGEHAMMER decided upon definitely as an operation for the spring of 1944."

The conversation then turned to the Pacific, where Roosevelt made a strong case that everything the Allies were planning relied on keeping China a "going concern." After short discussions covering Spain, Turkey, and taking some of the weight off Russia, Roosevelt adjourned the meeting. Marshall left the room a happy man; Roosevelt had bent but he had not broken. The next morning the Combined Chiefs, without Churchill or Roosevelt present, took up their rhetorical cudgels to go at it again. Leahy opened the proceedings by reading the American assessment of the operations planned for the rest of 1943 and 1944. Taken aback by the comprehensiveness of the American paper, Brooke's only response was to ask that he and the rest of the British chiefs be given time to study it. He then recited from his own six-page memorandum outlining the British position for the same time period. He spoke eloquently of British plans to "definitely assess the desirability" of operations in northern France, after which, if and only if they were found "desirable," they planned to carefully examine if such operations were "possible." This was the Brooke that Marshall and the JCS had planned for. It would be a fight to the finish.

There was no changing anyone else's mind, but that did not stop each team's papers from flying about the room. The British pushed for an invasion of Italy, for they firmly held that bombing alone could not knock Italy out of the war. The Americans held firm for invading northern Europe; forcing the British to counter with the claim that invading Italy would draw off German divisions, making a future attack on northern Europe easier. Doubling down, the British chiefs claimed that if the Allies also took Sardinia and Corsica even more German divisions would be tied down guarding southern France. The Americans, all of them seasoned poker players, kept their eyes fixed on the pot; no matter what the British bet they saw it and raised them one invasion of northern Europe.

Brooke could not understand why Marshall failed to comprehend that the British scheme increased the chance of success in northern France, as the invasion would face less resistance if the Germans were worn out and tied down elsewhere. For Brooke, the American Joint Chiefs still appeared to be very much in need of his tutelage. But to the American Joint Chiefs, the British, despite victory in North Africa, seemed frightened of the "vaunted" Wehrmacht, and too prone to let the "ghosts of the Somme" play on their minds.

When Brooke announced he had no confidence that a 1944 invasion would succeed, even if operations in the Mediterranean were shut down, Marshall declared, "Now we are getting to the heart of the matter." Brooke replied that all they would get for their troubles was a lodgment of twenty divisions, followed by a prolonged stalemate in front of continental-sized forces of fifty or a hundred divisions. He was adamant that it was essential to set the right conditions before an invasion. Marshall was equally inflexible, stating, "We are now at a crossroads—if we [are] committed to the Mediterranean, . . . it mean[s] a prolonged struggle and one which [is] not acceptable to the United States." The Joint Chiefs then declared that they were ready to take their army and head to the Pacific, where they said they were "still permitted to win the war."

An entry in General Brooke's diary demonstrates that the British did not consider this an empty threat: "The Americans are taking up the attitude that we led them down the garden path taking them to North Africa! That at Casablanca we again misled them by inducing them to attack Sicily!! And now they are not going to be led astray again. Added to that the swing towards the Pacific is stronger than ever and before long they will be urging that we should defeat Japan first!"

Obviously, nothing was concluded before the meeting adjourned.

The parties were still stalemated when Roosevelt declared that he and Churchill would take a weekend break at Shangri-La. The most memorable event of the weekend outing was Churchill's en-route recitation of John Greenleaf Whittier's poem about Barbara Frietchie: "'Shoot, if you must, this old gray head, / But spare your country's flag,' she said." Both men used the weekend to relax, Roosevelt by fishing and working on his stamp collection, and Churchill by watching as the president fished.

The Combined Chiefs met on Friday and again Saturday morning, but when no progress was made, Marshall took the entire party to Colonial Williamsburg. John D. Rockefeller had been asked to assist in the preparations, and he did his best—which given his wealth was substantial—to make the outing a success. His club in New York cooked the terrapin à la Maryland; the cream was hand-carried by his butler from Rockefeller's New York farm; and the best cheeses and fruits were bought up from the best shops. Brooke relaxed by indulging his favorite pastime: bird-watching. The others took walks, played croquet, or in Air Chief Marshal Portal's case dove into a pool wearing an overlarge bathing suit, and emerged sans suit. It was a pleasant respite for all, but the truce ended on Sunday afternoon. By Monday morning the staffs went back to their personal war, leaving Stimson dismayed by the deadlock, but glad to see that "the President seemed to be holding out."

By Wednesday afternoon Marshall was exhausted and showing the strain. He was holding as many as four meetings a day, many of them so hot that staff officers were ordered from the room, to allow the chiefs to fight it out in private. Between meetings, Marshall complained bitterly about Senator Albert "Happy" Chandler. The senator had vehemently opposed the "Germany first" strategy, and during Senate hearings he had said that the Joint Chiefs secretly supported his position of taking on Japan first. When he heard what Chandler said, Marshall exploded in outrage.

Stimson tried to calm him, but Marshall was beside himself, claiming that Chandler had launched "a personal attack" on his reputation. Stimson finally had to bring him up with a sharp and formal rebuke: "General Marshall, it would be quite impossible for Senator Chandler to destroy or even in any degree impair your reputation or character, so let's drop the subject." Marshall soon recovered and joined Stimson in a laugh. But Stimson remained worried, writing later, "I have it constantly on my mind—how much depends on keeping his [Marshall's] physical and mental poise. On him, more than anyone in government, I think rests the fortunes of the United States in this war."

The Joint Chiefs (minus the British) met early on May 19, but they were not optimistic. King opened the discussion, saying that "the British simply would not invade the Continent in the spring of 1944 and that we must get realistic about it." Even Marshall was showing signs of doubt, admitting for the first time "that ROUNDUP in the spring of 1944 was a logistical impossibility." Still he was determined to do something in France—possibly with just twenty divisions—and the Joint Chiefs agreed to press their British counterparts hard in their next meeting.

But this was the day everything changed. Before the Americans could even begin their full-court press, the British suddenly agreed to cease focusing on what Stimson called "the little points" and said they would consider the "big point." Marshall then made an observation that he had not brought up in his earlier meeting with the American chiefs, mentioning that he had read a British planning paper stating that if Mediterranean operations were conducted post Sicily it would still be possible to conduct an invasion of northern Europe on April 1, 1944. Brooke did not argue the point, stating that such a date was possible only if further Mediterranean operations drew off German forces. He then amended the April 1 date to May or June, but that was close enough for the Americans.

Sensing they were near an agreement, Marshall cleared the room, leaving only the chiefs, Dill, and a secretary, who dared not pick up his pen. As one historian said: "The Chief of Staff was going to squeeze an agreement and he wanted no witnesses." When the British committed to May 1, 1944, as a firm date for the invasion of northern France, Marshall, suddenly a font of generosity, said that in the meantime he and the rest of the Joint Chiefs would agree to knocking Italy out of the war, assuming the invasion of Sicily was rapidly concluded. Brooke, for his part, failed to get a firm commitment to invade Italy, but it was close enough. As he wrote later, approving the unsatisfactory agreement was "far better than a break-up of the conference." But Marshall was elated. He had a firm date for the invasion of Europe, and though the British only agreed to invading France with twenty divisions—in effect, a super-SLEDGEHAMMER—the scale of the operation could be adjusted later. Marshall had also gotten the British to commit to taking seven battle-hardened divisions out of the Mediterranean in the fall, ensuring that there was now a clear path to shutting down the Mediterranean "suction pump."

The remainder of the conference was mostly given over to securing bases in the Azores and discussions over operations in Burma and assisting China. Though these prolonged debates often got heated, nothing of permanence was concluded. Moreover, the American preoccupation with China would soon come to an end, as China's centrality to America's Pacific calculations was about to dramatically change.

Roosevelt and Churchill readily approved the plans, leaving only one important job: someone had to tell Stalin the disappointing news that there would not be a second front in 1943. For hours he and Churchill worked on various drafts of their joint statement to Stalin. In the end, Churchill said he would take it with him to Algiers and work on it during his travels. At Churchill's insistence and with Roosevelt's concurrence, General Marshall accompanied the prime minister on his trip. Churchill had planned to work on Marshall to approve further operations in the Mediterranean, but Marshall postponed the flood of Churchillian rhetoric by offering to fix the letter to Stalin. Marshall worked on it for about two hours, and the completed document was approved by the president and prime minister without changes.

Before heading to Algiers with the prime minister, Marshall had planned to take a much-needed few days off before heading out to tour the Pacific with King. Traveling with Churchill had cost him his rest, and his Pacific tour was postponed. When he heard Marshall was being denied a short vacation, Stimson was almost beside himself with rage, writing of Churchill: "He is going to take Marshall along with him in order to work on him to yield on a number of points that Marshall has held out on . . . to think of picking out the strongest man there is in America, and Marshall is surely that. . . . The one on whom the fate of the war depends, and then to deprive him on a gamble of a much-needed opportunity to recoup his strength by about three days' rest."

But Marshall had long ago developed a technique to divert Churchill from his intent. Early in their acquaintance Marshall had been awed by Churchill's near-photographic memory. Once Churchill had eyed Marshall reading a book about a former prime minister and on impulse had begun striding about the room reciting verbatim the minister's speeches. At a later date, when Marshall wanted to avoid talking strategy during a dinner party, he had asked the prime minister his thoughts about the eminent Victorian historian Lord Macaulay. On cue, Churchill sprung up and began reciting voluminous passages from Macaulay as he tramped about the room. During the trip to Algiers, Marshall asked about the impeachment of Warren Hastings, governor general of India in the late 1700s. When Churchill had exhausted that topic Marshall moved on to Rudolf Hess, and then the abdication of Edward VIII and his marriage to Wallis Simpson. Such diversions worked for a plane ride, but Churchill had a purpose and he would not be dissuaded. For the next several days Marshall and Eisenhower were the prime recipients of voluminous rhetoric, debate, cajoling, and argument, all aimed at getting a firm commitment to invade Italy. In the end, Churchill, seizing on Eisenhower's agreement to recommend an invasion if operations in Sicily went well, assumed he had won his points. In reality, Marshall had decided to conserve his strength and did so by ceasing to argue with a prime minister who liked nothing better than to debate until morning, after which he went for a nap as everyone else began a full day of work.

As Churchill scolded the American generals, Roosevelt, unbeknownst to Churchill, was attempting to conduct some private diplomacy with Stalin, and he decided to wait a week before forwarding the note informing Stalin there would be no second front in 1943.

Also without Churchill's knowledge, Roosevelt had tried before the Trident Conference to arrange a one-on-one meeting with Stalin. That attempt had failed, but Roosevelt tried again during the conference, sending the former American ambassador Joseph Davies to ask Stalin for a meeting in person. Davies reported that he had to wade through substantial distrust, but he returned with a letter from Stalin agreeing to meet Roosevelt as early as June. Having not yet informed Stalin of the latest delay in establishing a second front, Roosevelt was apprehensive about the marshal's re-action. He found out soon enough. Upon learning there would be no second front in 1943, an enraged Stalin—who was watching the massive German buildup on both sides of the Kursk salient, heralding an imminent major German assault—recalled his ambassadors from London and Washington. The personal meeting was cancelled, and on June 11, Stalin sent his reply to Roosevelt. After listing all the past "lies" about an imminent second front, Stalin warned that the Soviet government found it impossible to agree with the decision and warned that it would "result in grave consequences for the future progress of the war." These were harsh words between allies, but Stalin was speaking as a man who knew that the war could still be lost. For Stalin, FDR and Churchill's message declaring there would be no second front that year could have but one meaning: his allies, as he had long suspected, were duplicitous and had finally revealed their ultimate desire to fight the war to the very last Russian.

Shocked at the vehemence of Stalin's reaction, Roosevelt wrote a molli-fying letter, telling Stalin that he understood his disappointment. Stalin coolly responded: "I have to tell you that this is simply not a matter of disappointment to the Soviet government, but a matter of preservation of its confidence in its Allies, which is subjected to hard trials." There matters were left to lie. A brilliant summer was starting in Russia, but storm clouds were gathering over the Alliance.

42

SHOWDOWN IN QUEBEC

MARSHALL EVENTUALLY ESCAPED FROM CHURCHILL'S GRASP, AND on June 7 he returned to Washington. He was pleased to inform Stimson that he had kept all the gains made during the Trident Conference. Stimson, though, remained unsure, believing that the British were "straining every nerve to lay a foundation throughout the Mediterranean area to support their empire after the war."

Wanting to get his own impression of where things stood with Churchill and his chiefs, Stimson arrived in Britain on July 11, 1943, just as Allied divisions were still wading ashore on Sicily. Before darkness fell the beaches were secure and Allied divisions were pressing inland. The next day he had dinner at 10 Downing Street with Churchill and Eden, where he outlined the "political danger of delaying" the second front and how Americans would not understand or approve of "further penetration of the eastern Mediterranean." Stimson mentioned that the American people "did not hate the Italians but took them rather as a joke as fighters," before reminding Churchill that Americans truly hated the Japanese, and that only through "an intellectual effort were they convinced that Germany was their most dangerous enemy." He concluded by reminding Churchill that he had confirmed his fidelity to the invasion plan "unless his military advisers could present him with a better opportunity." As if on cue, Eden began droning on about the benefits of "stimulating trouble in the Balkans." But before Stimson's temper exploded Churchill calmed his growing disquiet by renewing his pledge to support the BOLERO buildup with all his energy.

Over the next few days, however, Stimson's suspicions grew. The planning staff for the invasion, temporarily known as ROUNDHAMMER (soon changed to OVERLORD) and under the direction of British general Frederick E. Morgan, warned Stimson that if any additional resources were sent to the Mediterranean, or there were delays moving divisions to Britain, it would be fatal to any chance of a spring invasion. Morgan made it clear that on November 1, the seven divisions scheduled to depart the Mediterranean that fall had to be on ships. It was not enough for them to be in a rear area camp waiting for shipment. When Stimson brought these concerns to Churchill, the prime minister dissembled a bit by claiming that he had a message from the United States stating that Marshall fully supported an invasion of Italy at Salerno. Churchill's mirth over Marshall's warming to British plans added to Stimson's alarm.

Over dinner a few days later Stimson confronted the prime minister, telling him that he had spoken to Marshall and that the chief had only countenanced a landing at Salerno in the expectation of a quick march on Rome that would speed operations in the Mediterranean and allow for a rapid departure of divisions for Britain. Churchill then admitted that if he were commander in chief he would cancel ROUNDHAMMER, but as he had pledged his support, he would go through with it loyally. Stimson immediately understood that Churchill was still looking for some evasion that would allow him to break his pledge, and told him that his comment was "like hitting us in the eye." Churchill quickly replied: "Oh no, if we start anything we will go through with utmost effort." The word "if" was not lost on Stimson, but before he could answer, Churchill was once again going on about the virtues of an extended Mediterranean campaign. When he could get a word in, Stimson said that neither Marshall nor the Joint Chiefs viewed such a prospect favorably, and warned the prime minister that he was not allowing for the planning and preparation necessary to pull off an operation as vast as invading northern Europe. With Churchill appearing somewhat subdued Stimson reminded him that Marshall, the Joint Chiefs, and the president strongly desired an invasion in the spring.

But Churchill was far from subdued; he was just pausing to develop a new line of attack. Announcing that he was alarmed at the check British forces had suffered at Catania, Sicily, he warned that this once again demonstrated the superlative fighting skills of the Germans. "If he had fifty-thousand men ashore on the French Channel coast," Churchill went on, "he would not have an easy moment, because the Germans would rush up reinforcements and push them into the sea." Resorting to his most vivid and oft-used imagery, he next spoke about the disastrous effect of having the Channel filled with corpses of the defeated Allies. This stirred Stimson, and for the next few minutes the two men went at it "hammer and tongs," without either making an impression on the other.

Stimson reported to the President that "if pressed he [Churchill] would sincerely go ahead with the ROUNDHAMMER [OVERLORD] commitment, but that he was looking constantly and vigorously for an easy way to end the war without a cross-Channel assault." He then warned Roosevelt that they must be constantly on the lookout for Mediterranean diversions. Stimson was right to be suspicious. Just three days prior to looking Stimson in the eye and swearing fidelity to ROUNDHAMMER, Churchill told his Combined Chiefs that such an invasion in May was beyond Allied strength, and ordered them to start preparing for Operation JUPITER (Norway) and a maximum post-HUSKY invasion of Italy as far as the Po River, which would, he said, give them the option of attacking into southern France or Austria in 1944. Churchill admitted to his chiefs that he had led the Americans down a garden path but forgave himself by claiming that it was "a most beautiful path." That same day the British chiefs began appealing, on Eisenhower's behalf, for more reinforcement, as well as requesting that no more forces leave the Mediterranean before the needs of an invasion of the Italian mainland were better understood.

Clearly, it was time for a final showdown.

The need to arrive at a conclusion over invading Italy and the subsequent invasion of northern Europe was given additional impetus by the fall of Mussolini on July 24 and his arrest soon afterward. Allied planners suddenly eyed an opening to leap into Italy and quickly knock that nation out of the war. Even Marshall favored such an invasion, but not at the expense of invading France in 1944. The problem in the days leading up to the next Allied conference was that the American planners were divided on the issue, and even some of the other American chiefs were wavering. At the JCS meeting on July 26, Leahy announced: "In view of what happened in Italy yesterday, we may not mount OVERLORD," and suggested troops earmarked for OVERLORD be sent to the Mediterranean. A few days later,

Rear Admiral Cooke, representing the Joint Planning Staff, recommended that OVERLORD be made into an "opportunistic operation," as diverting forces for the buildup in Britain for what now appeared to be a contingency operation was ceding the initiative in other theaters to the Axis. Cooke, who never slept when there was a possibility of sending more forces to the Pacific, was immediately opposed by his Air Force and Army counterparts, Generals Kuter and Wedemeyer, who clearly did not believe there was any need to back away from OVERLORD.

At the JCS meeting on August 6, however, Admiral King threw his weight into the argument, stating that he believed BOLERO and SICKLE (the buildup of strategic airpower) were stockpiling resources needed in the Pacific, and since the British "were taking full counsel of their fears" he thought the "idea of OVERLORD should be permanently abandoned." Remarkably the minutes state that General Arnold "agreed" with King's point of view. Marshall was isolated. Not only were the British reluctant to launch OVERLORD, but some of his own planning staff and now the rest of the Joint Chiefs were lining up against him.

Two of General Morgan's key OVERLORD planners arrived from London just in the nick of time. Their briefing to the Joint Chiefs provided a much-needed optimistic assessment. Though none of the chiefs were immediately brought back to the true faith, the briefing gave them pause. When Marshall inquired about how the British chiefs truly felt about the invasion, he was told that every soldier, including General Morgan, was 100 percent behind OVERLORD, but he then went on: "[When the] Chief of the Imperial Staff [Brooke] and others come under the 'sun lamp' of the Prime Minister, it is obvious that the latter's attitude is reflected and everyone knows the Prime Minister is always looking into the Mediterranean and especially the Aegean." This confirmed what Marshall had long suspected, that there was only one person in Britain whom he need convince: Churchill. As for the American Joint Chiefs, King was coming around, and he now advocated that a report American planners were already preparing for their British counterparts be amended so as to leave less wiggle room for the British to postpone OVERLORD. With that minor victory, Marshall concluded the meeting and sent the planners to work on planning recommendations that would unify the Joint Chiefs.

The next day, the Joint Chiefs again discussed OVERLORD. King offered that if troops building up in Britain could be employed for other purposes, such as attacking Sweden (to get air bases closer to Germany), it might "take the curse off the BOLERO buildup." This referenced the old concern over leaving troops languishing for a year unused when there were so many pressing needs elsewhere. Marshall replied that if any of the forces were stripped out one might as well take all of them. The mood changed, however, when Admiral Cooke reported that Eisenhower believed he could knock Italy out of the war and advance to the Po River with just the troops currently in the Mediterranean, even after losing seven divisions for OVERLORD. With that the chiefs approved a position paper for presentation to the British, clearly stating that further Mediterranean operations were to be "strictly subordinated" to the cross-Channel assault, and that whenever there was a shortage of resources OVERLORD had an overriding priority.

The American chiefs were all in line. Only the president needed to be brought firmly aboard. Two days after the JCS meeting, on August 9, 1943, Marshall went to see Roosevelt. Though he felt more could be done in the Mediterranean, Roosevelt assured his general that he was "insistent on OVERLORD." Hoping to lock in the president's agreement, Stimson went to see him the next day. In the Oval Office, he handed Roosevelt a letter that made several key points, starting with his observation that Passchendaele and Dunkirk still hung too heavily on British imaginations, and that therefore it was beyond rational hope that a British commander would ever desire to cross the Channel and come to grips with the Germans. He then offered Marshall up as the only commander who could furnish the required military leadership. Finally, Stimson reiterated that all the British were offering was a series of pinpricks around the periphery of German power that would never "fool Stalin into the belief that we have kept our pledge" to open a second front.

Immediately after his meeting with Stimson, Roosevelt met with his Joint Chiefs. Stimson, who was invited to stay, recorded that "the President went the whole hog on the subject of ROUNDHAMMER," as he was still calling OVERLORD. Stimson, who Marshall later said would pray every night for OVERLORD's approval and success, found Roosevelt more definite than he had ever seen him. Roosevelt also said that he did not want to go further in Italy than Rome, and that before OVERLORD was launched he wanted American soldiers in Britain to outnumber the British, so as to justify naming an American commander. The chiefs left the meeting fully united and with their president solidly behind them.

Churchill, with a staff of two hundred, was already en route.

Quebec, much cooler than Washington in midsummer, was the chosen venue for the final showdown. The military chiefs and their staffs took over the Château Frontenac, with its glorious views of the St. Lawrence River. They got right to work hammering at each other for several days while Churchill and Roosevelt kept each other company at Hyde Park. When the two leaders arrived, both were housed in the Citadel on the Plains of Abraham, where the British had defeated the French and seized Canada in 1759.

Official meetings for what was code-named the Quadrant Conference commenced on August 14, and quickly got heated. Things were immediately complicated by the news that operations in Sicily were concluding and the Italian government was prepared to surrender if the Allies invaded and protected them from the Germans. This lent a new urgency to Italian operations, which Eisenhower said he could commence within a month (September 9). The British still agreed that OVERLORD was the priority, but hedged that it could only be launched after Italian operations had worn down German strength. For the British the sticking point was the term "overriding priority" in relation to the BOLERO buildup, which the Americans were absolutely determined to keep in the plan as a guarantee that resources were not everlastingly siphoned off to Italy.

British insistence on expanding operations north of Rome, at least as far as Milan, provoked King to what Leahy charitably referred to as "undiplomatic language." This time it was Brooke's turn to clear the room. He then went to work on Marshall, trying to convince him that OVERLORD's success rested on victory in northern Italy. He got nowhere, later lamenting: "It is quite impossible to argue with him as he does not even begin to see a strategic problem!" When Brooke persisted, Marshall threatened to leave a small corps in England and take the rest of the American army to the Pacific. After what Brooke called "three unpleasant hours," the meeting concluded.

Field Marshal Dill went to talk to Marshall, and then reported to Brooke that the American chief was unmanageable, irreconcilable, and threatening to resign if the British pressed their points. Brooke saw the danger. Just

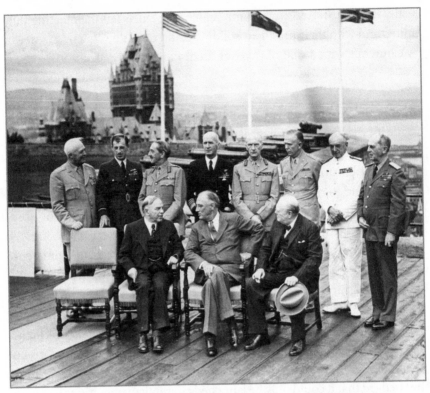

Standing, from left: General Hap Arnold, Marshal Charles Portal,
Marshal Alan Brooke, Admiral Ernest King, Marshal John Dill,
General George Marshall, Admiral Dudley Pound, and Admiral William Leahy.
Seated, from left: Canadian prime minister Mackenzie King,
President Franklin D. Roosevelt, and Prime Minister Winston Churchill.

that morning Churchill had told him that the command of OVERLORD, which the prime minister had promised to him, would go to an American—General Marshall. Brooke took the news hard, though he understood that as the Americans were now supplying most of the Allies' funding and combat forces they could demand the top commands as a right. It did not take much intellectual effort for Brooke to further extrapolate that if it came down to either his or Marshall's head rolling, he would be the one feeling the axe.

The next day the parties went at it again, but to no avail. Brooke got to the heart of the problem, boldly stating "that we are not trusting each other." Identifying the problem did not solve it, and after three more hours of heated debate they quit for the day. Brooke complained to his diary that Marshall had no strategic outlook, and King had only one thought: the Pacific. He did not believe he could stand much more.

On August 19, the parties went at it again, in what Brooke called a "poisonous day." Clearly, Brooke was never more eloquent than when he was employing new adjectives to describe his dealings with Americans. As soon as the room was cleared, the principals went at it. But this was the day Brooke broke. If the Americans agreed to remove the words "overriding priority," he agreed to give them everything they wanted.

The Americans agreed.

The deal started with OVERLORD being formally accepted as the Allies' top priority, with May 1 established as the definite invasion date. Moreover, Italian operations would be limited to those that could be undertaken only by the forces agreed to at the Trident Conference, which meant seven veteran divisions would soon leave the Mediterranean. The Americans also got British agreement for an invasion of southern France (ANVIL) to coincide with OVERLORD. At the time, the British likely assumed the required divisions would come from the United States. Only much later did they learn that the Americans planned to take them out of Italy. Finally, the

Marshal Charles Portal, General William Dean,
General Hap Arnold, and General George Marshall.

British gave in to King's demands, approving his plans for a campaign in the central Pacific and confirming that the goal was to prepare the theater so Japan could be defeated within a year of Germany's surrender.

As the conference drew to a close, a humorous incident helped dispel some of the toxic atmosphere. Lord Mountbatten, who had waited patiently for an opportunity, had the *Habbakuk* wheeled in. This was a typically British flight of fancy aimed at constructing an aircraft carrier out of pykrete—a mixture of ice and wood pulp—that would become an indestructible air base in the North Atlantic. To prove the *Habbakuk*'s resilience, Mountbatten proposed to shoot a regular cube of ice and then one of pykrete, and produced a revolver. Taking careful aim he shot the ice block, showering the chiefs with splinters of ice. Leveling his weapon once more he shot the *Habbakuk*. As he predicted, the bullet bounced off, ricocheting about like an angry bee and barely missing King's leg. Outside the door, where the dismissed planners had heard the last couple of hours of shouting, one wit said, "Good heavens, they've started shooting now!"

Once again, Churchill and Roosevelt quickly approved the deal, although Churchill had a few reservations. Few were happy with the final deal: Churchill wanted to attack Sumatra, though his own chiefs opposed him; the Americans wanted a major offensive in Burma, which the British resisted; and the British were far from happy that they were being bulldozed into invading northern Europe in less than nine months. Only King was truly happy. He had been green-lighted to launch his fleets, marines, and soldiers into the central Pacific; before him lay the Gilberts, Marshalls, Carolines, and Marianas. During the contests for these specks of land the American Navy would break the back of Japanese naval and air power.

The Allies now had a workable strategy, and probably the best one that could have been achieved. Rather remarkably, though, Churchill and Roosevelt had neglected to involve Stalin in their plans for Italy. They had kept him informed, but had not asked for his input. A miffed Stalin wrote on August 22 that he could no longer tolerate his two allies making agreements among themselves and only informing him later. The row that followed drove home the necessity for a meeting of the Big Three. An invitation was duly sent, and after some wrangling over location, Tehran was agreed on for later that year.

PART FIVE

ENDGAME

I just have a hunch that Stalin is not that kind of man. . . . He doesn't want anything but security for his country, and I think if I give him everything I possibly can and ask for nothing in return, noblesse oblige, he won't try to annex anything and will work with me for a world of democracy and peace.

President Franklin D. Roosevelt, conversation with
Ambassador William Bullitt, quoted in Life, *August 30, 1948, page 94*

43

THE BIG THREE IN TEHRAN

THE QUEBEC CONFERENCE HAD MOSTLY SETTLED THE DIRECTION of the war. There would be some backsliding by Churchill, and constant British attempts to get more resources for further endeavors in the Mediterranean, none of which amounted to much in the end. In one famous episode, Churchill and his chiefs pushed Marshall for an agreement to seize Rhodes in the eastern Mediterranean. After a long argument in which Marshall fought the British chiefs to a stalemate, Churchill intervened, exclaiming: "His Majesty's troops cannot sit idle. Muskets must flame." Marshall waited for a calm moment and in a soft voice ended the debate with a single comment: ". . . Not one American soldier is going to die on that goddamned beach." Further British backsliding was handled by the Joint Chiefs in an increasingly peremptory manner as the Americans began to comprehend that they were now the senior partner in the relationship and the British grudgingly conceded that in matters of strategy they were now in a subordinate role.

Two great battles of the Washington war were now mostly over. Byrnes was ruling the domestic front with an iron fist covered in soft velvet, and the strategic direction of the war was now set. From time to time Roosevelt would still don his referee hat, notably in the growing strategic argument in the Pacific between MacArthur's plan to win the war and that proposed by King and Nimitz. But from Quebec forward, Roosevelt, by degrees, focused his attention and energy on the postwar world. This was the final battle of the Washington war and it would be fought on multiple fronts, most of them far from the Capitol.

The first crucial part of this final battle rested on Roosevelt finding common cause with Stalin. FDR hoped to light a path along which the Soviet Union would be brought out of its perennial isolation and integrated into a peaceful world economy. To accomplish this, he embarked on November 12, 1943, aboard the USS *Iowa* on the first leg of his trip to Tehran for the first meeting of the Big Three.

With the war going well on all fronts he departed in an optimistic mood. The Red Army had stopped Germany's last major offensive at Kursk just as the Anglo-Americans were landing on Sicily. Since then the Russian juggernaut had continued rolling, and Kiev, the site of Russia's greatest defeat in 1941, had been retaken just a week earlier. As the Russian offensive gathered steam, the Allies had finally broken out of their beachheads in Italy and in early October had seized Naples. In the Pacific, the marines had assaulted Bougainville at the start of the month, and as Roosevelt traveled across the Atlantic they opened the Central Pacific Campaign by taking Makin and Tarawa atolls in the Gilbert Islands. Finally, and most crucially for Stalin, preparations for OVERLORD were moving apace, allowing Roosevelt to promise the long-awaited second front in the spring.

Roosevelt loved traveling on Navy ships, and in the *Iowa* he had a sailor's dream. It was the first of an entire class of super-battleships that were just starting to roll off the docks. In size and firepower there were few ships that could match her. Moreover, her captain, John McCrea, had been Roosevelt's naval aide for the previous couple of years and was keenly attuned to the president's requirements and desires. Traveling with Roosevelt were Hopkins, Marshall, King, Arnold, Leahy, and a select group of their key subordinates (Cooke, Handy, and Somervell). The *Iowa* was ready to depart as soon as the president boarded, but Roosevelt was under the sway of a seaman's superstition about leaving port on a Friday and ordered the ship under way at one minute after midnight.

The highlight of the crossing came on the second day out. Roosevelt was on deck, where he had been watching an antiaircraft exercise and enjoying the cacophony of over a hundred of the ship's guns firing live ammunition at distant balloons. Beside him, Hap Arnold, Pa Watson, and Harry Hopkins had just concluded a round of bets on the upcoming Texas A&M game. On the bridge, Captain McCrea was happy to both indulge and impress his former boss. Suddenly strict radio silence was broken: "Lion, Lion, torpedo heading your way"—Lion was *Iowa*'s code name.

"Full power, hard over starboard," McCrea shouted. Loudspeakers were already blaring "BATTLE STATIONS . . . BATTLE STATIONS . . . THIS IS NOT A DRILL. . . . REPEAT THIS IS NOT A DRILL." When Roosevelt learned a torpedo was coming at the ship, he asked his Secret Service guards to wheel him to the railing so he could watch. As he stared out at the waves there was a terrific blast behind the ship, where the torpedo exploded in the *Iowa's* wake. A shudder rippled through *Iowa's* nearly sixty thousand tons, causing McCrea to ask his executive officer if the ship had been hit. McCrea next radioed the captain of the USS *Porter*, the ship sending the warning, for the origination point of the torpedo, intending to send covering destroyers to hunt down and kill a supposed German submarine. After a minute's silence his speaker crackled with a sheepish reply: "We did it."

By this time an angry Admiral King was on the bridge. Anger turned to a white-hot flaming rage when he learned that a U.S. Navy destroyer had just fired on a U.S. Navy battleship that just happened to be carrying the president of the United States. He ordered all of the *Iowa's* massive 16-inch guns trained on the hapless *Porter*, and kept locked on target until he was certain the firing was an act of stupidity and not an assassination attempt. Eventually the matter was sorted out, and King ordered the *Porter's* entire crew placed under arrest—a naval first—and sent to Bermuda. Later in the war, the *Porter* would accidentally fire a 5-inch shell into the front yard of the base commandant in an Aleutian port, and was later credited with shooting down three "American" planes off Okinawa in 1945. Though a news blackout was ordered, the *Porter* became famous throughout the Navy and was invariably greeted with the signal: "DON'T SHOOT, WE'RE REPUBLICANS."

Later that day, a more settled King visited McCrea in his cabin. "You know, McCrea," King said, "I regard you as a good officer, but you have one outstanding weakness."

"Thank you," McCrea said. "I have inventoried myself often, and I came away with many self-appraised weaknesses. But since you say I have an outstanding weakness I am wondering if you would tell me what it is."

King replied, "Your big weakness, McCrea, is that you're not a son-of-a-bitch—and a good naval officer has to be a son-of-a-bitch."

McCrea let the statement lie there a moment before saying, "Admiral King, you are a good naval officer and universally regarded as such and I must say"—McCrea paused to look him dead in the eye—"I have never heard anyone refer to you as a son-of-a-bitch."

King stared in disbelief, stood, and stomped out of the cabin.

King then joined the other chiefs for discussions with the president. The list of topics covered during these conversations was remarkable for its variety: equipping a dozen French divisions, declaring Rome an open city, plans to protect the Galápagos Islands as a nature preserve (guarded by U.S. warships), distribution of *Reader's Digest* in Arabic, arrangements to appoint a supreme commander in the Mediterranean, and occupation zones in Germany. Equally remarkable is what does not appear on the various agendas—there are no discussions with the president about future strategy. The only exception in the record is the Joint Chiefs seeking presidential approval of a paper stating that the Americans would not get involved in Balkan operations. After reading it, Roosevelt simply said "Amen" and requested it be sent to the British immediately.

The one major point of contention during the voyage was which country would occupy what areas of Germany at the war's end. Roosevelt was not happy with plans to shunt the Americans off to Bavaria, where their lines of communication would have to travel through either the French or British zone. Rather, he wanted a zone in the northwest with access to ports. Roosevelt thought the British planners had assigned southern Germany to the United States based on political motivations, hoping to surround and isolate the Americans to keep America's influence in postwar Europe limited. Roosevelt clearly saw that such a situation would allow the other Allies to undercut every move the United States made within their assigned occupation area. At one point he became so irate over the planned occupation zones that he grabbed a map and drew out his own zones, which he handed to Marshall after the meeting. Roosevelt also raised some concerns about British plans to rehabilitate France as a great power, which he believed would take more than two decades to complete.

The rest of the trip was uneventful, with everyone spending more time trying to relax than they did thinking about the war. Arnold later commented on the "grand days without a worry in the world" as he tried to pick up a few extra dollars betting with Pa Watson and Harry Hopkins on the Texas A&M game. Hopkins, who had a chance to renew his intimacy with the president in the absence of his wife, worried about finding some cash to pay his meal bill on the *Iowa* ($11.25), after losing most of what he was carrying in marathon games of gin rummy. Luckily Roosevelt had raised his salary the previous year from $10,000 to $15,000.

After picking up substantially more naval escorts, and permanent air cover, the *Iowa* made its way through the Strait of Gibraltar and docked in Oran. From there, Roosevelt and his party made their way in successive stages to Cairo for a quick conference (Sextant) with Churchill and Chiang Kai-shek, held November 22–26. European strategy was not even discussed

Admiral Ernest King, Admiral William Leahy, President Franklin D. Roosevelt, General George Marshall, and General Laurence Kuter.

until the last meeting of the conference; rather, discussions were dominated by plans for the Far East and the Pacific. Chiang, heavily supported by his wife—who attended the military meetings in a dress that slit to the hipbone, which Brooke observed "exposed one of the most shapely of legs"—argued for as much of everything as he could get. But, in truth, Chiang was playing an increasingly weak hand. The Americans were still keen on keeping the Chinese fighting and pinning down Japanese divisions, and so put forth plans for operations in and around Burma. Talks broke down when the Chinese voiced a reluctance to engage in serious fighting for over a year, and upon American reluctance to use resources needed for OVERLORD and King's Pacific campaign for operations on the Asian mainland. Thus there was little left to offer Chiang.

Chiang then overplayed his hand. He would agree to plans and make demands, only to renege later and increase his demands. In the end, he got very little of what he came for. He was discovering the hard fact that the Americans no longer needed him. Previously, the Joint Chiefs had three major reasons for supporting China: pinning down Japanese troops on the Asian mainland; providing air bases for the strategic bombing of Japan; and providing manpower for the final great offensives that would wreck the Japanese Imperial Army. The last of these had already been negated, and the others soon would be.

On October 30, 1943, Secretary Hull had attended a banquet in the Catherine the Great Hall of the Kremlin. During the dinner, Stalin approached, and without any prompting he unequivocally declared that "when the Allies succeeded in defeating Germany, the Soviet Union would then join in defeating Japan." Hull was elated and cabled Roosevelt that night, using the Navy code for half of the message and the Army code for the other half. Stalin's commitment meant that soon after the fall of Berlin, Japan's armies on the Asian mainland would no longer face masses of ill-supplied and barely trained peasants, but instead the massed armored formations of the Red Army made expert in war and battle-hardened by four years of bloody combat against the Wehrmacht. In an instant, the necessity for Chinese manpower in the closing phases of the war evaporated.

Chinese armies were also becoming increasingly less crucial for the job of pinning Japanese forces to the mainland. As American submarines probed deeper into the Pacific they decimated the Japanese merchant marine. By the middle of 1944 the Japanese no longer had the ships to move large numbers of men. As for China replicating Britain's role as a gigantic bomber base, the Americans would soon discover that the Mariana Islands (Guam, Tinian, and Saipan) were more than adequate as large unsinkable aircraft carriers. Moreover, these islands in the central Pacific were far easier to supply than air bases in China. For now, China remained operationally useful, but it was no longer strategically crucial. As a result, there were major limits placed on the resources the Allies were willing to expend in this theater. To make up for the lack of support being offered, Roosevelt assured Chiang that China would be part of the Big Four at the end of the war. As Chiang had come to Cairo expecting deliverance, promises of increased status after the war were poor recompense for China's suffering.

For the moment, there was an excess of precious landing craft in the Mediterranean, and the Americans were willing to show their support for

China by using them to seize the Andaman Islands, in the Bay of Bengal, as a staging base for future operations in Burma. However, the British wanted those same ships to support Churchill's vision of extending operations into the Aegean and then the Balkans. The Americans were aghast, and the meeting, in Brooke's words, became "somewhat heated." According to other observers an exchange of insults between Brooke and King got King out of his chair and nearly brought him across the table. General Stilwell recorded in his diary that he was hoping King would sock Brooke. In any event, the landing craft were used for the Anzio invasion.

After the wreckage of the Combined Chiefs meeting was cleared, things calmed down somewhat for Thanksgiving. The British had thoughtfully secured a cathedral for religious services. There followed a Thanksgiving dinner hosted by the president, at which he expertly carved two turkeys he had brought with him from Washington. After dinner, there was some dancing, with Sarah Churchill, the only woman present, having her choice of partners, while Churchill whirled about the room with Pa Watson. Roosevelt concluded the evening with a toast: ". . . With the people of the United Kingdom in our family: we are a large family, and more united than before. I propose a toast to this unity, and may it long continue."

It didn't.

In fact, the fragile unity did not last through the next morning. When the Combined Chiefs met again on November 26 they had what Brooke called "the father and mother of all rows." Nothing was solved, but by now the Americans no longer cared if the British proposals were wrongheaded. As far as they were concerned British plans were becoming increasingly irrelevant. When Lord Moran, the apostle of Allied cooperation, approached Hopkins to alert him that Churchill was getting cold feet and many were wondering if OVERLORD would ever come off, Hopkins replied tersely that everyone on his side was ready for the Battle of Tehran: "You will find us lining up with the Russians."

The Americans were hardening to their purpose, and the British would be dragged along.

On the morning of November 27, Roosevelt boarded the *Sacred Cow*—the nickname for the plush C-54 reserved for presidential travel—and headed for Tehran. He was met at Gale Morghe Airport by the commander of

Somervell's Persian Gulf Service Command and whisked away to the American legation. Because of the distance from the Russian and British embassies, as well as a presumed assassination threat, Roosevelt was prevailed upon to accept the use of a villa on the Russian compound. Here security was airtight—even the NKVD-supplied maids were always well armed. Michael Reilly, head of Roosevelt's Secret Service detail, who became ill at ease if someone with a toothpick approached the president, was in a constant state of alarm over so many armed Russians in close proximity to his charge. Roosevelt later told his labor secretary, Frances Perkins, that he did not believe there was any plot, but it was clear that Stalin wanted him at the Russian Embassy, and he was only too happy to oblige. Every room was likely bugged, and prying eyes were everywhere, but that hardly mattered to Roosevelt. He was here to win Stalin over, and openness was one of his main calling cards.

Roosevelt once wrote to Churchill: "I know you will not mind my being brutally frank when I tell you that I think I can personally handle Stalin better than either your Foreign Office or my State Department. Stalin hates the guts of all your top people. He thinks he likes me better, and I hope he will continue to do so." Roosevelt had always possessed that master politician's certainty that through his own personal charm and magnetism he could sway anyone to his side. At Tehran, Roosevelt put the belief that he alone could reach Stalin on a personal level to the test, as he believed his plans for a postwar order had a much better chance for success if Stalin trusted his allies. But Stalin had once trusted Hitler—the 1940 Russo-German Non-Aggression Pact—and was determined not to make a similar mistake. As he once explained to the Yugoslav communist Milovan Djilas:

> Perhaps you think that just because we are the Allies of the English that we have forgotten who they are and who Churchill is. They find nothing sweeter than to trick their allies . . . Churchill is the kind who, if you don't watch him, will slip a kopeck out of your pocket. Yes, a kopeck out of your pocket! By God, a kopeck out of your pocket. And Roosevelt? Roosevelt is not like that. He dips his hand in only for bigger coins. But Churchill? Churchill—even for a kopeck.

Still, Roosevelt went to Tehran hoping to like Stalin and determined to do whatever it took to make Stalin like him. But after several days of failing to establish a personal rapport with the Soviet leader, the president was becoming discouraged. He complained that he had done everything Stalin had asked of him, yet Stalin remained "solemn, not smiling, stiff, and correct." Roosevelt said that he was unable to find "anything human to get a hold of." After days of official meetings and paperwork, Roosevelt was wondering about the wisdom of the trip.

Feeling that he had to "do something desperate," Roosevelt threw over Churchill. As Labor Secretary Frances Perkins remembered the president's retelling:

> I began almost as soon as we got into the conference room.... I lifted my hand up to cover a whisper "Winston is cranky this morning, he got up on the wrong side of the bed."
>
> A vague smile passed over Stalin's eyes and I decided I was on the right track. As soon as I sat down I began to tease Churchill about his Britishness, about John Bull, about his cigars, about his habits. It began to register with Stalin. Winston got red and scowled, and the more he did so, the more Stalin smiled. Finally Stalin broke out into a deep hearty guffaw... I kept it up until Stalin was laughing with me, and it was then that I called him Uncle Joe.... From that time on... the ice was broken and we talked like men and brothers.

Unfortunately, Eleanor had never warned Churchill about her husband's affinity for discarding people when they "no longer fulfilled a purpose of his." His thoughts were no longer on the ally who had been at his side since America's entry into the war, for he knew Britain would end the conflict a spent power. The future, as Roosevelt saw it, was a world dominated by the power of the United States and the Soviet Union. Optimistically he believed that by force of will he could bridge the chasm between each nation's political and economic systems to ensure a continuing harmony. Stalin, however, was not so easily enticed, and even if he had never heard Lord Palmerston's warning—"We have no eternal allies, and we have no perpetual enemies. Our interests are eternal and perpetual, and those interests it is our duty to follow"—he certainly abided by it.

The next morning, Roosevelt, knowing Churchill was hoping to entice him into sending forces to the Adriatic, refused a private meeting. Having no desire to go down the Mediterranean rabbit hole again, Roosevelt forwent a last opportunity to get Churchill squarely behind OVERLORD. It might have failed, but by not trying, Roosevelt, by default, opted to bare the Anglo-American differences before Stalin and all but invited him to become the arbitrator. After snubbing Churchill, Roosevelt was more than happy to welcome the marshal into his quarters for their first private meeting. As Stalin entered, the president greeted him: "I am glad to see you. I have tried for a long time to bring this about." And so he had, and, as a result, despite the fact that the United States would surely finish the war as the most powerful nation on earth in both economic and military terms, Roosevelt placed himself in the role of supplicant. He even began the meeting with a gift, declaring that when the war ended the United States would have far more merchant ships than it could possibly use, and proposing to donate the surplus to the Soviet Union. Stalin said he appreciated it and neatly pocketed the prize, without a return offering.

The official record states that Roosevelt and Stalin then came to complete agreement on two major points: that France should not be reconstructed as a powerful nation for many years, and that after a period of international trusteeship, French Indochina should receive its independence at war's end. Roosevelt appears to have not yet grasped that with Germany prostrate, only a powerful France could act as a European counterweight to Russian influence on the Continent. That fact was not lost on Stalin, who most certainly did not want a reconstructed France, possibly fielding a hundred or more combat divisions and vying with the USSR for influence in central Europe. So far, Stalin must have been very pleased, as the conference was barely fifteen minutes old and he was already being offered far more than he dared request. Though it does not appear in the official record the remainder of the conversation was mostly given over to Roosevelt explaining America's federalist system and America's "good neighbor policy" to the Soviet leader. If he was hinting that Stalin would do well to consider similar policies for his own nation, it was lost on Stalin.

At the first official meeting of the Big Three, Roosevelt, the youngest of them, ventured to open the proceedings by greeting his elders and then welcoming Stalin to the "family circle." Churchill then noted that this meeting represented the greatest concentration of power the world had ever seen, leaving Stalin to finish the greetings with the hope that this "fraternal meeting" would use its power wisely. Roosevelt then took the floor and briefed the status of the Pacific war. When he was done, Stalin interrupted to say, while still doodling on his pad, how much he appreciated everything the United States was doing in the Pacific, and only the titanic struggle with Germany was keeping him from entering that war. A cheered Roosevelt went on to discuss a series of possible future operations in the Mediterranean. A concerned Hopkins scribbled a note to King: "Who's promoting this Adriatic business that the President continually returns to?" King answered, "As far as I know it is his own idea."

Roosevelt's Mediterranean opening was all Churchill needed to take off running. For much of the remainder of the first session, Churchill, while paying lip service to OVERLORD, listed the benefits of a wide assortment of Mediterranean positions he was considering. Stalin was having none of it. The only operation in the Mediterranean he was interested in—attacking southern France in support of OVERLORD—was not high on Churchill's agenda. Stalin did not consider any of the other operations worthwhile, and went so far as to suggest leaving just ten divisions in Italy and forgoing the capture of Rome.

Nothing Churchill suggested made a dent in Stalin's thinking; he was impervious to any scheme that delayed OVERLORD. Stalin stated that he did not consider scattering British and American forces as a wise course and insisted that OVERLORD be the basis of operations in 1944 and that everything else be considered a diversion from the main effort. Roosevelt quickly fell into line and declared himself opposed to anything that delayed OVERLORD. He then suggested that the staffs begin working out plans for an attack on southern France, in support of the far larger invasion of northern France. Marshall, who had missed the meeting because he received the wrong start time and was out touring Tehran, would have been greatly heartened.

Hap Arnold, who typically sat silently when the Big Three were involved, recorded his impression:

> Three truly great men—The Prime Minister trying to outshine—perhaps better—carrying on in true form.—The President, reserved, listening, and enjoying the meeting, talking when he thinks necessary, master of the situation. Stalin the man of steel, fearless, brilliant mind, quick of thought and repartee, ruthless—a great leader, courage of his

convictions as indicated by his half humorous, half scathing remarks about the British—The PM and Brooke. I doubt either was ever talked to like that before.

At the meeting's close, a disheartened Churchill was intercepted by Lord Moran, who asked "whether anything had gone wrong." Churchill gruffly replied, "A bloody lot has gone wrong," before moving on. Churchill, like Roosevelt, placed tremendous faith in his ability to win people over to his side of an argument. It was disconcerting to him to lose a debate as decisively as he had this one.

For the rest of the day and well into the formal dinner Roosevelt hosted that evening, Churchill remained in a sour mood. The dinner itself was rather uneventful. Stalin, picking up Roosevelt's earlier comments about France, started the conversation by stating that he thought the French political class was rotten to the core and should all be punished as criminal collaborators with the Nazis. Roosevelt agreed and hastened to add that no Frenchmen over the age of forty should be allowed into any future French government. Where this would leave de Gaulle and the rest of the Free French leadership was never addressed. When Churchill suggested that the treatment of Germany was more crucial to the peace of Europe than how France was rehabilitated, Stalin proposed that Germany be put under tight controls and all its territory east of the Oder River be handed over to Poland. Stalin also stated his belief that the Allies would have to occupy Germany for a long time, as he said there was no hope of changing German character. As evidence of the average German's need for control he told a story about a 1907 mass meeting of communists in Leipzig. Two hundred German workers, sworn to overthrow the state and all its institutions, had failed to appear. The reason: There was no one at the train station to punch the tickets permitting them to leave the platform. It was then Stalin understood that the communist world revolution, contrary to Marx's thinking, would not start in Germany. The story amused both Churchill and Roosevelt, who voiced no objections to Stalin's postwar proposals for Germany.

At the next day's meeting of the Combined Chiefs, including, for the first time, Stalin's military chief, the incompetent but politically loyal Marshal Kliment Voroshilov, Brooke threw every one of his well-honed arguments for continuing operations in the Mediterranean against a Soviet general who could not have cared less. To every point Brooke made, Voroshilov had but a single response: OVERLORD is the priority, and must not be delayed. When Brooke forced the Red Army marshal to expand on his position, Voroshilov said that he thought as a military man the same as all other military men: "OVERLORD is the most important operation and that all other operations . . . must be planned to assist OVERLORD and not hinder it." When cornered, Voroshilov would simply tell his audience that Marshal Stalin had declared OVERLORD as the leading Allied priority. General Marshall was pleased with such unexpectedly strong support for his position, though he did find it necessary to explain to Voroshilov that crossing the English Channel was far more complex and dangerous than a river crossing, and that any reverse would be a catastrophe that might take years to recover from.

While the Combined Chiefs were meeting, Roosevelt, after once again turning down Churchill's request for a private get-together, met with Stalin. Roosevelt took the opportunity to discuss at some length his plans for a postwar organization, based on the United Nations, for the preservation of world peace. Stalin listened politely but balked at the idea of the Four Policemen—the United States, Britain, the Soviet Union, and China—saying many other nations would not agree. He was particularly troubled by the addition of China, which he did not believe would be a great power at war's end. Stalin then offered an alternative that was close to what Churchill advocated: regional committees—one for Europe, one for the Americas, and one for the Far East. Roosevelt said that he doubted Congress would approve the committee structure, and then went on to detail how he thought the Four Policemen could maintain the peace, giving no thought to how to cope with the problem of one of the Big Four breaking the peace. Stalin declared himself unconvinced, and Roosevelt soon found himself trading parts of the world where the great powers would maintain bases from which they could act decisively against any future threats.

Before the second plenary session began there was pause for a ceremony. Churchill, wearing his Royal Air Force uniform and acting on behalf of King George VI, presented a bejeweled ceremonial sword—the Sword of Stalingrad—to Stalin, while a Red Army band played "God Save the King" and "The Internationale." Stalin, apparently moved by the gift, kissed the sword before presenting it to Roosevelt to examine. As the ceremony closed, Stalin handed the sword to Voroshilov, who, not expecting the handoff, dropped it on his own foot.

Immediately after the presentation ceremony, the principals gathered for the second plenary meeting. Stalin went right for the jugular, asking who would command OVERLORD. Both Roosevelt and Churchill confirmed what Stalin already knew, that they had not decided on an overall commander. Stalin bluntly retorted, "Then nothing will come out of these operations." The discussion got progressively more animated until Churchill promised he and Roosevelt would have an answer for Stalin within two weeks. Stalin quieted, giving Churchill an opening to launch into another impassioned monologue detailing the benefits of further Mediterranean operations. After patiently sitting through the prime minister's extended oratory, Stalin finally brought him up short. He first offered a few brief comments on some specifics of Churchill's proposals, then bluntly stated that none of these were important matters: "If we are here to discuss military questions . . . we, the USSR, find OVERLORD the most important and decisive." Churchill and Brooke, used to the largely civil debates they had had with Roosevelt and the Joint Chiefs, were taken aback by the stark bluntness of the Soviet dictator. They had forgotten that Stalin was the only survivor of a selection system mired in Darwinian brutality, where a single misstep meant death. Once he had decided on a path, Stalin was incapable of elegant political discussion. Churchill had once referred to Hopkins as "Lord Root of the Matter," but compared to Stalin, Hopkins was a piker.

When Stalin directly asked Churchill if he fully supported OVERLORD, or was just saying so "in order to satisfy the USSR," Churchill was compelled to reply that if the proper conditions were set, ". . . he firmly believed it would be England's duty to hurl every ounce of strength she had across the Channel at the Germans."

At the official dinner that night, Stalin trod the path Roosevelt had led him to, and started making jokes at Churchill's expense. Despite maintaining a friendly manner, every remark he addressed to Churchill had a sharp edge, and no opportunity was lost to get a dig in at Churchill's expense. At one point, Stalin said that at least 50,000 and perhaps 100,000 German leaders "must be physically liquidated" and the Allies must hold strategic bases around the world. To which Roosevelt jokingly said that he put the figure at 49,000, and then, more seriously, he said that the bases should be held in trusteeship.

Incensed, Churchill warned that he would not countenance the "cold blooded execution of soldiers who had fought for their country." Churchill took Stalin's threat seriously, and it is incredible that Roosevelt treated it as a joking matter given that he was well aware that the Soviets had executed at least 10,000 Polish officers, and perhaps twice that many, in the Katyn Forest in 1940. Churchill continued, stating that Britain did not desire any new territory or bases, but intended to hold what it had. Mentioning Singapore and Hong Kong, he told Stalin that "nothing would be taken from England without war." Stalin kept at Churchill until the prime minister stormed off to compose himself. He was only in the garden a few moments when a smiling Stalin approached, assuring him that it had all been a joke.

The remainder of the conference was anticlimactic. Under orders from both Roosevelt and Churchill to fix a date for OVERLORD that would please Stalin, the Combined Chiefs did as ordered. After a long discussion about when to remove landing craft from the Mediterranean they decided that the invasion would take place during the month of May 1944, and that there would be a supporting invasion of southern France at approximately the same time.

After celebrating Churchill's sixty-ninth birthday that evening, Roosevelt made the last toast: "We have proved here in Tehran that the varying ideals of our nations can come together in a harmonious whole, moving unitedly for the common good of ourselves and the world. So, as we leave this historic gathering, we can see in the sky, for the first time, that traditional symbol of hope, the rainbow."

Before the conference's final meeting, Roosevelt asked Stalin for another one-on-one, this time to clear up a bit of domestic politics. Roosevelt informed Stalin that, if the war was still raging in late 1944, he would feel compelled to run for office one more time. Then, after telling Stalin that he agreed with most of Stalin's position on Poland, he asked for some changes to the proposed border. He then explained that he could make no agreements about Poland at Tehran or even the following winter, as there were six or seven million Americans of Polish extraction and "as a practical man he did not want to lose their vote." Stalin said that he understood, encouraging Roosevelt to continue. He told Stalin that he also had many voters of

Lithuanian, Latvian, and Estonian heritage to concern himself with, and then pointedly asked if Stalin could see that those states had a referendum after the war, so that the will of the people could be heard. Roosevelt concluded with a metaphorical wink, saying that he was "personally confident that the people would vote to join the Soviet Union." This was Roosevelt at his most Machiavellian, and Stalin was not slow to pick up the meaning, replying that some "propaganda work [on the subject populations] needed to be done."

The last meeting of the conference, on December 1, 1943, was focused primarily upon political questions such as postwar borders. Roosevelt again made a pitch for a referendum in the Baltic states that Stalin indulged while promising nothing. There was a long discussion of the Polish borders, involving the Soviets and the British, but Roosevelt, though present, did not participate. As he told Stalin, the topic was political dynamite and he was not going to touch it until the next election was safely behind him. This was unfortunate, as the time to make a deal with Stalin, if there ever was one, was before the Red Army occupied the country. By waiting until after the Red Army crossed and moved beyond the Vistula River, the Anglo-Americans lost most of their bargaining power. At the end of 1943, America, through Lend-Lease, was supplying over half of the Soviet Union's motor vehicles and planes, and American oil was keeping it all moving, not to mention millions of tons of foodstuffs and seeds that kept many Russians from starving. At Tehran, America had real leverage, but by the end of 1944, with the end of the war in sight, Russian needs would be far less, as would America's leverage. Here we have a true case of the imperatives of the Washington war, impacting the lives of tens of millions who would soon find themselves under ruthless Soviet domination for most of the next five decades.

44

THE GRIND

WHEN THE ANGLO-AMERICAN PARTY ARRIVED BACK IN CAIRO THE old arguments continued. But this time, decisions came quickly. The British tried to balk on their commitment to ANVIL (the invasion of southern France), but the Americans held their feet to the fire by promising to find the landing craft required. As a result, Roosevelt was forced to back out of his recent promises to Chiang Kai-shek to launch major assaults in Burma and the Andaman Islands, so that those resources could be applied to ANVIL.

Both Churchill and Roosevelt also spent considerable time working on Turkish president Ismet Inönü, who arrived in Cairo on December 4, but to no avail. His demands for Turkey's entry into the war were, as he knew, far beyond what the Allies could supply during the buildup for OVER-LORD.

The final big decision made by Roosevelt was choosing OVERLORD's commander. Hopkins, Stimson, Churchill, and Stalin had wanted Marshall to have the job. Even Roosevelt wanted to give the job to Marshall. They realized, although many Americans did not, that while everyone remembered Pershing and Grant, few Americans could name the chief of staff back in Washington during the Civil War and World War I. Opposed to Marshall's selection were the rest of the Joint Chiefs, particularly King, who thought Marshall was indispensable in his current role. On the other hand, the press had already made much of the perception that Marshall's stepping down to take command of OVERLORD would be a punishment. But this the president could handle or explain. What really mattered was what Roosevelt thought, and though he believed Marshall deserved the command, he had grown used to having the general in Washington. Though they were never personally close, Roosevelt considered him the indispensable man. Moreover, the Tehran Conference had put one major reason for giving Marshall the command behind him. Stimson had argued for months that only Marshall could see the project through against entrenched British opposition. But Stalin's firm support for OVERLORD, and the resulting British capitulation on the timing, made the invasion a certainty, with or without Marshall's presence in Britain.

Roosevelt still hesitated. He sent Hopkins to sound out Marshall as to his own desires. Marshall, despite having told his aide to prepare for a move and the fact that his wife was already moving personal furniture out of their official residence, told Hopkins that "he would go along whole-heartedly with whatever decision the President made." Marshall's biographer, Forrest Pogue, suspects that Roosevelt knew his man and expected he would reply as he did, thereby giving Roosevelt an open door to keep him in Washington. The next day Roosevelt met with Marshall in his villa and repeated the question. Marshall gave the president the same answer he had given Hopkins, leaving Roosevelt to ponder the problem a bit longer. FDR concluded the conversation by stating, "I feel I could not sleep at night with you out of the country." Hence Roosevelt selected Eisenhower as supreme commander for the invasion of northern Europe.

Stimson wrote an apropos evaluation of the Tehran Conference, after reading the complete minutes on December 5, 1943: "I thank the Lord that Stalin was there. In my opinion he saved the day. He was direct and strong, and brushed away the diversion attempts of the Prime Minister with a vigor which rejoiced my soul."

For all practical purposes all of the old issues of the Washington war were by the start of 1944 settled, for better or worse, or at least in the care of someone who could keep them from blowing up into renewed feuds. But a new phase of the relentless internecine war was already percolating; this time the battle was over the immediate postwar future. These issues had been on a low simmer for the first half of 1944, as everyone's focus turned to the battlefronts. There were, however, other reasons for Washington's quiescence. Soon after the Tehran Conference Hopkins fell seriously ill. He would spend the next seven months in a hospital bed, returning to work in July 1944. There remained some sporadic infighting on the production front, but most of the more troublesome players had left the scene, and Jimmy Byrnes was taming what remained. Moreover, the greatest production challenges had been overcome and American industry was now burying the Axis powers under an avalanche of matériel. As 1943 wound down no one was worried about how to get more war production. Rather, the best minds were focused on when to start shutting down war production, and how and when to start the reconversion of industry to peacetime pursuits. Not only was industry hitting full stride, but the Joint Chiefs now had the firm strategic direction they craved. As such, they had put their collective heads down and were getting on with running the war. But the last and most crucial reason for the Washington slowdown was that Roosevelt was a very sick man, and in dire need of a rest.

On March 27, 1944, the president checked into Bethesda Naval Hospital for a full checkup. This time he was examined by a cardiac specialist, Dr. Howard Bruenn. Though the president never displayed any curiosity about the findings, Bruenn diagnosed hypertension and congestive heart failure, along with other cardiac-related ailments. He prescribed digitalis, ten hours of sleep a night, regular naps, a diet, and less smoking. Roosevelt's daughter, Anna, took it upon herself to make sure he stayed on his regimen. Under her guidance, Roosevelt's health markedly improved, but he remained in need of a long rest. Roosevelt decided that the best place to get it was Baruch's estate at Hobcaw, South Carolina, where Hopkins had recuperated a few years before. Hobcaw was the perfect spot for a long rest. It was sixty miles from Charleston, overlooked the Waccamaw River, and was surrounded by twenty-three thousand acres of woods and fields. To make sure the focus stayed on rest and relaxation, Baruch never installed a phone. Roosevelt arrived in secrecy on Easter Sunday and spent his days fishing up and down the Black and Waccamaw Rivers on a fifty-four-foot Coast Guard patrol boat—always under a canopy of blimps and patrol planes. He also trolled for bluefish in the Atlantic, sunned himself, and slept ten to twelve hours a day. Baruch, though he made himself scarce most of the time, took the opportunities offered to mend an old friendship, and even looked the other way when FDR's former lover, Lucy Rutherfurd, came to visit. Roosevelt, who had intended to stay two weeks, remained almost a month. The one sad moment of his vacation was when news of the death of Secretary of the Navy Frank Knox arrived. Roosevelt pleaded illness as an excuse to skip the funeral.

Vacation notwithstanding, the war ground on, and Roosevelt was sent several updates a day. At the time, the reports were so good that Roosevelt had trouble believing them. Before his departure, the Air Force undertook Operation ARGUMENT, popularly known as the Big Week. The purpose was to break the Luftwaffe's back by attacking the German aircraft industry and forcing the Luftwaffe to come up and defend it. In under a week the Eighth Air Force dropped more bombs than it had during its first year of operation. Moreover, as they were now being escorted by swarms of long-range fighters, bomber losses fell dramatically. This was the beginning of a series of great air battles that crippled the Luftwaffe, giving Anglo-American forces air dominance of Europe's skies in the crucial months after D-Day.

In the Soviet Union, winter was ending and the powerful Red Army was coming out of a short hibernation. At the start of the year, the Russians had broken the nine-hundred-day encirclement of Leningrad, and by early April they had retaken Odessa on the Black Sea. Over the next two months the Red Army coiled up for the most powerful Soviet strike of the war: Operation BAGRATION, which would support the Normandy invasion in June 1944 and annihilate approximately twenty Wehrmacht divisions in under a month. In the Pacific, U.S. forces had taken the Marshall Islands, while land-based and naval airpower had wrecked the massive Japanese bases at Rabaul and Truk. At the same time, MacArthur's forces were making steady progress in New Guinea.

On May 8, 1944, Roosevelt returned to Washington. Vice Admiral Ross T. McIntire, his personal physician, announced that the president had "shaken off his winter sniffles and bronchitis," and declared: "I am perfectly satisfied with his physical condition . . . excellent shape . . . and as strong as he was a year ago." McIntire was lying; Roosevelt was a very ill man. He was, of course, buoyed by the war reports, but weighed down by the great test that was still before him and the country. The invasion of northern France was less than a month off, and Roosevelt was feeling the tension. He had intended to be in Britain when the assault began, but his fragile health forced him to cancel.

Just before the invasion, Roosevelt escaped Washington to spend the weekend at Pa Watson's home in Charlottesville, Virginia. There he worked on his speech for D-Day, using a simple theme Anna had suggested—start with a prayer. Returning to the White House, Roosevelt on June 5 went on national radio to announce the capture of Rome. Even as he spoke thousands of Allied ships and paratrooper-laden aircraft were making their way in the rain to the Normandy coast. Roosevelt gave no hint of what the next day would bring, as he praised the courage of the soldiers fighting in Italy.

At 3:00 A.M. on June 6, 1944, Marshall called the White House. The operator put him through to Eleanor, who went to wake her husband. Marshall reported that the landings were a success and the troops were beginning to move inland. Roosevelt remained awake, and at 4:00 A.M. he ordered the White House operator to call the staff and tell them to come to work. Stimson woke at that same hour and heard the news on his radio. He then took a short nap before heading to the office. Roosevelt met with congressional leaders before 10:00 A.M., and with the Joint Chiefs immediately after. By midafternoon, Roosevelt was sure that all the landings were a success, and though casualties had been high, they were well below estimates. That night he made another national address—reciting the prayer he and Anna had written a couple of days before.

Less than two weeks later Nimitz launched his assault on Saipan—D-Day in the Pacific—and waited for the inevitable Japanese counterstrike. When it came the Navy destroyed three Japanese fleet carriers and over 600 aircraft in what became known as "the Great Marianas Turkey Shoot." The United States lost 125 planes, the bulk of them ditching into the sea when they ran out of fuel returning to their carriers. Capturing Saipan brought, for the first time, every Japanese city within range of American B-29 bombers stationed on Saipan and nearby islands. Soon Japan would be enduring a horrific and sustained air bombardment that would reduce almost all of its great cities to ashes.

Several days later, on June 23, the Russians launched Operation BAGRATION, attacking along a 450-mile front in an offensive that doomed the Wehrmacht's Army Group Center. Within two months the Red Army had advanced into Poland and broken the back of German military power. It was a defeat from which the Wehrmacht would never recover. In the process, the Soviets suffered nearly three-quarters of a million casualties, or approximately triple what the Anglo-American forces suffered from D-Day until the breakout from Normandy at the end of July.

45

ELECTION 1944:

SURVEYING THE FIELD

A S AMERICA AND HER ALLIES WERE CLEARLY WINNING THE WAR, Roosevelt's attention turned to winning the 1944 presidential election. Unlike 1940, there was no mystery as to whether Roosevelt would run. The two-term taboo was shattered and no one doubted Roosevelt was planning for an unprecedented fourth term. The real drama this time around centered on who would be on the ticket with him. This was a matter of more than casual interest to Roosevelt's intimates. For even if most Americans were in the dark, no one close to Roosevelt was fooling themselves about his health or ability to live out another term.

Before the president officially threw his hat in the ring he wanted to know who he would be facing. Wendell Willkie wanted a second try, but the Republican Party was not having him. Why would they, as he had spent most of the past three years insulting much of the party's establishment? Whenever he met persons whose support was crucial to his chances, he was fond of telling them that they could take him or leave him—they left him. In a bid to talk over the party establishment, Willkie, as the primaries approached, went on a whirlwind tour of key states. In Wisconsin, however, he went to a luncheon with a roomful of potential supporters, many of them men who had given freely to his 1940 campaign. Then in a strange act of self-defenestration, Willkie took the podium and announced: "I don't know whether you are going to support me or not and I don't give a damn. You're a bunch of political liabilities anyway." Rarely does a political candidate so thoroughly crush his chances as Willkie did that evening. Roosevelt, however, was sorry to see Willkie's chances for the nomination implode, as he genuinely liked him and had reason to be concerned about the other two candidates.

In the Pacific, General MacArthur was waiting to be called. Publicly he remained aloof from politics, but in private letters he made known his willingness to serve if drafted. He remained a favorite of congressional Republicans and could count on the strong backing of the Hearst-McCormick-Patterson press, all of which had spent the past decade condemning the New Deal and hating Roosevelt. Led by Senator Arthur Vandenberg, who detested Willkie, a small group of congressional Republicans began a "quiet boomlet" for the general. There were reasons for hope, as some polls had MacArthur about even with Willkie and Dewey combined. What MacArthur did not realize was that this popularity was based on his being and remaining a victorious general, and that was unlikely to translate into votes at the ballot box.

Roosevelt watched the MacArthur surge like a hawk, but never appeared particularly bothered by it. From the start, he assumed that the bubble would eventually be pricked and the MacArthur movement would fade away. That did not stop him from preparing to meet the challenger. He knew that any campaign MacArthur ran had to be based on just a few points: that Roosevelt had failed to prepare the nation for war, that he had abandoned the Philippines, and that he had erred in his Germany-first strategy. Roosevelt was also sure that MacArthur would document Roosevelt's supposed failings by releasing copies of the memos that had poured into the War Department, detailing every slight MacArthur had endured and every grievance he had. But Roosevelt had a trump card in the form of a stenographic transcript of a conversation between MacArthur and Admiral Thomas Hart the day before Pearl Harbor. In it MacArthur boasted that he could hold the Philippines without further reinforcement, and said, "My greatest security lies in Japan's inability to launch an air attack on our islands." This was a particularly inopportune thing to say just before a Japanese air attack crippled MacArthur's own air force. As further insurance, Roosevelt announced that he was going to Hawaii to meet with both of his Pacific commanders—Nimitz and MacArthur—demonstrating in a series of photo opportunities who worked for whom.

For the most part, though, Roosevelt had no respect for MacArthur's political ability, and was certain the challenger would wilt under the hot lights of a presidential campaign. In the end, MacArthur's candidacy blew up when a supposed supporter, Congressman Arthur L. Miller, released two letters in which MacArthur denounced the New Deal—still wildly popular among most Americans. The Roosevelt machine wasted little time making sure MacArthur's views on the New Deal were fed into nearly every paper in the country. Instantly, the MacArthur bubble began hissing air, and MacArthur soon publicly asked that no action be taken that would link his name in any way with the nomination, stating: "I do not covet it nor would I accept it." If not exactly Shermanesque, it was enough.

Only one man was left standing, New York governor Thomas E. Dewey, and on June 28, the Republicans made him their candidate for president. Dewey came close to unanimous approval, receiving 1,056 votes out of 1,057. Wisconsin delegate Grant A. Ritter, who was pledged to MacArthur, stubbornly refused to vote for anyone else. He did, however, vote for "Honest" John Bricker, a dyed-in-the-wool party man, whom Dewey had selected as his running mate. It was an inauspicious start, as Bricker added nothing to the ticket and had famously been described as having a "stellar brain—a huge black void with a few clichés floating around." Dewey made an even worse choice when he convinced the party to make his friend Herbert Brownell its national chairman, whereupon Brownell went to work coordinating one of the worst-run campaigns in American political history. But many considered that the worst damage done to Dewey's chances came from the sharp wit of Teddy Roosevelt's daughter, Alice Longworth, who despite being a Republican asked: "How can you vote for a man who looks like the bridegroom on a wedding cake?"

On July 11, Roosevelt announced that though he did not want to run, his duty compelled him to do so. There was just over a week until the Democratic convention and Roosevelt's announcement gave no hints on who he wanted as a running mate. Earlier in the year he had indicated that he remained happy with Wallace, but that was a position few in the party and no one in his inner circle, except Eleanor, shared. Wallace's long bitter fight with Jesse Jones had inflicted huge political damage, which was compounded by a new FBI report (that Roosevelt did not believe but did not want to see made public) that Wallace, if not a Communist Party member himself, certainly displayed sympathy for their cause. As early as 1943, leaders of the Democratic National Committee made common cause with Roosevelt's gatekeeper, Pa Watson—who detested Wallace—to admit a steady stream of anti-Wallace politicos to the Oval Office and keep Wallace supporters at a distance.

In June, Roosevelt invited Edward Flynn, Bronx party boss and the man who ran his 1940 campaign, to Washington to get his views on Wallace. Flynn told the president that he personally liked Wallace before informing him that he had canvassed the country, and the only support for Wallace came from big labor. Moreover, if Wallace ran, the president would lose so many independents that he could easily lose crucial states. FDR often discounted the opinions of others, but at his core Roosevelt was a political animal. He could count votes as well as Flynn and so he accepted Flynn's analysis. From the moment Flynn informed Roosevelt that the only votes the vice president could bring the ticket were ones already in FDR's pocket, Wallace was doomed.

Roosevelt, true to form, did not want to break the news to a loyal ally and handed the job over to Rosenman and Ickes. When they went to see him, Wallace, who had just returned from a long trip to China, sensed their purpose and refused to meet with them until he saw Roosevelt. When Pa Watson told him that Roosevelt preferred he talk to Rosenman and Ickes before meeting with him, Wallace reluctantly invited the two men to lunch. Together they tried to convince the vice president to withdraw from the ticket, but Wallace would not consider such a move until he spoke with Roosevelt.

That afternoon, Wallace met with FDR, who went into considerable detail on everything he had been hearing from party officials about Wallace costing the ticket as many as three million votes. Roosevelt threw up every objection to Wallace staying on the ticket he could come up with, but refused to do the one thing that would discourage the vice president: he never asked him to withdraw his name from consideration. Roosevelt, in fact, did just the opposite, and said that he still wanted Wallace as a running mate and would make a statement to that effect. Wallace left feeling encouraged to stay in the fight. In all his years as a cabinet officer and then vice president, Wallace apparently never learned anything about the president's ways. Unable to fire people who were loyal to him, Roosevelt expected them to divine his desires and act appropriately. Wallace, however, with the same stubborn obtuseness that had kept him in a losing struggle with Jesse Jones, refused to grasp Roosevelt's intent, despite a steady stream of visitors, sent by Roosevelt, begging him to withdraw.

The next day, July 11, Wallace had lunch with the president. This time he spoke Roosevelt's language—plain, hard, name-calling, delegate-counting politics. He told Roosevelt that he was sure of 290 delegates at the convention, far higher than any other potential candidate. He then named and bitterly denounced the men who were "lying" to the president, before reminding FDR that the Democratic hold over the important black vote was slipping, and that was a constituency where he had strong support. At three o'clock Wallace left the White House with Roosevelt's promise to support him on the ticket.

What Wallace did not know was that just two weeks before, Roosevelt had promised Jimmy Byrnes the job. While at Shangri-La, Roosevelt had said that he had talked it over with party chairman Robert Hannegan, and they both wanted him to be the convention chairman and the vice presidential candidate. Byrnes later wrote that the president appeared "sincere in wanting me as a running mate, and I found myself beginning to think seriously about it."

Later that evening, after Wallace had departed, the good and great of the Democratic Party—Robert Hannegan, Chicago mayor Ed Kelly, former party chairman Ed Flynn, party treasurer Edwin Pauley, and megafundraiser George Allen—trooped into Roosevelt's office. Pauley later wrote a long memo to Rosenman about his recollections of the campaign to dump Wallace. In it he said, speaking for all at the meeting:

> My own intensive activities in this regard were occasioned by my conviction that Henry Wallace was not a fit man to be President of the United States; and by my belief, on the basis of observations, that President Roosevelt would not live much longer.
>
> I felt, therefore, that I could make no greater individual contribution to the Nation's good than to do everything in my power to protect it from Wallace during the war. My preconvention slogan was "You are not nominating a Vice President of the United States, but a President."

For several hours the assembled party leaders discussed and discarded various possibilities. Wallace's name was thrown into contention, but his chances died a quick death, as he had no supporters among the visitors, and Roosevelt offered him no defense. Byrnes's name was put forward and was quashed just as quickly. Perceived as an unreconstructed southerner, everyone feared that Byrnes would alienate the black vote. Moreover, Catholics did not like him because he had lapsed in the faith. More crucially, labor hated him, and after all the troubles Roosevelt had recently had with labor, he was not going to run with a man whose candidacy might be the straw that sent millions of labor votes to the Republicans for a generation.

So it went: Senator Barkley, good man but too old; Hull, too old, and besides, Roosevelt planned on dumping him after the election (Hull died first); even Jesse Jones's name was considered, but Roosevelt remained miffed over his treatment of Wallace. Roosevelt finally suggested Supreme Court Justice William O. Douglas. There was dead silence, as no one in the room wanted Douglas any more than they wanted Wallace. The president sensed the lack of enthusiasm and moved on. Hannegan then suggested Truman, who had done a fine job reducing waste during the war, and who, despite being associated with Kansas City's Pendergast machine, was considered incorruptible. Everyone fell in behind this suggestion, and the president finally looked at Hannegan and said: "Bob, I think everyone else wants Truman. If that is the case, it is Truman." Hannegan tarried as the room emptied. Knowing how Roosevelt worked, Hannegan asked him for a written statement to that effect, and Roosevelt wrote out that "he would be glad to run" with either Douglas or Truman.

Byrnes, who had decided to run and lined up Truman to nominate him, was visibly upset when Hannegan told him the results of the meeting. Calling Roosevelt, who was at Hyde Park, Byrnes asked him if he truly preferred Truman first and Douglas second. Roosevelt parsed his words, claiming that he had not meant to imply he "preferred" either man, but would be "glad" to run with one or the other. Roosevelt then continued, "After all, Jimmy, you are close to me personally . . . I hardly know Truman. Douglas is a good poker partner. He is good in a poker game and tells good stories." Byrnes, unaware that Hannegan had a note from the president, ended the call convinced that Roosevelt had not yet declared a preference for anyone. He then walked down a few doors from his office to consult with Hopkins, who had recently returned from the hospital. Hopkins informed him that Roosevelt had said that if he (Byrnes) entered the race he would be nominated.

The confusion had not been cleared up when Roosevelt boarded his train for a trip to California, en route to Hawaii for consultations with Nimitz and MacArthur. He specifically asked the engineer to time the trip so that he would not reach the West Coast until the convention had nominated him for a fourth term. When the train stopped in Chicago, Hannegan boarded to tell Roosevelt that the convention was in an uproar and he simply must make his intentions known. Roosevelt appeared indifferent to who ran with him, but apparently signed another note saying he would be fine with Douglas or Truman. Hannegan put it in his pocket without looking at it. When he finally did, he was mortified to find Douglas's name alongside Truman's. He and Ed Pauley decided to tell the convention that they had a letter from Roosevelt saying he wanted Truman, but not to release it. The trick worked; by the time copies were released it was too late for the Douglas forces to mobilize.

Wallace was also in town, holding a letter in which Roosevelt stated he personally would vote to nominate Wallace, but just as clearly telling the delegates they must make their own decision—a kiss of death that Wallace was too obtuse to recognize. Byrnes was also in Chicago, still convinced that he was Roosevelt's chosen successor. He was not alone; many others were just as certain Byrnes was already the vice president in waiting. But when Ed Flynn complained that he would cost Roosevelt 200,000 black votes in New York, losing the state and probably the election, things began to change. When big labor jumped into the fight to blackball him, Byrnes read the writing on the wall. Later, when Hannegan told him that he had spoken to Roosevelt by phone and that the president was withdrawing his support, rather than try and overcome a labor veto, Byrnes threw in the towel and returned to Washington. Bitter, but the consummate politician, Byrnes told his supporters to get behind Truman, and during the campaign he strongly backed the ticket. Still, he never forgave Roosevelt for the double cross, later writing to Senator Wheeler: "To him men were so many tools to be used for the accomplishment of some good purpose. Certainly, he played upon the ambitions of men as an artist would play upon the strings of a musical instrument."

With Byrnes pushed aside, Truman was finally convinced to enter his name into nomination, but only after being allowed to overhear a telephone conversation between Roosevelt and Hannegan. Roosevelt asked Hannegan: "Have you got the fellow lined up yet?" When Hannegan told him no, Roosevelt shouted: "Well, tell the Senator that if he wants to break up the Democratic party by staying out he can: but he knows as well as I what that might mean at this dangerous time in the world. If he wants to do it, anyway, then let him go ahead." It had all been neatly rehearsed beforehand, and it had just the effect Roosevelt expected; Truman, who previously had no idea he was under consideration, gave in, saying, "I guess I'll have to take it." The rest was pure power politics, and Wallace never knew what hit him.

After Roosevelt addressed the convention from his train car, Wallace went for the brass ring, as a "spontaneous" demonstration for Wallace broke out. Supporters rushed the floor chanting his name, just as a huge pipe organ began playing "Iowa"—Wallace's home state. It seemed that the entire hall was clamoring for Wallace. It was a masterstroke, but it was not enough. The Truman forces had been warned that Wallace's supporters had counterfeited tickets to the convention and would be present in force. When they started their chant, Hannegan and his team were ready. Mayor Kelly declared the stadium was filled beyond capacity and ordered his police and fire departments to close it. Ed Pauley sent one of his larger men with an axe to destroy the organ, but the organ player ceased playing when his precious instrument was threatened. Soon thereafter, Hannegan adjourned the convention for the night.

The next morning, Hannegan kept a tight hold on the tickets, ensuring that the number of Wallace supporters on the main floor would be a bare minimum, while Mayor Kelly dispatched Chicago's police to keep anyone wearing a Wallace pin out of the galleries. Hundreds more police guarded the stadium's doors, keeping Wallace's supporters from crashing the gates and shouting their man to victory. Wallace still had enough support to outpoll Truman by over a hundred votes on the first ballot, but that was before the party bosses went to work. All day, arms were twisted, deals were made, and everyone was reminded that Roosevelt no longer wanted Wallace on the ticket—and it was never wise to cross the president on political matters. Truman won the second ballot in a landslide, 1031–105.

46

PACIFIC OVERTURES

O N THE DAY OF TRUMAN'S NOMINATION, ROOSEVELT LEFT SAN Diego on the heavy cruiser USS *Baltimore,* heading for Honolulu. The trip was uneventful, except for Roosevelt's puzzlement over his black Scottish terrier Fala's loss of hair. It was soon discovered that Fala had learned that he could acquire numerous delicacies by visiting the crew quarters. The price for these snacks was paid in locks of hair, as he was shorn nearly hairless by sailors taking clips as souvenirs. On July 26, the *Baltimore* began its entry into Pearl Harbor, as destroyers circled, constantly pinging for enemy submarines. In port were six carriers, at least three battleships, dozens of destroyers, and over two hundred support ships. Even Roosevelt, an old Navy man, was impressed at the assembled might surrounding him, which represented only a small fraction of the great fleets at sea. At the rails of the ships were thousands of sailors standing at attention in gleaming white uniforms. Roosevelt, repeatedly doffing his fedora, very much enjoyed the spectacle.

As soon as FDR's ship docked, Admiral Nimitz and a large part of his top staff boarded to greet the president. The only officer missing was MacArthur, who had landed an hour before but went to take a bath first. When Roosevelt asked his whereabouts, Nimitz stared in embarrassed silence. Just when the admiral was about to give up and disembark, MacArthur, the great showman, condescended to make his appearance. Speeding onto the wharf with sirens wailing, in a grand touring car hastily procured from a notorious whorehouse madam, he pulled up beside the *Baltimore.* MacArthur, wearing a heavy leather bomber jacket despite the heat, bounded up the gangplank to greet the president. The greeting was amicable, and numerous pictures, which would be deployed effectively in the coming election campaign, were taken. Later, MacArthur fumed to aides about being called to Hawaii, and away from directing the war, solely to be used for presidential photo opportunities. If that was the case, and it was surely part of Roosevelt's reason for coming to Hawaii, the president used him in much the same way the next day, when he took a long tour of the island's military installations. The one event where Roosevelt forbade cameras was when he insisted on being wheeled through the hospital wards of men who had lost one or more limbs. Presidential assistant Sam Rosenman said that Roosevelt wanted to show by his own example that it was possible to rise above their potential bitterness and physical handicaps and still achieve great things in life. When he finally left the hospital, Roosevelt was close to tears.

That evening, Roosevelt met with his two senior Pacific commanders in a spacious room in the Holmes Villa overlooking Waikiki Beach. They had a simple question to answer: where next? With the Marianas in American hands and B-29s now rolling off assembly lines in large numbers, the Air Force would soon begin the sustained strategic bombing of the Japanese home islands. What Roosevelt wanted was a plan on how to next employ the mighty land and naval forces gathered in the Pacific to hasten Japan's surrender.

Nimitz, despite his own reservations about King's strategic ideas, repeated what King had told him to say, and laid out a plan to isolate and bypass the Philippines and strike straight for Formosa. Strategically, Nimitz claimed that taking Formosa would allow the Americans to assist the Chinese on the mainland and also interdict Japan's access to its southern supply zone. Such an attack across the central Pacific would, however, have the secondary effect of closing down MacArthur's theater.

MacArthur did not discuss strategy, as from any rational military viewpoint Formosa was a far superior objective than the Philippines. Marshall, who many historians have claimed backed MacArthur in this debate, had in actuality tried to warn MacArthur away from the Philippines. In late June, Marshall had addressed the issue with Stimson, stating that taking MacArthur's chosen course meant taking the slow way; and that it would have his forces butting heads with the large army that Japan had accumulated in the Philippines. Marshall did not want to bog down an entire army for months, when it was easier to just jump over the Philippines to the more strategically important Formosa. Two days after his talk with Stimson, Marshall wrote to MacArthur laying out his misgivings in detail and concluding: "We must be careful not to allow our personal feelings and Philippine political considerations to override our great objective which is the early conclusion of our war with the Japanese." Even as he wrote, Marshall knew better: MacArthur was temperamentally incapable of putting aside his personal feelings.

Unable to speak to the strategic merits, MacArthur hinged his position on honor, trying to strike an emotional chord within Roosevelt. He argued that America had a responsibility to the Filipino people, and that the early capture of the islands would rescue many thousands of American POWs, who were known to be enduring horrific treatment. He then told the president that American public opinion would rightfully condemn him if seventeen million Christian Filipinos were abandoned to the Japanese, and warned Roosevelt that he would pay a price at the ballot box for such a decision. Another version of this event, reproduced in many volumes, comes from MacArthur's postwar writings. He states that during a private meeting with Roosevelt he warned that the American people would desert him if he left American prisoners to languish. The clear but unspoken implication was that if Roosevelt did not approve operations in the Philippines, MacArthur himself would make sure it was a campaign issue. In any event, Roosevelt did not come to an immediate decision. Only on August 9, 1944, did Roosevelt write to tell his general that when he returned to Washington he would push for extensive operations in the Philippines.

Less than a month after returning to Washington, Roosevelt was once again heading to Quebec for another conference with Churchill (Octagon). His trip to Hawaii had shown America that he remained an active war leader, and a second Quebec Conference would solidify that image. Both men arrived at the train station at nearly the same moment, driving the protocol experts into fits. As Churchill's train pulled onto a siding at Wolfe's Cove, Quebec, Roosevelt was there to greet him, sitting in an open car, his eyes shaded by a big Panama hat. "Hello, I'm glad to see you," he called. "Eleanor is here. Did you have a nice trip?" Churchill replied with his own small talk: "We had three beautiful days." Then turning to the assembled reporters Churchill exclaimed: "Victory is everywhere."

Such was the mood of the conference. There were no major strategic military decisions left to take, and in fact, the biggest military row of the conference revolved around who would be in on the kill. On September 13, 1944, when the Combined Chiefs met with Roosevelt and Churchill, the prime minister declared that there were certain elements putting out that Britain would take "no share in the war against Japan." Churchill first offered to send 500–1,000 bombers to join in the air assault on Japan. When Arnold demurred for logistical reasons, Churchill replied: "With all of your airdromes you would not deny me a mere pittance of a few." When the prime minister claimed that a refusal would leave the British people unable to hold their heads up in public, Roosevelt nodded his acceptance and the deal was done.

Churchill then offered the British main fleet for operations against Japan as soon as Germany was defeated. Roosevelt replied "that the offer was accepted on the largest possible scale." A surly King, despite much prodding, refused to commit to their employment. An exasperated Churchill finally exclaimed, "An offer has been made; is it accepted?" Roosevelt replied that it had been.

The next day the Combined Chiefs met without the president and the prime minister, opening a door for King to say what he dared not say in front of the president. He did not want the British fleet in the central Pacific. As King saw it, the Pacific was an American Navy show, and he did not need British help. In fact, King thought the British would be a nuisance. They had no experience with American methods in the Pacific, they would have to adapt to a very different type of war than they were fighting in Europe, but most crucially, King did not want to use the American "fleet train" to replenish British ships. When Admiral Cunningham assured them that they would have their own fleet train with them, King changed gambits, stating that the "practicality of employing these forces would be a matter of discussion." Leahy brought King up short with a reminder that the president had already accepted the British offer, and all he needed from King was "where and when."

When the British were finally employed at Okinawa, British Task Force 57 comprised thirty ships, including four aircraft carriers. Because their decks were armored (American carriers had wood decks) they proved highly resistant to kamikaze attacks. One American quipped: "When a kamikaze hits a U.S. carrier it means 6 months of repair at Pearl. When a kamikaze hits a Limey carrier it's just a case of 'Sweepers, man your brooms.'"

47

THE MORGENTHAU PLAN

THE SECOND MAJOR DISPUTE AT QUEBEC WAS OVER THE TREATMENT of Germany after the war. At stake was the so-called Morgenthau Plan, which aimed at deindustrializing Germany and turning it into a pastoral paradise. This fight had begun several months earlier when a number of agency and military teams began working on the problem. Hull, for instance, had a State Department team working on it, and they were advising a soft peace that allowed for a rapid rebuilding of the German economy. As Roosevelt had not bothered to share the agreements made during the Tehran Conference with his cabinet, neither Hull nor anyone else at State knew that the president had already agreed to the partition of Germany. Without that knowledge, the State Department advocated an occupation for as long as necessary but no partition.

In Britain a European Advisory Commission (EAC) had been established in 1943 to study the German question and present recommendations. The commission had come to no firm conclusions, but the American representative, Ambassador Winant, hoped peace would lead to a disarmed, economically strong, democratic Germany. Also in Europe, General Eisenhower's headquarters, in the absence of guidance, produced its own instructions—the "Handbook for Military Government in Germany." The handbook called for purging the Nazis, but also for maintaining the German administrative system, and the rehabilitation of sufficient German industry to make Germany self-supporting and capable of contributing to the larger European economy.

None of this meant much, as Roosevelt had not approved any of the plans. In fact, as far as anyone could tell he appeared supremely disinterested in the entire topic for much of the war. His philosophy was to focus on winning first, and then worry about the peace later. When he did speak on the topic, his overriding idea was permanent German disarmament and the destruction of the Prussian military caste so that it could never again threaten European peace. As late as October 1944, during the struggle over the Morgenthau Plan, he wrote to Hull that "I think it is all very well for us to make all kinds of preparations for the treatment of Germany . . . but speed on these matters is not essential at the present moment . . . I dislike making detailed plans for a country which we do not yet occupy."

This was the state of affairs when Morgenthau, on August 6, 1944, flew to Britain. During the flight, Harry Dexter White, assistant secretary of the treasury and Soviet spy, handed Morgenthau a copy of the State Department's plan for postwar Germany, knowing his boss, who favored a hard peace, would hate it. Once in Britain, Morgenthau received copies of the EAC's proposals and a copy of the "Handbook for Military Government in Germany."

Morgenthau was appalled. After all the destruction and misery Germany had caused, he expected the Allies to coalesce around some form of Carthaginian peace. In his diaries, Morgenthau claims that one of his first stops in Britain was to see Eisenhower, and he was pleased to see him in agreement with Morgenthau's own plans. According to the secretary, when he asked how the Germans should be treated, Eisenhower told him that "they should be treated sternly and that they should be allowed to stew in their own juice." Eisenhower's memoirs tell a different story, stating that while Germany must be held accountable and its capacity to wage future wars eliminated, it would be a "folly" to wreck its economy in such a way that it could not support itself or pay reparations.

When he got back to Washington on August 17, Morgenthau first went to see Hull and found out that he knew very little of what was going on. When Morgenthau told him that he had learned from Churchill that Roosevelt had already agreed to partition the country, Hull gasped his reply: "Henry, this is the first time I have ever heard this. I have never been permitted to see the minutes of the Tehran Conference." Morgenthau reports that Hull just kept repeating over and over: "I have asked and I have not been allowed to see them." Hull went on to complain that when it came to postwar Germany he was not told anything. Morgenthau replied that although Germany's postwar treatment was not within his writ, "as an American citizen . . . I am going to stick my nose into it until it is all right." Two days later, believing he had Hull's full support for a tough-on-Germany policy, Morgenthau went to see the president.

Morgenthau got only thirty minutes with Roosevelt, and he had a hard time getting the president to move past a prolonged discussion of Britain's financial position. FDR was apparently dumbfounded to discover Britain was nearly broke. What he would have thought had he known that Morgenthau's deputy, Harry Dexter White, was responsible, likely on Soviet orders, for the Treasury policies that kept Britain on the edge of bankruptcy can only be guessed. Eventually Morgenthau got to the topic of postwar Germany and chastised Roosevelt for keeping the Tehran Conference agreements secret. According to Morgenthau, Roosevelt looked embarrassed but offered no excuses or explanations. When Morgenthau told him about the easy terms in all the various postwar plans circulating, FDR appeared shocked, saying, "We have to be tough with Germany and I mean the German people not just the Nazis. We either have to castrate the German people or you have to treat them in such a way that they can't just go on reproducing people who want to continue the way they have in the past." Satisfied that the president shared his own opinions about treating Germany harshly, Morgenthau once again plunged the Treasury Department into affairs that were none of its business and assigned a team led by Harry Dexter White to work on the problem.

On August 23, Morgenthau had lunch with Stimson and McCloy. The Stimson diary for that day says only that it was a most satisfactory talk, but gives no details. Morgenthau's diaries are more interesting. He reports that Stimson had not thought the matter through, so he gave him some of his own ideas. The first of these ideas was removing all German children from their parents and having them brought up in Allied military-run schools, where they could learn about democracy. Warming to his topic, Morgenthau next brought up the possibility of removing all industry from Germany and returning the country to a pre-industrial state of small landowners. Stimson replied that such a thing might have worked back in 1860 when Germany had a much smaller population, but for it to work today you might have to take a lot of people out of Germany. Morgenthau was not put off, replying, "Well, that is not nearly as bad as sending them to gas chambers."

In the meantime, within the Treasury, Harry Dexter White, who had strongly supported Morgenthau's efforts, worked on the Morgenthau Plan, the goal of which was the destruction of the German nation. As one British politician later commented, "It fell to White to clothe a bad thesis with an appearance of intellectual respectability." But it was a task White relished, as he, more than anyone, was pushing Morgenthau to treat Germany as harshly as possible. One can capture a glimpse of White's approach from directions he gave to Treasury economist Edward Bernstein. When asked to prepare a study on how much steel production capacity Germany should be allowed to keep after the war, Bernstein argued that Germany should keep sufficient capacity to aid in the rebuilding of Europe. White, however, told Bernstein, "We're not interested in having any German steel production. We want you to give us economic reasons to remove all of their capacity." When White presented the finished plan to Morgenthau, he told him that he had discussed the plan with Lord Maynard Keynes and had gotten the British economist's full agreement. This was important, as it was Keynes, in his pamphlet *The Economic Consequences of the Peace*, who had laid bare the stupidity of the post–World War I settlement at Versailles.

In truth, Keynes was appalled by the plan, writing to his friend the chancellor of the exchequer Sir John Anderson:

> Morgenthau started off on this before coming to our main business . . . When Harry White broached the same subject I took the line that all plans relating to Germany which I had seen so far struck me as equally bad, and the only matter I was concerned with was that it should not be the British Treasury which had to pay reparations or support Germany. I gathered that the plan is not quite as crude as it appeared in the reports from Quebec. All the same it seems pretty mad, and I asked White how the inhabitants of the Ruhr were to be kept from starvation; he said that there would have to be bread lines but on a very low level of subsistence. When I asked if the British, as being responsible for that area, would also be responsible for the bread, he said that the U.S. Treasury would if necessary pay for the bread, provided always it was on a very low level of subsistence. So whilst the hills are being turned into a sheep run, the valleys will be filled for some years to

come with a closely packed bread line on a very low level of subsistence at American expense. How am I to keep a straight face when it comes to a round table talk I cannot imagine.

It got worse. When asked if there was anything that might be done to reduce the number of Germans who would require feeding by soup kitchens, White proposed moving millions of German men to Africa to work as slave labor on massive construction projects. At another point, when told that thirty million would starve to death if his plans were enacted, White replied that he had done his own calculations and that the figure was closer to eighteen million dead, which he found acceptable. If anyone fits Hannah Arendt's concept of the "banality of evil," it is White. He was the perfect bureaucrat willing to sacrifice millions to a hideous death by slow starvation in pursuit of established policy goals. One could easily picture White fitting in at the Wannsee Conference, where Hitler's henchmen planned the details of the Final Solution. How much of White's written plan was dictated by his Soviet masters remains hotly debated, but it is a certainty that there was nothing in White's formulations that Stalin would have found troubling. It is, after all, reflective of how they treated East Germany after the war.

On September 2, 1944, White presented the Treasury Department's plan to Hull, who surprised him by calling it a plan of blind vengeance and castigated White for failing to see that by killing Germany he was putting a stake through the heart of Europe. At the same time, Morgenthau was briefing the plan to the president over tea. Roosevelt first said it would be enough to forbid any German from ever again wearing a uniform and to outlaw marching. But, by the end of their talk, Morgenthau was convinced that FDR was in full agreement with his plans. As he was leaving he told Eleanor: "I am convinced that the President wants to do the right thing in regard to the Germans, but he hasn't got the time to look into it thoroughly, and everything that has been done so far is useless, so some of us have to do it for him."

On September 4, Stimson had dinner with Morgenthau and White. Despite everyone acknowledging that sharp issues were arising over the treatment of Germany, Stimson thought it a pleasant dinner, and matters were discussed with "temperance and good will." Stimson did, however, record that "Morgenthau is, not unnaturally, very bitter and as he is not thoroughly trained in history or even economics it became very apparent that he would plunge out for a treatment of Germany which I feel sure would be unwise."

But a few days later, on September 5, Stimson learned that Hull too was apparently coming around to Treasury's way of thinking. For when Stimson met with Hull, Morgenthau, and Hopkins on September 5, his diary records his shock at discovering "Hull was as bitter as Morgenthau" and ready to "dump all of his principles." A dumbfounded Stimson also recorded that Hull "wished to wreck completely the immense Ruhr-Saar region of Germany and turn it into second-rate agricultural land, regardless of all that meant . . . to the welfare of the entire continent." As Stimson saw it, Hull was now standing with those aiming to prostrate Germany for all eternity.

He thus found himself a minority of one when he, Morgenthau, Hopkins, and Hull took up Germany's future with the president the next day. Stimson was horrified to hear Roosevelt talking about how happily and peacefully the Germans could live being fed from soup kitchens. Roosevelt continued this discourse with notions of how happily his pioneer ancestors had lived unburdened of the luxuries modern society deems necessary. Almost unbelievably, Roosevelt's nostalgia was driving a decision toward reducing Germany to a pastureland, as if the Industrial Revolution had never happened. When their meeting ended, Stimson recorded that he had never had a more unpleasant meeting, and then went to compose a long memorandum to Roosevelt, concluding with this:

> I cannot treat as realistic the suggestion that such an area [Germany] in the present economic condition of the world can be turned into a nonproductive "ghost territory." . . . I can conceive of endeavoring to meet the misuse which Germany has recently made of their [heavy industries] production . . . but I cannot conceive of turning such a gift of nature into a dust heap . . . By such economic mistakes I cannot but feel that you would also be poisoning the springs out of which we hope that the future peace of the world can be maintained.

FDR, preparing to depart for Quebec, did not make any final decisions then, nor did he do so during a short final meeting on December 9, but it was apparent that he was leaning toward the Morgenthau solution, having written to Hull: "I do not want them to starve to death . . . if they need food to keep body and soul together . . . they should be fed three times a day with soup from Army soup kitchens . . . The fact that they are a defeated nation, collectively and individually, must be so imposed upon them that they will hesitate to start any new war." By this time, Hull was again reversing his position, as he was angered over Treasury's trying to usurp the State Department's roles and responsibilities. Unfortunately, due to illness, Hull was increasingly just a bystander in this debate.

After quickly disposing of most of the military matters at Quebec, Roosevelt asked Morgenthau to come up and join them. Stimson was horrified that Morgenthau would be positioned to expound his views without anyone present to counter them, and believed Roosevelt was planning to recommend to Churchill only the most radical proposals for Germany's future. That night he wrote: "I cannot believe that he will follow Morgenthau's views. If he does it will certainly be a disaster." Felix Frankfurter agreed, telling Stimson: "Not to worry over it; it would not go anywhere and the President himself would catch all of the errors and would see that the spirit was all wrong." Stimson was not so sure.

Churchill, upon hearing Morgenthau out, was dumbfounded by the proposal and grew increasingly agitated as he took in its details. Then turning loose "the full flood of his rhetoric, sarcasm and violence," he told Morgenthau that his plan would chain Europe to a German corpse. Calling Morgenthau's proposals "unnatural, unchristian, and unnecessary," Churchill ended the discussion in a highly emotional state. The following week Morgenthau told Treasury colleagues that Churchill "was violent in the most foul language." Long after the encounter Morgenthau wrote down his memory of an event that obviously still troubled him: "He [Churchill] was slumped in his chair, his language biting, his flow incessant, his manner merciless. I have never had such a verbal lashing in my life . . . I went unhappily to bed, just the same and spent a sleepless night."

The next morning, Churchill, much to Morgenthau's amazement, had reversed himself. He now supported Morgenthau's plan nearly in its entirety. The reasons for this sudden change of heart are unclear. It is worth noting, however, that a couple of days earlier Roosevelt had delayed approving Lend-Lease's postwar extension, which Britain absolutely needed if it was to have any hope of salvaging its war-torn economy. At the time, a desperate Churchill grabbed Roosevelt and asked: "What must I do? Get on my hind legs and beg like Fala?" So, despite his rage over Morgenthau's plan, Churchill was standing upon a weak foundation. When he left that night he was accompanied by one of his advisers, Lord Cherwell (Frederick A. Lindemann). Cherwell was both sympathetic to the Morgenthau Plan and responsible for negotiating with the U.S. Treasury for continued Lend-Lease and financial support at the war's end. There is little doubt that Cherwell went to work on Churchill with some combination of two arguments: that Britain could profitably take over a deindustrialized Germany's markets, and that Britain could not secure necessary postwar loans from the United States if it did not accede to the U.S. Treasury's plan. The only reason Churchill ever provided for his change of heart was an unsatisfactory comment in his multivolume history of the war: "At first I violently opposed this idea. But the President, with Mr. Morgenthau—*from whom we had much to ask*—were so insistent, that in the end we agreed to consider it."

The only British opponent of the plan was now Anthony Eden, who jumped on Churchill with "hobnailed boots," insisting: "You can't stand for this. Why, you and I publicly had just spoken the opposite way. You can't stand for this." Churchill replied with an edged snarl: "Well, if it gets down to the question of whether I am for the German people or the English people, I am for the English people, and you can be for whomever you want." Churchill then warned Eden not to go back to the War Cabinet and stir up opposition, which is exactly what Eden proceeded to do. Soon thereafter Roosevelt and Churchill both signed a memorandum of agreement that was in all major respects a restatement of the Morgenthau Plan. The secretary of the treasury had won; Germany would be turned into pastureland.

Morgenthau and Roosevelt's threats—veiled and unveiled—may have roped in Churchill, but they had not reckoned with Stimson, a profoundly moral man, who remained unalterably opposed to the plan. When informed of the agreement he wrote: "I have yet to meet a man who is not horrified with the 'Carthaginian' attitude of the Treasury. It is Semitism gone wild for vengeance and if it is ultimately carried out . . . it will lay the seeds for another war in the next generation." With decades of Washington experience behind him, Stimson had developed into a wily and dangerous political infighter. After learning that an agreement had been made, he took the first step in unleashing a masterpiece of bureaucratic warfare: a long memorandum to the president. In it Stimson mixed the moral with the practical, making a strong case against the systematic deprivation of seventy million souls, as well as the damage such a program would do to the European economy. He then had the memo leaked.

Soon thereafter the entire Morgenthau Plan was leaked, by persons unknown, to those elements of the press often hostile to FDR, where it received a thorough lambasting from all quarters. In his diary Stimson merely noted that "the pack is in full cry," before telling Hull that such press coverage was to be expected. *Time* magazine, for instance, said that the plan fell just short of ordering sterilization for all Germans, and other papers and journals were not as gentle. Roosevelt knew he was in trouble when Dewey's reelection team made the plan an electoral issue, claiming that the plan to "dispose of the German people after the war" was stiffening German resistance and causing thousands of needless American casualties. German propaganda was, in fact, making much of Morgenthau's plan, as radio broadcasts repeatedly blared: "The occupation of the Reich by Americans and British would be as horrible as by the Bolsheviks. Morgenthau is outdoing Clemenceau . . . Clemenceau said there were 23,000,000 Germans too many—Morgenthau wants to see 43,000,000 Germans exterminated."

Stimson bided his time, letting the press and Republicans do his work for him. On September 27, he took a week off. But he was interrupted on his first day of rest by a call from the president. Stimson recorded: "He had just come back from an absence and was evidently under the influence of the impact of criticism which has followed his decision to follow Morgenthau's advice." Getting hammered in the press and in the polls, Roosevelt realized "he had made a false step" and was now looking for a way to back away from the plan. He told Stimson that he never wanted Germany made into a purely agricultural country, and that his underlying motive was only to provide a broke Britain enough business that it would not fall into an economic depression. Stimson politely thanked Roosevelt for some birthday roses he had sent a few days before and let the presidential fabrications go unremarked.

On October 3, Stimson lunched with a tired and worn-looking president. Eventually the discussion drifted to Germany's postwar treatment.

Stimson recorded that Roosevelt "grinned and looked naughty and said 'Henry Morgenthau pulled a boner.'" Roosevelt then went on about his intent to help Britain economically, and that he never meant to destroy Germany. Stimson, a bit annoyed at this rewriting of history, pulled out and read the document Roosevelt had approved. After he read it, Stimson reported, the president was "staggered" and said he "had no idea how he had initialed it."

With that the Morgenthau Plan died as if it had never existed. At a press conference, a few days later, FDR announced that he had asked foreign economic administrator Leo Crowley to advise him on postwar economic policies toward Germany. When asked if that meant the cabinet split was healed, Roosevelt replied, "That was all a newspaper story."

"No foundation to the stories at all?" a reporter queried.

Roosevelt answered with some gruffness: "Every story that came out was essentially untrue in its basic facts."

In that instant, the great debate over Germany's future had not only ended, but Roosevelt declared it had never happened. In various forms, some of the plan's ideas persisted through to the end of the war. They only finally died when President Truman, never a fan of Morgenthau, opted to leave him behind when he departed for the Potsdam Conference. Germany's, or at least West Germany's, fate was eventually decided by facts on the ground. The Army, with a war in Japan still to attend to, had no interest in pushing Germany into chaos, and placed the country in the capable hands of General Lucius Clay, last seen in this book arguing with Donald Nelson over cuts to Army procurement. Despite some interagency bickering with the State Department, Clay quickly took charge and began stabilizing German politics and economics.

Unfortunately, Clay, despite his many good qualities as an administrator and problem-solver, had no idea how to rebuild a war-torn economy. The German economic miracle, therefore, did not truly start for two years, when German economic chief Ludwig Erhard freed all prices and in a single stroke reinstituted a market economy. His actions met a storm of disapproval, particularly from professional economists. A worried Clay called Erhard to his office and told him that all of his economic advisers were telling him that freeing prices was lunacy. Erhard replied, "General, my advisors say the same thing. We must ignore them." Clay did so. Within a week previously scarce commodities reappeared on store shelves and the German economy was reborn.

The final, and in many ways most crucial, influence on Germany's economic recovery was the advent of the Cold War. Almost overnight Germany found itself transformed from a defeated enemy into a front-line ally in the battle with communism. There was no further talk of reparations and punishment, as a weak Germany was no longer in the interest of the West, which wanted a strong power in central Europe capable of deterring and possibly fighting the Soviet Union.

48

THE CHAMP

HAVING THE MORGENTHAU PLAN SAVAGED IN THE PRESS HAD given the Republicans a fighting chance in the election, as it gave credence to their repeated claims that Roosevelt was mismanaging the war. Republicans were also hitting the mark on issues such as the country being run by tired old men who were destroying the free-enterprise system that had made America great. One issue that seemed to particularly resonate was based on a false rumor. When Roosevelt was returning after meeting Nimitz and MacArthur in Hawaii, he had stopped to inspect bases in the Aleutians. A rumor began that Roosevelt had forgotten his dog, Fala, and ordered a destroyer sent back to retrieve him. The Republicans seized on it as an example of Rooseveltian entitlement, spending millions in taxpayer funds and diverting a warship from other duties to pick up and deliver the presidential dog. Taken together it was all having an effect: Dewey's poll numbers were rising and Roosevelt's were plunging.

Democratic strategists were begging the president to give up on his early version of the Rose Garden strategy and to come out fighting. Roosevelt obliged them, announcing a series of speeches, starting with the Teamsters on September 23 at Washington's Statler Hotel, where he made mincemeat of the Republicans. He reminded his audience, in a speech heard by millions on the radio, of the closed banks, the soup lines, the foreclosures, and the other tremendous hardships of the Depression. He invited Americans to join him in remembering how they had fought tough times together, to think of the gains and the setbacks, and most of all to recall that it was he, Roosevelt, who had been trying everything to get the economy moving again while Republicans fought him tooth and nail. He then lambasted Republicans who accused him of not preparing the nation for war. He told them that even Goebbels would not try that falsehood, and reminded the nation that it was Republican leaders who tried to block every attempt he had made to warn and prepare the nation.

But he saved his most damaging rhetorical salvo to the end, when he rose in righteous indignation in defense of Fala. After providing evidence to the press earlier of the untruthfulness of the story, Roosevelt now used it without mercy to destroy the Dewey campaign. It is worth quoting his defense of Fala in full, because in the two minutes it took to deliver, Roosevelt won the election. In a mock-serious voice and in a sad tone, Roosevelt drew his audience into what they thought was a confidential story of inner hurt.

> These Republican leaders have not been content with attacks on me, or my wife, or on my sons. No, not content with that, they now include my little dog, Fala. Well, of course, I don't resent attacks, and my family doesn't resent attacks—but Fala does resent them.
>
> You know, Fala is Scotch, and being a Scottie, as soon as he learned that the Republican fiction writers, in Congress and out, had concocted a story that I had left him behind on the Aleutian Islands and had sent a destroyer back to find him—at a cost to the taxpayers of two or three, or eight or twenty million dollars—his Scotch soul was furious.
>
> He has not been the same dog since. I am accustomed to hearing malicious falsehoods about myself—such as that old, worm-eaten chestnut that I have represented myself as indispensable. But I think I have a right to resent, to object to, libelous statements about my dog.

Rare is the opponent who can withstand ridicule.

Time reported: "The Champ had swung a full roundhouse blow. And it was plain . . . that the challenger had been hit hard—as plain as when a boxer drops his gloves and his eyes glaze." Four more speeches and a fifty-mile drive in an open car along New York City streets in the pouring rain (to demonstrate he remained in good health) and it was all over. When it officially ended, Roosevelt had captured 53.5 percent of the vote to Dewey's 46 percent. The "graceless" Dewey did not concede until 3:16 A.M., and only then did Roosevelt go to bed, but not before telling his secretary, Bill Hassett, "I still think he is a son of a bitch."

Roosevelt had earned another four years in office, but he had less than six months to live.

The election was close enough that had it come just six weeks later reports from the front might have given more credence to Republican claims that Roosevelt was mismanaging the war. Just as the invasion of the Philippines in late October buoyed Roosevelt's campaign, so the great German gamble in the Ardennes—the Battle of the Bulge—might have sunk it. Launched on December 16, 1944, the Wehrmacht's panzers—protected by low clouds from air attack—drove hard for the Meuse River, desperately trying to re-create the glory days of 1940. For many anxious days, Roosevelt, joined by Leahy, would stay in the map room watching as the pins representing German formations continually moved westward. But this was 1944, and the battle-hardened American army was far superior to the hapless French forces overrun in the same forest almost five years before.

This was an army that knew how to fight and defeat a penetration: hold the shoulders, contest every road junction, and counterattack. The southern shoulder held easily, but there were anxious moments in the north, where the 2nd and 99th Infantry Divisions held the Elsenborn Ridge against the Sixth Panzer Army. In the center, the Americans, recovering far more quickly from the initial shock than the Germans thought possible, dug in and held the vital road junction at St. Vith until December 21, destroying the carefully crafted German timetable. At the same time, the 101st Airborne Division passed into legend as it stubbornly held the town of Bastogne against overwhelming odds. As the 101st held, help was on the way, as Patton, a mere ninety-six hours after the German attack started, halted his own offensive, turned a large part of the Third Army ninety degrees, and hurled it against the flank of the German advance.

49

YALTA AND THE END

B Y THE TIME ROOSEVELT DELIVERED HIS STATE OF THE UNION
Address to Congress on January 6, 1945, the German attack was spent,
as powerful Allied counterattacks eliminated the Bulge. So, rather than
look back, Roosevelt was able to draw his audience's attention to the future, concluding his address by saying:

> This new year of 1945 can be the greatest year of achievement in
> human history...
>
> Most important of all—1945 can and must see the substantial begin-
> ning of the organization of world peace. This organization must be the
> fulfillment of the promise for which men have fought and died in this
> war. It must be the justification of all the sacrifices that have been
> made—of all the dreadful misery that this world has endured.

To accomplish this goal Roosevelt needed Stalin fully aboard, and that
meant one more conference of the Big Three. So, just two days after his
fourth inauguration, on January 22, 1945, Roosevelt boarded the USS
Quincy for the first leg of a trip to the Crimea. With him was his daughter,
Anna, chosen over Eleanor, who desperately wanted to go; Admiral Leahy;
Pa Watson; and an assortment of lesser aides. Also invited was Jimmy
Byrnes, whom Roosevelt was trying to appease after removing him from
the vice-presidential race and then not nominating him for secretary of
state when Hull resigned for health reasons. Waiting for them in Malta, the
Quincy's first stop, were Churchill; Hopkins; the new secretary of state,

Edward Stettinius; Ambassador to the Soviet Union Averell Harriman; and the Combined Chiefs.

Roosevelt was not a well man, and almost everyone who saw him noted how much he had deteriorated in just a few weeks. Typically a sea voyage would act as a tonic for his body and spirit, but not this time. Moreover, Hopkins, too, was very sick through much of the conference and could barely participate. He would be left in North Africa recovering as the rest

From left: Anna Boettiger, Sarah Churchill,
President Franklin D. Roosevelt, ship's captain, Harry Hopkins.

of the party made its way back to the United States. Finally, Roosevelt's friend and gatekeeper for much of his presidency, Pa Watson, died during the return trip. The Republican claim that the Roosevelt administration was nothing but a group of old sick men was beginning to look like a lot more than just election-year tripe.

While Roosevelt made his way across the Atlantic, the Combined Chiefs met to discuss operations to bring the war to a conclusion. During the conversations a terrific row, not reflected in the minutes, took place over which plan for crossing the Rhine and entering Germany would be approved. Before the chiefs were separate plans from Eisenhower and his subordinate, Field Marshal Montgomery. General Marshall later said that the debate was very hot and called it a "very acid meeting." At stake was whether Montgomery would be allowed to close on and cross the Rhine as the primary effort, while the American forces stood down; or whether, as Eisenhower wished, both the American and British armies would close on the Rhine together. The matter was finally decided in favor of Eisenhower's position, but not until there were threats from Eisenhower and Marshall to resign, as well as an offer to bring the entire matter to the president and prime minister. In any event, this last great squabble among the chiefs was made moot when General Omar Bradley's American troops seized an intact bridge across the Rhine at Remagen and started crossing in large numbers.

As the *Quincy* berthed in Grand Harbour Valetta on February 2, it was watched from across the harbor by Churchill aboard the light cruiser HMS *Sirius*. It had barely docked when a long list of visitors started queuing up to see the president. Roosevelt was further fatigued by hosting a small dinner that night, which included the prime minister. Exhausted, FDR turned in early, and before dawn was aboard the *Sacred Cow* heading for the Crimea. Escorted by five fighters, which had joined his plane over Athens, the president landed at Saki Air Field just after noon. After enduring five more hours in a car, a worn-out Roosevelt was put up in the czar's bedroom suite in the Livadia Palace—the Romanovs' summer retreat before 1917 and a tuberculosis hospital after that. For most of the past two years the palace had been a German command center, and they had thoroughly looted and ruined the grounds prior to their hasty departure. All that remained of its prior grandeur were two paintings that the Soviets hung in Roosevelt's room.

As the Yalta discussions got under way they ranged far and wide, but Roosevelt was concerned with only three items: Poland, Soviet entry in the war against Japan, and the organization of the United Nations. The first session out of a total of eight between the Big Three focused on the current military situation and the immediate prospects for the future. For the most part the parties took turns boasting to each other how well they were doing. As they did so the domestic peace among Roosevelt's entourage was crumbling, as Byrnes had been excluded from the first meeting. His name was not on the entry list, and the Soviet guards had refused to admit him. Embarrassed, Byrnes stalked back to his room and said he would not come to dinner. Roosevelt's daughter talked him into attending, but not before he had a showdown with Roosevelt.

In a rage, Byrnes said that he had not come just for the ride. Roosevelt attempted to soothe him with some of his famed charm, but Byrnes had long ago become immune. Byrnes then threatened Roosevelt, telling FDR that if he was excluded again, he would not lift a finger to get Roosevelt's Yalta deals through a conservative Congress—the kiss of death.

This was a threat Roosevelt could not, and did not, ignore. Byrnes boasts in his memoirs that from that point on he had lunch and dinner with the president every day and met privately with Roosevelt before every dinner. Stalin later said of Byrnes that "he was the most honest looking horse thief he had ever met."

Unexpectedly, many of the issues that the Americans thought would be major stumbling blocks were decided rather easily. The first issue on the agenda was reparations. Stalin had one of his representatives brief a detailed plan to strip Germany bare. After a lengthy give-and-take, Churchill said, "If you wish a horse to pull a wagon you would at least have to give it fodder." Stalin agreed, but warned that "care should be taken that the horse did not turn around and kick you." It was then agreed that the Russians, as they had suffered the most, would get the bulk of any reparations. The Russians threw out a figure of $20 billion total, of which they would get $10 billion. The principle was agreed to, but the final number was thrown to a committee for future discussion. Interestingly, smaller nations were not included. Poland, for instance, had suffered horribly, but was not included in the reparations discussions. Obviously, as far as the Big Three were concerned, reparations were for the major powers to divvy up, and the smaller nations would have to settle for scraps. It was also agreed that everyone favored the dismemberment of Germany, but when Stalin detected some wavering among his Big Three colleagues that too was sent to committee. Finally, at Churchill's urging, and because Stalin and Roosevelt did not care much about the issue, France was admitted to the Allied Control Commission that would run occupied Germany.

Most crucially, from Roosevelt's viewpoint, the Russians compromised on plans for the United Nations. Final agreement had been held up at the Dumbarton Oaks Conference by Soviet insistence on sixteen votes in the

General Assembly, and the USSR's fear that it could be isolated in the Security Council. Stalin became particularly incensed when he related how tiny Finland, with the connivance of France and Britain, had the Soviet Union expelled from the League of Nations. Stalin, as he drank toasts with vodka he had ordered watered down, said he was fine with protecting the rights of small nations, but he would not allow them to dictate to the large powers. To this Churchill replied, "The eagle should permit the small birds to sing, and care not for wherefore they sang."

The next day, however, the Soviets had a new position. They would agree to the voting procedures for the Security Council, and reduced their claims for seats in the General Assembly to just three: Russia, Ukraine, and

President Franklin D. Roosevelt and Prime Minister Winston Churchill.

Belarus. Roosevelt, unwilling to see the conference break down over so minor a point, and believing that the General Assembly had no real power, instructed his negotiators to agree to the demand. At Byrnes's urging, Roosevelt went back and told Stalin that America would need three votes also. Without them the United Nations might founder in Congress, much as the League of Nations had twenty years before. Both Stalin and Churchill agreed to the request, but the United States never exercised its right to three votes.

Next on the agenda was Poland. For three days Roosevelt and Churchill worked on Stalin, but they had no leverage. There was one overriding reality determining Poland's fate: the Red Army, at tremendous cost, had occupied the country. Where the Red Army was, so ran the writ of the Soviet Union. Consequently, Stalin was free to place a communist government—the Lublin Poles—in power in Warsaw. Moreover, after seeing German forces use Poland as a high-speed avenue of approach into Russia twice in twenty-five years, Stalin was loath to agree to anything that weakened Russia's hold on its new buffer state.

Churchill acknowledged the weak Anglo-American bargaining position from the start, telling his personal secretary, Jock Colville: "Make no mistake, all the Balkans except Greece is going to be Bolshevized; and there is nothing I can do to prevent it. There is nothing I can do for poor Poland either." Roosevelt also knew he was playing a weak hand, telling senators in January, "Occupying forces had the power where their arms were present . . . the Russians had the power in eastern Europe. That it was quite impossible to have a break with them and that, therefore, the only practicable course was to use what influence we had to ameliorate the situation." Unfortunately the Anglo-Americans had precious little influence.

All that Roosevelt could hope for was to get as much out of Stalin as his limited bargaining power allowed, while never neglecting the fact that his Joint Chiefs considered Russia's entry into the Pacific war as vital to success. Over several bargaining sessions, Stalin relented on several points, but the definitions of his terms of agreement were so nebulous that he truly gave away nothing. After looking over the agreement, Leahy turned to Roosevelt and said: "Mr. President, this is so elastic that the Russians can stretch it all the way from Yalta to Washington without ever technically breaking it." Roosevelt replied, "I know, Bill—I know it. But it's the best I can do for Poland at this time."

The final major point, Soviet entry into the war against Japan, was rapidly settled in a private meeting between Stalin and Roosevelt. The Red Army would move against the Japanese within two or three months of Germany's surrender. In return, Roosevelt promised the Soviets that the status quo in Outer Mongolia (Soviet-controlled) would be preserved; the southern part of Sakhalin (lost to Japan in 1904) would be returned, with all adjacent islands; possession of Port Arthur and Dairen on lease restored, along with the rights to the railroads leading to these ports; and finally, that the Kuril Islands would be handed over to the Soviet Union. Despite the fact that most of these demands would come at China's expense, Roosevelt agreed to all of them without ever consulting China. There is no starker example of how little China counted in U.S. strategic calculations by 1945.

On this note, the Yalta Conference drew to a rapid conclusion. Since

From left: Vyacheslav Molotov, Averell Harriman, Joseph Stalin,
Air Marshal Sergei Khudyakov.

then it has been a matter of tremendous debate: Was Roosevelt swindled, was he too ill to negotiate properly, did he give in to the Soviets too easily, could he have gotten a better deal? There is not much that can be added to the literature on this topic, and without new evidence few minds can be changed by any argument presented here. But there are crucial points to be made.

First, Roosevelt was a very ill man, but the evidence presented by his doctors and all those who saw him in action agree that his performance was unhampered by illness. He sometimes rambled, and once in a while was forgetful, but Admiral Leahy's observations reflect what most everyone there observed: "It was my feeling that Roosevelt had conducted the Crimean Conference with great skill and that his personality dominated the discussions . . . The President looked fatigued as we left, but so did we all."

As to whether Roosevelt, or anyone else, could have gotten a better deal—the answer is undoubtedly not. Nothing could do away with the fact that the Red Army was in Poland, and would soon occupy the rest of eastern Europe. There was no way to reverse that on-the-ground fact without waging a renewed war with the Soviets. While some crazies may have thought well of that idea, there was no appetite among the great masses of Americans or Britons to turn on a wartime ally and run the butcher's bill up by more untold millions. The problem was never with the agreement. The ultimate fault and blame lies with Stalin, who violated the agreement as he saw fit.

Given this, why is the Yalta Conference still considered the conference of lies and deceits? Much of this is the result of how Roosevelt sold the conference once he got home. Speaking in front of Congress on March 1, he focused his presentation on the most agreeable parts and interpretations. He totally left out the agreements made to get Russia into the war against Japan. This, however, was justified on security grounds, as it would have been irresponsible to alert the Japanese of the approaching Red Storm. Still, once the agreements were revealed they fed on the perception that there remained a "Pandora's Box of Yalta secrets" that compromised U.S. interests. This perception had begun when the White House, in late March, was forced to admit that Roosevelt had agreed to the Soviets' having three votes in the United Nations General Assembly. As *Time* magazine reported it: "The Big Three had practiced to deceive their Allies and the world. Roosevelt, Churchill and Stalin had made a secret bargain on voting in the postwar World Assembly—and kept it secret. The bargain was bad enough, but the deceit was worse."

Why Roosevelt deemed it necessary to keep this from Congress and the American people has never been adequately explained. It was an unforced error, as the agreement could have been explained in practical terms—we needed the Soviets in the war against Japan to save thousands of American lives. But the damage was done. When the secrecy was added to Soviet bad faith, the Yalta Conference could not help but become a lightning rod for political controversy that stretches to the present day.

On April 5, Roosevelt explained to reporters his thinking about why he agreed to giving the Soviets three votes, without explaining why he kept it a secret. The interview concluded as follows:

Roosevelt: I told Stettinius to forget about it. I am not awfully
keen for three votes in the Assembly. It is the little fellow who
needs votes in the Assembly.
Reporter: They don't decide anything, do they?
Roosevelt: No.

By this time Roosevelt had only a week to live.

The president had gone to Warm Springs for a much-needed rest. On
the eve of his death, Morgenthau drove two hours from Florida, where he
was staying with his ill wife, to have dinner with the president. As he wrote:
"I was terribly shocked when I saw him. I found that he had aged terrifi-
cally and looked very haggard. His hands shook so that he started to knock
glasses over." Morgenthau was still trying to sell the president on his plan
for a hard peace for Germany when Roosevelt's female guests, including
Lucy Rutherfurd, entered the room, ending the conversation.

The next morning he appeared much better. But just after 1:00 P.M. he
complained of a terrific pain in the back of his neck. A few minutes later
the president slipped into a coma and died in his bed at 3:35.

In 1932, the columnist Walter Lippmann wrote: "Franklin D. Roosevelt is a
highly impressionable person, without a firm grasp of public affairs and
without strong convictions. He is an amiable man with many philan-
thropic impulses, but he is not the dangerous enemy of anything. He is too
eager to please . . . Franklin D. Roosevelt is no crusader. He is no tribune of
the people. He is no enemy of entrenched privilege. The notion that Wall
Street fears him is preposterous. He is no crusader. . . . He is a pleasant man
who, without any important qualifications for the office, would very much
like to be President."

Few commentators have so misjudged his man. Was Roosevelt a great
president? I will leave his actions prior to the Second World War to the
judgment of others. But World War II challenged Americans to rise to
greatness. Many measured up, but those who were there would agree that
Roosevelt led the way and throughout the war stood at the pinnacle of
events.

He was still there when his part in the Washington war ended.

* * *

The Washington war continued, as it has for all of the decades since. But the next phase of the war would have a different president leading a new supporting cast. For the most part, they would not argue over the conduct of the war, with the dropping of the atomic bomb being a possible exception. Their Washington war would revolve around a new contest: the Cold War.

ACKNOWLEDGMENTS

First and foremost, I want to thank my wife, Sharon. Without her unstinting support and constant deliveries of high-energy drinks, morsels of food, and heaps of affection, this book would likely have never been finished.

I also want to thank my agent, Eric Lupfer, and my editor, Tracy Devine, who were a constant well of support and inspiration throughout the entire writing process. A special thanks goes to editor Emily Hartley, who picked the book up and carried it across the goal line. Susanna Sturgis is to be thanked and congratulated for a magnificent job copyediting what I "mistakenly" thought was a finished manuscript.

I also want to thank historians John Gooch, Williamson Murray, and Robert Citino for reviewing the manuscript and making many hundreds of suggestions and recommendations that hugely enhanced the quality of this book. Of course, any remaining manuscript errors are entirely my fault. I also want to thank a good friend, Major (retired) Mike McManus, who, while not a professional historian, has absorbed more knowledge of World War II than any person I know. His insights were invaluable.

My thanks as well to the superb team at Ballantine Bantam Dell/Random House: Lexi Batsides, Steve Messina, Virginia Norey, Carlos Beltrán, Mary Moates, Colleen Nuccio, Mark Maguire, Kim Hovey, Jennifer Hershey, Kara Welsh, and Gina Centrello.

Finally, I want to thank my bosses at the Marine Corps War College—Brigadier General William Bowers, Colonel David Eskelund, and Rebecca Johnson—who provided me an immense amount of much-appreciated support as I completed this manuscript.

Source Notes

Part One: Preparing the Battlefield

1: Inching Toward War

3 **"You must not talk that way to the President"** General Douglas MacArthur, *Reminiscences* (McGraw-Hill, 1964), p. 101.

4 **"I could not come out and say a war was coming"** James Roosevelt, *My Parents: A Differing View*, as quoted in Susan Dunn, *1940: FDR, Willkie, Lindbergh, Hitler—the Election amid the Storm* (Yale University Press, 2013), p. 328.

4 **"merchants of death"** Arthur M. Schlesinger, Jr., and Roger Bruns, eds., *Congress Investigates: A Documented History, 1792–1974*, vol. 4 (New York: Chelsea House Publishers, 1975), p. 2749.

5 **Moreover, he persuaded FDR to make the speech** Cordell Hull, *The Memoirs of Cordell Hull*, vol. 1 (Macmillan, 1948), p. 544.

5 **He then asked for the peaceful nations** Robert Dallek, *Franklin D. Roosevelt and American Foreign Policy, 1932–1945* (Oxford University Press, 1979), p. 148.

5 **"Quarantine Speech"** The speech can be listened to here: https://archive.org/details/FDRQuarantineSpeech.

5 **"Keep America Out of War"** Cordell Hull, *The Memoirs of Cordell Hull*, vol. 1 (Macmillan, 1948), p. 545.

5 **Rather he was trying to set an attitude** Dorothy Borg, "Notes on Roosevelt's 'Quarantine' Speech," *Political Science Quarterly* 72, no. 3 (September 1957), pp. 405–433.

5 **"dismayed by the widespread violence of the attacks"** Sumner Welles, *Seven Decisions That Shaped History* (Harper & Brothers, 1951), p. 13.

5 **"I frankly thought there would be more criticism"** *The Secret Diary of Harold L. Ickes*, vol. 1, *The First Thousand Days* (Simon & Schuster, 1954), p. 232.

5 **"Frankly I do not believe any of these newspapers"** Franklin Delano Roosevelt, *F.D.R.: His Personal Letters, 1928–1945*, vol. 1 (Duell, Sloan and Pearce, 1950), p. 726. For an excellent analysis of the aftermath of the "Quarantine Speech" see John McV. Haight, Jr., "Roosevelt and the Aftermath of the Quarantine Speech," *The Review of Politics* 24, no. 2 (April 1962): 233–259.

7 **"Boys, here is where I cash in my chips"** David Robertson, *Sly and Able: A Political Biography of James F. Byrnes* (W. W. Norton, 1994), p. 254.

8 **Afterward, financier Bernard Baruch** Jordan A. Schwarz, *The Speculator: Bernard Baruch in Washington, 1917–1965* (University of North Carolina Press, 1981), p. 319.

8 **When rumors of his plans to get rid of members of his own party leaked** Robertson, *Sly and Able*, p. 270.

9 **"We'll forget about it"** James F. Byrnes, *All in One Lifetime* (Harper & Brothers, 1958), p. 104.

9 **Even as Roosevelt was consumed** François R. Velde, "The Recession of 1937: A Cautionary Tale," *Economic Perspectives* 33, no. 4 (2009): 16–37. See http://papers.ssrn.com/sol3/papers.cfm?abstract_id=1523267.

10 **"punch drunk from the punishment"** Kenneth S. Davis, *FDR*, vol. 4, *Into the Storm, 1937–1940* (Random House, 1993), p. 107.

2: WARS ARE WON IN THE DETAILS

12 **Unfortunately, while Congress accepted** Rodney A. Grunes, "The Institutional Presidency," in William D. Pederson, ed., *A Companion to Franklin Roosevelt* (Wiley-Blackwell, 2011), p. 376.

12 **Byrnes, after reading the letter** James F. Byrnes, *All in One Lifetime* (Harper & Brothers, 1958), p. 106.

3: ROOSEVELT FINDS A WAR CONSIGLIERE

15 **Why was Hopkins chosen for this role?** Robert Sherwood, *Roosevelt and Hopkins: An Intimate History* (Harper & Brothers, 1948), p. 100.

16 **She sued for divorce and was awarded** Henry H. Adams, *Harry Hopkins* (G. P. Putnam's Sons, 1977), pp. 44–45.

16 **"Cultivate the President's family"** Michael Hiltzik, *The New Deal* (Free Press, 2012), p. 161.

16 **"a mind like a razor, a tongue like a skinning knife"** As quoted in Hiltzik, *The New Deal*, p. 161.

17 **"He did not bore FDR, ever"** Christopher D. O'Sullivan, *Harry Hopkins: FDR's Envoy to Churchill and Stalin* (Rowman & Littlefield, 2015), p. 53.

17 **although he was a rabid New Dealer** Rosenman Oral History, FDR Library: Oral Histories, Box 2.

18   "Hopkins was given to confident self-righteousness"   Hiltzik, *The New Deal*, p. 160.

20   The ship's paper, *The Blue Bonnet*   Sherwood, *Roosevelt and Hopkins*, pp. 78–79.

4: EARLY MANEUVERS

22   Hull firmly believed war could only be avoided   John Morton Blum, *From the Morgenthau Diaries: Years of Urgency, 1938–1941* (Houghton Mifflin, 1965), p. 44.

23   "tickled pink that the President is thinking"   Ibid., p. 46.

24   Waiting for them in the president's office   Also present were Solicitor General Robert H. Jackson and Colonel James Burns, an ordnance officer who worked as a liaison between the White House and the army chief of staff's office.

25   "informal conversations with the President"   Forrest C. Pogue, *George C. Marshall*, vol. 1, *Education of a General, 1880–1939* (Penguin, 1991), p. 325.

25   "a little sketch . . . is the most effective"   Ibid., p. 325 (emphasis added).

25   For their first one-on-one meeting   For the remainder of this book the Army Air Corps will be referred to as the "air force," despite the fact that the independent Air Force did not come into existence until 1947.

27   When the armistice was declared   Thomas N. Coffey, *Hap: The Story of the U.S. Air Force and the Man Who Built It; General Henry H. "Hap" Arnold* (Viking Press, 1982), p. 93.

28   In his memoirs, Arnold mentions a smear   H. H. Arnold, *Global Mission* (Harper & Brothers, 1949), p. 171.

29   "That is exactly what I want"   Blum, *From the Morgenthau Diaries: Years of Urgency, 1938–1941*, p. 70.

29   Over the next year the production   Conrad Black, *Franklin Delano Roosevelt: Champion of Freedom* (PublicAffairs, 2003), p. 502.

5: HOT DOGS AT HYDE PARK

30   In the end, all Roosevelt felt able to do   For a copy of this letter see http://www.jewishvirtuallibrary.org/jsource/ww2/fdr041439.html. To see Hitler commentary on the letter to the Reichstag, see https://www.youtube.com/watch?v=XUIYZwSHheA.

31   Equally important, the senators' comments   Conrad Black presents an excellent overview of Roosevelt's political maneuvering at the time. See Conrad Black, *Franklin Delano Roosevelt: Champion of Freedom* (PublicAffairs, 2003), pp. 516–520.

31   Only Germany's absence from the Court of Peace   Ibid., p. 522.

32 **"Frankly, I think it would be an excellent thing"** Elliott Roosevelt, ed., *F.D.R.: His Personal Letters, 1928–1945,* vol. 2 (Duell, Sloan and Pearce, 1950), p. 806.

34 **"I'm sure he would come to the conclusion"** Joseph Alsop and Robert Kintner, *American White Paper: The Story of American Diplomacy and the Second World War* (Simon & Schuster, 1940), p. 45.

34 **"more reliable than those of the State Department"** Ibid., p. 45.

34 **"Well, Captain, we might as well face facts"** Ibid., p. 46.

Part Two: Opening Rounds

6: First Salvos

37 **"Well, Bill, it has come at last"** Joseph Alsop and Robert Kintner, *American White Paper: The Story of American Diplomacy and the Second World War* (Simon & Schuster, 1940), pp. 58–70.

37 **"I not only sincerely hope so"** Kenneth S. Davis, *FDR,* vol. 4, *Into the Storm* (Random House, 1993), p. 488.

38 **"Speak for England, Arthur!"** Donald Cameron Watt, *How War Came: The Immediate Origins of the Second World War, 1938–1939* (Pantheon, 1990), pp. 578–579.

38 **"I wonder how long we are prepared"** Lynne Olson, *Troublesome Young Men: The Rebels Who Brought Churchill to Power and Helped Save England* (Farrar, Straus and Giroux, 2008), p. 209.

38 **"I have said not once but many times"** Fireside Chat 14: on the European War (September 3, 1939), at https://millercenter.org/the-presidency/presidential-speeches/september-3-1939-fireside-chat-14-european-war.

40 **"Let no group assume the exclusive"** The American Presidency Project, "Message to Congress Urging Repeal of the Neutrality Law, September 21, 1939."

40 **"a wanton encouragement of aggression"** Henry L. Stimson and Mc-George Bundy, *On Active Service in Peace and War* (Harper, 1947), p. 317.

42 **Perhaps he already saw that no less** Conrad Black, *Franklin Delano Roosevelt: Champion of Freedom* (PublicAffairs, 2003), pp. 540–541.

7: The State Department at War . . . with Itself

43 **"a personal record of no runs–no hits–no errors"** Robert Sherwood, *Roosevelt and Hopkins: An Intimate History* (Harper & Brothers, 1948), p. 135.

45 **A rumor, current at the time** Thomas Raymond Church, "The Hull-Welles Controversy," unpublished thesis, University of Texas, 1968.

46 **"Welles was first and foremost tough minded"** *Time,* August 11, 1941.

47 **"stabbed in the heart by an icicle"** Ibid.

48   **"In general, I was not a social intimate"**   Cordell Hull, *The Memoirs of Cordell Hull*, vol. 1 (Macmillan, 1948), p. 199.

49   **"You would think I had been pouring tea"**   Michael Fullilove, *Rendezvous with Destiny: How Five Extraordinary Men Took America into the War and into the World* (Penguin, 2013), p. 33.

50   **According to Bullitt's deputy**   Benjamin Welles, *Sumner Welles: FDR's Global Strategist* (St. Martin's Press, 1997), p. 245.

50   **The next day, after hearing**   Welles's complete report to the president is available in FDR Library, Welles Papers, Box 155.

50   **She had no better luck**   Fullilove, *Rendezvous with Destiny*, p. 37.

51   **"I can assure you that Germany's aim"**   Welles report to the president, p. 49.

51   **"Germany would strengthen"**   Ibid., p. 54.

51   **The first Parisians he met**   Fullilove, *Rendezvous with Destiny*, p. 48.

52   **"the destruction of Hitlerism"**   Welles report to the president, p. 83.

8: BLITZKRIEG

55   **"I suppose that Churchill was the best man"**   Harold Ickes, *The Lowering Cloud: The Secret Diary of Harold L. Ickes* (Simon & Schuster, 1955), p. 176.

55   **"Many New Dealers have bored Roosevelt"**   Sherwood, *Roosevelt and Hopkins*, p. 2.

55   **"Hopkins had an almost feminine sensitivity"**   Ibid., p. 2.

56   **"that he was there . . . He lived there"**   Rosenman Oral History, FDR Library: Oral Histories, Box 2.

56   **"During the years when Harry was at the height"**   Ibid.

56   **"Someday you may be sitting where I am now"**   Sherwood, *Roosevelt and Hopkins*, pp. 2–3.

57   **"extend to the opponents of force"**   For a copy of the entire speech, see https://www.mtholyoke.edu/acad/intrel/WorldWar2/fdr19.htm.

9: ROOSEVELT'S GENERAL

59   **"black spot on my boyhood"**   Marshall Foundation, Lexington, VA—Pogue interviews.

62   **The issue was finally forced**   Mark Stoler, *George C. Marshall: Soldier-Statesman of the American Century* (Twayne, 1989), p. 62.

62   **"he was all out for a total effort"**   Sherwood, *Roosevelt and Hopkins*, p. 113.

63   **"You came before us without even a piece"**   Forrest C. Pogue, *George C. Marshall*, vol. 2, *Ordeal and Hope, 1939–1942* (Viking Press, 1966), p. 28.

63   **"It makes me dizzy if we don't get it"**   Blum, *From the Morgenthau Diaries: Years of Urgency, 1938–1941*, p. 139.

63   "His respect for Marshall and his confidence"   Ibid., p. 139.

64   "Well, I still think you are wrong"   Ibid., p. 140.

10: A RELUCTANT INDUSTRIAL COMPLEX

65   German field marshal Paul von Hindenburg   Paul von Hindenburg, *Out of My Life*, vol. 2 (Harper & Brothers, 1921), p. 124.

66   "Here, one month was a blood-sweating"   Donald Nelson, *The Arsenal of Democracy* (Harcourt Brace and Company, 1946), p. 32.

66   Articles such as those by Charles Beard   Earl A. Molander, "Historical Antecedents of Military-Industrial Criticism," *Military Affairs* 40, no. 2 (April 1976): 59–63.

66   "more of a court than a congressional"   Robert Byrd, C. Hall, and Mary Sharon, *Senate, 1789–1989*, vol. 1, *Addresses on the History of the United States Senate* (Government Printing Office, 1988), p. 487.

66   "I confidently predict that when the Senate"   Ibid., p. 487.

67   "Some checker-playing, beer-drinking"   James Ledbetter, *Unwarranted Influence: Dwight D. Eisenhower and the Military Industrial Complex* (Yale University Press, 2011), p. 15.

67   Senator Harry Truman later called the committee   Harry S. Truman, *Memoirs of Harry S. Truman: Years of Decision*, vol. 1 (Da Capo Press, 1986), p. 190.

67   "if you are going to go to war"   Stimson Diaries, August 26, 1940.

11: THE SPHINX

72   "he has not the same zest"   Kenneth S. Davis, *FDR*, vol. 4, *Into the Storm* (Random House, 1993), p. 533.

72   "sincere statement of untruth"   Ibid., p. 594.

72   "Too many promises will be extracted"   Susan Dunn, *1940: FDR, Willkie, Lindbergh, Hitler—the Election Amid the Storm* (Yale University Press, 2013), p. 136.

74   "I like him. He is the kind of man"   Frances Perkins, *The Roosevelt I Knew* (Viking Press, 1946), p. 133.

75   "For God's sake, do you want a president"   David Robertson, *Sly and Able: A Political Biography of James F. Byrnes* (W. W. Norton, 1994), pp. 293–294.

75   "Don't do it, Henry"   Charles Peters, *Five Days in Philadelphia: The Amazing "We Want Willkie!" Convention of 1940 and How It Freed FDR to Save the Western World* (PublicAffairs, 2005), p. 150.

75   "If Willkie is an amateur"   Dunn, *1940*, p. 81.

78   The Germans did not know their man   Ibid., p. 117.

12: REPUBLICANS SEIZE THE WAR DEPARTMENT

80   "He appeared, in critical or confusing times"   Elting E. Morrison, *Turmoil and Tradition: A Study of the Life and Times of Henry L. Stimson* (History Book Club, 2003), p. 479.

80   "statesman incognito"   John G. Clifford, "Grenville Clark and the Origins of Selective Service," *The Review of Politics* 35, no. 1 (January 1973): 17–40.

81   But, two weeks later, when he and Hopkins did meet   Sherwood, *Roosevelt and Hopkins*, p. 157.

81   Somewhat buoyed by Roosevelt's tacit endorsement   Morrison, *Turmoil and Tradition*, p. 480.

84   As many of those who had served with him   Keith E. Eiler, *Mobilizing America: Robert P. Patterson and the War Effort 1940–1945* (Cornell University Press, 1997), pp. 11–30.

85   "had a great sympathy for people"   Doris Kearns Goodwin, *No Ordinary Time: Franklin & Eleanor Roosevelt; The Home Front in World War II* (Simon & Schuster, 1994), p. 23.

86   "broke down and cried like a baby"   Kenneth S. Davis, *FDR*, vol. 4, *Into the Storm* (Random House, 1993), p. 575.

86   "toughest man in Washington"   Eiler, *Mobilizing America*, pp. 19–23.

87   "force unqualified by reasonable doubt"   Morrison, *Turmoil and Tradition*, p. 492.

13: YOUR BOYS ARE NOT GOING TO BE SENT
INTO ANY FOREIGN WARS

89   "Immediate needs now are"   Warren F. Kimball, ed., *Churchill and Roosevelt: The Complete Correspondence*, vol. 1 (Princeton University Press, 1984), p. 37.

89   "It has now become most urgent"   Ibid., p. 45.

90   Roosevelt liked it and brought the scheme up   Stimson Diaries, August 2, 1940.

90   "very much encouraged"   Stimson Diaries, August 15, 1940.

90   The matter was discussed   Stimson Diaries, August 16, 1940.

92   "Roosevelt wants to put a lien on the fleet"   William Manchester and Paul Reid, *The Last Lion: Winston Spencer Churchill, Defender of the Realm, 1940–1965* (Little, Brown, 2012), p. 156.

93   "If his promise to keep our boys out"   James MacGregor Burns, *Roosevelt: The Lion and the Fox* (Harcourt, Brace & World, 1956), p. 443.

93   "I hope you will make some speeches"   Goodwin, *No Ordinary Time*, p. 182.

94   The "dear guru" letters   Burns, *Roosevelt: The Lion and the Fox*, p. 448.

94   **He proclaimed it a "remarkable somersault"**   Ibid., p. 448.

94   **Soon thereafter, a telegram from Ed Flynn**   Davis, *FDR*, vol. 4, *Into the Storm*, p. 620.

94   **"Evidently, you've got to say it again"**   Burns, *Roosevelt: The Lion and the Fox*, p. 448.

95   **"It's not necessary. If we're attacked"**   Sherwood, *Roosevelt and Hopkins*, p. 191.

95   **"Roosevelt with his known faults"**   Lynne Olson, *Those Angry Days: Roosevelt, Lindbergh, and America's Fight over World War II, 1939–1941* (Random House, 2013), p. 263.

14: Business Gets Its Field Marshals

97   **He was a huge man, a former boxer**   Many of the personal descriptions of individuals in this book are drawn from W. M. Kiplinger's book, *Washington Is Like That* (Harper & Brothers, 1942).

100   **His tremendous drive, steel-trap memory**   Matthew Josephson, *Sidney Hillman, Statesman of American Labor* (Doubleday, 1952).

101   **He was a big man, "allergic to exercise"**   Kiplinger, *Washington Is Like That*, p. 441.

101   **"He was pleasant, patient and conciliatory"**   David Brinkley, *Washington Goes to War* (Alfred A. Knopf, 1988), p. 66.

102   **On Washington's hottest days**   Ibid., p. 55.

102   **"just be a period in which Germany"**   Henderson presentation to the Industrial War College, "Organization and Administrative Problems of the Price Administrator" (April 1950). National Defense University Library at Fort McNair, Washington, D.C.

103   **"Just look at Leon"**   FDR Library, Henderson Diary, Henderson Papers, Box 36.

103   **As Knudsen (business) and Hillman (labor)**   Eliot Janeway, *The Struggle for Survival* (Weybright and Talley, 1951), p. 154.

104   **Henderson, for once, was satisfied**   Henderson presentation to the Industrial War College, "Organization and Administrative Problems of the Price Administrator" (April 1950). NDU Library at Fort McNair, Washington, D.C.

104   **"Biblically big"**   "The Cabinet: Emperor Jones," *Time*, January 13, 1941.

104   **Despite Knudsen's continual declarations**   Steven Fenberg, *Unprecedented Power: Jesse Jones, Capitalism, and the Common Good* (Texas A&M Press, 2001), p. 371.

106   **"there was no line of business"**   Ibid., p. 345.

106   **"admiring friends"**   *Time*, January 25, 1937.

107   **"take a bodyguard with him"**   George Vincent Sweeting, "Building the Arsenal of Democracy: The Government's Role in Expansion of Industrial Ca-

pacity, 1940 to 1945," unpublished dissertation, Columbia University, 1994, p. 138.

107 **"collection of tough-minded younger men"** Janeway, *The Struggle for Survival*, p. 133.

107 **While Jones bargained for the best deal** Ibid., p. 133.

108 **"howl and an uproar from Leon"** Stimson Diaries, October 16, 1940.

108 **"industry would not work"** Stimson Diaries, December 17, 1940.

109 **"the President has been advised"** Stimson Diaries, December 18, 1940.

109 **Both men took the meeting** Ibid.

109 **"Conferences with the President"** Ibid.

110 **"Czar, Poobah or Akhoond of Swat"** Franklin D. Roosevelt, *Complete Presidential Press Conferences of Franklin D. Roosevelt*, 25 vols. (Da Capo Press, 1972), pp. 622–631.

15: BANKROLLING BRITAIN

111 **"So far as he [Roosevelt] is concerned"** Sherwood, *Hopkins and Roosevelt*, p. 224.

112 **"Might it not be possible"** Davis, *FDR*, vol. 4, *Into the Storm*, p. 48.

113 **"That man's effort is flagging"** Manchester and Reid, *The Last Lion*, p. 202.

115 **"the most dreadful four hours"** Michael R. Beschloss, *Kennedy and Roosevelt: The Uneasy Alliance* (W. W. Norton, 1980), p. 231.

115 **They discussed the possibility of the United States** Stimson Diaries, December 3, 1940.

116 **His waking hours were devoted to fishing** Sherwood, *Roosevelt and Hopkins*, p. 223.

116 **"the most important of his life"** Winston S. Churchill, *The Second World War*, vol. 2, *Their Finest Hour* (Houghton Mifflin, 1949), p. 558.

116 **"if anything," but he thought it unwise** Sherwood, *Roosevelt and Hopkins*, p. 224.

116 **"He didn't seem to have any clear idea"** Ibid., p. 224.

117 **"What I am trying to do"** Ibid., p. 225.

117 **"Of course not, I only want"** Black, *Franklin Delano Roosevelt*, p. 605.

117 **Churchill did his best to make amends** Joseph P. Lash, *Roosevelt and Churchill 1939–1941: The Partnership That Saved the West* (W. W. Norton, 1976), p. 264.

118 **"The people of Europe"** The entire speech is available at https://www.mtholyoke.edu/acad/intrel/WorldWar2/arsenal.htm.

119 **"the most untruthful, the most dastardly"** James MacGregor Burns, *Roosevelt: The Soldier of Freedom, 1940–1945* (Harcourt Brace Jovanovich, 1970), p. 44.

119   *Though, too, sail on*   Sherwood, *Roosevelt and Hopkins*, p. 234.

120   **Willkie's trip was so successful**   Lynne Olson, *Those Angry Days: Roosevelt, Lindbergh, and America's Fight Over World War II, 1939–1941* (Random House, 2013), p. 282.

120   **"It was a bit of campaign oratory"**   Davis, *FDR*, vol. 4, *Into the Storm*, p. 118.

121   **"Harry, if you are going to London"**   Henry H. Adams, *Harry Hopkins* (G. P. Putnam's Sons, 1977), p. 200.

122   **"I guess you could say"**   Sherwood, *Roosevelt and Hopkins*, p. 289.

123   **"rotund, smiling—red faced"**   Ibid., p. 238.

123   **As British intelligence had been listening**   Manchester and Reid, *The Last Lion*, p. 278.

123   **"Neither the President or myself care"**   Sherwood, *Roosevelt and Hopkins*, p. 289.

123   **"The people here are amazing"**   Ibid., p. 245.

124   **"My husband is fighting in North Africa"**   FDR Library, Hopkins Papers, Sherwood Files, Box 304.

125   **"Are they going to hold out?"**   Adams, *Harry Hopkins*, p. 210.

126   **"Apparently the first thing"**   Christopher D. O'Sullivan, *Harry Hopkins: FDR's Envoy to Churchill and Stalin* (Rowman & Littlefield, 2014), p. 53.

126   **"It was Byrnes who made the voting checks"**   As quoted in David Robertson, *Sly and Able: A Political Biography of James F. Byrnes* (W. W. Norton, 1994), pp. 96–297.

16: COLORS BECOME RAINBOWS

128   **In his view, the German threat**   For the fate of the Rainbow plans see Mark S. Watson, *Chief of Staff: Prewar Plans and Preparations* (Chief of Military History, United States Army, 1950), pp. 13–108.

128   **The president, who consistently demonstrated**   Maurice Matloff and Edwin Snell, *Strategic Planning for Coalition Warfare: 1943–1944* (Center of Military History, United States Army, 1953), p. 20.

128   **"Are we not forced into reframing"**   Lawrence Guyer, *The Joint Chiefs and the War in Europe*, National Archives, Box 218, Section 1, pp. 1–70.

129   **"day and night for ten consecutive days"**   Letter, Admiral Stark to Admiral J. O. Richardson, Records of the Joint Committee on Pearl Harbor: Exhibits (1946), p. 971.

129   **By November 2, 1940, he was happy enough**   Mitchell Simpson, *Harold R. Stark: Architect of Victory, 1939–1945* (University of South Carolina Press, 1989), p. 66.

129   **"we might not *lose everywhere*"**   Matloff and Snell, *Strategic Planning for Coalition Warfare*, p. 25 (emphasis added).

129 **Accordingly, Stark's memo set out possible options** President's Secretary's File (PSF), 1933–1945: Box 4, Navy Department: Plan Dog Case file (FDR Library).

130 **Though Stark's assessment laid out four options** According to Guyer's unpublished history, *The Joint Chiefs and the War in Europe,* the first drafts of this document had five choices: 1. War with Japan in which we have no allies; 2. War with Japan with the British Empire and the Netherlands as allies; 3. War with Japan in which it is aided by Italy and we have no allies; 4. War with Germany and Italy in which Japan would not be initially involved and in which we would be allied with the British; 5. Remaining out of the war and dedicating ourselves exclusively to building up our defense of the Western Hemisphere, plus continued matériel support to Britain.

131 **"British leadership has not had the competence"** Guyer, *The Joint Chiefs and the War in Europe,* Section 1, p. 31.

131 **Perhaps the comments of the chief** Alanbrooke's true name was Alan Francis Brooke. His title was 1st Viscount Alanbrooke. The names Brooke and Alanbrooke are often used interchangeably; this history will use the former name, unless his title or rank is used at the same time.

131 **"Half of our Corps and Divisional Commanders"** Alex Danchev and Daniel Todman, eds., *War Diaries, 1939–1945: Field Marshal Lord Alanbrooke* (Weidenfeld & Nicolson, 2001), p. 243.

132 **"afford nor do we need to entrust"** Matloff and Snell, *Strategic Planning for Coalition Warfare,* p. 29; and Watson, *Chief of Staff: Prewar Plans and Preparations,* pp. 10–112.

133 **"nibbling away at the fringes of German power"** Guyer, *The Joint Chiefs and the War in Europe,* Section 1, p. 40.

133 **This agreement was later integrated** "United States–British Staff Conversation Report, ABC-1, March 27, 1941" in Steven T. Ross, *U.S. War Plans: 1938–1945* (Routledge, 1997), pp. 67–101.

17: HAMLET FINDS AN ADMIRAL

136 **The cabinet burst into a roar of laughter** Stimson Diaries, April 25, 1941.

138 **"It takes three years to build a ship"** Winston Churchill, *The Second World War,* vol. 3, *The Grand Alliance* (Boston: Houghton Mifflin, 1985), p. 265.

139 **The cheered all-outers** Samuel Rosenman, *Working with Roosevelt* (Da Capo Press, 1972), p. 283.

139 **Stimson, Knox, and Morgenthau wanted Roosevelt** Stimson Diaries, May 23, 1941.

139 **Based on this Manichaean outlook** Stimson Diaries, May 24, 1941.

139 **"waiting for the accidental shot"** Stimson Diaries, May 23, 1941.

139 **"The people must not be brought to combat evil"** Burns, *Roosevelt: The Soldier of Freedom,* p. 91.

139   "waiting to be pushed into a situation"   Ibid., p. 92.

140   Stimson claimed the only benefit   Stimson Diaries, May 6, 1941.

140   "He [Stark] is a timid and ineffective man"   Ibid.

140   "Endowed with a superior intellect"   Samuel Eliot Morison, *History of United States Naval Operations in World War II*, vol. 1, *The Battle of the Atlantic, September 1939–May 1943* (University of Illinois Press, 2001), p. 115.

140   "meaner than hell . . ."   Robert William Love, Jr., *The Chiefs of Naval Operations* (Naval Institute Press, 1980), p. 140.

141   "Once convinced he had the right answer"   Thomas B. Buell, *Master of Sea Power: A Biography of Fleet Admiral Ernest J. King* (Little, Brown, 1980), p. 11.

18: *DRANG NACH OSTEN*

144   Having seen what Germany did   Guyer, *The Joint Chiefs and the War in Europe*, Section 1, p. 67.

144   British strategists agreed, but were grateful   *General Strategy Review of the British Chiefs of Staff*, July 31, 1941, as quoted in Lawrence Guyer, *The Joint Chiefs and the War in Europe*, Section 1, p. 68.

144   "This precious and unforeseen period"   Stimson Diaries, June 23, 1941.

146   "treat Mr. Hopkins with the identical confidence"   Susan Butler, ed., *My Dear Mr. Stalin: The Complete Correspondence of Franklin Roosevelt and Joseph V. Stalin* (Yale University Press, 2008), p. 36.

146   Not an empty diplomatic word passed   Hopkins Papers, Sherwood Files: FDR Library, Box 306. This report of the meeting comes from notes and a draft article Hopkins was writing for *The American Magazine*.

147   During this first meeting Stalin   Hopkins Papers, Sherwood Files: FDR Library, Box 306.

148   Hopkins was forced to explain   Ibid.

148   "learn the Germans can be killed"   Ibid.

149   Growing visibly angrier as he spoke   Ickes, *The Lowering Cloud*, pp. 392–393.

149   Embarrassed in front of other cabinet members   Stimson Diaries, August 1, 1941.

149   In fact, Ambassador Oumansky   Stimson Diaries, July 31, 1941.

149   "I am sick and tired"   Davis, *FDR*, vol. 4, *Into the Storm*, p. 253.

149   "I didn't get half a chance with him"   Stimson Diaries, August 1, 1941.

150   "You are going to let plain hatred"   Pogue interview, Tape 10. http://marshallfoundation.org/library/wp-content/uploads/sites/16/2014/05/Marshall_Interview_Tape10.pdf.

19: Rendezvous at Sea

152 **When he had downtime** Hopkins Papers, Sherwood Files, Box 306.

152 **"There is a wild rumor"** Stimson Diaries, August 6, 1941.

153 **"At last we have gotten together"** Jean Edward Smith, *FDR* (Random House, 2008), p. 500.

154 **"Every word seemed to stir the heart"** Churchill, *The Second World War*, vol. 3, *The Grand Alliance*, p. 384.

155 **"wrong war, in the wrong ocean"** Burns, *Roosevelt: The Soldier of Freedom*, p. 150.

155 **After much debate and several rewrites** For a copy see http://avalon.law .yale.edu/wwii/atlantic.asp.

155 **"He was really incapable of a personal friendship"** Goodwin, *No Ordinary Time*, p. 304.

155 **"Each imagines that he is indispensable"** Ibid., p. 204.

156 **"I propose writing to you personally"** George Marshall, *The Papers of George Catlett Marshall*, vol. 2, *"We Cannot Delay," July 1, 1939–December 6, 1941* (Johns Hopkins University Press, 1986), pp. 602–604.

20: Production Battles

158 **America, he claimed, would have only months** Maury Klein, *A Call to Arms: Mobilizing America for World War II* (Bloomsbury Press, 2013), p. 193.

159 **"He's a Democrat!"** Public Papers of the Presidents of the United States: F. D. Roosevelt, 1941, vol. 10 (Government Printing Office, 1941), p. 116.

160 **"I was rather discouraged by his attitude"** Stimson Diaries, May 29, 1941.

162 **A compromise was then quickly brokered** Author interview with David Ginsburg on October 11, 2007. David Ginsburg was Leon Henderson's deputy during this period and later was general counsel to the Office of Price Administration.

163 **"all balled up on all of these initials"** Brinkley, *Washington Goes to War*, p. 107.

165 **"the whole industrial might of the United States"** Donald Nelson, *The Arsenal of Democracy* (Harcourt Brace and Company, 1946), p. 130.

166 **To influence Roosevelt, he befriended** Robert Nathan, "GNP and Military Mobilization," *Journal of Evolutionary Economics* 4, no. 1 (March 1994): 9.

166 **"We know you want"** Nelson, *The Arsenal of Democracy*, pp. 130–134.

167 **"Consolidated Balance Sheet"** I have not been able to find a complete copy of this document. For those interested, I have found a copy of the first sixty pages in the FDR Library; see the President's Secretary's File (PSF), 1933–1945, Box 82. A cover letter on the copy sent to the president, with commentary and examples, can be found at FDR Library, Hopkins Papers, Sherwood Files, Box 304.

168   **"they are fine and sincere"**   FDR Library, Henderson Diary, Henderson Papers, Box 36.

168   **"When I asked them about military requirements"**   Nathan, "GNP and Military Mobilization," p. 12.

21: WAR IN THE PACIFIC

170   **"They hate us"**   William L. Langer and S. Everett Gleason, *The Undeclared War: 1940–1941* (Harper & Brothers, 1953), p. 466.

171   **Marshall and Stark concurred**   David M. Kennedy, *Freedom from Fear: The American People in Depression and War, 1929–1945* (Oxford University Press, 2005), p. 506.

171   **"the Japs are having a real drag down"**   Harold Ickes, *The Lowering Cloud: The Secret Diary of Harold L. Ickes* (Simon & Schuster, 1955), p. 567 (emphasis added).

172   **Roosevelt, however, failed to issue an order**   Waldo Heinrichs, *Threshold of War: Franklin D. Roosevelt & American Entry into World War II* (Oxford University Press, 1988), pp. 161–178.

173   **Nomura was almost deaf**   Burns, *Roosevelt: The Soldier of Freedom*, p. 134.

174   **"There were few misunderstandings"**   Ibid., p. 155.

175   **When Stimson told him it contained reports**   Stimson Diaries, November 26, 1941.

176   **Hopkins later reported that Hull**   Sherwood, *Roosevelt and Hopkins*, p. 431.

176   **"no cussing out could have been stronger"**   Hull, *The Memoirs of Cordell Hull*, vol. 1, pp. 196–197.

177   **This sage advice caused Churchill to pause**   W. Averell Harriman and Elie Abel, *Special Envoy to Churchill and Stalin, 1941–1946* (Random House, 1975), pp. 111–112.

177   **Churchill soon signed off**   Churchill, *The Second World War*, vol. 3, *The Grand Alliance*, p. 608.

178   **"War with Japan"**   Michael E. Ruane, "'WAR!' How a Stunned Media Broke the Pearl Harbor News," *The Washington Post*, December 6, 2011.

178   **"For God's sake why were the ships tied up"**   Goodwin, *No Ordinary Time*, p. 292.

180   **"I have fought every trend"**   Robert Byrd, C. Hall, and Mary Sharon, *Senate, 1789–1989*, vol. 1, *Addresses on the History of the United States Senate* (Government Printing Office, 1988), p. 518.

180   **The escort was considered necessary**   Brinkley, *Washington Goes to War*, p. 91.

181   **"Hull is certain the Japs are planning"**   Stimson Diaries, December 7, 1941.

181   **"What is the significance"**   Forrest C. Pogue, *George C. Marshall*, vol. 2, *Ordeal and Hope* (Viking Press, 1966), p. 229.

181 **"be on the alert accordingly"** Ibid., p. 229.

182 **In fact, Marshall was talking to Short** Ibid., p. 230.

PART THREE: THE BEGINNING

22: A CITY AT WAR

187 **When he went before Congress** Robert Dallek, *Franklin Roosevelt and American Foreign Policy, 1932–1945* (Oxford University Press, 1979), p. 312.

188 **"The news is bad but will be better"** Kimball, *Churchill and Roosevelt*, p. 286.

188 **"It seemed like a completely changed world"** Henry L. Stimson and McGeorge Bundy, *On Active Service in Peace and War*, p. 317.

188 **But it was a transformation** Much of this description of Washington during the war years is drawn from W. M. Kiplinger's book *Washington Is Like That* (Harper Brothers, 1942).

190 **"twelve years, Mrs. Nesbitt"** Laura Shapiro, "The First Kitchen," *The New Yorker* (November 22, 2010). See http://www.newyorker.com/magazine/2010/11/22/the-first-kitchen.

194 **By mid-1942 the director** Brinkley, *Washington Goes to War*, p. 77.

194 **In any case, the police** Ibid., p. 76.

23: CHURCHILL COMES TO TOWN—ARCADIA CONFERENCE

196 **Churchill was given the Lincoln Bedroom** Smith, *FDR*, p. 543.

197 **Roosevelt, impressed by Churchill's ability** Black, *Franklin Delano Roosevelt*, p. 704.

197 **"I must have a tumbler"** Goodwin, *No Ordinary Time*, p. 302.

197 **"The Prime Minister of Britain has nothing"** Sherwood, *Roosevelt and Hopkins*, p. 442.

198 **"Let the children have their night of fun"** Black, *Franklin Delano Roosevelt*, p. 705.

198 **"I have no doubt whatever"** Ibid., p. 704.

198 **"What kind of people"** Sherwood, *Roosevelt and Hopkins*, p. 458.

199 **"Some chicken . . . some neck"** Ibid., p. 443.

200 **In the final analysis** Diane K. DeWaters, *The World War II Conferences in Washington, D.C. and Quebec City: Franklin D. Roosevelt and Winston S. Churchill*, unpublished dissertation, University of Texas, 2008, p. 5.

200 **"degree of secretarial license"** Alex Danchev, *Establishing the Anglo-American Alliance* (Brassey's, 1990), p. 7.

200 **"I know damn well it isn't"** General Thomas T. Handy, *Handy Oral History* (U.S. Army Military History Institute, Carlisle, PA).

203 "I was struck by the fact"   Churchill, *The Second World War,* vol. 3, *The Grand Alliance,* p. 668.

203 "he did not seem to have full access"   Ibid., p. 668.

203 "would have to take my resignation"   Stimson Diaries, December 25, 1941.

203 "that a paper had been going around"   Ibid.

203 After first recounting the Allied experiences   Minutes of the Arcadia Conference, Meeting, December 25, 1941, p. 3, at https://history.state.gov /historicaldocuments/frus1941-43/comp1.

204 An impressed Stimson later said   Stimson Diaries, December 28, 1941.

204 "You should work on Churchill"   FDR Library, Hopkins Papers, Box 136.

204 Churchill exploded, saying that he would not stand   Sherwood, *Roosevelt and Hopkins,* p. 457.

208 "an association strikingly lacking in empathy"   John Keegan, *Churchill's Generals* (Grove Press, 1991), p. 51.

208 "A position of great honor"   Ibid., p. 52.

208 "the handsomest man in town"   *Time,* August 10, 1942.

210 But before they made a plan   Stimson Diaries, January 2, 1942.

210 "this assignment virtually closed his career"   Larry Bland, ed., *The Papers of George Catlett Marshall,* vol. 3 (Johns Hopkins University Press, 1991), p. 57.

210 "Still working the China problem"   Robert H. Ferrell, *The Eisenhower Diaries* (W. W. Norton, 1981), p. 42.

211 "General, I don't give a damn"   Mark Perry, *Partners in Command: George Marshall and Dwight Eisenhower in War and Peace* (Penguin, 2007), pp. 58–59.

211 "There was a sense of Hitler's doom being sealed"   Goodwin, *No Ordinary Time,* p. 312.

212 "It is fun to be in the same decade with you"   Ibid., p. 313.

24: BUREAUCRATIC ROADKILL

213 "as America was four times Britain's size"   Norman Beasley, *Knudsen: A Biography* (McGraw-Hill, 1947), p. 335.

213 Beaverbrook made his deliberatively provocative statement   Nelson, *Arsenal of Democracy,* pp. 186–189.

214 "Let no man say it cannot be done"   Roosevelt's State of the Union Address, January 6, 1942.

214 "Ickes was dissatisfied with Knudsen"   Stimson Diaries, May 12, 1941.

214 "Knudsen was slow and lacked initiative"   Ibid.

214 "whoever takes this job"   Janeway, *The Struggle for Survival,* p. 217.

215 "You will run again"   Ibid., p. 217.

215 Others in the SPAB leadership   Ibid., p. 216.

216   "Look here, judge"   Beasley, *Knudsen,* pp. 341–342.

217   **Jones went to Knudsen's home**   Arthur Herman, *Freedom's Forge: How American Business Produced Victory in World War II* (Random House, 2012), p. 166.

217   **Patterson was in favor of the idea**   Stimson Diaries, May 29, 1941 (emphasis added).

217   **Stimson had to be persuaded**   Stimson Diaries, January 15, 1942.

218   **That meant increasing America's**   Comments by Robert Nathan on Stacy May report of December 4, 1941, National Archives, Record Group 179, Box 1.

218   **In comparison with these organizations' charters**   Janeway, *The Struggle for Survival,* p. 226.

218   **"The Chairman's . . . *decisions shall be final*"**   Executive Order 9024, January 16, 1942, National Archives, Record Group 179.2.1 (emphasis added).

218   **Before the ink had dried**   "The United States at War: Development and Administration of the War Program," Bureau of the Budget, Historical Reports on War Administration, 1946, p. 107.

218   **"Somervell is quietly hot-tempered"**   "Streamlining the Army," *Time,* March 9, 1942.

219   **"He was an instrument"**   John Kennedy Ohl, *Supplying the Troops: General Somervell and American Logistics in WWII* (Northern Illinois University Press, 1994), p. 4.

219   **Nelson liked to persuade people**   John Lord O'Brian, Oral History Project, Columbia University, pp. 548–551. Quoted in Calvin Lee Christman, "Ferdinand Eberstadt and Economic Mobilization for War, 1941–1943," PhD dissertation, Ohio State University, 1971, pp. 89–91.

219   **Remarkably, Leon Henderson, who would belatedly**   Author interview with David Ginsburg (Leon Henderson's legal assistant at OPM) on October 11, 2007.

220   **"Somervell would come into a meeting"**   Nathan, "GNP and Military Mobilization."

222   **"'The only trouble with that plant'"**   *The New Republic,* April 13, 1942, p. 487.

25: A BITTER SEASON

223   **"In all the war, I never received"**   Churchill, *The Second World War,* vol. 3, *The Grand Alliance,* p. 620.

223   **"I think we got a hell of a beating"**   Barbara Tuchman, *Stilwell and the American Experience in China, 1941–1945* (Macmillan, 1970), p. 300.

224   **He was, however, as dumbfounded**   Mark Perry, *Partners in Command* (Penguin, 2007), p. 11.

224   **Eisenhower returned several hours later**   Ed Cray, *General of the Army: George C. Marshall, Soldier and Statesman* (W. W. Norton, 1990), p. 265.

224   **Marshall, agreeing that the Philippines**   Stephen E. Ambrose, *Eisenhower: Soldier and President* (Simon & Schuster, 1991), p. 61.

225   **"looks like MacArthur is losing his nerve"**   Robert H. Ferrell, *The Eisenhower Diaries* (W. W. Norton, 1981), p. 46.

225   **"the plan of President Quezon"**   Louis Morton, *Strategy and Command: The First Two Years* (Washington, DC: Center of Military History, United States Army, 1962), p. 190.

225   **"ghastly in their responsibility"**   Stimson Diaries, February 9, 1942.

225   **"I immediately discarded everything"**   Pogue, *George C. Marshall,* vol. 2, *Ordeal and Hope,* pp. 247–248.

226   **"It was a pretty hard day"**   Stimson Diaries, February 10, 1942.

226   **"I therefore give you"**   MacArthur Papers, Record Group 2, MacArthur Memorial Archives and Library.

226   **This transaction is still shrouded in mystery**   This story was first broken only in 1979 by Carol Petillo. See Carol M. Petillo, "Douglas MacArthur and Manuel Quezon: A Note on an Imperial Bond," *Pacific Historical Review* 48, no. 1 (February 1979): 107–117. Confirmation was later published by MacArthur's stenographer, who had written up most of the documents; see Paul P. Rogers, "MacArthur, Quezon, and Executive Order Number One: Another View," *Pacific Historical Review* 52, no. 1 (February 1983): 93–100.

228   **"The trouble, Admiral, is"**   Williamson Murray and Allan Millett, *A War to Be Won* (Harvard University Press, 2000), p. 250.

229   **"The loss by submarines"**   Ernest J. King and Walter Muir Whitehill, *Fleet Admiral King: A Naval Record* (W. W. Norton, 1952), pp. 455–456.

229   **In fact, his main biographer**   Buell, *Master of Sea Power.*

230   **General Stilwell, then commanding**   Joseph W. Stilwell and Theodore H. White, eds., *The Stilwell Papers* (Da Capo Press, 1991), p. 8.

230   **In fact, once the decision to intern**   Goodwin, *No Ordinary Time,* p. 322.

230   **During their first conversation on the topic**   Stimson Diaries, February 11, 1942.

230   **"General DeWitt [Fourth Army commander] is anxious"**   Stimson Diaries, February 19, 1942.

231   **"we have carte blanche to do what we want"**   Stetson Conn, "The Decision to Evacuate the Japanese from the Pacific Coast," in Greenfield, *Command Decisions* (Center of Military History, 1960), p. 143.

231   **"We shall maintain our connection"**   The "Magic Background of Pearl Harbor," Department of Defense, Message No. 174.

231   **"If it is a question"**   Kai Bird, *The Chairman: John J. McCloy & the Making of the American Establishment* (Simon & Schuster, 1992), pp. 149–150.

231   **"I am afraid of no easy solution"**   Ibid., p. 151.

232   **As for Roosevelt's in-house conscience, Eleanor**   *Collier's,* October 16,

1941, pp. 18–21. https://www2.gwu.edu/~erpapers/documents/articles /challengetoamerican.cfm.

232 **"If Stimson had insisted"**   Francis Biddle, *In Brief Authority* (Doubleday, 1962), p. 226.

26: Joint Chiefs

233 **"This war can't be won with men"**   Sherwood, *Roosevelt and Hopkins,* p. 492.

236 **Marshall ended by telling the president**   Pogue interviews with Marshall; see Tape 15, February 14, 1957: http://marshallfoundation.org/library/wp -content/uploads/sites/16/2014/05/Tape_15.pdf.

237 **"I took him in the room"**   Pogue interview, February 15, 1957. See http:// marshallfoundation.org/library/wp-content/uploads/sites/16/2014/05 /Tape_15.pdf.

237 **"It would never have done"**   Pogue interview, February 14, 1957. See http:// marshallfoundation.org/library/wp-content/uploads/sites/16/2014/05 /Marshall_Interview_Tape15.pdf.

237 **"King . . . is an arbitrary, stubborn type"**   Ferrell, *The Eisenhower Diaries,* p. 50.

238 **"Admiral King came to see me"**   Pogue interviews, February 14, 1957: http://marshallfoundation.org/library/wp-content/uploads/sites/16/2014/05 /Tape_15.pdf.

238 **Its 174,000 men were poorly trained**   Eric Larrabee, *Commander in Chief: Franklin Delano Roosevelt, His Lieutenants and Their War* (Simon & Schuster, 1987), p. 114.

238 **"It remains to me a mystery"**   Winston S. Churchill, *The Second World War,* vol. 4, *The Hinge of Fate* (1950; Houghton Mifflin, 1985), p. 120.

240 **"I am going to put these men"**   Larrabee, *Commander in Chief,* p. 103.

27: Striking Back

242 **Captain F. S. Low, working on the Navy's operations staff**   Ernest J. King and Walter Muir Whitehill, *Fleet Admiral King: A Naval Record* (W. W. Norton, 1952), p. 376.

242 **When King brought the question to Arnold**   H. H. Arnold, *Global Mission* (Harper & Brothers, 1949), p. 298.

243 **"So far as Combined Fleet was concerned"**   As quoted in Andrew P. Stohlman, "The Doolittle Raid in History and Memory," master's thesis, University of Nebraska, 1999.

244 **What they could not figure out**   Lawrence Guyer, *The Joint Chiefs and the War in Europe,* Section 3, p. 4 (pages are not numbered in this section of the document).

244   **Roosevelt, in two long messages**   Kimball, *Churchill and Roosevelt,* pp. 390–400.

245   **"We've got to go to Europe and fight"**   Ferrell, *The Eisenhower Diaries,* p. 44.

245   **As early as February, Eisenhower**   Matloff and Snell, *Strategic Planning for Coalition Warfare,* p. 179.

245   **On March 25, Eisenhower**   Ibid., pp. 118–183.

245   **"In my talks with McCloy"**   Stimson Diaries, February 24, 1942.

245   **"I doubt any single thing"**   Sherwood, *Roosevelt and Hopkins,* p. 519.

245   **Roosevelt had himself sent**   Kimball, *Churchill and Roosevelt,* p. 399.

245   **The one uncertain element was King**   Guyer, *The Joint Chiefs and the War in Europe,* Section 3, p. 11.

246   **Roosevelt agreed**   Stimson Diaries, March 25, 1942.

246   **Hopkins also cabled Churchill**   FDR Library, Hopkins Papers, Box 136.

247   **"I liked what I saw of Marshall"**   Danchev and Todman, *War Diaries, 1939–1945,* p. 246.

247   **Marshall was equally unimpressed**   Sherwood, *Roosevelt and Hopkins,* p. 523.

248   **"fighting against the 'ghosts of the Somme'"**   Pogue interview, October 5, 1956.

248   **"virtually accepted the proposals"**   Pogue, *George C. Marshall,* vol. 2, *Ordeal and Hope,* p. 318.

248   **The next day he cabled Stimson**   Ibid., p. 318.

249   **"come clean much sooner than we did"**   Danchev and Todman, *War Diaries, 1939–1945,* p. 249.

249   **"I discovered that he had not studied"**   Ibid., p. 249.

249   **"appreciated that his [Marshall's] strategic ability"**   Ibid., p. 249.

28: DESERTING THE BEAR

254   **"Dickie [Lord Mountbatten] will explain to you"**   Kimball, *Churchill and Roosevelt,* p. 494.

254   **"As urgent as the mounting of BOLERO may be"**   Guyer, *The Joint Chiefs and the War in Europe,* Section 3, pp. 25–28.

255   **"If such is not the case"**   Guyer, *The Joint Chiefs and the War in Europe,* Section 3, p. 28. The President's Secretary's File (PSF), 1933–1945, Box 4, FDR Library.

255   **"I regard it as essential"**   Ibid., p. 29.

255   **"it might be better to consider"**   Ibid., p. 31. These statements were made at the White House conference on May 5, 1942.

256   **After requesting a straight answer**   *Foreign Relations of the United States, 1942,* vol. 3, p. 577: https://uwdc.library.wisc.edu/collections/frus/.

256   **Marshall with no hesitation replied, "Yes"**   Sherwood, *Roosevelt and Hopkins,* pp. 561–565.

29: STOPPING THE TIDE

259   **"We could reverse our rush of reinforcements"**   Stimson Diaries, June 7, 1942.

260   **But it was not until Field Marshal Dill**   FDR Library, Hopkins Papers, Box 194.

261   **"It looked like he [Roosevelt] was going"**   Stimson Diaries, June 17, 1942.

261   **Knox refrained from the debate**   Ibid.

261   **King's silence was not unusual**   George Elsey, a young officer who worked in the White House map room, said that "King was a sonofabitch to everyone he dealt with. But whenever he was in front of Roosevelt he turned into an obsequious dolt. It made me quite sick." Author's interview with George Elsey, July 12, 2014.

261   **"King wobbled around"**   Stimson Diaries, Wednesday, June 17, 1942.

262   **Stimson thought it a "foolish exercise"**   Ibid.

262   **"We were largely trying"**   Pogue interviews (notes), November 5, 1956.

262   **When it was complete**   Stimson Diaries, June 19, 1942. The President's Secretary's File (PSF), 1933–1945, Box 4, FDR Library.

262   **With their unanimous support**   Stimson Diaries, June 19, 1942.

262   **"no responsible British military authority"**   Churchill, *The Second World War,* vol. 4, *The Hinge of Fate,* p. 342.

263   **"strongly in favor of concentrating"**   Guyer, *The Joint Chiefs and the War in Europe,* Section 3, p. 49.

263   **Marshall was gratified to gain Brooke's support**   Danchev and Todman, *War Diaries, 1939–1945,* pp. 266–268.

263   **Marshall reiterated that opening**   Guyer, *The Joint Chiefs and the War in Europe,* Section 3, p. 50.

263   **"We fear the worst"**   Danchev and Todman, *War Diaries, 1939–1945,* p. 268.

263   **Neither the War nor the Navy secretary**   Stimson Diaries, June 21, 1942.

264   **Roosevelt then invited Marshall to speak**   Ibid.

264   **"This was one of the heaviest blows"**   Churchill, *The Second World War,* vol. 4, *The Hinge of Fate,* p. 383.

264   **"Nevertheless if the British need"**   Ibid., p. 383.

265   **Marshall reveled in the idea**   Pogue interviews, November 19, 1956. See http://marshallfoundation.org/library/wp-content/uploads/sites/16/2014/05/Tape_18.pdf.

265   **By this time, Marshall realized**   Stimson Diaries, June 22, 1942, and June 23, 1942. See also J. R. M. Butler, *Grand Strategy,* vol. 3, *June 1941–August 1942* (Her Majesty's Stationery Office, 1964), p. 629.

265   "preparations for BOLERO on as large a scale"   Butler, *Grand Strategy,* vol. 3, p. 627. Also see Guyer, *The Joint Chiefs and the War in Europe,* Section 3, p. 54.

265   "possibilities for GYMNAST"   Butler, *Grand Strategy,* vol. 3, p. 627.

265   "If, on the other hand, detailed examination shows"   Ibid., p. 628.

266   "the Day of the Dupes"   Ibid., p. 627.

266   "a large American force to cover everything"   Stimson Diaries, June 22, 1942.

266   "overthrow everything they had been planning for"   Ibid.

266   "failed to see that a leader"   Pogue interviews, November 13, 1956.

267   The Germans had spent all their time   Stimson Diaries, June 22, 1942.

267   "shrank from the image"   Ibid.

267   Convinced that ROUNDUP would not be made in 1943   Ibid.

267   "was talking of the most critical situations"   Ibid.

267   Stimson was not so sure   Sherwood, *Roosevelt and Hopkins,* p. 591.

268   "this has all along been in harmony"   Kimball, *Churchill and Roosevelt,* pp. 520–521.

30: ON TRACK

269   Dill was so taken aback   Gordon A. Harrison, *Cross-Channel Attack* (Army Center of Military History, 1951), p. 27. See also Stimson Diaries, July 12, 1942.

270   King expressed himself   24th Meeting of JCS, July 10, 1942, National Archives, Record Group 218.

270   "it was impossible to fulfill naval commitments"   Ibid.

270   As a result, the Joint Chiefs forwarded a memorandum   Stimson Diaries, July 10, 1942. For a complete copy of the memorandum see King and Whitehill, *Fleet Admiral King,* pp. 398–399.

270   "if the United States is to engage"   Guyer, *The Joint Chiefs and the War in Europe,* Section 3, p. 122. The entire memo is reproduced in Appendix E to chapter 3.

270   He concluded by emphasizing   Ibid.

270   After King had added a "little more punch to it"   Stimson Diaries, July 12, 1942.

271   "The trouble is neither he [Churchill]"   Ibid.

272   He had been a widower since 1937   *Time,* July 13, 1942.

272   FDR's attraction ended when   Curt Gentry, *J. Edgar Hoover: The Man and His Secrets* (W. W. Norton, 2001), p. 311.

273   According to Robert Sherwood   Sherwood, *Roosevelt and Hopkins,* p. 600.

273   "we would take up our dishes and go home"   Stimson Diaries, July 15, 1942.

273 **To all concerned he made it clear** Hayes, *The History of the Joint Chiefs in World War II*, p. 152.

273 **Despite this, both Marshall and Stimson thought** Stimson Diaries, July 15, 1942.

273 **That evening, Roosevelt had a long talk** Robert Sherwood, *Roosevelt and Hopkins*, p. 602.

273 **To make sure he got what he wanted** Appendix F to chapter 3 in Guyer, *The Joint Chiefs and the War in Europe*, Section 3. See also the President's Secretary's File (PSF), 1933–1945, Box 4, FDR Library.

274 **Rather, he wanted to stay home with Louise** Robert Sherwood, *Roosevelt and Hopkins*, p. 607.

274 **"It will be a queer party"** Danchev and Todman, *War Diaries, 1939–1945*, p. 280.

275 **They had what they wanted for 1942** The entire memo is reproduced in Appendix G to chapter 3 in Guyer's *The Joint Chiefs and the War in Europe*, Section 3.

275 **"more evil the President's decision appears to be"** Stimson Diaries, July 26, 1942.

275 **"British leaders have lost their nerve"** Stimson Diaries, July 27, 1942.

275 **"had made the decision"** Matloff and Snell, *Strategic Planning for Coalition Warfare*, p. 284.

276 **"The President has the happy faculty"** Stimson Diaries, August 6, 1942.

276 **He strongly advised Stimson** Stimson Diaries, July 10, 1942.

276 **"I am just a little disturbed about TORCH"** Matloff and Snell, *Strategic Planning for Coalition Warfare*, p. 295.

277 **"Okay, full blast"** Kimball, *Churchill and Roosevelt*, p. 520.

277 **"I found that he fully agreed with me"** Stimson Diaries, September 28, 1942.

277 **After hours of lambasting, Churchill erupted** Churchill, *The Second World War*, vol. 4, *The Hinge of Fate*, pp. 494–497; W. Averell Harriman and Elie Abel, *Special Envoy to Churchill and Stalin, 1941–1946* (Random House, 1975), pp. 149–167.

277 **"Your words are of no importance"** Harriman and Abel, *Special Envoy*, p. 157.

277 **"Now they know the worst"** Kimball, *Churchill and Roosevelt*, p. 572.

31: THE GREAT FEASIBILITY DISPUTE

279 **"In the Battle of Washington"** Sherwood, *Roosevelt and Hopkins*, p. 631.

280 **Instead, he got all-out war** 77th Congress, 1st Session, Special Senate Committee investigating the National Defense Program, Hearings, April 21, 1942, pt. 12, pp. 508–509.

281   **Every day, dozens of field teams**   *Time,* February 9, 1942.

281   **Nathan's constant prodding inevitably led**   *Industrial Mobilization for War: History of the War Production Board and Predecessor Agencies* (Government Printing Office, 1947), p. 240.

282   **In bold language, the Army was told**   Memorandum from Stacy May to Donald Nelson, December 4, 1941, "Planning Committee Document," National Archives, Record Group 179, Box 1.

282   **"never in the long history of combat"**   Klein, *A Call to Arms,* p. 435.

282   **If the program was going to be salvaged**   Minutes of the Planning Committee, March 16, 1942, National Archives, Record Group 179, Box 4.

283   **Nelson sent the note**   Roosevelt Safe Files, FDR Library, Hyde Park. See http://docs.fdrlibrary.marist.edu/psf/box3/a43kk01.html.

283   **Unbeknownst to Nelson, General Marshall**   Ibid.

283   **Nathan was clearly losing the fight**   John Brigante, "The Feasibility Dispute: Determination of War Production Objectives for 1942–1943," an unpublished case study by the Committee on Public Administration Cases, 1950, p. 53.

284   **How they thought the military would acquiesce**   JCS minutes, October 20, 1942, National Archives, Record Group 218.

284   **In a break with protocol**   Brigante, "The Feasibility Dispute," p. 84.

284   **"To me this is an inchoate mass of words"**   FDR Library, Hopkins Papers, Box 234.

285   **Somervell concluded by stating**   National Archives, Minutes of War Production Board, October 6, 1942; National Archives, Record Group 179.2.2, Box 3.

287   **Kuznets then chimed in with the idea**   Minutes of the War Production Board, October 6, 1942.

287   **"If we say that the objectives"**   Memorandum from Simon Kuznets to the Planning Committee, "Proposals for Adjustment of the Program," October 8, 1942, Minutes of the Planning Committee, April 8, 1942, National Archives, Record Group 179, Box 4.

287   **The Joint Chiefs took up the matter**   JCS minutes, October 20, 1942, National Archives, Record Group 218.

288   **"About as well as or better"**   Author interview with David Ginsburg on October 11, 2007.

288   **"Into the Army as a private last week"**   *Time,* May 10, 1943.

32: NO RUBBER, NO WAR

290   **By the end of 1941 the nation had stockpiled**   Paul Wendt, "The Control of Rubber in World War II," *Southern Economic Journal* 13, no. 3 (January 1947): 203–227.

291   **The next day, Roosevelt joked with reporters**   William M. Tuttle, Jr., "The Birth of an Industry: The Synthetic Rubber 'Mess' in World War II," *Technology and Culture* 22, no. 1 (January 1981): 35–67.

291   **To meet an expected need of 600,000 tons**   Nelson, *The Arsenal of Democracy*, p. 294.

292   **"We find the existing situation"**   FDR Library, Hopkins Papers, Box 230.

292   **"would take his coat off"**   *Time*, February 15, 1943.

293   **But once again, when offered**   Herman Miles Somers, *Presidential Agency, OWMR: The Office of War Mobilization and Reconversion* (Greenwood Press, 1950), p. 28.

293   **The dispute turned nasty**   *Time*, August 7, 1944.

294   **His replacement, the equally tough-minded Bradley Dewey**   *Time*, August 7, 1944.

294   **From Pearl Harbor until the end of the war**   Paul A. C. Koistinen, *Arsenal of World War II* (University Press of Kansas, 2004), p. 259.

294   **"Ickes is now captain of our souls"**   *Time*, June 9, 1941.

296   **But Henderson stuck to his guns**   *Time*, May 18, 1942.

296   **Initially the WPB proposed limiting vehicles**   Bruce Catton, *The War Lords of Washington* (Greenwood Press, 1948), p. 159.

297   **Henderson then rattled off the facts**   Ibid., p. 162.

298   **During one of General Marshall's TORCH briefings**   Pogue interviews, October 5, 1956.

298   **When Roosevelt airily asked**   Evelyn M. Cherpak, ed., *The Memoirs of Admiral H. Kent Hewitt* (Naval War College Press, 2004), p. 146.

298   **"Sir, all I want to tell you is this"**   Rick Atkinson, *An Army at Dawn: The War in North Africa, 1942–1943* (Henry Holt, 2002), p. 31.

299   **"A great politician is not of necessity"**   Martin Blumenson, *The Patton Papers: 1940–1945* (Da Capo Press, 1996), p. 94.

299   **James Farley, until recently one of Roosevelt's closest confidants**   *Time*, November 16, 1942.

299   **His only private comment**   William D. Hassett, *Off the Record with FDR, 1942–1945* (Rutgers University Press, 1958), p. 135.

299   **His only public comment**   *The New York Times*, November 7, 1942.

PART FOUR: NEW FRONTS

33: TORCH

304   **"We have landed in North Africa"**   Grace Tully, *F.D.R., My Boss* (Charles Scribner's Sons, 1949), pp. 263–264.

304   **"What remains of the honor of France"**   Burns, *Roosevelt: The Soldier of Freedom*, p. 296.

304   "If Norway were invaded"   *Time,* November 30, 1942.

305   "Prostitutes are used; they are seldom loved"   *The Nation,* November 21, 1942, pp. 529–530.

305   Distressed, Roosevelt refused to talk   Rosenman, *Working with Roosevelt,* p. 364.

305   Stimson thought that "Morgenthau was sunk"   Stimson Diaries, November 16, 1942.

305   After reading the group the entirety   Ibid.

307   At the time, Frankfurter considered it a "cruel thing"   John Morton Blum, ed., *From the Morgenthau Diaries: Years of War, 1941–1945* (Houghton Mifflin, 1967), November 17, 1942. See http://www.fdrlibrary.marist.edu /_resources/images/morg/md0845.pdf, pp. 190A–190B.

307   "I said he was a most ruthless person"   Ibid., pp. 190A–190B.

307   "It was typical of Frankfurter"   Ibid., p. 190C.

308   At 11:00 P.M., Roosevelt called to tell Stimson   Stimson Diaries, November 16, 1942.

308   As pressure mounted Hopkins prevailed on Roosevelt   FDR Library, Map Room Papers, 1941–1945, Box 3.

308   As for the present situation   Franklin D. Roosevelt's Statement on North African Policy: November 17, 1942. See http://avalon.law.yale.edu/wwii /north-af.asp.

308   In a personal message to Eisenhower   Burns, *Roosevelt: The Soldier of Freedom,* p. 297.

308   "My children it is permitted you"   FDR Library, Map Room Papers, 1941–1945, Box 3.

308   There is no question that Darlan understood   Eisenhower to Marshall, November 24, 1942, NA/RG 165 [OCS, 381 TORCH]; Marshall Foundation, http://marshallfoundation.org/library/memorandum-for-the-president-64/.

309   "relieved the Allies of their embarrassment"   Churchill, *The Second World War,* vol. 4, *The Hinge of Fate,* p. 578.

34: NEW HANDS AT THE HELM

312   Thus, Henderson became the target   Davis, *FDR,* p. 602.

312   "My lack of politeness"   *Time,* December 21, 1942.

312   "I belong to the group"   Ibid.

312   By mid-1942 Americans had $84 billion   *Time,* August 31, 1942.

313   In a stern message to Congress   A transcript of this Fireside Chat (September 7, 1942) is available at http://millercenter.org/president/fdRoosevelt /speeches/speech-3328.

313   In a stroke Roosevelt had denied   *Time,* September 7, 1942.

313   Congress grumbled, debated, swore, and fought   *Time,* October 12, 1942.

313 "the office was important, but less so" James F. Byrnes, *Speaking Frankly* (Harper & Brothers, 1947), p. 18.

313 "Suppose," said Catton, "you and I had an argument" Catton, *The War Lords of Washington*, p. 203.

314 "Harry," Byrnes said, "stay the hell out of my business" Sherwood, *Roosevelt and Hopkins*, p. 614.

314 He was also hated by Congress Brinkley, *Washington Goes to War*, p. 133.

314 On December 8, 1942, he resigned Klein, *A Call to Arms*, p. 467.

314 When he eventually went to New York *Time*, December 6, 1943.

315 In his eyes, the problem was Donald Nelson Stimson Diaries, July 20, 1942.

315 Nelson's incapacity for the job Ibid.

315 Stimson, in his diary, said Stimson Diaries, July 22, 1942.

316 The entire first half of the meeting Ibid.

316 He was wounded, promoted to captain *Time*, September 28, 1942.

317 "a remarkably blunt and forceful character" Janeway, *The Struggle for Survival*, pp. 238–239.

318 Swope was kind enough *Time*, September 28, 1942.

318 "Then you're Joe So-and-So" Catton, *The War Lords of Washington*, p. 242.

318 But he was not without some negative traits Koistinen, *Arsenal of World War II*, p. 329.

318 "CMP flooded the fighting fronts with firepower" Janeway, *The Struggle for Survival*, pp. 238–239.

319 "the bitterest fight I ever had" Nelson, *The Arsenal of Democracy*, p. 383.

319 "would take from the Army and Navy" Stimson Diaries, November 23, 1942.

319 As it was, Stimson believed "he was crazy to try it" Stimson Diaries, November 25, 1942.

319 He only wished that they had not picked him Nelson, *The Arsenal of Democracy*, p. 384.

319 Still, he was sure Stimson Diaries, November 23, 1942.

320 Roosevelt told him that was a good idea Stimson Diaries, November 25, 1942.

320 "He is a weak man" Stimson Diaries, November 26, 1942.

320 "Well. If you need me, come to Poppa" Nelson, *The Arsenal of Democracy*, p. 385.

321 New Dealers were soon putting it about Washington *The New York Times*, February 14, 1943.

321 "Nelson is not the man" *Time*, February 15, 1943.

321 Byrnes closed by reminding Roosevelt Byrnes, *All in One Lifetime*, pp. 172–173.

323 "I will fight to hold my job" *The New York Times,* March 3, 1943.

323 One observer punned that Nelson's problem *The New York Times,* February 17, 1943.

323 Once told by Stimson and Hopkins Stimson Diaries, February 18, 1943.

324 Neither man ever brought up the WPB chairmanship Bernard M. Baruch, *Baruch: The Public Years* (Holt, Rinehart and Winston, 1960), p. 316.

35: Byrnes Cast upon Troubled Waters

326 On May 14, he sent Roosevelt a letter FDR Library, President's Secretary's File, 1933–1945, James F. Byrnes, 1942–1945, Box 132.

326 But as journalists repeatedly pointed out *Time,* February 15, 1943.

326 "discussion of the over-all legal authority" As quoted in Herman Miles Somers, *Presidential Agency, OWMR: The Office of War Mobilization and Reconversion* (Greenwood Press, 1950), p. 37.

326 "Tinkering, tinkering, always tinkering" *Time,* February 15, 1943.

327 Byrnes continually warned his staff Somers, *Presidential Agency, OWMR,* p. 58.

327 "Byrnes, unlike too many timid czars before him" *Time,* June 21, 1943.

328 In July 1941, Roosevelt, looking for important work Executive Order 8839, dated July 30, 1941.

328 "it bore all the earmarks of futility" Dean Acheson, *Present at the Creation: My Years in the State Department* (W. W. Norton, 1969), p. 40.

328 Perkins was a stocky, slit-eyed, tweedy *Time,* August 25, 1941.

328 Acheson described him Acheson, *Present at the Creation,* pp. 40–41.

328 Within months of its coming into existence *Time,* April 27, 1942.

329 Rather, Hopkins, Jones, Hull, and others Donald G. Stevens, "Organizing for Economic Defense: Henry Wallace and the Board of Economic Warfare's Foreign Policy Initiatives, 1942," *Presidential Studies Quarterly* 26, no. 4 (Fall 1996).

329 Hull sent Dean Acheson to represent him Stimson Diaries, July 16, 1942.

329 This was particularly true Nelson, *Arsenal of Democracy,* pp. 267–268.

329 As Jones put it, though the president ordered him Jesse Jones, *Fifty Billion Dollars: My Thirteen Years with the RFC* (Macmillan, 1951), p. 489.

330 Wallace accused Jones of obstructing Ibid., p. 489.

330 On April 23, FDR had everyone in Stevens, "Organizing for Economic Defense."

330 "We knew that if you knew" Cordell Hull, *The Memoirs of Cordell Hull,* vol. 2 (Macmillan, 1948), pp. 1156–1157.

331 "A Washington saying of the past decade" *Time,* August 9, 1943.

331 But after months of back-and-forth bickering Jones, *Fifty Billion Dollars,* p. 492.

331 **But before that proposal could move forward** Gregory A. Fossedal, *Our Finest Hour: Will Clayton, the Marshall Plan and the Triumph of Democracy* (Hoover Institution Press, 1993), p. 93.

331 **"We are helpless when Jesse Jones"** Fenberg, *Unprecedented Power,* p. 455.

332 **He had been visiting Capitol Hill for months** *Time,* July 12, 1943.

333 **"I'm 69 now, but if I can't handle that little shit"** Ibid.

333 **"[Wallace's] tirade is so filled with malice"** Ibid.

333 **"that when he said his prayers that night"** Jones, *Fifty Billion Dollars,* p. 496.

333 **Byrnes claimed that he ended the meeting** Robertson, *Sly and Able,* p. 328.

333 **"They lived in peace but a short time"** John William Partin, "Assistant President for the Home Front: James F. Byrnes and World War II," unpublished dissertation, University of Florida, 1977.

334 **His top assistant, Milo Perkins, went down fighting** John C. Culver and John Hyde, *American Dreamer: The Life and Times of Henry A. Wallace* (W. W. Norton, 2001), p. 309.

334 **"If you have a disagreement with another agency"** Byrnes, *All in One Lifetime,* pp. 193–194.

36: A NON-UNITED FRONT

336 **Marshall further stated that before any further operations** Notes taken at meeting in the Executive Office of the President, November 25, 1942; JCS Records, National Archives, Record Group 218.

336 **In fact, Roosevelt had cabled Churchill** FDR Library, Map Room Papers, 1941–1945, Box 3.

337 **At that time, Leahy told the other chiefs** JCS minutes, July 10, 1942, National Archives, Record Group 218.

337 **This time Marshall appeared back in form** Notes taken at meeting in the Executive Office of the President, December 10, 1942; JCS Records, National Archives, Record Group 218.

338 **Failing that, even the preparations** Matloff and Snell, *Strategic Planning for Coalition Warfare,* pp. 363–382; see Guyer, *The Joint Chiefs and the War in Europe,* Section 3, pp. 137.

338 **On December 11, Embick's Joint Strategic Survey Committee** Guyer, *The Joint Chiefs and the War in Europe,* Section 3, pp. 159–160.

339 **These recommendations were discussed** Ibid., pp. 159–163.

339 **He concluded that conference** Ibid., p. 162.

340 **The point was made moot** FDR Library, Map Room Papers, 1941–1945, Box 8.

340 **"I prefer a comfortable oasis"** FDR Library, Map Room Papers, 1941–1945, Box 3.

340 **"Allow me to express my confidence"** FDR Library, Map Room Papers, 1941–1945, Box 8.

341 **After stating that Stalin might be suffering** Notes taken at meeting in the Executive Office of the President, January 7, 1943; JCS Records, National Archives, Record Group 218.

341 **"There is not a united front on that subject"** Ibid.

341 **He said he personally favored operations** Ibid.

342 **When asked what difficulties could be expected** Ibid.

342 **Just as crucially, when the great "feasibility dispute" ended** Memorandum from Somervell to Marshall, Joint U.S. Staff Planners' Directive J.P.S. 57/1/D, September 17, 1942, "Strength of Army for 1943," Somervell Desk File, National Archives, Record Group 160. See also Somervell Desk File, National Archives, Record Group 160, Box 6.

342 **Because of Somervell's reluctance** Dr. Robert R. Palmer, "The Mobilization of the Ground Army. The Army Ground Forces. Study No. 4," Historical Section—Army Ground Forces 1946, p. 11.

37: CASABLANCA

344 **"They swarmed down on us like locusts"** Albert Wedemeyer, *Wedemeyer Reports!* (Henry Holt, 1958), p. 192.

344 **The avalanche of papers caught** JCS minutes, May 8, 1943, National Archives, Record Group 218.

344 **When he could give no strategic rationale** Danchev and Todman, *War Diaries, 1939–1945*, p. 359.

345 **"The whole process is made more difficult"** Ibid., p. 360.

347 **"We are in the position of a testator"** Cray, *General of the Army*, p. 361.

347 **"You know that you must come to some agreement"** Danchev and Todman, *War Diaries, 1939–1945*, p. 362.

347 **By this time, Marshall had already agreed** Forrest Pogue, *George C. Marshall*, vol. 3, *Organizer of Victory* (Viking Press, 1973), p. 29.

348 **But when faced with a united** Guyer, *The Joint Chiefs and the War in Europe*, Section 3, p. 195.

349 **"We came, we listened, we were conquered"** Ray S. Cline, *Washington Command Post: The Operations Division* (Center of Military History, United States Army, 1959), pp. 236–237.

349 **And it is in this debate that the Americans** FDR Library, Map Room Papers, 1941–1945: Box 26; and Fredrick Aandahl, William M. Franklin, and William Slany, eds., *Foreign Relations of the United States, The Conferences at Washington, 1941–1942, and Casablanca, 1943* (Government Printing Office, 1958).

350 **His neck was in a noose and he knew it** Harry C. Butcher, *My Three Years with Eisenhower* (Simon & Schuster, 1946), p. 243.

350 "generals can make mistakes and be fired"   Sherwood, *Roosevelt and Hopkins*, p. 677.

351 "Look at him!"   Lord Moran, *Churchill: Struggle for Survival; Taken from the Diaries of Lord Moran* (Houghton Mifflin, 1966), p. 88.

351 "I almost laughed in his face"   Hassett, *Off the Record with FDR, 1942–1945*, p. 153.

352 But this is belied by the fact   Sherwood, *Roosevelt and Hopkins*, pp. 694–695.

353 "Negotiation with Hitler was impossible"   Ibid., p. 696.

353 "If anything happened to that man"   Larrabee, *Commander in Chief*, p. 39.

354 This pronouncement was followed up   FDR Library, Map Room Papers, 1941–1945, Box 8.

38: MAN—AND WOMAN—POWER

356 In general, each of these parties   Janeway, *The Struggle for Survival*, pp. 248–249.

356 For instance, getting approval   Stimson and Bundy, *On Active Service in Peace and War*, p. 474.

357 By the middle of 1942   *Time*, September 14, 1942.

357 But faced with intense demands   Committee of Records of War Administration, *The United States at War* (Da Capo Press, 1972), pp. 177–178.

357 Although disliked by most   Kiplinger, *Washington Is Like That*, p. 443.

357 He was a handsome man   Dean J. Kotlowski, *Paul V. McNutt and the Age of FDR* (Indiana University Press, 2015), p. 293.

357 "he has got more out of a head of platinum hair"   *Life*, January 29, 1940.

359 "a lot of callow New Dealers"   Kotlowski, *Paul V. McNutt and the Age of FDR*, p. 253.

359 "Harry, I've been robbing your roost"   Stimson Diaries, December 11, 1942.

359 That night Stimson confided to his diary   Stimson Diaries, December 9, 1942.

360 "I had fine soldiers in my company"   Klein, *A Call to Arms*, p. 341.

361 Through executive orders, and as a result   Byron Fairchild and Jonathan Grossman, *The Army and Industrial Manpower* (Center of Military History, 1988), p. 160.

361 The order caused an immediate uproar   Albert A. Blum, "Work or Fight: The Use of the Draft as a Manpower Sanction During the Second World War," *Industrial and Labor Relations Review* 16, no. 3 (April 1963): 366–380.

361 Baruch went directly to Roosevelt   Baruch, *Baruch: The Public Years*, p. 327.

361 Warming to his topic, he scolded the president   Ibid., p. 327.

362   **One, first proposed by Representative Clare Boothe Luce**   Blum, "Work or Fight."

362   **Roosevelt then took his turn at the problem**   Rosenman, *Working with Roosevelt*, p. 411.

363   **When the brutal and often sadistic**   Jacob Vander Meulen, "West Coast Labor Aircraft and an American Military-Industrial Complex, 1935–1941." See https://depts.washington.edu/pcls/documents/research/VanderMeulen _WestCoastAircraft.pdf.

365   **The government promptly seized the pits**   FDR Library, Address of the President to the Coal Miners, May 2, 1942. See http://docs.fdrlibrary.marist .edu/050243.html.

366   **So many people saw Ickes as their salvation**   Geoffrey Perret, *Days of Sadness, Years of Triumph: The American People, 1939–1945* (Coward, McCann & Geoghegan, 1973), p. 308.

367   **He had gotten them their pay raise**   *Time*, July 5, 1943.

368   **According to Byrnes, Roosevelt's opening gambit**   Byrnes, *All in One Lifetime*, p. 200.

368   **While the publicity accorded the coal and rail strikes**   Perret, *Days of Sadness, Years of Triumph*, p. 308.

368   **As the deadline approached**   Stimson Diaries, December 23, 1943.

369   **According to Stimson, Marshall had told him**   Stimson Diaries, December 31, 1943.

369   **Marshall was so upset at the entire state**   Byrnes, *All in One Lifetime*, p. 201.

369   **There he learned that Roosevelt**   Stimson Diaries, December 27, 1943.

369   **In a rare display of temper**   Cray, *General of the Army*, p. 442.

369   **Six other railroad heads were also made colonels**   *Time*, January 10, 1940.

39: THE JEWISH QUESTION

372   **"Roosevelt acted in the face of strong"**   Gerhard Weinberg, "The Allies and the Holocaust," in *The Holocaust in History: The Known, the Unknown, the Disputed, and the Reexamined*, ed. Michael Berenbaum and Abraham Peck (Indiana University Press, 1998), pp. 480–491.

373   **"Received alarming report about plan being discussed"**   For a copy of the cable, see http://nationalarchives.gov.uk/documents/education/britain-and -the-holocaust-prep-pack.pdf (Document 2).

373   **The cable was sent with a notation**   For a copy of the cable and notations, see http://www.alliedpowersholocaust.org/wp-content/uploads/2015 /03/1942-August-Reigner-Telegram.pdf.

374   **It was the first and last time Roosevelt would meet**   Richard Breitman and Allan J. Lichtman, *FDR and the Jews* (Harvard University Press, 2013), pp. 209–210.

375   **"I do want you to know"**   Cable from Stephen Wise to Franklin Roosevelt; FDR Library: Documents Related to the Holocaust and Refugees, 1933–1945, Box 1, Personal File 19.

375   **If, however, one is looking**   Neil Rolde, *Breckinridge Long, American Eichmann??? An Enquiry into the Character of the Man Who Denied Visas to the Jews* (Polar Bear & Company, 2013).

375   **"I do not need to tell you"**   J. Robert Moskin, *American Statecraft: The Story of the U.S. Foreign Service* (Thomas Dunne Books, 2013), p. 417.

376   **"We can delay and effectively stop"**   A copy of this memo can be seen at https://www.facinghistory.org/rescuers/breckinridge-long-memorandum.

377   **And despite writing that their "appeal for asylum"**   Fred L. Israel, *The War Diary of Breckinridge Long: Selections from the Years 1939–1944* (University of Nebraska Press, 1966), p. 282.

377   **"I caught him in a trap"**   Harry J. Cargas, *Voices from the Holocaust* (University Press of Kentucky, 1992), p. 63.

378   **"The new Nazi policy is to kill Jews"**   OSS Report, March 17, 1943. Map Room Papers; MR 203(12); Sec. 1; OSS Numbered Bulletins, March–May 1943, Box 72.

379   **"All I can do is put this thing"**   Morgenthau Diaries, vol. 688–pt. 1: Jewish Refugees, May 7–December 9, 1943, pp. 111–118. See http://www.fdrlibrary.marist.edu/archives/collections/franklin/index.php?p=collections/findingaid&id=159&q=&rootcontentid=72431.

379   **"I know that is so"**   Morgenthau Diaries, vol. 688–pt. 2: Jewish Refugees, December 13–December 31, 1943.

379   **In explicit detail the report spelled out**   Breitman and Lichtman, *FDR and the Jews*, p. 234.

380   **When Morgenthau reminded the president**   Ibid., p. 191.

380   **"This much is certain, however"**   Morgenthau Diaries, vol. 694, January 14–January 17, 1944. A copy of the entire report can be found starting at page 110.

380   **"I think it's wonderful"**   Blum, *The Morgenthau Diaries: Years of War*, p. 222.

382   **McCloy did not offer a lot of hope**   Breitman and Lichtman, *FDR and the Jews*, p. 282.

382   **"The most effective relief to victims"**   Ibid., p. 282. For a copy of the entire message see http://www.jewishvirtuallibrary.org/jsource/Holocaust/airaction.html.

382   **On July 4, McCloy delivered the bad news**   War Refugee Board Records; Projects and Documents File; Measures Directed Toward Halting Persecutions; Hungary No. 5, Box 42. See http://www.fdrlibrary.marist.edu/archives/pdfs/holocaust.pdf (Document #9).

382   **As the Allies bombed industrial targets**   Stuart G. Erdheim, "Could the Allies Have Bombed Auschwitz-Birkenau?" *Holocaust and Genocide Studies* (Fall 1997): 129–170.

382 **The forty-page report contained the testimony** A copy of the report can be found here: http://www.holocaustresearchproject.org/othercamps /auschproto.html.

383 **He may have belonged to clubs** Bird, *The Chairman,* pp. 222–223.

383 **"central obsession, the life's mission"** Ambassador William J. vanden Heuvel, Keynote Address, Fifth Annual Franklin and Eleanor Roosevelt Distinguished Lecture, October 17, 1996. Roosevelt University, Chicago.

384 **"The idea that men dedicated to the killing program"** Gerhard Weinberg, "The Allies and the Holocaust," in *The Holocaust and History: The Known, the Unknown, the Disputed, and the Reexamined,* ed. Michael Berenbaum and Abraham Peck (Indiana University Press, 1998), p. 490.

385 **"How ironic that our greatest president"** Ambassador William J. vanden Heuvel, Keynote Address, Fifth Annual Franklin and Eleanor Roosevelt Distinguished Lecture, October 17, 1996. Roosevelt University, Chicago.

385 **"To see the whole works go up in fire"** Elie Wiesel, *Night* (Bantam Books, 1982), p. 59.

40: AULD LANG SYNE

387 **Many men over the years** Goodwin, *No Ordinary Time,* p. 204.

387 **After renting out her Seattle home** *Time,* May 29, 1944.

389 **As Bullitt could not attack the president** Robert Murphy, *Diplomat Among Warriors: The Unique World of a Foreign Service Expert* (Doubleday, 1964), p. 35.

389 **Roosevelt was planning cabinet-level changes** Ickes, *The Lowering Cloud,* pp. 343–344.

390 **The porter reported the incident** H. W. Brands, *Traitor to His Class: The Privileged Life and Radical Presidency of Franklin Delano Roosevelt* (Anchor, 2009), pp. 749–750.

390 **Visibly upset at his visitor's impertinence** Fullilove, *Rendezvous with Destiny,* p. 231.

390 **"Bill ought to go to hell for that"** Blum, *The Price of Vision: The Diary of Henry A. Wallace, 1942–1946* (Houghton Mifflin, 1973), p. 383.

390 **Throughout this period, Secretary Hull's resentment** Thomas Raymond Church, "The Hull-Welles Controversy," unpublished dissertation, University of Texas, 1968, p. 211.

390 **In September 1942 Hull discussed the accusations** Israel, *The War Diary of Breckinridge Long,* p. 281.

391 **In June 1943, Hull broached the subject** Benjamin Welles, *Sumner Welles: FDR's Global Strategist* (St. Martin's Press, 1997), pp. 343–346.

391 **"conflicting personalities, and lack of cohesive policy"** *The New York Times,* August 4, 1943.

391 "the State Department will function smoothly" *The New York Times*, August 6, 1943.

391 Stalin had just agreed Hull, *The Memoirs of Cordell Hull*, vol. 2, pp. 1227–1230.

392 Feigning reluctance to get between old friends Byrnes, *All in One Lifetime*, pp. 196–198.

392 "Saint Peter is at the gate" Dallek, *Franklin Roosevelt and American Foreign Policy*, p. 421.

392 The president's stenographer, Dorothy Brady Geoffrey C. Ward, *Closest Companion: The Unknown Story of the Intimate Friendship Between Franklin Roosevelt and Margaret Suckley* (Simon & Schuster, 2009), p. 244.

392 Only too late did he learn Brands, *Traitor to His Class*, p. 751.

41: STORM CLOUDS OVER THE ALLIANCE

395 Roosevelt was unconvinced JCS minutes of meeting at the White House, April 6, 1943, National Archives, Record Group 218.

396 "Madame Chiang stepped to the rostrum" *Time*, March 1, 1943.

396 Eden found the discourse fascinating Anthony Eden (Earl of Avon), *The Eden Memoirs: The Reckoning* (Houghton Mifflin, 1965), p. 433.

396 Interestingly the Joint Chiefs were never present JCS minutes, April 13, 1943, National Archives, Record Group 218.

397 "felt so sure of himself disposing" Eden, *The Eden Memoirs: The Reckoning*, p. 433.

399 In the past, the Americans had been buried Guyer, *The Joint Chiefs and the War in Europe*, Section C, p. 405.

399 To make sure they were ready Ibid., p. 411.

399 Admiral Charles M. Cooke, who often represented King JCS minutes, April 27, 1943, National Archives, Record Group 218.

399 "Husky was an end in itself" JCS minutes of meeting at the White House, April 6, 1943, National Archives, Record Group 218.

400 "We will do well avoiding preliminary skirmishes" JCS minutes, April 27, 1943, National Archives, Record Group 218.

400 He escorted Churchill, with his hundred-person staff *The Foreign Relations of the United States: The Third Washington Conference; Preliminary Papers*, pp. 1–23: https://uwdc.library.wisc.edu/collections/frus/.

400 The Trident Conference started The complete papers and minutes for this meeting have recently been published online, see http://www.ibiblio.org/hyperwar/Dip/Conf/Trident/TRIDENT.PDF.

400 "The collapse of Italy would cause a chill" Ibid., pp. 26–27.

401 "we only need to break even" Ibid., p. 27.

401 "Given the large armies and naval force available" Ibid., p. 27.

401 "We have talked about ROUNDUP and SLEDGEHAMMER" Ibid., p. 29.

402 He spoke eloquently of British plans *The Foreign Relations of the United States: The Third Washington Conference*, pp. 223–227.

402 The British pushed for an invasion of Italy Ibid., p. 41.

403 "The Americans are taking up" Danchev and Todman, *War Diaries, 1939–1945*, p. 405.

403 The most memorable event of the weekend outing Sherwood, *Roosevelt and Hopkins*, p. 729.

403 Both men used the weekend to relax Churchill, *The Second World War*, vol. 4, *The Hinge of Fate*, pp. 795–798.

403 The others took walks Pogue, *George C. Marshall*, vol. 3, *Organizer of Victory*, pp. 202–203.

403 By Monday morning the staffs went back Stimson Diaries, May 17, 1943.

404 Marshall soon recovered and joined Stimson in a laugh Stimson Diaries, May 19, 1943.

404 "I have it constantly on my mind" Ibid.

404 Even Marshall was showing signs of doubt JCS minutes, May 19, 1943, National Archives, Record Group 218.

404 But this was the day everything changed *The Foreign Relations of the United States: The Third Washington Conference*, pp. 112–123.

404 He then amended the April 1 date Ibid., p. 101.

404 "The Chief of Staff was going to squeeze" Cray, *General of the Army*, p. 396.

405 "far better than a break-up of the conference" Danchev and Todman, *War Diaries, 1939–1945*, p. 407.

406 Once Churchill had eyed Marshall reading Pogue interviews, Tape 19: http://marshallfoundation.org/library/wp-content/uploads/sites/16/2014/05/Tape_19.pdf.

406 On cue, Churchill sprung up Andrew Roberts, *Masters and Commanders: How Roosevelt, Churchill, Marshall and Alanbrooke Won the War in the West* (Alan Lane, 2008), p. 374.

406 When Churchill had exhausted that topic Pogue interviews, Tape 19: http://marshallfoundation.org/library/wp-content/uploads/sites/16/2014/05/Tape_19.pdf.

406 In reality, Marshall had decided to conserve his strength Mark Stoler, *The Politics of the Second Front: American Military Planning and Diplomacy in Coalition Warfare, 1941–1943* (Greenwood Press, 1977), p. 98.

406 Davies reported that he had to wade through FDR Library, Map Room Papers, 1941–1945, Box 8.

406 Having not yet informed Stalin Stalin had assumed the military rank and title of marshal after the victory at Stalingrad.

407 **After listing all the past "lies"** FDR Library, Map Room Papers, 1941–1945, Box 8.

407 **"I have to tell you that this is simply"** Ibid.

42: Showdown in Quebec

408 **He was pleased to inform Stimson** Stimson Diaries, June 8, 1943.

408 **Stimson, though, remained unsure** Stimson Diaries, June 1, 1943.

408 **The next day he had dinner at 10 Downing Street** Stimson Diaries, July 12, 1943.

408 **"did not hate the Italians"** Stimson Diaries: Report to the President. This report is placed after August 4, 1943, in the diaries.

408 **He concluded by reminding Churchill** Ibid.

408 **But before Stimson's temper exploded** Stimson Diaries, July 12, 1943.

409 **The word "if" was not lost on Stimson** Stimson Diaries, July 22, 1943.

409 **"If he had fifty-thousand men ashore"** Stimson Diaries: Report to the President.

410 **This stirred Stimson, and for the next few minutes** Ibid.

410 **Churchill admitted to his chiefs** Stoler, *Politics of the Second Front*, p. 99.

410 **"In view of what happened in Italy yesterday"** JCS minutes, July 26, 1943, National Archives, Record Group 218.

410 **A few days later, Rear Admiral Cooke** Stoler, *Politics of the Second Front*, p. 102.

411 **At the JCS meeting on August 6** JCS meeting, August 6, 1943, National Archives, Record Group 218.

411 **"[When the] Chief of the Imperial Staff [Brooke] and others"** Ibid.

411 **King offered that if troops building up in Britain** JCS meeting, August 7, 1943, National Archives, Record Group 218.

412 **This referenced the old concern** Ibid.

412 **The mood changed, however** Ibid.

412 **With that the chiefs approved a position paper** C.C.S. 303: Strategic Concept for the Defeat of Axis in Europe, see *The Foreign Relations of the United States: The Conferences at Washington and Quebec, 1943*, pp. 472–482.

412 **Though he felt more could be done** Matloff, *Strategic Planning for Coalition Warfare: 1943–1944*, p. 211.

412 **Finally, Stimson reiterated** Stimson Diaries, August 10, 1943. Also see *The Foreign Relations of the United States: The Conferences at Washington and Quebec, 1943*, pp. 496–498.

412 **"the President went the whole hog"** Stimson Diaries, August 19, 1943.

412 **Roosevelt also said that he did not want** JCS meeting with the president, August 10, 1943. For a transcript see *The Foreign Relations of the United States: The Conferences at Washington and Quebec, 1943*, pp. 498–504.

413 **Official meetings for what was code-named** *Foreign Relations of the United States: The Conferences at Washington and Quebec, 1943*, pp. 849–967.

413 **British insistence on expanding operations** William D. Leahy, *I Was There* (McGraw-Hill, 1950).

413 **"It is quite impossible to argue with him"** Danchev and Todman, *War Diaries, 1939–1945*, p. 442.

414 **Brooke took the news hard** Ibid., p. 441.

415 **He did not believe he could stand much more** Ibid., p. 443.

416 **"Good heavens, they've started shooting now!"** Ibid., pp. 445–446.

PART FIVE: ENDGAME

43: THE BIG THREE IN TEHRAN

419 **"Not one American soldier is going to die"** Larry I. Bland, ed., *George C. Marshall: Interviews and Reminiscences for Forrest Pogue* (Lexington, 1996), p.13.

420 **Beside him, Hap Arnold, Pa Watson, and Harry Hopkins** Library of Congress, Henry Arnold Papers, Reel 3.

421 **He ordered all of the *Iowa*'s massive 16-inch guns** John McCrea, unpublished autobiography, FDR Library, McCrea Papers, 1942–1943.

421 **"DON'T SHOOT, WE'RE REPUBLICANS"** Kit Bonner, "The Ill-Fated USS William D. Porter," *The Retired Officer Magazine* (March 1994).

421 **"Admiral King, you are a good naval officer"** John McCrea, unpublished autobiography, FDR Library, McCrea Papers, 1942–1943.

422 **After reading it, Roosevelt simply said "Amen"** JCS minutes, Meeting with the President, November 15, 1943.

422 **Roosevelt clearly saw that such a situation** JCS minutes, Meeting with the President, November 19, 1943.

422 **Roosevelt also raised some concerns** Ibid.

422 **Hopkins, who had a chance to renew his intimacy** Arnold Papers, Library of Congress, Reel 3.

423 **Thus there was little left to offer Chiang** *Foreign Relations of the United States: The Conferences at Cairo and Tehran, 1943*, pp. 304–366. See http://digicoll.library.wisc.edu/cgi-bin/FRUS/FRUS-idx?type=header&id=FRUS.FRUS1943CairoTehran.

424 **In an instant, the necessity for Chinese manpower** Hull, *The Memoirs of Cordell Hull*, vol. 2, pp. 1308–1318.

425 **The Americans were aghast** Danchev and Todman, *War Diaries, 1939–1945*, p. 478.

425 **General Stilwell recorded in his diary** Roberts, *Masters and Commanders*, p. 437.

425   **After dinner, there was some dancing**   Lynne Olson, *Citizens of London: The Americans Who Stood with Britain in Its Darkest, Finest Hour* (Random House, 2010), p. 303.

425   **"With the people of the United Kingdom in our family"**   Goodwin, *No Ordinary Time*, p. 302.

425   **When the Combined Chiefs met again**   Danchev and Todman, *War Diaries, 1939–1945*, p. 481.

425   **"You will find us lining up with the Russians"**   Moran, *Churchill: Struggle for Survival*, p. 142.

426   **Roosevelt later told his labor secretary**   Perkins, *The Roosevelt I Knew*, pp. 82–85.

426   **"I know you will not mind"**   FDR Library, Map Room Papers, 1941–1945, Box 2.

426   **"Perhaps you think that just because we are the Allies"**   Milovan Djilas, *Conversations with Stalin* (Harcourt Brace, 1963), p. 73.

427   **After days of official meetings and paperwork**   Perkins, *The Roosevelt I Knew*, pp. 82–85.

427   **"I began almost as soon"**   Ibid., pp. 84–85.

427   **"We have no eternal allies"**   Lord Palmerston, British Prime Minister, 1855–1858 and 1859–1865, in a speech in the House of Commons, March 1, 1848.

428   **"I am glad to see you"**   *Foreign Relations of the United States: The Conferences at Washington and Quebec, 1943*, pp. 482–486.

428   **Though it does not appear**   Forrest Davis, "What Really Happened in Tehran," *Saturday Evening Post* (May 13, 1944), pp. 12–41. This was a two-part series. The second part was published on May 20, 1944.

428   **Churchill then noted that this meeting represented**   *Foreign Relations of the United States: The Conferences at Washington and Quebec, 1943*, p. 487.

429   **"As far as I know it is his own idea"**   Sherwood, *Roosevelt and Hopkins*, p. 780.

429   **Stalin stated that he did not consider scattering**   Minutes of Combined Chiefs Meeting, November 29, 1943, *Foreign Relations of the United States: The Conferences at Washington and Quebec, 1943*, p. 505.

429   **He then suggested that the staffs begin working**   Ibid., p. 507.

429   **"Three truly great men"**   FDR Library, Henry Arnold Papers, Reel 3.

430   **It was disconcerting to him to lose a debate**   Moran, *Churchill: Struggle for Survival*, p. 164.

430   **The reason: There was no one at the train**   *Foreign Relations of the United States: The Conferences at Washington and Quebec, 1943*, p. 514.

431   **Stalin declared himself unconvinced**   Dallek, *Franklin Roosevelt and American Foreign Policy, 1932–1945*, pp. 434–435.

432   **"If we are here to discuss military questions"**   *Foreign Relations of the United States: The Conferences at Washington and Quebec, 1943*, pp. 540–552.

432   **"he firmly believed it would be England's duty"**   Ibid., p. 552.

432   **To which Roosevelt jokingly said**   Ibid., p. 554.

433   **Incensed, Churchill warned**   Ibid., p. 554.

433   **Mentioning Singapore and Hong Kong**   Ibid., p. 554.

433   **"We have proved here in Tehran"**   Ibid., p. 585.

433   **He then explained that he could make**   Ibid., p. 594.

434   **This was Roosevelt at his most Machiavellian**   Ibid., p. 595.

44: THE GRIND

435   **When the Anglo-American party arrived**   *Foreign Relations of the United States: The Conferences at Washington and Quebec, 1943*, pp. 675–764.

436   **Marshall, despite having told his aide**   Sherwood, *Roosevelt and Hopkins*, p. 803.

436   **"I feel I could not sleep at night"**   Cray, *General of the Army*, p. 13.

436   **"I thank the Lord that Stalin was there"**   Stimson Diaries, December 5, 1943.

437   **Roosevelt, who had intended to stay two weeks**   Baruch, *Baruch: The Public Years*, p. 336.

438   **"I am perfectly satisfied with his physical condition"**   *Time*, May 15, 1944.

439   **Roosevelt remained awake**   Hassett, *Off the Record with FDR, 1942–1945*, p. 248.

439   **He then took a short nap**   Stimson Diaries, June 6, 1944.

45: ELECTION 1944: SURVEYING THE FIELD

440   **"I don't know whether you are going to support me or not"**   Donald Bruce Johnson, *The Republican Party and Wendell Willkie* (University of Illinois Press, 1960), p. 251.

441   **In the Pacific, General MacArthur**   Philip J. Briggs, "General MacArthur and the Presidential Election of 1944," *Presidential Studies Quarterly* 22, no. 1 (Winter 1992): 31–46.

441   **"My greatest security lies in Japan's inability"**   Jim Bishop, *FDR's Last Year: April 1944–April 1945* (William Morrow, 1974), p. 69.

442   **In the end, MacArthur's candidacy blew up**   Stanley Weintraub, *Final Victory: FDR's Extraordinary World War II Presidential Campaign* (Da Capo Press, 2012), p. 78.

442   **"I do not covet it nor would I accept it"**   *Life*, May 8, 1944, p. 113.

442   **Wisconsin delegate Grant A. Ritter**   *Time*, July 10, 1944.

442   **"How can you vote for a man"**   Ibid.

443   **As early as 1943, leaders of the Democratic National Committee**   Ed Pauley, Memo on the Truman Nomination, FDR Library, Rosenman Papers, Box 8.

443   **Together they tried to convince the vice president**   Blum, *Price of Vision*, pp. 360–374.

444   **At three o'clock Wallace left the White House**   *Time*, July 24, 1944.

444   **Byrnes later wrote that the president appeared**   Byrnes, *All in One Lifetime*, p. 221.

444   **Later that evening, after Wallace had departed**   Rosenman, *Working with Roosevelt*, pp. 444–446.

444   **"My own intensive activities in this regard"**   FDR Library, Rosenman Papers, Box 8.

445   **There was dead silence**   Ed Pauley, Memo on the Truman Nomination, FDR Library, Rosenman Papers, Box 8.

445   **"Bob, I think everyone else wants Truman"**   Ibid.

445   **Knowing how Roosevelt worked**   Byrnes, *All in One Lifetime*, p. 225.

445   **Hopkins informed him**   Ibid.

446   **The trick worked**   Ed Pauley, Memo on the Truman Nomination, FDR Library, Rosenman Papers, Box 8.

446   **"To him men were so many tools"**   Robertson, *Sly and Able*, pp. 360–361.

447   **"I guess I'll have to take it"**   Rosenman, *Working with Roosevelt*, p. 451.

447   **When they started their chant**   Ed Pauley, Memo on the Truman Nomination, FDR Library, Rosenman Papers, Box 8.

447   **Soon thereafter, Hannegan adjourned the convention**   Ibid.

46: PACIFIC OVERTURES

448   **The price for these snacks was paid**   Rosenman, *Working with Roosevelt*, p. 456.

449   **When he finally left the hospital**   Ibid., p. 459.

449   **Marshall did not want to bog down**   Stimson Diaries, June 22, 1944.

450   **"We must be careful not to allow"**   Pogue, *George C. Marshall*, vol. 3, *Organizer of Victory*, p. 444.

450   **Even as he wrote, Marshall knew better**   Pogue interviews, Tape 12, November 21, 1956: http://marshallfoundation.org/library/wp-content/uploads/sites/16/2014/05/Tape_12.pdf.

451   **On September 13, 1944**   Combined Chiefs of Staff Meeting, September 13, 1944; *Foreign Relations of the United States: The Conferences at Quebec, 1944*, see http://images.library.wisc.edu/FRUS/EFacs/1944/reference/frus.frus1944.i0012.pdf.

451   **"With all of your airdromes"**   FDR Library, Henry Arnold Papers, Reel 3.

451   **"When a kamikaze hits a U.S. carrier"**   Nicholas E. Sarantakes, "The Short but Brilliant Life of the British Pacific Fleet," *Joint Force Quarterly*, Issue 40 (First Quarter 2006): 85–91.

47: THE MORGENTHAU PLAN

454   "I think it is all very well for us"   Hull, *Memoirs of Cordell Hull,* vol. 2, p. 1621.

454   "they should be treated sternly"   Morgenthau Diaries, Book 763, August 16–18, 1944, p. 202 (FDR Library); see http://www.fdrlibrary.marist.edu /_resources/images/morg/md1056.pdf.

454   Eisenhower's memoirs tell a different story   Dwight D. Eisenhower, *Crusade in Europe* (Doubleday, 1948), p. 287.

454   "I have asked and I have not been allowed"   Morgenthau Diaries, Book 763, p. 204 (FDR Library); see http://www.fdrlibrary.marist.edu/_resources /images/morg/md1056.pdf.

455   "as an American citizen"   Ibid.

455   Two days later, believing he had Hull's full support   Morgenthau Diaries, Book 763, August 18, 1944, pp. 202–205.

455   "We have to be tough with Germany"   Blum, *The Morgenthau Diaries: Years of War, 1941–1945*, p. 346.

456   "Well, that is not nearly as bad"   Morgenthau Diaries, August 23–24, 1944, p. 15. See http://www.fdrlibrary.marist.edu/archives/collections/franklin /index.php?p=collections/findingaid&id=535.

456   In the meantime, within the Treasury   Diane Manchester, "Development of Postwar Policy in Germany," *Western Political Quarterly* 17, no. 1 (March 1964): 109–116.

456   "It fell to White to clothe a bad thesis"   David Rees, *Harry Dexter White: A Study in Paradox* (Conrad, McCann & Geoghegan, 1973), p. 248.

456   "We're not interested"   Georg Schild, *Bretton Woods and Dumbarton Oaks* (St. Martin's Press, 1995).

456   "Morgenthau started off on this"   Donald Moggridge, *Maynard Keynes: An Economist's Biography* (Routledge, 1992), p. 776.

457   One could easily picture White   The above two paragraphs are taken from the author's volume, *The Making of Peace* (Cambridge University Press, 2009), pp. 293–322.

457   On September 2, 1944   Hull, *The Memoirs of Cordell Hull,* vol. 2, p. 1606.

457   But, by the end of their talk, Morgenthau was convinced   Morgenthau Diaries, September 2, 1944. See http://www.fdrlibrary.marist.edu/_resources /images/morg/mpd17.pdf.

457   "I am convinced that the President"   Ibid.

457   "Morgenthau is, not unnaturally, very bitter"   Stimson Diaries, September 4, 1944.

458   "wished to wreck completely"   Stimson Diaries, September 5, 1944.

458   Roosevelt continued this discourse   Stimson Diaries, September 6, 1944.

458   "I cannot treat as realistic"   This memorandum is in the Stimson Diaries, after September 5, 1944.

459   **"I do not want them to starve to death"**   Hull, *The Memoirs of Cordell Hull*, vol. 2, p. 1603.

459   **"I cannot believe that he will follow"**   Stimson Diaries, September 13, 1944.

459   **"Not to worry over it"**   Stimson Diaries, September 11, 1944.

459   **Then turning loose "the full flood"**   *Foreign Relations of the United States, The Conferences at Quebec, 1944*, pp. 325–326.

459   **Churchill "was violent"**   Morgenthau Diaries, vol. 773, FDR Library.

459   **"He [Churchill] was slumped in his chair"**   *Foreign Relations of the United States, The Conferences at Quebec, 1944*, pp. 325–326.

459   **"What must I do?"**   John Morton Blum, *Roosevelt and Morgenthau: A Revision and Condensation of the Morgenthau Diaries* (Houghton Mifflin, 1970), p. 599.

460   **"At first I violently opposed this idea"**   Winston S. Churchill, *The Second World War*, vol. 6, *Triumph and Tragedy* (Houghton Mifflin, 1953), p. 156 (emphasis added).

460   **"You can't stand for this"**   Morgenthau Diaries, September 15–19, 1944, p. 209.

460   **"Well, if it gets down to the question"**   Ibid., p. 209.

461   **In it Stimson mixed the moral**   The memorandum is included in full in the Stimson Diaries, after September 19, 1944.

461   **Soon thereafter the entire Morgenthau Plan was leaked**   Stimson Diaries, September 25, 1944.

461   ***Time* magazine, for instance**   *Time*, October 2, 1944.

461   **Roosevelt knew he was in trouble**   *The New York Times*, November 5, 1944.

461   **Getting hammered in the press**   Stimson Diaries, September 27, 1944.

462   **After he read it, Stimson reported**   Stimson Diaries, October 3, 1944.

462   **Within a week**   Daniel Yergin, *The Commanding Heights: The Battle for the World Economy* (Free Press, 2002).

48: THE CHAMP

465   **"These Republican leaders"**   This segment of the speech and its impact on his audience can be viewed here: https://www.youtube.com/watch?v=qqt7b9veFo8.

466   **"I still think he is a son of a bitch"**   Hassett, *Off the Record with FDR, 1942–1945*, p. 294.

49: YALTA AND THE END

469   **Before the chiefs were separate plans**   *Foreign Relations of the United States, Conferences at Malta and Yalta, 1945*. Meeting transcripts can be viewed

at http://images.library.wisc.edu/FRUS/EFacs/1945/reference/frus.frus1945.i0011.pdf.

469 **General Marshall later said that the debate** Pogue interviews, Tape 13: http://marshallfoundation.org/library/wp-content/uploads/sites/16/2014/05/Tape_13.pdf; and Pogue interviews, Tape 18: http://marshallfoundation.org/library/wp-content/uploads/sites/16/2014/05/Tape_18.pdf.

469 **All that remained of its prior grandeur** *Foreign Relations of the United States, Conferences at Malta and Yalta, 1945,* p. 551.

469 **As the Yalta discussions got under way** Burns, *Roosevelt: The Soldier of Freedom,* p. 565.

470 **Byrnes then threatened Roosevelt** Robertson, *Sly and Able,* p. 383.

470 **Byrnes boasts in his memoirs** Byrnes, *All in One Lifetime,* p. 259.

470 **"he was the most honest"** Robertson, *Sly and Able,* p. 383.

470 **"care should be taken"** *Foreign Relations of the United States, Conferences at Malta and Yalta, 1945,* p. 621. See http://images.library.wisc.edu/FRUS/EFacs/1945/reference/frus.frus1945.i0012.pdf.

472 **"Make no mistake"** John Colville, *The Fringes of Power: The Incredible Inside Story of Winston Churchill During WW II* (Lyons Press, 2002), p. 555.

472 **"Occupying forces had the power"** Edward Stettinius, as quoted in Dallek, *Franklin Roosevelt and American Foreign Policy,* pp. 507–508.

472 **"I know, Bill—I know it"** Leahy, *I Was There,* pp. 315–316.

473 **"It was my feeling that Roosevelt"** Ibid., p. 321.

474 **"Pandora's Box of Yalta secrets"** Kennedy, *Freedom from Fear,* p. 806.

474 **"The Big Three had practiced to deceive their Allies"** *Time,* April 9, 1945.

474 **When the secrecy was added** S. M. Plokhy, *Yalta: The Price of Peace* (Viking, 2010).

474 **The interview concluded** Rosenman, *Working with Roosevelt,* p. 541.

475 **"I was terribly shocked"** Blum, *Roosevelt and Morgenthau,* pp. 628–630.

475 **"Franklin D. Roosevelt is a highly impressionable person"** Walter Lippmann, *Interpretations, 1931–1932* (Macmillan, 1932), pp. 260–262, as quoted in David M. Kennedy, *Freedom from Fear: The American People in Depression and War, 1929–1945* (Oxford University Press, 2005), p. 101; and *Time,* April 23, 1945.

BIBLIOGRAPHY

Aandahl, Fredrick, William M. Franklin, and William Slany, eds. *Foreign Relations of the United States: The Conferences at Washington, 1941–1942, and Casablanca, 1943*. Washington, DC: United States Government Printing Office, 1958.

Abramson, Rudy. *Spanning the Century: The Life of W. Averell Harriman*. New York: William Morrow, 1992.

Acheson, Dean. *Present at the Creation: My Years in the State Department*. New York: W. W. Norton, 1969.

Adams, Henry H. *Harry Hopkins: A Biography*. New York: G. P. Putnam's Sons, 1977.

Adams, Stephen B. *Mr. Kaiser Goes to Washington: The Rise of a Government Entrepreneur*. Chapel Hill: University of North Carolina Press, 1997.

Aglion, Raoul. *Roosevelt & de Gaulle: Allies in Conflict, a Personal Conflict*. New York: The Free Press, 1988.

Alanbrooke, Alan Brooke, Viscount. *Alanbrooke War Diaries, 1939–1945: Field Marshall Lord Alanbrooke*, eds. Alex Danchev and Dan Todman. London: Weidenfeld & Nicolson, 1998.

Ambrose, Stephen E. *Eisenhower: Soldier and President*. New York: Simon & Schuster, 1991.

Armstrong, Anne. *Unconditional Surrender: The Impact of the Casablanca Policy on World War II*. New Brunswick, NJ: Rutgers University Press, 1961.

Arnold, Henry H. *Global Mission*. New York: Harper & Brothers, 1949.

Asbell, Bernard. *The FDR Memoirs*. Garden City, NY: Doubleday, 1973.

Astley, Joan Bright. *The Inner Circle: A View of War at the Top*. Boston: Little, Brown, 1971.

Baldwin, Hanson W. *The Crucial Years: 1939–1941*. New York: Harper & Row, 1976.

———. *The Price of Power*. New York: Harper & Brothers, 1948.

Barber, Noel. *The Week France Fell*. New York: Stein & Day, 1976.

Barnard, Ellsworth. *Wendell Willkie: Fighter for Freedom*. Marquette: Northern Michigan University Press, 1966.

Barnes, Joseph. *Willkie*. New York: Simon & Schuster, 1952.

Barnett, Correlli. *The Lords of War: Supreme Leadership from Lincoln to Churchill*. London: Pen and Sword, 2013.

Baruch, Bernard M. *Baruch: The Public Years*. New York: Holt, Rinehart & Winston, 1960.

———. *My Own Story*. New York: Henry Holt, 1957.

Basch, Antonin. *The New Economic Warfare*. New York: Columbia University Press, 1941.

Beard, Charles A. *President Roosevelt and the Coming of the War, 1941*. New Haven, CT: Yale University Press, 1948.

Beasley, Norman. *Knudsen: A Biography*. New York: McGraw-Hill Book Company, 1947.

Bercuson, David, and Holger Herwig. *One Christmas in Washington: The Secret Meeting Between Roosevelt and Churchill That Changed the World*. Woodstock, NY: Overlook Press, 2005.

Berthon, Simon. *Allies at War: The Bitter Rivalry Among Churchill, Roosevelt and de Gaulle*. New York: Carroll & Graf, 2001.

———. *Warlords*. Cambridge, MA: Da Capo Press, 2006.

Beschloss, Michael R. *Kennedy and Roosevelt: The Uneasy Alliance*. New York: W. W. Norton, 1980.

———. *The Conquerors: Roosevelt, Truman and the Destruction of Hitler's Germany, 1944–1945*. New York: Simon & Schuster, 2002.

Biddle, Francis. *In Brief Authority*. Garden City, NY: Doubleday, 1948.

Bird, Kai. *The Chairman: John J. McCloy & the Making of the American Establishment*. New York: Simon & Schuster, 1992.

Bishop, Jim. *FDR's Last Year*. New York: William Morrow, 1974.

Black, Conrad. *Franklin Delano Roosevelt: Champion of Freedom*. New York: Public-Affairs, 2003.

Blake, I. George. *Paul V. McNutt: Portrait of a Hoosier Statesman*. Indianapolis: Central Publishing Co., 1966.

Bland, Larry I., ed. *George C. Marshall: Interviews and Reminiscences for Forrest C. Pogue*. Lanham, MD: Lexington, 1996.

Blum, John Morton. *Roosevelt and Morgenthau*. Boston: Houghton Mifflin, 1970.

———. *V Was for Victory*. New York: Harcourt, 1976.

———, ed. *From the Morgenthau Diaries: Years of Urgency, 1938–1941*. Boston: Houghton Mifflin, 1965.

———, ed. *From the Morgenthau Diaries, Years of War, 1941–1945*. Boston: Houghton Mifflin, 1967.

———, ed. *The Price of Vision: The Diary of Henry A. Wallace, 1942–1946*. Boston: Houghton Mifflin, 1973.

Blumenson, Martin. *The Patton Papers: 1940–1945*. New York: Da Capo Press, 1996.

Bohlen, Charles. *Witness to History, 1929–1969*. New York: W. W. Norton, 1973.

Borneman, Walter R. *The Admirals: Nimitz, Halsey, Leahy, and King—the Five-Star Admirals Who Won the War at Sea*. Boston: Little, Brown, 2012.

Brands, H. W. *Traitor to His Class: The Privileged Life and Radical Presidency of Franklin Delano Roosevelt*. New York: Anchor, 2009.

Breitman, Richard, and Allan J. Lichtman. *FDR and the Jews*. Cambridge, MA: Belknap Press of Harvard University Press, 2013.

Brigante, John E. *The Feasibility Dispute: Determination of War Production Objectives for 1942 and 1943*. Washington, DC: Committee on Public Administration Cases, 1950.

Brinkley, Alan. *The End of Reform: New Deal Liberalism in Recession and War*. New York: Alfred A. Knopf, 1995.

Brinkley, David. *Washington Goes to War*. New York: Alfred A. Knopf, 1988.

Brinkley, Douglas, ed. *Dean Acheson and the Making of U.S. Foreign Policy*. New York: St. Martin's Press, 1993.

Brodhurst, Robin. *Churchill's Anchor: Admiral of the Fleet Sir Dudley Pound*. Barnsley, UK: Leo Cooper, 2000.

Bryant, Arthur, ed. *The Turn of the Tide: A History of the War Years Based on the Diaries of Field-Marshal Lord Alanbrooke, Chief of the Imperial General Staff*. Garden City, NY: Doubleday, 1957.

———, ed. *Triumph in the West: A History of the War Years Based on the Diaries of Field-Marshal Lord Alanbrooke, Chief of the Imperial General Staff*. Garden City, NY: Doubleday, 1959.

Buell, Thomas B. *Master of Sea Power: A Biography of Fleet Admiral Ernest J. King*. Boston: Little, Brown, 1980.

Bullitt, Orville H., ed. *For the President, Personal and Secret: Correspondence Between Franklin D. Roosevelt and William C. Bullitt*. Boston: Houghton Mifflin, 1972.

Burns, James MacGregor. *Leadership*. New York: Harper & Row, 1978.

———. *Roosevelt: The Soldier of Freedom*. Vol. 2, *1940–1945*. New York: Harcourt Brace Jovanovich, 1970.

———. *Roosevelt: The Lion and the Fox*. New York: Harcourt, Brace & World, 1956.

Bush, Vannevar. *Modern Arms and Free Men*. New York: Simon & Schuster, 1949.

———. *Pieces of the Action*. New York: William Morrow, 1970.

Butcher, Harry C. *My Three Years with Eisenhower*. New York: Simon & Schuster, 1946.

Butler, J. R. M. *Grand Strategy*. Vol. 3, *June 1941–August 1942*. London: Her Majesty's Stationery Office, 1964.

Byrnes, James F. *All in One Lifetime*. New York: Harper & Brothers, 1958.

———. *Speaking Frankly*. New York and London: Harper & Brothers, 1947.

Callahan, Raymond. *Churchill and His Generals*. Lawrence: University Press of Kansas, 2007.

Campbell, Thomas M., and George C. Herring. *The Diaries of Edward R. Stettinius, Jr., 1943–1946*. New York: New Viewpoints, 1975.

Catton, Bruce. *The War Lords of Washington*. Westport, CT: Greenwood Press, 1948.

Church, Thomas Raymond. "The Hull-Welles Controversy." PhD dissertation, University of Texas, 1968.

Churchill, Winston S. *The Second World War*. Vol. 2, *Their Finest Hour*. Boston: Houghton Mifflin, 1985.

———. *The Second World War*. Vol. 3, *The Grand Alliance*. Boston: Houghton Mifflin, 1985.

———. *The Second World War*. Vol. 4, *The Hinge of Fate*. Boston: Houghton Mifflin, 1985.

———. *The Second World War*. Vol. 5, *Closing the Ring*. Boston: Houghton Mifflin, 1985.

———. *The Second World War*. Vol. 6, *Triumph and Tragedy*. Boston: Houghton Mifflin, 1985.

Clemens, Diane Shaver. *Yalta*. New York: Oxford University Press, 1970.

Clifford, Clark, with Richard Holbrooke. *Counsel to the President: A Memoir*. New York: Random House, 1991.

Coffey, Thomas N. *Hap: The Story of the U.S. Air Force and the Man Who Built It: General Henry H. "Hap" Arnold*. New York: Viking Press, 1982.

Cole, Wayne S. *America First: The Battle Against Intervention, 1940–1941*. Madison: University of Wisconsin Press, 1953.

———. *Charles A. Lindbergh and the Battle Against American Intervention in World War II*. New York: Harcourt Brace Jovanovich, 1974.

Colville, Sir John Rupert. *Footprints in Time: Memories*. Norwich, UK: Michael Russell, 1984.

———. *Fringes of Power: 10 Downing Street Diaries, 1939–1955*. New York: W. W. Norton, 1985.

———. *The Fringes of Power: The Incredible Inside Story of Winston Churchill During World War II*. Guilford, CT: Lyons Press, 1985.

Conn, Stetson. "The Decision to Evacuate the Japanese from the Pacific Coast." In *Command Decisions*, edited by Kent Roberts Greenfield. Washington, DC: Center of Military History, United States Army, 1960.

Connery, Robert H. *The Navy and the Industrial Mobilization in World War II*. Princeton, NJ: Princeton University Press, 1951.

Conway, Ed. *The Summit: Bretton Woods, 1944: J. M. Keynes and the Reshaping of the Global Economy*. New York: Pegasus Books, 2015.

Costigliola, Frank. *Roosevelt's Lost Alliances: How Personal Politics Helped Start the Cold War*. Princeton, NJ: Princeton University Press, 2012.

Cousins, Norman, and J. Garry Clifford, eds. *Memoirs of a Man: Grenville Clark*. New York: W. W. Norton, 1975.

Craig, R. Bruce. *Treasonable Doubt: The Harry Dexter White Spy Case*. Lawrence: University Press of Kansas, 2004.

Cray, Ed. *General of the Army: George C. Marshall, Soldier and Statesman*. New York: W. W. Norton, 1990.

Crum, William L., et. al. *Fiscal Planning for Total War*. New York: National Bureau of Economic Research, 1942.

Culver, John C., and John Hyde. *American Dreamer: A Life of Henry Wallace*. New York: W. W. Norton, 2000.

Dallek, Robert. *Franklin D. Roosevelt and American Foreign Policy, 1932–1945*. New York: Oxford University Press, 1979.

Danchev, Alex. "'Dilly-Dally,' or Having the Last Word: Field Marshall Sir John Dill and Prime Minister Churchill," *Journal of Contemporary History* 22 (1987).

———. *Very Special Relationship: Field-Marshall Sir John Dill and the Anglo-American Alliance, 1941–44*. London: Brassey's Defence Publishers, 1986.

Danchev, Alex, and Daniel Todman, eds. *War Diaries, 1939–1945: Field Marshal Lord Alanbrooke*. London: Phoenix, 2002.

Davies, Norman. *No Simple Victory: World War II in Europe, 1939–1945*. New York: Viking, 2007.

———. *Rising '44: The Battle for Warsaw*. New York: Viking Penguin, 2004.

Davis, Kenneth S. *FDR*. Vol. 1, *The Beckoning of Destiny, 1882–1928*. New York: G. P. Putnam's Sons, 1972.

———. *FDR*. Vol. 2, *The New York Years, 1928–1933*. New York: Random House, 1986.

———. *FDR*. Vol. 3, *The New Deal Years, 1933–1937*. New York: Random House, 1986.

———. *FDR*. Vol. 4, *Into the Storm, 1937–1940*. New York: Random House, 1993.

———. *FDR*. Vol. 5, *The War President, 1940–1943*. New York: Random House, 2000.

Deane, John R. *The Strange Alliance: The Story of Our Efforts at Wartime Cooperation with Russia*. Bloomington: Indiana University Press, 1973.

De Gaulle, Charles. *War Memoirs: The Call to Honour, 1940–1942*. New York: Viking Press, 1955.

D'Este, Carlo. *Eisenhower: A Soldier's Life*. New York: Henry Holt, 2002.

———. *Warlord: A Life of Winston Churchill at War, 1874–1945*. New York: Harper-Collins, 2008.

Dewaters, Diane K. "The World War II Conferences in Washington, DC, and Quebec City." PhD dissertation, University of Texas at Arlington, 2008.

Dickinson, Matthew J. *Bitter Harvest: FDR, Presidential Power, and the Growth of the Presidential Branch*. New York: Cambridge University Press, 1997.

Dilks, David. *Churchill and Company*. New York: I. B. Tauris, 2012.

————, ed. *The Diaries of Sir Alexander Cadogan, O.M., 1938–1945*. New York: G. P. Putnam's Sons, 1972.

Dobbs, Michael. *Six Months in 1945: FDR, Stalin, Churchill, and Truman—from World War to Cold War*. New York: Alfred A. Knopf, 2012.

Dobson, Alan P. *U.S. Wartime Aid to Britain*. London: Croom Helm, 1986.

Drummond, Jones. *The Role of the Office of Civilian Requirements in the Office of Production Management of the War Production Board, January 1941 to November 1945*, Historical Reports on War Administration, War Production Board, Special Study No. 20, Civilian Production Administration. Washington, DC: Civilian Production Administration, Bureau of Demobilization, 1946.

Dunn, Dennis J. *Caught Between Roosevelt and Stalin: America's Ambassadors to Moscow*. Lexington: University Press of Kentucky, 1998.

Dunn, Susan. *1940: FDR, Willkie, Lindbergh, Hitler—the Election amid the Storm*. New Haven, CT: Yale University Press, 2013.

Dunne, Gerald T. *Grenville Clark: Public Citizen*. New York: Farrar, Straus and Giroux, 1986.

Eden, Anthony (the Earl of Avon). *The Eden Memoirs: The Reckoning*. Boston: Houghton Mifflin, 1965.

Eiler, Keith E. *Mobilizing America: Robert P. Patterson and the War Effort, 1940–1945*. Ithaca, NY: Cornell University Press, 1997.

Eisenhower, Dwight D. *At Ease: Stories I Tell to Friends*. Cape Cod, MA: Eastern Acorn Press, 1981.

————. *Crusade in Europe*. Garden City, NY: Doubleday, 1948.

————. *The Eisenhower Diaries*. New York: W. W. Norton, 1981.

Eisenhower, John S. D. *Allies: Pearl Harbor to D-day*. Garden City, NY: Doubleday, 1982.

————. *General Ike: A Personal Reminiscence*. New York: The Free Press, 2003.

Ellis, John. *World War II: A Statistical Survey*. New York: Facts on File, 1993.

Eubank, Keith. *Summit at Teheran*. New York: William Morrow, 1985.

Evans, Richard. *The Third Reich at War*. New York: Penguin Press, 2009.

Fairchild, Byron, and Jonathan Grossman. *The Army and Industrial Manpower*. Washington, DC: Center of Military History, United States Army, 1988.

Farley, James. *The Roosevelt Years*. New York: Whittlesey House, 1948.

Fenberg, Steven. *Unprecedented Power: Jesse Jones, Capitalism, and the Common Good*. College Station: Texas A&M University Press, 2011.

Fenno, Richard. *The Yalta Conference*. Boston: Heath, 1955.

Ferrell, Robert H. *Choosing Truman: The Democratic Convention of 1944*. Columbia: University of Missouri Press, 1994.

————. *The Dying President: Franklin D. Roosevelt, 1944–1945*. Columbia: University of Missouri Press, 1998.

Finney, Burnham. *Arsenal of Democracy: How Industry Builds Our Defense*. New York: McGraw-Hill, 1941.

Fish, Hamilton. *FDR: The Other Side of the Coin*. New York: Vantage Press, 1976.

Fleming, Thomas. *The New Dealers' War: Franklin D. Roosevelt and the War Within World War II*. New York: Basic Books, 2001.

Flynn, George Q. *The Mess in Washington: Manpower Mobilization in World War II*. Westport, CT: Greenwood Press, 1966.

Fossedal, Gregory A. *Our Finest Hour: Will Clayton, the Marshall Plan, and the Triumph of Democracy*. Stanford, CA: Hoover Institution Press, 1993.

Foster, Mark S. *Henry J. Kaiser: Builder in the Modern American West*. Austin: University of Texas Press, 1989.

Frankfurter, Felix. *From the Diaries of Felix Frankfurter*. Edited by Joseph P. Lash. New York: W. W. Norton, 1975.

Franklin D. Roosevelt Presidential Library, Map Room Papers, 1941–1945, Box 3.

Fraser, David. *Alanbrooke*. London: Hamlyn Paperback, 1983.

Freidel, Frank. *FDR*. Vol. 1, *The Apprenticeship*. Boston: Little, Brown, 1952.

———. *FDR*. Vol. 2, *The Ordeal*. Boston: Little, Brown, 1954.

———. *FDR*. Vol. 3, *The Triumph*. Boston: Little, Brown, 1956.

———. *FDR*. Vol. 4, *Launching the New Deal*. Boston: Little, Brown, 1973.

———. *Franklin D. Roosevelt: A Rendezvous with Destiny*. Boston: Little, Brown, 1990.

Fromkin, David. "Churchill's Way: The Great Convergence of Britain and the United States," *World Policy Journal* 15, no. 1 (Spring 1998).

Fullilove, Michael. *Rendezvous with Destiny: How Five Extraordinary Men Took America into the War and into the World*. New York: Penguin Press, 2013.

Galbraith, John Kenneth. *A Life in Our Times: Memoirs*. Boston: Houghton Mifflin, 1981.

Gardner, Richard N. *Sterling Dollar Diplomacy: Anglo-American Collaboration in the Reconstruction of Multilateral Trade*. Madison: University of Wisconsin Press, 1964.

Gellman, Irwin. *Secret Affairs: Franklin Roosevelt, Cordell Hull and Sumner Welles*. Baltimore: Johns Hopkins University Press, 1995.

Gilbert, Martin S. *Churchill and America*. New York: The Free Press, 2008.

———. *Winston S. Churchill*. Vol. 6, *Finest Hour, 1939–1941*. Boston: Houghton Mifflin, 1983.

———. *Winston S. Churchill*. Vol. 7, *Road to Victory, 1941–1945*. Boston: Houghton Mifflin, 1986.

Goodwin, Doris Kearns. *No Ordinary Time: Franklin & Eleanor Roosevelt; The Home Front in World War II*. New York: Simon & Schuster, 1994.

Gould, Jean, and Lorena Hickok. *Walter Reuther: Labor's Rugged Individualist*. New York: Dodd, Mead, 1972.

Grant, James. *Bernard M. Baruch: The Adventures of a Wall Street Legend*. New York: Simon & Schuster, 1983.

Gropman, Alan, ed. *The Big "L": American Logistics in World War II.* Washington, DC: National Defense University Press, 1997.

Groves, Leslie. *Now It Can Be Told: The Story of the Manhattan Project.* New York: Harper & Brothers, 1962.

Hamilton, Nigel. *Montgomery, D-Day Commander.* Washington, DC: Potomac Books, 2007.

———. *The Mantle of Command.* Boston: Houghton Mifflin Harcourt, 2014.

Hand, Samuel B. *Counsel and Advise: A Political Biography of Samuel I. Rosenman.* New York: Garland Publishing, 1979.

Harbutt, Fraser J. "Churchill, Hopkins, and the 'Other' Americans: An Alternative Perspective on Anglo-American Relations, 1941–1945." *International History Review* 8, no. 2 (May 1986).

———. *Yalta 1945: Europe and America at the Crossroads.* Cambridge: Cambridge University Press, 2010.

Harriman, W. Averell, and Elie Abel. *Special Envoy to Churchill and Stalin, 1941–1946.* New York: Random House, 1975.

Hassett, William D. *Off the Record with FDR, 1942–1945.* New Brunswick, NJ: Rutgers University Press, 1958.

Hastings, Max. *Inferno: The World at War, 1939–1945.* New York: Alfred A. Knopf, 2011.

———. *Overlord: D-Day and the Battle for Normandy.* New York: Simon & Schuster, 1984.

——— *Winston's War: Churchill, 1940–1945.* New York: Vintage, 2011.

Hayes, Grace Person. *The History of the Joint Chiefs of Staff in World War II: The War Against Japan.* Annapolis, MD: Naval Institute Press, 1982.

Heinrichs, Waldo. *Threshold of War: Franklin D. Roosevelt & American Entry into World War II.* Oxford: Oxford University Press, 1988.

Hickok, Lorena. *The Road to the White House: FDR; The Pre-Presidential Years.* New York: Scholastic Book Services, 1962.

Hirsch, H. N. *The Enigma of Felix Frankfurter.* New York: Basic Books, 1981.

Hodgson, Godfrey. *The Colonel: The Life and Wars of Henry Stimson, 1867–1950.* New York: Alfred A. Knopf, 1990.

Hooks, Gregory. *Forging the Industrial-Military Complex: World War II's Battle of the Potomac.* Urbana: University of Illinois Press, 1991.

Hoopes, Townsend, and Douglas Brinkley. *Driven Patriot: The Life and Times of James Forrestal.* New York: Alfred A. Knopf, 1992.

Hull, Cordell. *The Memoirs of Cordell Hull.* 2 vols. New York: Macmillan, 1948.

Hyman, Sidney. *Marriner S. Eccles: Private Entrepreneur and Public Servant.* Palo Alto, CA: Graduate School of Business, Stanford University, 1976.

Ickes, Harold L. *The Autobiography of a Curmudgeon.* New York: Reynal & Hitchcock, 1943.

———. *The Secret Diary of Harold L. Ickes.* Vol. 1, *The First Thousand Days, 1933–1936.* New York: Simon & Schuster, 1953.

———. *The Secret Diary of Harold L. Ickes*. Vol. 3, *The Lowering Clouds, 1939–1941*. New York: Simon & Schuster, 1954.

Isaacson, Walter, and Evan Thomas. *The Wise Men: Six Friends and the World They Made*. New York: Simon & Schuster, 1986.

Ismay, Lord General Hastings. *The Memoirs of General Lord Ismay*. New York: Viking Press, 1960.

Israel, Fred L., ed. *The War Diary of Breckinridge Long: Selections from the Years 1939–1944*. Lincoln: University of Nebraska Press, 1966.

Janeway, Eliot. *The Struggle for Survival*. New Haven, CT: Weybright and Talley, 1951.

Jeffries, John W. *Wartime America: The World War II Home Front*. Arlington Heights, IL: Harlan Davidson, 1986.

Jenkins, Roy. *Churchill: A Biography*. New York: Farrar, Straus and Giroux, 2001.

———. *Franklin Delano Roosevelt*. New York: Times Books, 2003.

Jones, Jesse. *Fifty Billion Dollars: My Thirteen Years with the Reconstruction Finance Corporation, 1932–1945*. New York: Macmillan, 1951.

Jordan, Jonathan W. *American Warlords: How Roosevelt's High Command Led America to Victory in World War II*. New York: NAL Caliber, 2015.

Kaiser, David. *No End Save Victory: How FDR Led the Nation into War*. New York: Basic Books, 2014.

Keegan, John. *The Second World War*. New York: Penguin Books, 1990.

Kennan, George F. *American Diplomacy, 1900–1950*. New York: New American Library, 1951.

———. *Memoirs, 1925–1950*. Boston: Little, Brown, 1967.

Kennedy, David M. *Freedom from Fear: The American People in Depression and War, 1929–1945*. New York: Oxford University Press, 2005.

Ketchum, Richard M. *The Borrowed Years, 1938–1941: America on the Way to War*. New York: Random House, 1989.

Kimball, Warren F., ed. *Churchill and Roosevelt: The Complete Correspondence*. 3 vols. Princeton, NJ: Princeton University Press, 1984.

———, ed. *Forged in War: Roosevelt, Churchill, and the Second World War*. New York: William Morrow, 1997.

———, ed. *Swords or Ploughshares? The Morgenthau Plan for Defeated Nazi Germany, 1943–1946*. Philadelphia: Lippincott, 1976.

———, ed. *The Juggler: Franklin Roosevelt as Wartime Statesman*. Princeton, NJ: Princeton University Press, 1991.

———. *The Most Unsordid Act: Lend-Lease, 1939–1941*. Baltimore: Johns Hopkins University Press, 1969.

King, Ernest J., and Walter Muir Whitehill. *Fleet Admiral King: A Naval Record*. New York: W. W. Norton, 1952.

Kiplinger, W. M. *Washington Is Like That*. New York: Harper & Brothers, 1942.

Klein, Maury. *A Call to Arms: Mobilizing America for World War II*. New York: Bloomsbury Press, 2013.

Koistinen, Paul A. C. *Arsenal of World War II: The Political Economy of American Warfare, 1939–1945*. Lawrence: University of Kansas Press, 2004.

Kotlowski, Dean J. *Paul V. McNutt and the Age of FDR*. Bloomington: Indiana University Press, 2015.

Kubek, Anthony. "The Morgenthau Plan and the Problem of Policy Perversion." *Journal of Historical Review* 9, no. 3 (Fall 1989).

Kuznets, Simon. *National Product in Wartime*. New York: National Bureau of Economic Research, 1945.

Lacey, Jim. *Keep from All Thoughtful Men: How U.S. Economists Won World War II*. Annapolis, MD: Naval Institute Press, 2011.

Lamb, Richard. *Churchill as War Leader*. New York: Carroll & Graf, 1991.

Langer, William L., and S. Everett Gleason. *The Undeclared War: 1939–1940*. New York: Harper & Brothers, 1952–1953.

Larrabee, Eric. *Commander in Chief: Franklin Delano Roosevelt, His Lieutenants and Their War*. New York: Harper and Row, 1987.

Lash, Joseph P. *Dealers and Dreamers*. Garden City, NY: Doubleday, 1988.

———. *Eleanor and Franklin: The Story of Their Relationship*. New York: W. W. Norton, 1971.

———, ed. *From the Diaries of Felix Frankfurter*. New York: W. W. Norton, 1975.

———. *Love, Eleanor: Eleanor Roosevelt and Her Friends*. Garden City, NY: Doubleday, 1982.

———. *Roosevelt and Churchill, 1939–1941: The Partnership That Saved the West*. New York: W. W. Norton, 1975.

Leahy, William D. *I Was There: The Personal Story of the Chief of Staff to Presidents Roosevelt and Truman Based on His Notes and Diaries Made at the Time*. New York: Whittlesey House, 1950.

Levy, Herbert. *Henry Morgenthau, Jr.: The Remarkable Life of FDR's Secretary of the Treasury*. New York: Skyhorse Publishing, 2010.

Lindbergh, Charles A. *The Wartime Journals of Charles A. Lindbergh*. New York: Harcourt Brace Jovanovich, 1970.

Love, Robert William, Jr. *The Chiefs of Naval Operations*. Annapolis, MD: Naval Institute Press, 1980.

MacArthur, Douglas. *Reminiscences*. New York: McGraw-Hill, 1964.

Mackenzie, Compton. *Mr. Roosevelt*. New York: Dutton, 1944.

Macmillan, Harold. *The Blast of War, 1939–1945*. New York: Harper & Row, 1968.

———. *War Diaries: Politics and War in the Mediterranean: January 1943–May 1945*. London: Macmillan, 1984.

Maisky, Ivan. *Memoirs of a Soviet Ambassador, 1939–1943*. London: Hutchinson, 1967.

Manchester, William. *American Caesar: Douglas MacArthur, 1880–1964*. Boston: Little, Brown, 1978.

———. *The Last Lion: Winston Spencer Churchill: Alone, 1932–1940*. Boston: Little, Brown, 1983.

Manchester, William, and Paul Reid. *The Last Lion: Winston Spencer Churchill, Defender of the Realm, 1949–1965*. Boston: Little, Brown, 2012.

Marcus, Sheldon. *Father Coughlin: The Tumultuous Life of the Priest of the Little Flower*. Boston: Little, Brown, 1973.

Marshall, George Catlett. *The Papers of George Catlett Marshall*. Vol. 1, "The Soldierly Spirit," December 1880–June 1939, edited by Larry Bland. Baltimore: Johns Hopkins University Press, 1981.

———. *The Papers of George Catlett Marshall*. Vol. 2, We Cannot Delay, July 1, 1939–December 6, 1941, edited by Larry Bland. Baltimore: Johns Hopkins University Press, 1981.

Marshall, Katherine Tupper. *Together: Annals of an Army Wife*. New York: Tupper & Love, 1946.

Marshall Foundation, Lexington, VA—Pogue Interviews: http://marshallfoundation.org/library/documents/Tape_1.pdf.

Martin, George. *Madame Secretary: Frances Perkins*. Boston: Houghton Mifflin, 1976.

Matloff, Maurice, and Edwin Snell. *Strategic Planning for Coalition Warfare: 1941–1942*. Washington, DC: Center of Military History, United States Army, 1953.

———. *Strategic Planning for Coalition Warfare: 1943–1944*. Washington, DC: Center of Military History, United States Army, 1959.

Mayers, David. *FDR's Ambassadors and the Diplomacy of Crisis: From the Rise of Hitler to the End of World War II*. New York: Cambridge University Press, 2013.

Mayle, Paul D. *Eureka Summit: Agreement in Principle and the Big Three at Tehran, 1943*. Newark: University of Delaware Press, 1987.

McGrane, Reginald C. *The Facilities and Construction Program of the War Production Board and Predecessor Agencies, May 1940 to May 1945*. Washington, DC: United States Government Printing Office, 1945.

McIntire, Ross T. *White House Physician*. New York: G. P. Putnam's Sons, 1946.

McJimsey, George. *Harry Hopkins: Ally of the Poor and Defender of Democracy*. Cambridge, MA: Harvard University Press, 1987.

McNeill, William Hardy. *America, Britain, and Russia: Their Co-operation and Conflict, 1941–1946*. New York: Johnson Reprint Corporation, 1970.

Meacham, Jon. *Franklin and Winston: An Intimate Portrait of an Epic Friendship*. New York: Random House, 2004.

Miller, Nathan. *FDR: An Intimate History*. Garden City, NY: Doubleday, 1983.

Milward, Alan S. *War, Economy, and Society*. Berkeley: University of California Press, 1977.

Miscamble, Wilson D. *From Roosevelt to Truman: Potsdam, Hiroshima, and the Cold War*. Cambridge: Cambridge University Press, 2007.

Monnet, Jean. *Jean Monnet's Memoirs*. Garden City, NY: Doubleday, 1978.

Moran, Lord. *Churchill: Taken from the Diaries of Lord Moran*. Boston: Houghton Mifflin, 1966.

Morgan, Ted. *FDR: A Biography*. New York: Simon & Schuster, 1985.

Morgenthau, Henry, Sr. *All in a Life Time*. Garden City, NY: Doubleday, 1926.

Morgenthau, Henry, III. *Mostly Morgenthaus: A Family History*. Boston: Ticknor and Fields, 1991.

Morison, Elting E. *Turmoil and Tradition: A Study of the Life and Times of Henry L. Stimson*. New York: History Book Club, 2003.

Morison, Samuel Eliot. *The History of United States Naval Operations in World War II*. 15 vols. Boston: Little, Brown, 1947–1962.

Morse, Arthur D. *While Six Million Died: A Chronicle of American Apathy*. Woodstock, NY: Overlook Press, 1983.

Morton, Louis. "Germany First: The Basic Concept of Allied Strategy in World War II." In *Command Decisions*, edited by Kent Roberts Greenfield. Washington, DC: Center of Military History, United States Army, 1960.

———. *Strategy and Command: The First Two Years*. Washington, DC: Center of Military History, United States Army, 1962.

Moseley, Leonard. *Marshall: Hero for Our Times*. New York: Hearst Books, 1982.

Moskin, J. Robert. *American Statecraft: The Story of the U.S. Foreign Service*. New York: Thomas Dunne Books, 2013.

Murphy, Bruce Allen. *The Brandeis-Frankfurter Connection: The Secret Political Activities of Two Supreme Court Justices*. New York: Oxford University Press, 1982.

Murphy, Robert. *Diplomat Among Warriors*. Garden City, NY: Doubleday, 1964.

Neal, Steve. *Dark Horse: A Biography of Wendell Willkie*. Garden City, NY: Doubleday, 1984.

Nelson, Donald. *The Arsenal of Democracy*. New York: Harcourt Brace, 1946.

Nesbitt, Henrietta. *White House Diary*. Garden City, NY: Doubleday, 1948.

Novick, David, Melvin Anshen, and W. C. Truppner. *Wartime Production Controls*. New York: Columbia University Press, 1949.

O'Connor, Raymond. *Diplomacy for Victory: Franklin Roosevelt and Unconditional Surrender*. New York: W. W. Norton, 1971.

Ohl, John Kennedy. *Supplying the Troops: General Somervell and American Logistics in WWII*. DeKalb: Northern Illinois University Press, 1994.

Olson, Lynne. *Citizens of London: The Americans Who Stood with Britain in Its Darkest, Finest Hour*. New York: Random House, 2011.

———. *Those Angry Days: Roosevelt, Lindbergh, and America's Fight over World War II, 1939–1941*. New York: Random House, 2013.

———. *Troublesome Young Men: The Rebels Who Brought Churchill to Power and Helped Save England*. New York: Farrar, Straus and Giroux, 2007.

O'Neill, William L. *A Democracy at War: America's Fight at Home and Abroad in World War II*. New York: The Free Press, 1993.

O'Sullivan, Christopher D. *Harry Hopkins: FDR's Envoy to Churchill and Stalin.* Lanham, MD: Rowman & Littlefield, 2015.

Overy, Richard. *Why the Allies Won.* New York: W. W. Norton, 1995.

Parrish, Thomas. *Berlin in the Balance: 1945–1949.* Reading, MA: Addison-Wesley, 1998.

———. *Roosevelt and Marshall: Partners in Politics and War, the Personal Story.* New York: William Morrow, 1989.

———. *To Keep the British Isles Afloat: FDR's Men in Churchill's London, 1941.* New York: Smithsonian Books/Collins, 2009.

Perkins, Frances. *The Roosevelt I Knew.* New York: Viking, 1946.

Perret, Geoffrey. *Days of Sadness, Years of Triumph: The American People, 1939–1945.* New York: Coward, McCann & Geoghegan, 1973.

Perry, Mark. *Partners in Command: George Marshall and Dwight Eisenhower in War and Peace.* New York: Penguin, 2008.

Persico, Joseph. *Franklin and Lucy: Mrs. Rutherfurd and the Other Remarkable Women in Roosevelt's Life.* New York: Random House, 2008.

———. *Roosevelt's Centurions: FDR and the Commanders He Led to Victory in World War II.* New York: Random House, 2013.

———. *Roosevelt's Secret War: FDR and World War II Espionage.* New York: Random House, 2001.

Phillips, Cabell. *The 1940s: Decade of Triumph and Trouble.* New York: Macmillan, 1975.

Phillips, Harlan B., ed. *Felix Frankfurter Reminisces.* New York: Reynal and Company, 1960.

Picknett, Lynn, Clive Prince, and Stephen Prior. *Friendly Fire: The Secret War Between the Allies.* Edinburgh: Mainstream Publishing, 2005.

Pilpel, Robert H. *Churchill in America, 1895–1961.* New York: Harcourt Brace Jovanovich, 1976.

Pitt, Barrie. *Churchill and the Generals.* London: Sidgwick & Jackson, 1981.

Plokhy, S. M. *Yalta: The Price of Peace.* New York: Viking, 2010.

Pogue, Forrest C. *George C. Marshall.* 4 vols. New York: Viking Press, 1963.

Polenberg, Richard. *War and Society: The United States, 1941–1945.* Philadelphia: J. B. Lippincott, 1972.

Pyle, Ernie. *Brave Men.* New York: Henry Holt, 1944.

Rees, David. *Harry Dexter White: A Study in Paradox.* New York: Coward, McCann & Geoghegan, 1973.

Rhodes, Richard. *The Making of the Atomic Bomb.* New York: Simon & Schuster, 1986.

Robertson, David. *Sly and Able: A Political Biography of James F. Byrnes.* New York: W. W. Norton, 1994.

Rolde, Neil. *Breckinridge Long, American Eichmann??? An Enquiry into the Character of the Man Who Denied Visas to the Jews.* Solon, ME: Polar Bear & Company, 2013.

Roosevelt, Eleanor. *This I Remember*. New York: Harper & Brothers, 1949.

Roosevelt, Elliott. *As He Saw It*. New York: Duell, Sloan & Pearce, 1946.

Roosevelt, Elliott, and James Brough. *An Untold Story: The Roosevelts of Hyde Park*. New York: Putnam, 1973.

———. *A Rendezvous with Destiny: The Roosevelts of the White House*. New York: Putnam, 1975.

Roosevelt, Franklin D. *Public Papers and Addresses of Franklin D. Roosevelt*. Edited by Samuel I. Rosenman. 4 vols. New York: Macmillan, 1941–1945.

———. *Complete Presidential Press Conferences of Franklin D. Roosevelt*. 25 vols. New York: Da Capo Press, 1972.

———. *FDR: His Personal Letters, 1928–1945*. 4 vols. New York: Duell, Sloan, and Pearce, 1950.

———. *Public Papers and Addresses of President Franklin D. Roosevelt*. 13 vols. New York: Random House, 1928–1945.

———. *Roosevelt and Frankfurter: Their Correspondence, 1928–1945*. Annotated by Max Freedman. Boston: Little, Brown, 1967.

Rosenman, Samuel I. *Working with Roosevelt*. New York: Da Capo Press, 1972.

Schlesinger, Arthur M., Jr. *The Age of Roosevelt*. 3 vols. Boston: Houghton Mifflin, 1957, 1959, 1960.

Schmitz, David F. *Henry L. Stimson: The First Wise Man*. Wilmington, DE: Scholarly Resources, 2001.

Schwarz, Jordan A. *The Speculator: Bernard M. Baruch in Washington, 1917–1965*. Chapel Hill: University of North Carolina Press, 1981.

Seidman, Joel. *American Labor from Defense to Reconversion*. Chicago: University of Chicago Press, 1953.

Sherwood, Robert E. *Roosevelt and Hopkins: An Intimate History*. New York: Harper & Brothers, 1948.

Shirer, William L. *The Rise and Fall of the Third Reich*. New York: Simon & Schuster, 1960.

Skidelsky, Robert. *John Maynard Keynes: Fighting for Freedom, 1938–1946*. New York: Viking, 2001.

Smith, Jean Edward. *FDR*. New York: Random House, 2008.

Somers, Herman Miles. *Presidential Agency: OWMR; the Office of War Mobilization and Reconversion*. Westport, CT: Greenwood Press, 1950.

Steel, Ronald. *Walter Lippmann and the American Century*. Boston: Little, Brown, 1980.

Stettinius, Edward R. *The Diaries of Edward R. Stettinius Jr., 1943–1946*. Edited by Thomas M. Campbell and George C. Herring. New York: New Viewpoints, 1975.

Stimson, Henry L., and McGeorge Bundy. *On Active Service in Peace and War*. New York: Harper & Brothers, 1947.

Stoler, Mark A. *Allies and Adversaries: The Joint Chiefs of Staff, the Grand Alliance, and U.S. Strategy in World War II*. Chapel Hill: University of North Carolina Press, 2000.

———. *George C. Marshall: Soldier-Statesman of the American Century.* New York: Twayne, 1989.

———. *The Politics of the Second Front: American Military Planning and Diplomacy in Coalition Warfare, 1941–1943.* Westport, CT: Greenwood Press, 1977.

Sweeting, George Vincent. "Building the Arsenal of Democracy: The Governments' Role in Expansion of Industrial Capacity, 1940 to 1945." Unpublished dissertation, Columbia University, 1994.

Taylor, A. J. P. *Beaverbrook.* New York: Simon & Schuster, 1972.

Terkel, Studs. *The Good War.* New York: Pantheon Books, 1984.

Time magazine. "The Cabinet: Emperor Jones." National Affairs, January 13, 1941.

Tooze, Alan. *Wages of Destruction: The Making and Breaking of the Nazi Economy.* London: Allen Lane, 2006.

Tosi-Lacey, Sharon. *Pacific Blitzkrieg: World War II in the Central Pacific.* Denton: University of North Texas Press, 2013.

Tull, Charles J. *Father Coughlin and the New Deal.* Syracuse, NY: Syracuse University Press, 1965.

Tully, Grace. *F.D.R., My Boss.* New York: C. Scribner's Sons, 1949.

Tuttle, Dwight William. *Harry L. Hopkins and Anglo-American-Soviet Relations, 1941–1945.* New York: Garland Publishing, 1983.

United States Bureau of the Budget. *The United States at War.* Washington, DC: United States Government Printing Office, 1946.

United States Office of Management and Budget. *The United States at War: Development and Administration of the War Program by the Federal Government.* New York: Da Capo Press, 1972.

Van Dormael, Armand. *Bretton Woods: Birth of a Monetary System.* London: Macmillan, 1978.

Vatter, Harold G. *The U.S. Economy in World War II.* New York: Columbia University Press, 1985.

Wallace, Henry A. *The Price of Vision: The Diary of Henry A. Wallace, 1942–1946.* Boston: Houghton Mifflin, 1973.

Ward, Geoffrey C. *Closest Companion: The Unknown Story of the Intimate Friendship Between Franklin Roosevelt and Margaret Suckley.* New York: Simon & Schuster, 2009.

Warken, Philip W. *A History of the National Resources Planning Board.* New York: Garland Publishing, 1979.

Warner, Emily Smith, with Hawthorne Daniel. *The Happy Warrior.* Garden City, NY: Doubleday, 1956.

Watkins, T. H. *Righteous Pilgrim: The Life and Times of Harold I. Ickes, 1874–1952.* New York: Henry Holt, 1990.

Watson, Mark S. *Chief of Staff: Prewar Planning and Preparations.* Washington, DC: Center of Military History, United States Army, 1950.

Watt, Donald Cameron. *How War Came.* New York: Pantheon, 1989.

Wedemeyer, A. C. *Wedemeyer Reports!* New York: Henry Holt, 1958.

Weinberg, Gerhard. *A World at Arms: A Global History of World War II.* New York: Cambridge University Press, 1994.

———. "The Allies and the Holocaust." In *The Holocaust and History: The Known, the Unknown, the Disputed, and the Reexamined,* edited by Michael Berenbaum and Abraham Peck. Bloomington: Indiana University Press, 1998.

Welles, Benjamin. *Sumner Welles: FDR's Global Strategist.* New York: St. Martin's Press, 1997.

Welles, Sumner. *Seven Decisions That Shaped History.* New York: Harper & Brothers, 1951.

———. *The Time for Decision.* New York: Harper & Brothers, 1944.

Wilmot, Chester. *The Struggle for Europe.* London: Collins, 1952.

Winik, Jay. *1944: FDR and the Year That Changed History.* New York: Simon & Schuster, 2015.

Winkler, Allan M. *Home Front U.S.A.: America During World War II.* Wheeling, IL: Harlan Davidson, 2000.

Woolner, David, ed. *The Second Quebec Conference Revisited: Waging War, Formulating Peace: Canada, Great Britain and the United States in 1944–1945.* New York: St. Martin's, 1998.

PHOTOGRAPH CREDITS

Page 74: Library of Congress, Prints & Photographs Division, FSA/OWI Collection, reproduction number LC-USE6-D-002159

Page 76: Library of Congress, Prints & Photographs Division, Bachrach Collection, reproduction number BIOG FILE—Willkie, Wendell Lewis, 1892–1944 <item>

Page 77: Library of Congress, Prints & Photographs Division, Harris & Ewing Collection, reproduction number LC-H22-D-2958

Page 83: Library of Congress, Prints & Photographs Division, Harris & Ewing Collection, reproduction number LC-H22-D-5479

Page 84: Harry S. Truman Library & Museum, accession number 64-04-03

Page 86: Library of Congress, Prints & Photographs Division, Harris & Ewing Collection, reproduction number LC-H22-D-9268

Page 89: Library of Congress, Prints & Photographs Division, FSA/OWI Collection, reproduction number LC-USW33-029456-C

Page 91: Library of Congress, Prints & Photographs Division, Harris & Ewing Collection, reproduction number LC-H22-D-5479

Page 97: Library of Congress, Prints & Photographs Division, Harris & Ewing Collection, reproduction number LC-H22-D-6688

Page 98: Library of Congress, Prints & Photographs Division, Harris & Ewing Collection, reproduction number LC-H22-D-9351

Page 99: Library of Congress, Prints & Photographs Division, FSA/OWI Collection, reproduction number LC-USE6-D-000963

Page 100: Library of Congress, Prints & Photographs Division, FSA/OWI Collection, reproduction number LC-USE6-D-005120

Page 101: Library of Congress, Prints & Photographs Division, Harris & Ewing Collection, reproduction number LC-H22-D-4580

Page 105: Library of Congress, Prints & Photographs Division, Harris & Ewing Collection, reproduction number LC-H22-D-6568

Page 114: Library of Congress, Prints & Photographs Division, Harris & Ewing Collection, reproduction number LC-H22-D-2348

Page 117: Library of Congress, Prints & Photographs Division, Harris & Ewing Collection, reproduction number LC-H22-D-6912

Page 122: Library of Congress, Prints & Photographs Division, NYWT&S Collection, reproduction number, NYWTS—BIOG—Hopkins, Harry L.—Presidential Advisor—Dead [item]

Page 125: Library of Congress, Prints & Photographs Division, FSA/OWI Collection, reproduction number LC-USE6-D-000965

Page 136: Library of Congress, Prints & Photographs Division, Harris & Ewing Collection, reproduction number LC-H21-C-481

Page 142: Credit: General Dean Collection, United States Army Heritage and Education Center, Carlisle, PA

Page 147: Library of Congress, Prints & Photographs Division, Office of War Information, Overseas Picture Division, reproduction number LC-USZ62-132802

Page 153: National Museum of the U.S. Navy, officially a U.S. Navy Photograph, now in the collections of the National Archives, accession number 80-G-26848

Page 163: Library of Congress, Prints & Photographs Division, FSA/OWI Collection, reproduction number LC-USE6-D-001022

Page 166: Library of Congress, Prints & Photographs Division, FSA/OWI Collection, reproduction number LC-USE6-D-000668

Page 201: Credit: General Dean Collection, United States Army Heritage and Education Center, Carlisle, PA

Page 209: Library of Congress, Prints & Photographs Division, FSA/OWI Collection, reproduction number LC-USE6-D-009430

Page 215: Library of Congress, Prints & Photographs Division, FSA/OWI Collection, reproduction number LC-USE613-D-000192

Page 220: Library of Congress, Prints & Photographs Division, Harris & Ewing Collection, reproduction number LC-H22-D-9254

Page 221: Library of Congress, Prints & Photographs Division, FSA/OWI Collection, reproduction number LC-USE6-D-002445

Page 236: Library of Congress, Prints & Photographs Division, Harris & Ewing Collection, reproduction number LC-H22-D-6166

Page 271: Credit: General Dean Collection, United States Army Heritage and Education Center, Carlisle, PA

Page 291: Library of Congress, Prints & Photographs Division, Harris & Ewing Collection, reproduction number LC-H2-B-6886

Page 292: Library of Congress, Prints & Photographs Division, FSA/OWI Collection, reproduction number LC-USE6-D-003116-a

Page 293: Library of Congress, Prints & Photographs Division, FSA/OWI Collection, reproduction number LC-USE6-D-004759-a

Page 295: Library of Congress, Prints & Photographs Division, Harris & Ewing Collection, reproduction number LC-H22-D-8473

Page 306: Library of Congress, Prints & Photographs Division, Harris & Ewing Collection, reproduction number LC-H22-D-2370

Page 316: Library of Congress, Prints & Photographs Division, FSA/OWI Collection, reproduction number LC-USE6-D-005723-a

Page 317: Library of Congress, Prints & Photographs Division, FSA/OWI Collection, reproduction number LC-USE6-D-005888-a

Page 322: Library of Congress, Prints & Photographs Division, Harris & Ewing Collection, reproduction number LC-H22-D-4711

Page 329: Library of Congress, Prints & Photographs Division, FSA/OWI Collection, reproduction number LC-USW3-006467-D

Page 332: Library of Congress, Prints & Photographs Division, Harris & Ewing Collection, reproduction number LC-H2-B-5749

Page 345: Credit: General Dean Collection, United States Army Heritage and Education Center, Carlisle, PA

Page 346: Credit: General Dean Collection, United States Army Heritage and Education Center, Carlisle, PA

Page 358: Library of Congress, Prints & Photographs Division, Harris & Ewing Collection, reproduction number LC-H22-D-8550

Page 364: Library of Congress, Prints & Photographs Division, Harris & Ewing Collection, reproduction number LC-H22-D-7016

Page 366: Library of Congress, Prints & Photographs Division, Harris & Ewing Collection, reproduction number LC-H22-D-2076

Page 367: Library of Congress, Prints & Photographs Division, Harris & Ewing Collection, reproduction number LC-H22-D-1643

Page 376: Library of Congress, Prints & Photographs Division, Harris & Ewing Collection, reproduction number LC-H25-43370-CG

Page 388: Library of Congress, Prints & Photographs Division, Harris & Ewing Collection, reproduction number LC-H22-D-8968

Page 397: Credit: General Dean Collection, United States Army Heritage and Education Center, Carlisle, PA

Page 414: Credit: General Dean Collection, United States Army Heritage and Education Center, Carlisle, PA

Page 415: Credit: General Dean Collection, United States Army Heritage and Education Center, Carlisle, PA

Page 423: Credit: General Dean Collection, United States Army Heritage and Education Center, Carlisle, PA

Page 468: Credit: General Dean Collection, United States Army Heritage and Education Center, Carlisle, PA

Page 471: Credit: General Dean Collection, United States Army Heritage and Education Center, Carlisle, PA

Page 473: Credit: General Dean Collection, United States Army Heritage and Education Center, Carlisle, PA

INDEX

Page numbers of photographs appear in italics.

FDR = Franklin Delano Roosevelt

ABOUT THE AUTHOR

JAMES LACEY is the author of *The First Clash: The Miraculous Greek Victory at Marathon and Its Impact on Western Civilization, Moment of Battle: The Twenty Clashes That Changed the World, The Washington War: FDR's Inner Circle and the Politics of Power That Won World War II*, and many other works on military history. He is a widely published defense analyst who has written extensively on the war in Iraq and on the global war on terrorism. Having served more than a dozen years on active duty as an infantry officer, he recently retired from the Army Reserves. Lacey traveled with the 101st Airborne Division during the Iraq invasion as an embedded journalist for *Time* magazine, and his work has also appeared in *National Review, Foreign Affairs*, the *Journal of Military History*, and many other publications. He currently teaches at the Marine Corps War College and Georgetown University.